BCS '81

INFORMATION TECHNOLOGY FOR THE EIGHTIES

PROCEEDINGS OF THE CONFERENCE
ORGANIZED BY
THE BRITISH COMPUTER SOCIETY
LONDON, 1-3 JULY 1981

Edited by

R.D. Parslow

D1340781

Published by
Wiley Heyden Ltd
on behalf of
The British Computer Society

This reprint is being produced at such very short notice that there has been no opportunity for edition of the submitted preprints offered in the original edition. I must therefore apologise for the absence of full papers from several contributors and suggest that further information may be obtainable direct from the authors.

R.D. Parslow — 2 November 1983

First published 1981 by Heyden & Son Ltd.
Reprinted 1983, Copyright © Wiley Heyden Ltd.

ISBN 0 471 25946 2

Printed and bound by Page Bros (Norwich) Ltd, Mile Cross Lane, Norwich NR6 6SA

CONTENTS

CONTENTS

CONTENTS

INTRODUCING BCS '81

Gerry Fisher   Bob Parslow

BCS '81 is the latest in the line of biennial British Computer Society Conferences, formerly called Datafairs, which was interrupted slightly by Eurolfip '79 when we were hosts for all the European Societies. The Committees have attempted to produce a worthy set of sessions and the full texts of these are reported in this volume.

It is our aim to demonstrate that the British Computer Society is concerned with more than pushing forward the frontiers of computer science. The Society also gives great priority to the practical uses and social implications of the technology and to the personal and work development of computer professionals. Through this Conference and its Proceedings we trust that managers, analysts, programmers, academics and users in application fields will increase their knowledge both generally and in their own special interest areas.

We should particularly like to thank the authors for their work and participation, and also the Programme Committee and the Session Chairmen for the effort they have contributed.

G.A. Fisher
Chairman, Organizing Committee

R.D. Parslow
Editor
Chairman, Programme Committee

KEYNOTE SPEAKERS

John Anderson

Professor John Anderson studied medicine at the University of Durham, qualifying in 1950. He pursued his medical career in Newcastle and later in London, and held a Rockefeller Research Fellowship at Harvard University, USA. He became interested in medical computing in 1955 with the setting up of a computer laboratory using a Pegasus machine. Since then he has continued his interest in medical computing both in projects which are scientific and in relation to medical education and medical records at Kings College Hospital Medical School where he is Professor of Medicine. His contribution is entitled 'The Systematic Doctor'.

David Firnberg

David Firnberg is Managing Director of Urwick Nexos Limited, the information technology training and consultancy organisation, set up jointly by Urwick Orr and Partners, the management consultants and Nexos Office Systems, the NB backed office equipment specialists. Before joining Urwick Nexos in January 1980, David Firnberg was Director of the National Computing Centre for five years. He has become widely known as an author and broadcaster, and he also lectures extensively both nationally and internationally. He is a prominent figure on committees dealing with information technology standards and education, as well as many national and international bodies concerned with information technology policy. David Firnberg, who is a Fellow of the BCS and President of the Association of Project Managers, describes the progress towards 'The Electronic Office'.

Murray Laver

Murray Laver has been associated first with communications and then with computing throughout a career which started in 1935 and has included appointments as Head of the Computer Division of the Treasury (the precursor of the CTA), as Director of the Computer Division of the Ministry of Technology and as a member of the Post Office Board. In 1973 he retired to live in Sidmouth, but he remained a part-time member of the NRDC Board and a visiting Professor, Computer Laboratory, University of Newcastle upon Tyne. Well known as a prime-mover in the activities of BCS, Murray Laver gives one of his inimitable and far-reaching lectures, this one on the theme 'Politics and Policies for Computing and Communications'.

LIST OF CONTRIBUTORS

Abbatt, J., BCS Business Information Systems Specialist Group, UK (p. 751)
Adamczewski, B., Harris Computers, UK (p. 402)
Agosti, M., University of Padua, Italy (p. 559)
Anderson, J., King's College Hospital Medical School, UK (p. 159)
Arnold, E., Sussex University, UK (p. 148)
Bandler, W., University of Essex, UK (pp. 191, 483)
Bessant, J., University of Aston, Birmingham, UK (p. 107)
Bogod, J.L., The British Computer Society, UK (p. 591)
Bott, M.F., University College of Wales, UK (p. 652)
Bramer, M.A., The Open University, UK (p. 486)
Bridge, R.E., North Staffordshire Polytechnic, UK (p. 200)
Buxton, J.N., University of Warwick, UK (p. 1)
Cairns, D.J., Birkbeck College, UK (p. 227)
Campbell, C., BCS Business Information Systems Specialist Group, UK (p. 751)
Carmichael, J.W.S., ICL Corporate Information Systems, UK (p. 733)
Castell, S., Infolex Services, UK (p. 517)
Cousins, W.B., Computel, UK (p. 439)
Crookes, P., The Queen's University, Belfast, UK (p. 81)
Dalla Libera, F., University of Padua, Italy (p. 559)
Dickson, K., University of Aston, Birmingham, UK (p. 107)
Disney, C., F International, UK (p. 286)
Edmonds, E.A., Leicester Polytechnic, UK (p. 2)
Farrer, J., Royal Lancaster Infirmary, UK (p. 195)
Firnberg, D., Urwick Nexos, UK (p. 43)
Florentin, J.J., Birkbeck College, UK (p. 227)
Forrington, C.V.D., Corporate Business Systems, UK (p. 52)
Freedman, A.L., Plessey Radar, UK (p. 319)
Gaines, B.R., Middlesex Polytechnic, UK (p. 235)
Harivel, J., CAP Sogeti Logiciel, France (p. 529)
Huc, B., CAP Sogeti Logiciel, France (p. 34)
Huzan, E., Slough College of Higher Education, UK (p. 458)
Johnson, R.G., Thames Polytechnic, UK (p. 559)
Johnston, C.I., Aberdeen University, UK (p. 689)
Jones, A.H., BCS Business Information Systems Specialist Group, UK (p. 751)
Jones, G.O., Constructors John Brown, UK (p. 373)
Kohout, L.J., Brunel University, UK (pp. 191, 483)
Land, F.F., BCS Business Information Systems Specialist Group, UK (p. 751)
Lane, V.P., North East London Polytechnic, UK (p. 581)
Laver, F.J.M., BCS Past President, UK (p. 93)
Layzell, P.J., University of Manchester, UK (p. 16)

Levene, A.A., Systems Designers, UK (p. 343)
Malpas-Sands, C.A., A.T. Kearney, UK (p. 46)
McClinton, S.I., Ulster Polytechnic, UK (p. 303)
Menzies, D.C., Lloyds, UK (p. 703)
Morgan, L., National Computing Centre, UK (p. 452)
Myszko, J.M., International Computers, UK (p. 388)
Newman, S.I., Shared Medical Systems Corp., USA, (p. 207)
Peltu, M., Independent Consultant, UK (p. 124)
Pollitt, A.S., Huddersfield Polytechnic, UK (p. 546)
Presutto, E., York University, Canada (p. 424)
Race, J.P.A., Brunel University, UK (p. 134)
Rao, V.K., National University of Singapore, Singapore (p. 571)
Reade, C.M.P., Brunel University, UK (p. 675)
Roberts, J., Royal Lancaster Infirmary, UK (p. 195)
Sabatier, P., CAP Sogeti Logiciel, France (p. 253)
Saiady, C., The Hatfield Polytechnic, UK (p. 599)
Sale, A.E., Angusglow, UK (p. 660)
Schappo, A., Leicester Polytechnic, UK (p. 2)
Shaw, M.L.G., Middlesex Polytechnic, UK (p. 235)
Sheard, J.R., International General Electric Company of New York, UK (p. 171)
Smith, F.J., The Queen's Universiy, Belfast, UK (p. 81)
Stokes, A.V., The Hatfield Polytechnic, UK (p. 599)
Stone, A.S., Aberdeen University, UK (p. 689)
Tedd, M.D., SPL International, UK (p. 652)
Townley, H.M., BCS Committee for Disabled, UK (p. 612)
Townsend, R., Arthur Anderson, UK (p. 718)
Triance, J.M., University of Manchester, UK (p. 16)
Tully, C.J. University of York, UK (p. 273)
Warman, D.J., British Medical Data Systems, UK (p. 207)
Wexelblat, R.L., Sperry Univac, USA (p. 259)
Williams, P.W., UMIST, UK (p. 468)
Williamson, G.L., North Staffordshire Polytechnic, UK (p.200)
Wilson, I.R., University of Manchester, UK (p. 634)
Woodman, L.A., Willis Faber & Dumas, UK (p. 66)
Wyld, B.A., Urwick Orr & Partners, UK (p. 303)

The STONEMAN Project and Support Systems for Ada: Summary

J. N. Buxton

University of Warwick, UK

The first phase of the Ada development for the DoD was the language design effort. This was initiated by a series of documents which set forth the requirements on the new language (IRONMAN, STEELMAN) and competitive designs were submitted. After evaluations, one was chosen and named "Ada".

The second and current phase of the effort is the provision of an integrated software environment for the production of high-quality and reliable software in Ada. Such an environment must offer support throughout the software life cycle from the requirements stage through to long-term maintenance and the necessary incremental growth and change which is undergone by long-lined software.

This phase has also been addressed by the production of a series of requirements documents culminating in the "STONEMAN". The "STONEMAN" lays down the general requirements for Ada Programming Support Environments - APSEs. The three principal features of an APSE are the database, the communication interface and the toolset. The database acts as the central repository for information associated with each project throughout the project life cycle. The interface includes the command language which presents an interface to the user as well as system interfaces to the database and toolset. The toolset contains an integrated set of tools to support program development, maintenance and configuration control.

A further goal of great importance is that of portability, both of user programs and of software tools within the APSE. The STONEMAN, therefore, also outlines an approach to portability by giving requirements for two lower levels within the APSE; the Kernel (KAPSE) and the minimal useful toolset (MAPSE).

The presentation will discuss the main features of APSEs as required by STONEMAN and will outline current developments.

An Interactive Raster Graphics Language

A. Schappo
(*Research Student*)
and
E. A. Edmonds
(*Reader in Computing*)

Leicester Polytechnic, UK

This paper describes an interactive graphics system and traces its development from a Vector based system to a Raster based system using a read/write bit map. By use of an extensible user interface command language and an extensible set of graphic primitives, higher level graphic commands can be built. To achieve this aim the user has the ability to define procedures which consist of calls to sets of these graphic primitives.

Furthermore, the read/write bit map enables the graphic primitives to effectively see the current state of the bit map. The consequence of this is that it becomes feasible for a user to define procedures which will handle shapes in a manner consistent with that users visual interpretation of those shapes.

1. INTRODUCTION

This paper describes the philosophy and implementation of an interactive graphics system called GOLL(1). The system has existed in two distinct states. viz

a) The Vector System. This system was implemented as an undergraduate final year project and named GOLL.
b) The Raster System. This system is an extension of the original GOLL and was named RGOLL.

The system has developed in two stages and therefore the paper will describe, respectively, GOLL and RGOLL.

The system provides a software environment for our computer graphics research work and a particular feature is the ease with which new work can be incorporated into it. The development of GOLL into RGOLL is an example of such a change.

2. ORIGINAL SYSTEM

2.1 CONCEPT OF GOLL

Goll is an acronym for Graphically Oriented Learning Language. Its original intended purpose was to teach naive computer users (with the emphasis being upon middle/secondary school children) some of the basic principles of programming computers. The basic principles being, in this case, structure, recursion, procedures and logic flow.

Logo(2), which was used successfully at Edinburgh University, supplied the initial stimulus to the development of GOLL. Logo users have the ability to direct the movements of a turtle on a drawing medium. The turtle is equipped with a pen and the user can instruct the turtle to raise or lower the pen onto the drawing medium. Thus a trace of the turtles path can be engraved on the drawing medium. Goll makes use of the same principle except that the user directs a point.

2.2 WHY GOLL?

Any activity can be made more interesting if that activity produces tangible results. In addition, if those results are appealing to the person doing that activity then it would encourage participation in that activity.

To facilitate these aims GOLL produces line drawings as a direct result of the efforts of the user. It is envisaged that, to a naive user, a drawing would be more appealing and meaningful than would be text output or abstract computations. Thus (or it seems evident that) a naive user would be encouraged to explore and make full use of the capabilities of GOLL in order to obtain more appealing results ie. better drawings.

2.3 WHAT DOES GOLL DO?

Given that the aim of the user is to achieve maximum drawing power, then GOLL provides the environment and facilities to achieve this aim. The interface to the user is provided by a simple interpretive

language and a simple operating system. The core of the language
consists of three basic graphic commands which can, respectively;

a) draw a straight line of a specified distance.
b) move a specified distance without drawing.
c) turn a specified angle.

From these basic commands the user can build up procedures consisting
of sequences of these basic components. The user can accumulate a
library of procedures and thus increase his/her drawing power.
Effectively the user has the ability to define a higher level graphics
language than the basic language provided by GOLL. In summary what we
have is a line drawing, user directed picture generator.

2.4 LANGUAGE

2.4.1 BASICS
The user must be provided with a means of communicating with and
instructing GOLL. Therefore a simple language has been defined and
translation and interpretive systems implemented for the language.

The language includes three basic drawing commands:

a) DRAW <expression>
b) MOVE <expression>
c) TURN <direction> <expression>
where
a) draws a straight line <expression> units in length.
b) moves in a straight line <expression> units in length without
   drawing.
c) turns <expression> degrees in the specified direction, clockwise or
   anticlockwise.

<expression> is a simple arithmetic expression consisting of at most
two operands and 'unit' is a GOLL measurement of length which is
dependent on the device being used. These statements can be executed
directly to draw simple straight line pictures.

A basic concept of drawing pictures is that all movements of the pen
are relative to the current direction of travel and the current
position. Current point therefore has two attributes: current
position and current direction. Execution of any of the basic
commands described above will result in current position and/or
current direction being updated. The importance of this methodology
is that a picture is described using its intrinsic properties rather
than its extrinsic properties ie. taking the example of a square, it
would be described as a series of DRAWS and TURNS instead of by
reference to an external frame of reference.

The drawing area is bounded by a Frame of Reference. This frame
measures 260 by 200 GOLL units and any attempt to draw beyond this
frame would be classified as an error. The initial conditions for
drawing are with the pen at the left hand bottom corner of the frame
(origin) and the initial direction of travel along the horizontal axis.
Refer to the appendix for the full repertoire of basic commands
available.

2.4.2 PROCEDURES

The next stage is to allow the user to define sequences of instructions as a unit which can be manipulated and executed as a unit.
This unit is called a procedure in GOLL terminology. So, for instance, the user could define a procedure which would draw a square of a given size.

The next logical step is to allow the user to generalise a procedure instead of writing a new procedure for every possible shape required. This is achieved by defining parameters through which values can be passed to a procedure. Thus a procedure which draws squares can be generalised by including a parameter which passes the size of the square to be drawn.

Procedures calls can be nested and the depth of nesting is only limited by the Software Stack size. The user could therefore breakdown a picture into component parts and write procedures with a 1:1 correspondence between procedure and picture component. All parameter passing is call by value. Thus a procedure can cause some graphic change on execution but can return no information to the user or calling procedure. Considering that GOLL procedures are purely generative call by value was found to be sufficient.

2.4.3 RECURSION

A user may define a procedure that, directly or indirectly, calls itself. Recursion introduces the ability to draw algorithmic patterns. The procedures defined below illustrate the use of a simple condition to control recursion and nested procedure calls. Entry into recursion is on truth of the condition and exit from recursion is on falsity of the condition.

```
TO   ROTESQ SIZE ANGLE LIMIT DEC
       SQ SIZE
       TURN CLOCKWISE ANGLE
       IF SIZE GREATER LIMIT ROTESQ SIZE-DEC ANGLE LIMIT DEC
       SQ SIZE
       TURN CLOCKWISE ANGLE
DONE
```

```
TO   SQ SIZE          TO   SIDE SIZE
       SIDE SIZE              DRAW SIZE
       SIDE SIZE              TURN CLOCKWISE 90
       SIDE SIZE      DONE
       SIDE SIZE
DONE
```

2.4.4 OTHER SYSTEM COMMANDS

The remaining GOLL commands will be described briefly. The syntactic structure of the commands can be found in the Appendix.

a) CLEAR. Clear the screen and origin the current point.
b) ORIGIN. Set current point position to bottom left hand corner of the Frame of Reference and current point direction positively along the x axis.
c) SAVE. Saves a named procedure in the library for use at another

session.

d) FORGET. Removes a named procedure from the library.

e) LIST/PRINT. Lists or prints the source code of a named procedure.

f) LIST/PRINT DIRECTORY. Lists or prints the names of all procedures existent in the users library where LIST writes to the terminal and PRINT writes to the line-printer.

3. RASTER BASED SYSTEM

Initial exploration of using GOLL on a Raster System was conducted on a PDP8 computer with a black/white bit map.(5) It has now been moved onto a colour system but still uses basically a binery colouring system. The raster based GOLL is henceforth called RGOLL.

3.1 HARDWARE ENVIRONMENT

The Raster System (7) hardware (that hardware relevant to this paper) consists of:

a) Cromemco System Three micro computer with 64 K immediate access memory.

b) Dual disk drive unit with approximately half megabyte storage capacity per disk.

c) VDU as the user interface.

d) B6700 mainframe computer.

e) Colour Television with a definition of 400 x 300.

f) Raster Graphics Unit. This consists of:

1) 128K dedicated refresh memory with 4 bits per pixel.

2) Palette memory which holds 16 colours with 4 bits for each of the primary colours.

3) 8085 processor acting as controller and interface to the cromemco.

g) Joystick.

3.2 SOFTWARE ENVIRONMENT

RGOLL is still resident on the B6700 but all calls to GINO-F have been removed. Graphic routines have been written as primitives resident on the Cromenco. Each primitive is intended to be as independent as possible so that block building techniques can be used. This objective is not always achievable, as will be seen, and primitives sometimes have to call other primitives. The user though, by using RGOLL statements, will regard each primitive as independent. RGOLL, under direction, fires off a primitive and awaits termination of the primitive. Thus RGOLL's graphic capabilities depend entirely on the type of primitives available and as will be seen these primitives explore primarily the use of bit map image representation.

3.3 EFFECTS OF NEW ENVIRONMENT

Fundamentally, the new environment enables the user to interact with the image. In addition to creating RGOLL picture generating procedures the user can manipulate images on the display screen. In effect, the interactiveness of the system is increased since the user is given the ability to tailor the image directly rather than change a procedure to obtain the desired results.

3.4 BIT MAP REPRESENTATION

By use of the bit map (read/write raster refresh memory) RGOLL has
acquired another sense, that of seeing. Furthermore, RGOLL is seeing,
not a symbolic representation of an image but instead a direct
representation of the image the user sees. We, therefore, have
available in the bit map an image that is accessible and understandable
(to a limited extent). Without this bit map image GOLL would, in
order to see the image, have to either

a) have the ability to analyse the procedures used to generate a
   particular image.
   or
b) Maintain a complex data structure that represents the current state
   of the display image. Furthermore it would have to analyse the
   components of a procedure generated image in order to allow partial
   manipulation.

The user, as stated, has the ability to directly tailor the images
being displayed. The word image is being used, in this case, to mean
the whole display area.

The actual operation of the primitives deal with shapes of a limited
type. A shape, in this case is defined as a set of pixels that:

a) have the same colour value (black/white).
b) each pixel in the set is connected to every other pixel in the set.

The black region of figure 3.1 is a primitive shape because all the
pixels are connected to each other whether directly or indirectly.

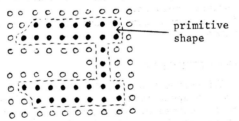

primitive
shape

figure 3.1

3.5 GRAPHIC PRIMITIVES

Apart from the primitives required for the original system the
following are also available. It is important to note that they
operate directly on the bit map and do not rely on some structured
representation of the image.

a) Cursor Mode - Switching into local cursor mode enables the user to
   move a cursor using a joystick leaving a trail invisible, black,
   white or complementary. The joystick is used as a direction
   indicator rather than a positioning device. The user can thus move
   the current position, draw a shape on the screen or modify existing
   shapes. Exiting from this mode will update RGOLL with the new
   coordinates.

b) FILL (6) - By use of the bit map only, the interior of a closed
   boundary can be filled in to form a solid region. Given the

outlined ring shape of fig 3.2a and a starting point a fill
operation would result in the solid ring of fig 3.2b.

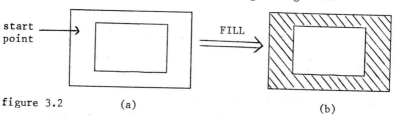

start
point   FILL

figure 3.2   (a)   (b)

c) SAVE - This primitive saves a shape existing at the current
   position onto diskette as a literal bit map pattern and colour.
   FILL is called to find the shape and so the user sees the shape
   being filled in. The SAVE operation restores the original shape so
   it is a non destructive SAVE. It introduces the ability to save
   shapes other than as RGOLL generative procedures.

d) DEPOSIT - Restores a diskette saved shape into the bit map at the
   current position.

e) EXPAND - For each invocation of this primitive a region boundary
   is extended uniformly by a one pixel depth. (Figure 3.3) FILL again
   is called in order to find the region existing at the current
   location but instead of complementing the colour a third temporary
   colour is used to fill in. This allows expand to distinguish
   between that which has been filled in and that which is non shape.
   Therefore for each pixel filled in we do:-
       Look at neighbours.
   If any neighbour has a complementary colour include that neighbour
   in the expanded shape.

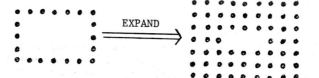

                                    EXPAND

figure 3.3

f) SHRINK - For each invocation of this primitive a region boundary is
   reduced by a one pixel depth. (figure 3.4). Shrink uses FILL in
   the same manner as the expand operation.

   For each pixel filled in do:-
       Look at neighbours
       If any neighbour has a complementary colour exclude the pixel
       from the Shrinked shape.

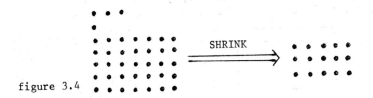

figure 3.4

3.6 RGOLL DEFINED GRAPHIC FUNCTIONS

Given the block building capabilities of RGOLL the user can now, using the basic set of primitives, construct higher level graphic functions. These functions can be defined such that they operate in accordance with the way in which the user interprets the picture.

In order to manipulate shapes locally the most obvious basic functions to be defined would be MOVESHAPE and COPYSHAPE. These could be defined using the following procedures:

```
TO MOVESHAPE           TO COPYSHAPE
    SAVE SHAPE             SAVE SHAPE
    FILL                  CURSOR MODE
    CURSOR MODE           DEPOSIT
    DEPOSIT            DONE
DONE
```

In the above procedures it is assumed, before invoking the appropriate procedure that the current position is within the shape to be manipulated. CURSOR MODE is used to locate the new position as it is assumed that finding the new location is an interactive process. COPYSHAPE could also be modified to make several copies by including a parameter for number of copies. The only difference between the two procedures is that MOVESHAPE has a FILL command to remove the shape once picked up.

3.7 INTERPRETATION OF PICTURE

A user may wish to manipulate shapes according to his/her interpretation. Take the simple case of a rectangular outline boundary of black pixels enclosing an interior of white pixels and the rectangular region is to be manipulated. If the region is to be moved then should the boundary be included or excluded?

Procedures to take account of both cases could be defined as follows:

```
TO MOVE EXCLUSIVE      TO MOVE INCLUSIVE
    SAVE SHAPE            FILL
    INVERT               SAVE SHAPE
    CURSOR MODE          CURSOR MODE
    DEPOSIT              DEPOSIT
DONE                  DONE
```

MOVE EXCLUSIVE will save all interior white pixels, invert the colour to black, move to new location and deposit the shape (Assuming white background).

MOVE INCLUSIVE will FILL in the white interior to black thereby
creating a new solid region including the boundary. This new region
is then manipulated.

The procedures, defined above, take no account of what shape is left
behind.

3.8 BOUNDARY EXTRACTION

Given a region it may be required to extract its boundaries (8).
Here again there are two cases: complementary boundary and internal
boundary (figure 3.5).

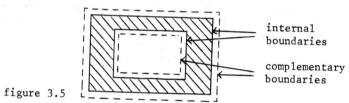

internal
boundaries

complementary
boundaries

figure 3.5

Execution of the following procedures would result in the appropriate
boundary being displayed.

```
TO FIND COMPLEMENTARY BOUNDARY        TO FIND INTERNAL BOUNDARY
    SAVE SHAPE                            SAVE SHAPE 1
    INVERT                                SHRINK
    EXPAND                                SAVE SHAPE 2
    DEPOSIT                               INVERT 2
DONE                                      DEPOSIT 1
                                          DEPOSIT 2
                                      DONE
```

In the procedure FIND INTERNAL BOUNDARY the facility to save a named
shape is introduced. In all other cases a default name is used.

3.9 FIGURE ON GROUND

The shapes of figure 3.6 could be interpreted as a white figure on a
black background (8). Each shape could be handled seperately but to
deal with both figure and ground a procedure could be defined as
follows:

```
TO FIGURE ON GROUND
    SAVE SHAPE 1
    FILL
    SAVE SHAPE 2
      |
    DEPOSIT 2
    DEPOSIT 1
DONE
```

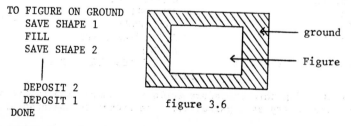

ground

Figure

figure 3.6

The white interior is saved as shape 1. This would then be filled to

black which effectively reveals the ground as though the figure had
been lifted off. The ground is then saved as shape 2. After some
undefined operation(s) the shapes are deposited. The ground is seen
as being laid down first followed by the figure being placed on top of
it.

3.10 COMPLEX SHAPES

Given a set of shapes existing in the bit map there is no intrinsic or
structured relationship between any of them. The user on the other
hand may perceive a relationship between a set of these shapes. The
four seperate shapes of figure 3.7 could, for instance, be perceived
as being related or as an entity. Any operations on these shapes
would then have to treat them as being performed on the entity. The
primitives available would not be capable of dealing with the four
shapes as an entity.

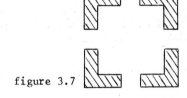

figure 3.7

Take, for example, the operation of MOVING the entity of figure 3.7.
The user would go through four cycles of:
                    a) point to shape
                    b) save shape
                    c) point to new location
                    d) deposit shape
for each component of the entity. This would though, most likely,
lead to the moved entity having incorrect relationship between its
components.

Using the facilities of RGOLL we could instead define a procedural
relationship between the components to produce an entity move. The
procedure MOVECOMPLEXSHAPE, defined below, would, with user
interaction, achieve this objective.

```
TO MOVECOMPLEXSHAPE N                TO MCS2 DX DY N
    REMEMBER X1 Y1                       CURSOR MODE
    SAVE SHAPE                           REMEMBER X1 Y1
    CURSOR MODE      .                   SAVE SHAPE
    REMEMBER X2 Y2                       GOTO X1+DX Y1+DY
    DEPOSIT                              DEPOSIT
    IF N>1 MCS2 X2-X1 Y2-Y1 N-1          IF N>1 MCS2 DX DY N-1
DONE                                 DONE
```

The user when invoking this procedure would also supply the number of
components of the entity as a parameter. The procedure operates as
follows:
a) Move first component and in so doing record offset to new location

from original location.
b) Point to the remaining N-1 components (in any order) which will
individually be moved to a new location retaining its correct relative
position to the first component.

4.   IMPLEMENTATION

The diagram shown in figure 4.1 illustrates the implementation method.
RGOLL is broken down into its software components and the Raster
System into its hardware components. The arrows indicate direction of
flow of data and commands.

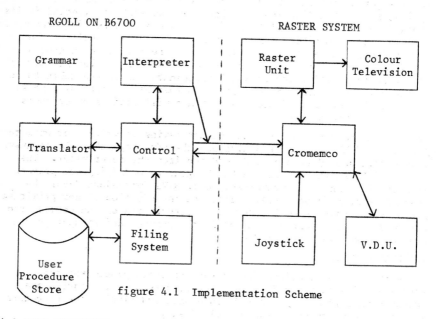

figure 4.1   Implementation Scheme

4.1 USER INTERFACE

The user talks to RGOLL using the V.D.U. and for this process the
Cromemco is invisible. Processing of a user command will result in
either
a) text output by RGOLL displayed at V.D.U. or
b) a graphic primitive being fired off by RGOLL which will produce a
change in the bit map and hence the television display. On
completion of the primitive RGOLL is informed of new position, if
required, and errors, if any.

4.2 CONTROL

The main task of the control component is to switch between the three
basic modes of operation.
a) directly executable mode.
   Source input is accepted from the user, translated into a string of

tokens, interpreted and executed.
b) procedure definition mode.
   Source input is translated and then stored in the users library
   under the appropriate procedure name.
c) procedure execution mode.
   The token form of a statement is taken from the users library,
   interpreted and executed. Recursion and procedure nesting is
   handled using a Software Stack.

4.3 TRANSLATION

The task of translation is performed by the Synics package (3).
Synics is a syntax directed translator and as such is directed in its
translation by a pre-defined grammar. The synics-directing grammar is
defined using a modified BNF notation. The grammar specifies the
syntactic structures to be recognised and the output to be generated
by Synics upon recognition of a syntactic construct. The grammar in
this case is a definition of RGOLL statements and of the token to be
generated. The grammar is defined such that all strings will parse
successfully but invalid RGOLL statements will produce error codes
instead of token strings.

Apart from the obvious advantage of not having to write a program to
translate RGOLL statements Synics has the advantage that the language
does attain some degree of independence from the interpreter. The
format of RGOLL statements can be changed, by modifying the grammar,
without affecting the interpreter. e.g. SAVE (procedure) could be
changed to KEEP (procedure). Also, the introduction of new primitive
graphics commands is well ordered. A description of the command and
its internal form must be entered in the grammar and an appropriate
procedure provided for the Cromemco.

4.4 FILING SYSTEM

The Filing System provides for storage of users procedures and
retrieval of procedures for execution or display. Procedures are
accessed individually on user defined name and within each procedure
each statement can be accessed individually.

The store is divided conceptually into temporary and permanent store
areas. Temporary store is used as a dynamic workarea which is
existent for the duration of a session and permanent store is used to
retain procedures between sessions. A newly created procedure is
placed in temporary store and will only be made permanent if the user
issues a SAVE command.

The dynamic store is provided by use of a Leicester Polytechnic
implementation of List-Processor - N (4). The basic structure of the
store is a list of procedures and for each procedure there are lists
for source statements and token strings.

5. CONCLUSIONS

As we have stated, RGOLL provides a software environment for our

research activities in interactive raster graphics. Although it
started life as GOLL, a language for a certain class of end-user,
it is now primarily a development tool for our own use.
Our developments are incorporated into RGOLL in one of two ways.
Either a primitive graphics routine is written for the micro-computer
and the grammar of RGOLL extended to provide a corresponding primitive
command or an RGOLL procedure is defined to effect the operation. In
this way a unified system is maintained which is dynamic but always
upwards compatible.

The implementation of languages for end-users is also quite feasible
in RGOLL. Where these require extentions to the non-graphics
primitives of the language we may introduce them in a similar way to
in the introduction of non primitive graphics commands, except that
their interpretation would take place in the B6700.

APPENDIX

The syntax for both GOLL and RGOLL is defined below using a modified
BNF notation. The definition is an abstracted and hopefully more
understandable version of the grammar used as input to the Synics
Translator system. This definition shows all valid statements and
excludes syntax error detection and semantic directives for
generating output.

```
<Line> = <comment-line>|<goll-statement>
<goll-statement> = <utility-statement>|<definition-statement>|
                   <executable-statement>
<utility-statement> = 'SAVE'<procedure-name> |'FORGET'<procedure-name>|
                      'LIST' 'DIRECTORY'| 'PRINT' 'DIRECTORY'|
                      'LIST'<procedure-name>|'PRINT'<procedure-name>|
                      'END'
<definition-statement> = 'TO'<procedure-name><TO-parameter-list>|
                         'DONE'
<executable-statement> = <conditional-part><executable-part>|
                         <executable-part>
<conditional-part> = 'IF'<exp><relational-op><exp>
<executable-part> = <graph-statement>|<assignment-statement>|
                    <call-statement>
<graph-statement> = 'REMEMBER'<identifier><identifier>|'CURSOR''MODE'|
                    'FILL'|'SHRINK'|'EXPAND'|'INVERT'<digit>|
                    'SAVE''SHAPE'<digit>|'DEPOSIT'<digit>| 'INVERT'|
                    'SAVE''SHAPE'|'DEPOSIT'|'MOVE'<exp>|'DRAW'<exp> |
                    'TURN''CLOCKWISE'<exp>|'TURN''ANTICLOCKWISE'<exp>|
                    'TURN''C'<exp>|'TURN''A'<exp>|'CLEAR'|'ORIGIN'
<assignment-statement> = 'LET'<identifier> '=' <exp>
<call-statement> = <procedure-name><call-parameter-list>
<TO-parameter-list> = [<identifier>]₀⁶
<call-parameter-list> = [<exp>]₀⁶
<exp> = <unary-unit><arithmetic-operator><unary-unit>|<unary-unit>
```

```
<unary-unit> = '+'<variable>|'-'<variable>|<variable>
<arithmetic-operator> = '+'|'-'|'*'|'/'
<relational-op> = 'EQUALS'|'NOT''EQUALS'|'NOT''EQUAL'|'LESS'|
                  'NOT''LESS'|'GREATER'|'NOT''GREATER'
<procedure-name> = <identifier>
<variable> = <identifier>|<constant>
<identifier> = <letter>[<letter>|<digit>]⁵₀
```

$$<constant> = [<digit>]_1^4$$

REFERENCES

(1) A. Bowdin, E.A. Edmonds, A. Schappo.
    GOLL: A simple graphics language
    Man-Computer Interaction Research Group Report No. 31
    Leicester Polytechnic 1980.

(2) C.D. McArthur.
    LOGO: USER GUIDE AND REFERENCE MANUAL
    Bionics Research Reports: No. 14
    Bionics Research Laboratory
    School of Artificial Intelligence
    University of Edinburgh.

(3) E.A. Edmonds, S. Guest.
    SYNICS: A Fortran subroutine package for translation
    Man-Computer Interaction Research Group Report No. 6
    Leicester Polytechnic 1978.

(4) D.W. Dray.
    Dynamic storage for Fortran programs
    Sig plan Notices. pp. 2-10. Sept. 1974.

(5) E.A. Edmonds, S.A.R. Scrivener, L.A. Thomas.
    Improving image generation and structuring using Raster Graphics.
    Proceedings CAD 78
    Brighton 14-16 March 1978 pp. 223-229.

(6) E.A. Edmonds, A. Schappo, S.A.R. Scrivener.
    Graphics without data structures
    Proceedings CAD 80
    Brighton 31 March - 2 April 1980 pp. 138-145.

(7) The Colour Raster Graphics System
    Man-Computer Interaction Research Group Report No. 34
    Leicester Polytechnic 1981.

(8) S.A.R. Scrivener, E.A. Edmonds.
    Pictorial Properties in Raster Graphics: Classification and Use.
    Proceedings COMPUTER GRAPHICS 80
    Brighton 13-15 August 1980 pp. 423-433.

Choose Your Own COBOL

J. M. Triance and P. J. Layzell

Computation Department, University of Manchester,
Institute of Science and Technology, UK

A great deal of effort is expended by CODASYL and ANSI to improve COBOL. This effort has been directed mainly to responding to the needs of the times (e.g. structured programming and screen handling) and improving the portability of COBOL. In pursuing these worthwhile goals the assumption has been made that it is possible to produce a single programming language to satisfy the needs of all COBOL users.

This paper

- demonstrates the invalidity of this assumption

- establishes the actual language requirements of the individual user

- investigates the available methods of satisfying these requirements.

1. THE CURRENT STATE OF COBOL VARIABILITY

A study of programs written in COBOL reveals that they are in fact
written in different dialects of COBOL. The variations are introduced
at four levels:

the standard permits considerable variation. ANS74 COBOL [1]
recognises more than 100,000 versions of Standard COBOL. In addition
to this the implementor is permitted to extend the language and is
required to fill in some gaps left in the specfications. This is
discussed at length elsewhere [2].

the implementor takes full advantage of the freedom offered by the
Standard and sometimes helps himself to more freedom. A recent survey
of mainframe compilers [3] reveals that only 11% of the Procedure
Division formats had the same syntax in all ten compilers investigated.

the user frequently makes further variations by banning some features
and adding others (often with the help of a pre-processor). The
1980/81 International Directory of Software [4] reveals 91 different
COBOL pre-processors in use in more than 8000 installations. A
survey of UK COBOL Users [5] revealed that 43% of them were using at
least one pre-processor.

the programmer usually uses a restricted subset of the language
available: avoiding features which he/she has not learned or which
have given trouble at some time in the past. Many programmers also
have their own set of rules for such things as indentation and naming
conventions (in the cases where these are not rigorously controlled
by the installations).

Thus the COBOL language used by the programmer is not pure Standard
COBOL. It is not even the COBOL language provided by the compiler
supplier. It is the language supported by the compiler with some
extensions and some restrictions. Some of these variations are
historical accidents which could be removed by a well designed
rigorously enforced Standard. Others result from personal preferences
and perhaps should be removed for the sake of conformity within an
installation.

Other variations can however be justified because they result from

- the applications area

- the computer hardware/software used

- the programming techniques used.

Some examples of variations in COBOL are

- different naming conventions: while most installations encourage meaningful data-names one large installation is known to use precisely 6 characters for all data-names.

- report writer: in the user survey [5], of the users commenting on the use of the report writer, one-third said that their compilers did not support it but they want it, whilst the remaining two-thirds have the facility, but never use it.

- nested IF's: the user survey revealed that some users ban nested IF's while others regard them as essential for well structured programs.

In addition to the preferences for and against features which are part of the Standard there is a requirement for features which are specific to applications. Because it cannot easily be fulfilled with the software currently available users often fail to recognise this requirement.

Imagine if specialists such as doctors, plumbers and computer professionals were required to speak in the subset of English which is in everyday use. They would not be able to use terms such as stethoscope, compression joint or virtual store. Instead they would have to give a usually lengthy description which was understandable to the layman, even when they were talking to fellow professionals. This is what COBOL requires of its users. The language cannot readily be extended with accounting, banking or statistical processing terms.

Thus the requirements for COBOL vary, so also do the implementations of COBOL. However, little effort is made to match the users' requirements with the various implementations. Most users are expected to make do with the version of COBOL available on their machine: no more, no less. We would however be appalled if our computer supplier offered us only a standard hardware configuration. We expect to be able to choose the amount of store and the peripherals we attach - we even expect to attach peripherals from other suppliers. Why should not we likewise be able to configure the language we use?

While we wait for the compiler supplier to offer us this facility there are a number of ways in which we can do our own enhancing. Restrictions on COBOL can be enforced manually or by pre-processors and extensions can be supported by translating them into COBOL which is acceptable to the compiler.

2.   THE USERS' REQUIREMENTS

Before investigating the various approaches to language enhancement we will analyse the users' requirements.

The User Survey [5] identifies the following categories of language enhancement.

2.1 Shorthand

This is the use of a string of characters (which is not valid COBOL text) in place of a longer string of characters (which is valid COBOL text). e.g. CSR in place of COMPUTATIONAL SYNCHRONIZED RIGHT.

Sometimes the meaning of the orignal string depends on the context in which it appears.

2.2 Local Extensions

An example of this category is the INITIALIZE statement which is to be introduced in the next Standard [11]. It can be used to initalise all numeric items to zero and alphanumeric items to spaces within a specified group item. Thus for the following table:

```
1     BRAND-TABLE.
3     BRAND-ITEM              OCCURS 20.
  5   BRAND-NAME  PIC X(15).
  5   BRAND-SALES PIC 9(5).
```

the following statement

```
    INITIALIZE BRAND-TABLE
```

is equivalent to the following Standard COBOL

```
1     BRAND-NO    PIC 99.
      .
      .
      .
    MOVE 1 TO BRAND-NO.
INITIALISE-BRAND-TABLE.
    IF BRAND-NO NOT > 20
      MOVE SPACES TO BRAND-NAME (BRAND-NO)
      MOVE ZERO TO BRAND-SALES (BRAND-NO)
      ADD 1 TO BRAND-NO
      GO TO INITIALISE-BRAND-TABLE.
```

This differs from shorthand in that

- the extension contains variable information (the identifier BRAND-TABLE)

- the action of the extension depends on coding elsewhere in the program (the definition of BRAND-TABLE)

- the equivalent COBOL will not necessarily all appear in the same position in the program as the extension (the définition of BRAND-NO appears in the Working Storage Section).

2.3 Structured Programming

The main enhancements in this category are
- a terminator, such as END-IF, for conditional statements
- a multi-branch (case type) statement
- an in-line looping construct

These differ from local extensions in that each extension consists of
two or more parts (e.g. IF with the corresponding END-IF) separated
by an arbitrarily long piece of COBOL text. The situation is
complicated by the fact that the COBOL text may contain other
extensions of the same type (e.g. a nested IF).

2.4 Major New Features

These consist of a set of interrelated extensions. In some cases they
depend on features specified outside the program. The main examples
quoted in the User Survey are:
- database
- telecommunications
- report writer
- data validation

2.5 Installation Standards

These have the effect of reducing the freedom of the programmer by
imposing additional rules. Examples in the survey are:

- program layout rules
- naming conventions
- the banning of certain features (such as GO TO, ALTER and the
  CORRESPONDING option)

The program layout rules can only be enforced by a process which can
detect the position of each item on a line and remember information
about the layout of the previous line.

Naming conventions require the ability of the enforcing process to
recognise different categories of word and the context in which they
appear.

When banning features there is a requirement to issue diagnostic
messages. In simple cases like GO TO the recognition is straightforward. In other cases it is necessary to check the context or
study other parts of the program before deciding whether a piece of
code should be banned. Examples involving these problems are the
limiting of IF Statements to three levels of nesting and permitting
only one EXIT PROGRAM in a subprogram.

3. CRITERIA FOR LANGUAGE ENHANCEMENT

The enhancements discussed in the previous section can be implemented by a variety of mechanisms. This section establishes a set of criteria to help judge the suitability of these mechanisms: the criteria are

<u>High level support</u>: the enhancement should be supported to the same level as that provided by a good compiler. This includes reliability, full syntax checking and comprehensive error reporting and recovery.

<u>Portability</u>: the use of enhancements should not reduce the portability of the programs in which they are used. Portability is usually maintained by translating any extensions into Standard COBOL and by writing any enhancement supporting software in COBOL.

<u>Readable and Writable Syntax</u>: the mechanism should permit the most appropriate syntax for any extension. In particular long or obscure syntax should not be forced upon the user.

4. METHODS OF ENHANCEMENT

Three distinct approaches can be identified for the enhancement of COBOL by the user:

Use COBOL Itself

CALL can be used to execute a subroutine which performs the function of a new feature. COPY and the new REPLACE statement can be used to substitiute one piece of the COBOL source text by another.

Use People

Programs can be written in extended COBOL and then translated by hand into COBOL acceptable to the compiler. This process is fairly common with Program Design Languages (such as pseudo code or schematic logic).

Use Pre-Processors

With this approach programs written in extended COBOL are submitted to a pre-processor which translates them into COBOL acceptable to the compiler.

The pre-processors can be classified as

- <u>off the shelf</u>: a pre-processor supporting a pre-specified set of features

- <u>home made</u>: if a suitable pre-processor does not exist or is too expensive users can write their own

- programmable: the pre-processor can be programmed to support a variety of features

- made to measure: users state their requirements and are supplied with a pre-processor which meets them.

So far in this section we have concentrated on extensions to COBOL. Pre-processors and people can also be used for restricting the COBOL used. CALL, COPY & REPLACE are unsuitable for this purpose.

We will now look at each of these approaches and investigate their suitability for each type of enhancement.

5. USING COBOL TO ENHANCE ITSELF

The advantage of using COBOL features (CALL, COPY & REPLACE) to enhance COBOL are

- immediate availability

- no extra expenditure

- nothing new to learn

- the features are Standard (and therefore portable)

5.1 CALL

The CALL statement is used widely to extend COBOL although the fact that it is used for this purpose is often not recognised by the user. It is used for example for accessing data bases, communicating with remote devices, converting the formats of dates and performing tax calculations.

The point can best be demonstrated by using a CALL statement for a feature which already exists in most compilers. Take the following INSPECT statement:

```
INSPECT QUANTITY
   REPLACING LEADING SPECES BY ZEROS
```

When using a compiler which did not support INSPECT this statement could be implemented with a CALL "INSPECT" statement; e.g.

```
    MOVE 20 TO LENGTH-OF-ITEM
    MOVE "LEADING" TO INSPECT-MODE
    MOVE "NULL" TO DELIMIT-MODE
*   NO DELIMITER REQUIRED
    CALL "INSPECT" USING QUANTITY, LENGTH-OF-ITEM, SPACE-ITEM,
           ZERO-ITEM, INSPECT-MODE, DELIMIT-MODE,
```

As far as the programmer, who uses pre-written subroutines, is concerned, each CALL to a different subroutine is a different type of Procedure Division Statement. It has a format: e.g.

    <u>CALL</u> "INSPECT" <u>USING</u> identifier-1, identifier-2, identifier-3, identifier-4, identifier-5, identifier-6

It has syntax rules (in the above example the size and USAGE of the data items referenced by identifier-1, etc). There is also a description of its function and effect. So to the COBOL programmer CALL "INSPECT" is just another statement like ADD or MOVE. It is a different statement from CALL "CALCULATE-PAYE" because it has a different format and a completely different function, effect and set of syntax rules.

Thus CALL can be used as a means of extending the set of Procedure Division statements but it suffers from the following defects

- it is unreadable (in the above example, which was made as self-documenting as possible, it is not clear which item is being inspected, which one is replacing and which is being replaced)

- it cannot reference files, conditions, literals or imperative statements as parameters

- all parameters have to be specified even when some are irrelevant to a particular call (e.g. DELIMIT-MODE in the above example)

- there is minimal compile time checking of parameters (e.g. the compiler will not check that QUANTITY is USAGE DISPLAY)

- each parameter must have the same definition for each CALL statement referencing the subroutine (whereas in the INSPECT statement QUANTITY, for example, may be any length).

The major strength of CALL is that the called subroutine has at its disposal the full power of COBOL and, in some machines, other languages. This allows CALL to support local extensions and major new features albeit in a manner which is somewhat hostile to the COBOL programmer. It is not suitable for the other classes of enhancement.

5.2 COPY

COPY can be used to transfer lines of text into a COBOL program. Thus you can write

    COPY ACCOUNTS-RECORD

to transfer the whole record definition (of ACCOUNTS-RECORD) into the program or

```
COPY PRINT-ROUTINE
```

to transfer a whole routine (PRINT-ROUNTINE) into the program.

It can thus be used as a shorthand method of specifying, often very
large, pieces of source text.

The REPLACING option allows copy to be used for implementing local
extensions. For example the INSPECT Statement could be coded with
dummy identifiers (INSPECTED-ITEM, REPLACED-STRING, etc) and could
be copied in as follows

```
COPY INSPECT-ROUTINE
     REPLACING = = INSPECTED-ITEM = =    BY = = QUANTITY = =
               = = ITEM-LENGTH = =       BY = = 20 = =
               = = REPLACED-STRING = =   BY = = SPACES = =
               = = REPLACING STRING = =  BY = = ZEROS = =
               = = INSPECT MODE = =      BY = = "LEADING" = =
               = = DELIMIT-MODE = =      BY = = "NULL" = =
```

This is somewhat long-winded but is moderately readable once you
understand the REPLACING phrase.

COPY can thus be used for shorthand and local extensions. It is
unsuitable for structured programming, major new features and some
local extensions because of the following limitations.

- COPY's cannot be nested in most implementations

- the copied text all appears in the position in the program of the
   COPY statement (it is thus unsuitable for the INITIALIZE statement
   discussed earlier)

- the COPYING process is unintelligent (thus no conditional
   replacement is possible and COPY's cannot communicate with each
   other).

5.3 REPLACE

In the next standard [11] the replacement which is confined to copied
text can be applied to the whole program using the REPLACE statement.

For example the following REPLACE statement could be placed at the
start of the Data Division:

```
REPLACE = = CSR = =
    BY  = = COMPUTATIONAL SYNCHRONIZED RIGHT = =
```

This would cause all instances of CSR to be replaced by COMPUTATIONAL
SYNCHRONIZED RIGHT. Each replacement may be, activated and de-

activated at any point in the source program.

REPLACE is designed for shorthand and obviously fulfils that purpose.

5.4 Using People

The advantage of using people to translate or check enhancements to COBOL is that they are extremely flexible. They can, at short notice, support extremely involved changes to the language being used. The fatal flaw is that in general they are totally unreliable. They can be rather slow and expensive. For these reasons any enhancements which can be formalised are best automated.

Currently people are used reasonably extensively for

- translating structured programs (pseudo code, schematic logic, etc) into COBOL

- enforcing standards (the user survey [5] revealed that 76% of installations used manual methods of enforcement)

- translating local extensions into COBOL (e.g. data conversion, and check digit calculations)

- translating major features into COBOL (e.g. data validation, report writing)

5.5 Using Pre-Processors

The methods of enhancing COBOL discussed so far are used, to a large extent, for the casual enhancement of COBOL. Where installations have deliberately set out to provide an enhanced   language they have normally used pre-processors.

Pre-processors have the advantage that they can effectively cope with most extensions. Their main disadvantages are:

- they cost money

- they need to be supported (some more than others)

- the programmer is normally presented with two error listings (one from the pre-processor and one from the compiler)

- COBOL COPY cannot be freely used (but for this reason some pre-processors provide an equivalent facility)

- they are of variable quality (reference [6] gives some criteria for a good pre-processor)

- they consume machine time (though, by offering a better verion of
  COBOL, fewer compilations may in practice be needed)

5.6 Off the Shelf Pre-Processors

Off the shelf pre-processors exist for a great variety of COBOL
enhancements convering all the categories identified: shorthand, local
extensions, structured programming, major new features (such as
database, telecommunications, report writer, data validation and
debugging) and installation standards.

It they are well designed they can be effective and efficient. The
problems are

- each one is usually only supported on a restricted range of machines

- they might be incompatible with each other (the output from one is
  not acceptable to another)

- it is unlikely that the complete requirements of an installation
  can be met by any pre-processor (or set of compatible pre-
  processors).

5.7 Home Made Pre-Processors

There are two circumstances in which this approach might be considered.
One is if suitable pre-processors are not already in existence and the
other is if they do exist but are judged to be too expensive.

The advantage of a home made pre-processor is that it can be designed
to meet the precise requirements of the user. The disadvantages are
that, to some extent, the user is getting involved in program
language design and compiler writing both of which require special
expertise.

An indication of how difficult it is to extend a language as complex
as COBOL is the fact that CODASYL with some of the best COBOL brains
in the world at its disposal still on occasions produces unworkable
syntax.

Except for very straightforward enhancements, writing a pre-processor
is a difficult task involving lexical analysis, some syntax checking
and code generation. There are many examples of programmers under-
estimating the complexity of this task and as a result producing
unusable pre-processors. Some guidelines for intending authors of a
pre-processor are given in reference 6.

If the job is taken seriously then it is of course possible to produce
a satisfactory pre-processor. For anything more complicated than a
shorthand expander it is likely, however, to be appreciably more
expensive than buying an off the shelf pre-processor. It can also be

very difficult to change the pre-processor later to handle further
enhancements to COBOL even if these are apparently independent of the
features originally supported by the pre-processor.

5.8 Programmable Pre-Processors

An alternative method for users to meet their own requirements without
writing a complete pre-processor is to use a programmable pre-
processor. These are normally based on macros. Such pre-processors
will do the lexical analysis, will do some syntax checking and will
assist with the code generation.

There are two COBOL oriented macro pre-processors in common use -
Cobra and MetaCOBOL. Cobra [7] was developed by Plessey and is
currently marketed by Dataskil for use on ICL equipment. MetaCOBOL
[8] is an Applied Data Research (ADR) product for use on IBM
equipment. Their limitation to one make of computer will make them
unsuitable for many users although Cobra, since it is written in
COBOL, is capable of being transferred to other ranges of computer.

It is of course, possible to use a language independent macro
processor but these suffer from the severe disadvantage of not
understanding COBOL. They will not, for example, automatically
handle COBOL's continuation conventions or understand the rules of
area A and area B. With a sufficiently powerful macro processor this
knowledge could, with some difficulty, be programmed in. Alternatively, a fairly simple pre-processor could be used to take a standard
COBOL program and reformat it to make it acceptable to the macro
processor. Many such macro processors are totally unsuitable
because they cannot handle COBOL-like statements. One which can is
ML/1 [9] which is used widely (for other applications) and is designed
to be portable. It is available from its author Professor Peter
Brown, at the University of Kent.

All macro processors work on the principle of expressing each desired
enhancement as an independent routine (known as a macro). Each macro
states the format of the enhancement (the prototype), the text
(generated text) which is to replace each instance of the enhancement
in the source, and in the less simple cases, conditional code
generation. Beyond that the various macro processors differ
significantly.

The principle can be illustrated with a simple extension. Let us
assume that the single destination ADD (ADD A TO B) is already
supported by COBOL and we wish to support ADD with two destinations:

$$\underline{ADD} \left\{ \begin{array}{l} \text{identifier-1} \\ \text{literal} \end{array} \right\} \underline{TO}\ \text{identifier-2 identifier-3}$$

The way it will be supported is to recognise statements such as

```
ADD SALES TO DAY-TOTAL WEEK-TOTAL
```

and replace them by single destination ADD's. In this case

```
ADD SALES TO DAY-TOTAL
ADD SALES TO WEEK-TOTAL
```

When using macros we would specify a prototype corresponding to the format of the two-destination ADD. In MetaCOBOL we would express it:

```
ADD   &1(S, L)  TO   &2(S)   &3(S)
```

The arguments (i.e. the variable information) are represented by &1, &2 etc. S following an argument indicates that the argument may be a subscripted qualified data-name (i.e. an identifier), L indicates that it may be a literal.

The generated text is expressed by writing the constant text interspersed with arguments represented by &1, &2 etc:

```
ADD   &1  TO  &2
ADD   &1  TO  &3
```

The full macro definition in MetaCOBOL is:

```
SP  ADD   &1(S, L)  TO   &2(S)   &3(S):
      ADD  &1  TO  &2
      ADD  &1  TO  &3
```

In addition to the prototype and the generated text this macro definition contains

S to indicate String Macro (the string macros are the most powerful of three types of macro supported by MetaCOBOL),

P to indicate that this extension occurs only in the Procedure Division

: to terminate the prototype

It is not always possible to specify the prototype with such precision.

In MetaCOBOL more involved formats are handled by specifying as the prototype the first part of the format and reading the rest of the format. The read instruction and any other macro statements needed are interspersed with the generated text.

In ML/1 all the text between two delimiters is passed across as a single argument leaving the macro writer to do any validation and analysis of the arguments.

For more complicated macros it is necessary to specify instructions
which will be executed at macro execution time. COBOL programmers
will find this set of instructions rather limited for all three macro
processors under discussion. ADR has however recently enhanced the
MetaCOBOL macro writing language with a set of structured programming
constructs.

When used for this very specific application (the enhancement of COBOL)
ML/1 is obviously at a severe disadvantage. In addition to the
problems already mentioned ML/1 has no facilities for distributing
generated text to different parts of a COBOL program (such as Working
Storage items generated in support of a new Procedure Division feature).
On the other hand, Cobra and MetaCOBOL both have a variety of features
designed specifically for the COBOL context - MetaCOBOL for example
makes available to the macro all the attributes of the data items in
the program (the PICTURE, USAGE, etc.).

In its favour, ML/1 does automatically handle nested contructs (e.g.
nested IF's) which are more cumbersome to handle in Cobra and Meta-
COBOL.

The big advantage of the macro processors is that straightforward
enhancements can be supported very easily. Furthermore the
enhancements can be implemented independently. This offers great
benefits when a wide variety of langauge enhancements are required.
The independence can however cause problems when implementing a set of
closely related macros, but the macro schemes each have means of
communicating between macros which if used carefully do not impinge
unduly on the independence of other macros.

The COBOL oriented macro processors are likely to be the most
convenient method for users to enhance COBOL for themselves. ML/1 has
the advantage of availability, cheapness and its suitability for other
applications but for COBOL enhancement it compares unfavourably with
the COBOL oriented macro processors.

5.9 Made to Measure Pre-Processors

An alternative method of getting the precise version of COBOL required
is to have a "made to measure" pre-processor produced by a software
house. Three companies in the U.K. offer this service (all aimed
primarily at ICL users). They are:

Cobra Systems and Programming - based on the Cobra Macro Processor

Forward Computing - based on their MEL Macro Processor

S+PC - based on the Philtr-2 Pre-Processor

This approach is likely to be fairly expensive for a user whose
requirements differ from other users. It does however minimise the

the effort required of the user.

5.10 Summary

In this section we will attempt to summarise the preceding discussion
by means of two tables. Due to the diversity of the discussion these
tables should only be interpreted by reference to the remainder of
the paper. Table 1 gives a subjective assessment of the suitability
of the various approaches for each category of enhancement.

Approach	Category of Enhancement				
	Shorthand	Local Extns	S.P.	Major Features	Inst. Standards
CALL	-	*	-	*	-
COPY	**	*	-	-	-
REPLACE	***	-	-	-	-
Manual	*	*	*	*	*
Off-the-Shelf Pre-Processor	**	**	**	**	**
Home-Made Pre-Processor	**	**	**	**	**
Cobra	***	***	***	**	***
MetaCOBOL	***	***	***	**	***
ML/1	***	**	***	*	*
Made to Measure Pre-Processor	***	***	***	***	***

Table 1. Assessment of Various Approaches

Key: - totally unsuitable
       * not very suitable
      ** fairly suitable
     *** well suited

Local Extns   -   Local Extension
S.P.   -   Structured Programming
Inst. Standards -   Installation Standards

The main factors in these ratings are summarised in table 2

Approach	For	Against
CALL/COPY/REPLACE	availability, no software costs, nothing new to learn, portability	limited capabilities, poor readability and writability
Manual	extremely flexible, no software costs	high people cost, unreliable
Pre-Processors (general)	can support most desired enhancements	two source and error listings, added run time for compilations
Off the shelf Pre-Processors	cheapest and possibly most reliable form of pre-processors	restricted availability, unlikely to precisely match users requirements
Home Made Pre-Processor	flexible, can write in any language	major undertaking for user, many pitfalls
Programmable	very flexible, easier for user than "home made" approach	restricted availablity - only 2 COBOL oriented ones, programming language is limited, significant undertaking for user, danger of proliferation of COBOL dialects
Made to measure	precise match of requirements possible, least effort to user	high software costs

Table 2. Main factors

5.11 Conclusion

There is appreciable disatisfaction amongst users with the versions of
COBOL supported by their compilers. Many methods exist for users to
enhance their version of COBOL. Of these pre-processors represent
the only approach which can adequately cope with all the categories of
enhancement identified in the paper.

For users with standard requirements an off the shelf pre-processor
offers the best solution. For those with more specialist needs a
programmable or a made to measure pre-processor should be considered.

5.12 The Way Ahead

COBOL is not one language but a family of languages. Despite much
lip-service to standarisation many users prefer to deviate from the
Standard. Indeed many of the deviations are totally justified and
improvement to the Standard and the Standardisation process cannot
totally remove the need for this deviation.

There is a strong case for recognising this need and providing a
standard means of implementing variations in the COBOL language. This
could give the users the versions of COBOL they want without requiring
them to sacrifice portability.

This requirement has been recognised by the British Computer Society's
COBOL Specialist Group who have designed the COBOL Language
Enhancement Facility (CLEF) [10]. This has the flexibility of the
macro pre-processors while providing an improved language for the
specification of the enhancements.

The hope is that CLEF will become part of the Standard COBOL
specifications and thus become available to COBOL users.

5.13 Acknowledgements

Thanks are due to members of the BCS CLEF Working Party for their
valuable comments on the first draft of this paper. The paper was
produced as part of the UMIST "User Configuration of COBOL Compilers"
project which is sponsored by the Science Research Council.

REFERENCES

[1]   ANSI (1974), American National Standard Programming Language
      COBOL X3 .23-1974, American National Standards Institute.

[2]   TRIANCE, J.M. (1978), A Study of COBOL Portability,
      Computer Journal, Volume 21, Number 5.

[3]   TRIANCE, J.M. (1980), A Study of Mainframe COBOL Compiler
      Features, National Computing Centre (unpublished)

[4]   CUYB (1980), International Directory of Software 1980-1981,
      CUYB Publications Ltd.

[5]   LAYZELL, P.J. (1980), A Summary of Results of the BCS COBOL
      Users Questionnaire, Computation Department Report 257, UMIST.

[6]   TRIANCE, J.M. (1980), Structured Programming in COBOL - the
      Current Options, Computer Journal, Volume 23, Number 3.

[7]   ICL DATASKIL LIMITED (1974), 2900 COBRA Users Manual.

[8] ADR (1977), Macro Writing for the MetaCOBOL Specialist, SM5G-02-00, Princeton, New Jersey.

[9] BROWN, P.J. (1967), The ML/1 Macro Processor, Comm. ACM, Volume 10, Number 10.

[10] LAYZELL, P.J. (1980), CLEF Journal of Development, Computation Department Report 258, UMIST.

[11] ANSI (1981), Draft Proposed Reised X3.23 American National Standard Programming Language COBOL, American National Standards Institute.

A Portable PASCAL Compiler
for Multiple Target Computers

Bernard Huc

Cap Sogeti Logiciel,
Centre Technique de Grenoble,
Grenoble, France

A large amount of efforts are actually done for portability and realiability of the software. A way to guarantee portability is the use of a high level language as Pascal. The portability would be better if the same compiler is used for all the computers. Here is described a portable compiler for multiple target computers.
This compiler uses a structured description of each target computer and is written in Pascal (70%) and CPL1 (20%).

1.   IMPLEMENTED LANGUAGE

The implemented language is the PASCAL language defined by Nyklaus
Wirth (1). It had been modified according to the International
Standard (2) actually defined by the I.S.O.

Some extensions have been defined :
- Separate compilations
- Use of direct access files
- Initialization of global variables
- Use of a SUBSTR function, allowing manipulation of substrings.

Those extensions (except the last one) have been designed according
to the SOL project specifications (3). The choosen characters set is
the ASCII set.

An option of the compiler allows to check the conformance of the user
program with the International Standard.

2.   COMPILER ARCHITECTURE

The compiler has been designed to work in two passes

This first pass performs the lexicographic, syntaxic and semantic
analyses and the translation of the Pascal program into the assembly
language of the target computer.

The compiler, allowing generation of code for multiple target computers,
needs two kind of parameters : static and dynamic parameters.
a) Static parameters : those parameters describe the target computer
   and are used by both passes of the compiler.
b) Dynamic parameters : those parameters describe for each instruction
   of the intermediate language the algorithm used to produce an
   assembly language sequence.

Those parameters are included in a file associated to each target
computer. This file is used to initialize the compiler data before
the first pass and to allow the final generation before the second
pass.

The portability and the reliability of the compiler is guaranted by
the languages used in its development. The first pass is fully written
in Pascal and is the same for every host and every target computer.
(This stability implies the portability of the compiled program
according to the accepted language.) The second pass and the background
of the compiler are written in CPL1 (4) except for some sparse
critical parts which are written in the assembly language of the host
computer in order to optimize the compilation time.

It is interesting to note that the CPL1 compiler use the same
generation technics as the Pascal one. It is so obvious that some parts
of the two compilers are identical :
- the description file
- the second pass
- a part of the background

3.   TARGET COMPUTER STATIC DESCRIPTION

The first part of the parameters file gives to the compiler a
description of the target computer. The given parameters are of three
kinds :
- data description
- registers description
- assembly language caracteristics.

a) Data description
   Those informations give the description of the computer data (size
   of a word in bytes, size of a byte in bits, ...) and the description
   of the specific pascal data (size of an integer, size of a real,
   size of a Pascal pointer, size needed to code a file description,..)
b) Registers description
   For each register, the following informations are obtained from the
   file :
   . assembly name
   . functions (index, arithmetic,...)
   . size and boundary.
   On an other hand, a table describing the interactions between
   registers is produced for the first pass. This table will be used
   in the registers allocation to avoid conflicts for the registers
   usable for multiple functions (e.g. arithmetic and index, binary
   and floatting point,...).
c) Assembly language caracteristics
   The compiler needs to know some caracteristics of the assembly
   language as :
   . largest imediate constant
   . comment character
   . key words (if any)
   . size of the identifiers
   . etc.

Most of those informations are used by the first pass, the function
of the second pass being only to translate the instructions of the
intermediate language, using the algorithms given by the dynamic
parameters.

4. TARGET COMPUTER DYNAMIC DESCRIPTION

The translation, in the second pass, works by macro-generation. Each instruction of the intermediate language is a macro call. In the parameters file a macro definition is given for each kind of instruction. Those macro definitions are precompiled and ready to be used by the second pass. The compilation of those macros sets and their development are done using a processor called MACOMP (5).

5. THE INTERMEDIATE LANGUAGE

The Intermediate Language (IL) has been designed in order to make the second pass computer-independant. For this purpose the IL is very close to an assembly language and make easier the macro generation by avoiding the second pass to know the target computer organisation. On an other hand the IL has no structured instruction like "loop" or "case" ; all the structured Pascal instructions are translated using transfers and comparisons.

Each instruction of the IL is a macro call, composed of the macro name which gives its function and of a list of parameters. The number of parameters depends on the macro name.

The macro calls are classified into :
- name declarations
- space allocation
- memory initialization
- moves between register on memory
- moves in memory
- arithmetic operations
- boolean operations
- transfer instructions
- address computing
- conversions
- special sequence generations (prolog, epilog, etc..)

For the Pascal procedures, the calling, entry and return sequences are carried out using operators. Those operators are computer dependant and are integrated in the run-times package (cf §7).

The parameters of the macro have always the same syntax :
          L,ØP,T
where   L   is the length in bytes of the item
          ØP   is the description of the item
          T   is a character giving the class of the item.

The items handled by the IL are :
- registers   Type R
- numerics   Type N
- labels   Type L
- variables   others types

The item "Variables" is used for :
- the static variables
- the non-numeric Pascal contents which are generated with an internal
  assembly name
- the internal items generated by the compiler
- the Pascal local variables (those variables being rerenced via pointer
  registers or   static pointers).

The type of the variable indicates its addressing mode :
- static
- external
- based by a pointer register
- based by a static pointer
- based by an external pointer

The description field of the item (ØP) is used to complete the
addressing mode. The information which can occurs are :
- assembly name of the variable, the pointer or the register
- bytes displacement to be added
- index register to be used.

```
(1)   4,03,R
(2)   4,+27,N
(3)   4,Z.127,L
(4)   4,VALUE,S
(5)   12,(02,4,+8,N),A
(6)   8,(BASE,4,06,R,18),B
```

Fig.1 - Examples of "Variables"

(1)   REGISTER ## 3
(2)   NUMERIC CONSTANT 27
(3)   LABEL Z.127
(4)   STATIC VARIABLE VALUE (SIZE=4 BYTES)
(5)   ITEM BASED WITH POINTER REGISTER ## 2 AND WITH DISPLACEMENT
                                            8 BYTES
      (SIZE = 12 BYTES)
      ADDRESS = (R02) + 8
(6)   ITEM BASED WITH A STATIC POINTER, WITH A DISPLACEMENT OF 18 BYTES
      AND MODIFIED BY THE INDEX REGISTER ## 6 (SIZE + 8 BYTES)
      ADDRESS = (BASE) + 18 + (R06)

```
(1)   C151      4,VALUE,E,REF
(2)   C154      4,+2,N,4,F1F2F3F0,C
(3)   C154      4,+32,N
(4)   C22       4,03,R,4,(02,4,+88,N),A
(5)   C10       4,Z.123,L
(6)   C51       4,02,R,4,(BASE,4,06,R,18),B
(7)   C213      8,04,R,4,04,R
(8)   C07
(9)   C04       4,Z.123,L
```

Fig.2 - Examples of macro calls

(1) name generation
(2) memory initialization
(3) memory allocation
(4) add a memory item to a register
(5) transfer to a label
(6) load of a pointer register with the address of an item
(7) conversion of an integer register into a floatting point register
(8) epilog of a program
(9) label definition

6.   REGISTERS ALLOCATION

In the first pass, the compiler uses virtual registers classified
into :
- Integer registers
- Pointer registers
- Real registers
- Index registers
- Powerset registers.

Each virtual register is associated to a physical register via the
table obtained from the parameters file. However the powerset registers
are always pseudo registers and the pointer register either real
registers or pseudo registers according to the possibility of the
target computer.

Except for powerset and pointer registers, a same physical register
may tally with more than one virtual register. Those virtual registers
are so handled using allocation and desallocation primitives, working
according to the interaction table obtained from the target computer
static description. In order to generate the macro calls the names
table (cf. §3) is also used.

The handling of two kinds of virtual registers changes from one target
computer to an other :
- the index registers
- the pointer registers.

For the index registers, special macros are used to load and store them
and a special modification field (cf. §5) is used to indicate that a
variable is modified by a saved index registers. This mechanism is
particulary usefull for the computer having only one index register.
However, before using the index loading macro, the first pass has
sometimes to compute an index expression in an integer register ; it
is so obvious that, if it is possible, every integer register must
also be usable as index register to avoid superfluous moves between
registers.

The pointer registers are all physically independant from the others
registers. One of them, used to point the frame associated to the
current procedure, is never altered during the code generation. On
the computer poor in registers, pseudo registers may be used.
It is obvious that all those strategic rules are used only <u>inside</u>
the primitives.

7. IMPLEMENTATION OF A NEW COMPILER

The implementation of a "new" compiler for a new target computer needs
two tools :
- the parameters file
- a set of run times.

The constitution of the parameters file (static and dynamic) can be
performed in about 5 months with one people. However, those parameters
files existing for many computers and used by CPL1 (4) needs only some
slight modifications and are then performed in about 5 weeks.

The run- times writting is done using a "Run-Time Writer's guide".
It can be performed in about 3 months. This short delay is obtained
by the writting of about 50% of the run-times in PASCAL (I/O on text
files, dynamic allocation).

When the compiler needs to be carried on an other computer, some slight
modifications are to be performed in the critical sequences (written
in the assembly language of the host computer) and needs about
one month.

8. FIRST IMPLEMENTATIONS

The first implementation has been done by bootstrapping from a HB68
(MULTICS) (6) on a HB66 (GCOS).

Only the first pass was implemented on the HB68 ; on this computer,
the target computer description was simulated in PASCAL.

In the same time, the second pass and the background, yet existing on
HB66 was modified to accept the output from the HB68 (a file of macro
calls).

The full release on HB66 was obtained by auto-compiling the first
pass on HB68 and by macro-generation on HB66.
A second implementation was then performed on IBM/ØS.

BIBLIOGRAPHY

(1) "The Programming language PASCAL" ETH Zürich (revised report)
     July 1973 - N. WIRTH

(2) ISO DP/7185 (ISO/TC 97/SC 5 N565) (January 1981)

(3) Le Langage de programmation PASCAL - Specifications et mise en
     oeuvre (AFNOR-SOL 1980)

(4) CPL1 - Language Reference Manual - Version 4 (CAP SOGETI LOGICIEL
     Ref. GEN-1002-11) (1978)

(5) Macro language Reference Manual MACOMP X100 (CAP SOGETI LOGICIEL
     Ref. MAC 101-1) (1975)

(6) Presentation of a Pascal compiler under MULTICS (HLSUA Congress
     November 1980) J.P. FAUCHE, B. HUC, J.M. ATHANE

The Electronic Office: a General Introduction

David Firnberg

Managing Director, Urwick Nexos Limited, UK

Computers have been around now for about thirty years and, although most people are aware of them, computers have not had any marked effect on the structure of society or our way of life. Why should the next thirty years be any different?

This presentation argues that there is a discontinuity, and information technology in all its manifestations will have a far more marked effect in the years to come than heretofore. The reasons for this stem both from the nature of computing as it has existed so far, as well as from certain technical, social and economic imperatives that will help to mould the future.

By introducing the mass-produced motor car, Henry Ford started a process which has had ramifications for all facets of the western world. New industries, new geographical distribution, innumerable new jobs, new cultural mixing, all followed. The world thirty or forty years after the Model T is almost unrecognisable when compared with the world thirty or forty years before.

The 'chip' represents mass produced processing power. Up to now computers have been large and expensive, the preserve of substantial organisations, required specialist support and a protected environment. Mass produced processing power is changing all that.

The application can now dominate the technology! Mass produced processing power seeks out mass markets. What sells in a mass market is not technical sophistication but usability.   The products and systems which will sell are those which are easy to use and which users can associate with their needs rather than with the technology. Computing will become buried in a plethora of 'end user' devices, all of which will contain computing, but which relate to their own market place not the technology.

Whilst the inflationary cost of employing people continues upwards, the cost of employing information technology continues to fall at a great rate.   The drive for 'cost effectiveness' must bring about a change in the balance between what people do and what the technology does.

Energy costs, and therefore the cost of moving people, also continue upwards. At the same time, developments in telecommunications are bringing about improvements in the quality and reliability of moving information to people: thus another balance is changing - the balance between moving people and linking them through some telecommunications channel.

The next thirty years will see extraordinary changes in the ways in which information is processed. The impact of this - with its origins in the mass-produced 'chip' - is as difficult for us to anticipate as it would have been for the managers of the 20s to anticipate the manifold implications of mass produced motor cars.

No longer is information technology confined to the processing of the formal structure data in an organisation, it is rapidly invading the casual and informal exchange of information, the telephone conversations, office memos, conferences and meetings. The heart of these systems has moved away from the main frame computer to the communications processor managing the storage, editing and forwarding of the digital representation of all forms of information, voice, image and text as well as data.

The systems using these products are no respecter of organisational boundaries, thus to benefit fully, new policies are needed; policies that transcend the parochial boundaries of existing office services, and which take into account the interactions of information within the organisation as a whole as well as with the outside world. Policies which embrace the training of the people who are going to design these new systems and work with them, and the certainty that at some point of time the various devices are going to have to inter-communicate.

The technology is all around us, what we can already do technically transcends what we, as people, can comprehend, or what we, as people are prepared to accept. The real challenge is to build on information technology in order to make bureaucracies more human, and use technology to enhance the life of each individual.

Rational Office Automation

Clive E. Malpas-Sands

*Manager, Business Administration Group,
A. T. Kearney Limited, UK*

From a background outside the mainstream of equipment manufacturers, systems houses and users this paper is aimed at reflecting on some of the realities behind Office Automation. It aims to propose a more fundamental approach in posing not merely the questions what? and how? but also why? and when? Furthermore, it aims to relate the approach to that of value for money, not from the point of view of the equipment, but from the point of view of improved management and administrative effectiveness. Doing this involves taking a more pragmatic view than that which is frequently propounded to our clients - one indeed that appears initially less enthusiastic, but which, on the basis of research and experience here and in the States is more likely to yield tangible results.

In doing this the paper traces the development of the concept of the automated office, draws a distinction between mechanisation and automation and relates those to differences of perception between management and those selling the equipment and proposes finally a way forward.

HISTORICAL PERSPECTIVE

Since this paper treats office automation it must needs first be defined. Its definition is, in fact, as elusive as the goal it seeks to define. In the late 60's, any use of computers in offices was highly structured, high volume data processing concentrating primarily on producing paper faster than clerks could produce it. Gradually in the early 70's the idea of a paperless office began to take shape. Attention began to be focussed on tasks related to information as opposed to data transfer. At this point, the idea of the computer as a tool to support information management was born. From 1977 on we see the beginnings of the use of DP technology to support the information flow and underlying processes which produce and consume the information.

We may perhaps propose therefore a definition in that office automation is the utilisation of computer based systems to enhance the effectiveness and efficiency of people working in an operational or administration office.

WHAT'S NEW

There are five major ways in which OA is different from commercial data processing:-

1. The interleaving of structured and unstructured activities.

2. The extent and frequency of human intervention.

3. The low volumes of data involved.

4. The high demand for instant availability.

5. The distributed environment.

MECHANISATION OR AUTOMATION

We can see four stages of expansion in OA development:-

1. Initiation.

2. Expansion.

3. Formalisation.

4. Maturity.

In the first phase, with the prime movement toward, for example, word processors, as with the first stage of commercial dp the goal is the more efficient production of paper.

In the second phase, which few companies either here or in the USA have got beyond we see the mechanisation of office activities. Development is oriented toward tasks, the emphasis is on disjointed tools and mechanising devices. Users thus becomes confused between the apparently conflicting demands of word processing, electronic mail, electronic filing, calendar management, etc. Most dangerously of all this process attacks the method of carrying out tasks without considering the possibilities of worker alienation on the one hand or improvement of the whole process on the other.

Our researches show that management needs to be and is more concerned with what needs to be done than with how to do it.

This second phase is analogous in data processing development where largely unrelated independent batch systems with their own independent files were set up.

In the third phase we must start to consider a shift from task to function orientation, from the HOW? to the WHAT?, that incorporates the notion of process. It is at this point that mechanisation gives way to automation and the dichotomy opens between supplier, potential user and buyer.

In the fourth phase, that of maturity, the assimilation of the available technology into the organisation is completed, in much the same way as today telephone, telex, typewriter and photocopier are. It is a phase in which the work is completely redesigned and the available technology not used to do things differently but to do different things.

WHY AUTOMATE

It is here that we find the greatest divergence. Most managements will spend money to save money. In the production, distribution and product development areas it is frequently easier to identify what can be saved by spending where than it is in the amorphous area referred to variously as administration, management, overheads, or offices. Whatever one may think or know about office activities their functions ultimately are:-

.   Coordination
.   Communication
.   Control

These three functions in varying degrees are the prime objectives of all administrative staff. On these basis of our work in the area we have concluded that:-

. They are the areas where managers spend most of their time.

. They offer significant potential for improving managers' effectiveness and providing economies.

. They could, if improved by more efficient and timely communication techniques and technologies, support a broader span of control.

. They are highly automated in the plant, but hardly developed in the administration area.

. Their success is largely dependent on human factors which dictate a personal style which relates to the tools and techniques each manager uses.

. Managers and subordinates do not always agree on the effectiveness and adequacy of their systems.

. The most valuable resource for most managers is their own time.

Whether a company is going to be successful in the market place is less a result of the level of telephone expenses or the efficiency of its typists and clerks than the quality of the relationship its managers have with each other, their subordinates, superordinates and the outside world. The three functions of coordination, communication and control build this relationship.

KEY STEPS FOR SUCCESS IN INTRODUCING OFFICE AUTOMATION

The most important step in successful development of use of office automation is 'having clear objectives'. Whatever the objective (learning, cost analysis, human factors analysis, opportunity creation, cost reduction, etc.), it should be explicitly stated and agreed upon by all involved.

The second key step is involvement of two groups as outlined below:-

1. A top management steering committee should be established for planning and control of office automation as a whole and for coordination of separate projects.

2.   A project team composed of representatives from potential user groups, systems analysts, organisational analysts led by a strong team leader should be established.

This two-level planning approach includes some checks and balances to minimise the 'empire building' and 'tunnel vision' which often occur in data processing and other capital spending projects. It should not restrict the autonomy of departments or project teams to select and develop new applications which they determine to be relevant for their groups. It should advise these groups of the long-range implications of equipment acquisition, provide them with guidelines for equipment comparison and cost justification and help them develop communication protocols to ensure compatibility with appropriate networks.

The third key step is clear functional planning in advance of technological design or selection. Again, the temptation is to listen to the vendors or the press and decide that someone else's solution will work for you.

The fourth key step is the realisation by all involved that there will be a 'learning curve' and that systems should be continually improved in response to user experience and needs. There is no-one with the ultimate system now, nor will there be in the foreseeable future.

The fifth step is the total understanding and commitment of all participants in the pilot or operational test at the earliest stage of the project. People who have not been involved in early discussions and planning are very unlikely to contribute to its success. There is need for a great deal of well-designed user training from the start of the project.

The sixth step is professional training and user support, once the system is implemented. A rule of thumb is to spend 25% of the system cost on training for a pilot project. It has become common recently to conduct extensive testing of the functional definition of the system and even the user dialogue before the system is programmed or selected. 'Learn before you buy' are four words to the wise.

The seventh key step is to specify a flexible, powerful, reliable system. Flexibility ensures adaptability to user habits and preferences. Power ensures extensibility to accommodate the applications that you wish you had specified at the outset. Reliability is essential for user confidence and for effective testing.

The bottom line and eighth critical factor is that the system or
project genuinely serves the needs of the user group. If the value of
the service offered is marginal, so may be their commitment. It is
always best if a project addresses critical resource problems
experienced by an entire group of users.

OFFICEMAN:
A Design Approach
to the Electronic Office

C. V. D. Forrington

Managing Director, Corporate Business Systems Limited, UK

OFFICEMAN embraces a software product and a design
approach to the electronic office. It is based on
an evolutionary process involving feasibility study,
pilot systems and design experimentation, leading to
a full functional and technical specification of a
proposed operational system, without prior commitment
to a longer-term hardware and software strategy.

Experience in the early usage of the OFFICEMAN
approach indicates the effectiveness of user
participation in the design process and forms the
basis for the continuing development of the
software product.

1   INTRODUCTION

The concept of the 'electronic office' is now well established,
involving the merging of communications, computing and information
storage and retrieval techniques into a single developing
methodology. In order to achieve the full potential of the concept,
a number of formidable technical and behavioural problems remain to
be solved; however, worthwhile benefits are already being obtained
from the application of the techniques currently available.
In particular, organisations are beginning to identify and evaluate
the human as well as the technical aspects of the move from the
current 'paper-based' systems to the 'paperless' office of the
future.

OFFICEMAN is an approach to the design and implementation of the
electronic office which facilitates the early evaluation of the
potential benefits without involving a restrictive commitment to a
specific long-term systems or hardware strategy.

OFFICEMAN is based on digital computer techniques and hence is most
applicable to environments where the components of the information
system can be readily expressed in or converted to digitial formats.
In particular, it is aimed at environments where much of the
information is internally generated, such as memoranda, minutes,
action plans, etc., rather than generated externally in a wide
variety of formats.

2   THE OFFICEMAN SYSTEM

A   OUTLINE

The OFFICEMAN system comprises a number of software modules that can
be linked together, with or without modification or extension, to
provide a customised electronic office embracing the following
basic facilities :

- o   information storage and retrieval
- o   word processing
- o   the automated work desk
- o   electronic mailing
- o   linkages with other systems
- o   usage analysis

The system is shown schematically in Figure 1.

Figure 1   The OFFICEMAN System

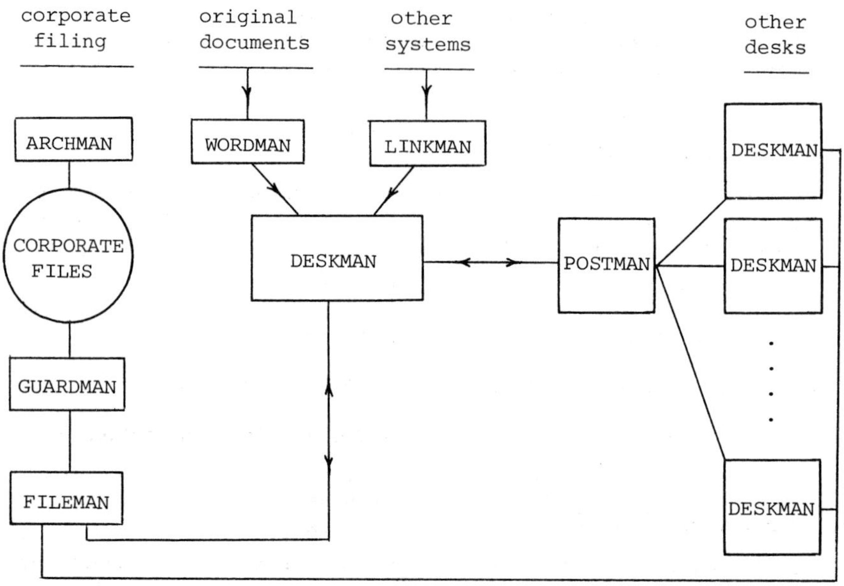

B   SYSTEM MODULES

The functions of the individual system modules are outlined below.

i   Information Storage and Retrieval

A corporate filing system is maintained which contains a single
entry of each source document within the system;   thus there is no
duplication of documents and hence storage and retrieval problems
are minimised.   The file is accessed and updated by the FILEMAN
program module, which services the needs of all the automated work
desks.   A security module, GUARDMAN, ensures that data can only be
accessed by desks with the appropriate privileges and thus provides
a system of data confidentiality.

A further program module, ARCHMAN, is concerned with the archiving
of file information once the system deems it to be no longer in
current use.

ii Word Processing

A comprehensive word processing system, WORDMAN, is used for the
input of original documents and for the amendment and updating of
'standard' documents. Standard documents may be defined for a
particular organisation and can incorporate complex formatting,
assembly and, if required, computational rules.

iii The Automated Work Desk

The automated work desk is the user's main contact with the system
and the area in which the major benefits from the electronic office
should arise. It comprises :

    o   an electronic in-tray and out-tray
    o   an electronic diary and check list
    o   an electronic personal filing system

The above are controlled through the DESKMAN program module.

A user-orientated outline of the operation is given in Section 3.

iv Electronic Mailing

The POSTMAN program module provides an electronic mailing system by
which information is communicated between work desks. This is
described in more detail in Section 3.

v   Linkages with Other Systems

OFFICEMAN may be linked with other systems in the organisation
through the LINKMAN program module. This takes information
generated by the external systems and converts it into standard
OFFICEMAN formats, and vice versa. Examples of other systems would
include :

    o   data processing systems on the same or different computers
          as OFFICEMAN
    o   external machine-readable inputs such as OCR or telex.

vi Usage Analysis

The system can monitor the usage of specified facilities so as to
provide information for the system designers and for the system
controllers.

3 OPERATION OF THE AUTOMATED WORK DESK

A GENERAL

A desk consists of a visual display unit and access to a printer.

Figure 2 The User Interface

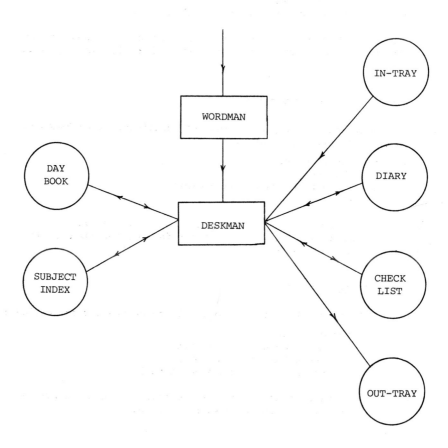

A user may perform the following basic functions :

    o   enter an original document
    o   examine his In-Tray
    o   file information from his In-Tray
    o   mail information to other desks
    o   examine his Out-Tray
    o   examine his personal files
    o   edit his personal files
    o   produce hard copy of information
    o   maintain his diary and check list
    o   interrogate other diaries and check lists.

The detail of how these functions are performed will depend on the
requirements of the particular organisation but will broadly be as
follows.

B ENTER AN ORIGINAL DOCUMENT

The document will be prepared using the facilities of WORDMAN and,
in particular, will designate :

    o   the originator
    o   the recipients
    o   the subject matter (keywords)
    o   the text.

The originator code, together with an internally-generated
reference number, form the unique file reference for the document
within the FILEMAN system.

C EXAMINE THE IN-TRAY

The contents of the In-Tray may be displayed on the screen, giving :

    o   the originator
    o   the date and time of receipt
    o   the subject matter (keyword)
    o   the priority (originator-assigned).

The user may thus display a particular document, request a printed
copy of it, acknowledge it or leave it pending.

D FILE INFORMATION FROM IN-TRAY

A document listed in the In-Tray will automatically be filed in the user's Daybook File and may optionally be filed in the originator-designated subject files and/or in user-designated files. Once it has been filed it will deleted from the In-Tray.

E MAIL INFORMATION

A document may be electronically mailed to another desk by assigning recipient codes and priorities to it. It will then be transferred to the user's Out-Tray and mailed to the recipients' In-Trays.

F EXAMINE THE OUT-TRAY

The user may display the contents of his Out-Tray in order to establish the status of his outgoing mail, i.e. whether and when it has been acknowledged and processed by the recipients.

G EXAMINE THE PERSONAL FILES

The user's personal files in fact only contain pointers to the Corporate File and thus do not entail any duplication of text. The personal files are split between :

     o   Daybook File
     o   Subject Files.

i Daybook File

This contains, in time and date sequence, all documents originated or received by the user. It may be interrogated to display the date, originator and subject matter (keywords). If necessary, a document may then be displayed or printed.

ii Subject Files

These are again kept in time and date order but, in this case, also within subject matter.

Thus the two types of file correspond directly with those normally associated with paper-based filing systems.

H EDIT SUBJECT FILES

Subject files may be edited by the user. The options in

- o   delete document
- o   copy to another subject file
- o   copy from Daybook File
- o   change the sequence in which documents are filed
- o   associate (cross-reference) documents within a file.

I PRODUCE PRINTED DOCUMENTS

At any stage the user may request a printed version of a
particular document. This will be produced immediately if the
particular desk has its own printer, or queued for printing on a
shared printer otherwise.

J MAINTAIN DIARY AND CHECK LIST

If required, a personal diary and/or check list may be maintained
by the user. These are filed separately from the main corporate
filing system and may be accessed by other user desks to identify
vacant times and dates for appointments, etc.

K INTERROGATE OTHER DIARIES AND CHECK LISTS

The user may, subject to having the necessary access privileges,
access other diaries and/or check lists for the purposes given in
J above.

4 EVOLUTIONARY DESIGN OF OFFICEMAN APPLICATIONS

OFFICEMAN is based on a staged approach to design and
implementation, as follows :

- o   feasibility study
- o   design and implementation of pilot system
- o   operation and evaluation of pilot system
- o   final design and implementation strategy
- o   implementation programme.

These steps are outlined below.

A FEASIBILITY STUDY

The feasibility study follows broadly the conventional lines
established for computer-based information systems, seeking
initially to identify areas in which cost-effective benefits can
be obtained within the limits of the available technologies and
within the constraints of the particular organisation. These
areas are then examined in some detail and incorporated into an
overall programme for further investigation and development. The
major difference in emphasis, however, is that there is likely to
be far less experience, both internal and external, to draw upon,
and hence the resulting programme will have a greater
'experimental' component than with most conventional data
processing systems. In particular, it will necessitate the
design and implementation of a pilot system (see B and C below).

B DESIGN AND IMPLEMENTATION OF PILOT SYSTEM

The pilot system should be designed to evaluate the proposed
functional design within a specific area of the development
programme, with particular reference to its functional
performance, user acceptability and achieved benefits. It need
not be overly concerned with the technical problems of
optimisation, nor with the organisational problems of scale.

As an example, consider a system for the generation, distribution
and filing of internal memoranda. A final operational system
might have a hundred or more users; however, a pilot system
might have only three or four. Also, the final system would have
significant sub-systems relating to information security,
archiving, etc., which do not affect the user directly and hence
need not be present in the pilot system.

Once designed, the pilot system is implemented using the OFFICEMAN
program modules, as described in Section 2.

An elapsed time of one-two months is usually sufficient for the
above design and implementation stage.

C OPERATION AND EVALUATION OF PILOT SYSTEM

Once implemented, the pilot system needs to be operated for a
sufficient length of time for a realistic evaluation to be made.
During the initial period of operation a number of areas for
immediate modification will be identified and these will be
incorporated. Other less urgent areas for improvement will be
noted for incorporation into the final design.

The evaluation of the pilot system needs to be related directly to performance criteria identified in the design stage.

An elapsed time of three-six months is usually sufficient for the purposes of system evaluation.

D   FINAL DESIGN AND IMPLEMENTATION STRATEGY

Once the functional design, user acceptance and benefits of the proposed system have been validated by means of the pilot system, the final design of the full system can be undertaken. This must take into account the technical problems of scale, security etc., and the organisational problems of more general introduction that were absent from the pilot system. It must also evaluate the most cost-effective implementation strategy and, in particular, the most appropriate equipment to be used, which will not necessarily correspond to that used for the pilot system.

The final design and implementation strategy stage will probably also require experimentation; however, this will be confined to the technical aspects of the strategy as the functional and user aspects have already been validated.

The elapsed time for the above stage will depend largely on the scale of the technical and organisational aspects but it is likely to be in the range six-nine months.

E   IMPLEMENTATION PROGRAMME

The full implementation programme is likely to be spread over at least a year; however, as with good conventional computing practice, it will be broken down into tangible stages of not more than six-nine months' duration.

Figure 3   OFFICEMAN Implementation on Central Processor

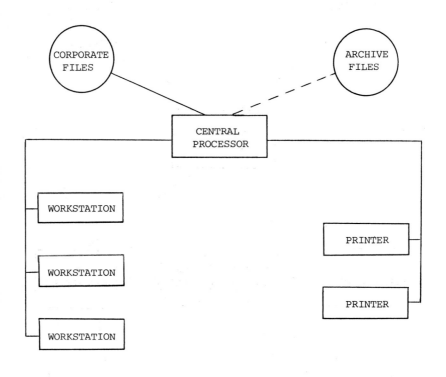

WORKSTATIONS

(screen or
screen + printer)

SHARED
PRINTERS

Figure 4   Distributed OFFICEMAN Implementation

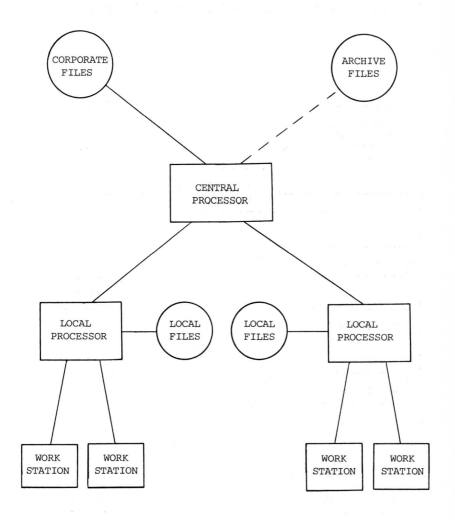

5   HARDWARE AND COMMUNICATIONS STRATEGIES

OFFICEMAN was initially written to operate on DEC PDP 11 computers
under the RSTS operating system, with a typical configuration as
shown in Figure 3. Workstations consist of a visual display unit
with or without an associated local printer. A number of shared
printers are also included. This form of implementation is
suitable for pilot systems and for operational systems where most of
the workstations are local to the processor; that is, within
standard cabling distances. Non-local workstations can be
connected through leased or dial-up lines.

For applications involving more than one major location a
distributed system is more appropriate, as illustrated in Figure 4.
Here, local files hold the local subject indices, with the
centralised files holding the corporate text files. The concept of
a 'pending tray' may also be introduced, leaving text files
currently of interest in local storage to reduce the communications
load between the local and central processors.

The software design of OFFICEMAN facilitates portability within the
DEC range, with DEC System/20 implementation already existing and a
VAX version planned. No immediate plans exist for non-DEC
implementations, although it is envisaged that OFFICEMAN
applications proven as pilot systems on DEC equipment will be
converted to other computers during the implementation of resulting
operational systems in those areas where corporate computing
strategy dictates that approach.

6   OPERATIONAL EXPERIENCE

The operational experience gained since the introduction of
OFFICEMAN in mid-1980 is summarised below.

A   PILOT SYSTEMS

Pilot systems have been implemented in a number of organisations,
including a major oil company, a multi-national textile group, a
university and a professional consultancy practice. A pattern of
operation has emerged as follows :

  MONTH 1   set up initial system based on standard
             OFFICEMAN facilities

  MONTH 2   use of initial system

  MONTH 3   review of usage and modification/extension
             of facilities based on user feedback

MONTH 4   use of modified/extended system and initial
definition of scope and characteristics of
an operational system.

To date, most of the modifications/extensions identified by users at
the first review point have concerned the setting-up of standard
documents corresponding to those in use in the existing manual
system and the simplification of the updating and distribution of
these documents. Such changes are usually introduced in a matter of
hours rather than days and take place without disruption to usage.

The second review has tended to concentrate on the interfaces between
the OFFICEMAN systems and other corporate systems, for example the
telex and the data-processing systems. At this point the user-led
design process for an operational system can be said to have started.

B   DESIGN AID

Pilot systems conducted as above have led to the use of OFFICEMAN as
a continuing design aid for an operational system. As well as
allowing functional designs to be tested and evaluated, OFFICEMAN has
proved of value in assessing the technical apsects of a particular
design. For example, response-time experiments can be conducted in
order to assess the response requirements of different groups of
users.   The end result of the design-aid mode of working will
usually be the functional and technical specification of a full
operational system.

C   OPERATIONAL SYSTEMS

Present usage of OFFICEMAN is limited to pilot systems and design aid
work, although the experience gained to date indicates that in many
cases it will also form the basis of the final operational system,
particularly if the use of DEC computers is within the organisation's
corporate computing strategy.

7   CONCLUSION

To date, OFFICEMAN has fulfilled its original design objectives and
in some areas exceeded them, particularly in its potential for full
operational systems. User acceptance has been high and, consequently,
their contribution to the design process has been very effective.

The future technical development of OFFICEMAN will be based mainly on
operational experience and it is hoped that this will lead eventually
to a powerful and comprehensive office automation product for
exploitation in UK and overseas markets.

Strategic Planning for Office Automation

L. A. Woodman

Executive Director, Willis Faber & Dumas, UK

The purpose of office automation is to provide more effective support for business operations. Strategic planning for office automation is an integral part of business strategic planning. It requires a thorough knowledge of the business; an understanding of the organisation, its development and philosophy; and an appreciation of the capability of emergent technology.

Traditionally, computers have been used in highly structured, logical environments; but a different approach is needed in offices because each one is unique, only partially structured and highly political. Carefully planned management of change is necessary to achieve complex transitions in office systems.

Office automation is a challenge to Systems and Data Processing people which requires adaptability from conventional methodology.

INTRODUCTION

We live in a world where everything we possess originates from
people and their use of natural resources. However, the number of
people producing goods and services is decreasing, whilst the number
of consumers is increasing, so to maintain or improve our standard
of living we need to produce more from less. This paper describes
how office automation can contribute, a method of approach, and the
pitfalls to be avoided.

AN OFFICE

An office is a system, a means by which something happens. Offices
only exist to provide support for business operations. This is
their mission. All offices are physically similar, being a
collection of people and equipment in a space together with
information and procedures, but each office has its own unique
mission.

Individual offices do not exist in a vacuum. All the offices in an
organisation form a series of networks, and each office is a node in
one or more networks. Data, time and space are the main attributes
of the interactions between them. Each office is an integrated part
of the information infrastructure which supports the business
operations of the whole organisation.

Offices are complex, sensitive systems and tend to be poorly
understood. Although office procedures may start off simple and
straightforward, they are constantly changing in minor ways. They
grow and evolve on a piecemeal basis to meet the needs of the
business and the needs of people who work there. This means that
major interventions in one part of an office system can have hidden
repercussions in other parts. Most office workers only understand a
narrow view of their own job, because this is how they were
trained. Few people understand what everyone else is doing and how
it all fits together.

Traditional, commercial data processing is oriented towards the
automated execution of high volume tasks which are straightforward,
uniform, repetitive and structured. Offices generally have a low
proportion of work in this category. Most office work is an
intricate, conditional mixture of structured repetitive tasks and
unstructured judgmental tasks, which are highly dependant on
interpersonal interactions. There is little uniformity between
offices.

Office procedures generally operate on an "input/processing/output" basis by receiving raw data which they use with their own records to produce information, decisions or products, in the form of messages and documents. Offices and networks have various levels of procedures, which have been categorised in this paper as: corporate decision making, products, functions, tasks and use of tools.

OFFICE AUTOMATION

Office automation should not be technology driven or confused with contemporary artifacts such as word processing or electronic mail. It should not be seen as a once-off exercise, but rather as an evolutionary process (8) using various techniques such as rationalisation of procedures (1), product line automation (2) and decision support systems (3) to respond to business needs and provide more effective support for business operations. The contribution of office automation to the work of an office is different at each level of detail:

Corporate Decision Making

This includes work such as defining corporate strategy, setting pricing policy, evaluating risks, negotiating terms etc. Machines can, and will continue to help people to do these jobs better, but it is unlikely machines will ever do the whole job, because business people use their judgment. This judgment is based on a wide range of factors, including years of practical experience, knowledge of the attitudes and aspirations of the people with whom they do business, knowledge of political and economic environments and knowledge of other related issues. It is an extremely complex process to put such diverse factors together to form a judgment.

The benefits of office automation at this level come from decision support systems which provide people with more meaningful information in order to expand their knowledge and to improve the quality of their decisions.

Products

The offices of manufacturing goods industries rarely produce their own products. Instead they provide support for products such as soap powder or motor cars which have been made in a factory. This is very different to the offices of service industries which generally make most of their own products, for example: letters of credit; portfolios of shares; insurance protection; and conveyancing of property. Products made by offices are abstract compared with the products made by manufacturing goods industries which are concrete. Customers perceive organisations with whom they do business, in terms of the organisation's products.

When businesses start, they are generally organised around their
product, supported by a small group of people in a single office.
However, as the business grows, the single office increases in size
until it becomes unwieldy and cumbersome. When this happens the
office tends to subdivide into a number of smaller offices linked by
a network. These in turn grow, subdivide and so on. Benefits from
economies of scale are generally sought from this subdivision
process, with separate functional departments being formed, such as
marketing, invoicing, purchasing and production control. With the
formation of networks there is a paradox however, because
"Parkinson" tends to set in.

Each functional department contributes towards the product, but
regardless of the individual efficiency of each department, the
effectiveness of producing the whole product depends on the
organisation structure of the offices and the interpersonal
relationships between them.

The main benefits of office automation at the product level, come
from integration of the separate functions and facilities enabling
the business to reorganise around its products. Other benefits come
from rationalisation of procedures and decision support systems.

Functions

Examples of functions include marketing, invoicing, purchasing and
production control. Functional departments are common in large
organisations and if larger than about twenty people they subdivide
into smaller sections and task groups such as typing pools. Each
group of people behave as an individual office. Complexity is
directly proportional to the number of offices and networks.

Subdivision into manageable size offices creates additional work.
Some extra jobs are necessary, for example: monitoring the progress
of products through each office and controlling the location of
documents; but others are unnecessary, for example alibi records,
and buck passing procedures. Most functional departments are
perceived within their organisation as cost generators rather than
profit centres. This may cause them to behave in a protective way
jealously guarding their own territory and creating their own self
importance through mythology and mystique. Thus it is essential to
rationalise office procedures before automating them, in order to
eliminate any protectionism and unnecessary work.

Rationalisation of procedures is where office automation can make
its greatest contribution at the functional level. Decision support
systems and partial product line automation can also increase the
effectiveness of functional level work.

Tasks

In order to accomplish a function, specific tasks have to be done,
such as record keeping, typing, communicating messages, and so on.
Individual jobs may comprise a single task or a combination of
tasks, and equally tasks may be done by one person or a small group
of people.

Although the mechanisation of individual tasks may improve the
efficiency of individual people it is unlikely to have much affect
on the effectiveness of business operations. Office automation
makes its greatest contribution with the integration of mechanised
tasks at the higher levels of product and function.

At the task level, rationalisation of procedures can generally
improve efficiency by making some tasks redundant, and simplifying
others.

Use of Tools

The tools of an office include telephones, typewriters, calculating
machines and filing cabinets. There has been considerable
innovation and increasing improvements in tools over the last twenty
years. Office automation is not concerned with tools as an end in
themselves but only as the means to the end of getting business done
in the most effective way.

Rationalisation of procedures may improve the use of tools.

To summarise, rationalisation of procedures is an essential
pre-requisite to automation, and the internal information gathered
from the product line is a desirable pre-requisite for most decision
support systems. The ratio of internal to external information used
by decision support systems is generally inversely proportional to
the level of work. The contribution of office automation to profits
varies at each level of work, according to the methods used:

	CONTRIBUTION TO PROFITS		
	Rationalisation	Automation	Decision Support
Corp decision making	-	-	High
Products	High	High	Medium
Functions	High	Medium	Low
Tasks	Medium	-	-
Use of tools	Low	-	-

STRATEGIC PLANNING

The purpose of strategic planning is not to produce a plan, it is to
think through what an organisation wants to achieve. The physical
plan is just a representation of the thinking process. The
perspective of strategic planning is business strategy within
corporate strategy. Business strategy is concerned with securing
and maintaining competitive success in a business area and is
largely market oriented; whereas corporate strategy addresses the
need for a competitive portfolio of business areas and is largely
finance oriented.

The major stages of strategic planning include: environmental
understanding, business analysis, strategy formulation, and
strategic anticipation.

Environmental Understanding addresses the relationships and
trends between the organisation and the various levels of
surrounding environment. It identifies competitive pressures,
critical factors for success, threats and opportunities.

Business Analysis defines the present position of self and
competitors in terms of objectives, products, markets,
technology and other key policy issues. It also identifies
major constraints, strengths and weaknesses.

Strategy Formulation identifies niches (product or market
segments which provide surplus resources or are competitively
secure), and competitive fronts (areas vulnerable to attack).
From this, offensive and defensive strategies can be formulated.

Strategic Anticipation estimates external competitive responses
through analysis of competitors strategy, political environment
and organisational processes; and internal responses from
staff. It may identify causes to iterate previous stages.

The business opportunities provided by office automation stem
primarily from the inverse price/performance trends between people
and equipment. As these opportunities can influence each stage in
the process described above, strategic planning for office
automation should not be considered as an isolated activity but
rather an integral part of business strategic planning.

The increasing size and complexity of business operations is
creating demands on offices for more extensive information, and
pressures to provide higher levels of service at less cost. To
respond to these pressures for change, requires significant
investment of human effort and capital expenditure. It involves
risk of lost investment, as well as possible damage to the current
situation. Investment in office automation is no different to any
other commercial investment and it should yield a similar return for
equivalent risk. Various strategies can be used to optimise the
payoffs and avoid the pitfalls.

OFFICE AUTOMATION STRATEGIES

There are many different strategies and variations of them, each of
which will only be appropriate in certain circumstances. Examples
of strategies include: greater productivity; increased
competitiveness; exploiting new markets; and improved quality of
lifestyle:

Greater Productivity

Productivity is normally measured as the ratio of output to input,
where output comprises goods and services and input comprises
manpower, money, and materials. The method of measuring
productivity and its contribution to the profit and loss account,
vary at each level of office work. The lower the level, the easier
it is to measure productivity, but the lower the contribution to
profits, for example the productivity of an individual office worker
is relatively insignificant compared with the effectiveness of the
whole business.

Corporate decision making productivity is extremely complex to
measure and depends on the profits in a particular environment
over a period of time. The value of improved information to the
quality of managerial decisions is very difficult to measure
objectively, and is generally assessed subjectively.

Product productivity is best measured as the ratio of revenue
earned to the cost of making the product. However, measures of
cost and revenue are rarely straightforward, for example: if
several functional departments contribute to a product, the cost
of it depends on how much resource each functional department
spends on it, which is probably a function of the management
accounting policy; revenue may depend on some products being
"lost leaders" for others and this is difficult to value. The
complexity of fair transfer pricing may outweigh its worth and
it may be more appropriate to use pragmatic measures of the
factors influencing revenue and cost.

Function productivity is measured as the ratio of output to cost
of resource used. The unit of output depends on the function,
for example: number of transactions; value of stock levels etc.
Without revenue, functional productivity is only a relative
measure of unit costs and only relates indirectly to profits.

Task productivity is simple to measure, for example: the number
of pages typed per typist per day. However, it is at such a low
level it is unlikely to have much affect on profits.

Tool productivity is even easier to measure and is generally
provided by suppliers of the equipment. Most suppliers have
their own measures which are rarely comparable. Tool
productivity is meaningless on its own and only contributes to
the extent that it affects the levels of work above.

Productivity can improve profits by reducing costs, avoiding costs
or increasing product value. There are several ways of increasing
productivity such as: less people producing the same volumes; the
same people producing more; reduced errors; faster throughput;
improved use of equipment; optimising the time and material value of
money; etc. Reorganisation is often needed to convert identified
benefits into real savings for example: creation of spare hours in
individual peoples jobs are meaningless until the work is aggregated
and the number of jobs reduced.

Increased Competitiveness

Improved client service can often increase competitiveness. Office
automation can contribute through: improved presentation, accuracy
and timeliness of documents; better information available for
advising and guiding clients; faster response to queries; etc. It
may also provide opportunities for enhancing existing products or
initiating new ones.

Increased productivity, improved client service and enhanced or new
products provide scope for making prices more competitive whilst
maintaining or increasing margins.

Exploiting New Markets

By defining products in terms of their markets and integrating
office automation strategy with business strategy, synergistic
business opportunities are likely to arise, for example:
teleconferencing can enable people to communicate across time zones
and could possibly change the nature of arbitrage between existing
markets.

Wealth is created from innovation and added value, by identifying
and capitalising unexploited markets, for example: fifty years ago
the television industry barely existed; and twenty five years ago
there was no photocopying market as we know it today. Office
automation may assist in identifying such opportunities.

Improved Quality of Lifestyle

People can make or break any system. The effectiveness of office
systems depends more on the motivation of the people who use them,
than on the excellence of their technical design. Thus people are
the most important part of any office system.

Individual people have their own measures of quality of lifestyle,
for example: job interest; recognition; achievement; dignity;
autonomy; freedom of choice, etc. These criteria and the values
individual people place upon them, are influenced by national and
corporate cultures. Although the principles are similar, the values
people place on quality of lifestyle vary considerably.

Greater understanding of people's needs and wider choices available
through office automation techniques, can provide opportunities for
improving the quality of lifestyle at the same time as more closely
aligning personal motivations with corporate goals.

MANAGEMENT OF CHANGE

However well strategic planning has been thought through, it will
make no positive contribution without proper management and
stabilisation of the required changes (4).

The initiative for office automation may originate from a number of
areas, such as Systems Development, Data Processing, Administrative
Services, or Operating Divisions. Wherever it comes from, all work
needs close co-ordination and management so that the most effective
use is made of skills and knowledge.

To effect change participation is needed from everyone involved
including local management, people whose jobs will alter, and those
skilled in office automation techniques and technology. Their time
is needed for study and analysis - to understand what each office
accomplishes and how they all fit together into the context of the
whole organisation; system design; and implementation.

There are three main areas of managing change, expanding the
knowledge and understanding of the people involved, developing the
skills of the participants, and managing the transitions of offices
systems:

Expanding Knowledge and Understanding

Technological evangelism tends to create friction and negative
energy which can be avoided if people learn about office automation
opportunities in a low key, gradual way. If their expectations are
managed realistically people perceive technology as just another
tool, and approach it in a common sense, unemotional way.

Expanding the knowledge and understanding of the people involved, is
not a once off activity, but a continuous, evolutionary process of
advising people with what is available and how they can benefit.
The need for knowledge and understanding varies at different levels
within an organisation and depends on the state of existing office
systems. The less familiar people are with the concepts of office
automation, the more important it is to avoid abstract
generalisations and focus on concrete examples that relate directly
to their work experience.

At the business goals level, a regular exchange of information is
needed between the people who plan strategy and those who understand
office automation opportunities. At the middle management level,
members of steering committees, user groups and so on can learn from
experimental projects, demonstrations, seminars or short courses.
At the lower levels there are many different ways of increasing
knowledge and understanding, for example: articles in the company
newspaper; organising family open days; competitions organised
through the sports club; lunch hour film shows; etc. Whatever ways
are chosen, the content must be aimed at the appropriate level of
knowledge for the audience.

Developing Skills

There are several ways of integrating knowledge and understanding
into normal work to help people develop skills from practical
experience, for example:

> On the job learning can be achieved by seconding technical data
> processing people to an operating area for a few months to
> physically do the range of different jobs there. This helps
> them understand what makes the place tick, and develops sound
> interpersonal relationships between the people. However, it
> requires tact, persistence, and data processing people able to
> emphathise, with perception and perspective, and no trace of
> arrogant elitism.

> Experimental projects run in an environment where people can
> learn for themselves in relaxed way, help them to understand
> technology and invent better ways of doing things by
> themselves. This can be achieved through the trial use of
> equipment and minimum bureaucracy. Although the systems
> developed by users will probably be technically inelegant, they
> will work, because their inventors will be committed to them.
> There are risks to this approach including oversold situations
> (where users demand facilities that the centre cannot support),
> and lack of control and co-ordination.

> Building prototypes as part of a planning process is common in
> scientific and engineering fields, but rare in commerce, and yet
> it provides a low cost, low risk way of testing out the
> practicalities of ideas and concepts, before a major investment
> is made. To be successful, the objectives must be clearly
> defined at the outset and prototypes should only be considered
> in areas where local management and staff recognise the scope
> for improvement in the work they do and are keen to achieve
> change. Implementation should aim to deliver practical, visible
> products within a six month time frame.

Mentoring can be used by employing an external organisation of specialists consultants. Staff who work alongside the specialist, should gain a "rub off" of the specialists skills. The main difficulty is in finding consultants of adequate calibre.

Managing the Transitions of Office Systems

Strategic planning defines what an organisation is aiming to achieve, but to make these achievements change will be necessary. Managing the transitions of office systems is an integral part of the study-analysis/design/implementation process.

There are six key stages to managing transitions (4), which need to be thought through before system design is started: defining the current, future and transition states, developing work programmes for managing the transition, evaluating the change effort and stabilisation.

As work progresses through the stages of design and implementation additional information often comes to light and other changes happen in the environment which have a bearing on earlier work. This means all work must be done in a practical, flexible and iterative way, so that it can be modified to be responsive to the needs of the business.

The current state needs to be clearly understood so that action plans are developed from a firm base. False assumptions about the current state can cause confusion, and negative energy that work against the change.

The future state is best described by a series of scenarios or pictures of what the new state will look like and how it will work. This provides a clear aiming point.

The transition state covers the choices on whether and how to make what individual changes. It identifies where and how, what interventions should be made, from an understanding of the varying degrees of readiness.

Work programmes identify specifically who needs to do what tasks by when, taking full consideration for contingencies, interdpendance of tasks and availability of resources.

Evaluation establishes criteria for measuring the success of the change.

Stabilisation is to ensure change is accepted and working satisfactorily.

PITFALLS TO AVOID

The main pitfalls are: ignorance and mythology; irrelevant goals, poor human relations; and inadequate management of change.

Ignorance and Mythology

Ignorance stems from: inadequate knowledge and understanding of the business goals; unrealistic expectations; and perceptions of office automation as a panacea. If strategic planning is neglected or poorly defined, (existing only in peoples minds and on miscellaneous papers) there will be a lack of coordination giving rise to differing perceptions and confusion instead of a common understanding. Full benefits from office automation will not be realised if corporate direction is unclear.

A number of companies are only investing in office automation because they see their competitors investing and they are afraid of falling behind. Operational management who abdicate responsibility to technical people are far less successful than those who invest their personal time in leading the initiatives.

Mythology stems from false assumptions such as: all offices are the same; offices exist to do office tasks such as filing and typing; office automation is about doing these tasks better and faster; office systems do not need to be cost justified; the bigger and better the equipment the more important and valuable the system; office automation is easy; and so on.

Ignorance and a belief in mythology can lead to irrelevant goals.

Irrelevant Goals

Any goal which does not focus on the business needs of the organisation is irrelevant, for example: the paperless office; the peopleless office; use of technology for its own sake; etc. The plethora of available equipment often leads people to confuse means with ends. Business effectiveness is unlikely to be improved by solutions searching for problems to solve.

Irrelevant goals lead to: overloads of information; neglect of materiality; inefficient methods; reduced control; lower productivity; and increased costs.

Goals that are irrelevant give rise to meaningless measures of
performance such as: increased keystrokes per minute; reduced number
of secretaries; increased professional productivity; etc. The only
meaningful measures of performance are those which are real in
business terms and influence the bottom line of the profit & loss
account.

Poor Human Relations

Neglect of people is generally unintentional but happens through
ignorance and the other pitfalls described above. A common failing
is to concentrate only on the technical, logical part of a system
and overlook the human behavioural side which is equally if not more
important.

Office systems comprise social and technical parts which although
independant relate to form a whole socio technical system (7). Any
imbalance between the socio and technical parts will reduce
effectiveness of the overall system.

Systems belong to the people who use them. People will not be
committed to systems unless they feel ownership. Change should
therefore originate from the people affected by it. Individuals who
are dissatisfied with the status quo will have a genuine felt need
for change, and be committed to it (5). Whereas those who are
comfortable with the status quo will tend to counter implement
change strategies in order to maintain the status quo.

Inadequate Management of Change

If change is not managed properly it can cause people to feel
threatened and generates negative attitudes as happened in the Times
newspapers disputes (6). Failure to manage change properly can
destroy the business.

CONCLUSION

Office automation can make a valuable contribution towards
increasing standards of living, but it needs to be seen in the right
perpective.

Companies do not want office automation, companies want to make
profits and office automation is simply a means to that end.

BIBLIOGRAPHY

1. Hammer, M., and Zisman, M.D., "Design and Implementation of
    Office Information Systems", Proceedings of the NYU Synposium on
    Automated Office Systems, May 1979.

2. Matteis, R., "The New Back Office Focuses on Customer Service",
    Havard Business Review, March - April 1979.

3. Keen, P.G.W. and Scott Morton, M.S., "Decision Support Systems:
    An Organisational Perspective", Addison Wesley, 1978.

4. Beckhard, R. and Harris, R.T., "Organisation Transitions:
    Managing Complex Change", Addison Wesley, 1977.

5. Keen, P.G.W., "The Politics of Change: the Role of the Change
    Agent", Auerbach, 1980.

6. Jacobs, E., "Stop Press, The Inside Story of the Times Dispute",
    Andre Deutsch, 1980.

7. Cummings, T.G., and Markus, M.L., "A Social-Technical Systems
    View of Organisations" (from: Cooper, C.L., Editor of
    "Behavioural Problems in Organisations", Prentice-Hall 1979).

8. Hammer, M., and Sirbu, M., "What is Office Automation?",
    MIT Laboratory for Computer Science, 1980.

An Office Document Retrieval System

P. Crookes
(*Programmer*)
and
F. J. Smith
(*Professor*)

*Department of Computer Science,
The Queen's University of Belfast, N. Ireland*

Free text information retrieval systems are almost all based
on large computers. Examples are STAIRS developed by IBM,
STATUS developed by AERE, Harwell and QUOBIRD (and more
recently QUILL) developed at Queen's University in Belfast.
These systems are too large and expensive for use in an
office alongside a word processor and they are based on a
technology which is being rapidly overtaken and replaced by
the development of the microprocessor, new storage media and
new software engineering techniques. We have therefore
undertaken a study at Queen's University on the design and
implementation of a free text information retrieval system
based on a microcomputer or microcomputers to be used either
alongside a separate word processor or along with a word
processor on the same microcomputer.

1.   INTRODUCTION

We believe that microcomputer based document retrieval systems will
soon begin to replace the filing cabinet in the automated office just
as the microcomputer driven word processor[1] is rapidly replacing both
the mechanical and electrical typewriter. To prove this we have
started to build such a system.

Before the rapid development of integrated circuit technology[2] in the
mid-1970's computer processing of documents and letters in an office
was scarcely viable and depended on terminals, linked to time sharing
services on large main frame computers. These were unreliable, not
entirely secure and too expensive to be practical. In contrast, the
microcomputer based word processor is extremely reliable, entirely
secure (provided no one is using special equipment to pick up the
electromagnetic radiation emanating from the VDU) and the price,
though still high, is competitive and falling. These word processors
are designed for the typing of reports, letters or series of similar
letters after corrections or changes are made. However, they do not
yet provide effective filing and retrieval services for the documents,
except for small numbers of documents.

Document retrieval at present, just like computer word processing ten
years ago, depends on terminals linked to timesharing services on
large computers. Examples of such document retrieval systems are
STATUS[3] developed by Atomic Energy Research Establishment at Harwell,
STAIRS[4] developed by IBM and QUOBIRD[5,6] (and more recently QUILL[7])
developed at the Queen's University of Belfast. The main frame
computers on which these systems depend break down often and give
poor responses when a large number of users are on-line at the same
time (i.e. at the very time when users need the service most). These
two unfortunate characteristics can only be eliminated by duplication
and underuse of the resource - this is expensive.

Large computers allow on-line systems to grow in size and complexity
to provide a wide range of facilities for a user, only a few of which
facilities he may need. Thus these systems become too large and
expensive to use in an office alongside a word processor and they are
based on a technology, the technology of timesharing of fast
sequential processors, which is being rapidly overtaken or replaced
by the development of the microprocessor and new inexpensive storage
media. We have therefore undertaken a study at Queen's University on
the design and implementation of an information retrieval system
based on a microcomputer or microcomputers to be used alongside a
separate word processor or sometimes on the same microcomputer as the
word processor.

2.   EARLIER WORK IN BELFAST

Two small on-line information retrieval systems have been designed
and implemented in the past in Belfast. The first was an early on-
line text retrieval system built in 1969, called QUOBIRD[5]. It was a

free text system (the documents were indexed with all the words in
the text) and its design was based on an inverted file structure. We
believe that it was one of the first free text inverted file systems.
Much attention was given to methods of accessing the disc[9] which gave
the system a quick response. The retrieval program and each of the
auxiliary programs resided in a central store of 48K characters, a
third or less the size of current systems, and although it was a very
early system which could draw on no previous experience, it could
quickly retrieve documents with almost the same recall as later
systems, though with lower precision. It was slower to use by the
professional or experienced user but it was simple and easy to use by
the non professional. It was used by Physicists[10] at the University
until about 1976 (until the finance to maintain the database ran out)
in spite of the inevitable frequent breakdowns of the mainframe
computer and the poor response when many terminals were attached.
With its small size this system showed that it is possible to write a
full text retrieval system for a small computer and that on-line
retrieval from such a small system can be effective when it is
designed from the beginning as a small system.

The second implementation of a small system in Belfast was a modified
form of the successor to QUOBIRD, called QUOBIRD 2, on a PDP 11/40
computer. QUOBIRD 2 was a large system with many facilities (perhaps
too many). It was marketed briefly by ICL on 1900 computers.
Although the PDP 11/40 was a much bigger computer than the microcomputers used in our present design, to put QUOBIRD 2 onto such a
computer proved possible only with a great deal of overlaying,
software paging and other modifications. Although it proved that a
full text retrieval system could be put on a large minicomputer (if
not a microcomputer), it also showed that the design needed changing
to suit the new computer architecture. To be successful a new design
was needed; the much modified QUOBIRD 2 on the PDP 11/40 was
therefore not completely finished and never used.

This experience indicated that it would have been unwise to try to
scale down our newest mainframe system QUILL[7] on a small office
computer. QUILL (Queen's University Interrogation of Legal
Literature) was designed as an experimental system to help teach
information retrieval to law students and to provide advanced
linguistic facilities for research on legal retrieval. It includes
many facilities such as synonyms, homographs, ambiguous words,
thesaurus, not all of which are needed in a small office system.
Thus we decided to begin a new design drawing on all of the
experience available to us on the earlier systems, but particularly
using the experience with the first small system at Belfast, QUOBIRD[11]
We plan to call the new system "Micro-BIRD".

3.   Micro-BIRD

3.1 Facilities
Micro-BIRD is an information system suitable for free text retrieval

from large files using a small office computer. It is designed to
have only the essential features of a text retrieval system while
allowing reliable and effective document retrieval by a person in an
office who is not experienced with computer systems. However,
inevitably, the small system is without some facilities found in the
large text retrieval systems such as STAIRS, STATUS or QUILL. In
practice we hope to prove that the lack of these extra facilities
will not be a serious drawback; many of them are cosmetic; more are
included as advanced facilities to speed up the work of the
professional information scientist or librarian and are not needed by
someone not trained as a scientist such as a lawyer (or his secretary)
in a small office. The system is also designed to use the most recent
technology: microprocessors, new high capacity discs and video tapes.
With the experience gained with large systems over the last 12 years
we hope to be able to minimise the restrictions to users brought
about by the physical constraints of the size of a small computer.

3.2 A separate or shared microprocessor

The system we envisage is one which is used alongside a wordprocessor
or a group of wordprocessors in a small to medium sized firm. It
would be used in the office for retrieval from internally produced
documents such as letters, memoranda, notes, reports, etc. It might
also be used for retrieval of other information purchased from some
central data bank. For example, for the lawyer it would be used
primarily for retrieval of Statute and Case law, forms and
precedents, text books and journal papers in some areas in which the
lawyer was specialising.

Since the retrieval system would be used alongside a wordprocessor,
some means of transmitting data from the wordprocessor to the
retrieval microcomputer would be essential. A communications ring[12]
using a coaxial cable would be suitable or completed documents could
be transferred on floppy discs. In a very small office the word
processing computer could itself be used for retrieval if spare time
was available. It would need enhancement by the addition of extra
store, a large extra disc unit and a fast input/output device. The
one machine would then have to be shared between the two functions.

In a medium sized office already using a minicomputer with shared
word processing and data processing terminals it should be possible
to run the retrieval system in parallel with the other systems on
the one computer. This may require a more sophisticated operating
system and since the information retrieval system would take up a
relatively large amount of store there would be a degradation in
performance unless the installation bought more store and more disc
space; the salesmen would soon be suggesting the next model in the
range! A computer doing two or three different things at the same
time is more prone to problems and is more difficult to use without
professional computer staff. Response times are also slower at busy
periods. With the rapid fall in the cost of microprocessors and the

parallel increase in the cost of software and staff, it will soon be
more cost effective to have a separate microprocessor dedicated to
free text information retrieval than to enhance a medium sized
system used already for data processing and word processing.
However, sharing of peripherals would be a possibility if they were
not already heavily used.

Although we are aiming at a separate system, there is no reason why
the software should not be implemented on a medium computer and time
shared with other activities. However, we do not expect that this is
the way in which our system will be used.

Whether standalone or time shared, we have made one other assumption
about our micro system. We assume that retrieval is a minor part of
the work in an office and since our system is designed for a small
firm it is unlikely that two vital retrieval operations have to be
attempted simultaneously. We expect that the second can always wait
till the first is finished and we can therefore avoid the
complications of writing the software to make it reentrant, i.e.,
accessible by several users simultaneously. This makes the task of
implementing such a system much easier.

4.   REPLACEMENT OF ON-LINE INFORMATION SYSTEMS

Successful information retrieval systems on microcomputers in an
office will have an additional second function, to provide
information services. These will be new services which will replace
existing on-line services.

There are a number of such on-line services. For example, LEXIS[13]
and EUROLEX[14] allow a lawyer, through a terminal, to access a large
remote database of Case and Statute law; this database consists of
documents which are indexed using every word in the text of the
documents. Similar services are available for searching for
abstracts in many libraries[15] through a terminal linked to the
database by telephone lines.

In a microcomputer system such as the one we propose, data would be
sent to each user in the post in the form of video tapes. The tape
would include both the text of the documents in the database and the
index, so that a user need only load the tape to his disc to make as
many searches as he requires. There would be no charge for
telephone lines, the very high cost of large mainframe computers
would be avoided, the response would be fast at all times of the day
and not just in the early morning, the system would be reliable and
almost always available.

One drawback is the time taken to load a 10 M byte disc from a
cassette video tape each time the subject of a search has to be
changed, about 15-20 minutes. However, it should only be a few
years before cassette tapes are replaced by large capacity video
discs[16]. With a capacity of 1,000 M bytes or more and low cost, it
is difficult to see how on-line computing can compete with a service

which posts video discs to its users, each of whom has his own microcomputer system.

It is worth observing that the centre producing these video discs need not use a large computer. A medium size minicomputer would be sufficient to keep the database up-to-date, including the inverted file or index; it would be necessary to have a number of video disc writers which would operate in parallel and would write the latest updates of the database to several users' discs simultaneously. Thus the capital cost of the centre need not be high.

5.   THE COMPUTER EQUIPMENT

We are aiming to produce a retrieval system which can work on an inexpensive small computer or microcomputer. This would need at least 48K immediate access store to hold the retrieval program, an exchangeable floppy disc for programs, compilers and working lists of documents, one large capacity disc, a visual display monitor, keyboard and printer. A link to a word processor would be essential; so would be a link to a fast input device such as a tape reader or high speed interface to a data base on another computer, to receive computer data in large quantities from elsewhere. In Belfast we can use either a link to the main frame computer or a video tape reader for input/output. The latter device uses the mass market for video cassette recorders to give us an inexpensive tape reader and a medium to hold a very large amount of data, up to about 100 M bytes on a standard video cassette.

Even this technology will be overtaken within a few years by the video disc. This will permit storage of 1000 Million characters or more on one disc, and the disc transports, because they will be mass produced to meet the needs of the high fidelity music market and video market, will be cheap enough to use on an office system. (Currently the price of a prototype is £50,000). We are designing our microsystem with such large and inexpensive mass data devices in mind. Whole databases produced on large computers will be capable of being made available on a few discs for use within an office. For example, all of U.K. Statute and Case law could be held on a small number of such discs, reproduced cheaply, and, we believe, any part retrieved very rapidly with an inexpensive micro-based office system such as the one we are building.

Initially our system is based on an Apple II microcomputer. The cost of such a system, including a 10 M byte Corvus disc and video tape recorder and printer is less than £12,000. The software will be written in UCSD Pascal which should make the system highly portable to other microcomputer systems. This is important as we do not expect that our final system will be operational on an Apple II.

The Apple II microprocessor is relatively slow. However, for a dedicated information retrieval system, processor time is not as critical as disc access time. Thus the slow processor speed of the

Apple II is not a major drawback to the design as long as it can access a disc quickly.

What does make the Apple II unsuitable for a fast information retrieval system is the small central store, limited by an address 16 bits long, i.e. limited to 64K bytes. The PASCAL compiler takes 16K leaving 48K bytes for the retrieval programs. This is small for such a program and this explains why there are not many of these programs already widely available. One called METER was described at a BCS-ACM conference in 1980. (Proceedings[17] are not yet available). We did build a system of this size previously in Belfast, QUOBIRD. However, it was in machine code which optimised the storage used. Our proposed micro system is written in UCSD PASCAL to make it machine independent and this inevitably does not use the storage as efficiently as a machine language program. By overlaying the programs this space is sufficient for the code, but only if small block sizes are used for the transfer of data to and from the disc. It is the small size of the blocks which limits the speed of the Apple II for large text databases.

However, for the development of the software and the testing of the system the Apple II microcomputer is sufficient and we know that the small size of the central store of cheap microcomputers is of short duration only: microcomputers with much larger stores will be available within 2 or 3 years.

We have therefore been careful not to introduce crippling restrictions on our system due to a shortage of store which will not be necessary in a few years time.

We have therefore aimed at a system with the maximum sophistication in the design and we have saved store by leaving out facilities (which can be included later) and by using minimum buffer sizes for disc handling. As we have stated, small buffers will slow down the system, but on the next implementation when more store is available the buffer sizes can be increased to make it faster.

We have also considered the possibility of saving store by using a separate microprocessor in parallel with the first. With the low cost of microprocessors such a solution is now possible; file handling and input/output could be handled by one microprocessor and all other processing by the second. We have not yet tried to implement such a system, but it does provide an alternative strategy. We are initially concentrating on a design for a cheap micro with (say) 256K bytes of store.

6.   DESIGN CHARACTERISTICS OF MICRO-BIRD

6.1 Text Structure

All data held in the system is stored as text, including titles, authors, headings, etc. Thus what is stored is exactly what is typed on the typewriter or keyboard. New line characters are also stored.

Text is made up of many natural units. The system structures the text of each document as a set of paragraphs, each paragraph made up of a set of sentences and each sentence made up of a set of words. For simplicity a title or heading is treated automatically as part of the following paragraph.

Division of the text into a wider number of natural units, for example into sections or subsections, is not possible and is one of the inevitable limitations of a small system. However, our experience suggests that this limitation is rarely of much significance to someone searching for information. The section or subsection numbers or headings are not lost: they are part of the text, included as part of the following paragraph.

6.2 Text File Directory

As we have stated, the text file is made up of a set of characters including new line characters. It is stored as a set of blocks each of which is a PASCAL record. A PASCAL definition of the data structures used in the construction of the textfile is outlined below:

```
TYPE TEXTRECORD = RECORD

                     TEXTBLOCK:PACKED ARRAY [0..BLOCKSIZE] OF CHAR

                  END;

VAR TEXTFILE:FILE OF TEXTRECORD;
```

The identifier BLOCKSIZE is a user determined constant.

6.3 Dictionary

The terms used to index the documents are held in a special dictionary file of PASCAL records (called WORDRECORD in the example below) made up of a set of fields which include the addresses of the lists of text references for each word (called REFADDRESS). They must be ordered and stored in block records on disc (called DICTBLOCK). They can be ordered in alphabetical order as an indexed sequential file or by a hashing algorithm (as in QUOBIRD) or both (as in QUILL). The indexed sequential approach is slower and takes more store to hold the dictionary block index. Having words in alphabetical order has the advantage that most synonyms have the same stem and are stored contiguous to one another. However, conservation of store is a prime consideration for a small system. We therefore use a hash generation technique on the letters of each word and put them in alphabetic order within each block. Stems as well as words may be stored.

A PASCAL description of the data structures used in the dictionary file is given below:

```
TYPE WORDSPELLING = STRING [12];
     ADDRESSONREFFILE = RECORD
                             REFBLOCK,
                             REFCHAR:INTEGER
                             END;

     WORDRECORD = RECORD
                      STATUS,
                      LENGTHOFWORD,
                      TOTALOCCURRENCES:INTEGER;
                      SPELLING:WORDSPELLING;
                      REFADDRESS:ADDRESSONREFFILE
                      END;

     DICTBLOCK = RECORD
                     WORDSINBLOCK,
                     BLKSIZE:INTEGER;
                     ARRAYOFWORDRECORD:ARRAY [1..MAXWORDSINBLOCK]
                                       OF WORDRECORD
                     END;

VAR  DICTINDEX:FILE OF DICTBLOCK;
```

6.4 REFERENCE FILE

References to the text are stored in a chain, each cell in the chain
holding a number of references. The cells are stored together in
blocks, each block being a PASCAL record. We believe that this
structure will give us the most rapid retrieval.

The PASCAL description of the data structures used in the
construction of the reference file is outlined below:

```
TYPE ADDRESSONREFFILE = RECORD
                              REFBLOCK,
                              REFCHAR:INTEGER
                         END;

     REFERENCE = RECORD
                     NOOFDOC,
                     NOOFPARA,
                     NOOFSENT,
                     NOOFWORD:INTEGER
                 END;

     CELLRECORD = RECORD
                      TOTALREFERENCES,
                      REFSINCELL:INTEGER;
                      PREVCELL,
                      NEXTCELL:ADDRESSONREFFILE;
                      REFDETAILS:ARRAY [1..MAXREF] OF REFERENCE
                  END;

     BLOCKOFREFERENCES = RECORD
                              CELL:ARRAY [0..MAXCELL] OF CELLRECORD
                         END;

  VAR  REFFILE:FILE OF BLOCKOFREFERENCES;
```

7.   CONCLUSION

The system described above has now been implemented and first
retrieval has been achieved from a small database. By the time of
the conference we should be able to retrieve from a moderately sized
database and obtain some information on the response times of the
system. Our initial experience with the system reinforces our view
that effective information retrieval can be achieved through the use
of inexpensive microcomputers.

ACKNOWLEDGEMENT

We wish to acknowledge support from the National Law Library Limited.
We would like to thank Mr. Daniel Flynn for his help with PASCAL on
the APPLE II microcomputer.

REFERENCES

1. K.R. James, "Word Processing into the '80s", Computers and
    Lawyers, Proceedings of the Conference held by the Society for
    Computers and Law, June 1978; F.J. Smith, "The Use of a Mini-
    Computer to aid Legislative Drafting", Computers and Law, No.8,
    5-6, 1976.

2. T. Forester (Editor), "The Microelectronics Revolution",
    Basil Blackwell, Oxford, 1980.

3. N.H. Price, C. Bye and G.B.F. Niblett, "On-line Searching of
    Council of Europe Conventions and Agreements - the STATUS
    project, a study in bi-lingual document retrieval", Inform.
    Stor. Retr. 10, 145-54, 1974.

4. S.E. Furth, "STAIRS : An Interactive Full Text Retrieval System",
    Automated Law Research: A collection of presentations delivered
    at the First National Conference on Automated Law Research,
    American Bar Association, 19-34, 1973.

5. L.D. Higgins and F.J. Smith, "On-line Subject Indexing and
    Retrieval", Program, 3, 147-156, 1969.

6. M. Carville, L.D. Higgins and F.J. Smith, "Interactive Reference
    Retrieval in Large Files", Inform. Stor. Retr., 7, 205-10, 1971.

7. C.M. Campbell and F.J. Smith, "Students Searching Legal Texts
    by Computer", Computers and Law, No. 11, 6-7, 1977.

8. F.W. Lancaster & E.G. Fayen, "Information Retrieval On-line",
    Ch.6, Melville Publishing Co., Los Angeles, California, 1973.

9. L.D. Higgins and F.J. Smith, "Disc Access Algorithms",
    Computer J., 14, 249-53, 1971.

10. M. Carville, "A Study in on-line Text Retrieval", Ph.D. Thesis,
    The Queen's University of Belfast, N. Ireland, 1976.

11. F.J. Smith, "The Small Computer and Law", Computers and Law,
    No. 16, 4-5, 1978.

12. C. Weitzman, "Distributed Micro/Minicomputer Systems",
    Prentice Hall, New Jersey, 60-79, 1980.

13. J.S. Rubin, "An Automated Research System", Automated Law
    Research: A collection of presentations delivered at the First
    National Conference on Automated Law Research, American Bar
    Association, 35-42, 1973.

14. "A European Law Centre Service", Newscast II,
    4 Bloomsbury Square, London WC1A 2RL, 1981.

15. J.L. Hall (Compiled by), "On-line Information Retrieval,
    1965-1976: Bibliography with a guide to On-line Data Bases and
    Systems", ASLIB, London, 1977.

16. R.D. Wooley, "Microcomputers and Videodiscs: New Dimension for
     Computer Based Education", Interface Age, 4, 79-82, 1979.

17. C. Landauer and C. Mah, "Message Extraction through Estimation
     of Relevance", Summary of Papers presented at the Third
     International Conference on Information Storage and Retrieval
     (Joint BCS and ACM Symposium), Cambridge, England, p 40, 1980.

Part 3
Computers and People

Politics and Policies for Computing and Communications

F. J. M. Laver, CBE FBCS

INTRODUCTION

Because there is no accepted general term covering the use of
electronics in telecommunications, computing, information, robotics
and automatic control, I shall lump them together as 'teletechnics'.
That word has three merits: it is brief, it is wholly Greek, and
its prefix reminds us that, until nanocomputers are routinely
implanted in our brains, even local computers have to communicate
with their users through terminals connected to transmission lines.
Isn't it sad that, at the end of all that subtle logic and clever
semi-conducting, we are forced back to the rude, slow, mechanics of
sound, signs and keyboards!

My subject is the question: why on earth doesn't the Government
wake up and do something about this, that or the other aspect of
teletechnics?   The responses sought by that despairing cry range
from the economic: more cash for research, or new product development; to the political: open up the operation of data networks,
or shut up the use of personal data.   They all assume that the
combination of computing and communications with programmed control
has quite exceptionally important implications.   That premise is
not self-evident, but this is not the occasion to debate its truth:
heathens may care to read one of the numerous tracts on the life to
come - in the age of cyber-informatics.   It is only fair to say
that many who write these prophecies adopt an evangelical, pop-
science, approach - all terabytes and Tomorrow's Utopia; while
others luxuriate in apocalyptic descriptions of impending doom.
Three books, however, I can recommend; the other two are: John
McHale's 'The Changing Information Environment', and MIT's study
'The Computer Age: A Twenty-year View'.

I shall assume that there will be social and economic effects of
some importance, and consider what Society or The State should do;
because my context is the United Kingdom, we can still usefully
separate these two fields of communal human action.   'Society' is
the ensemble of individuals and voluntary associations of all
kinds - you and me, software and systems houses, hardware manufacturers, professional institutions, trade unions and so on.
'The State' is the political unit to which we belong, by accident
of birth and failure to emigrate, and which has the function of
enacting laws whose application is universal, plus the power to
enforce our compliance.   Thomas Paine brought this distinction
into sharp focus when he wrote: "Society is produced by our wants,
and government by our wickedness."

The authority of our state has been delegated to an elected
government, which acts always within the law.   Changes in government action may, therefore, require changes in the law, and
politics begins here.   Debate between political parties is an
exothermic reaction which converts disagreed premises into dis-

agreed conclusions.   Nowhere is disagreement more marked than over
the proper role of the state in economic and social affairs, and it
has lately become the practice when the ruling party changes, for
the incoming government to reverse the principal economic acts of
its predecessors.

Unfortunately, the planning, design, construction and commissioning
of any large project are complex and interlocking activities which
require coherence of policy over periods that are long compared
with the average interval between general elections.   Aristotle
advised against extending the electoral cycle when he wrote: "It
is not easy for a person to do any great harm when his tenure of
office is short."   The remedy, therefore, is to devise some all-
party instrument to evolve and establish long-term national
objectives, and to help to steer the economic acts of government
with fewer, and less drastic changes of course.

Political inconstancy is an unwelcome and costly factor which delays
and diminishes the enjoyment, use and profit we could derive from
advances in teletechnics.   At present, the only election-proof
policies are those with multi-party support, thus, the protection of
human rights is a political aim on which we all agree.   Such
policies, however, tend to be somewhat pallid lowest-common-plati-
tudes, and more positive policies offering an immediate boost to
teletechnics provide much less secure foundations on which to build
and invest.   Governments are frequently urged to be bold and far-
seeing;   but boldness attracts opposition, and the vision of
politicians rarely extends beyond the relentlessly narrowing
electoral horizon.

It would be naive to overlook the influence of the struggle for
power between political parties, but indelicate to explore their
differences here;   nor could I guarantee to do so fairly.   Less
controversially, I shall list some helpful actions open to British
administrations, in a kind of menu from which our rulers might
select.   It is usually better for a government not to legislate
if it does not have to do so: there is no shortage of laws.
Moreover, the pressure of parliamentary business means that new
measures are rather more hastily drafted, and rather less critic-
ally examined, than is needed to control their side-effects.   To
take an obsolete, foreign, and therefore non-partisan, illustration
of these: prohibition in America unfortunately increased the output of gangster films, as well as reducing the input of alcohol.

Even when the state does not need to be involved as law-maker,
society may find it worthwhile to adopt voluntarily policies for
improving the health and promoting the growth of teletechnics.   We
have examples in BCS Codes of Practice and Conduct, in British
Standards, in the universities' acceptance of computing science as a
respectable - or, at least, an examinable - discipline, and so on.
The state can also influence society by its non-legislative actions,

as by its purchasing policy for teletechnics, by its own use of
computers, by the public pronouncements of Ministers and senior
officials, and by steering its actions delicately within existing
laws.

TELETECHNICS AND THE GOVERNMENT

It is convenient to note the policies and actions open to the
Government under eight heads.   None is novel, and several have
tried; but truly significant help for the development of teletechnics require a more coherent, and a very much more sustained
and energetic programme of support than has yet been offered in the
UK.

1. Election Proofing

   A stable economic environment requires all the political parties
   who are likely to form governments to share a firm commitment to
   producing and maintaining a British teletechnics industry able
   to compete strongly in international markets.   Without
   stability, firms cannot devise reliable long-term plans to guide
   their future growth; and without plans that respond to the real
   time scales of the industry, a firm's development consists of a
   succession of short-term expedients as it limps from crisis to
   crisis.

   But why should the political parties agree to support teletechnics when they agree about so little else?   The usual
   arguments are listed:

   (a) As a vital element of our national 'infrastructure'
       effective teletechnic systems are necessary to the
       efficiency of the whole of industry, commerce and govern-
       ment.

   (b) Teletechnics is a high-growth industry, with virtually
       unlimited scope for market development, and its success is
       a necessary component of national economic growth.

   (c) Teletechnics not only provides employment in itself, its
       technology makes an indispensable contribution to the
       competitiveness of other products - and therefore to employ-
       ment - in most other industries today.

   (d) We have amply demonstrated our skills in teletechnic
       invention and design, and cannot afford to bury this talent.

   (e) Teletechnics is the acme of high technology, and success in
       it proclaims our competence in advanced engineering - so
       helping to offset the Beefeater image of Britain.

(f) Teletechnic products have an exceptionally high import/
export conversion ratio, for they consume few raw materials
and little energy - software especially!

(g) Our balance of payments is further helped when our own
indispensable needs for teletechnic systems can be met by
domestic suppliers.

(h) Other countries, notably Japan and France, give massive
support to their teletechnic industries, and we need to
redress the balance if we are to match them in home and
overseas markets.

(i) The vital importance of teletechnics to Britain's industry,
and to national defence, requires strategic independence of
overseas sources, for these may falter in time of need, or
may fail to provide as advanced a technology as that available to their own industries: self-sufficiency in teletechnics removes a potential constraint on foreign policy.

In addition to these reasons, there are other economic and
social questions which may justify government intervention to
protect the public.

I should like to see BCS initiate discussions with the principal
political parties in order to:

- isolate a nucleus of aims and policies for the development and
control of teletechnics in Britain, which all parties accept;

- attach whatever priorities can be determined non-controversi-
ally, on social, economic or technological grounds;

- note where and how the individual policies and priorities of
each party differ.

Clarification of this kind could stake out a much needed patch
of firm ground on which to build the future growth of teletechnics.

2. Persuade and Induce

It is, of course, primarily the responsibility of the teletechnics industry to persuade potential customers, and induce
them to buy its wares. However, teletechnic systems -
computers especially - have acquired a putrid public image for
a number of reasons, which include:

(a) widespread fears that men and women will be displaced into
prolonged unemployment;

(b) the anxieties of vocal minority about personal privacy and
surveillance;

(c) the popular belief that teletechnics is much too complex
    for ordinary people to understand or influence, yet far too
    important to be trusted to the scheming of 'scientists';

(d) first-hand encounters with badly designed and poorly
    executed systems which have generated gross errors and
    degraded whatever services they have taken over.

These and other blemishes have been magnified by the media, in
part because conflict and disaster are judged more newsworthy
than harmony and success, but also because teletechnic specialists too often speak from the clouds in an opaque and esoteric
jargon.

The miasma of suspicion and fear is now too thick and too widespread to be dispersed by the sales cries of competing
suppliers.   The public needs systematic reassurance by a calm,
disinterested, and authoritative presentation of the facts.
Because this should not even seem to be a dose of official
bromide designed to induce docility, it cannot come directly
from the Government.   Perhaps the National Computing Centre
might extend its remit to cover the public at large, and
commission and publish, at cheap subsidised prices, a top-
flight series of books, articles, tapes and films.

The Government can bring its considerable influence to bear in
other ways:

  (i) Above all by the example it sets in using British hard-
      ware and software in its own teletechnic systems, civil
      and military.

 (ii) Through the encouragement of standardization by making
      more men, women and money available to speed the prepar-
      ation of international standards, and by insisting on
      their strict observance in its own purchases and oper-
      ations.

(iii) By setting up validation services, for example, to
      provide an independent audit of the design and operation
      of measures intended to protect security and privacy;
      certification of that kind could be invaluable as an aid
      to export sales.

 (iv) The most obvious form of promotion is by financial induce-
      ments to users, either by direct grants, or by tax reliefs
      coupled to investment in appropriate technology.

3. New Systems not Old

Hectic innovation will continue to dominate the market, and a

nation will succeed only when its teletechnic industry remains
acutely dissatisfied with its current products. The Government
has recognised the need to encourage the use of microprocessor
techniques, and backed its conviction with money. This commitment should be extended to the whole of teletechnics. In its
own work, the Government should always be ready to pioneer new
kinds of application, using British hardware wherever possible,
and British software always. It is important for Britain to
be competent in the manufacture of teletechnic hardware, but it
is absolutely essential that we beat the best in applying it.
Leading-edge innovation is not a natural, or comfortable,
posture for government departments; it is unlikely to allow
acceptance of the lowest tender, and the possibility of failure
cannot be eliminated. Any attempt to kill two birds with one
stone risks missing both and breaking a window.

Everyone will have novelties they would like to be supported:
mine appear below. In all of them, I would want to insist
that human needs remain paramount. Our new systems must be
'user-friendly', and must satisfy their operators with work that
is evidently useful, responsible, varied and not machine-paced.
Systems must be made for man, and never again vice versa. Five
items are especially important in my view:

(a) Viewdata for both open and restricted (public and private)
    use will be a key component of office work, and not for text
    alone; it should be pushed ahead as fast and as far as
    possible - or even faster, and certainly further.

(b) Electronic mail is an off-shoot of viewdata but distinct
    from it with its particular emphases on privacy, printing
    and cheapness.

(c) Federated computer systems linking machines of differing
    sizes and manufacture, in which centralization and de-
    centralization cease to have any meaning - an inevitable
    development where we have so much to learn.

(d) Secure systems in which data bases are conceptual not
    geographical, with all information widely dispersed - and
    thus insensitive to local failure, as in a hologram.

(e) Local work centres in which the white collar staffs of
    different, remote, employers share a common building, as the
    most practical form of telecommuting, and a way of returning
    employment opportunities to rural areas.

4. Help for the Suppliers

Governments cannot help industries, for industries are meta-
economic fictions; only firms exist. It is, however, thought

to be altogether more respectable to subsume help for an individual firm under a general theorem: no sooner do we admit the
need to help Messrs XYZ & Co than we perceive the national
importance of the corresponding 'industry'.   Teletechnics
covers three industrial components with different needs.

Telecommunications, the oldest, revolves around a public
utility whose funding by past governments has assumed very long
working lives for its equipment, and a correspondingly gentle
pace of technical development.   Automatic control has been
dominated by engineering products tailor-made for individual
customers.   Computing is young, brash, frenetic in innovation,
and fiercely competitive in selling general-purpose products -
readymade to fit no one in particular.   It is troublesome also
in the inevitable importance of software for, because that
intangible product depends much more on brain power than on
capital equipment, sfotware suppliers tend somewhat to tran-
sience - some at times have resembled statistical fluctuations
rather than durable entities; and that makes for difficulty
when commiting public funds.   Equally troublesome is the fact
that the sales potential for teletechnic products within Britain
is too small to support an economic scale of activity; exports
are essential.   In export sales particularly, the hardware
market resembles a war, for the competition is fierce and
unforgiving, and success may go to those with the big battal-
ions.   Software selling, however, is more like a game, with
winnings awarded for skill and experience; the small but
clever can still win.   The market for applications, systems and
packages, is a race where rewards are confined to those who stay
ahead of the field.

These diversities, compounded by the wide variety in size and
stability of the firms engaged, make general conclusions about
government support more than usually suspect.   What is required
is a flexible, rapid, response which can be sensitively adjusted
to each individual need; but such a course is inevitably wide
open to contentious criticism when public money is being
distributed, and when political points are up for the scoring.

Various methods have been used to support suppliers:

(a) Help with financing by loan guarantees, loans, equity parti-
    cipation, cash grants, tax relief on interest payments or on
    profits.

(b) Start-up finance for new firms producing innovative goods.

(c) Preference for home suppliers in public sector purchases -
    as in other countries.

(d) Exports have been assisted by credit guarantees; and could

be further helped by validating performance, because teletechnic systems are often bought by those who lack the
specialist skills required for testing or appraisal.

(e) Import controls have protected other new industries -
synthetic dye-stuffs and silks, for instance - they have
ranged from heavy import duties to complete prohibition;
Britain is, of course, exceptionally vulnerable to
reprisals.

This range of remedies suggests that no sovereign cure has been
found, and that governments will continue to treat each symptom
as it becomes acute.   Perhaps the only lesson is that there may
be a critical mass, a threshold below which aid is wasted.   A
Spanish proverb says: "He who gives quickly gives twice", so
giving twice as much twice as quickly may be eight times more
effective - the law is certainly non-linear.

5.   Forward to System Z

Teletechnics has a voracious appetite for innovation, and new-
product development is so heavy a drain on profits that a firm
whose earnings falter may be forced to cut back the development
work on which its long-term survival depends.   This vicious
circle operates with singular force in an industry where very
large firms can set a pace of advance that burns off smaller
rivals;   fortunately, they do not always succeed.   Government
help has been specifically directed to new-product development,
which it is important to distinguish from research.

Research has become a debased coin, which often means no more
than opening a reference book or two.   The place for real
research is in the universities where, indeed, the Government is
its principal patron.   Essentially, the results of research are
unpredictable - if not, we could save time and money by predicting them;   hence, say, 10% of research funds should be
allocated to long shots, most of which will miss or fizzle.   I
would like to see more money spent, on the principle of maximum
unfairness, to support the best workers in the fields listed
below:

(a) Artificial intelligence, in order to correct the Lighthill
deviation, which was as unfortunate as Airy's condemnation
of Babbage;   eminent scientists are hardly ever right when
they cry 'impossible'.

(b) Robotics exploiting the artificial intelligence it will need
to pass beyond automation with chips.

(c) The use of interactive systems with physiological sensors
and colour video plus audio displays for the treatment of

mental disability.

(d) The analysis of reliability so that we can design it into the massive teletechnic systems which will perform the vital functions of our society.

(e) Program validation as a separate study, although basic to system dependability.

(f) Improved programming and command language - an inexhaustible theme which is essential to the widest use of computers and urgently needed to contain the rapidly rising cost of software.

Product development and introduction are larger, much more expensive matters than research and involve skills not commonly available in universities, or congenial to academics.   They must be supported in industry, in the ways we have discussed. I would like to see this aid selectively enlarged in support of future winners.   Backing winners is a hazardous occupation, but I have marked my card:

(i) Systems using many processors, dispersed and local.

(ii) Parallelism in numerical and systems analysis for array processors;   for these must have a fruitful future in all fields of modelling.

(iii) Cheap, massive, content-addressable stores without moving parts;   for reliable, high-volume, easy-to-use files are the key to the dispersed, friendly systems we so badly need.

(iv) Convincing, cheap, encryption devices to allay the wretched fears of those who worry about privacy, and to provide confidentiality for commercial transactions.

6. Foundations

The development of teletechnics depends on many pre-coditions, for example on public order and stable government.   More specifically, it can prosper only if adequate supporting services are made available.   Of these, data communications - the most important - are provided by a state monopoly primarily concerned with the public telephone service.   While this arrangement continues, the Government must act to ensure that the development of data services does not lag.   It could do this by ministerial directive, but more probably by non-attributable arm-twisting, or by introducing alternative suppliers.   This needs careful thought, for little would be gained by removing British Telecom's telephone monopoly, nor by breaking up its

network of cable and radio channels - for private competitors
are much more likely to flock around the profitable inter-city
services than rush to provide a comprehensive national coverage.

The arguments for a monopoly of data terminals and switching
centres are less obvious; more capital for their development
might be forthcoming from private sources. Only the innocent
would expect this to reduce costs to the customers, but it might
increase the speed of provision, the range of facilities and the
pace of innovation. The public interest in access to, and the
adequacy of, privately-provided data-links would probably need
to be protected by regulation.

Teletext services, such as viewdata and whatever may be provided
by cable television, raise many complex issues of public policy.
Who should supply the information disseminated, and on what
terms? Should viewdata include electronic mail? Who will
watch over advertising, competition with local press and radio,
pornography, and so on? Should computing facilities be
offered, and on what terms? Teletext has immense potential and
correspondingly large problems but, as an essential component of
office systems, it is of crucial importance to the future of
teletechnics. We urgently need policies for the development
and control of these supporting services before their pattern
becomes set and unalterable.

7. Economics and Individuals

The greatest fear created by teletechnics flows from its
expected effects on employment, for it is almost always used to
reduce the unit costs of production or, as it is more usually
phrased, 'to increase productivity'. The social problems
arise from the down-grading of jobs by the de-skilling, close
monitoring and pace-setting which commonly accompany automation.

How acute these problems will become depends on the speed of
development in robotics and on whether the rate of economic
growth exceeds the rate of increase in productivity. For many
years, at least, technological unemployment will pose major
personal and social problems. Some have proposed to solve
these by work-sharing - by shortening the working week, increasing holidays, or offering sabbaticals or early retirement.
Superficially attractive, this course would stir up a hornet's
nest of its own. This whole area has deep and broad implications for social stability, for the provision of leisure
facilities, for education and for remedial re-education; but
few of the public utterances of politicians, employers or trade
unions give much confidence that acceptable policies will emerge
before crises develop and panic actions are taken.

8. Social Control

Those of us who have written about teletechnics and society are
open to a criticism which Gibbon applied in an earlier context,
namely that among the consequences which we foreshadow "some are
enumerated which innocence could not have suspected, and others
which reason cannot believe".   Even so, we have to take
seriously a list which can include:

(a) Personal privacy and liberty.

(b) Ethical and economic questions raised by artificial intelli-
    gence and robotics.

(c) Unequal access to information in teletechnic systems as
    between socio-economic groups, and between private persons
    and corporate bodies.

(d) Inability of the electorate, or their non-specialist repre-
    sentatives, to challenge decisions based on complex analyses
    and models.

(e) Social and economic consequences of industrial action by
    teletechnic staff, which is being intensified daily by the
    concentration of data storage and processing, and by heavy
    dependence on data links.

The state and society will each be forced to act sooner or later
to control the impact of these and other matters.   The
institutions of society include professional bodies for computing and electronics, fully equipped with new - almost unused -
codes of ethics and practice.   Their social control function is
weakened because membership is not a pre-requisite of practice.
Should it be made so, as in medicine?   I believe the answer is
"Yes", and that sensitive areas of work should be reserved to
licensed practitioners - to a kind of State Registered Tele-
technologist.   De-registration for unprofessional conduct, or
evident incompetence, would then powerfully reinforce the
promptings of conscience.

CODA

The rag bag of actual and potential policies set out above resembles
a herbalist's catalogue rather than a well-considered course of
thereapy.   Policy making in teletechnics is still very primitive,
and I fear that it will remain so unless we can convince others that
teletechnics really does raise serious issues for society and the
state, for the solutions we can propose inevitably involve time,
trouble and money.   Business users will not act unless they can be
satisfied that our remedies have cash value - say, in the avoidance

of future troubles.   Politicians will not act unless they are
convinced that doing something about teletechnics has votes value.
This is not mere cynicism, for a businessman who ignores cash soon
fails;   and a politician who neglects to ensure his own re-election
loses all power.

Part of our difficulty is lack of precision.   Old Testament
prophets were men of immense character - and very little use for
aftershave - who went about crying: "Woe!   Woe!"   In teletechnics, prophecy is easy - I have often done it;   but prediction
with actual numbers and dates is virtually impossible, for we are
dealing with genuine novelty - and, by definition, novelty is unpredictable   (predicting the rate of take-up also, is most uncertain
because we have in teletechnics a technology of universal application) which does not really matter because men and women lived and
loved long before computers.   When we attack honest uncertainty
limits to any prediction about teletechnics, our limit lines diverge
rapidly and fall off the edges of the graph paper.   There is a
paradox here: the more precise our prediction, the less accurate it
will be.

We have to accept that few professional politicians have any burning
desire to promote teletechnics - they know an unpopular cause when
they see one!   Nor do they seek the tedium of legislating to
control it, for the subject is too technical for the broad sweep of
rhetoric, or to fill the headlines.   It is, therefore, unlikely to
elbow its way into the brief and over-crowded programmes of
parliament.   Our only practical course is to plug away, gradually
educating our political masters and accepting that, for them at
least, teletechnics will never be an end in itself.   Politics is
where ends are chosen, and we must strive to persuade the choice-
makers that our work is changing the parameters of choice, and that
eventually they will be unable to avoid taking account of what we
have done.

Equally, we have to accept the limitations of action by the state.
Laws make no one good: they merely punish those who are found out.
Again, teletechnics is used in pursuit of economic goals, and legal
regulations will not convert profit maximers into altruists overnight.

How then should we set about our task?   I believe that the importance of BCS derives as much or more from what it can do for society
as from what it does for its members.   It can and should speak with
authority on all that we have been reviewing - once it has its own
lines of policy clear - for it will be listened to with much more
respect and belief than any individual expert.   Above all, it must
be seen to be reasonable and not fanatical.   If we are not to be
dismissed as politically naive, we have to recognise that teletechnics is only one, and far from the most politically important,

of a great many matters competing for the Government's attention.

Some, perhaps most, of you may be disappointed that I have made no attempt to formulate, or even to commend, a 'national strategy' for teletechnics, as the French and the Japanese have done.   This is not because I regard teletechnics as unimportant;   on the contrary, I believe it to be one of the four more important technological developments of this century - with nuclear energy, semiconductor electronics and genetic engineering.   Nor is my reticence due to a sudden access of modesty, although I would question any one person's competence across so wide a field.   I am, by nature, a meliorist not a revolutionary, and my restraint reflects a conviction that in teletechnics we are still in the very early days of our ignorance, so that we do well to be modest, content to advance step by step, but always forward.   British Governments, also, are suspicious of Grand Designs, especially when they have been worked out with irrefutable logic, and we may well rejoice that they are.

A Reassessment of the Impact of Computers on Employment

John Bessant and Keith Dickson

Research Fellows, Technology Policy Unit,
University of Aston in Birmingham, UK

The emergence of low cost, computing power in the 1970's gave rise to much discussion about a "microelectronics revolution". A major feature of this debate was a concern for the employment consequences of applying the new technology.

Whilst this enabled a well publicised and comprehensive debate to reach an amazingly large audience, much of the evidence on which the debate was based, was speculative, overgeneralised and lacking in empirical substance, thus allowing the more sensational aspects to gain the ascendancy.

Four years on, a reassessment of the predicted employment consequences is possible. With hindsight, it can be seen that the "revolution" has not yet occurred, due mainly to the economic environment but also in part to the adoption characteristics of those existing applications. Thus any employment effects have been either somewhat lessened, delayed or clouded by more severe recessionary effects. This is not suggesting that the employment impact will be less significant, but rather, it allows more time for further information gathering so that more substantial and comprehensive policies can be satisfactorily formulated to deal with the envisaged problems.

INTRODUCTION

During the 1970's the phrase "microelectronics revolution" began to be used with rapidly increasing frequency: the popular conception of the technology became distorted, extending at times to a vision of the entire future contained on a tiny integrated circuit. Two features of the technology were singled out for particular media attention: the potential for economic revival through its widespread application and the potential for massive employment displacement. The basic argument behind the former was that microelectronics could be programmed to handle almost any logical task and was at the same time incredibly cheap. Therefore it could be fitted to existing machinery to make it operate more efficiently, to new machines (especially robots) designed to take full advantage of its "wonder-features", into existing products to enhance their overall performance and into totally new products which would represent a great leap forward for the consumer society. All of this activity, so the argument went, was bound to revitalise the manufacturing and market bases of the country. The government in agreeing with this argument, were quick to seize the opportunity and commit resources to promoting the technology and its adoption - at the same time as most other governments.

There were reservations, however, being expressed about the adverse consequences this technology might be expected to have. Chief amongst these was that of employment displacement: if the factories of the future were to be automated to a high degree by the silicon chip, what was to happen to all the people who used to work in them? This argument was reinforced by (apparently) strongly supportive evidence from the experience of industries like cash registers, where the changeover from mechanical to electronic systems (with its accompanying product simplification and reliability improvement) brought with it massive reductions in the labour force required. Similar examples could be found in the fields of TV set manufacture and the proposed manufacture of all-electronic telecommunications equipment. Some examples of these often-quoted figures appear in table (1).

Table 1. Typical examples of job loss statistics

(a)   Cash registers

NCR, (USA) in 1970 employed 37,000 and in 1975 employed 18,000.

One plant, Dayton in Ohio, went from 15,000 to 1,500 employees during this period. Two W. German NCR plants between 1974 and 1977 cut from 4,200 to 400. In UK, operations cut from 3,000 employees on 4 sites in 1975 to 1,000 on 2 sites by 1978.

Source (Hines and Searle)[1]

Table 1 (continued)

(b)   Telecommunications equipment

    (i)   Employment figures: UK

	1973	93,300
	1974	88,000
	1976	75,000
	1979	64,900
Sweden (L.M. Ericsson)	1975	15,300
	1978	10,300
W. Germany (one Siemens plant)	1977	1,800
	1978	800
USA (Western Electric)	1970	39,200
	1976	19,000
	1980	17,400

    (ii)   In task related terms, the average number of people
required for assembly of switching systems is:

1975	Strowger & Crossbar	100
1977	TXE-4	40
1985	System X	4

    (iii) Maintenance also declines: Western Electric estimate
75% fewer needed for fault-finding, repairs, maintenance
and installation. In Canada, System X maintenance per
10,000 lines in 2 areas fell from 9.4 men to 3.75 and
from 11.0 to 1.70.
                              Source (ETUI)[2]

(c)   TV Manufacture

    (i)   Japanese Employment figures

	1972	1976
- Hitachi	9,000	4,300
- National	9,875	3,900
- Sony	4,498	2,278
- All 7 major manufacturers	48,000	25,000
- Sets produced	8.4m	10.5m

Source (ETUI)

    (ii)   UK Employment figures

1973	1976
69,600	45,800

Prophets of doom were quick to extrapolate these figures to produce
horrifying claims for the job-destroying potential of microelectronics. Visions of the future "information society" became
haunted by the spectre of a return to 1930's Depression conditions:
such fears were clearly in evidence in the titles of many articles
published on this theme. "Microelectronics - job killer?",
"Automatic unemployment", "Armageddon or Utopia", "The collapse of
work" and so on. Some claims appeared to be pure sensationalism
- e.g. Stonier,[3] who regularly predicted unemployment of 10 million
within ten years, largely due to the advent of microelectronics
technology. Others - for example Jenkins and Sherman[4] were more
politically motivated and designed to illustrate specific viewpoints (in their case, the trade unions).

It would be unfair to group all the material which appeared at this
time under these headings: however, the acute shortage of factual
information meant that even the best of reports was largely
speculation. The effect was that a mythology was built up
surrounding microelectronics and its employment displacing effects.
(Again, a prosaic example could be gleaned from the incidence of
jokes in the entertainment media which were based on the theme of
microchips replacing jobs, activities and even biological functions!)

Much of the public "fuss" about the technology dates back to 1977,
when the BBC "Horizon" programme, "Now the chips are down" was
first screened. This raised many of the above questions and issues
for the first time and was certainly responsible for triggering off
much of the subsequent interest and exposure which the technology
has received, (for example, at least two peak viewing time TV
series - "The mighty micro" and "The silicon factor").

Four years on, we feel that it will be useful to take stock of
"the revolution", and to review the actual employment consequences.
Much of the background for this comes from work carried out within
the British Computer Society's Specialist Group on Computers and
Employment, which has included the preparation of a major annotated
bibliography on the subject.

Before examining the employment aspects, it will be useful to
review the arguments behind the "revolutionary" application of
microelectronics.

The unlikely marriage

One of the common practices (when revolutionary fever was running
high) was to list the enormous potential embodied in microelectronics. When linked to other elements like advanced telecommunications, computing theory and so on, the resultant
information technology became a "miracle" solution for all needs.
Table 2 gives examples of this approach.

At the same time it was clear that manufacturing industry had a
major requirement in the area of control: potentially any
activity which involved information processing would be amenable
to automation using microelectronics.   In the case of the service
sector this was even more pronounced: Porat's survey of information
content indicated that activities like banking and insurance were
very largely based around information processing.   Table 2 gives
examples of both of these.

Table 2.   The Potential of microelectronics

(a)   Potential advantages of microelectronics

reductions in:	cost	increases in:	flexibility
	processing time		complexity
	size		reliability
	connections		systems integr- ation
	maintenance downtime		memory capacity
			compatability with communica- tions systems
			word length

(b)   Potential uses in manufacturing

- controlled movement of materials, components, products
- control of process variables
- shaping, cutting, mixing and moulding of materials
- assembly of components into sub-assemblies and finished
  products
- control of quality at all stages of manufacture via
  inspection, testing or analysis
- organisation of the manufacturing process, including
  design, stock control, despatch, maintenance, task
  allocation, etc.

Source (J. Bessant et al, 1980)[5]

Table 2 (continued)

(c)   Potential uses in the service sector

        - office automation - information storage and retrieval,
        conversion (e.g. via word processors) into paper copies,
        communication (via phone, mail, satellite, etc.)

        - banking - electronic funds transfer, automated cash
        dispensers, computer-based filing, etc.

        - insurance - computerised accounting, claims processing,
        etc., integrated renewal/collection/commission system.

        - transport - automatic fare collection, ticket vending,
        computerised reservations, parcels booking, automatic
        signalling and operation, etc.

        - retailing - point-of-sale terminals, stock control systems,
        anti-theft and security systems, direct debit shopping, etc.

        - telecommunications - electronic switching, microwave
        transmissions, viewdata systems, automated dialling and
        charging, etc.

        - postal services - electronic mail, computer sorting etc.

Given this enormous range of activities (with significant
information processing content) on the one hand and a new technology
offering fast, reliable, flexible and cheap computing power on the
other, it was almost inevitable that assumptions would be made
about their compatibility. Much was made of this potential
marriage and widespread and rapid diffusion of the technology was
expected.

The role of government

Nowhere did this "ideal marriage" argument find stronger support
than in government circles. Given the rundown in UK performance
over many years in manufacturing - much of it associated with old
plant and unsophisticated equipment - and the need to maintain
the competitiveness of the traditionally high performance skills
of the service sector (especially "invisible" exports like banking
and insurance), it was inevitable that microelectronics technology
would receive serious consideration. Added to the external
pressures generated by increasing 3rd World industrialisation and
the support of high technology by most other developed countries,
this became a strategic imperative. The extent to which government
is now committed to the "restorative" powers of microelectronics
can be seen in the often-publicised faith in the twin pillars of

UK economic regeneration - North Sea Oil and "the miracle chip".

The practical steps taken were based around a massive £300m aid
package: additionally other schemes were linked in - for example,
support for automated small batch production (ASP), for robotics,
for instrumentation, for education, and so on. However, it is
important to note that the vast majority of this support was
promotional in nature: little was done in respect of developing
strategies to cope with the consequences of adoption.

Nevertheless, the concern about employment could not be ignored:
in addition to various rather loose policy statements about how to
cope with job displacement (e.g. early retirement, shorter working
week etc.), some urgent fact-finding research was commissioned.
In particular, the Manpower Services Commission report[6] was one of
the most comprehensive government efforts to examine the employment
question but even this tended to take an optimistic line.

The Role of the Trade Unions

For the Trade Unions, the problem was more complex for it posed a
dilemma of conflicting possibilities. On the one hand, they have
always supported industrial investment policies aimed at improving
the manufacturing base of the country in order to arrest the
decline of our industrial competitiveness and microelectronics
was seen as one such major investment opportunity. Yet, on the
other hand, they were wary of the employment implications since
their prime responsibility lay in protecting the jobs, and job
content, of their members.

Their initial response was essentially a cautious one, issuing
a number of "holding" policy statements concerning ways in which
employment effects should be dealt with. At the same time, several
unions were quick to initiate research programmes in order to
provide factual material as a basis for future policy-making.
This resulted in the publication of many reports into several
areas of employment like those on office work by APEX, telecommunications by POEU, white-collar work by ASTMS and AUEW (TASS),
etc., whilst organisations like ETUI and FIET gave European and
international perspectives. (7), (8), (9), (10), (11).

The research culminated in the TUC report, "Employment and Technology" (12) which provided a realistic national strategy based on
"technology agreements" in which employers and unions could
negotiate the conditions under which new technology would be
introduced.

These well researched and considered responses certainly indicated
the level of concern felt by the unions and reflected the enormity
of the employment problems posed by the new technology as seen from
the unions' perspective.

The problem was not just seen as a quantitative one, for the unions
quite rightly saw the qualitative implications as well - ranging
from differing effects on various skills and levels of employment,
changes in occupational structures, the implications for work
monitoring, supervision, health and safety, to possible demarcation
disputes between unions. The more perceptive unions predicted
that the first effects would be felt by women clerical workers,
since office equipment could be more easily modernized and they
were a fragmented and more vulnerable workforce.

Of all the interest groups involved in the whole debate, the unions
have provided the most comprehensive strategy towards technological
change.

Other interested parties

Manufacturing companies often appeared keen to adopt the new
technology for the obvious well-publicised economic reasons but
surveys carried out under the government awareness scheme indicated
that the level of appreciation of the technology and its
implications was very superficial. Anyhow, there was minimal
collective interest amongst firms for pursuing the subject since
different industrial sectors, and even individual firms within the
same sector, were prepared to embrace quite different strategies
for their own particular requirements.

Research institutions and universities did perceive the significance
of the debate and several began empirically based research projects.
But such research has taken a long time to surface partly due to
the nature of the enquiry but also because of the often cautious
and theoretical approach taken.

The economic concept of Kondratiev, or long wave, cycles was often
introduced into these studies. This description of historical
cycles of booms and recessions are often associated with major
periods of technological changes as well as being linked to
employment trends. Freeman,[13] for example, saw microelectronics
as the "heartland" technology of the upward surge of the next
cycle.

Political parties or their associated research bodies also entered
the debate and their reports showed marked similarities in the
policies for promoting the technology but with a divergence of
views concerning proposals to deal with the wider social effects.
Much depended, it appears, on which party was in power at the time
of publication.

The employment arguments

So what were the arguments about employment and the new technology?
There are several which we shall briefly discuss here:

(i)   product simplification: the development of cheap integrated
        circuitry means that mechanical and electromechanical logic
        systems can be replaced by electronic ones. Almost
        inevitably this will mean fewer parts in a given product,
        so requiring less assembly labour. Such simplification
        also permits automation of remaining assembly tasks.

(ii)   reliability and ease of maintenance: simplification of the
        product is also likely to reduce the number of moving
        parts and thus increase reliability. Maintenance is also
        simplified through modular design, self-diagnostics, etc.

(iii)   on-line monitoring of processes: on-line systems provide
        information and analysis on demand, when and where
        required. Such systems remove much of the need for manual
        supervision, progress chasing etc.

(iv)   automated assembly, robotics, etc.: combinations of
        mechanical/hydraulic/electromechanical actuators and
        microelectronics-based information processing capability
        can replace labour, particularly for repetitive, low-
        skilled activities.

(v)   automated test equipment: using microelectronics-based
        systems gives increases in speed, accuracy, consistency
        and reliability of testing, leading to the likely
        displacement of manual testing.

(vi)   computer-aided design: implies replacement of draughtsman
        and designer skills.

(vii)   automated handling systems: implies reduction in the need
        for manual storekeeping and distribution skills.

(viii) office automation: the high information content of office
        work makes it a prime target for substitution of labour by
        information processing technologies. This is especially
        true as the integration of elements of office systems -

(viii) continued

   e.g. word processors, computer files, intelligent copiers,
   electronic mail and so on - begins to take place.

 (ix) banking systems/EFT: automated facilities for banking
   and insurance transactions - particularly the concept of
   electronic funds transfer - will certainly reduce the
   need for cash transactions and so bring about reductions
   in staff like bank tellers and insurance clerks.

In numerical terms, a number of figures were presented to illustrate
the extent of these employment displacement areas: table 1 gives
some examples. At first sight these give considerable cause for
concern, particularly in the service sector. However, closer
examination suggests that many of these early reports were
exaggerated and taken out of context, or else the same reports
and figures were repeatedly used, thus masking their isolated
nature. Other criticisms include the fact that many of the
predictions made involved making a number of quite significant
and unjustifiable assumptions about the way things were likely to
proceed in the future. Overall it became clear that carefully
researched and balanced information was in short supply but badly
needed.

Four years on

Having criticised early reports and commentary for lack of factual
information, it would be nice to report that the position has now
changed. Sadly this is not the case: despite a number of
valuable reports (e.g. Green et al,[14] Bird,[15] Swords-
Isherwood and Senker,[16])
the level of speculation as to the employment effects of microelectronics remains high. More seriously, the descent into
recession has brought with it such serious unemployment that it
has totally distorted "normal" employment patterns thus making it
very difficult to attribute any direct causal links between new
technology and job loss.

At the same time, it is clear that the climate has changed. Microelectronics is no longer seen in such a revolutionary role but
increasingly as just one more increment in the overall pattern of
innovation eg IFAC.[17] Certainly the rate of take-up - particularly in
the manufacturing sector - has been much slower than expected,
and thus the employment effects far less devastating than had been
predicted. Without going into detail (but see Bessant 1980,[18]
Bessant and Dickson 1981[19] for more information) the range of problems
encountered in industrial adoption suggest that the "marriage"
between manufacturing and the chip is going to involve a long
courtship. (See table 3 for examples).

Having said that, there are changes taking place - especially where
new plant is constructed and the full "systems" advantage implicit
in the technology can be exploited, rather than the piecemeal
applications which have characterised the bulk of investment so far.
(The new Metro line at BL, Longbridge, is an example of high level
automation, exploiting the systems approach on a new site).

In the service sector, the effects have been more widespread -
partly because of the high information content of many activities
in this area, and partly because of the comparative ease with
which new equipment can be introduced on an incremental basis
rather than a more costly total systems change.

As far as figures for actual labour displacement are concerned,
these are, as previously noted, hard to obtain especially in the
context of recession. It is somewhat easier to identify likely
trends and table   gives a few examples. More valuable, perhaps,
would be descriptive information regarding changes in job content
as a result of the adoption of new technology - but there are few
examples available. Downing's [20] **work on changing**
women's role in offices, Swords-Isherwood and Senker's on skills
changes in engineering, and Gilchrist and Shenkin's [21] on typesetting
jobs (albeit very recent example).

Another important consideration is the relationship this technology
bears to the international division of labour. In the growing
industrialisation of the developing world, microelectronics
technology is likely to play a significant role in both increasing
the rate of industrialization and through its part in a defensive
high technology strategy adopted by the developed countries. In
either case, the use of this technology will have significant
employment consequences for these countries, a topic which has
been the focus of several studies (e.g. Hoffman and Rush, [22]
Rada, [23] Jacobsson. [24])

Concluding discussion

It is clear that the "revolution" has not yet taken place. Given
the historical perspective, one might add "again" to that statement,
for there have been previous episodes concerning computers and
employment, viz the automation debates of the '50's and '60's.
However we believe that it would be wrong to assume that the
threats posed in the present episode are also insignificant. It
is more realistic to see the rate rather than the direction of
technical change having altered; ultimately the employment and
other social effects will emerge, but meanwhile there is some
further time to examine policy options and so respond more
effectively.

Table 3.   Influences on adoption of microprocessors by
           manufacturing industry

 (i) innovation-related factors
   - costs
   - reliability
   - maintainability
   - compatibility
   - complexity
   - contribution to: labour saving, energy saving,
    materials saving, product quality improvement,
    product variety improvement and other perceived
    advantages
   - perceived risks of adoption

 (ii) organisation-related factors
   - size
   - structure
   - availability of skilled resources
   - access to training
   - tradition of innovation
   - industrial relations
   - presence of key figures ("champions", "gatekeepers",
                etc.)
   - introduction strategies
   - availability of capital and other resources
   - presence of technically competent management
   - age of plant
   - likely changes in work patterns

 (iii) environment-related factors
   - economic climate
   - behaviour of competitors
   - relationship to supplier firms
   - role of government
   - market characteristics
   - state of labour market

Hitherto, the responses have taken one of the following forms:-

(i)   "We've seen it all before". Like the earlier automation debates, the belief is that it will sort itself out eventually. However, the differences now are two-fold; firstly, the degree of technological integration and pervasiveness today are much more significant, and secondly, the economic expansion of those previous periods is no longer with us.

(ii)   Non-adoption, or rather, if microelectronics is such a threat to employment, then why bother? But the fact is that estimates suggest that the sort of economic growth (even without the assistance of microelectronics) the U.K. would need just to return to "normal" employment, is clearly an improbable task under present circumstances.

(iii)   service sector absorption: one view of the employment problem has been to see it in terms of an inevitable shift towards the "post-industrial" society (Bell,[25] Gershuny[26]) this implies a drift from manufacturing to services as the basis for employment. Implicit in this is the assumption that the service sector has a vast absorptive employment capability: whilst this may be true in the ideal sense - in that activities like health and welfare services could absorb large numbers of people - it is less clear in practice how it would operate. Commentators using this argument point to the recent growth in service sector employment (e.g. Porat) - but what they fail to point out is that the bulk of this has been in fields like banking and insurance. Since it is these sectors which are under most threat from information technology, it is difficult to see how they would provide absorptive capacity: indeed, it is only as a consequence of their rapid growth recently that they have been able to avoid employment displacement!

(iv)   new jobs: another common argument is that new technologies create new industries around new products and this generates new jobs to replace those displaced. Examples include the production of TV games, microelectronic components and assemblies, computers and controllers, and so on. The problem with these is that none of them is a labour-intensive process, and is based far more around capital-intensive, high-technology equipment. Secondly, the skills likely to be needed in these new areas are different and of a higher order than those made available through

employment displacement. Thus the number and type of jobs
likely to emerge from this area will be poorly matched to the
large number of unemployed displaced onto the labour market by
adoption of microelectronics elsewhere.

We have argued that the rate of diffusion of information technology
is slower than had been expected, and consequently there is a
space of time available to improve on policies aimed at dealing
with the technology's impact. The foregoing are clearly examples
of a failure to appreciate the likely employment implications:
when coupled to the strongly promotional emphasis which existing
policies have had regarding this technology, it is clear that
there is a need for significant change.

A policy to help adapt to rather than adopt information
technology is not simple to design and is anyway beyond the scope
of this paper. However, we have tried to outline in skeleton
form areas of concern which require further attention: these
appear in table 4.

Table 4.   Some relevant policy-making areas for adapting to
           information technology.

   (i)   Skills/education: need to ensure adequate provision
         for training at all levels from school upwards
         (including use of advanced training technology).
         - closer monitoring of needs and improved feedback
         mechanisms for training agencies.
         - more specific support to ITB's, ITB liaison with
         companies and in-company training schemes.
         - increased commitment to training support (financial
         and resources).
         - possible closer monitoring of the labour market
         aimed at better matching of supply and demand.

   (ii) Information/awareness: need for continuing awareness
         development (as under MAP scheme) but aimed at other
         groups apart from management.
         - guidance/advice for firms requiring support for the
         management of change as well as its technological
         aspects. (Especially in areas like training, job
         design and enrichment, relocation of labour,
         development of suitable new support policies in
         maintenance, and so on).

(iii)   <u>Industrial relations</u>: need to support a move from
single union collective bargaining towards site-wide
(company-wide technology agreements).
- support for independent research aimed at
establishing a common information base from which
such technology agreements could be developed.
- extension of options for coping with labour
displacement - e.g. early retirement, shorter working
week, sabbatical leave, job sharing and so on.

References

(1)   C. Hines and G. Searle, "Automatic unemployment", Earth
Resources Research Ltd., London, 1971.

(2)   J. Evans, "Microelectronics and Employment in Europe in
the 1980's", European Trade Union Institute, Brussels,
Belgium, 1979.

(3)   T. Stonier, "The silicon chip, education and employment",
Advice, $\underline{7}$(3), pp.1-6, 1979.

(4)   C. Jenkins and B. Sherman, "The collapse of work",
Eyre Methuen, London, 1979.

(5)   J. Bessant, E. Braun and R. Moseley, "Microelectronics
in Manufacturing Industry: The Rate of Diffusion"
in T. Forester (ed.) "The Microelectronics Revolution",
Blackwells, Oxford, 1980.

(6)   J. Sleigh et al., "The Manpower Implications of Micro-
electronic Technology", Dept. of Employment Manpower
Study Group, HMSO, London, 1980.

(7)   APEX, "Office Technology: The Trade Union Response",
Association of Professional, Executive and Computer
Staff, London, 1979.

(8)   P.O.E.U., "The Modernisation of Telecommunications",
Post Office Engineering Union, London, 1979.

(9)   ASTMS, "Technological Change and Collective Bargaining",
ASTMS Discussion Document, 1979.

(10)   AUEW (TASS), "New Technology: A Guide for Negotiators",
A TASS Policy Statement, London, 1980.

(11)   FIET, "Computers and Work", International Federation of
        Commercial, Clerical and Technical Employees, Geneva,
        1979.

(12)   TUC, "Employment and Technology", Report by TUC General
        Council to Congress, 1979.

(13)   C. Freeman, "Technical change and unemployment", paper
        delivered at "Science, technology and public policy :
        an international perspective" Conference, University
        of New South Wales, Australia, December, 1977.

(14)   K. Green et al., "The Effects of Microelectronics
        Technologies on Employment Prospects: A Case Study
        of Tameside Gower Press, Farnborough, 1980.

(15)   E. Bird, "Information Technology in the Office: The
        Impact of Women's Jobs", Equal Opportunities Commission,
        1980.

(16)   N. Swords-Isherwood and P. Senker, "Microelectronics and
        the Engineering Industry - the Need for Skills", Frances
        Pinter Publishers, London, 1980.

(17)   IFAC, Workshop on "Automation, demand for work and the
        economy", Aston University, 7-9 May, 1980.

(18)   J. Bessant, "Influential factors in the adoption of
        manufacturing innovation", Working Paper Technology
        Policy Unit, University of Aston, 1980.

(19)   J. Bessant and K. Dickson, "Issues in the adoption of micro-
        electronics", Frances Pinter, London, (forthcoming
        1981).

(20)   H. Downing, "Word Processors and the Oppression of Women"
        in T. Forester (ed.), "The Microelectronics Revolution",
        Blackwell, Oxford, 1980.

(21)   B. Gilchrist and A. Shenkin, "Disappearing Jobs: The
        Impact of Computers on Employment", The Futurist,
        Vol. 15, No. 1, pp.44-50, February 1981.

(22)   K. Hoffman and H. Rush, "Microelectronics and industrial-
        isation in the Third World: some emerging issues",
        Occasional Paper, Science Policy Research Unit,
        University of Sussex, 1980.

(23)   J. Rada, "The impact of microelectronics", I.L.O.,
        Geneva, 1980.

(24)   S. Jacobsson, "Microelectronics, technical change and
        employment in less-developed countries", (mimeo)
        Research Policy Institute, University of Lund,
        Sweden, 1979.

(25)   D. Bell, "The coming of post-industrial society",
        Basic Books, New York, 1973, and Heinemann, London,
        1974.

(26)   J. Gershuny, "After industrial society?", Macmillan,
        London, 1978.

The Industrial Relations Challenge to Computer Professionals

Malcolm Peltu

Independent Consultant, UK

The implementation of computer-based systems are frequently at the forefront of industrial relations negotiations and disputes. Unions are pressing to have a say in the systems design, analysis and evaluation process. Management want computing professionals to exhibit greater empathy with real corporate, user and operator needs. Management and unions both recognise the importance of behavioural and human sciences in determining the effectiveness of a system and would like the work of computing professionals to be more accessible to non-technical staff.

All this creates an additional challenge to DP staff who are already faced with rapid technological developments. Computing professionals must start to learn new skills in behavioural and human sciences or, at least, recognise where the expertise of a human factors engineer is needed. DP staff must come out from their smokescreen of jargon-generated mystification and take more responsibility for the way their work affects other people's jobs, health and happiness.

1. THE RESPONSIBILITIES OF THE COMPUTING PROFESSIONAL

Computing professionals are paid to provide certain technical
skills as their primary occupation. Although the systems designed
and implemented by computing professionals have an impact on the
lives, jobs and well being of other people, responsibility for
the success or failure of a system stays officially with the
management who set the objectives and who have the final say in
accepting the suitability of the system.

Until the availability of low cost personal computer systems in the
late 1970s, computing professionals could argue that their position
as a relatively highly paid technical elite was justified because of
the rarity of their basic skills, such as programming and systems
analysis. The 'elite' status was perpetuated by the way DP staff
usually stayed as a breed apart from the rest of the organisations
for which they worked. The computing professional has tended to
perceive his or her career progress in terms of computing rather
than the activity of the organisation for which they work.

The personal computer showed that programming could be child's play.
They also put computing power into the hands of managers who began
to question the mystique, the excuses for project delays, the
general remoteness which had previously characterised the relationship between the user and the computing profession.

In many ways, the apparent simplicity of personal computing is
illusory and the need to develop well designed, reliable programs
is intrinsically more complex, subject to delays and requires more
specialist skills than typical personal computing tasks.

This paper, however, is more concerned with the nature of the
perception of computing professionals held by people involved
directly or indirectly in the use or impact of a computer system.

For many staff, the computing professional is an agent of change;
change that could destroy, deskill or dehumanise their job. Computing
professionals speak an apparently strange language. At a time of
high unemployment, relatively young computer staff are seen to be
in a priviledged, secure job; moreover, a job which frequently
defines (or eliminates) the jobs of others.

The computing professional has been seen by some managers, staff and
unions as having power without responsibility. When challenged
about a poorly designed system, the computing professional could
claim it was the fault of the management in setting the objectives.
The skill of the computing professional is computing, they claim,
not behavioural and human science tasks like job design, organisational behaviour, staff motivation, industrial psychology, etc.

Yet most tasks undertaken by computing professionals involve some form of interaction between people and machines. I believe it has been an abdication of responsibility for the computing 'profession' and 'industry' (the two terms are often synonymous) to take so long to recognise that human factor engineering, ergonomics, industrial psychology and related disciplines should be regarded as important basic elements in the training and expected expertise of anyone paid to develop or implement computer-based equipment and services.

Like architects who live in comfortable luxury houses but design tower blocks unfit for human habitation, computing professionals have sometimes used their priviledged and relatively luxurious jobs to create working conditions they themselves would not put up with for a day. Dr John Long of the Applied Psychology Unit of the Medical Research Council in Cambridge participated with IBM on a study into the psychological aspects of people/computer communications. He was appalled by what he found when talking to staff working on live online systems.

"We now look back on some of the industrial methods of the last century as imposing inhuman working conditions. Yet we seem to ignore the fact that computers have created many modern analogies," he commented (1).

Surely it is time that computing professionals took responsibility for the human consequences of their 'technical work'.

2. THE INDUSTRIAL RELATIONS IMPACT OF COMPUTING

The employment impact of technological innovation is not new; it goes back to the invention of the wheel and beyond. The most popular image of 'automation', however, was created by Charlie Chaplin in Modern Times — man becoming a cog in a gigantic machine. This image is a negative interpretation of a technique known as Scientific Management or Taylorism, after its originator, Frederick W Taylor, an early 20th Century behavioural scientist.

Taylorism subdivides work into units with relatively well defined inputs and quantified outputs. The worker's job is to achieve the output targets set with very little room for independent decision making; the worker's rewards are primarily the money received for reaching the required targets. Proponents of Taylorism claim that this approach provides a controlled way of achieving business objectives and satisfying basic worker needs. Critics claim it leads to alienation and dehumanisation of work.

After the Second World War, particularly in Scandinavia, new approaches to work organisation were developed which emphasised job enrichment, the importance of working in groups rather than in isolated units, greater staff involvement in the decision making process affecting the quality of the working environment (2).

In the 1970s, as the impact of computing across a wide spectrum of activities became evident, the Scandinavian approach to industrial democracy and work design was applied to the introduction of computer-based services.

In 1977, for example, the Norwegian national representative bodies for unions and management concluded a 'technology agreement' which provided the framework for introducing 'new technology'. This included two principles which impinge directly on the work of computing professionals. First, employees would be consulted about any technological innovation as early as possible. Second, staff could appoint a data steward to represent their views on the technical systems design team. The Norwegian Working Environment Act in the same year brought the force of law to bear in trying to ensure that computers do not cause a deterioration in the working environment, job satisfaction, etc.

Specific attention has been focused on the health and safety factors in the design of Visual Display Units (VDUs). In 1978, Sweden became the first country to issue national directives relating to VDUs,through a document Reading of Display Screens. More recently national guidelines have been drawn up in West Germany. There are also many well documented research projects and recommended guidelines covering physical factors, like screen and keyboard design, operator fatigue, the need for rest periods, suitable lighting, etc. (3, 4, 5, 6, 7).

Despite the known results of human factors engineering and ergonomics research, many computer professionals and managers responsible for implementing computer systems create unnecessary human discomfort and operational inefficiency because of ignorance of this research or a failure to insist that suppliers satisfy the required criteria.

D. Doran of British Airways, one of the world's first and largest users of VDUs, states firmly (4): "The discomfort created by many VDUs can cause (for the operator) resentment, complaint, eye-strain, etc and (for the employer) restrictions on use, lack of performance, claims for concessions, etc and, perhaps, largely abortive expenditure on piecemeal palliatives. The discomfort is the cumulative, perhaps synergistic, effect of several problems. But there already exist solutions, either complete or partial, to most of these problems....

"Exchanging experience and perfecting knowledge is certainly important but it is equally important to devise means of informing VDU customers that many of the problems are unnecessary so that they can persuade VDU manufacturers to put theory into practice by adopting known solutions to unnecessary environmental burdens."

Attention amongst management and unions has been moving away from
the relatively well-quantified area of equipment ergonomics and the
physical environment to the more nebulous but crucial questions
about organisational behaviour, job design, staff motivation, etc.
From the staff point of view, the prime fear is that some of the
most dehumanising aspects of Taylorism will be repeated with office
automation. For managers, the main concern is to identify those
behavioural science factors which can help to improve the
productivity and effectiveness of electronic information systems.

There is considerable evidence from the first wave of office automation in the last four or five years that the requirements of both
sides can be met by a more human-centred approach to systems design.
Firstly, it is clear that there is a tendency towards Taylorism
in some forms of word processor implementations. Francis McMahon
for example, has conducted a study of some of the major users of
word processors in Britain for Birkbeck College, London (8). She
concluded that many word processor operators were virtually
"automotons" and that word processing jobs are as "fragmented as
an assembly line in a car factory."

At the same time, there is evidence that such production line office
systems run by alienated, unmotivated staff do not produce the
required productivity improvements. For example, Jim Driscoll of the
Alfred P Sloan School of Management at the Massachusetts Institute
of Technology says that office automation designs which emphasise
the hardware and software technologies "portend very little
improvement in the productivity of office workers" (9) However,
he believes that if office systems designers draw on the "long
standing tradition of behavioural science research", a new
organisation design can be developed to take maximum advantage of
the automation of an office.

"Such a design will coordinate the social organisation and the tasks
of office workers in a more participative and informal organisational climate. Such a design can reasonably be expected to develop
a more motivated, committed and produtive office workforce," he says.

In addition to physical health and safety questions and organisation
and job design, there is another factor which places computer-based
systems at the forefront of modern industrial relations: the fear
of unemployment.

In the UK, it was the potential link between microelectronics and
job losses which alerted the nation - including the unions - to the
significance of information technology. This lead to a great deal
of research amongst unions and culminated in the publication of
a 10-point plan by the TUC (10). This plan suggest the main
elements in what has become known as Technology Agreements.

Technology Agreements have now become a focus for discussion throughout the world for creating a framework within which to analyse and
negotiate the terms under which technological innovation takes place.

3. THE TUC 10-POINT TECHNOLOGY AGREEMENT PLAN

The following is a summary of the TUC plan which has formed the
basis for New Technology Agreement proposals by individual unions.
Although few actual agreements cover the full ten points, this
summary encapsulates the major issues at stake. I have ordered these
points so that the first five are those of most relevance to
computing professionals.

-Status quo: no new technology before agreement. Full consultation and agreement should be reached before major decisions
are taken such as choice of equipment or systems design approach.

-Information to staff in plain language. As part of consultation
procedure, staff should have access at an early stage to full
information about the objectives and nature of the system.
Such information should be presented in jargon-free language.

-Staff/union representative on systems design team. Specially
trained technology representative (equivalent to Scandinavian
data steward) to participate in technical design. Staff/unions
to have say in data protection and work measurement aspects.

-No deterioration in quality of the working environment. Covers
all the ergonomic and behavioural science factors discussed in
section 2 above.

-Adequate training and retraining. Part of a planned approach to
staff redeployment, more flexible career opportunities and
overcoming shortages of skilled staff.

-No redundancy or planned redundancy with priority to staff
redeployment and relocation.

-Reduction in working hours as way of sharing productivity
benefits.

-No disruption of pay structures and grading schemes. As information technology cuts across so many job categories and organisation structures, care needs to be taken to adapt personnel
policies without putting some groups at a sudden disadvantage
or destroying procedures developed over many years of negoti-
ation.

-Greater inter-union collaboration and rationalisation. The
all-pervasive nature of information technology cuts across
current union structures. This could lead to a rationalisation

of the highly fragmented nature of British industrial relations.

-Constant monitoring of agreements by joint management/union
team.

4. THE IMPACT ON COMPUTING PROFESSIONALS

An international white collar union, FIET, has explictly stated
that one of the objectives of Technology Agreements should be to
"Challenge the attitudes of DP professionals and put the view of
those affected in daily work." And, taken together, the first
four points in the TUC plan could have a profound effect on the
systems design, analysis and implementation process.

The status quo clause, staff consultation and priority given to
the quality of the working environment add constraints to the
traditional working methods of computing professionals. The need
to provide information clearly and in a language easily understandable to those without specialist technical knowledge will open
up computing activities to a more comprehensive and systematic
method of scrutiny by non-technical users (management and staff.)

It will no longer be possible to hide poor, thoughtless design
behind a smokescreen of technical mystique and jargon. If implemented in a positive environment, staff representation on the technical
team should mean that resultant design is both more effective
and humane because the final system should
                    -give higher priority to human factors
                    -be closer to real world needs rather than the formal
                     view of managers and systems analysts that relate more
                     to paper definitions than real actions
                    -provide a more satisfying, efficient working environ-
                     ment.

Of course, if there are negative industrial relations attitudes
the status quo clause could be used to block innovation;
consultation could become an excuse for delay; the technology
representative could use the technical design team as an extension
of management/union confrontation and may not even truly represent
the views of the staff.

In practice, most computing professionals will not be faced with
the full force of the TUC plan. But many managers agree with some
of the major concepts, such as more priority to human factors,
more non-jargon communications and better consultantion. The TUC
approach also has a great deal in common with developments
elsewhere in the world.

The International Labour Organisation, for example, represents

the views of governments, managers and unions throughout the world.
It has produced a set of guidelines (11) which follow the general
trend of the Scandinavian and TUC approaches. These advisory
conclusions include:

>   —workers and their representatives should be consulted
>   before decisions likely to affect their employment and
>   working conditions are made;
>   -close co-operation and effective communication should
>   prevail throughout the process of the introduction of
>   change;
>   —workers' representatives or organisations should bear in
>   mind the possibility of consulting experts to assist them;
>   —regard should be given to types of work organisation which
>   promote job satisfaction and higher skills.

The attitudes and implications of Technology Agreements are therefore
unlikely to be a temporary, isolated fad.They fit firmly into
the mainstream of industrial relations developments and evokes
sympathetic chords in management as well as unions.

The industrial relations impact will force computer professionals
to re-examine their responsibilities, priorities and working
methods. They will be made aware of the human consequences of
the decisions they take in a more direct way than before.

The priority that will be given to human factors is a threat and
a challenge. The threat is to the insensitive,introverted, lazy
technical attitudes and the jargon-spiked defences which have
unfortunately characterised a great deal of the work done by
computing professionals.

The challenge and the opportunity come for those computing
professionals who look on the more open, human-centred approach
as a chance to gain new human factors skills and thereby to extend
the scope, satisfaction and effectiveness of their work.

5. CONCLUSION

Computer-based information technology is an important and potentially explosive factor in industrial relations. The unions
have responded by adopting a coherent and increasingly co-ordinated
set of plans, focused around Technology Agreements. At the same
time, managers and users are giving more emphasis   to human
factors, behavioural science and other related areas as a way
of getting more value for money out of the technology.

As a result, computing professionals will be put under pressure to
accept human and organisational factors as an intrinsic part of
their responsibilities. They will have to open up the technical
processes to greater non-technical scrutiny.

Unless computing professionals become more sensitive to personal
and organisational needs, they could exacerbate existing poor
industrial relations or prevent or delay the creation of a co-operative attitude to technological innovation. Those professionals
who do add behavioural and human science skills to their technical
expertise could enhance their work enrichment and status in the
organisation. Those who do not could find some of their more
interesting work usurped by human factors engineers, industrial
psychologists, etc.

My personal view is that computing professionals have had it too
easy for too long. They have had comfortable, secure jobs and
could wield a great deal of power without ever taking direct
responsibility for the consequences. If their 'professionalism'
were to be regarded in the same context as civil engineers or
doctors, few who are 'professionals' in terms of being a 'hired
hand' would qualify.

The computing citadel has now been breached. On the technical
front, microelectronics has placed computing power in the hands of
users. And all levels of user are demanding that computing professionals should explain and justify their work in plain language.

At last computing professionals are   being forced to realise that
they must tread softly lest they trample on other peoples jobs and
lives. Those who grasp the new opportunities will be rewarded.
Those who fail to face reality will find themselves washed up in
a technical backwater.

6. REFERENCES

(1) Making a match between man and machine by Malcolm Peltu (Inter-
     national Management, McGraw-Hill, September 1979)

(2) The quality of working life in Western and Easter Europe
     edited by Cary L Cooper and Enid Mumford (Associated Business
     Press, 1979)

(3) Visual Display Terminals A manual covering ergonomics, work-
     place design, health and safety, task organisation by
     A Cakir, D J Hart, T F M Stewart (John Wiley & Sons, 1979)

(4) Ergonomic Aspects of Visual Display Terminals edited by
     E Grandjean and E Vigliani (Taylor & Francis, 1980)

(5) Designing Systems for People by L Damodaran, A Simpson and
     P Wilson (National Computing Centre, 1980)

(6) Guide to Health Hazards of Visual Display Units (Association of
     Scientific, Technical and Managerial Staffs -ASTMS)

(7) <u>Office Technology</u> (Association of Professional, Executive, Clerical and Computer Staff – APEX, 1980)

(8) <u>Word Processing – its effects on female employment</u> by Frances McMahon in proceedings of 1980 International Word Processing conference (Online Conferences)

(9) <u>The Capacity to Absorb Change</u> by Jim Driscoll in proceedings of conference Towards the Automated Office (ISL, 1979)

(10)<u>Employment and Technology</u> (TUC, 1979)

(11)<u>ILO Conclusions on New Technology</u> (International Federation of Commercial, Clerical, Professional and Technical Employees – FIET, 1981)

- - - - - - -

Are There Senses in which a Computer may Properly be Held Responsible for its Actions?

J. P. A. Race

Computer Science, Brunel University, UK

It is argued that there are practical reasons for treating computer systems as moral and legal agents, and that commonsense, philosophy, and English law can accommodate an extension of the class of responsible entities to include computers.

Certain proposals are made for putting this into effect: in particular, how sanctions (punishment, restitution of damages) may be applied to a computer system found liable in a criminal or civil case.

1. INTRODUCTION

Let us consider a wrong which was brought about by the
agency of

  a hammer,

  a tiger,

  a human being,

  a computer.

If a crime is committed or injury caused through the
agency of a hammer, it is obviously absurd to indict the
hammer. The right person to pursue through the courts
will be the wielder of the hammer.

If a tiger mauls a child, we may certainly say without
being called naive, that the tiger was responsible, and it
will very likely be punished summarily but not brought to
court. We will however rapidly extend its responsibility
to cover its owner and trainer, and seek to punish and/or
extract damages from them.

Now let us suppose a human being, acting as an agent for
another party, commits a crime or becomes liable to civil
action. Again, he may properly be termed responsible,
and unlike the tiger, may well be taken to court and
punished or made to pay damages. As he was an agent, it
is also quite likely his bosses or instructors may be
held liable as well as, or possibly instead of, him.

Finally we consider a wrong committed, prima facie, by a
computer. The consequences are likely to be as serious,
or more so, as those of a misapplied hammer, something the
delay to the Space Shuttle launch on April 10th 1981,
demonstrates. But so far, it is regarded as naive to say,

      'It was the computer's fault!'

Many people will in practice say exactly that, and feel
that this is a reasonable remark to make, whereas it
would have been silly to say, like a child, 'it was the
hammer's fault', in the earlier example. We feel that
if we can reasonably say 'it was the tiger's fault', (so
long as we do not thereby exclude others from responsibility), then we are allowed to say 'it was the computer's
fault', with the same proviso. Surely the computer was at

least as responsible and competent an agent as a tiger,
and possibly as a human being, since it is probably doing
a job which formerly required human ability to carry out.

Yet at the moment our natural reaction, to say 'It was the
computer's fault', will be laughed at. The sophisticated
will argue that we are naive. They point out, a computer
is inanimate, like a hammer: we should not even consider
the notion of responsibility in connection with either,
but turn immediately to the human beings involved, the
programmers, operators, compiler writers, maintenance
engineers, sponsors, consultants, hardware designers...
and try to apportion liability among them. (A difficult
task, compared with that of getting the owner of the
hammer or the tiger into the dock).

Such critics of our 'It was the computer's fault' are
themselves naive. We are quite correct in our instinct to
start by blaming the computer, for the following reasons:

> The computer system may be indeed liable, and no
> one else. The progam may have been correctly design-
> ed and arranged to adapt to circumstances, but on
> this occasion the adaptation led it astray. The
> human beings involved acted in good faith to the best
> of their ability, and are not liable. Yet a blame-
> worthy thing happened. Therefore the non-human
> system must be blamed, unless we call the happening
> an Act of God, which we would never do if a human
> being had been involved instead of a computer.

> The computer system may evade responsibilty wholly or
> in part, because of negligence or deliberate action
> on the part of one or all of the human beings
> involved. But we have to start somewhere, and by
> calling to account the agent - the computer - which
> is prima facie responsible, the process of finding a
> culprit, fails safe. We shall see later how the
> computer may be expected to defend itself by inculp-
> ating others, and how it can make amends if found
> wholly or partly liable.

I argue therefore that our instinctive reaction to blame
the computer system itself is both desirable from a
prudential point of view, to safeguard a plaintiff or
prosecutor against an infinite regress in trying to assign
responsibility, and logically defensible, because a
computer is much closer to being a moral and legal agent
than, say, tigers or children, whom we are quite correct

to call blameworthy in appropriate circumstances.

The rest of this paper discusses the legal and philosoph-
ical implications in greater depth, and finishes by pro-
posing some mechanisms for making the notion of 'liable
computer systems' more practicable.

2. COMMONSENSE

In this section I try to describe the type of computer
system I have in mind when arguing that we must ascribe
responsibility to it, and go on to suggest what the
attitude of Aristotle's 'reasonable man' will be towards
it. This pragmatic individual is the cornerstone of much
English law and philosophy, and if we can show that he
is content to accept that a computer can be regarded as
an individual with at least some moral and legal aspects,
we are well on the way to convincing our philosophers and
lawyers to accept the idea as well.

First, one ought, I suppose, to define what we mean by a
computer system. What is intended here is one particular
combination of hardware, software, and data, such that its
functional behaviour is different from any other system.
It follows that a computer system may exist in two places
at once, for example, if two copies of the same program
run on functionally similar machines with initially
identical data files. These might be regarded rather like
'identical twins', or cloned individuals. However, if
they hold data, and the data becomes different over time,
as is likely if they are not just parts of one system
which is duplexed for security purposes, then they are
different individuals. The reason for making this point
is that if a computer system is made up of multiple
identical units, maybe scattered geographically, any
action taken against it because of misbehaviour will be
taken against all its elements, since they are not autonomous individuals but parts of a whole. If however their
functional behaviour has changed over time because they
have processed different data (as in the case, say, of
computers for medical diagnosis with inbuilt learning
mechanisms based on their local experience), then each
becomes a system in its own right and a failing in one is
not automatically a signal for action against all, any
more than the twin of a murderer should be hanged as well.

One may note that unlike human twins, two systems might
regain functional identity and become effectively a single
system again, if they pool their experiences. At all
events, I am trying to show that some care will be needed

to define what an individual really is, when a computer
system comes to be treated as a (responsible) individual
as is recommended in this paper.

The next point to make is that the decision to treat
computer systems, as described above, as moral and legal
individuals, is not the same decision as that of deciding
whether 'computers are intelligent'. It is true that a
a minimum degree of intelligence is required, but in
ancient Rome, for example, a slave, however intelligent,
did not have any legal existence: he was the property of
his master, who was held liable for his slave's mistakes.
Naturally, the master would take it out of the slave,
just as a man who is fined when his dog bites the postman
will give it a good hiding. But as time went by, the
Romans freed their more competent slaves, just as we
shall free our computers: not for humanitarian, but for
purely practical reasons: both give of their best when
allowed responsibility for their actions. (Buckland).

No, the characteristic of the computer systems under
discussion is not so much intelligence, as the ability to
rationalise, that is, to give an ccount of their actions,
and to construct courses of action using powerful planning
procedures, like Terry Winograd's SHRDLU (as reported,
for example, in Boden, M. A., 'Artificial Intelligence
and Natural Man', Harvester Books, Hassocks, UK, 1977).

Such systems are now being developed for practical use,
for example to help prospectors find oil and minerals, or
doctors to diagnose illness. In some cases the system
is not much more than a really sophisticated database,
which does not 'reason' so much as build up a library of
useful facts, and search for appropriate ones in each
new situation. The behaviour of such an 'expert system'
can save lives, or exploration costs. But of course, it
will also cost lives and money if it makes errors.

Let us suppose such an exploration-assistance system was
programmed by A and installed by B, who gave it an
initial database D, which it added to by asking questions
of people P and satellites S. One day it recommends to a
client C he should drill for oil in Piccadilly Circus:
C does this at enormous expense, and finds no oil at all.
If this computer system had been a human consultant, the
oil man C would very likely have sued it for negligence,
or, if it had been his own employee, interviewed it with a
view to dismissing it. A similar situation should
apply here, and the essential ingredient is that the
computer system must be able to defend itself by giving a
SHRDLU-like justification of its actions:

C (client): 'Why did you recommend drilling in
Piccadilly Circus?'

Z (the computer system):   'Because the ratio of
probable return to probable cost appeared highest
at that location.'

C: 'What led you to believe the probable return was
high?'

Z: 'Geologically the location is such that if oil is
present, the quantity would be 1bn barrels, plus or
minus 10%, with a confidence of 95%.'

C: 'But what was the probability you found for there
being oil there?'

Z: '.1, so that the weighted expectation was 100m
barrels.'   /

C: 'What was your evidence for your figure of .1?'

Z: 'I spoke directly to S, a geosat, and consulted
certain human experts P, and their views correlated
to a factor of .9.'

C: 'Why did you not indicate that the expected oil
find was based on low probability multiplied by high
estimates of oil-if-present?'

Z: 'A programmed me to give such a warning, but also
to reduce the threshold for such warnings in the
light of experience, which I have done.'

This dialogue could obviously continue for some time, and
one can imagine that the outcome could be quite complex:
S and P are in the clear, A may be somewhat to blame in
his programming of Z or in his initial database D, C himself should perhaps have had this discussion with Z before
buying up Piccadilly and drilling, and Z appears to have
been wrong in reducing its warning threshold. True, this
propensity to reduce the threshold was ultimately programmed in Z by A, but the decision was actually taken by
Z. We must blame Z so that Z can do better next time. C's
reactions at the end of this dialogue will go into Z's D
as further data for directing Z's behaviour. This may be
termed the rehabilitative aspect of punishment, to be
discussed further in the next section.

The above dialogue is one which has been achieved already
in SHRDLU-type systems which can rehearse or recall their
solution protocols through dependency nets until the
original axioms or external data are reached. Advice-
giving medical systems are another example of what we are
concerned with here - and their advice may be even more
important than Z's, to uproot Eros. Note that the actual
computation in these programs may not be particularly
brilliant (any more than the commander of a nuclear
submarine need be an Einstein when deciding whether to
fire his missiles). Z, in its system for finding oil,
simply followed the rule, 'recommend x, where x is a
mmember of the set of possible locations L, if for all y in
L, where y $\neq$ x, the probability of a strike multiplied by
the expected amount for x, is greater than that for y.'

It is Z's ability to explain this, not to carry it out,
which makes it a responsible agent - an advice-giving
system which can give an account of its (in this case
simple) reasoning. And this makes it accountable.

We are talking about responsibility: no need to put Z to
Turing's test to show a human level of intelligence. In
fact, as pointed out by Turing's brother (letter,
Observer, 12 April, 1981), a computer like Z will make a
poor showing at writing a sonnet, but that doesn't stop us
from treating it as a responsible agent. Few submarine
captains write good sonnets either, or clerks, or
public corporations, yet all these entities have responsibilities in law.

No discussion on the moral position of computers should
be thought complete without mention of Asimov's 'Laws of
Robotics'. Since lawyers and philosophers may object if
they are discussed in the sections on law and philosophy,
it may be better to consider them here. His laws are:

1. A robot may not injure a human being, or, through
inaction, allow a human being to come to harm;

2. A robot must obey the orders given it by human
beings except where such orders would conflict with
the First Law;

3. A robot must protect its own existence as long
as such protection does not conflict with the First
or Second Laws.

At first sight one might say, these laws are so obviously
appropriate, can we not simply build them into our
systems and thereby avoid all the tangled questions of
responsibility we are raising here? Unfortunately, we
cannot. It is practically impossible to calculate in
every situation whether an action might lead to someone's
eventual injury. Like a human being faced with the Ten
Commandments, the computer may do the best it can, but may
still make errors, because its original programming
(sin !) caused it to mistake situations or the right
action to take, and in these cases it will commit faults
which need investigating and possibly punishing. Of
course Asimov himself would not have been able to write
his stories if his Laws were adequate to specify robot
behaviour completely, with no more to be said!

In the next session we shall see that from the legal point
of view, computers are if anything more, rather than less,
well-qualified to be considered responsible agents than
human beings.

3.   ENGLISH LAW

Our law is not so much founded on axioms as on precedents
which are reasonably consistent and beneficial, but above
all, pragmatic. If through better nutrition, girls mature
earlier, the age of consent is reduced. Cats are 'of a
feral nature' and their actions are not the responsibility
of their owners, unlike those of dogs. So the law would
not be concerned if a plaintiff or a defendant was made of
titanium from the neck down, nor even if titanium from the
neck up, if, despite such a drastic prosthesis, the individual's behaviour indicated he or she - or it - was a
responsible agent. However, there are two aspects which
need investigation in a little depth: liability, and
punishment.

It is a principle of our law that to be convicted, someone
must have 'mens rea', that is to say, 'a guilty mind',
(James). But this does not mean that the law requires
definite evidence of a Cartesian soul within the defendant
or to observe a shifty look in his eyes. 'Mind' is taken
by the law much in the behavioural sense of Ryle, and the
whole expression should be interpreted as meaning that the
defendant carried out his action intending the consequences. It is not even necessary for the defendant
to be aware the results of his action would be criminal,
since 'ignorantia juris haud excusat' (ignorance of the
law is no excuse).

Now the behaviour of a correctly working computer system
with the ability to set up goals, work out strategies for
attaining them, and, on demand, provide explanations,
(as can be done by SHRDLU and its modern successors),
is supremely rational and a fine example of the mens rea
in operation. What the computer does, is very definitely
intentional: it works out what it will do and how it is
going to do it. Nevertheless we may feel that it may be
absolved from blame in some circumstances, if its
responsibility can be shown to be diminished by one of the
admissible factors. We shall see that it may indeed be so
diminished, but not just because the entity involved is
a computer system, rather, because in particular circumstances, defences similar to those open to a human being
are also open to it. The defences to consider are:

> Mistake. A computer might argue that it turned off a
> patient's oxygen in the belief that the cylinder cont-
> ained carbon dioxide. Hence, a malfunctioning sensor
> may be an adequate defence, but only if it was
> reasonable for the system not to have cross-checked
> the sensor, which in such vital matters one would
> expect it to do.

> Duress, that is, another person forced the system to
> act as it did. Since computers cannot be threatened
> with violence, this excuse either refers to physical
> over-riding of its authority, or, more subtly, to
> the possibility that a computer system might be
> thought of as under duress from the person who pro-
> grammed it. However, human beings cannot evade re-
> sponsibility on the grounds that 'I have inherited my
> father's ungovernable temper and was taught to be
> anti-social by him', for example. It may be an
> extenuating circumstance which will affect the
> punishment, but it does not affect the question of
> guilt.

> Self-defence. In other words, the Third Asimov Law.
> It would seem to me that this might indeed be a valid
> defence, if the Third Law had been incorporated in
> the system: for example, a medical computer might
> shut down a subsystem to avoid overloading its power
> supply, and as a consequence, an unfortunate event
> occurred. However, it would have to show that the
> likely consequences of its action to other parties
> appeared minor compared to the consequences to itself
> if it did not switch off, just as a car driver who
> swerved into a dog to avoid a cow might get off even
> the apparent dog turned out to be a child.

Necessity. This is 'duress by circumstances' and
once again results in extenuation rather than total
exculpation. The subject of free will is dealt with
in the next section.

Incapacity. People of Unsound mind, Drunken Persons,
Minors and Corporations may plead incapacity. But
computers are singularly free from madness or drunk-
enness. They may perhaps plead a voltage fluctuation
which disabled them at the crucial time. However, it
is not an excuse open to them on the grounds that
they are incapable all the time, because computers
are, now, most of the time, capable. (Nor is a bad
program a form of incapacity any more than bad
inclinations are in a man.)

Minors escape criminal responsibility because they
are judged incapable of forming a proper intent, but
as we have seen, a computer can indeed form an intent
in a most rational, deliberate way. Secondly,
minors may be incapable of certain (principally
sexual) crimes, and no doubt a computer would have
a strong defence to a charge of rape, which as James
points out, is unlikely to succeed against a corporation. However, corporations can indeed be held
criminally as well as civilly responsible, for con-
spiracy for example, and this is a strong point in
favour of the case I have made that the law does not
insist that you have to be made of flesh and blood
before you can be held to be a responsible agent.
It is interesting to note that the scope of corporate
responsibility has widened of late.

We now turn to the question of punishment. Our first reaction to the idea of 'punishing' a computer will very
likely be similar to that of Sidney Smith, who, on seeing
a little girl stroking a tortoise, said 'You might just as
well stroke the dome of St Paul's to please the Dean and
Chapter'. Yet if one looks more closely at punishment, it
seems a perfectly appropriate term to use in the case of a
computer system found guilty of an act which in a human
being would certainly be termed criminal. Nor is the fact
that a computer cannot feel physical pain a big stumbling
block, since a judge would not hesitate to punish a man
suffering from total anaesthesia. Nor is punishment today
a question of inflicting physical pain, at least here.

There are three aspects of punishment:

Retribution: the need for society to get its revenge
on the wrong-doer: a basically irrational (but
quite understandable) emotional response.   If this
means pushing a computer over a cliff after it has
driven someone to suicide through sending them wrong
electricity bills, we can understand it, and there is
still such a retributive element in our make-up.   It
may not do much good, but it gets the hate out of
our systems.

Rehabilitation.   In this sense, the aim of punishment
is to improve the individual for his own sake and
that of society.   In the case of a computer, this
may involve re-programming or the indication to the
computer that its previous response had been wrong,
so that this reprimand is stored as a new parameter
value to adjust its future behaviour.   The fact that
we did not use a cat-o'-nine-tails or the brig does
not mean what we did was not punishment, any more
than it is not punishment - of a severe kind - if a
court-martial reprimands an officer who runs a
frigate aground.

Deterrence.   The fact that Z is punished should be
communicated to other computer systems working on
similar things.   They would be like a family of chess
programs: if one is defeated as a result of a
flaw in an opening, all others should be informed.
Through the increasingly wide use of networks
(Martin) this is now technically feasible, and one
can envisage a Prestel-like clearing house of law-
reports made available for the type of computer
system we have been describing, and a procedure for
down-line-loading program modifications in those
cases we examined earlier, where the computer system
consisted of a set of 'cloned' parts of one individual, all of which must be corrected/punished.

Lastly in this section we should consider the case where
a computer is involved as a principal in a civil suit:
punishment is not involved, but restitution of damages is.
In the past one would have thought it bizarre for the
mechanical agent to be the actual defendant, yet as was
said at the outset, our big problem with computers is that
unlike hammers, it is very hard for a plaintiff to find
any human being to accept responsibility for their bad
behaviour.   So he should be able to sue them, just as a
corporation may be sued, and for much the same reason.

4. PHILOSOPHY

I hope I have shown that commonsense and English law are
receptive to the idea that computer systems can and should
be treated as accountable, responsible entities. But it
might be objected that although for pragmatic reasons this
may come about, computers are fundamentally inanimate and
inhuman, and therefore can never be real moral agents.

Philosophers such as Teilhard de Chardin and Lucas
certainly ascribe a special status to mankind, not shared
by the rest of creation. Teilhard de Chardin supposes a
quantum jump - hominisation - during mankind's evolution.
Lucas argues that men transcend machines because men can
perceive truths which as a consequence of Godel's theorem,
machines cannot. But Kenny, a lawyer and philosopher,
considers that a deterministic view of human action is not
inconsistent with men having free will (hence the fact
that machines are determinate does not automatically stop
them from having enough freedom to be classed as moral
agents, though this is my gloss on his remarks, not his.)
In a recent issue of Mind, Langford considers a solitary,
fabulous guinea-pig called Fido, and discusses whether an
observer would consider its behaviour purposive. In the
same issue, Gustafson looks at intentional action from
a more linguistic point of view.

Lawden considers the phenomenon of consciousness to be
an important criterion for deciding whether an entity
should be classed as intelligent, and presumably responsible: a view which suffers from our difficulty in defining consciousness in any but circular terms.

If one looks at the arguments of such philosophers,
to see if they shed light on the question whether it is
reasonable to speak of computers having responsibility,
one is likely to come to the conclusion that the philosophers are divided and our view is at least defensible.
Indeed, the determinists are on our side and the anti-
determinists have not ruled out the possibility of
determinate machines being allowed 'second class' responsibility at least, like tigers and children, for practical
reasons:

Most determinists now would assert that human behaviour
is entirely governed by starting conditions and subsequent
experience, but that this does not rule out and might even
support free will and responsibility for actions. It
seems that by the same arguments they would have to admit

computers into the ranks of resposible entities, provided
they could not only form intentions but also explain them,
which, as we have seen, they can.

Even if a non-determinist view is taken and we say that
man has a special status, on some metaphysical grounds,
this does not logically exclude the possibility that other,
determinate entities should be allowed responsibility too.

5.   PROPOSALS

Computer systems should be designed to include the
ability to give an account of the bases of their
actions, as 'expert systems' do now, and, at a more
mundane level, commercial systems do with in inbuilt
'audit trail'.

Our instinct to 'blame the computer' when it makes
errors should be elevated to a policy. It should be
possible to take civil or criminal action against it
in circumstances in which a human agent would also
have been taken to court.

Based on the system's own account of events, and
other evidence, responsibility will be assigned and
judgement given.

Where the responsibility is laid at the computer's
door, the basis for its behaviour (program or data)
will be altered .

To provide for restitution of damages when a system
is successfully sued in a civil action, it should
not be a 'man of straw' but would hold money reserves
or insurance.

6. REFERENCES

Arbib, M. A., 'Brains, Machines and Mathematics', McGraw-Hill, New York, 1964

Asimov, I, 'The Rest of the Robots', Granada, London, 1968

Ayer, A. J., 'The Central Questions of Philosophy', Weidenfeld and Nicolson, London, 1973

Buckland, W. W., 'The Roman Law of Slavery', quoted in Oxford Classical Dictionary, OUP, 1949

Devlin, K., (Department of Law, Brunel University), letter, 1981.

Gustafson, D., 'Passivity and Activity in Intentional Actions', Mind, Aberdeen, Jan 81

James, P. S., 'Introduction to English Law', Butterworths, London, 1979

Kenny, A., 'Will, Freedom and Power', Blackwell, Oxford, 1975

Kenny, A., 'Freewill and Responsibility', Routledge and Kegan Paul, London, 1978

Kent, W., 'Data and Reality', North-Holland, Amsterdam 1978

Langford, G., 'The Nature of Purpose', Mind, Aberdeen, Jan 81

Lawden, D. F., New Scientist p476, London, 4 Sept 1969

Lucas, J. R., 'The Freedom of the Will', OUP, 1970

Martin, J., 'The Wired Society', Prentice-Hall, New Jersey, 1978

Race, J. P. A., letter, New Scientist, London, 18 Sept 1969

Ryle, G., 'The Concept of Mind', Hutchinsons, London 1949

Teilhard de Chardin, P., 'The Phenomenon of Man', Collins, London, 1960

The Manpower Implications of Computer-aided Design in the UK Engineering Industry

Erik Arnold

Fellow, Science Policy Research Unit,
Sussex University, UK

The industry supplying computer-aided design (CAD) equipment is growing rapidly and competition affects the shape of the technology on offer. Research in progress at the Science Policy Research Unit analyses CAD use in some engineering sectors and suggests that it can reduce demand for design staff and some craft workers. Competition in the engineering industry could also be affected.

INTRODUCTION

This paper presents initial findings of research in progress at the Science Policy Research Unit, Sussex University, into the manpower implications of computer-aided design in the UK engineering industry. The work is sponsored by the Engineering Industry Training Board and the support of the Board is gratefully acknowledged.*

The research method involves the use of structured interviews. At the time of writing, interviews have been conducted with design management in firms using Computer-Aided Design (CAD) in a sample of engineering sectors. It is intended that discussions also be held with non-users of CAD in order to gain a better understanding of the role of CAD in competition. Manufacturers and suppliers of CAD equipment have been interviewed in order to gain an understanding both of directions of technical change and the nature of competition among these firms, whose policies and products are likely to affect future CAD usage. Some trade unionists have also been consulted.

The use of computer aids in engineering design is not novel, computers having long been used in 'number-crunching' applications such as stress analysis and in data processing applications such as parts listing. The more general use of graphics, however, is a fairly recent development. The research — and, hence, this paper — is primarily concerned with the more restricted sense of CAD as 'graphics-based CAD'.

COMPETITION AND TECHNICAL CHANGE

CAD user firms, like the suppliers, are in competition. Study of the competitive process is likely to provide explanations of why CAD is adopted. In general, SPRU research has tended to suggest that new production technology is _permissive_ of changes in the way firms use labour, rather than determining such changes.(1) Shortages of particular skills can _prevent_ firms using new technologies(2), as can the resistance of the labour force to technical change. The

---

* Thanks are also due to Dr. Raphael Kaplinski of the Institute of Development Studies at Sussex University in co-operation with whose work for the United Nations Industrial Development Organisation some of the research was done; to Mike Cooley; and to the firms, managements and trades unionists who so generously gave their time and effort during the interviews.

Errors of fact and interpretation are, of course, the responsibility of the author.

effects of the use of new technology will be related to firms'
motives in introducing it. Similarly, decisions not to acquire will
be grounded in firms' strategies and tactics, and in the constraints
operating upon them.

The traditional approach to the study of the manpower implications of
technological change is to assume the availability of a new
technology, establish its area of maximum application, assume a rate
of diffusion, and then make predictions on this basis. But the logic
of the relation between a technology and user firms becomes
comprehensible only when the characteristics of the firms' 'world'
are understood, and this world consists essentially of a market and
of competitor firms. The situation of engineering firms, as
potential users of CAD, is crudely represented in Figure 1.

Figure 1   The Engineering Firm and its Environment

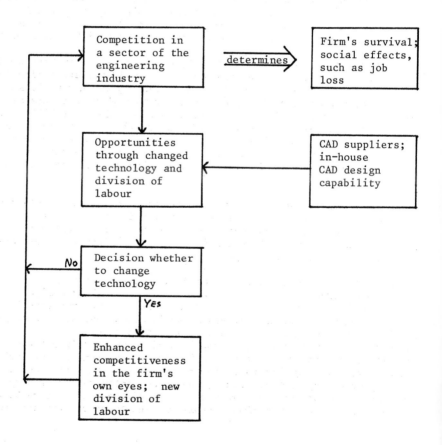

THE SUPPLY SIDE

CAD has its roots in the work done during the 1950s and 1960s on
numerical control (NC) for machine tools. Research was funded by the
Aerospace Industries Association and the Department of Defense in the
USA on NC techniques during the 1960s, and a Department of Defense
symposium in 1968 coined the phrase 'CAD-CAM' (Computer-Aided Design
- Computer-Aided Manufacturing) to describe the interfacing of
computerised design aids with NC production techniques. Mainframe-
based graphics systems were in use in the US aerospace and motor
industries by the mid 1960s, but only with the emergence of the
storage display tube were the problems of refreshing graphics using a
mainframe computer resolved.

By about 1970, the availability of minicomputers and storage tubes
suggested the feasibility of cheaper and more generally available
graphics-based CAD, but the problems of structuring data to run vast
CAD programs on minicomputers were considerable. A turnkey CAD
market only began to emerge at the end of the 1970s, although the
major companies supplying this equipment were established in 1968-70.

The turnkey CAD market is dominated by Computervision, in both the US
and Europe. Computervision hold 35% of the world market, followed by
Calma and Applicon with about 14% each. The top seven suppliers held
92% of the market in 1980, so the industry is highly concentrated.
Industry turnover tripled in two years to $510 million in 1980, and
is expected to quadruple to $2.2 billion by 1984.(3) The rapid rates
of growth of CAD manufacturers in the recent past has led to cash
flow difficulties. Calma was bought by United Telecommunications in
1978 for $17 million, and sold to, General Electric (of the USA) in
1980 for $170 million.(4)

Barriers to entry into the industry are formidable. One manufacturer
claims to have written 13 million lines of software; another claims
to have a thousand person-years similarly embodied in software.
General Electric intend to put a further $170 million into software
at Calma over the next five years.

Some of the CAD suppliers established their early strength in
integrated circuit (IC) and printed circuit board (PCB) design software, and have since been concerned to diversify into mechanical
engineering applications. Others began in mechanical or cartographic
applications and have sought to diversify into electronics.
Competition between the major suppliers of turnkey equipment now
hinges substantially on the generality of application of their software. Arguably, this results from their selling the 'features' of
their products against each other, and consequently the major suppliers
see themselves as being 'up-market'. Many of their sales have been to
'blue chip' companies or their suppliers, and there are few systems

on the market which are within the financial grasp of smaller user
firms. There may, therefore, be scope for new entrants following
a 'little league'(5) strategy of selling cheaper specialist systems
dedicated to particular design tasks.

The established way of modelling mechanical designs has been to
represent them in the form of a 'wire frame'. Work has been in
progress for a number of years (some of it in the UK, which is
dominated by the American suppliers) on developing 'solid', or
'volumetric', modelling techniques. Some people in the CAD industry
suggest that this work is maturing and could form the basis of new
entry, circumventing the barriers erected by the established makers'
investment in software. Solid models have yet, however, to make a
significant impact on the market, and it is not clear how they would
compete with the generality of the established vendors' software
libraries.

The use of minicomputers instead of mainframes has perhaps been one
of the major achievements of the turnkey manufacturers.
Characteristically, their equipment shares a 16-bit minicomputer
between a small number of workstations. Use of a minicomputer,
however, severely limits the number of workstations and results in
considerable degradation of system performance if number-crunching
(such as finite element analysis) is run concurrently with drawing.
Latterly, the tendency has been to view the optimal CAD system as a
satellite of the mainframe, with the mainframe handling number-
crunching and data processing associated with maintaining the firm's
engineering data base. The next stage of hardware development
involves 32-bit minicomputer-based stand-alone workstations,
communicating with a minicomputer or a mainframe. Raster displays
are being offered - often colour - and these seem likely to displace
storage tubes to some extent.

USER SECTORS

CAD was used for Printed Circuit Board (PCB) and integrated circuit
(IC) design. PCB work is pervading the engineering industry because
of the increasing use of electronic controls, hence there is a demand
for PCB layout facilities in systems otherwise used in mechanical
applications. Computer boards are now so complex that it is
impractical to lay them out by hand, and machine-drawn artwork is
often needed because of the fineness and complexity of lines on the
boards. One electronics firm said that for boards of 'moderate
complexity' a productivity ratio (ratio of output per unit time using
CAD to manual output) of at least 2:1 was achieved, and other
estimates were higher. PCB routing makes heavy demands on processing,
and was often run separately from other work in turnkey systems
(e.g. overnight). Productivity ratios are not very meaningful in
complex PCB design, as CAD is increasingly an entry ticket into this

work. This may tend to exclude small firms, although there are now some small dedicated PCB design systems on the market.

Discussants said that IC designs of Large Scale Integration (LSI) or larger were not feasible without CAD. Two IC makers have so far been visited, both of whom had developed systems in house, and felt they had been forced to make the running on CAD because of the lack of products in the market. Each felt it had been possible to develop and monopolise aspects of technical capability through in house development. Design aids were said to be lagging behind testing aids and the scale of integration feasible in production processes. CAD was helpful in developing chips from standard hard or soft elements (for example in uncommitted logic arrays). Graphics is a relatively small part of the repertoire of computer-aided techniques increasingly needed to design, simulate, and test ICs, but increasing chip complexity increases the need for and use of a broad range of CAD techniques, and provides barriers to entry operating in favour of established firms. In IC manufacture, CAD is more of an engineer's tool than in PCB work, where specialist PCB layout draughtspeople already exist.

The car industry was one of the earliest users of CAD. Applications in body design and aerodynamics have been important in the past, and body designers are in short supply. Work on components is also important. Some car components are approaching 'maturity', and CAD helps to reduce design times and improve designs under conditions of diminishing returns to design effort. Weight reduction for fuel economy is an important example. Some new work such as crash simulation has become possible, and design investigations can be more intensive.

Car and component firms are becoming increasingly interdependent. Joint engine development is becoming a feature of the car industry, for example. Communication between firms via CAD output in digital form is beginning, although this is inhibited in the UK by the low penetration of CAD in some areas. This may affect firms supplying the car industry. In general, however, established barriers to entry are so high (and the difficulties of car makers so considerable) that CAD is unlikely to affect competition, especially as all established mass production car firms are already users.

Process and other plant suppliers design or supply machines to tender. In the process plant firms, employment varies a great deal with the workload and a heavy reliance is placed on contract labour, both in design and drawing. Reduced use of contract labour was a stated objective in all firms visited, although this might reduce flexibility. Process plant are usually 'one-offs', although an element of design modularity is creeping in. Mistakes are very expensive to correct on site, and CAD helps reduce design errors.

Better 3D conceptualisation, for example, helps eliminate situations where pipes are designed to pass through obstacles (such as other pipes). CAD offers a major competitive advantage in the preparation of fuller and better-costed tenders for work. Examples were cited of rapid tender preparation resulting in contracts being awarded at the expense of competitors who were not users of CAD. Users appear likely to maintain design employment, at the expense of non-users and contract workers.

Other engineering sectors are being explored, but data are so far patchy.

CAD USE

This paper is a report on work still in progress in the UK. Coverage of sectors is patchy at this stage, and limited by the fact that discussions with non-users of CAD have yet to take place. Nonetheless a number of tentative findings emerge from the work to date.

The turnkey CAD makers are mostly based in the USA, and are growing at a phenomenal rate. Many UK users have found that their distance from the American headquarters of supplier firms led to relatively poor service, particularly in terms of software support. US manufacturers' UK branches are newly established, and the UK personnel often have limited CAD experience, hence users claim that they often have to tell suppliers what to do, rather than the other way about. A number of users said that it was necessary to go directly to US headquarters if serious problems arose.

Potential users often gain more from visiting installations than suppliers, and a small number of key personalities have emerged in the user population who influence the extent and type of diffusion of CAD strongly in the UK. One user, who had benefitted from Department of Industry 'seed money' for CAD, was particularly important in promoting the diffusion of CAD. To this extent, the Department's money was spent wisely, but the benefits to the UK are limited by the absence of a substantial UK turnkey manufacturer.

It was evident that some of the users were not entirely sure why they had acquired CAD, and a number had discovered major benefits only after intallation. In at least three cases, CAD had been bought to 'keep up with the Joneses' because a major competitor had introduced CAD already. Clearly, there remains a great deal of scope in the UK for management learning about CAD.

Firms using CAD systems designed and built in house were found only in the electronics and car industries. In each case, the firms were long-standing CAD users who made the equipment themselves before turnkey offerings appeared. Two turnkey users had abandoned in-house systems because turnkey products were better and cheaper. An IC manufacturer had developed design and simulation software, but bought in a turnkey system for graphics work.

More recent users of CAD had all rejected the idea of in-house development, even in those cases where at least some of the relevant expertise already existed in the firm. Turnkey systems were generally seen as superior to in-house developments, although they were in some cases enhanced by in-house software work.

Established CAD users - notably those who had developed their own systems - found that their own efforts to refine and add to existing software tended to 'lock' them into their current system or supplier. Some users were selling back specialised software they had developed to their CAD suppliers, or exchanging it for more software. A number of discussants thought that this would be an important source of CAD software improvements in the future, as it overcame the problem of the suppliers' lack of experience in the problems of users in different sectors.

In applications where CAD is used mostly as a draughting tool, the largest productivity gains are achieved where it is possible to modularise designs. Drawing then becomes a question of combining predefined modules from a library and making appropriate adjustments (sometimes including scaling). This use of a CAD database essentially to produce variations on a standardised theme is only productive where the design element, proper, is almost wholly absent from the process of drawing production. Genuine design work is done for new 'generations' of the standardised products.

One use of CAD prevalent across many sectors is in 'nesting', where the object is to maximise the use of a raw material which can be treated as two dimensional. Applications extend from sheet metal cutting, beyond engineering into shoe sole and upper cutting, cloth cutting, and positioning houses on housing estates.

The extent to which firms were concerned with a formal cost-benefit treatment of the CAD investment decision is highly variable. In electronics, where CAD is a prerequisite for some products, cost-benefit analysis was not an issue. However, in the older mass-production car industry, this type of treatment of the CAD investment decision was seen as important, despite the degree to which it was felt that there was no choice about whether to acquire CAD techniques. In process and other plant firms, where costs tend to be considered more in relation to particular projects than in relation to a flow of production, the economic justification of CAD was taken very seriously. CAD was used in these firms primarily as a draughting tool in order to get increased labour productivity as early as possible; the jobs of the protagonists were often at risk if anticipated benefits were not achieved. In one firm, however, where CAD was seen as the only way to stay in business, the cost-benefit treatment was muted. Not all

anticipated benefits are achieved. One firm was visited after the
end of the planned payback period for CAD, but the system appeared
to have made no contribution to output as yet.

SKILLS AND LABOUR

CAD has provoked a broad range of attitudes. One turnkey user visited
appeared to encompass the full range in the three members of the
drawing office staff. The designer regarded the system as a useful
adjunct which freed him from routine aspects of his work and allowed
him to be more creative. One of the draughtsmen preferred working
with CAD to using a board, but thought he would tire of it eventually.
The other described CAD as an "electronic deskiller". On a board,
he saw his drawings as pictures, recognisable as his by his style and
the quality of his work. With the CAD system, everyone's work looked
alike and there was no scope for individual flair.

Management often thought that trades unions were 'Luddite' in
relation to CAD. Of 17 users visited, 12 were unionised and 5 were
not. Of the unionised firms, only two had experienced industrial
relations difficulties in relation to CAD: in one firm there was a
brief strike, and in the other the equipment was 'blacked' for a
time. It appeared, however, that rather than objecting to the
technology itself - which was generally seen as a good thing likely to
improve the firm's competitiveness and protect employment - trades
unions were using CAD as a bargaining chip in the more familiar
process of attempting to extract more money from a reluctant management. In some firms, management were surprised at the ease with which
they had 'got CAD past the union', while other discussants suggested
that the unions had a better understanding of the need for CAD than
many senior engineering managers.

CAD is a special case of Information Technology, and information is
the means whereby firms are managed and controlled. The design
function provides a motive for a centralisation which would maximise
the portion of the production squence which falls under the firm's
(the designer's) control, and therefore the opportunity for
optimising designs. Potential systems effects of CAD include tighter
management control over design and production, and the movement of
elements of skill and decision-making upstream from craft workers and
into the design area. The links through to CAM are crucial in this
respect. In one example, NC data output from a CAD system was used
to machine a mould. This replaced the pattern-maker's work,
including the process of 'blending by eye' between the sections
through the mould shown on the drawing provided. As a result, the
designer's control over the mould shape - which was critical to the
performance of the finished product - was increased because the
pattern-maker's particular skill and decision-making no longer
intervened.

The scope for links between CAD and computer-controlled machining (CAD-CAM) appear to be enormous. But making the link between CAD and CAM is much more difficult than it appears at first glance. It requires substantial planning, investment, managerial ability, determination and courage still to implement a successful and comprehensive CAD-CAM system. Many of the problems identified by Senker et al. in 1976 still need to be overcome.(6) Nevertheless, some progress is being made in the direction of CAD-CAM. For example, two firms bought NC machine tools because they already had CAD; a third firm used CAD to prove manually produced NC tapes. Aspects of pattern and model making were replaced by output from CAD systems. The increased accuracy afforded by CAD and NC machine tools reduced the amount of fitting work in some cases. One machine maker said that "fitters used to be issued with a hammer, a file, and a pair of running shoes" to keep up with production. But now components designed on CAD systems and produced on NC machine tools are more likely to fit first time.

Claims of productivity ratios of about 3:1 in draughting were common among firms interviewed. In the last year or so of recession, the long-standing shortage of draughtspeople has disappeared in many - but not all - areas, but computer-aided draughting has generally been introduced in the context of, and sometimes as a response to, skill shortage. No cases were found of draughting redundancies following the introduction of CAD, but most installations were still in an early (and partly experimental) phase. The use of contract labour went down in some cases, and a few of the discussants expected job loss in the future when their firm made more extensive use of CAD. Where firms were successful and growing, as was often the case with CAD users, employment effects of CAD were masked, and the technology has been responsible for 'jobless growth' in the output of some drawing offices.

Most managers said that the best CAD operators were already good draughtsmen, but there were also people using CAD satisfactorily without drawing board experience. Management tended to seek aptitude and interest in potential operators, rather than formal qualifications. CAD tended to promote flexitime and shift working to keep the equipment in use, and both managers and operators said that work tended to become machine-paced - that it "cut out the chit-chat" in the drawing office.

In design, proper, there was no evidence of job loss. Better designs were said to be produced with CAD than without. Management standards and standardisation of components and designs were more easily imposed on CAD than on manual design. Cooley argues that the range of solutions open to designers is narrowed by the use of CAD, and that poorer designs result. Depending on the criterion of 'goodness' adopted, this is not necessarily inconsistent with the findings of this research.

CONCLUSIONS

CAD has been used only in part to break the bottleneck of skill
shortage in engineering design and drawing, and it offers many other
advantages to users. In two cases, firm survival was acutely
threatened by a historical failure to invest in innovation, and CAD
appears to have saved the situation. In these cases, job loss was
clearly avoided by the use of CAD. Elsewhere, there are signs that
the technology may reduce the demand for draughting labour, initially
affecting contract workers. In certain sectors CAD gives users a
clear competitive edge, and this may result in job loss from non-
users. This pattern is not clear, however, for all sectors.

Craft workers downstream from the design process are threatened by
CAD-CAM links, but these are often difficult to make and there has
yet to be any substantial impact. The autonomous process of NC
machine tool diffusion has had a far greater impact on employment.

Insofar as CAD offers competitive advantages, firms will have little
option as to whether to make use of it. This seems likely to change
the character of competition - and the competitors - in some sectors.

REFERENCES

1. R. M. Bell, Changing Technology and Manpower Requirements in the
    Engineering Industry, Engineering Industry Training Board Research
    Report No. 3, Sussex University Press in association with EITB,
    1972.

2. P. Senker, C. Huggett, R. M. Bell, and E. Sciberras,
    Technological Change, Structural Change and Manpower in the UK
    Toolmaking Industry, EITB Research Paper, No. 2, 1976, p.52.

3. The Economist, 6th December 1980.

4. Business Week, 22nd December 1980.

5. E. Sciberras, Multinational Electronics Companies and National
    Economic Policies, Contemporary Studies in Economic and
    Financial Analysis, Vol. 6., Greenwich, Conn.: JAI Press, 1977.

6. P. Senker, C. Huggett, R. M. Bell, and E. Sciberras,
    Technological Change, Structural Change and Manpower in the UK
    Toolmaking Industry, EITB Research Paper No. 2, 1976, pp.16-17.

The 'Systematic' Doctor

J. Anderson

Professor of Medicine,
King's College Hospital Medical School, UK

The arrival of the 'systematic' doctor, who uses
medical information systems and supporting technology with
advantage is awaited. Some of the challenges in relation
to medical theory, medical specialisation and technology,
medical care and records and medical education are outlined. By reviewing briefly the course of progress, a
framework is given to indicate possible future developments of medical information and computerised technology.

Introduction.

The developments in medicine that have been taking place in the past two decades will change medical practice and training. The 'systematic' doctor will evolve who will accept and use automation and information processing extensively in his practice whether it be in primary care or in hospital. Developments in medical informatics are producing radical changes in our system of investigating patients for structural and functional defects and are having an impact on our information and knowledge based systems. This has put pressure on medical theory to extend and develop to meet the new challenges of informatics. Both logical and statistical methodologies have been pressed into use.

For society to create and accept the systematic doctor it is useful to have a brief review of the development of medical theory, medical specialisation and technology, medical care, medical education and relate these to new developments in informatics. Changes in medicine seem to occur in quantum jumps and the last two decades of this century will be no exception. The medical profession tends to be conservative, but with the telecommunications revolution data bases can be accessed quickly anywhere in the world and this alters the approach to the medical literature.

The pressure of change towards the 'systematic' doctor will come not only from technological advances in communication and information science, but from the realisation that the expansion of knowledge and theory is becoming such that it is no longer within the power of anyone doctor to carry in his memory or to use all the knowledge that is available for patient care. There are more than 20,000 medical journals in the world today and the number is increasing at least at a linear rate. Moreover, it has become obvious that we are neglecting our learning opportunities in patient care because of the limitations and inadequacies of our present pen and paper methods of recording and analysing relevant medical data. Our present medical record libraries in every hospital rival those of the complete universities at the turn of the present century.

On the other hand there is a risk of being inundated
by complexity and care has to be taken not to fall into
the chasm of bottomless data. It is easy to have automatic machines to record data from our patients not only
hour by hour, minute by minute, second by second, milli-
second by milli-second, but what are we to do with it and
how are we going to ascertain both change and relevance.
In many areas of medical investigation technology has to
address itself to these questions. New tools exist, but
we must also build into our information systems a mechanism for forgetting, that will delete the irrelevant and
preserve that which will be useful.

Medical Theory.

Medical theory is not a well recognised entity.
Although it has been around for nearly two thousand years,
few pay attention to its development and change. Because
it is cognitively based, to date it has relied much upon
concept and logic rather than on mathematical science.
It has tended to be left to a few interested teachers to
recognise its importance and to review its development.
It, however, is the foundation on which medical practice
is built and around which our educational systems grow
and develop.

It began with Hippocrates who as the father of medicine
separated it from religion nearly two thousand years ago
in Greece by developing the concept of prognosis. By the
use of his 'aphorisms' describing clinical data, he was
able to foretell the future of the patient thus establishing his prognosis. It is true that in those days
fevers were of dominant importance and it was necessary,
for example, to separate out the future of patients with
malaria from that of tuberculosis which ran a different
course and had a different prognosis. The importance of
this theoretical step cannot be overestimated and it
relied on observation for nothing was known about causat-
ion or pathology. Galen of Pergamon also used animal
experiments to develop theories of normal bodily functions
which were based on observation and which were to last
for over a thousand years.[1]

The development of the concept of diagnosis by Thomas
Sydenham flowed not only from his ideas of the natural
history or course of disease, but from the desire to
classify epidemic fevers so as to understand epidemics of
his time. Classificatory systems for diagnosis received
a great impetus from the work of Linnaeus, the great
Swedish botanist, who published in the 18th century his
classification of plants. The French School of Medicine
under Broussais and Pinel and others later pushed forward
the classification of disease by symptoms. They had to
await the development of pathology and bacteriology in the
latter half of the 19th century for important developments
about aetiology in relation to diagnosis.

The work of Claude Bernard in France and Cannon at the
beginning of the first world war created the concept of
homeostasis. This suggested man was in a steady state
which was an open system with agencies acting or about to
act to maintain stability. The process of diagnosis now
had to take into account not only the possible causes,
but the responding systems. Following the second world
war our ideas of feedback and control further extended
this theoretical development. (2).

The development of theories for investigating disease
awaited not only progress in medical technology which
followed the discovery of the microscope, the stethoscope
and the development of radiology, biochemistry and pathology, but also that which gave rise to the concept of
deviation from the normal by changes in structure and
function. Thus in radiology we have the concept of a
normal x-ray of the chest or abdomen and in biochemistry
we have the concept of a normal range of values for a
normal population. This has been extended recently to
the concept of the patient specific normal range for
interpreting normal biochemical and haematological data.
For some time we have also realised the implications of
false negative and false positive data transferring ideas
from the statistical techniques developed for preventive
medicine earlier in the century.

Medical theory in relation to therapy has been slow to
develop and for the greater part of two thousand years it

has largely been empirical and dependent on prevailing fashion. The concept of the controlled clinical trial put paid to blood letting over a century ago and the art form of the phlebotomist's bleeding bowl disappeared. In the present century the pharmaceutical industry has produced drugs that alter the natural balance of control either in the direction of alleviating symptoms such as pain or curing infectious disease both by killing or inhibiting the growth of invading organisms and enhancing the bodies defences.

The management of disease in both the individual patient and the community has depended on the development of theories of control and appropriate tools for surveillance. With the development of mathematics in the 18th century it was possible for Farr to describe the rise and fall of the epidemics of disease of his day. Fisher and Karl Pearson developed techniques to assess the significance of observations both for the individual patient and for collected data giving new insights into the problems of measurement in disease. Patient management has become important both from the need for a continuing patient service and the clinical necessity of using the concepts of cost effectiveness and cost benefit.

There are now pressures for better statements and definition of medical theory now that new analytical tools are available. The possibility of extending medical theory using some of the tools of medical informatics exist.

Medical Specialisation and Technology.

Medicine has developed specialisation in the clinical and laboratory fields. Specialties such as paediatrics and geriatrics have arisen because of the need for special care situations in these age groups. Others have arisen around body systems such as cardiology. Specialisation has divided pathology into morbid anatomy, microbiology, haematology and clinical biochemistry.

In the midst of this specialisation process the role of the generalist both in family practice and hospital care has remained to deal with whole man problems and the

difficulties that are created by too rigid a specialisation. Perhaps specialisation has gone far enough and it
is now time to recognise that the reasons for the process
need to be explored as the portion of national talent and
resources that can be devoted to the medical area is not
without limit.

One of the potent factors fuelling the demand for
specialisation is the fixed capacity of human memory for
detail and so far our ability to extend and enlarge this
capability has not been great. We have already had to
accept that the undergraduate period of training cannot
encompass all the relevant knowledge of all medical
specialties although it should provide a firm general
educational basis for further specialisation. Thus there
is a need for new ways of dealing with and organising the
exploding information system. This is an essential
requirement for the last two decades of the 20th century.

Medical Care and Records.

Medical care has increased both in extent, direction
and purpose and is continually evolving in response to
perceived needs and demand. Some of this pressure is
undoubtedly medically oriented and demand for new tools
and technology arises more from doctors than from the
patient. The medical services industry addresses its
selling effort in the appropriate direction. These rapid
changes in the pattern of medical care have worried
administrators and governments who have sought means of
managing the expenditure of resources in new directions.
Not only have they had to contend with increases in the
investigation of patients disorders, but also the therapeutic revolution has made great demands on both medical care
and record systems. Drugs themselves are not an outright
benefit and it is necessary to carefully weigh the desired
therapeutic effect against the unwanted side-effects.

Medical records are centuries old and have reflected
the theoretical and practical issues of medicine of the
day. While primarily existing as an aid-memoire for the
doctor and for communication purposes, they have performed
diverse functions in relation both to medico-legal and
educational purposes. Indeed one of the new medical

record designs, the problem oriented record, was devised
to improve the training of doctors. Because of the
diverse objectives of medical care and medical records it
has been difficult to get an overall view.

While medical specialisation was minimal some consensus
about medical records appeared. With the increasing
complexity of care there have come divergencies in the
format and recording of clinical states which reflect
different views of clinical care as they deal with
different aspects of specialisation. Already the limitations of the single unique medical paper record which
encompasses only the hospital part of the illness of a
particular patient are familiar to us all. The problems
of continuity of records in family care are also growing.

Because much of the format and data content of medical
records reflects medical decisions and actions which are
based on medical theory and knowledge, we need to have
better analytic systems for control. Otherwise the
medical record becomes an impossible monster. (3).

Medical Education.

Medical education must reflect the changes and
vicissitudes of professional life. The teaching of the
art and science of medicine has not been an easy task
especially during a period of medical change. The difficulties both in relation to the scientific content and
the state of the art have been reflected by the number of
investigators and commissions trying to produce order out
of complexity and to keep medical education on a progressive and productive path.

The need to integrate learning for the student has
become much more important with the knowledge explosion
and the necessary procedures by which we might ensure this
have been slow to arrive. Now that we are more conscious
of the complexity of our knowledge base, perhaps a better
understanding of teaching difficulties might be achieved.
Not only is it necessary to appreciate the difficulties
of the knowledge situation, but we must also appreciate
that the learning rate of our students is not ever increasing and cannot be expected to keep up with the

exponential explosion in knowledge. (4).

Just as we now need specialisation containment, so we need more radical recognition of what is essential to be learned and the techniques for supporting memory based activities. It is counter-productive to go on increasing the load of our students in medical schools without informing them of new ideas and principles which they may use to deal with complexity.

Further education has similar problems in relation to general and specialist training both in family and hospital medicine. Non-university colleges have assumed the role of setting standards and examinations and these are accepted as part of postgraduate training and consequently an essential part of the career pathways. Nevertheless, the need to use new approaches and tools to ensure clinical conpetency is a pressing problem.

The Role of Informatics in dealing with the Problems.

The medical scene has been defined overall so that the potential benefits of medical informatics might be viewed and the critical areas it would impact. Naturally, such descriptions must involve future predictions based on the contributions that are possible from medical informatics and also the development of medicine itself, so that we may have a systematic doctor. Certainly there will be a need to classify and extend medical theory to deal with the problems that beset us. The use of modelling and simulation techniques may help us towards this goal and may reveal the inadequacies of medical theory as it exists at present.

Already the exploration of automated systems for diagnosis and prognosis has revealed some of the cognitive, logical and mathematical difficulties that are encountered. While extensive knowledge data bases are essential a more detailed investigation of the diagnostic process and how different pieces of evidence are used becomes necessary. (1). Attention has to be paid to the intermediate decision pathways when moving towards an accurate diagnosis and the use of logical methods of exclusion which tend to focus on a limited number of

alternative diagnoses or prognostic possibilities. While
it may be difficult to classify fully common disorders,
another part of the diagnostic problem relates to having
knowledge of some 10 - 15,000 rare disorders which are
only encountered occasionally during a doctor's life time.
Here memorising all different diagnoses may be extremely
difficult and the use of online large data bases describing rare diagnoses would be very useful.

While we have some knowledge of the use of expert
systems, these need developing and testing before doctors
would place a great deal of reliance on their usefulness.
In recent years new models of diagnosis have been
suggested and they may be useful in different areas of
medicine and have the potential to yield new insights into
the complex situations encountered in old age. (5).

In therapy the situation is just as complex and there
are often challenging situations for the doctor in relation to the interaction of drugs and disease. Not only
does the taking of drugs and other therapy relieve the
main symptoms or change the course of an illness which is
the desired effect, but there also may be side effects and
interactions which in some occasions are quite serious.
Because of the diversity of human structure and function,
it is necessary to accept that therapy has to be carefully
applied to the individual. Thus judgement as well as
knowledge is required for adequate therapy.

New drug information systems can offer the doctor the
ability to consult data bases about interactions of drugs
and their side effects. It is also possible to convey
this information to the patient from the information
system. Thus knowledge can be given to both parties in
the therapeutic relationship. Information systems are
also useful in assessing the actions of drugs especially
in collecting and processing the necessary data from
controlled clinical trials and from clinical records.

The demand for increasing specialisation and sub-
specialisation undoubtedly arises because of the large
knowledge base required of the doctor. Support from
information systems and the existence of large data bases
goes some way towards retarding extension of specialicism

and makes it possible for the doctor to encompass wider
areas of care. Information support can assist clinical
decision making and also improve the usage of medical
technology.

So far expert advisory systems using knowledge data
bases have been only developed to a limited extent. (6).
Once their potential is realised there will no doubt be a
great deal of effort made to create more comprehensive
systems. However, a great deal of effort is required to
design and implement these aid systems. It may be that
they are not cost-effective at present though very useful.

With the development of telecommunications it is
possible to access the expert systems in any country, but
as yet the difficulty in the United Kingdom is that the
means of accessing are not readily available in the
clinical situation. Nevertheless, if we are to halt the
progress of specialisation and change practice, we need
to have both knowledge and decision support systems.
This would greatly increase the area of effectiveness of
individual doctors.

The need for information support in relation to the
teaching of concepts and the use of an extensive knowledge base is now recognised. Also computers can be
useful in aiding rote learning as they do not tire.
Comprehension can be helped by presenting data in
different ways to the learner. The use of graphics,
moving scenes and other ways of presentation can improve
understanding.

Acceptance of computerised systems in medical education
today has been slow except in relation to using then as
tools for marking multiple choice questionnaires. Nevertheless, technology also needs development for at the
present time while it can automatically produce results in
the laboratory, it is not possible to make these available
on computerised systems for immediate use by the clinical
doctor. Indeed, the laboratory revolution merely churns
out more and more paper which relies on hand-driven
systems to convey the result to doctors either at the bedside or in family practice. Also we may improve the

present difficulty of interpretation of data by changing
its presentation to the doctor.

One of the major difficulties to date has been for
medical informatics to produce adequate and cost-effective
solutions to the medical record problem. There has been
little progress both in system analysis and design of the
specialised records which are an urgent need. It is not
possible to find an overall blanket solution to this
problem. Nevertheless, there are difficulties in dealing
with the multitude of purposes for which medical data is
collected and used. All too often the importance of
feedback in the immediate care cycle is forgotten and the
thought of creating data for preventive action tends to
dominate the caring aspects. Thus a comprehensive view
of care is necessary if we are not to make further errors.
Analyses of medical records can be used for modelling and
simulating clinical situations. Records can also act as
support base for decision making systems and doctors must
now begin to use their data storing potential. Because of
the need for thorough systems analysis and design, computer aided systems of learning are difficult to create.
Nevertheless they offer a great potential to master the
use of a large knowledge base of medical records and apply
it to clinical problems.

Naturally, medical education must relate to the use of
medical support systems if doctors are going to accept
these both in relation to diagnosis, prognosis, investigation, therapy and management. All too often it is
assumed that such support is not necessary and that if
the doctor works harder and harder, he can gain the same
benefit. Nevertheless, the necessity for providing knowledge base support systems to deal with complexity is
being recognised.

In relation to decision making aids, such procedures
must be able to be investigated by the doctor who must be
able to trace the logical development of the advice given
and check the operations carried out. This demands more
sophisticated systems. Nevertheless, it is quite certain
that doctors cannot even comprehend the whole range of
knowledge available unless such support systems become
generally accepted and available.

Conclusions.

The challenges are such in medicine that the systematic doctor will be trained and created in the near future and he will be reliant much more than his precedessor on advances in medical informatics. Hopefully he will grow up with such systems during his training period. As yet we have to admit that these are rather elementary and far from ideal.

Medical information systems are at a stage where it is possible to foresee such developments, but they will only be implemented if they are likely to be accepted by those who work in the system. It is no use creating large data bases for use if they are going to be ignored or extensive decision aids if they are not going to be accepted. The important aspect of such systems is to give the doctor the help and information he needs at the time it is required and not at some other pre-arranged time which seems to be optimal for the system but not for the doctor.

The challenges the systematic doctor has to meet are complex and difficult. Nevertheless, the tools to deal with some of these are at hand and the opportunities must be grasped. Who is for the systematic doctor ?

References

1. Anderson, J. (1970) Information Processing of Medical Records, p.3-13 ed. Anderson, J., Forsythe, J.M., pub. North Holland.

2. Llewelyn, D.E.H., Anderson, J. (1980) Med. Informatics 5, 267-80.

3. de Heaulme, M., Anderson, J. (1978) Med. Informatics 3, 37-50.

4. Anderson, J., Graham, A. (1980) Med. Educ. 14, 4-7.

5. Cooper, D.J., Graham, A., Anderson, J. (1976) 541-8, Medical Data Processing ed. Laudet, N., Anderson, J., Begon, F., Taylor & Francis London.

6. Lenoir, P., Charles, G. (1980) Med. Informatics 5, 281-9.

Digitally Dependent Medical Imaging

J. R. Sheard

*Sales Support Manager,
International General Electric Company
of New York Limited, UK*

Medical Imaging, developing since 1895 now includes CT, Ultra-sound and the Gamma Camera. These developments depend in various ways on the availability of low cost mini- and micro-computers.

Conventional x-ray systems can now make use of the micro-computer to improve efficiency of use; the mini-computer has brought the benefits of digital techniques to conventional x-ray.

In radiotherapy treatment planning the mini-computer has not only simplified the preparation of treatment plans but has also provided a link to CT.

This paper surveys these developments and discusses their dependence on mini- and micro-computers.

DIGITALLY DEPENDENT MEDICAL IMAGING

Introduction

The purpose of this paper is to summarise development of the use
of digital logic applied to medical imaging. The term digital
logic is used rather than "computing" because it acknowledges the
increasing use of dispersed micro-processors and avoids confusion
with traditional data processing.

Medical imaging started with Roentgen's discovery in 1895 of the
translucency of body tissue to x-radiation. Today there are
imaging techniques in use based on

    a)   Ionising Radiation (x-ray)
    b)   Ultrasonic radiation (ultrasound)
    c)   Isotope scintillation (nuclear medicine).

In addition to the above there are developments in nuclear
magnetic resonance (NMR) which is still in the experimental
stage and outside the scope of this paper.

1.   Computed Tomography

The most outstanding application of digital methods to medical
imaging is in the use of x-ray technology for computed tomography
(CT). In the main current applications of this technique, x-rays
in the form of a fanned beam which typically will be forty to
fifty degrees in the xy direction and between one and fifteen
millimetres in the z direction, produce data by scanning a
patient's body or head as in fig. 1.

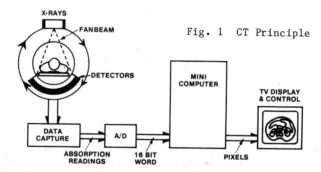

Fig. 1 CT Principle

Nobel prize winner, G. Hounsfield of U.K., perceived that an x-ray picture of a transverse section of patient anatomy could be built up using a computer thereby increasing very considerably the amount of information that could be obtained from an x-ray image. The process is illustrated by fig. 1 and the results at figs. 2A and 2B.

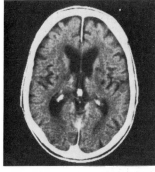

Fig. 2a
CT Scan
of Head

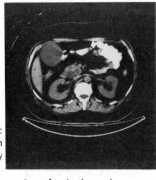

Fig. 2b
CT Scan
of Body

After the x-rays have passed through the patient's body, the level of absorption is measured by scintillating crystal or ionising gas detectors and the resultant signals amplified, and after A/D conversion, are passed to a computer. A large number of transverse views are taken and the computer reconstructs the image, usually using a technique known as back projection. The technique allows the interior of the skull and body to be examined without the need for invasive surgery.

The principles of CT have been described extensively in the literature and typical references are given at the end of this paper, (1 2 3 4). It is important to remember, however, that CT computing is entirely dependent upon the availability of the mini-computer; each image requires several hundred thousand calculations, which must be completed within a few seconds.

The computer dependence and complexity of a modern system is illustrated by the block diagram at fig. 3.

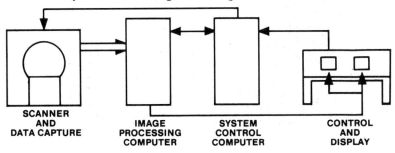

SCANNER
AND
DATA CAPTURE

IMAGE
PROCESSING
COMPUTER

SYSTEM
CONTROL
COMPUTER

CONTROL
AND
DISPLAY

Fig. 3 Contemporary CT System

In this system, there will be input to the image reconstruction
computer upwards of 200,000 to 300,000 readings from the
detectors during a scan as short as 3 - 4 seconds. Each reading
will be in the form of a sixteen bit word and within 20 - 30
seconds or less an image will be generated of very high
resolution. A dedicated array processor is frequently used as
image processor and the image is presented on a TV screen.
Typically, system control will be by mini-computer with a fast
semi conductor memory of 64K 16 bit words or more, with hard disc
capacity of up to 192 mbytes and peripherals including printer,
magnetic tape and floppy discs.

For the purpose of this paper, the basic computer dependent CT
system will be regarded as "standard and only latest
developments discussed which depend very heavily upon digital
processing.

Typical of contemporary development is the generation of images
of sections in the sagittal and coronal planes along the z axis
of the slices derived from the x and y axis information, contained in the normal CT slice images. This is achieved by trans-
forming the data along the x,y axis and individual components of
a z axis slice with results illustrated by fig. 4.

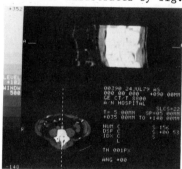

Fig. 4   Section Reconstruction

The basic technique is clearly capable of development; for
instance, sections at angles between the sagittal and coronal can
be generated. With appropriate software and adequate digital
storage the rotational techniques used in CAD could be applied.
The digital capability which make the technique possible is the
availability of fast cheap storage and fast processing provided
by the modern mini-computer.

Another very important CT based development for the clinician is
so called dynamic scanning. If an iodine based x-ray opaque
liquid (contrast media) is injected into the patient, CT images
of the blood rich part of the anatomy will be enhanced. The
clinician may wish to use this technique to study blood-flow

patterns in the patient's head
which he can do with a dynamic
series of scans taken sequentially, collecting the data as the
scans occur and processing the
sequence as a batch at the end of
the dynamic scan sequence as
illustrated by fig. 5. The
computer can take pixel density
values across the image (a pixel
is a picture element) and present
these as a histogram, from which
the clinician can deduce the rate
of blood migration.

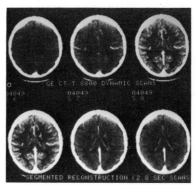

Fig. 5   Dynamic Scan

A further important development in CT is the use of digitised
x-ray images. As the resolution of CT systems and positioning
precision increases, exact location of the scan area becomes
very important. By holding the scan beam fixed and moving the
patient in the z axis, output of the
detectors can be processed to form a
very high grade x-ray type image as
fig. 6. Software can be used to set
the position of the patient table so
that there will be exact correlation
between slice selection and slice
scanning.

There are other examples of digitally
dependent imaging developments in CT,
including highlighting selected ranges
of absorption values, forming
statistical calculations on selected

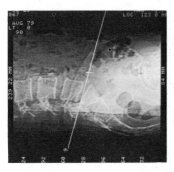

Fig. 6   Digital X-Ray View   parts of the image, applying different
algorithms for processing images and
other techniques currently being developed jointly by clinical
users and manufacturer.

Summarising, in CT, the computer is being used to generate images
and then further applied to extract from the images, far more
data than can be obtained by simple visual inspection. The
latter principle is increasingly being used in other areas of
digitally based imaging.

2. Conventional X-Ray

The availability of micro-processors in the last few years has resulted in their application to conventional x-ray techniques.

In taking an x-ray image, the main factors of technique involved are:-

The kVp (peak kilovoltage), which determines the energy or the "penetrating power" of the radiation.

The current in mA, which determines number of photons generated in a given unit of time at a given kVp.

The exposure length in seconds, which determines the total quantity of photons.

In addition to the technique factors, there are a number of options which can be selected in relation to the x-ray taken and the particular procedure being used by the Radiologist.

Using micro-processors it is not difficult to both pre-program and store, combinations of techniques and in particular their relation to particular requirements. The small physical size of the micro-processor allows it to be incorporated in the electronics of the x-ray system control console. The result can be a set of control buttons as in fig. 7 which indicate to the system the details of the patient to be x-rayed and allow selection of suitable technique factors.

The availability of micro-processor capability can be further exploited to develop sophisticated interlock and control procedures. This relates particularly to other aspects of radiographic technique using fluorography, cinematography and photography. Fluorography, for example, uses a television system to view the image, as fig. 8, and is particularly important for real time examination of dynamic anatomy such as the digestive system.

Fig. 7 Micro Processor Control of X-Ray System

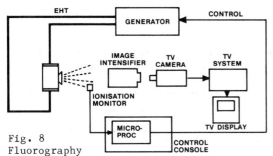

Fig. 8
Fluorography

The maintenance of image brightness and contrast and the relation of technique factors to film characteristics are very important. This can be achieved by using the micro-processor as part of a servo-system controlling the x-ray generator, to maintain the required and pre-set requirements as shown in fig. 8.

From the above very brief description it can be seen that even Roentgen's basic techniques are now being made more effective by digitally dependent methods.

3. Ultrasound

Engineers, making use of ultrasonic techniques will be familiar with the very useful properties of the piezo electric crystal transducer. 'piezi electric' refers to the inter-dependence of mechanical stresses and generation of electrical output. Deformation of a piezo electric crystal produces an electric output; conversely applying an electrical input causes deformation of the crystal. This property makes it possible to produce a transducer which generates ultrasonic pulses and then 'reads' or detects returning reflections of these pulses. One of the initial applications of ultrasound was to generate ultrasonic pulses for detecting defects such as cracks and voids in solid materials.

In using ultrasound for medical imaging the transducer is applied to the skin of a patient so that images can be obtained of internal structure. The system is effective because the human body is in a sense, a series of voids, formed of different densities of tissue. (Refs. 5,6)

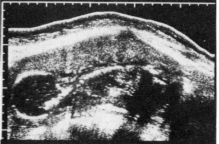

Fig. 9 Ultra Sound Obstetrics

The application of this form of imaging tends to overlap with that of CT in particular and x-ray to some extent, but there are specific areas in which it is particularly useful. An important specialist application area is in obstetrics. See fig. 9.

Considering how digital techniques can be applied to ultrasound imaging, there is a basic distinction in the image generation systems between static B scan and real-time displays. For B scanning, the transducer is a single piezo electric element attached to a moving arm, which can be used to generate x,y co-ordinate information, to produce a static picture. In the real-time situation a special form of transducer is used which generates a line of pulses by using either a series of individual transducers (typically 64) or a rotating scanner.

In the case of the static B scan system, digital techniques are particularly appropriate since the image can be digitised, stored in a matrix, displayed and manipulated under micro-processor control.

A typical system will be as fig. 10 in which a transducer is passed across the patient's body and the arm to which it is attached moves potentiometers to provide x and y co-ordinate information, so establishing the position in space of the transducer at a particular instant. The reflected or echo information is placed into the digital storage matrix at an address determined by the x and y co-ordinate information so that an image can be built up and input to a TV display system. Matrix size will correspond to the number of pixels (picture elements) in the display matrix and the range of grey scale information will be dependent on the number of bits available for each pixel. Typically, a storage matrix would be 512 x 512 x 5 bits. The diagram at fig. 10 also illustrates that the digital control functions can be shared between two micro-processors, one for control of the system and the other for scan conversion of the image into digital form and storage.

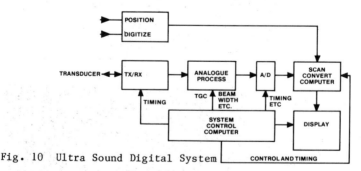

Fig. 10   Ultra Sound Digital System

The system computer can be used for controlling various compensation functions such as gain control in relation to depth of penetration of the patient (TGC) to compensate for signal attenuation. There also has to be compensation to achieve an effectively uniformly homogenous beam cross-section. In addition there are many other more subtle corrections, compensations and post-receiver processing activities.

In total there will be a large amount of software which can be enhanced and modified as developments create the need. Since the software will probably be stored in PROMS (Programmable Read Only Memories) not only is the system flexible and highly adaptable but software changes are relatively easy to implement.

4. Nuclear Medicine

The next area to consider is scintillation imaging; the equipment generally being known as a gamma camera and the technique, Nuclear Medicine. The system is well documented (ref. 7) and the basic process is to inject into the patient's body a radio-isotope having a short half-life which will be taken up by the organ or tissue to be examined.

Radioactivity from the isotope is "scanned" by a detector system which uses a crystal responding to the mainly gamma radiating particles.

The camera principles are illustrated at fig. 11 and a typical detector head would consist of a thallium doped sodium iodide crystal which will generate light photons (scintillations) in response to the radiation (similar principle to some types of detectors used for CT.) The light output from the crystal will be captured by a matrix of photo multipliers to provide an adequate level of input to the camera display system.

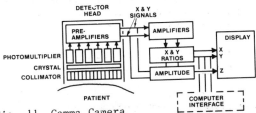

Fig. 11 Gamma Camera

To define accurately the spatial position of the emission source, a lead collimator with holes or hexagonal matrix of foil is interposed between the detector crystal and the patient. The whole assembly is enclosed to form a complete unit as can be seen at fig. 12.

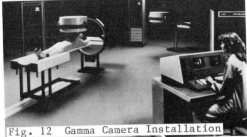

Fig. 12 Gamma Camera Installation

Different types and sizes of detector heads are used for specific purposes and inter-changeable collimators are available for emission particles of different energy levels.

The overall system illustrated by fig. 11 shows a basic camera arrangement in which x and y signals provide spatial positional information on particle source and z information on particle generation. The radiation source will generally have three dimensions, but the image can only be displayed in two.

In its simplest form the camera is an analogue device with an image displayed on a screen; image storage can be by photographic film.

The basic gamma camera, however, captures a large amount of dynamic information which requires digital techniques for processing and display.

A modern nuclear medicine system with the addition of the post-camera processing facilities can therefore be represented as fig. 13.

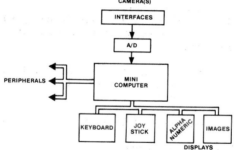

Fig. 13   Gamma Camera Digital Processing

Such a system can provide a large amount of dynamic information. For instance with the gamma camera linked to a sophisticated digital processing system, the movement of the heart can be studied by injection of the isotope material; the data derived by the camera being gated, processed and displayed dynamically. Alternative methods of heart study by x-ray use arterial catheter insertion.

From a data processing aspect the additional processing system is likely to have an outline specification as follows:-

        Memory; 64k, 16 bit words
        Busses; I/O and memory
        Interrupt structure; 16 priority levels
        Memory; MOS with 400 Ns cycle time

Hard disc; 12.5mb
Floppy disc; 1.26 mb

Camera Interface including;
provision for two cameras, software selectable
2 high speed 12 bit A/D convertors
Acquisition sub-system with direct memory accesses
Digital buffering at 64 levels
Data matrix choice of 64 x 64, 128 x 128 or
     265 x 256
Real-time clock
Physiological trigger system (x2)

The range of software packages will include:-

Heart activity
Lung perfusion
Renal functions
Brain, bloodflow
Section reconstruction
Acquisition protocols
Image Reconstruction
ECT (Emission Computerised Tomography)
and a wide range of other display and processing
functions.

The digital processing system, as shown in fig. 12 will have a
dual display for text and image and a number of sophistications
to help the operator such as:-

Data and image storage directly accessible

Windowing of images
Peripherals such as:-
    Printer/plotter
    Magnetic tape
    Floppy disc

In addition successive issues of software are expected to become
available; this is particularly important since currently, a
great deal of development is taking place.

5. Digital Radiography and Fluorography

Earlier in this paper, reference was made to the use of micro-
processors to control conventional x-ray systems and earlier in
discussing CT, fig. 6 showed an x-ray picture, built up by
software from digitised input.

There are a number of advantages in digital x-ray techniques, many of which will be evident to data-processing specialists and others which are particularly important to the Radiologist.

General advantages of the digitally based radiograph are expected to be as summarised below:-

> Improved low contrast detectability
> Improved contrast differentiation
> Accurate and interactive processing
> Synchronised diagnostic procedures
> Flexible image display
> Digital storage of raw data and images.

The sum result of the above should be the ability to produce better image quality (and/or employ less invasive procedures) and improved display benefits for numerous types of radiographic and fluorographic examinations.

Currently there are two methods in use to produce digital x-ray images:-

> scanned projection (as described under CT)
> digital fluorography

an earlier method of digitising from film has nowadays effectively been abandoned.

Scanned projection is an adaptation of the CT scanning principle with a modified CT scanning system held static but still pulsed, whilst the patient is moved with precision through the scan field.

Each time the system is pulsed, the detector system and computer processing produces one line of x-ray image; successive lines are built up as the patient is progressed along the z axis.

An alternative method is digital fluorography in which the x-ray image is digitised then processed and displayed on a t.v. screen as in fig. 14. An important application of this technique is in angiography; examination of the circulatory system of the body.

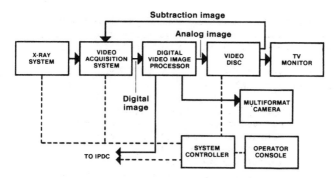

Fig. 14   Digital Fluorography

Digital radiography x-ray can contribute to this form of
examination by the use of dual energy x-ray techniques. If the
x-ray EHT generator is pulsed, successive pulses can be at two
different voltage levels. This allows two separate images to be
taken at intervals which are sufficiently rapid to be effectively
at the same time and digital techniques allow these to be stored
independently within the computer.

At different energy levels, absorption characteristics of dense
materials such as bone have smaller differences than softer
tissue. By using computer subtraction methods, selective
presentation of the images is possible. An example of dual
energy angiography is illustrated at fig. 15.

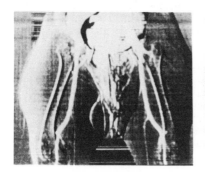 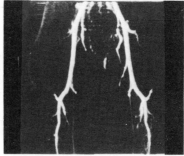

Fig. 15   Dual Energy Angiography

Since digital x-ray techniques have particular application to
vascular x-ray studies, it is logical to apply digital techniques
to specialist vascular x-ray equipment such as fig. 16.

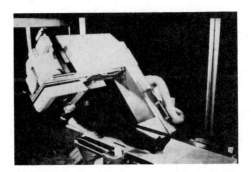

Fig. 16   Vascular X-Ray

Since a digital fluorography system, as illustrated at fig. 14, includes a computer, the digital techniques for both x-ray images and system control (as discussed previously under 2) can be combined.

The techniques described in this section on digital radiography, and which are described in the literature, (refs. 8,9,10) are already being applied to equipment commercially available or currently in production planning for commercial availability. The data-processing specialist will note that the overall problems of a high resolution digital fluorographic system are mainly in the production of the video information, on which the final image quality will depend, rather than the digital processing.

5.   Radio Therapy Treatment Planning

Although not strictly digitally dependent imaging, a mention of Radio Therapy Treatment Planning is used to conclude this paper, because modern techniques in RTP are both digitally based and directly related to digitally dependent imaging.

A method of cancer treatment in use for a number of years is the bombardment of tumours by high energy radiation (ref.11). The radiation is obtained from linear accelerators, high activity isotopes or x-ray generators. By using well established methods, a field map can be drawn of the radiating source as in fig 17 and if required, the shape of the field contours can be modified by using absorption wedges, or shaped by collimation.

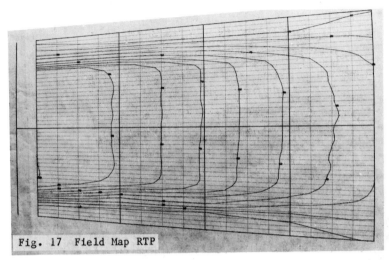

Fig. 17   Field Map RTP

In generating a treatment plan, the object is to achieve a
concentration of energy at the tumour, maintain a low radiation
level in surrounding tissue and avoid radiation of susceptible
areas such as eyes, spine and delicate organs. Traditionally,
this planning has been achieved by a combination of skill and
experience using arithmetical and graphical methods.

Availability of the mini computer, provides fast efficient
methods of storing and manipulating data and tables and the
printer plotter and VDU, of displaying results. In a typical
planning system the computer can store the data and the patient
outline is set up on a special plotting table, provided as a
peripheral to the planning computer.

An important principle in RTP is that of inhomogeneity; allowing
for different levels of tissue radiation absorption in the
patient's body. The absorption level of, for example, bone and
lung tissue will be different.

The sophistication of mini computer based planning systems
reached a peak with the RAD 8 system which was developed at the
Marsden Hospital in England (ref.12). The RAD 8 was subsequently
marketed as a commercially available system.

There are two notable aspects of these systems; the necessity for
an accurate measure of patient outline and the need for
simplification of the inhomogeneity for calculation purposes;
usually it is limited for say two to three absorption levels.

An increasingly used clinical tool in both diagnosing and treatment monitoring of cancer is the CT scanner. It is logical
therefore to develop systems with a closer link between the CT

scanning and the RTP
systems. Such a system
is illustrated in use in
fig. 18; it was developed
from the RAD 8 but uses a
CT scan as source data
(refs.13,14).

In use, the system shown
in fig. 18 has as basic
reference input to the
planning computer an
image from the CT
scanner, transferred
either on a floppy disc
or magnetic tape.

Software is used to define the patient outline which will be
accurately representative of that which will appear to the
treatment system; accuracies of a few millimetres are sought and
the shape of the scanner table must be the same as the treatment
platter to avoid organ displacement within the patient's body.
In the case of treatment of the head, a transparent plastic shell
is moulded which ensures accuracy of repetitive positioning.

An important advantage of the CT based system is that the actual
CT absorption values are used to define inhomogeneity between
tissues rather than the two to three values typically used in non
CT planning.

The system is highly interactive, making the best use of both the
operator's time and skill; use of two screens allow alphanumeric
information on one, and planning graphics on the other. In
addition to the keyboard for calling up software options, a
lightpen is used to call up planning facilities by addressing
visual keys on the screen. The lightpen is also used to indicate
specific positions on the plan where modifications are to be
made. Finally, the plan can be output to a printer plotter to
provide a documentary record of the patient treatment plan, fig.
19. As the patient's treatment progresses, interaction with the
CT scanner will continue, as the effect of the treatment is
monitored.

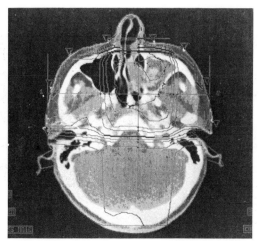

Fig. 19   RTP Printout

Summary

It will be evident from the survey covered by this paper that
availability of cheap compact digital processor power has
resulted in a wide range of largely complimentary methods of
imaging areas within the human body.   In the last few years the
mini-computer has been supplemented in the medical imaging field
by low cost programable micro-processors which makes feasible,
dispersed processing.   Imaging of large quantities of rapidly
produced data has been possible by mini array processors.

The imaging techniques range from those entirely dependent on
digital processing such as CT, through use of micro-processors to
enhance efficiency and stretch the use of the existing techniques
in radiography and ultrasonography.

In addition, digital techniques are now providing new ways of
using x-rays and of processing the results.

In nuclear medicine, the mini-computer is encouraging development
of dynamic examination methods and of extracting and recording
the maximum amount of information from a given amount of data -
this is in the best tradition of data processing!

The patient benefits directly from this expansion of digital
imaging techniques; more accurate and rapid diagnosis followed by
more precise monitoring of subsequent treatment.   In particular
the techniques become increasingly less invasive; that is they
give less discomfort and pain to the patient.

It is particularly heartening that there is no sign of a slowing down in the application of digital processing techniques to medical imaging. NMR will be yet another digitally dependent and complementary technique to become available in the next year or so.

No doubt, as this century nears its close there will be other digital dependent imaging systems and doctors will become increasingly understanding of and receptive to these new techniques. This is good for the patient who will increasingly continue to benefit.

REFERENCE   LIST

1. Computerized Transverse Axial Scanning (Tomography):
    Part 1. Description of System
    G.N. Hounsfield
    December 1973.

2. Theory of Image Reconstruction in Computed Tomography
    R.A. Brooks & G. Di Chiro
    Radiology, December 1975.

3. Principles of Computer Assisted Tomography (CAT) in
     Radiographic and Radioisotopic Imaging
    R.A. Brooks & G. Di Chiro
    Phys.Med.Biol., 1976, Vol.21,no.5.

4. Picture Processing in Computed Tomography
    M. Bergstrom & R. Sundman
    Am J Roentgenol, July 1976.

5. Ultrasound in Medical Diagnosis
    G.B. Devey & P.N.T. Wells
    Scientific American, May 1978.

6. Physical Principles of Ultrasonic Diagnosis
    New York Academic Press, 1969.

7. Information Processing in Research and Routine Nuclear
     Cardiology
    C.N. de Graaf, P.P. van Rijk & O.Ying Lie
    First Congress of the European Federation for Medical
     Informatics Cambridge, September 1978.

8. A Digital Video Image Processor for Real Time Subtraction
     Imaging
    R.A. Kruger, C.A. Mistretta, J. Lancaster, T.L. Houk,
     M.M. Goodsitt, S.J. Riederer, J. Hicks, J.F. Sackett,
     A.B. Crummy, & D. Flemming
    Optical Engineering, November/December 1978.

9. Intravenous Angiography Using Computerized Fluoroscopy.
    IEEE Transactions on Nuclear Science, June 1980.

10. Digital Videoangiography
    C.A. Mistretta
    Diagnostic Imaging, January 1981.

11. Principles of Radiation Therapy
    T.J. Deeley
    Butterworths London, 1976.

12. An Interactive Digital Computer System for Radiotherapy
    Treatment Planning
    R.E. Bentley & J. Milan
    British Journal of Radiology, November 1971.

13. The Direct Use of CT Numbers in Radiotherapy Dosage
    Calculations for Inhomogeneous Media
    R.P. Parker, P.A. Hobday & K.J. Cassell
    Phys.Med.Biol., April 1979.

14. Computed Tomography Applied to Radiotherapy Treatment
    Planning: Techniques and Results
    P.A. Hobday, N.J. Hodson, J. Husband, R.P. Parker &
    J.S. Macdonald
    Radiology, November 1979.

The Identification of Hierarchies in Symptoms and Patients through Computation of Fuzzy Triangle Products and Closures

W. Bandler

Department of Mathematics,
University of Essex, Colchester CO4 3SQ, UK

L. J. Kohout

Department of Computer Science,
Brunel University, Uxbridge UB8 3PH, UK

Recently developed Fuzzy Relational Theory is called upon to frame and answer problems, arising from real-world data, involving the degree to which certain symptoms imply others, and the degree to which the condition of certain patients is subsumed in that of others.

The triangle product, developed by the authors, is shown to offer a useful resolution of these questions. It has been built into a program suite which goes on to test the degree to which a hierarchy is truly present in the data, and, when this degree is high enough, prepares the information for the drawing of the appropriate Hasse diagram.

191

Almost all non-trivial realistic decision processes require approximate reasoning. Information is incomplete or excessive (requiring interpolation or summarization); objectives or standards are imperfectly clear; interconnections are to a great extent a matter of surmise. The recent development of Fuzzy Relational Theory has had a greatdeal of success in formalizing (and thereby rendering computable) the kind of reasoning which human beings actually use -- and use remarkably well -- in organizing their pictures of the real world.

The authors have made[1,2] an intensive study of the _fuzzy implication operators_ by which propositions are connected in approximate reasoning, and explored the characteristic flavour which each such operator gives to the rational process. They have furthermore developed[2,4,5,6] new _triangle products_ of relations, reflecting in a global way the application of these operators upon atomic statements.

Important in the motivation of this work all along has been the desire to analyse in a meaningful way actual data obtained by the second author from the observation, over an extended period, of a number of Parkinsonial patients undergoing a course of physiotherapy[3,4,6]. There the problem arose of determining the degree to which the attribution of a certain feature (healthy or symptomatic) to a patient implied the attribution of other features -- in other words, the determination of the dependency relation among the features. The dual problem arose at the same time, namely, that of arranging the patients in a pseudo-hierarchy according to the severity of certain emotional symptoms.

Briefly, these problems may be summarized as follows. For each member $\underline{a}$ of a set A of therapists, at each time $\underline{t}$ of a set T of observation-days, there was given a binary fuzzy relation $R^{(a,t)}$, from a set C of constructs to a set P of patients, of which the ij-component $R_{ij}^{(a,t)}$ is the degree to which (by that therapist at that time) construct C_i was attributed to patient $\underline{P}_j$. The converse relation $R^{(a,t)-1}$ then has this same degree as its ji-component. (It should be clear that, in the interests of simplicity and clarity, we are focussing upon binary projections of what is actually a quaternary relation.)

The first problem can then be phrased, 'To what extent does the

attribution (by a at t) of C_i imply the attribution (by a' at t')
of C_k?' (Here a' and t' may or may not differ from a and t.) A
satisfactory answer is provided by the ik-component of the triangle product relation $V = R^{(a,t)} \lhd R^{(a',t')-1}$, given by the
mean degree (over all patients P_j) to which $R_{ij}^{(a,t)}$ implies $R_{kj}^{(a',t')}$,
that is,

$$V_{ik} = \frac{1}{N_j} \sum_j (R_{ij}^{(a,t)} \rightarrow R_{jk}^{(a',t')-1}).$$

Here the arrow represents any one of the fuzzy implication operators, and gives to the expression in brackets a fuzzy falue
(in the closed interval from 0 to 1) as a function of the values
of the two terms it connects.

The second problem similarly becomes, 'To what extent does the
attribution (by a at t) of constructs to P_j imply their attribution (by a' at t') to P_m?' It is answered by the jm-compo-
nent of $U = R^{(a,t)-1} \lhd R^{(a',t')}$ given by a mean over all the
C_k, namely

$$U_{jm} = \frac{1}{N_k} \sum_k (R_{jk}^{(a,t)-1} \rightarrow R_{km}^{(a',t')}).$$

The authors have developed a program suite written in Pascal
for tackling these problems and, of course others of the same
type. the program user has his choice of any or all of the
potentially useful implication operators (arrow operators) so
far discovered. In terms of each of the operators chosen the
program calculates the fuzzy matrix of dependencies (both among
constructs and among patients) and analyses it at four different
levels ('alpha cuts') of intensity. At each level, the degree
to which the relation is a pre-order is calculated, and whenever
this degree exceeds a given criterion, the pre-order to which
the data tend (the local pre-order closure of the relation) is
processed in optimal fashion: first the equivalence classes of
its symmetric interior are found, and then for the induced true
order on them, there is found the 'Hasse matrix' from which the
corresponding Hasse diagram may be drawn. These are the hierarchies, of constructs (or classes of constructs), for example, of
symptoms, on the one hand, and of patients (or classes of patients), on the other, to which the title of this paper refers.

It is intended to illustrate the presentation of this paper with
a number of the Hasse diagrams produced in the manner described,
providing easily viewed and significant comparisons among the

hierarchies resulting from different operators, different observers, different intensity levels, etc.

While work on diagnostic applications has barely begun, some
of the possibilities in that direction will already be clear to
the reader.

References:

1. Bandler, W. and Kohout, L.J., Fuzzy power sets and fuzzy
   implication operators. Fuzzy Sets and Systems, 4, (1980),
   13-30.

2. Bandler, W. and Kohout, L.J., Semantics of implication ope-
   rators and fuzzy relational products. Intl. J. Man-Machine
   Studies, 12 (1980), 89-116. Reprinted in Mamdani, E.H. and
   Gaines, B.R., eds., Fuzzy Reasoning and Its Applications,
   London: Academic Press, 1981.

3. Bandler, W. and Kohout, L.J., The use of new relational products in clinical modelling. General Systems Research:
   a Science, a Methodology, a Technology (Proc. 1979 North
   American Meeting of the SGSR) Louisville, Kentucky: SGSR,
   1979, 240-246.

4. Bandler, W. and Kohout, L.J., Application of fuzzy logics
   to computer protection structures. Proc. Ninth Intl. Symposium on Multiple-Valued Logic, New York: IEEE, 79CH 1408-
   4C, 200-207.

5. Bandler, W. and Kohout, L.J., Activity structures and their
   protection. Proc. 1979 International Meeting of the SGSR.
   Louisville, Kentucky: SGSR, 1980, 239-244.

6. Bandler, W. and Kohout, L.J., Fuzzy relational products as
   a tool for the analysis and synthesis of complex natural
   and artificial systems. Wang, S.K. and Chang, P.P., eds.,
   Fuzzy Sets: Theory and Applications to Policy Analysis and
   Information Systems, New York: Plenum Press, 1980, 341-367.

EMG Analysis: Clinical Pattern Recognition and Computing Methods Used

John Farrer and Jean Roberts

Royal Lancaster Infirmary, UK

The analysis of the signals from muscle responses to stimuli is a complex problem. Outputs have previously been captured and assessed visually using a digital averager wired up to the patient. Our studies are progressive and in a field where computer assistance has been rarely used previously.

The methods we have employed are discussed. The aims of the study are to aid clinical recognition of certain medical conditions and to build up a database of trends to aid in the teaching of future electromyography technicians.

INTRODUCTION

In an earlier paper (9) we defined the reasons for employing
computer analysis of EMG outputs from patients. Two thousand
signals are sampled over a two or three hundred millesecond period
from the area of the body under study in order to detect any
deviation of reaction from expected norms. The precision of these
signals is not fully appreciable visually on an oscilloscope or
audibly. Mathematical problems have to be overcome in the analysis
of the graph of output responses.

Phase 1 is to produce the general profile of the signal. For this
the number of crossings of a mid-point (or mid-range) were
determined. We considered the possibility of a mid-area in the
central section of the output set up by visual assessment of a
graphical printout of the signals. This proved to give no
significant different results from taking the midpoint between
maximum and minimum signals so the latter method is now used as
the value can be calculated mathematically and no prior graph is
required.

MATHEMATICAL ASSESSMENT

Recognition of a change of direction is simple. Consideration of
what is a significant change level is more difficult. A percentage
calculated from the signal range between maximum and minimum can be
applied to requested signal levels. The above protocol will not
detect slow turning, low signal "sine waves" - however most nerve
signals involve rapid changes (if any).

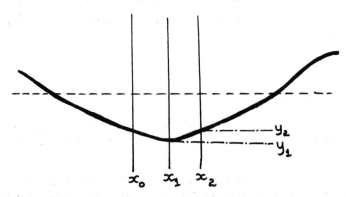

FIG. 1 : 'TURN' AT x_1 IS NOT SIGNIFICANT:
$(y_1 - y_2)$ IS SMALL.

A further approach is to define a "turn" as being a significant
change in levels across n signals - this procedure has to discount
any non-significant "noise." Visual detection of all but the
minimally significant turns is possible from the computer output
but the mathematical quantification proved difficult.

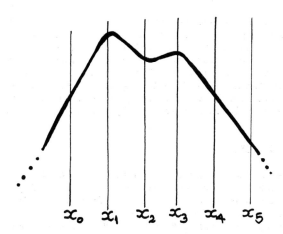

FIG. 2: CHANGE OF DIRECTION DETECTED : x_1
SIGNIFICANCE OF TURN ESTABLISHED: $x_1 - x_5$
NON SIGNIFICANT 'NOISE' DISCOUNTED : x_3

CLINICAL ASSESSMENT

On average three patients per week are having EMG analyses in our
District General Hospital. Patients are referred for EMG studies
from various Clinics.

Many Neurological Clinics at larger hospitals have their own
apparatus and conduct tests as required. Smaller hospitals such as
this may have a part time department and referrals from Orthopaedic,
Physiotherapy, Ear Nose and Throat, Neurologists and Clinical

Physicians and Paediatricians with differing requests.

The technical measurement of nerve conduction velocities is a large part of the testing but this aspect is relatively clear cut and can be extended to involve the Central Nervous System as well as the Limbs.

Difficulty arises in the diagnosis of conditions affecting Muscles and Neuromuscular systems. It is these latter where signal processing is required to reinforce or replace the "judgment" of the Physician and gather a library of comparability for interchange of standards by which to measure diseases.

CONCLUSION

Technology is developing very rapidly. The precision of instruments is now at the level whereby signals can be analyzed throughout the body and over large areas and distances across the skin.

Consideration of identified clinical patterns will aid the diagnosis of patient conditions and assist in the teaching of EMG analysis skills. It is felt that once perfected the analysis techniques may be applied to any other signal processing procedures within Health Care including Electrocardiography and Electroencephalography.

ACKNOWLEDGEMENTS

Thanks to Dr. Peter Harvey, Consultant Pathologist, Royal Lancaster Infirmary for his constructive criticism and enthusiastic support and for providing equipment for data capture. We acknowledge the continued support of Mr. H. Carr B.E.M. District Administrator and his team. The help of the Electronics Department, Royal Lancaster Infirmary is greatly appreciated. We would also like to thank the patients taking part in this study and Mrs Isabel Walker who typed this for us.

REFERENCES AND FURTHER READING

1. GOODGOLD J., EBERSTEIN A. Electrodiagnosis of Neuromuscular Diseases 2nd Edition (1980) Williams & Wilkins, Baltimore.

2. CORAL-66 Language specifications. Ferranti Computer Systems Limited.

3. TOWNSEND H.R.A. Some Uses of Microcomputers in Health Care. British Computer Society Seminar, London July, 1980.

4. WILLISON R.G. Analysis of electrical activity in health and dystrophic muscle in man. J. Neurol. Neurosurg. Psychia., 27 386-394 1964.

5. KAISER E., and PETERSON I., Muscle action potentials studied by
    frequency analysis and duration measurement. Acta Neurol. Scan.
    41 213-236, 1965

6. RATHJEN R., SIMONS D.G., and PETERSON C.R. Computer analysis of
    the duration of motor-unit potentials. Arch. Phys. Med., 49
    524-527 1968

7. BERGMANS J. Computer assisted on line measurement of motor unit
    potential parameters in human electromyography 11 1610181 1971

8. MOOSA A. and BROWN B.H., Quantitative electromyography: a new
    analogue technique for detecting changes in action potential
    duration. J. Neurol. Neurosurg. Psychiat. 35 216-220 1972.

9. FARRER J., ROBERTS J. A Simple Method of EMG Analysis to
    determine Patterns for use in the Recognition of Clinical
    Conditions. A Preliminary Report. Medical Informatics
    In Press.

Complete Computer System for General Practitioners

R. E. Bridge and G. L. Williamson

North Staffordshire Polytechnic, UK

A fully integrated computing solution at the primary care level is still in its infancy. It is likely that a large proportion of the country's general practices will be using computers in the next few years. What they will use them for is the subject of energetic debate in the medical profession.

The impact of computers in general and microcomputers in particular
has been dramatic. Few areas of business and technology have not
been affected. The use of computers in the health service has been
until recently confined to work at the regional centres such as the
South West Regional Health Authority at Exeter and the North Staffs
Royal Infirmary at Hartshill, Stoke-on-Trent.

The computing departments at a number of Polytechnics have had
students complete their industrial training period at such centres
and had graduates join these centres in full time employment. A
degree of interest in computer assistance in case history, detail
matching for organ transplants and so on has evolved.

A further development at Polytechnics has been the growth of work
linked with industry and other organizations usually of an advisory
nature, variously termed consultancy, development, collaborative
ventures, joint ventures etc. In particular smaller organizations
are finding useful information available at Polytechnics through
specialized short courses in low level and high level programming
languages, systems analysis and applications. The links forged are
sometimes extended to encompass advice on a full systems design and
implementation by Polytechnic staff.

It is against this background that the authors became interested in
a venture with a local G.P's practice. We are all no doubt aware
how busy these skilled people are, the fact that appointments are
necessary for patients in many practices illustrates one effort made
by the G.P's to improve efficiency. Computer based records would
appear to offer increased efficiency in the area of appointments,
visits, clinics etc. At least four improvements over a manual
system are:
records held in compact storage form with back-up copies also
occupying little volume; immediate recall of any patient details
from an age/sex/name/address type register; automatic transfer to an
accounts file of any expense or payment; various statistics and
listings such as "at risk" patients produced on demand.

A very low cost microcomputer system would facilitate the four
improvements mentioned above. However much clerical work and
handling of records is still required if the system only provides
"batch" access to records. Much greater efficiency is gained by
having the computer held records available to the doctor(s) and
receptionist(s) when they most need them, that is during surgery or
appointment time respectively. Interactive working is then possible
with decisions taken according to the information available. Data
captured is automatically filed such that no note making is necessary
after a surgery consultation or a telephone call to the receptionist.

A fully integrated computing solution at the primary care level is
still in its infancy. It is likely that a large proportion of the
country's general practices will be using computers in the next few

years. What they will use them for is the subject of energetic
debate in the medical profession.

Our view regarding the prime requirement for any system is that it is
acceptable to the doctors. They will use a computer system only if
it means they can give a better service. To be acceptable it will
have to be easy to use, unobtrusive, inexpensive and capable of
storage and handling information better than existing methods.

Most parties agree that better records mean better care. A major
hurdle is the funding of general practice systems. General
practitioners are independent contractors to the Health Service, they
are not paid a salary but derive their income from a fee for each
patient on their lists plus payments for special services such as
vaccinations and contraception. They pay their own bills, including
wages for ancillary staff, but receive 70% of the cost of secretarial
services from the N.H.S. It seems most unlikely that individual
doctors will be willing to pay for computer systems, so some form of
Government finance may be inevitable.

Using a computer should undoubtedly increase a doctor's revenue, as
a result of accurate logging of services rendered, and an increase
in these services through screening and recall procedures. The move
to computers at the primary care level is indicative of the trend
towards preventive medicine. A computer system permits doctors
access to information they could not otherwise use.

A suitable microcomputer implementation evolves as needing two or
more terminals, visual display units (VDUs) with keyboards, a
processor with backing storage (floppy discs or hard discs), printer,
multiuser operating system and suitable software. A number of
systems designed as a range ensures that one doctor practices
upwards are catered for with enhancements to any system as required.
Further, a single user system can be expanded to a number of
concurrent users without the need to re-enter any data or replace
hardware already in use. In the initial system the hardware is
configured as one processor (the one selected is the D.T.C. 8085-2,
64K bytes RAM and DMA), floppy discs, terminals and printer.

Two sources of information were used principally to establish
overall guidelines and details. Firstly, meeting with the doctors
at a local group practice and secondly study of relevant literature.
For the latter the Royal College of General Practitioners' occasional
paper 13 "Computers in Primary Care" June 1980 is fundamental, whilst
publications such as "Computer audit of repeat prescribing" by Dr.
K. Bolden in the Mims Magazine March 1981 are useful. Many other
useful articles are available from "Doctors" periodicals and
journals and tend to be in accord with concept of the "driving force
coming from the periphery" as argued by P. Hammersley in his article
"The Impact of Microcomputer Systems on Commercial Data Processing",
in the BCS Computer Journal February 1981.

In general a good measure of agreement was achieved at the meetings

concerning what was wanted and what could realistically be provided.
For example, one point was, how much data can be stored? Doctors
tended to agree that many case history notes could be reduced in
volume. It is noted however that in certain circumstances detailed
and ongoing notes are necessary and provision for this has to be
made. Another point established was that of the possible danger of
the delete action. We have included this action in the file
maintenance operations, the deleted record is, in fact, archived.
During periodic housekeeping, archived records are transferred to a
separate floppy disc. Inspection or printout from this disc answers
questions such as "did we once have a Mr. J.G. Brown as a patient"?

The use of a computer terminal in the doctor's surgery to record
patient contact raises a number of problems. The patient might be
upset by the presence of the terminal although they are frequently
seen in use on television. The doctor might be apprehensive about
the terminal or at least its use, this is a question of suitable
software and care in the design of the interface. Possibly the
most important problem is time, time to assimulate the details of
the patient displayed at the beginning of the contact and the time
required to insert any details about the present condition of the
patient. The former requires a neat display layout of the required
data, the latter requires a system with a minimum number of keying
operations for the doctor.

The retrieval of patient details is generally made using the key
already stored in the booking file for this session whether the
patient be next-on-the-list or out-of-sequence. The insertion of a
drug name or an illness only requires the first few characters,
the system then reads down from file the full name for display and
confirmation by the doctor. Most input is prompted and optional.
The patient detail file may be noted as requiring attention at a
later time to remove out of date items to a history file with or
without a printer listing.

The patient past history would be kept on floppy discs together with
the N.H.S. reference number. When a patient leaves the practice
either a printer listing of all entries for this patient may be
made or with suitable modems at each telephone it could be
transmitted directly to the new doctor's practice. This implies
that both doctors have a computer which will accept a modem
connection. There is obviously the problem of the expense of the
modem and telephone time but this would be a more sensible solution
than sending a floppy disc through the post to the new doctor. Even
if he has the same type of computer, the adjustment of its floppy
disc drive might not be the same as the source computer's and the
disc unreadable. If the computer is a different type it is most
unlikely that it will be compatible. Further and more important,
the modem would allow information to be passed to and from a
hospital or any other institution about a patient requiring a visit,
examination, results etc., with any information required to go with

the message being set up in a file ready for sending or access by the hospital etc., when they are ready to receive the information.

The possibility of passing information directly from computer to computer implies some requirement for standardisation of details to be passed. This could all be controlled at the surgery by the doctor only inserting items into the output file which are specifically required to be transferred for a hospital appointment for example. The means of identification of the patient i.e. N.H.S. reference number and possibly name and address, would have to be present. This is easily re-organised into the appropriate order for onward transmission provided it is all present in one of the original files of the system. Equally, by using a special output file it is not possible for outsiders to access all the data on a particular patient, only the created output file is made available external subject to some password control.

APPENDIX

OUTLINE OF SOME OF THE MENUS

START MENU

1. FOR USE BY DOCTOR
2. FOR USE BY RECEPTIONIST
3. TERMINATE

RECEPTIONIST MENU

1. INSERT OR CHANGE INFORMATION
2. INFORMATION IS WANTED
3. DEPOSIT MESSAGE IN RECEPTIONIST/DOCTOR'S DIARY
4. REMOVE MESSAGE FROM DIARY
5. RETURN TO START

DOCTOR MENU

1. RUN SURGERY
2. ENTER CALLS COMPLETED
3. INSERT OR CHANGE PAYMENTS DETAILS
4. SINGLE PATIENT DETAIL CHECKING/REDUCTION
5. CONFERENCE/SPECIFIC PATIENT DETAIL FILE REDUCTION
6. DEPOSIT MESSAGE IN DOCTOR/RECEPTIONIST'S DIARY
7. REMOVE MESSAGE FROM DIARY
8. RETURN TO START

INSERT OR CHANGE INFORMATION MENU

1. TO INSERT A NEW PATIENT
2. MAKE A SURGERY APPOINTMENT
3. CANCEL OR CHANGE APPOINTMENT
4. MAKE APPOINTMENT FOR VISIT
5. CANCEL OR CHANGE VISIT APPOINTMENT
6. INSERT DRUG DETAILS
7. REPEAT PRESCRIPTIONS
8. INSERT ILLNESS
9. CHANGE ACTION

APPENDIX (CONT)

<u>WHEN INFORMATION IS WANTED MENU</u>

1. PRINT SURGERY LIST
2. DISPLAY &/OR PRINT VISITS LIST
3. PRINT MONTH'S ACCOUNT
4. INFORMATION & STATISTICS
5. PRINT PATIENT HISTORY FILE
6. PRINT DRUG LIST OF SYSTEM
7. CREATE BLANK DOCTOR'S SURGERY LIST
8. PRINT REPEAT PRESCRIPTIONS
9. CHANGE ACTION

Taking COMMAND of Hospital Patient Care

Shelly I. Newman

Manager of Systems Development,
Shared Medical Systems Corporation, USA

Dennis J. Warman

Technical Analyst, British Medical Data Systems Limited, UK

Computerisation in the highly complex field of hospital
patient care poses challenges to any database management
system. Shared Medical Systems in the U.S.A. has
developed enhancements and proprietary software that
optimise system 2000's performance in this environment
and support the COMMAND patient care product. The
COMMAND System software is available in the United
Kingdom through British Medical Data Systems Limited.

System 2000 enhancements are described in this paper
that we at Shared Medical Systems created to support our
database applications, particularly the COMMAND patient
care system. The COMMAND application will be described
in a moment, but first, we would like to give some idea
of the operating environment in which this system is
now used. Some statistics on the size of the client
base, hardware, traffic, and applications are provided
below:

Client Base: 500 Hospitals

Hardware: 2 IBM 168 AP's with 12 megabytes each

                 1 IBM 3033 with 8 megabytes
                 (all run under MVS operating system)

                 60 billion bytes of on-line disk storage

                 140,000 miles of leased telephone line

                 5,000 + terminals

Traffic: 2 million transactions/day
                 1.5 billion characters/day through the
                 network (includes reports transmitted)
                 25 million frames/month of microfiche

Application: 5 Management Control Systems
                 5 Resource Control Systems
                 2 Patient Care Systems
                 4500 Installed Applications

On this scale even a slight increase or decrease in
processing efficiency is multipled several times until
it becomes a significant factor. It is, therefore,
imperative that we optimise every aspect of processing
the vast amount of data that flows through our systems;
in doing so we have developed some techniques that may
interest other system 2000's users. These enhancements
allow us to take command of the processing so we can
give the end user command of his data.

Since the early 1970's Shared Medical Systems has used
System 2000 for a variety of hospital applications:

- Inventory — This database contains hospital
  inventory data and is used for
  on-line enquiry. Updates are in
  batch mode.

- Personnel — The hospital's personnel files
  are on-line for enquiry and
  report-generation. There is no
  on-line updating; the database
  is loaded periodically from
  conventional files updated in
  batch mode.

- Internal — Our own multi-application data
  base contains job flow
  schedules, customer information,
  engineering specifications, and
  other internal data.

- Report Catalogue— This is basically a free form
  stores all report specifications
  and uses passwords for our
  entire customer base.

- COMMAND — Storing patient and related
  information, the COMMAND databases (there are 18) are the
  largest and most complex. We
  will discuss COMMAND
  requirements and internal
  structure after examining data
  entry and retrieval
  requirements.

Data can enter the System network from any terminal
throughout the hospital, as shown in FIGURE 1. These
could be located in the Data Processing Department,
Admissions Office, Ward or Professional and Technical
Department. It is entered once, checked by the hospital
mini-computer and then transmitted to Shared Medical's
central computer centre where it must pass another
stringent check before being passed to its destination.
The target file could be the COMMAND database or another
application file, or both. Since information is entered
only once, there is a very high rate of elements updated
to transactions submitted (about 20:1). Currently the
system updates 2,000,000 data elements per day, based on
100,000 COMMAND update transactions per day.

Once a month, data is moved from the COMMAND active file
to the historical file; since each hospital may specify
their own data retention periods. Most hospitals choose
to keep several years worth of data for reporting in
the historical file. The historical file, unlike the
active file is not available for on-line enquiry.

To meet heavy reporting requirements Shared Medical
Systems developed a fast mechanism that takes a snapshot
of the database. Reports are extracted from this file
in batch mode by Mark IV and our Ad-Hoc Reporting
System.

COMMAND is Shared Medical Systems offering for patient
care data accumulation, storage and retrieval. Today
the system described processes:

  - Over 1000 on-line reports and Enquiries Daily
  - Over 100,000 transactions daily
  - Over 900 megabytes of data on-line

Our product is called COMMAND because it gives the
hospital COMMAND of their data and the ability to meet
the many, often conflicting, demands from government
agencies or medical researchers in the most effective
way. To meet these requirements COMMAND keeps the
hospital data:

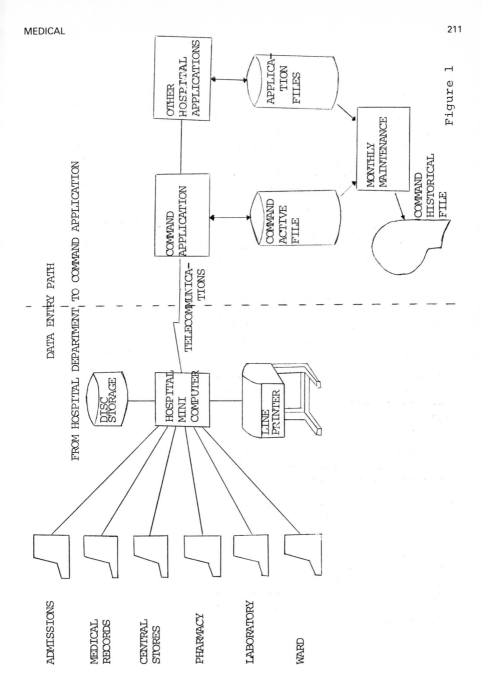

DATA ENTRY PATH

FROM HOSPITAL DEPARTMENT TO COMMAND APPLICATION

Figure 1

Consistant and Accurate - Data must be consistant; data
on a VDU screen must not contradict the same information
in a printed report. COMMAND provides multiple real
time data entry points but a single storage. Beyond
this, data integration is ensured by using data entered
to the COMMAND database to automatically update related
conventional files. But data consistancy is of no use
if the data is not accurate. Data must meet stringent
physical and logical edit requirements.

A hospital having accurate and consistant data
wants that information to be -

Flexible - The hospital cannot satisfy the varied
hospital and external demands for specialised reporting
by being locked into a fixed set of reports. Such
reports would require a manual search to select and
organise the data that is really needed. COMMAND offers
three types of reports: Standard, Custom and Ad-Hoc.

Over 150 Standard reports may be adapted through user
selected options to reflect the organisation and
procedures of the individual hospitals. Shared Medical
Systems programmers are available to prepare custom
reports that address requirements that the standard
reports, even with this option, cannot handle.

The company creates relatively few custom reports, due
in part to the success of Ad-Hoc Reporting, a COMMAND
option that allows end users; Medical Researchers,
Nurses, or Regional, Area and District Administrators to
enter report specifications in a simple English-like
format. Learning to use Ad-Hoc is not like learning a
specialised report generator language; no programmer
intervention is required to generate reports that can
draw on the COMMAND database and historical file for
statistical tabulation and detailed lists. Data element
selection, sorting sequence, etc. are all up to the
user.

Flexibility means more than adaptable reporting; the
hospital must be able to change to a new drug coding
system, add new procedures, and so forth, without a
major disruption of operations. COMMAND provides this
flexibility. By selecting "profile options", a user can
choose the features he needs; this enables COMMAND to
serve both small hospitals and more sophisticated
univeristy teaching institutions.

Economical - COMMAND has saved hospitals money by
reducing clerical overhead and work duplication and by
providing current information that management can use to
improve operations.

We've discussed the hospital requirements and indicated
how COMMAND meets them. This paper will now focus on
the internal characteristics and data structure of
COMMAND. At that time we will be in a position to
examine the COMMAND processing requirements and the
system 2000 support mechanisms that address them.

Although the applications that run against the database
continually are changing, the basic COMMAND data
structure has remained stable. Three data trees -
consultant, room, and patient - contain 350 data
elements. Some elements such as patient name, sex, and
age, are single valued. For others there are descendent
repeating groups.

Data definitions are general, allowing a variety of data
to be recorded under a common definition. For example,
under Problems and Treatments, anaesthesia,
consultation, tissues studies, medication, symptoms and
other classifications can be entered with the
responsible consultant or technician identification.

Many fields are derived, minimising the data entry task.
For example, a valid procedure code prompts COMMAND to
automatically generate statistical category, procedure
class, and description. For the primary surgical
procedure, the preoperative stay is automatically
derived as the difference between admission date and
procedure date.

Data is overlayed only when a specific change or delete
transaction is entered. Unintentional data destruction
is thereby prevented.

Most data is recorded with both a process date and time
and an effective date and time. This allows analysis of
delays in getting data into what is intended to be a
real time system.

As FIGURE 2 suggests, the repeating groups allow a wide range of pertinent data to be entered as many times as necessary to form a complete patient record. The repeating groups contain:

- patient data   - age, sex, patient origin, admission date, and other single valued elements.

- relatives   - name, address, and phone number of the refering G.P; other medical institutions that the patient is going to or coming from; follow up addresses for the patient, guardian, etc.

- problems and treatments   - any number of entries recorded in any number of categories together with the identity of the person responsible.

- special handling   - a flag and date stamp to mark those patients enrolled in a special study of medications, diagnoses, etc.

- service summary - the detailed consultant orders - lab test, radiology procedures, supplies, medications, etc. The detailed treatment record - 2 ECG's 4 glucose tolerance tests, a specific anti-biotic, etc. - can be recorded.

- bed state history   - a record of the changes in beds, attending consultants, hospital speciality or departments. This is used to track and analyse the movement of a patient through a hospital.

- certification   - the recorded determination of the medical necessity, care level and adequacy of hospital care.

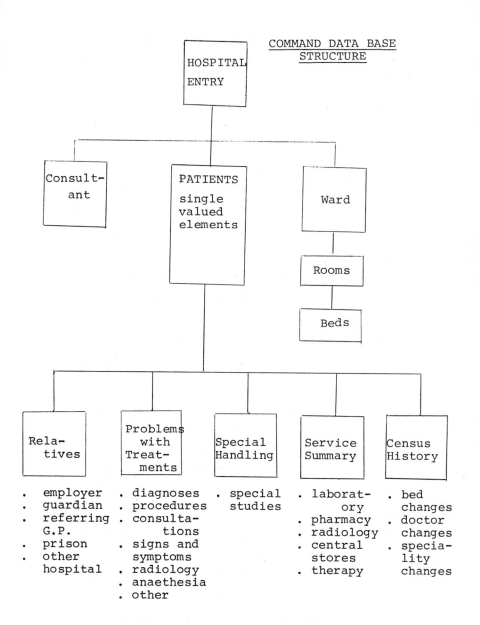

Figure 2

In delivering our COMMAND product our support mechanisms
and enhancements are important. These facilities are
grouped under seven headings and are explained in detail
in the following section. They are:

- System 2000 Internal Organisation and Management
- Backup and Restore
- Resource Management
- Application Development Flexibility
- Extend Reporting Facilities
- Secure and Integrity Provisions
- Performance Monitoring

S2K INTERNAL ORGANISATION AND MANAGEMENT encompass

. Horizontal Padding   - which keeps data
organised by hospital
within the database,
reducing retrieval
time and simplifying
access.

. Repeating Group Control   - which allow us to go
  Nodes   directly to the
desired repeating
group type.

. "GETD WHERE..."   - which facilitates
updates by pointing
to the next available
space.

. Buffer Management Tuner   - which provides buffer
specifications suited
to each application.

HORIZONTAL PADDING

At the end of each month we move "complete" patient
records from the active file to the historical file.
As mentioned, it is up to the hospital to decide when a
patient record is complete.

Typically the database (active file) will shrink to
about 1/4 its pre-transfer size. This could leave us
with a database such as that shows in (FIGURE 3) with 2
records for hospital A,3 for hospital B,5 for C, etc.

Adding records sequentially as they are entered
throughout the month could result in (FIGURE 4's)
arrangement. Extracting data for a particular hospital
would become increasingly time consuming as the month
wears on. To avoid this, we pad the database to allow
for the anticipated new records (FIGURE 5). The
resultant data contiguity supports fast path retrieval
and contributes to improved system performance.

HORIZONTAL PADDING

FIGURE 3.   FIGURE 4.   FIGURE 5.

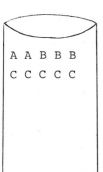
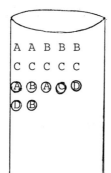
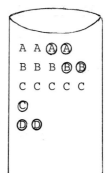

REPEAT GROUP CONTROL NODES

For each hospital there are three data trees:
Consultant, Room, and Patient. Each data tree has
multiple occurences, each with its data contiguous
within the hospital record.

To access patient data by first going through all
occurences of the consultant and room trees would be a
lengthy process. Again we looked for a fast path to
preserve availability and response time. The use of
control nodes allows us to reach the appropriate tree
before we begin searching. This approach has saved a
considerable amount of CPU time.

"GETD WHERE"

The underlying principle for this is, as for the
previous items, fast access. Suppose we are updating
and want to enter a new procedure in the patient's
"Problems and Treatments" repeating group. Horizontal
Padding ensures that we'll get to the correct hospital
quickly; the RC Control Nodes help us to locate the
patient tree. The patient record then contains a
pointer to the next free space in each of its repeating
groups. We pass over the filled problems and
treatments elements without having to read them. Our
record is written in the free space and the pointer is
incremented to indicate the next available element.

BUFFER MANAGEMENT TUNER

For COMMAND buffer management was the most important
aspect of System 2000 Release 2.70. This facility
brought our I/O rates down to an acceptable level. As
mentioned earlier, COMMAND is not the only System 2000
application. Inventory, Personnel, etc., access some
of the same file types, and each has a different buffer
requirements. Even within a single application, some
variations in buffer policy are desirable. We have,
therefore, built a "tuner" into the buffer manager to
make it more flexible. Rather than impose a compromise
on the applications by setting a single buffer level
that fully satisfies none of them, we can process each
application without over or underbuffing.

BACK/RESTORE includes

-        Concurrent Save/Restore/Apply - which addresses
         the availability problems encountered when several
         databases must be backed up and restored.

-        Automatic Recovery - which reduces operator
         intervention for recoveries.

-        File Seven Utilization Monitor - which keeps tabs
         on file 7 (up-date audit file) usage to avoid
         filling the file.

CONCURRENT SAVE/RESTORE/APPLY

Concurrency in our backup/restore operations helps maintain high COMMAND availability. Shared Medical Systems has between 45 and 50 on-line databases. If backup and restore were serialized, a system hang could result in hospitals being locked out for a half day while we do restores. This is obviously unacceptable in an environment where availability is crucial.

To eliminate this possibility, we have made backup/restore operations concurrent. We could have left these functions in the MVS multiuser address space; instead, to further increase efficiency, we put them in the individual user addresses spaces Since database Y recovery does not depend on completion of database X recovery, lockouts are drastically reduced.

The APPLY function applies updates since the previous back-up; since it is a standalone System 2000 function running in the user's address space, we can have several users doing APPLY concurrently for different databases.

Recoveries are automatic; we have virtually eliminated operator intervention. The supporting mechanisms include a Checkpoint Subsystem, damage assessment routines, and automatic job submission utilities. Recovery jobs are restorable, manual intervention is necessary only in catastrophic cases.

The Checkpoint Subsystem is a generalised (not COMMAND specific) facility that allows a number of jobs to write checkpoint data to a common file and to quickly access desired records, across multiple CPU's through user defined keywords.

The damage assesment routines determine whether and to what extent recovery is necessary. The routines interrogate the databases to determine physical damage and compare the cycle numbers to the checkpointed cycle numbers to determine logical damage.

The automatic job submission utilities use information from the damage assessment routines to decide which jobs must be run. These jobs are automatically initiated.

To illustrate the interaction of these recovery mechanisms we will see how they handle an abend in a Transaction Processing program (TPP) subtask:

1.   The Transaction processing Program
            generates and submits the damage
            assessment routines.

2.   The damage assessment routines examine the
            database for physical and logical damage.

3.   If damage is present, the automatic job
            submission utilities submit the
            appropriate recovery job.

4.   Once the database is restored to its
            checkpointed cycle number, the recovery
            job releases the resource.

5.   The Transaction Processing Program again
            has access to the resource for On-line
            processing.

FILE SEVEN UTILIZATION MONITOR

We maintain a "file seven" update audit file for each
database. In allocating file size we naturally want to
have sufficient, but not unnecessary space available.
The monitor automatically generates reports showing the
utilization percentage of each file seven. When our
predetermined thresholds are exceeded we allocate more
space.

RESOURCE MANAGEMENT

The Resource Management Subsystem is the primary Shared
Medical mechanism for controlling and protecting system
resources, including files, hardware, and databases.
Each request to access or update an RMS resource must
be cleared by the RMS Reserve/Release mechanism. RMS
works across CPU's and is effective with sequential,
ISAM, and VSAM files. The subsystem can provide access
on a shared (read only) or exclusive (update) basis,
and is called for any updates or access to the database whether in foreground or batch mode.

The Resource Management Subsystem is essential to the
recovery procedures just described. Without it we
could not have multiple address spaces simultaneously
accessing a database, nor could we do concurrent
recoveries. RMS ensures that only the recovery job
accesses the damaged database.

APPLICATION DEVELOPMENT FLEXIBILITY is based on an
integrated set of software components that support
rapid development of application modifications. These
include:

- Preprocessors - which are similar to the
  MRI preprocessors but have some additional
  features.

- Component Definition Dictionary - which
  contains schema definitions.

- Data Management Subsystem which provides
  record and data management functions.

PREPROCESSORS

Our preprocessors support COBOL and PL1, as do the MRI
preprocessors. Beyond this, they support our
Transaction Processing Program environment through
special data manipulation facilities. One example is
Global Working Storage, which allows data to be passed
from one transaction module to another, reducing System
2000 data retrieval requirements. Access to non System
2000 data is also supported, using System 2000 syntax.

Our data Entry Language, as an integral part of the
preprocessors, supports automatic generation of modules
that perform logical and physical data edits. Entry of
data element characteristics and relationships result
in the generation of edit routines with no procedural
coding required.

COMPONENT DEFINITION DICTIONARY

The Component Definition Dictionary, accessed by the
preprocessors at compile time, is our subschema
definition repository. Each element is defined only
once but many appear in several schemata. The
component definition dictionary, itself a System 2000
database, minimizes programming errors and promotes
naming standardization and data consistency. Data
Manager, a generalized, formal Data Dictionary
Directory, will eventually replace our System 2000
specific Component Definition Dictionary.

DATA MANAGEMENT SUBSYSTEM

Data Management Subsystem is the interface between our
preprocessors and the MultiUser Interface.   Data
Management Subsystem reformats control blocks, maps
passwords and databases (e.g., production databases
to test databases for nonauthorized users), and
performs schema maintenance chores.   It also promotes
availability by shutting down in an orderly manner when
errors occur.

For conventional ISAM and VSAM files, Data Management
Subsystem's data management functions include an
Environment Description facility (allowing users to
tailor the input/output environment for optimal
processing) and Mode change commands that can optimize
processing for bursts of record insertion.

Data Management Subsystem also facilitates record
retrieval and modification and structure modification.
Through key values, we can rerieve isolated records or
LOCATE all qualified records into a logical subfile for
sequential retrieval.   Records may be inserted into or
deleted from System 2000 databases;   entire trees or
subtrees may be deleted.

EXTENDED REPORTING FACILITIES are provided by

- Report Catalog System   which contains
  report specifications for free form report
  generating mechanisms.

- Fast Unload   which increases availability
  by sidestepping the System 2000 retrieval
  process.

- Ad-Hoc which allows end users to define
  and schedule their own reports without
  Shared Medical Systems involvement.

REPORT CATALOG SYSTEM

The Report Catalog System is a generalized report
definition repository that contains all System 2000
string definitions.   We do not keep any of the 150
COMMAND strings in the COMMAND database definition;
this would be unfeasible because we would have to put
all strings in each use of the 18 COMMAND databases.
The Report Catalog System allows the association of
user dependent information with a string, and is used
for other free form report processing languages.

Report Catalog System also has   built in funtions that extend report generalization capabilities for application programmers and hospital end users. For example, the Report Catalog System dynamically translates a report specification of "last month" to provide data on the month prior to that in which the report is run.

FAST UNLOAD

Fast Unload is a specialized program that reads database files directly to produce a "frozen" copy of a System 2000 data base without going through System 2000. It takes advantage of System 2000 files structures to produce its snapshot in one fourth the time required by a Procedural Language program.

Fast Unload is run every night; standard COMMAND reports are then produced from the snapshot in batch mode, while the database itself remains available for hospital enquiry and update. Creating reports from a database copy has the additional advantage of ensuring that all reports from the various applications balance.

AD-HOC REPORTING

Ad-Hoc Reporting allows end users to design, test, catalog, schedule, and generate their own reports without programmer intervention. Ad-Hoc is a batch mode interpretive report processor. Through access to the historical file, hospitals can examine up to ten times the amount of data available on-line.

There are two types of Ad-Hoc reports: statistical cross tabulations and detail lists. Ad-Hoc has been enthusiastically received by the user community since it simplifies preparation of the elaborate and specialized reports often needed.

Ad-Hoc offers both felxibility with high performance, a rare combination among reporting packages. Enhancements currently under development, including a GRAPH function, will significantly increase Ad-Hoc's capability.

SECURITY AND INTEGRITY are supported by
  .   Functional Restriction)
  .   User Defined Passwords)   Security

  .   System 2000 COMMAND Type Restrictions)
  .   Fast Unload Integrity Checks   ) Integrity

FUNCTIONAL RESTRICTIONS

Through Message Processing, functional restrictions are imposed on user terminals. Functions may be restricted by terminal identification, user access code, and password. No hospital can access another institution's data without permission; within a hospital, data access is restricted as specified by the hospital.

USER DEFINED PASSWORDS

Passwords for database access are user defined and are generally broken down by application. The user passwords are not defined within the many System 2000 databases, but are stored together by the report Catalog System. This reduces redundancy, allows more flexibility in password updating, and increases the total number of passwords possible. A user password is necessary to establish a working session at a terminal.

SYSTEM 2000 COMMAND TYPE RESTRICTIONS

To maintain data integrity we have imposed some restrictions on the System 2000 command types. COMMAND end users enter strings only; all System 2000 commands are screened out by our teleprocessing interface.

FAST UNLOAD INTEGRITY CHECKS

We perform Data Integrity checks as part of the daily data base backup. Data is verified as it is unloaded before the actual backup to tape. In this way we have been able to trap hardware and software failures that could have allowed bad data to contaminate the system.

PERFORMANCE MONITORING is continous through

- General Monitoring System which is a real time monitor and alert system.

- System Resource Utilization which is a set of routines that capture data on resource consumption and issue reports.

Most of the mechanisms described thus far are based on the need to maintain availability, flexibility and so forth. Influencing the design of the systems is the standing requirements that they be efficient tools that allow us to offer COMMAND at a competitive price. The two performance aids described here help maintain overall processing efficiency.

GENERAL MONITORING SYSTEM

The General Monitoring System constantly strobes queues for pieces of work left undone and alerts operators and programmers to any processing problems it identifies. The system likewise strobes the Resource Management Subsystem tables to identify work that is taking too long. Thresholds are determined for each transaction's processing time. Through a table containing job identifiers, transaction types, and other pertinent data, the General Monitoring System can tell operators which jobs are running slower that they should. A dynamic system, the General Monitoring System often alerts us to problems that can be corrected without the end user ever knowing there was a problem.

SYSTEM RESOURCE UTILIZATION

The System Resource Utilization mechanisms comprise data collection routines and an offline reporting system that produces weekly graphs and reports that show critical system resource consumption data. This material allows ongoing analysis of system performance.

The routines are capable of tracking resource usage down to the smallest indivisible unit, e.g., a Procedural Language opcode or a Natural Language command. System Resource Utilization is used both to uncover problems and to optimize application code. The result is a finely tuned System 2000 COMMAND environment.

SUMMARY

This paper has centered on identifiying and addressing needs. We pointed out that the hospital needs systems that are accurate, available, flexible, and secure, all at an economical price. COMMAND meets these end user needs; its own parallel needs are met by System 2000 and the support mechanisms we have described.

Part 5
Man–Machine Interaction

Human Factors and Program Flexibility

D. J. Cairns and J. J. Florentin

*Department of Computer Science,
Birkbeck College, University of London, UK*

Users of highly interactive systems for non-routine processing
almost always ask for a succession of modifications and
extensions to their systems. These requests are probably not
an indication of the poor quality of the system but must be
accepted as an inevitable outcome of human factors effects.
A programming maintenance approach must be developed to allow
flexible change and extension. It is suggested that existing
data dictionary techniques of system maintenance must be
complemented by suitable program structures based on 'virtual
interfaces'. Experience with a preliminary ad hoc approach
is described.

Introduction

We have designed and implemented several interactive systems for
financial analysis. These systems allow professionally qualified
financial analysts to access the computer directly through a VDU/
keyboard terminal, and to carry out non-routine processing of data
from a database of various investment projects. The results of
their analyses can be viewed either on the VDU screen, or on well-
formatted print-outs. Over a number of years we have received
continuing requests to modify and enhance these systems. This work
of modification has become a considerable undertaking and we believe
it to be important to understand how these requests originate, and
to develop further technical approaches to carrying out system and
software changes.

Briefly, we believe that these requests for changes arise because
of the human factors situation of our users, and they are thus not
specific to our computer system designs. Such requests will arise
whenever users are closely involved with the computer through their
terminals, and have some personal choice in the way that the computer
is used to aid their work. Systems of this kind have been called
'Decision Support Systems' [1]. Any similar system must be designed
from the outset to allow modifications and, as we describe later,
to allow demonstrations of intended modifications.

Modifying a large software system (30,000-60,000 lines of high level
code) can be an expensive and unrewarding experience. In a rough
and ad hoc manner we have developed data dictionary and application
generator aids. But we have further found it essential to design
our software in a particular way so as to make the best use of these
aids.

This paper first summarises briefly the human factors origins of the
requests for changes that we receive, and suggests that these
circumstances are widespread enough to demand special systems design
techniques. Next we describe an approach to software design which
is aimed at maximising the effectiveness of software implementation
aids.

Human factors in decision support systems

The users of our systems are analysts with specialised financial and
business knowledge. The projects they are concerned with often have
a high   financial value, and they are frequently involved with
discussions with non-specialists and with specialists representing
outside interests. They have considerable scope for deciding what
kind of analysis is appropriate for each individual project, and
they will be careful in selecting the manner of presentation of

results to different audiences.

The most obvious way in which demands for changes arise are:

- new projects come along which invite analysis along lines not
  provided in the original system;

- new projects, or new client contacts, come along and it is thought
  that the results of analysis should be presented in formats not
  available in the existing system.

However, a more subtle call for change comes from the fact that the
analysts' understanding of the power of the computer grows. The
analysts perceive new methods of analysis and presentation which were
not apparent to them previously. It is noticeable that their self-
confidence in their capability to exploit the computer grows after
about two years' use, and this extra confidence can lead to a
re-thinking of the way in which they utilise the computer.

The above remarks show how the human milieu gives rise to demands for
change. At the same time human factors also demand a certain
conservatism. Once a complex operational procedure has been learnt
people do not abandon it lightly; once certain screen layouts have
become familiar, new layouts with substantially the same information
could be irritating. Thus changes must preserve the distinctive
character and appearance of the system, in much the same way that
a newspaper must retain its distinctive character and appearance.

What kinds of change are wanted

The changes that are requested are of many different kinds. The
simplest changes affect (directly) only one data item, usually by
changing a definition, for example, lengthening a name field. These
changes usually lead immediately to changes in the validity rules for
that item. The repercussions of a change to a simple data item can
be manifold. Several data declarations in programs must be amended,
then file formats, screens, data entry forms and print-outs must be
reconsidered. The user manual must also be amended.

Techniques for handling changes to simple data items are fairly well
developed, and depend on a data dictionary [2], which is a cross-
referenced index showing where each data item is used, and its
connections with other data items.

More complex changes involve the introduction of new operations, such
as calculating new financial indices, or the introduction of further
data items to give a more complete description of the projects.

When users ask for changes they often put forward suggestions which
are vague in significant details, or which are impracticable in their
proposed form. It is therefore almost essential to be able to

demonstrate terminal operating procedures, displays and print-outs, before installing the changes fully.

Using a data dictionary

Data dictionaries are usually stored and maintained by computer, but they can be used subsequently with varying levels of computer assistance. In the simplest situations modifications can be transferred by computer directly from the modified dictionary entries to programs. There is an inherent limit to the automation of the modification process; the limit is caused by the fact that many system interfaces – data forms, VDU screens and print-out paper – are of fixed size. When larger data fields have to be placed in these interfaces it is not possible to re-format them automatically. The appearance of these interfaces is often very important to the users, and it is necessary to re-format manually. It is clear that the manual reformatting of the system interfaces should be carried out in conjunction with the demonstration to users.

An application generator for system interfaces

The system interfaces – screens, data entry forms and print-outs – can be produced by application generators. We have devised an ad hoc application generator which is based on word processing. Screens of text can be manipulated with word processor conventions and these texts can be stored and used as the basis of screens, print-outs or data entry forms. The generator can also be used to produce the text of user manuals.

This aid leads to programs which produce the screens and print-outs.

A 'change' procedure

Using the ad hoc data dictionary and application generator our procedure for carrying out changes is:

- decide on change requirements

- document the changes in temporary mode in the ad hoc data dictionary

- identify the interfaces to be changed

- reformat the interfaces using the application generator in demonstration mode

- demonstrate the new interface to the users

- correct the original request for change, if necessary, and repeat the demonstration

- install the changes when they have been approved.

Program structure and change aids

In the literature describing data dictionaries and application
generators the programs eventually produced with their aid may have
any arbitrary structure. We have found that to facilitate changes
it is best to structure the programs so that interfaces are
controlled by specific portions of program. The approach is to
separate the portions of program which generate the data to be
displayed from those portions which control the format of
presentation. The programs which control presentation can be called
'virtual screens' or 'virtual print-outs', that is, 'virtual
interfaces'. These presentation control programs are the ones which
have to be inspected when changes are made. Further they can be
driven by test routines to produce demonstrations. Figure 1
illustrates the required structure.

Interfaces are often made up of several sections, for example, a main
heading showing the date and major activity, followed by another
section showing the project title, and a third section showing local
data. Data can be produced and formatted in sections except that
the format control is split into sections, and the sections are
combined by an overall display control (see Figure 2).

A virtual interface may hold several variants of one format, for
example, a main data entry screen might have several variants when
it is re-displayed to show error conditions. Similarly, a print-out
may have variants such as 'end of week' and 'end of month' reports.
In the design main interfaces are first identified and the variants
are developed at a later stage.

An example of the use of the virtual interface

The virtual interface used in conjunction with a data dictionary was
found to be valuable in a system where the number of stored data
items increased considerably over a few years. Originally a small
number of data items was used, and their values were entered into
the computer piecemeal by the analysts. Eventually the number of
items to be entered grew to about 300 and it was necessary to
introduce data entry forms so that data could be gathered together
systematically before going to the terminal. All the data items and
the entry screen routines were known. It was possible to adapt the
routines to print the data entry forms to correspond with the screens
and to produce the correct spacing for users to write in the data.
An initial attempt to produce the 25 forms by hand was tedious and
led to errors.

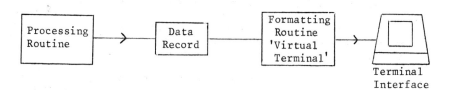

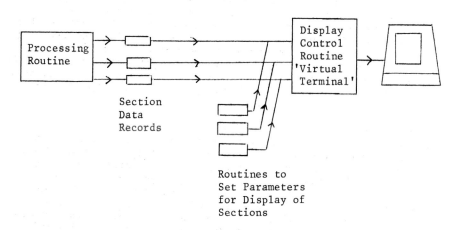

Fig. 2.

When the data entry forms were shown to the users they asked for layout amendments, and also decided that further data items were to be added. Using our ad hoc system it was comparatively easy to demonstrate the modified forms quickly, and also to be sure that changes made at the level of the forms would be accurately reflected back into the file, program and screen specifications. The speed of reaction was a significant advantage from the human factors viewpoint and increased the effectiveness of the demonstration.

Another benefit of the use of aids is that consistent presentations of particular data items were gained, for example, the same range of formats for dates were accepted in every interface.

Implementation of the program structure

Virtual interfaces appear at an early stage of system design. Our systems have been written in a greatly extended Basic, and the transliteration of the limited structures available has been unsatisfactory. It seems that a faithful representation of the virtual interface could only be obtained in a programming system which allowed modules of programs to run concurrently, each maintaining its own data, and intercommunicating with other modules by exchanging messages. Programming systems of this kind have long been used for applications which handle real-time interrupts, but these languages have not been acceptable for data processing. At the present time it is a possibility that ADA [3] could be accepted as a concurrent process language for data processing if only file and database facilities were added.

In ADA virtual interfaces would be tasks. Data would be passed through packages where some arrangement for synchronising the data transfer would have to be made. The processing routines would also be tasks. However, there are some problems of programming style: one is that the number of tasks would be large, and each interface would have to be activated and de-activated frequently. It seems that ADA is intended to have a few tasks which are activated and de-activated infrequently. Note that the notion of virtual terminal discussed in [4] is a logical representation of a physical terminal. The virtual terminal exists for the entire time that the system is active; it carries various screen formats. By contrast the virtual interfaces discussed here carry only one screen, and exist only during specific system operations.

Other possible uses of a concurrent program system to aid human factors

If a concurrent programming language were available for data processing then a number of other structures useful for human

factors purposes could be constructed. One useful structure would be
a 'context' process which would keep a record of the various
collections of data currently being used by an analyst. The
interactive computer dialogue can then be adjusted so that the
computer apparently 'knows' what the analyst is doing. This keeping
of context information is a feature of our systems which has been
welcomed by users.

Conclusion

It has been suggested that highly interactive systems
characteristically give rise to requests for modification and
extensions. If these requests are to be met in an economical
fashion then automatic aids to system maintenance are needed. To
make these aids fully effective it is necessary to design
appropriate program module and routine structures. An important
program structure is a 'virtual interface'. These interfaces usually
need manual attention when changes are made because of visual
appearances and the limitations of display devices.

A programming language providing concurrent processes which was also
suitable for data processing would be very suitable for
implementing the program structure.

Acknowledgement

We acknowledge the support of the Science Research Council for work
on interactive dialogue design.

Bibliography

[1]   Alter, S. 'A Taxonomy of Decision Support Systems', Sloan
          Management Review, April 1977, pp.39-56

[2]   Report of the Data Dictionary Systems Working Party of the
          British Computer Society, London 1977

[3]   ADA Documentation Centre, Department of Computer Science,
          University of York

[4]   Brinch Hausen, P. 'The Architecture of Concurrent Programs',
          Prentice-Hall Inc., New Jersey 1977

The Personal Computer and the Personal Scientist

Mildred L. G. Shaw and Brian R. Gaines

Middlesex Polytechnic and
Centre for Man–Computer Studies, UK

There are a number of techniques used in psychiatric practice and
management study which have been in the past dependent on their
administration by experts, generally psychologists specializing in
these techniques. Recently, the advent of low-cost personal
computers with good user interfaces such as graphic displays has
made it straightforward to take these techniques directly from the
laboratory to the real world. In this paper we suggest that this
is an example of the emancipatory use of the computer to aid
people in dealing with a complex world. We illustrate our
discussion with examples of a range of powerful clinical and
management tools now transferred to the personal computer and
originating from the work of George Kelly on Personal Construct
Psychology. Kelly's techniques are widely applicable to all those
interested in modelling their own approach to life, those of
others, and the inter-relationships between them. We also argue
that their are significant features of person-computer interaction
that goes beyond those possible in person-person interaction. In
conlusion we suggest that a key role for the personal computer may
be seen as a symbiotic one with a person in emancipating his
cognition by aiding the comprehension and control of an
increasingly complex environment.

INTRODUCTION

There are a number of techniques used in psychiatric practice and
management study which have been in the past dependent on their
administration by **experts,** generally psychologists specializing in
these techniques. Not only is the expert required to administer the
material but also to analyse and interpret the results, and this has
greatly limited the range of application of the techniques. In the
last decade computer-based systems for the administration and analysis
of these techniques have been developed and demonstrated to be
effective in the laboratory and clinical trials (Elithorn & Telford
1969, Gedye & Miller 1969, Elwood 1972a,b,c, Klinge & Rodiewicz 1976).
The use of interactive computer systems to undertake interviews
previously performed by medical practitioners has proved very
acceptable to patients (Card et al 1974, Lucas 1977) and it has even
proved possible for the computer to act as an effective therapist in
some situations (Stodolsky 1970).

Recently, the advent of low-cost **personal computers** with good user
interfaces such as graphic displays has made it straightforward to
take these techniques directly from the laboratory to the real world.
The new personal computers are very well suited to this type of
application since many have been designed as comfortable, homely
workstations that are not technologically awesome to the user. The
availability of rapid access to quite powerful computing facilities
makes it possible to incorporate on-line analysis and to feed back to
the user information that might be only intuitively available to a
human administrator. The availability of low-cost graphic printing
devices makes it possible to present the results of the analysis in a
readily assimilable form. Thus, there is much in the new technology
that enhances the techniques and goes beyond what is possible with
human administration.

It is probably too early yet to discern the long-term impact of this
de-professionalization of powerful techniques for analysing and
modifying human behaviour. Perhaps there will be none -- we all too
readily subscribe to the mystique with which the professions surround
themselves and believe that their magic is more powerful than it
actually turns out to be. However, we are now at a fascinating nexus
where it is possible to encapsulate the **expert** within the computer and
even outperform him in many respects, and there are no cost
constraints to making the resultant systems widely available. In this
paper we discuss these topics, analysing the advantages and
disadvantages of the computer in this context compared with the human
expert.

We illustrate our discussion with an example from a range of powerful
clinical and management tools now transferred to the personal computer
and originating from the work of George Kelly (1955) on **Personal
Construct Psychology.** His techniques are widely applicable to all
those interested in modelling their own approach to life, those of
others, and the inter-relationships between them.

PERSONAL COMPUTERS AND THE COMPLEXITY OF LIFE

In examining the role of the computer as encapsulating an expert we
see a far greater potential than the mere automation of established
techniques. There is a more fundamental impact on society in aiding
individuals to cope with the complexity of modern life, a role of
greater significance for the computer than any so far played. Luhmann
(1979) in his work on **Trust and Power** postulates **complexity-reduction**
as the fundamental motivation for all our social institutions. He
notes:

"The world is overwhelmingly complex for every kind of real
system... Its possibilities exceed those to which the system has the
capacity to respond. A system locates itself in a selectively
constituted 'environment' and will disintegrate in the case of
disjunction between environment and 'world'. Human beings, however,
and they alone, are conscious of the world's complexity and
therefore of the possibility of selecting their enviroment --
something which poses fundamental questions of self-preservation.
Man has the capacity to comprehend the world, can see alternatives,
possibilities, can realize his own ignorance, and can perceive
himself as one who must make decisions." (Luhmann 1979 p.6)

He goes on to note the added complexity of inter-personal
relationships:

"we invoke a whole new dimension of complexity: the subjective
'I-ness' of other human beings which we experience (perceive) and
understand. Since other people have their own first-hand access to
the world and can experience things differently they may
consequently be a source of profound insecurity for me." (Luhmann
1979 p.6-7)

De Bono (1979) sees the computer as playing an important role in
complexity reduction:

"By great good fortune, and just in time, we have to hand a device
that can rescue us from the mass of complexity. That device is the
computer. The computer will be to the organisation revolution what
steam power was to the industrial revolution. The computer can extend
our organizing power in the same way as steam extended muscle
power...... Of course we have to ensure that the result is more human
rather than less human. Similarly we have to use the computer to
reduce complexity rather than to increase complexity, by making it
possible to cope with increased complexity." (De Bono 1979, pp.18-19)

The theme of Luhmann's and De Bono's remarks is not a new one. For
example, Wiener (1950) emphasizes it in his **Human Use of Human Beings;**
Licklider (1968) foresaw the development of a form of **man-computer
symbiosis;** Gaines (1979) has compared the computer as an 'engine' for

moving around and conquering Popper's (1974) **world 3** of information
and theory with the mechanical engines used to move around and conquer
his **world 1** of the physical environment. More recently Toffler (1980)
has seen information technology as supporting a **third wave** that takes
us beyond agricultural and industrial societies to one of greater
individual freedom and participation. It is only with the advent of
the personal computer that the technology underlying these predictions
has become manifest. The overall scenario predicted may be summarized
as:

* 1 individuals are becoming dominated in their thoughts and actions
    by the organizational structures of an increasingly complex
    world;
* 2 individual decision-making is increasingly restricted because
    the basis for comprehending the ramifications and consequences
    of decisions is too complex for most people;
* 3 only a few are capable of being truly individualistic in moving
    within society's framework;
* 4 most give in and are driven by the organization rather than
    driving it;
* 5 some opt out destructively rebelling against the complete social
    order.

However there is also seen to be an alternative scenario in which 1
and 2 still hold but the numbers of people in category 3 is greatly
increased at the expense of categories 4 and 5 because the personal
computer is available to interface between the person and the complex
society in which he is embedded.

This may seem to exagerate the possible importance of the computer.
However, already many of the programs being made widely available at
low cost to those who have computers in the home are ones which enable
them to come directly to grips with a complex world without going
through the experts normally required to mediate on their behalf. Some
programs replace the professional adviser such as those which perform
accounting functions, evaluate stock portfolios or allow elaborate
business plans to be evaluated. These have obvious derivations from
the mainframe computing services of yesterday but there is innovation
in their availability on low-cost interactive systems in the home.
Other programs allow the clerk who acts as gatekeeper to information
to be by-passed such as those which give access to bank accounts and
transport timetables. Some of the programs give access to expertize of
a acientifically substantiated nature such as those on diet and
nutrition whereas for others which cast horoscopes or deal tarot cards
the basis of the expertise is less well-founded but nonetheless real
to the users. Even 'adventure' games may be seen as providing personal
access to a learning environment in a simulated fantasy world that has
many of the aspects of real life.

Such applications also give a very different image of the use of the
computer from the current stereotype in which it is usually seen as a
technical cognitive tool (Habermas 1968) to exert authority over man.

We see the computer being used in what Habermas calls an **emancipatory cognitive** role to give greater freedom to the individual rather than further restrict it. In this respect, the emphasis on the truly personal computer is a significant one. It is not the 'computer utility' (Parkhill 1966), the global network, into which everyone connects -- that is too open to central control. It is rather the individual machine with its own capabilities for computation and storage that is part of a person rather than part of his environment. Thus **a key role for the personal computer may be seen as a symbiotic one with a person in emancipating his cognition by aiding the comprehension and control of an increasingly complex environment.**

There have been developed computer programs that play an **emancipatory** role in presenting to a person the structure underlying their thinking and interpersonal interactions. Mulhall's (1977) PRI essentially generates a state-transition diagram enabling someone to see the sequential nature of their social behaviour: that when they take one action it leads to someone else taking another, them taking a third, and so on, until they arrive at desirable or undesirable consequences. The PRI has been used successfully in a form of psychotherapy that emancipates the patient by presenting to him a comprehensible account of what is a complex, and emotionally loaded range of situations. In the context of management decision-making Boxer's NIPPER (1979) is an interactive program to make apparent the constructs underlying a preference relationship. In both clinical and management studies Slater's (1976) INGRID program has been used to give a map of personal semantic space which can be presented to a person to help him comprehend his own thought processes (Easterby-Smith 1981). Shaw (1980) presents a range of programs for eliciting and analysing both personal and group meaning: PEGASUS for interactively eliciting personal constructs; FOCUS for presenting the structure underlying the constructs; PEGASUS-BANK for allowing one person to interact with the constructs of another, e.g. an expert; CORE for deriving a relation between two grids; SOCIOGRIDS for deriving the shared constructs in a group of people; and ARGUS for eliciting a set of grids simultaneously from one person in several different roles.

All of these programs are emancipatory in that they feed back to a person information about his own behaviour, thought processes and relationships to others. They do not give rules, guidelines or other normative behavioural modifications, or any form of 'answer'. Their effects and impact come only from the greater understanding that the user may derive from them. Such an approach is suggested by Kelly's (1955) personal construct psychology and in the next section we discuss the theory, its role in computing and programs deriving from this.

THE PERSONAL SCIENTIST

George Kelly commenced his studies as an engineer but moved into
clinical psychology and developed a radically different approach to
the subject that emphasized the questing nature of the individual and
the idiosyncratic content of our models of the world. Kelly put
forward the idea of an individual as what Shaw (1980) terms a **personal
scientist** using **personal constructs** as filters through which he
perceives events:

> "Man looks at his world through transparent templets which he
> creates and then attempts to fit over the realities of which the
> world is composed." (Kelly 1955 pp.8-9)

He emphasizes the role of these constructs in our predicting and
controlling the world and their status as personal conjectures rather
than reality-derived absolutes:

> "Constructs are used for predictions of things to come, and the
> world keeps on rolling on and revealing these predictions to be
> either correct or misleading. This fact provides the basis for the
> revision of constructs and, eventually, of whole construct systems."
> (Kelly 1955 p.14)

Thus, making explicit the construct structures in use and identifying
their strengths and weaknesses is a key process in aiding man's coping
with a complex world. In psychiatry the assumption is that problems
may often be related to the construct system through which the patient
is viewing the world. In general we may expect many problems of
knowledge, decision and action, both fundamental as in science and
applied as in management, to be similarly related to the construct
systems in use.

A variety of approaches has been taken to the elicitation of personal
construct systems. As well as theoretical foundations, Kelly (1955)
also proposed a methodology for the elicitation of personal constructs
using a **repertory grid.** He assumed that constructs were bipolar and
binary so that an element would be construed as being assigned to one
or other of the poles of a construct. To elicit the constructs
themselves Kelly used triads of elements and asked for some basis on
which one element differed from the other pair in the triad, i.e. how
could the elements in the triad be construed so that two were similar
in some way and the other differed in that same way. The grid obtained
of elements against constructs is essentially a binary matrix in which
each element is assigned to one or the other of the poles of a
construct. An extension generally adopted is to allow multi-point
rating scales to be used bewtween the poles. Kelly notes that the
repertory grid may be used and analysed in a number of ways, notably
through some form of factoring that makes apparent relationships
between constructs. Since its original description there have been
many applications of the repertory grid and developments from it
(Bannister & Fransella 1971, Slater 1976, Shaw 1980, Gaines & Shaw

1981).

Figure 1 shows a repertory grid elicited from a person contemplating a change of employment: the elements are different jobs and the constructs are significant distinctions between them. A '1' in the matrix indicates that the left-hand description on the row applies to the element on that column; a '5' that the right-hand description applies; and intermediate values that the element lies between the two descriptions. This grid was derived by the computer program PEGASUS (Program Elicits Grids And Sorts Using Similarities, Shaw 1980) which elicits a grid interactively from an individual, simultaneously acting as a psychological reflector for heightening his awareness and deepening his understanding of himself and his processes. This is done by continual commentary on related elements or constructs, together with the encouragement to differentiate between them.

```
                * 1  2  3  4  5  6  7  8  9
                ******************************
 know what it is 1 * 1  1  5  5  3  2  5  2  1 * 1 unknown
        exciting 2 * 5  1  2  5  1  1  2  1  3 * 2 doesn't excite me
  changes little 3 * 1  1  1  3  5  1  5  3  1 * 3 changes everything
     done before 4 * 1  4  5  5  4  2  4  4  2 * 4 totally new
can work at home 5 * 4  4  1  5  4  3  3  2  1 * 5 have to go out
   work with team 6 * 1  1  2  2  1  5  5  2  4 * 6 on my own
   more free time 7 * 3  3  3  5  1  1  1  1  1 * 7 not much free time
    probably dull 8 * 1  4  3  1  4  2  5  5  3 * 8 varied & interesting
                 * *  *  *  *  *  *  *  *    unemployment
                 * *  *  *  *  *  *  *    ideal job
                 * *  *  *  *  *  *    consultancy US
                 * *  *  *  *  *    consultancy UK
                 * *  *  *  *    US teaching
                 * *  *  *    government
                 * *  *    company
                 * *    another department
                 *    my job now
```

Figure 1 Grid Elicited by PEGASUS from Person Thinking of Changing Job

Before choosing his elements the user is asked to think about his purpose for eliciting the grid. Here it was stated to be "to decide whether to change my job". This is of great importance for the interaction which is to follow, since the elements are dependent on the purpose and the constructs are dependent on the elements. By using combinations of reviewing the purpose and adding and deleting constructs and elements, a depth of interaction can be achieved which could not at first be envisioned. The user is given the opportunity to reflect on his understanding of the topic and to examine and explore his thoughts and feelings in an atmosphere of heightened awareness of personal knowing. His perception may be changed in a way which by other means can take much time to accomplish.

The program is divided into six main sections and these are

illustrated here through the elicitation of the grid in Figure 1. The
first section is the **Basic Grid** in which explanation of grids and the
use of the terminal are given, and the first four constructs elicited.
Before the user chooses his elements he is asked to think about his
purpose which defines the universe of discourse and enables him to
choose elements which are relevant and representative of the topic
area since the choice of elements largely determines the depth of
interaction which can be achieved. This is shown in the following
dialogue with PEGASUS in which computer output is in upper case and
the responses in lower case.

THIS IS A PROGRAM TO ELICIT A KELLY REPERTORY GRID.
PLEASE READ CAREFULLY EVERYTHING THAT IS PRINTED AND
MAKE SURE YOU UNDERSTAND WHAT YOU HAVE TO DO.
A REPERTORY GRID IS A TECHNIQUE DEVISED BY KELLY TO
HELP YOU EXPLORE THE DIMENSIONS OF YOUR THINKING.

YOU MUST DECIDE ON A PURPOSE FOR DOING THE GRID AND
KEEP THIS IN MIND WHEN YOU CHOOSE THE ELEMENTS--THE
THINGS YOU ARE GOING TO THINK ABOUT DURING THE PROGRAM.
THESE ELEMENTS WILL THEN BE USED TO ELICIT CONSTRUCTS.

THIS PROGRAM INCORPORATES FOUR VERSIONS OF PEGASUS.
  1. A PEGASUS GRID ELICITATION STARTING A NEW GRID;
  2. A STRAIGHT KELLY REPERTORY GRID ELICITATION
     WITHOUT COMMENTARY (MIN-PEG);
  3. A PEGASUS GRID ELICITATION USING A STORED BANK
     OF CONSTRUCTS (PEG-BANK);
  4. A PEGASUS GRID ELICITATION WITH PART ALREADY
     ELICITED BY YOU RECENTLY (PRE-PEG).
WHAT IS THE NUMBER OF THE VERSION YOU WISH TO USE ?1

TYPE IN ON ONE LINE YOUR PURPOSE FOR DOING THIS GRID

  ?to decide whether to change my job

NAME SIX ELEMENTS.
YOU MUST CHOOSE A SET OF SIX ELEMENTS KEEPING IN MIND
WHY YOU WANT TO DO THIS GRID. THEY COULD BE PEOPLE, EVENTS,
PIECES OF MUSIC, PICTURES, BOOKS, OR WHAT YOU WANT BUT
WHATEVER YOU CHOOSE THEY MUST BE OF THE SAME TYPE AND
EACH MUST BE WELL KNOWN TO YOU. TRY TO CHOOSE SPECIFIC
THINGS. NOW TYPE EACH ONE AFTER EACH QUESTION MARK.
DO NOT FORGET TO PRESS THE RETURN KEY AFTER EACH.

ELEMENT 1   ?my job now
ELEMENT 2   ?another department
ELEMENT 3   ?company
ELEMENT 4   ?government
ELEMENT 5   ?US teaching
ELEMENT 6   ?consultancy UK

The conventional method is then used to elicit the first few
constructs, that is to present a triad of elements to be divided into
a pair and a singleton indicating the poles of the construct. After
the user has named the poles the computer assigns a 1 to the pair and
a 5 to the singleton, and he has then to assign ratings from 1 to 5 to
each of the other elements. These are then retyped in groups to
highlight the relative position of each element with respect to the
others, and an option to change the ratings is given. This is shown in
the following dialogue with PEGASUS.

TRIAD FOR ELICITATION OF CONSTRUCT 1
  1 my job now
  2 another department
  3 company

NAME THE PAIR

CAN YOU CHOOSE TWO OF THIS TRIAD OF ELEMENTS WHICH ARE IN
SOME WAY ALIKE AND DIFFERENT FROM THE OTHER ONE.
TYPE IN THE NUMBERS OF THE PAIR ONE AFTER EACH QUESTION
MARK. DONT FORGET TO PRESS THE RETURN KEY AFTER EACH.

   ?1
   ?2

NAME THE POLES OF YOUR CONSTRUCT

NOW I WANT YOU TO THINK ABOUT WHAT YOU HAVE IN MIND WHEN YOU
SEPARATE THE PAIR FROM THE OTHER ONE.HOW CAN YOU DESCRIBE
THE TWO ENDS OR POLES OF THE SCALE WHICH DISCRIMINATE
my job now AND another department FROM company
JUST TYPE ONE OR TWO WORDS FOR EACH POLE TO REMIND YOU WHAT
YOU ARE THINKING OR FEELING WHEN YOU USE THIS CONSTRUCT.

LEFT POLE RATED 1 -- ?know what it is
RIGHT POLE RATED 5 -- ?unknown

TYPE IN THE RATINGS

NOW IF my job now AND another department ARE
ASSIGNED THE VALUE 1 AND company IS ASSIGNED THE VALUE   5
ACCORDING TO HOW YOU FEEL ABOUT THEM PLEASE ASSIGN TO EACH
OF THE OTHER ELEMENTS IN TURN A PROVISIONAL VALUE FROM 1 TO 5

  1 my job now   1
  2 another department   1
  3 company   5
  4 government   ?5
  5 US teaching   ?3
  6 consultancy UK   ?2

POLE 1 --know what it is

```
1 my job now           1
2 another department   1

6 consultancy UK       2

5 US teaching          3

3 company              5
4 government           5
```

POLE 5 --unknown

DO YOU WANT TO CHANGE ANY OF THESE VALUES ? no
DO YOU WANT TO CHANGE THE POLE NAMES ?no

The second section, **Construct Match,** provides feedback when two
constructs are highly related. The user is first asked to add an
element which is either at pole 1 on the first construct and pole 5 on
the second or vice versa. If he can add a new element it must be rated
on all the constructs so far elicited, but if he cannot split the two
constructs this way he is asked if he would like to delete a
construct, combine two constructs into one, or just carry on. Feedback
from a construct match is shown in the following dialogu.

THE TWO CONSTRUCTS YOU CALLED
 1 know what it is--unknown
 4 done before--totally new
ARE MATCHED AT THE 66 PERCENT LEVEL.
THIS MEANS THAT MOST OF THE TIME YOU ARE SAYING
know what it is YOU ARE ALSO SAYING done before
AND MOST OF THE TIME YOU ARE SAYING
unknown YOU ARE ALSO SAYING totally new

THINK OF ANOTHER ELEMENT WHICH IS EITHER
know what it is AND totally new
OR done before AND unknown
IF YOU REALLY CANNOT DO THIS THEN JUST PRESS RETURN AFTER
THE FIRST QUESTION MARK BUT PLEASE TRY. THEN YOU MUST GIVE
THIS ELEMENT A RATING VALUE ON EACH CONSTRUCT IN TURN.
AFTER EACH QUESTION MARK TYPE A VALUE FROM 1 TO 5
WHAT IS YOUR ELEMENT ?consultancy US
RATINGS :

know what it is--unknown ?5
exciting--doesn't excite me ?2
doesn't affect other things--changes everything ?5
done before--totally new ?4

DO YOU WANT TO CHANGE ANY OF THESE VALUES ?no

It is interesting that the user here does not do as the computer asks
in the ratings assigned but does add a new element. This illustrates
the role of the feedback in stimulating the user's own thought
processes rather than directing them in ways determined by the
program.

When four constructs have been entered, the program moves into the
third section, **Element Match,** and begins to calculate matching scores
between elements. Each element is matched with every other on the
basis of the ratings used, and a comment made on the highest match if
it meets the set criterion. The first choice offered is to add a new
construct on which the two elements are placed at opposite poles, and
then all the elements must be rated in the usual way. Alternatively an
element may be deleted, or no action may be taken. Feedback from a
element match is shown in the following dialogue with PEGASUS.

```
THE TWO ELEMENTS   2 another department AND   6 consultancy UK
ARE MATCHED AT THE   80 PERCENT LEVEL.
THIS MEANS THAT SO FAR YOU HAVE NOT DISTINGUISHED
BETWEEN another department AND consultancy UK
DO YOU WANT TO SPLIT THESE ?yes
HELP ?yes
THINK OF A CONSTRUCT WHICH SEPARATES THESE
TWO ELEMENTS AND THEN KEEPING THIS IN MIND
ACCORDING TO HOW YOU FEEL ABOUT THEM PLEASE ASSIGN TO EACH
OF THE OTHER ELEMENTS IN TURN A PROVISIONAL VALUE FROM 1 TO 5
NAME THE POLES OF YOUR CONSTRUCT
LEFT POLE RATED 1 -- ?work with team
RIGHT POLE RATED 5 -- ?on my own
TYPE IN THE RATINGS


2 another department   1
6 consultancy UK        5
1 my job now           ?1
3 company              ?2
4 government           ?2
5 US teaching          ?1
7 consultancy US       ?5


POLE 1 --work with team

1 my job now           1
2 another department   1
5 US teaching          1

3 company              2
4 government           2

6 consultancy UK       5
7 consultancy US       5

POLE 5 --on my own
```

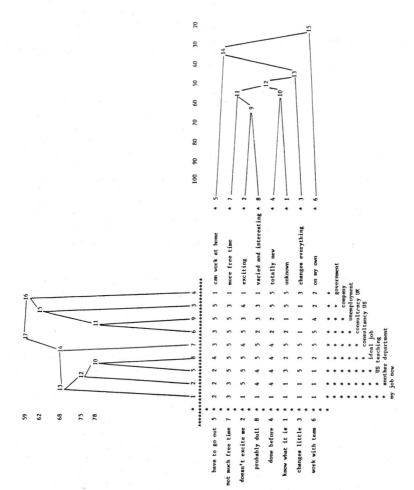

Figure 2 FOCUS Hierarchical Cluster Analysis of the Grid of Figure 1

Section four allows the user to **Finish** at this stage in the cycle.
Section five, **Review,** gives the choice of adjusting or redefining the
purpose, and altering the level of match on which feedback commentary
is given. There is an opportunity to see a focused version of the grid
to date, and to delete any element or construct which is felt to be
unsatisfactory in any way. In the sixth section, **Alternative
Elicitation,** the user is given the freedom to add an element or to add
a construct without using a triad if he so wishes. For example in the
elicitation shown the element 'ideal job' was added in this way.

When the grid reaches the maximum size allowed, or if the user chooses
to finish before that, the results are analysed using the FOCUS
procedure as shown in Figure 2. This is a two-way hierarchical cluster
analytic technique which systematically reorders the rows of
constructs and columns of elements to produce a focused grid which
shows the least variation between adjacent constructs and adjacent
elements. The printout shows the trees of the elements and constructs
as well as the focused grid with the element and construct labels. It
can be seen that the element 'ideal job' matches most closely to 'US
teaching' and that 'unemployment' and 'consultancy UK' have similar
characteristics. It can also be seen that constructs 7, 2, 8, 4 and 1
form a related cluster with 5, 3 and 6 only loosely linked in. Since
the PEGASUS feedback encourages the separation of constructs very
close matches are rare.

As a PEGASUS elicitation proceeds this FOCUS algorithm is used to
offer to the user a possible explanation and interpretation of his
meaning system in the terms of the similar patterns he uses in
supposedly different circumstances. Cross-references are mapped across
the grid and exhibited to the user in such a way as to offer him the
facility to reconsider and change anything he feels to be
inappropriate, which in turn enables him to be more aware of the links
he is implicitly holding in his cognitive model. Here the conversation
can be seen as a feedback loop with the computer acting as an
emancipator by re-presenting the content of the conversation and the
implicit links within it. In this way the participative analysis
extracts and presents the essence of the personally meaningful
relationships in the grid. It may well be impossible for a person to
derive such relationships themselves without help -- for example, the
studies of Michalski and Chilausky (1980) on expert systems show that
inductive algorithms are better at extracting the rules for an
expert's decision than the expert himself is at expressing them.

THE ROLE OF THE PERSONAL COMPUTER

It would be easy to assume that such interactive programs are merely
more convenient ways of eliciting construct systems through extensions
of the repertory grid and do not themselves add anything qualitatively
new to the process. However, such an assumption would be missing
certain crucial psychological factors in the person-computer situation

13.

and its differences from the person-person situation. We have observed informally in making PEGASUS available to a wide range of people in a variety of situations that those coming to it for the first time often seem to find it a very dramatic experience. They react to it intensely and become gripped by the interactive process of construct elicitation. They also feel that they are learning something new from the process and are prepared to use this in determining their actions.

Probably such involvement is also significant in the elicitation of construct systems by people rather than computer interaction. However, we believe there are certain quite fundamental differences when the elicitation is done in such a way that interpersonal interaction is clearly absent. In particular, when a person is feeding back comments and guidance it is a natural and ready assumption that they are injecting the constructs rather than eliciting them. It is easy to believe that the elicited constructs do not come from oneself but that one is in a tutorial or debating situation with another person. One has to be persuaded that this is not so and the persuasion has to be stronger the more striking and significant the constructs elicited. However, when a computer is the tool by which one's construct structure is being reflected or laid bare then such an assumption of outside injection and interference is far less tenable.

When constructs are being elicited by a computer program then one is more likely to accept that it is precisely and only oneself that is being portrayed. We 'trust' a computer program to be doing just what it appears to be doing without deeper motivations and without attempting to persuade us to its point of view. No-one is telling you anything -- you are seeing, in interacting with PEGASUS, possibly for the first time the basis for your own thought processes. Very often extreme surprise is the first reaction -- the person had not thought that he was viewing the world in the way portrayed. If another person were eliciting the construct structure then the surprise would be taken by the subject as an indication that the elicitor was incorrect and followed by a process of ignoring him or arguing with him. With computer elicitation the reflected structures are accepted as being self-generated and the surprise leads to a motivation to know more.

That this knowledge can be totally private to oneself is another important feature of interaction with the computer. We do not like, as Kelly put it, to be "caught with our constructs down". When another person is involved we are more reluctant to expose and explore our constructs the more surprising they are -- perhaps because the surprise is often the result of a conflict between our ostensive value judgements and the basis of our behaviour. Or it may just be sloppy verbal behaviour -- that we are naming two distinct constructs with the same label -- a scientist found that he was using the word 'time' to label several different constructs and generating confusion in his arguments because of this.

Another reason that we are reluctant to explore construct structures freely in interacting with another person, particularly a professional person, is that we are acutely aware of the possible 'waste' of their time. This phenomenon has been noted (Card et al 1974) as accounting for a major part of the preferences expressed by patients to be interviewed through an interactive computer program rather than their doctor. There are many pressures and artefacts of interpersonal relationships that can totally obscure and undermine such reflective processes as we require in the elicitation of personal constructs. Adams (1979) has put this argument in reverse in noting that children learn quickly to play games on a personal computer and conjecturing that this is because of the lack of interpersonal complications.

These are some of the key psychological factors in which the use of a personal computer for the elicitation of constructs is significantly different from previous manual techniques. They can be summed up by noting that one can see one's reflection most effectively in a stream if one is sure that no-one else's reflection is mixed up in it (and that no-one else is muddying the waters).

There are technical factors also, however, that add new dimensions to the computer elicitation of constructs. The most notable is that already demonstrated in PEGASUS -- that relationships between constructs may be inferred instantly and queried with the user. This immediate analysis and feedback is a key factor in most applications of interactive computers and can go way beyond what any manual analysis can accomplish. Instant feedback whilst one remembers one's line of reasoning is very different from delayed analyses that arrive at a later time when the entire context of the replies one has been giving may have been forgotten. Construct structures in particular have a high degree of context-dependence -- it is often precisely the relationship between the structures elicited and the role we are adopting in answering the questions that elicit them which is of prime interest to us. Using Wolff's (1976) vocabulary, we **surrender** ourselves to a particular role and become a 'physicist', a 'manager', a 'father', etc., and it is the analysis of our construal of the world in the specific role which we are attempting to **catch.**

In terms of this discussion it seems reasonable to suggest that one takes an existential view of the phenomenon of computer elicitation of personal constructs regardless of one's view of Kelly's theory and methodologies based on it. The computer interaction is in itself a meaningful and significant experience for many people and they gain from it. Perhaps it is only that introspection is not a skill developed by most current educational systems -- we promote the 'received view' of knowledge and act as teachers to bring the minds of students into conformity with our consensual models of reality. What you think does not matter in itself -- only that it does not deviate from what it is 'correct' to think. It is a novel experience for many people to realize that there are actually individualistic thought processes going on within them. It is even more novel for them to realize that these condition 'reality' and that different approaches to life and different reactions to the same circumstances may be ascribed to different construals of reality.

CONCLUSIONS

We have argued in this paper for a highly significant role for the
personal computer in enabling an individual to operate effectively in
his role as **personal scientist** in coming to interact with an
increasingly complex world. We have illustrated the argument with
examples of interaction with a computer program that **emancipates the
cognition** of a person involved in a decision-making process. We have
also argued that the role of the computer is an essential one which
goes beyond that which another person might supply. In conclusion we
can only note that it is early yet to determine whether the role we
see for the computer is coming to pass. Current programs are primitive
and restricted by technology, our knowledge of psychology and our
creative imaginations. We hope that this paper will encourage the
further exploration of the development and application of **man-computer
symbiotic systems.**

REFERENCES

Adams, J.
   1979 "Pet Behaviour." **Practical Computing** 2: 29.

Bannister, D. & Fransella, F.
   1971 **Inquiring Man.** Penguin, UK.

Boxer, P.J.
   1979 "Reflective analysis." **International Journal of Man-Machine
   Studies** 5: 547-584.

Card, W.I., Nicholson, M., Crean, G.P., Watkinson, G., Evans, C.R.,
   Wilson, J. & Russell, D.
   1974 "A Comparison of Doctor and Computer Interrogation of
   Patients." **Int. J. Biomedical Computing** 5: 175-187.

DeBono, E.
   1979 **Future Positive.** Maurice Temple Smith, London.

Easterby-Smith, M.
   1981 "The design, analysis and interpretation of repertory grids."
   in **Personal Construct Technology.** (ed. M.L.G.Shaw) Academic
   Press, London.

Elithorn, A. & Telford, A.
   1969 "Computer analysis of intellectual skills." **International
   Journal of Man-Machine Studies** 1: 189-209.

Elwood, D.L.
   1972a "Test retest reliability and cost analyses of automated and
        face to face intelligence testing." **International Journal of
        Man-Machine Studies** 4: 1-22.

   1972b "Automated WAIS testing correlated with face-to-face testing:
        a validity study." **International Journal of Man-Machine Studies**
        4: 129-137.

   1972c "Automated versus face-to-face intelligence testing:
        comparison of test-retest reliabilities." **International Journal
        of Man-Machine Studies** 4: 363-369.

Gaines, B.R.
   1979 "Computers and society: the basis for a systemic model."
        **Improving the Human Condition: Quality and Stability in Social
        Systems.** Society for General Systems Research, Kentucky.
        523-530.

Gaines, B.R. & Shaw, M.L.G.
   1981 "New directions in the analysis and interactive elicitation of
        personal construct systems." in **Personal Construct Technology.**
        (ed. M.L.G.Shaw) Academic Press, London.

Gedye, J.L. & Miller, E.
   1969 "The automation of psychological assessment." **International
        Journal of Man-Machine Studies** 1: 237-262.

Habermas, J.
   1968 **Knowledge and Human Interests.** Heineman, London.

Kelly, G.A.
   1955 **The Psychology of Personal Constructs.** Norton, New York.

Klinge, V. & Rodziewicz, T.
   1976 "Automated and manual intelligence testing of the Peabody
        Picture Vocabulary Test on a psychiatric adolescent
        population." **International Journal of Man-Machine Studies** 8:
        243-246.

Licklider, J.C.R.
   1968 "Man-Computer Symbiosis." in **Conversational Computers.** J.Wiley,
        New York.

Lucas, R.W.
   1977 "A study of patients' attitudes to computer interrogation."
        International Journal of Man-Machine Studies 9: 69-86.

Luhmann, N.
   1979 **Trust and Power.** John Wiley, Chichester.

Mulhall, D.J.
   1977 "The representations of personal relationships: an automated
        system." **International Journal of Man-Machine Studies** 9:
        315-335.

Michalski, R.S. & Chilausky, R.L.
   1980 "Knowledge acquisition by encoding expert rules versus computer
        induction from examples: a case study involving soybean
        pathology." **International Journal of Man-Machine Studies** 12:
        63-87.

Parkhill, D.F.
   1966 **The Challenge of the Computer Utility.** Addison-Wesley, Mass.

Popper, K.
   1974 "Autobiography of Karl Popper." in **The Philosophy of Karl
        Popper.** (ed. P.A.Schilpp) Open Court, Illinois.

Shaw, M.L.G.
   1980 **On Becoming a Personal Scientist.** Academic Press, London.

Slater, P. (ed.)
   1976 **Dimensions of Intrapersonal Space.** Vol.1. Wiley, London.

Stodolsky, D.
   1970 "The computer as a psychotherapist." **International Journal of
        Man-Machine Studies** 2: 327-350.

Toffler, A.
   1980 **The Third Wave.** Bantam Books, New York.

Wiener, N.
   1950 **The Human Use of Human Beings.** Houghton Mifflin.

Wolff, K.H.
   1976 **Surrender and Catch.** D.Reidel, Holland.

The New Generation Natural Language Systems

P. Sabatier

Engineer, CAP Sogeti Logiciel, France

Natural language is becoming a possible interface between casual
users and very large database systems. We discuss the main aspects
of the new generation of systems involving this facility owing to
an interesting natural language subset, metalinguistic abilities
and expert interfaces.

Slowly but surely, natural language is becoming a possible method of
communication between the general public and the computer, in
particular in the formulation of queries over very large distribued
databases. Today non-technical users should not have to know
technicalities on how to formulate their questions; and the way of
using the terminal should remain unaffected when the user deals with
different types of service and data.

The introduction of natural language looks like being an important
step with a fruitful social impact. The consultation of data will
spread rapidly, once this facility is established.

Systems which retrieve information requested in natural language
from a database have long been a subject of study by computer
scientists, from a variety of different viewpoints.

Historically, we can distinguish two generations before 1975.

The first generation (1959-1965, 15 or 16 systems), that of -word
generation-, uses a large thesaurus of words, but without a
linguistic model of sentence; in its place there is a poor syntactic
analysis based on keywords and statistical methods.

Abandoning these including techniques, the second generation
systems (1965-1975, 80 systems, Wood's LUNAR, Winograd's SHRDLU,
Waltz's PLANES, Plath's REQUEST) introduced parsers for basic and
transformational grammars (syntactic analysis), semantic relations
and networks (semantic analysis), frames, scripts, scenarios,
information and data representation (representations for cognition)
and high level programming languages such as Hewitt's PLANNER. But
in their internal configuration, these systems are incomplete and
diverse. Word governement is too important. In fact, users have to
learn a special language (quasi-natural) to ask their questions : the
linguistic coverage of the interface is too narrow and strongly
bound to the specific domain of the database. Such systems are in
consequence not transportable to other applications without costly
changes. In general, the systems of the second generation were
poorly talktative, explicit and sympathetic with the user; in other
words, not convivial : the user was expected to be very familiar
with the domain of the system (discourse, nomenclature, structure
of the database), and not the contrary, ie. the program thoroughly
familiar with the user's language.

Since 1975, a new generation of systems is appeared, drawing lessons
from the preceding one, and developping the following main aspects :
    - an interesting natural language subset;
    - metalinguistic abilities, faciliting the definition of new
      syntactic structures and words, and the explanations about the
      linguistic competence of the system;

- expert interfaces, in which the system tries to understand what the user really wants, anticipates answers for next related questions, asks him precisions, explains what it can do and how.

1. AN INTERESTING NATURAL LANGUAGE SUBSET

Instructive experiences have been and are presently made at the Artificial Intelligence Group of Marseille where Prof. Colmerauer (1979) delimits and studies a natural language subset (C'sNLS, hereafter) that serves as starting point of many applications, such as the consultation, creation and updating of sophisticated databases. This subset, at first circumscribed to French, has been sucessfully transported to other languages (English, Spanish and Portuguese, in particular) owing to a rigorously defined semantics expliciting a logical system underlying natural language.

C'sNLS has a simple and natural syntax, containing the fundamental structures of a given language : declarative sentence; yes-no and wh-questions; relative, coordinate, negative and elliptic clauses; pronouns and articles (a, an, the, some, many, several, few, every, all the, each, each of, no, ...). C'sNLS is entirely independent of its linguistic application, ie. of the domain of the database. Its semantics deals with these invariant elements and the fundamental role played by articles in the quantification hierarchy problem.

In this framework, each sentence is transformed into a logical sentence, -its meaning-, where each of its constituent parts corresponds to the sense of individual words. It is required that the logical sentence has one truth value over the database domain defined if only if the natural language sentence has the same truth value. The method of transformation consists in considering
- elementary statements based on proper nouns;
- properties with n arguments corresponding to each verb, adjective and noun;
- each article A as a three-branched quantifier : a variable X related to two formulae E1 and E2, such for A X such that E1, it is true that E2;
- precedence rules for governing the relatives scopes of the quantifiers, defining the hierarchy among the subject of a verb and its different complements, and between a noun and its complements.

Relative to an appropriate database, each sentence is interpreted with one of three truth values (true, false, meaningless) to allow handling of presuppositions. Specific answers are generated for meaningful questions only, ie. with true presuppositions.

2. METALINGUISTIC ABILITY AND EXPERT INTERFACES

An important aspect of some of the new systems lies in their ability to discourse on their linguistic competence. Generally, the metalinguistic consciousness of the primary ones was limited to point out incorrect sentences and unknown words. Now, we find systems which are able to
- localize grammatical and spelling mistakes;
- point out parts of a sentence they can't understand;
- force analysis of an ill-formed string;
- disambiguate sentences, asking the user for full particulars about it.

Natural language processors must be able to explicit the syntactic structures they accept, and to provide the user the possibility for extending their competence, defining new strings and words, through a natural interaction,of course. Metalinguistic ability is delicate to compute. Mainly, the coverage of its language subset is not easy to delimit, the casual user not being expected to be very familiar with high linguistic terminology.

The metalinguistic ability is in fact part of a more general capability, that one might call "introspection aptitude". Systems are nowdays expected to be able to describe themselves, revealing the content of their database and the fundamental principles and mechanisms set in action. At any time during the current interaction, the user may ask the system for justifying its last results and how they were achieved. Such an aptitude requires expert interfaces, acting between the user and the computing facilities, which try to understand what he really wants and suitting him with answers, thanks to fexible control structures.

Interesting experience in this domain is presently processing by Prof. Moniz Pereira at the New University of Lisbon (Portugal) and by Texas Instruments (Hendler and al., 1981) in U.S.A.

3. OUR CONTRIBUTION

Recently, we have built at CAP Sogeti Logiciel a database system with a natural language interface. The domain of the application is a subset of a French civil service consisting in different types of dependent organisms, with their staff (names, functions, ranks and titles),addresses and telephone numbers.

Entirely written in Roussel's PROLOG, a new high level Artificial Intelligence language, -a very simple but surprisingly powerful language in which programs can be written quickly with few errors-,

our system contains five modules : Supervisor, Word, Grammar,
Evaluation and Database. Database is the only application dependent
module; by changing it, our system is transportable to other domains.

Supervisor is the high level control structure of all the processors
acting during a dialogue, calling Word, Grammar, -deciding upon the
linguistic output to accept or refuse the question-, Evaluation for
accepted questions, and Database for retrieving the appropriated
answer.

By consulting the dictionary of required lexical items, Word
transforms the list of characters of the user's question into a list
of words and associated syntactic categories (verb, noun, ...). When
a character or a word is unknown, Supervisor points it out and awaits
a new query from the user.

Grammar handles the interesting rules of C's NLS, analysing each
question, representing them in a logical sentence that contains all
the information needed by Evaluation. At this step, Supervisor
localizes grammatical mistakes and ill-formed questions, inviting
the user to correct them.

Evaluation interprets the logical sentence corresponding to the
question and decomposing it into meaningful information atoms, and
evaluating them by consulting Database. At this point, any
meaningless query is detected.

Database contains facts and general laws about the application,
defined as sets of relations and represented in predicate logic
sentences, which are directly processed by PROLOG through Supervisor.

Our system is able to understand simple questions of the following
type,

- Quelle est la fonction de M. K. ?
  (What is the function of M. K. ?)

- Est-ce que M. K. est chef de département ?
  (Is M. K. a head of department ?)

- Quel est le grade de chaque adjoint au chef de service ?
  (What is the rank of each assistant of a head of service ?)

- Est-ce que le département X fait partie du service Y ?
  (Is the department X a part of the service Y ?)

- Combien de personnes dépendent de M. K. ?
  (How many persons are serving under M. K.?)

- Où se trouve le département X ?
  (What is the address of the department X ?)

or more complex queries as,

- Quels sont les organismes qu'aucune personne ne dirge ?
  (What are the organisms that no one manages ?)

- Que dirige chaque personne qu'aucun chef de bureau ne commande?
  (What does each person manage whom no head clerk commands ?)

- Quels sont les titres de chaque chef dont les departements ne
  font pas partie du service Y ?
  (What are the titles of each head whose départments are not
  part of the service Y ?)

Putting by the attractive implementation of C's NLS, the grammar and
the domain of discourse of our system can be easily extended, thanks
to a large modularity. We are presently working to endow our system
with a generous metalinguistic consciousness, trying to solve the
problems pointed out above.

CONCLUSION

I believe that the research we are doing on natural language interface
is quite important to the success of the development of databases
consultable by casual users. I hope that a such natural interactive
facility will have an happy social impact, even if the applications
are not all paradisiac. Truly, if we want that computers become
convivial, we'd better be learning them to understand natural
language.

REFERENCES

Colmerauer A., Un sous-ensemble interessant du français, RAIRO, 13, 4,
Dunod, Paris, 1979.

Hendler J., Kehler T., Michaelis P., Philipps B., Ross K., Tennant H.,
Issues in the development of natural language front-ends, National
Computer Conference, Chicago, 1981.

Tennant H., Evaluation of natural language processors, Ph.D. Thesis,
University of Illinois, 1981.

Design of Systems for Interaction between Humans and Computers

Richard L. Wexelblat

Director, Software Research, Sperry Univac,
Blue Bell, PA 19424, USA

To create a successful computer-based system, the designer must take into account not only the system's function but also the human factors of the user interface.

There is no set of firm rules to be followed in such a design but here are some principles and guidelines that will assist the designer.

> The painter draws with his eyes, not with his hands. What-
> ever he sees, if he sees it clear, he can put down. The
> putting of it down requires, perhaps, much care and labor,
> but no more muscular agility than it takes for him to write
> his name. Seeing clear is the important thing.
>   -- Maurice Grosser, The Painter's Eye

1. Why systems succeed and why they fail

Interaction between people and computers is primarily linguistic.
Although many versatile and ingenious devices have been invented to
help in this interaction, communication still requires words, phrases,
and sentences. The success of a computer-based system is as much due
to the user interface as to the function. Absence of a learnable,
usable interface can doom a system to failure. Furthermore
learnability and usability must be designed in from the beginning.

Nietzsche wrote, "A traveller who had seen many countries and peoples
and several continents was asked what human traits he had found
everywhere; and he answered: people are inclined to laziness." This,
I believe, is the key to systems design. If a system is difficult to
learn or difficult to use, people will not use it. If it is easier do
the job the old way -- or maybe not to do the job at all -- then the
system will not be used.

A system must behave in a reasonable fashion. James Martin [1973]
points out that a system whose behavior is not reasonable (he uses the
word "natural") will lead to bewilderment, then annoyance, criticism,
and perhaps rejection of the system by its intended users. When use
of a system leads to frustration, rejection follows. Later, I will
describe my definition of "reasonable" in more precise terms.

All too often the potential users of a system have no say whatever in
defining how the system will behave. It's not enough for a proposed
system to meet its functional goals. Sometimes an excellent user
interface is not enough. The design must take into account the way
the users did the task before the new system came along. Changes in
procedures, changes in the way people think about doing their task
must be taken into account or people will ignore, misuse, or just
plain hate the new ways.

I remember two computer-based systems developed at Bell Labs while I
was working there in the 1970s: One was a maintenance overseer for
switching equipment. It gave the "craftsmen" periodic reports on how
the equipment was working. It diagnosed many problems and warned of
many potential problems that might arise.

The second was the Directory Scope Analysis Program, (DSAP), best
described through an example: Given the calling frequencies for
residence-to-residence calls between all central offices in a
geographic area, how many different residential telephone directories
should there be; who should be listed in each; and who should receive
a copy of each? The goal was to minimize cost, first by reducing the
number of directory pages printed and distributed, and second, by
reducing the frequency of Directory Assistance calls.

The maintenance system printed long messages on a noisy Model 33 Teletype. It demanded attention and required responses in a fairly complicated notation. It did not differentiate among informative (Everything's ok), cautionary (Error level on Trunk 35 above normal), and serious (Rack 8 has caught fire) messages. Each message had the same format and each required the same complex form of response. The program did not use the particular vocabulary, the jargon, of the craftsman. The result, of course, was that the TTY-33 was pushed to the side. The most junior person was taught the minimum necessary to make it shut up. The output was used seldom, if at all.

DSAP, by its nature, was an approximating tool. It too, was rather verbose, though its office-located terminals were quieter than the TTY-33. Outputs were printed only on request, however. By a stroke of genius or of good luck, DSAP was designed not to compute a figure it could easily have found: the number of unique directories. Given the number of different directories desired, DSAP would find the inclusion and distribution patterns to minimize cost. Letting the user choose the number of directories was crucial to acceptance. Before DSAP, the job was done manually. After years on the job, people advanced to the level where they could choose the number of directories in an area. No computer was going to take this power away from them. And DSAP didn't. The user asked for figures for various numbers of directories and chose the lowest cost among them. Several hours of "human time" were added to the task (and, it turned out, a good bit of computer time saved). But the users were happy. They still had their status and the computer became their powerful helper, not their master.

These two anecdotes are examples of the "little things mean a lot" school of ergonomics. As is usual with anecdotes, no firm conclusions can be drawn. Yet, when you study the causes of success and failure of consumer products, economic policies, military systems, etc. the human factors are very often the basis for the results.

2. Ease of use

The first question to ask about a system design is, "Does it do the job?" Too often, however, doing the job is the sole criterion. We should ask whether a system is easy to use and whether it is enjoyable to use. The designer of a computer-based system must balance many competing requirements. The system must be able to perform its assigned task. It must be reliable; that is, it must run for a long time without error. It must be robust. (Computer people have adopted the word "robust" to describe software that continues to perform its task despite errors in input or operation.)

And again, it must be easy to use.

The design requirements of reliability, function, and ease of use apply across many quite different areas of design. Basic principles of design also span many areas. How delightful it would be if the design process were algorithmic. It isn't. Design is as much a part of the Arts as of the Sciences; a branch of architecture, perhaps more than a branch of engineering.

As Roger Bacon wrote 700 years ago, "There are two modes of knowing, those of argument and experience." They are complementary to one another; neither is reducible to the other; and their simultaneous working may be incompatible. One mode is verbal and rational, sequential in operation, orderly; the other is intuitive, tacit, diffuse in operation, less logical and neat, a mode we often devalue, culturally, personally, and even psychologically. [Ornstein, 1972]

I characterize the "argument" mode as the engineering component of design and the "experience" mode as the architecture. Nowadays we can teach a budding artist all about paints, brushes, color, composition, and contrast. But we cannot teach a person to become an artist. Similarly in the computer field we can teach all of the tools of the programming trade: structured programming, top-down implementation, abstract data structuring (apply "buzzwords" at will). Nevertheless, the Chief Programmer is still a virtuoso.

The simultaneous working of argument and experience is possible when the argument part is learned and so thoroughly ingrained as to be applied at the subconscious level. An artist who must think consciously about how to mix and apply paint will be distracted from the artistic to the technical aspects of applying oil to canvas. When the use of the tools and materials is second nature, the artistic will be able to take control -- if the talent is there.

3. The Process of Design

Attempts have been made over the years to capture the essence of the process of design. One of my favorite books on the subject is an informal, fast moving treatise called The Universal Traveler. The authors, Don Koberg and Jim Bagnall, characterize design by the following sequence of steps:

Accept situation -- To state initial intentions. To accept the problem as a challenge; to give up our autonomy to the problem and allow the problem to become our process.

Analyse -- To get to know the ins and outs of the problem; to discover what the world of the problem looks like.

Define -- To decide what we believe to be the main issues of the problem; to conceptualize and to clarify our major goals concerning the problem situation.

Ideate -- To search out all the ways of possibly getting to the major goals. Alternatives.

Select -- To compare our goals as defined with our possible ways of
  getting there. Determining best ways to go.

Implement -- To give action or physical form to our selected "best
  ways".

Evaluate -- To determine the effects or ramifications as well as the
  degree of progress of our design activity.

The steps may be taken in sequence or in parallel. In the design of
computer-based systems, as the true intent of the system is made
clear, the problem statement will be subject to refinements that
result in loops among the first two or three steps. This <u>should</u> lead
to a precise specification in the third step. It seems the fate of
designers of computer-based systems to be continually refining
specifications. If changes are not the result of consciously made
design decisions, disaster will ensue. Applying the above steps to
computer system design, we have:

ACCEPTING THE SITUATION. The designer of the human-machine interface
should take the problem statement as given and not try to solve a
different problem. Many major difficulties arise from misconstruing
the problem as "just a special instance of a more general problem,"
leading to an attempt to try to solve the general problem.
Recognizing that a problem is nearly (but not quite) the same as a
problem previously solved and trying to warp the prior solution to fit
the new situation can create trouble as well.

This is not to say that a general solution or a modification of a
prior solution will never work. The point is that such a conclusion
should come at a much later point in the design process.

ANALYSIS. In this formulation, analysis is not only looking at the
problem and devising solutions, but also considering the context, the
world around. Not only must the system be taken into account, but
also users and their training and skill, terminal hardware,
environment, and any other relevant factors.

DEFINITION. Put down, in some useful form as precisely as possible,
what your system is to do and at least some ideas on how it will do
it. Include not only the function but also assumptions about the
behavior of the operating environment. Now the goals can be made
precise. Now "outsiders" may validly begin to comment on, and perhaps
to influence, the design criteria and goals.

Ideally, the definition should use a formal specification mechanism.
In practice, any means will do so long as the designer and the
potential user can agree on the content.

It is important to write down assumptions about the behavior of the
system. First, documented assumptions give meaning to the concept of

robustness (the ability of a system to perform despite violations of assumptions in the specifications). Second, they are, to a large extent, what determines the ease of use or the lack of it.

IDEATION. Ideation refers to achieving a full grasp of the problem and thinking it through to a solution. Any problem worth working on probably has many approaches to solutions. There may, indeed, be several acceptable alternative solutions. Some problems may have no acceptable solution at all. Beware of easy answers.

Given the goals for the system to be designed, as many avenues of approach as possible should be explored. It is best to have a small group of people working together. The size depends on the problem. Four or five is probably about enough at this point in the design. One is too few. The "Chief Programmer Team" approach to systems design indicates that an initial team of two has been successful in many actual projects [Baker, 1972]. The synergy of people working together is crucial to success in design. It is better to have two people jointly working on solving two problems than to have two people each working separately on a separate problem.

SELECTION. More people are needed in the selection process than in prior phases. Design trade-offs may be in order. "Management considerations" -- a euphemism for pragmatics -- are applied and the practical is derived from the ideal. The cold light of day is applied to the dreams of the previous night and the small (it is to be hoped) design team will have to justify their approaches to a larger, interested, audience.

Now is the time to question assumptions. If the eventual users have not been actively involved, now is the time to get them involved. Now is the time to make sure that the problem that is being solved is the problem that needed to be solved. The solution that is most promising is selected. The designers, however, must not fall so in love with their creation that they are unwilling to change or compromise.

The initial team must commit their designs to writing. Alternatives and design decisions must also be documented. Too often, incompletely thought through ideas will be presented verbally, argued, accepted, and the various members of the design and review teams will go off with their own separate ideas of what has been decided. Without written specifications, there is no way to be certain what is to be done. Without written plans, there is no way to determine what has been decided.

IMPLEMENTATION. For a computer system, implementation is the process of going from a detailed specification to running code -- from a precise and unambiguous specification to a complete, debugged, fully documented program. The details of software systems implementation can be found in many books and articles. This topic is beyond the scope of the present essay.

Soundness can be overdone. For the novice, completeness is much more
important than soundness. Given a reasonably simple syntax and
straightforward semantics, the beginner would probably prefer to have
errors (gently and politely) pointed out, not automatically fixed.

NATURALNESS. Command and response must be natural for the user.
Naturalness is in the eye, ear, and psyche of the user. A thorough
study of the proposed functions of a system, its hardware and software
realization, and its potential users is necessary for any hope of
achieving naturalness. Secondary considerations such as training,
prior experience, physical environment, and documentation must be
taken into account, too.

REASONABLENESS. According to G. K. Chesterton, "The real trouble with
this world of ours is not that it is an unreasonable world, nor even
that it is a reasonable one. The commonest kind of trouble is that it
is nearly reasonable, but not quite." If somehow, all of the other
design criteria were achieved then perhaps systems would be
reasonable. The "real world" being what it is, it is neither
economically nor technically feasible to have a system complete,
consistent, sound, and natural. "Reasonableness" is the term I apply
to the compromise among these four attributes that will permit the
system to be usable even though not perfect. Reasonableness can be
attained only through interaction among designer, implementer,
documenter, and user.

Perhaps each designer should make a checklist of what is reasonable
and what is not -- an open ended list -- and apply these items to each
design on an ad hoc basis. Here are some of the items on my list:

Long keywords are reasonable when there is also a reasonable
abbreviation convention.

Reserved words are not reasonable at all. PASCAL implementations all
seem to have reserved keywords, although from the original definition
of PASCAL, there seems to be no' such requirement [Jensen and Wirth,
1975]. For a special "treat," in TRS-80 BASIC, try to use a variable
name that contains a keyword, SIFT, for example. It turns out that
reserved words on the TRS-80 also apply to substrings of variable
names!

Responses to questions should have reasonable freedom. Y and N (also
y and n) should be permitted for yes and no. If the response is not
yes, don't assume that the answer is no. Nor vice versa. Here is a
typical sequence that adds a bit of reasonableness at the cost of a
few extra lines of code:

```
print "Do you want to continue?"
do until(yes-or-no)
   print "Continue? (yes or no; enter ? for more info.)"
end do
```

where yes-or-no is a function that accepts the user response and
returns true if yes or no has been entered and false otherwise. A
reasonable system will let the user answer "?" or "help" to any query
to find out more about the question. This may prove somewhat
inefficient, but it certainly is handy.

> The great emphasis that modern management puts on efficiency is a
> powerful element which militates against the improvement of design
> in the corporation. For a management executive to question the
> sanctity of efficiency in modern business takes great courage
> because top management has been taught to literally worship at the
> shrine of efficiency. [Walter Hoving, quoted in Schutte, 1975]

A design overly concerned with efficiency from the very start is
doomed to fail. Although efficiency is a pragmatic concern that
cannot be avoided, it should take close to last place in the array of
design criteria. Efficiency is one of the few attributes that can be
worked in after the other design criteria are satisfied. Probably a
very small minority of system designers hold this opinion. Pity.

One final note on design criteria: innovation and novelty. The
designer still acts subjectively. Until a system is tried in the
field, no one can really assess its success. We all try to insert
some special part of our own feelings, likes, and dislikes into the
systems we design. Novelty for its own sake should be avoided.
Changing the way people do things should be undertaken only with
careful forethought. Remember that people are lazy. They make do.
They form habits and don't like to change what they have learned to be
successful for new methods claimed to be better. Note also:

> Until more research work is undertaken we can do little better than
> follow the advice of Palladio who in the 16th century, wrote:
> "Although variety and things new may please everyone, yet they ought
> not to be done contrary to that which reason dictates." [Black,
> 1975]

6. Human Factors

Psychology and the study of Human Factors can begin to unravel the
mysteries of ease of use by reliably identifying what the user will
generally do and by reliably identifying different classes of users.

The birth of Human Factors as a separate discipline probably dates
from the early 1940s when, during World War II, methodology for
control, instrument, and display design was greatly needed.
Minimizing the effect of fatigue on an operator and designing
equipment to avoid fatigue became a goal. Boredom can resemble
fatigue, decreasing performance and increasing errors. Fatigue and
boredom can be fought by appealing to the user's curiosity: the
natural tendency toward new and different things. Combatting boredom
by abetting curiosity can be achieved easily in a learning situation
through feedback and reinforcement mechanisms.

Research (and inspiration) are needed. I have seen two systems that attempted to provide variance. The first was a system that provided witty remarks at fairly inappropriate times, usually following an error in input: "Goofed again, dummy?" Mechanized repartee, perhaps amusing at first, quickly palls. Repetition leads to frustration and annoyance, especially when the user can't avoid it. The result is the opposite of what was intended. Users, instead of being amused, are infuriated.

Another example is a computer system that kept the operator informed of system activities by a continuous display of messages. Occasionally, a request for action was missed as there was really no motivation for the operators to watch the screen. Even highlighting requests in double-size font didn't help, since they were infrequent and watching the screen was boring. Someone testing a new split-screen technique added a dynamically updated set of statistics to the display: number of jobs run, users active, tapes and disks requested, lines printed, etc. Whenever an operator response was required, the status stopped changing and a reminder was displayed. The dynamic display was so interesting that there was usually someone watching. Few messages were missed thereafter.

Anxiety is a significant contributor to task performance. Extroverts seem to work better under tension; introverts do better without. If performance is graphed against anxiety the curve is an inverted U with poorer performance at both low and high anxiety and better performance in the middle. How can we use this aspect of human behavior in an on-line computer system? Unrelieved tension creates anxiety. Some tension is naturally present since the user is probably anxious to get the job done. The potential for additional tension is always available since slow response time seems an omnipresent flaw in on-line systems. Tension could be decreased by providing bursts of good response, even in a heavily loaded system. Errors can be both a cause and an effect of tension. Tension and the error rate could be reduced by good on-line user assistance.

I do not recommend the blatant manipulation of the user by the computer. Rather, I am suggesting that studies be made to determine whether the known interdependency of anxiety and performance can be used to design systems that minimize needless anxiety while maximizing performance.

7. Psychological testing: some preliminary results

My own Software Research group at Sperry Univac has been doing some research into psychological questions relating to ease of use. To give an idea of the sorts of data that can be obtained, I report here on a few of our experiments. [Schneider and Hirsh-Pasek, 1981]

ABBREVIATION IN LIMITED LEXICONS. Users of computer systems tend to use limited subsets of the command language: 10 to 15 commands.

Given this fact, what strategy for providing keyword abbreviations is best? In a controlled experiment, preliminary results indicate that for forming the abbreviation from the full word, simple truncation (e.g. first 4 letters) is best. For retrieving the full term from the abbreviation, phonic abbreviation (e.g. dcl for declare, xqt for execute) appears optimal. Both are better than the other tested alternatives: a simple vowel drop and minimum to distinguish.

If final results lead to different recommendations for generation and for retrieval, designers will have a difficult task when choosing an abbreviation convention. An obvious suggestion is that systems generate phonic abbreviations, but accept truncation as well.

LINE NUMBERING STRATEGIES. In response to a request from a design group, Schneider and Hirsh-Pasek tested two alternatives for extendable text line numbering: fractional (nnnnn.dddddd...) and hierarchical (aaa.bbb.ccc. ...).

Subjects were tested for rapidity and accuracy of line insertion and new number creation. Preliminary results show that for searching, the fractional convention is preferred. For insertion, the methods are roughly equivalent. Error rate is the same for both. However, fractional seems to require fewer keystrokes than hierarchical.

DELIMITER CHOICES IN COMMAND SYNTAX. What cognitive functions are involved in processing commands? Given that most command structures have a verb followed by a series of arguments and options, there are many variations. Should arguments and options be intermixed or separate? How do you identify and punctuate them? For example, is LIST=NO preferred to NOLIST as the converse of LIST?

No results are yet available, but we have already gained insight into the problems of measuring cognition (and the problems of designing complex experiments). It appears that two levels of delimiter (one to separate groups, another to separate items in the groups) is best.

Other studies are planned. The most encouraging aspect of the work goes beyond the actual results. Development groups becoming interested in the project are suggesting new areas for tests. We may not be able to guarantee ease of use. We can, however, reduce error and user fatigue and boredom. We can provide a basis for rational choice.

7. User levels

Users are not all alike. Schneider and Hirsh-Pasek have been working on a classification of users and have proposed this hierarchy:

```
                                                 Expert
                                      Advanced/
                          Intermediate/
                  Novice/
          Parrot/
```

The Parrot memorizes some command sequences and uses them exclusively.
The Novice has just begun to use the computer or is an infrequent
user. The Intermediate understands function but probably has small
grasp of the interactions of the parts of the system. The Advanced
user fully understands the function and the command language. The
Expert extends the system. Evolution from stage to stage depends
mostly upon frequency of use and user interest in learning more.
Progress is as much a function of task and intelligence as of
motivation.

Users refuse to sit still and be classified. The draft of this essay
was created by a text formatter implemented in PL/I on the UNIVAC
1100. I am an expert in PL/I, an advanced user of the formatter, and
an intermediate user of the 1100 command language. This creates an
asymmetry as I try to make changes and improvements to the formatter.
Although I can create the appropriate PL/I code fairly easily, I
usually cannot install the changes without help from a systems expert.

It is difficult to design a system to satisfy both novice and advanced
user. Many have tried, few have succeeded.

9. Conclusion

A study of the psychological foundations of human factors will provide
an excellent perspective for the system designer. Still, there is
much to be done in the way of research into the ways that people and
computers can talk to each other.

English is not yet the answer. Although great strides have been made
recently in natural language interaction, too much work still remains.
It is premature to assume that JCL will be replaced by English. So
far, it seems that natural language is good for asking questions of
the computer. Giving commands in English is still far in the future.

Probably the most useful attitude for the designer to take is that of
a sceptic. All design decisions should be questioned and justified.
Nothing can be taken for granted. "Because we've always done it that
way" is no more acceptable a reason for making a change than it is for
avoiding a change. Potential users must be involved in the design
from the beginning. Design each system not as if you were to be the
user, but as if the user is to be your boss.

10. References

Baker, F. T. 1972. Chief programmer team management of production programming. IBM System J. 11,1, 56-73.

Black, Sir Misha. 1955. The designer and manager syndrome. The art of design management, Thomas F. Schutte, ed. New York: Tiffany & Co. pp. 41-57.

Jensen, Kathleen and Niklaus Wirth. 1975. PASCAL user manual and report. New York: Springer Verlag.

Koberg, Don and Jim Bagnall. 1973. The universal traveler. Los Altos CA: Kauffman.

Martin, James. 1973. Design of man-computer dialogues. Englewood Cliffs NJ: Prentice Hall. (See esp. pp. 25-33)

Ornstein, Robert E. 1972. The psychology of consciousness. San Francisco CA: W. H. Freeman and Co.

Schneider, Michael L. and Kathy Hirsh-Pasek. 1981. Unpublished memoranda and drafts of papers to be published.

Schneider, Michael L., Richard L. Wexelblat, and Michael S. Jende. 1980. Designing control languages from the user's perspective. Command language directions, D. Beech, ed. New York: North Holland.

Schutte, Thomas F., ed. 1955. The art of design management. New York: Tiffany & Co.

11. Acknowledgements

Prof. Kathy Hirsh-Pasek and Dr. Michael L. Schneider provided background information on the psychological aspects of Human Factors and generously permitted me to draw from their preliminary research findings. Thanks also to my wife, Geraldine, who helps reduce the obfuscation level of my prose.

# # #

Part 6
Education

Government, Industry, Universities:
a Fractured Triangle

Colin J. Tully

*Lecturer, Department of Computer Science,
University of York, UK*

A bold expansion of university courses in computer science
should be an important component of a national policy for
information technology. There is a notable and growing
shortage of specialist skills in industry, but universities
are in no position to respond to the educational need. An
action programme appropriate to the crisis is proposed.

INTRODUCTION

Before discussing my theme, I want to set it in a context.   The
context is the 1980s and the 1990s, and the process in this country
throughout those decades of adopting, and adapting to, information
technology.

There is no need, at BCS81, to define, explain or defend the term
information technology, nor to spend time depicting how it (IT) may
affect the economic performance of the nation and the lives of individual citizens — our wealth, welfare and well-being.   Probably no two
delegates to this Conference would share the same views on these
matters, yet I dare say we all share the recognition that they are of
critical importance.

We all know that IT will be pervasive, and that how we use it will
influence the cost, efficiency and quality both of products and
production processes, and of manual, clerical, secretarial,
professional, managerial and administrative activities.   The chips
indeed are down: the game is on, and the game will proceed by means of
a multitude of decisions, ranging in scope from the vast to the trivial,
made by cabinets and boards and unions and ordinary men and women.

To come to my theme: it concerns a small subset of the decisions that
are to be made.   I mean decisions about the role of universities in
educating information technology specialists at a professional level.
These decisions must be taken quickly and must be got right.   At
present, there is little sign that any decisions, even wrong ones, are
to be taken at all.   My purpose is to provide some information on the
matter and to initiate and stimulate argument.

The latter purpose should not prove too difficult.   Universities and
scholarship, teachers and students alike, command at best grudging
respect; and within the computing community there is no shortage of
those who would say that there are ample numbers of computer science
graduates and that they are useless anyway.

If I refer only to universities, it is partly for simplicity and partly
because I know about them best.   But I must stress that much of what I
say applies equally to polytechnics.   I have close contacts with
several computer science departments in polytechnics, and certainly
they do an excellent job both at the professional (degree) level and at
the technician level.   And if the universities have problems, the
polytechnics' may if anything be worse.

For similar reasons I refer only to the discipline of computer science
— which by no means is because I think other disciplines are not
relevant to information technology.   Nevertheless, computer science —
the study of programmable devices and their use — must be regarded as
the central discipline.

A final constraint on my theme is that I refer only to the teaching
work of university computer science departments, not to research.   That
is not to say that there are no problems of making sure that enough
research of the right kind is carried out, and that its results are

effectively transferred to industry and government; but I think these problems are less severe, better understood and more likely to be solved than those to do with teaching. Nevertheless I am uncomfortably aware that many academics regard the inseparability of teaching and research as an article of faith, and that I may appear to be wrenching siamese twins apart.

To refer globally, as I do in the title and shall subsequently in the paper, to government and industry is shamefully to oversimplify. For instance, the word industry conceals the fundamental difference between users and suppliers of information technology, and the special roles of the City and the media. Government has a user role as well as its role of policy-making and funding with which I am chiefly concerned. Both industry and government are involved in education, as well as the universities. I have omitted any mention of professional bodies. I hope, in the interests of brevity, these oversimplifications will be forgiven.

ANALYSIS OF FAILURE

a) Government

Government is responsible for both information technology policy and education policy.

The appointment of a Minister of State at the Department of Industry with responsibility for information technology was a very big step forward, especially since the present Minister argued strongly before his appointment that a national strategy in this field was imperative. This brings to an end the lamentable state of affairs that the UK government directed its attention only to the protection of the domestic hardware industry and to computer use throughout the civil service, and (in contrast to our major competitors) had no policy concerning the effective use of computers in industry.

We must, however, regret (a) that the Minister has other responsibilities than information technology (as if that were not enough), (b) that it is not at all clear what power, if any, he has to influence and coordinate policy in other departments, such as the DES, where that may impinge on information technology.

Kenneth Baker has announced that he sees his role as being both missionary and salesman, which smacks rather too much of talking and rather too little of getting things done. So far as managing UK Limited goes, the government is happy tampering with enterprises according to the prevailing political dogma, but it is all too bashful about exercising enterprise itself in those areas where it alone can.

Cutting excessive expenditure on current account is one thing; failure to make necessary investment expenditure is quite another, and something for which government often self-righteously rebukes industry. As the Director of the NCC, David Fairbairn, wrote recently: there is "a critical quantum of support and assistance for which a national response is required. It will be little short of a tragedy if the United Kingdom, alone amongst the nations which have significant computing industries, fails to provide that vital element" [1]. Information technology is an area where energetic government entrepreneurship, involving money, is necessary.

It is a cliché to say that education is an investment for the country's future; but it is none the less true, and it is an investment that must largely be determined and funded by government. As in all state enterprises, there is a lot of waste in education, and it is right that it should bear its part of the cuts. Cutting costs is not incompatible with intelligent investment, however; and rapid technological change implies adaptation in education, which implies resources.

It could be said that talk of education as an investment is not just a cliché, it is little more than empty words: what is the return on that investment? I should happily accept that objection if it implied the need for greater control over educational innovation and its effects.

How about the intersection of these two areas of government responsibility — information technology and education? Sir Peter Carey, of the DoI, has reportedly referred to the "large-scale programme" being mounted, and had apparently in mind the MAP and micros in schools schemes. Perhaps these seem large-scale to our civil servants; but they seem chicken-feed in comparison to the scale of the problem. Furthermore, they totally ignore industry's requirements for people whose education covers a range of systems skills and is sound enough to enable them to adapt successfully to technological change over the next ten to twenty years.

The French understand this. The Prime Minister, Raymond Barre, commissioned a report on "La formation des specialistes informaticiens". Its author, Jacques Tebeka, subtitled it "La revolution informatique ne peut s'accomplir sans informaticiens" [2].

Amongst the welter of reports produced by or for government, unions, etc., the majority make no mention of this issue. Even the notable exceptions give it little emphasis.

The study carried out by the Science Policy Research Unit, Sussex University, for the DoI's CSERB (Computers, Systems and Electronics Requirements Board), authored by Iann Barron and Ray Curnow, said: "A programme is required to generate relevant degree courses in universities .... Such a programme must be regarded as urgent" [3].

The Cabinet Office's ACARD (Advisory Council for Applied Research and Development) has referred to the problem in two reports, on Technological change and on Information technology. It said: "Government cannot afford to delay in making resources available to produce more graduates with the skills required to take advantage of the market opportunities we foresee" [4]. "The benefit that the United Kingdom derives from IT in the coming decade will depend more on education, training, work attitudes, the investment climate and regulatory systems .... than on advances in technical knowledge." "Government, its agencies concerned with training, and educational bodies at all levels, should examine the provision of education and training courses in IT-related subjects" [5].

The study carried out by the Institute of Manpower Studies, Sussex University, for NEDO's Electronic Computers Sector Working Party, said: "We are .... worried by the poor supply of higher degrees in .... system-related disciplines. The seed-corn for their expansion in universities and polytechnics .... would seem to be excessively small. What must be guarded against absolutely is the consideration of any short-term cuts in these activities" [6].

Government has resolutely ignored this advice. Perhaps that is not surprising, since to accept it would involve innovatory planning and energetic execution, whereas government has recently seemed intent only on economics and reacting to immediate and unavoidable problems.

b) Industry

Industry, if it is to make effective use of IT, needs skilled manpower (at professional and technician levels) and well-informed management (able to make good decisions).

The responsibility for meeting this need lies both with educational institutions in the public sector (with which this paper is concerned) and with bodies involved in industrial training (with which this paper is not concerned). The need is certainly immediate: the Institute of Manpower Studies report [6], referred to above, provides a much-needed authoritative estimate of shortfall. But the need is also long-term: the IMS report predicts that things will get worse, not better, in the absence of remedial measures. The educational sector cannot do much to meet immediate needs, because by its very nature it has slow response times; but if the gap between manpower supply and demand is not to increase, and is even to be reduced throughout this decade, then the role of universities in particular cannot be ignored.

The IMS report is fairly pessimistic about this. The problem of serious shortages of engineering/systems/software skills "is unlikely to be fully resolved in this century. Because of inherited attitudes (to engineering), a persistent national 'generalist' culture disruption in the schools system, and future demographic trends, the opportunity has passed. It is already too late, and — as Finniston implies — the problem is so great that it is impossible to over-react" [6].

It is worth summarising some of the other points made in this very important report.

● Shortages of skilled manpower are a major constraint on the spread of IT.

● Insofar as IT has job-creating potential, these shortages will reduce the rate at which unemployment levels can be reduced.

● There is some evidence that employers are guilty of "educational overkill" — that is, seeking qualifications that are higher than is necessary for given positions.

(Comment: this may account for a good deal of the mutual
dissatisfaction between employers and computer science graduates.
However, some employers know quite well what they are doing: the
initial period as a humble programmer is merely an apprenticeship,
and they are interested in graduates' long-term potential.
Other employers, who know less well what they are doing, are
certainly guilty of wasting talent which could be better used
elsewhere.)

●   The report (probably rightly) doubts whether developments in
     systems and software methods will increase the productivity of
     skilled manpower sufficiently to have a significant impact on the
     gap between supply and demand in the foreseeable future.

     (Comment: my own view is that, even if progress is faster than
     we anticipate at present, and software tools do serve to improve
     productivity, they will also serve to increase the level of skills
     which will be needed.)

●   The report estimates current levels of manpower, current short-
     falls, and levels and shortfalls to 1985.

     (Comment: by necessity it concentrates on the traditional jobs
     in the supplier and user sectors — those largely associated with
     data processing. It almost certainly fails to account for large
     and diverse requirements for special skills as IT spreads through-
     out the economy.)

So far we have discussed the problem of advanced IT-related skills.
What about the problem of well-informed management?   Management will
less and less be able to keep IT at arm's length.   Decisions about IT
in products and processes will be unavoidable; and ability to discuss
information systems will become as essential as ability to read a
balance sheet or draw up a budget.   We are talking about something
more far-reaching than merely using an electronic office terminal —
however important that step may be in weaning managers toward IT.

Again, the educational and training need is both immediate and long-
term.   Immediately, well-designed appreciation courses, in sufficient
volume, could have a most productive effect (provided managers
attended them).

For the long-term, in which universities have a role to play, four
needs may be identified.   (1) There is a need for all those leaving
the educational system, at whatever level, to have some basic understanding of IT and its uses.   The current effort in schools in this
direction is inadequate, and in universities is non-existent.
(2) University courses in management (undergraduate and graduate)
should include a significant amount of mandatory material on IT and
should also include further optional material.   (3) The throughput of
computer science and other IT-related courses should be sufficient to
enable graduates to take non-IT-specialist jobs (without thereby
leaving specialist posts unfilled).   (4) The resources for teaching
information systems as a major variant of computer science should be
increased from their present paltry level.

Although the Finniston Report [7] was directed specifically toward the
problems of the formation of engineers in manufacturing industry, a
great deal of its analysis is directly applicable to the field of IT
— in particular, its discussion of the lack of commitment by British
industry to education and training.   There is, of course, one big
difference between the position as described by Finniston and our own:
in traditional engineering there are established professional bodies,
which is hardly so (*pace* the organisers of this Conference) in our own
case.   It is hard to say which side is better off.   Certainly the
professional bodies in engineering have acted as a deterrent to the
implementation of Finniston.   On the other hand, they certainly perform an important function in influencing university courses and in
organising subsequent training in industry.

I cannot suppress the comment that I find two things astonishing about
the BCS: its apathy toward Finniston, and its inertia in the face of
the educational and training problem which this paper discusses.

We are in recession and industry is under pressure.   Even when that
has not been the case, industry has never shown much enthusiasm for
expenditure on education and training — like government, it regards
them as a cost rather than as an investment.   Industry will come
under more pressure, however — recession or no recession — the longer
it delays getting to grips with IT and with the manpower shortages that
are slowing down the process of innovation.   Some firms at the leading
edge recognise this, and they are beginning to make approaches to
universities.   How well-prepared are the universities to respond?

c)   Universities

In brief, British universities have rather less than 300,000 students
and rather more than 30,000 academic staff — a ratio of less than
10:1 across all subjects.   Their annual budget is about £1 billion.

The 1960s saw considerable growth.   Some people, looking back across
student unrest and The History Man, would say that the growth was too
great.   I would rather say that, in the best tradition of academic
autonomy in this country, it was uncontrolled.   An unique opportunity
to shift the balance in higher education toward science, engineering,
technology and management, to create prestige institutions in these
fields such as exist abroad, and to adopt new patterns of teaching and
links with industry — this opportunity was lost.   Academics were
allowed to follow their own predilections, and as a result the system
grew but it changed little.

Even after that growth, it should be noted, we send a smaller proportion
of our school-leavers to university, and for a shorter period, than our
main competitors.

Funds for university teaching come mostly from the University Grants
Committee (UGC), a body interposed between the DES and the universities
in order to preserve the latter's autonomy.   The UGC receives a block
sum from government, which it distributes between universities;   each
university in turn receives a block sum, which in general it is free to

spend as it will.   With this system, the UGC is by no means devoid of
influence on the direction of individual universities;   but its
influence is discreet and indirect.

It is not clear how the universities will accomplish the necessary cuts
over the next few years.   Perhaps 3,000 teaching posts might need to
go — equivalent to closing several universities.   If teaching
standards are preserved, and if there is no increase in "productivity"
(which is hard to achieve in the short-term and without investment),
then student numbers must fall, several years before the bulge has
finally passed through the universities.

Let us now turn to the position of computer science in these circumstances.

Computer science is taught in most universities.   For historical
reasons which it is unnecessary to elaborate, the large majority of
departments are small, with ten or fewer teaching staff.   It is not
possible to give accurate numbers of students and staff, because (a)
official statistics generally do not recognise computer science as a
separate subject, (b) in some universities the teaching staff are
members of a larger department, (c) many students read computer science
in combination with another subject.   There are two things that can
safely be said, however, which will give some indication of how things
are.

First, computer science (together with history) has the eighth largest
number of applicants for entry to university next October.   It follows
medicine;   law;   electrical, civil and mechanical engineering;
English;   and business and management studies.   It is ahead of (for
instance) mathematics, economics, each of the natural sciences,
psychology, accountancy and French.   Two facts I am fairly sure of:
there are about 900 history teachers in universities, and there are
fewer than 400 computer science teachers.   That is a rough indication
that, if we are to cope with the numbers applying, we need to double
the number of teachers.

Second, I have already mentioned that the student-staff ratio is
generally around 10:1.   In the department in which I teach, it is at
present worse than 16:1, and it will certainly become worse still
unless either we take draconian measures to cut our intake or we
succeed in attracting enough private funding to support one or more new
posts.   I believe that the position is similar in other departments
which are suffering for having designed successful courses which attract
students and match the needs of industry.   Now 16:1 is worse than the
pupil:teacher ratio in Scottish secondary schools and approaching the
English ratio.   Other departments at York (like sociology) have ratios
around 9:1.   A polytechnic was recently reported as having a ratio in
sociology (should polytechnics be teaching sociology?) of 4:1.

May I indulge myself for a moment?   The head of my department is
responsible not only for teaching and research but also for the
provision of a computer service for the whole university: his is not,
therefore, a full-time teaching/research role.   Leaving the service
function aside, however, there are in the department seven teaching

staff and seven full-time research staff (funded by the Science Research Council and working on real-time language projects). The professor and these fourteen people are served by four technicians and one-and-a-half secretaries; as a result, for instance, almost everyone does almost all their own typing. The teaching staff (seven plus the part-time professor) are responsible for over 150 under-graduates (some single-subject, some in combination with other subjects), 14 full-time and 5 part-time research students. All teaching staff are required by contract to carry out research. There is a very big administrative load, spread across the few teaching staff, of processing applications, interviewing applicants, curriculum development (a continuous process in computer science), setting and marking examinations and continuous assessments, serving as external examiners, serving on committees, timetabling, etc. Teaching is done not only through lectures but in practicals, small-group tutorials, individual project supervision, etc.

If there is an excuse for that burst of self-indulgence, it is to combat the notion that all academics are pampered, idle and low in productivity, and (more specifically) to support the claim that computer science needs special treatment.

It needs specially favourable student-staff ratios, because it is a rapidly changing subject (probably more rapidly changing than any other) and because (as in other branches of engineering and technology) industrial contact is essential.

The UGC has persistently regarded computer science as a branch of mathematics. This has meant that, as the subject developed, universities tended to provide resources to computer science at roughly the same level as to mathematics — meaning no laboratories, no technicians, departmental grant per student at a fraction of the amount for the natural sciences and engineering, and so on. The fact that the UGC is currently involved in a cautious reappraisal of its position, is of little use. It is too late: universities will not be able to increase the resources for computer science by the large amounts necessary, *unless* the UGC departs from its almost unvarying practice and earmarks funds for the purpose.

A comment is necessary on the excellent provision of computing facilities in British universities that has been achieved by the Computer Board. These facilities are intended to serve the whole academic community in any university (like the library or any other central service). The Computer Board has so far been specific in limiting their use, for instance, for specialist teaching and research in computer science. Computer science departments, in other words, do not have a kind of hidden subsidy through the provision of the Computer Board: computing power for teaching, quite rightly, is regarded as something which must largely be provided for out of departmental allocations.

Another misconception must be removed. "If you want more money", people say, "get out into the market place and earn it". There are two things wrong with that argument. The resources of time and money

are not there to meet the set-up costs of such an operation.   Even if
they were, it would be madness to try to support the long-term activity
of teaching undergraduate and graduate students with essentially casual
income, subject to the changing conditions of the market place.

The picture, then, is of a rather large number of rather small departments, all under-provisioned, some groaning under the strain of massive
excess demand.   The total national resource is deficient by 400 - 500
teachers, who would be able to increase throughput by about 1500
graduates per year.   Reading the IMS report gives no cause to worry
that such a number would be in any way excessive.

David Butler was recently reported as calling for the foundation of a
"Systems University".   (In a similar vein, Barron and Curnow [3]
proposed an Institute for Information Technology, though its
objectives were limited to research and development.)   While I believe
these monolithic proposals are wrong, Butler is certainly right in his
assessment of the scale of the problem, which is equivalent to the need
for a medium-size university dedicated to teaching and research in
information technology.

DESIGN FOR SUCCESS

The problem analysis has been lengthy.   The proposals for a solution
will be shorter, and can in fact by summed up in one sentence.

A small number of departments (university or polytechnic) should be
selected for rapid expansion, to offer courses for at least one thousand
students a year in total, funded by earmarked grants, set up and run in
full collaboration with industry.

May I elaborate that proposal with the following points.

1)   The proposal seems to be preferable to David Butler's notion of a
      single giant new institution.   The French may go in for such
      approaches: we, it seems, do not — perhaps for good reasons.
      Courses in six to ten different departments would give competition,
      variety, and the chance for unsuccessful ventures to be wound up
      and replaced elsewhere.

2)   The initiative should come from the UGC — but the UGC should
      (indeed must) take the opportunity to operate in a manner to which
      it is unaccustomed.   It should appoint a small group of people
      from the academic and industrial worlds, who (a) know a great deal
      about information technology, (b) are energetic and used to getting
      results.   This group should be seconded full-time, with full
      support, to the task of preparing a specification of requirements
      for courses in information technology, at undergraduate and
      graduate levels, which would be both of high academic quality and
      of manifest value to employers.

3)   The selection of departments to run courses should be made by
      inviting tenders against the specification of requirements.
      (This is similar to the process used for awarding research grants.)

In their tenders departments should be required to give an estimate of costs.

4) Where a contract was awarded, it would be supported by directly earmarked funding.

5) The progress of the whole scheme, after award of contracts, should be monitored by a small part-time standing committee of the UGC, which should include high-level representation from industry. A management committee, including external academics and industrial representatives, should be responsible for the general direction of each course.

6) While an individual department would undertake primary responsibility for each course, it would be highly desirable for there to be collaboration between different departments in planning and running it. Such collaboration could be with departments of the same discipline elsewhere, or with departments of other disciplines in the same university or elsewhere. Overseas collaboration should not be excluded. Obvious types of collaboration would be between computer science and electronics, or between computer science and management science in the field of information systems studies.

7) Government involvement, from the DES or the DoI or both, should be minimal. It should lay down broad policy guidelines, exercise broad control — and provide the money. The return on its investment should be safeguarded by building in genuine and effective participation by industry.

8) In addition to the consultative role already proposed, industry should give support through sponsorships, sandwich places, provision of project work, staff exchanges or joint appointments.

Professor John Brown (Department of Electrical Engineering, Imperial College) has put the point well. "The academic sector requires authoritative advice on the nature and content of the courses needed to make students fully alive to everything that the term productivity denotes. It also requires expert practitioners to teach these subjects, in a way which leaves students in no doubt of their importance. Both tasks, provision of advice and participation in teaching, require a tighter coupling between industry and education than exists at present in our engineering colleges. Such coupling can, I believe, only be achieved by a very large increase in appointments shared equally between a teaching institution and an engineering organisation. There are plenty of precedents for such an arrangment — it is commonplace in many European countries — and it applies in the UK for other professions, notably medicine, but also architecture, accountancy and law." [8]

9) Industry, perhaps through the CBI, might set up a body with the objectives of encouraging and supporting IT education. The Foundation for Management Education could be a model for this.

10) Government could add to its involvement by offering generous tax incentives to firms which give financial support to IT education.

Do all the responsibilities fall on industry and government? What about universities? Our task is to sell such an idea to academic boards of somewhat conservative bent, to maintain academic standards against some of the wilder suggestions likely to come from industry, AND to get on and deliver the goods.

CONCLUSION

Earlier in this paper I allowed myself to whine about some of the difficulties facing the department in which I work. I should like now to look on the brighter side.

We enjoy tremendous demand for entry to our courses — nearly twenty applicants for each place. (On the gloomy side, we have to turn away many excellent candidates.) Those we accept are extremely good students, and have often, incidentally, done most impressive work at school in electronics or with micros. Our graduates are in considerable demand from employers. We have received more than £½ million in research grants over the last few years. We have frequent approaches from industry, enquiring about software products, seeking advice or expressing interest in development contracts; we are usually unable to give a positive response. Members of the department are active in various national and international organisations. We are energetically pursuing ideas for a new industrially-sponsored course and for the setting up of a financially self--supporting institute to handle all industrial liaison activities.

That is not a picture of a privileged group of dons, pursuing ivory-tower research, unaware and uncaring of the realities and needs of the user community. It is a picture of a department which is hampered by lack of resources of all kinds from fully carrying out the function it believes it should be serving.

Also, of course, it is not a picture of an unique department. Much the same could be said about a number of other computer science departments.

I believe that one of the reasons for the success of the USA in computing has been the productive relationships that have existed between government, industry and universities. That triangle in Britain is a fractured one. I believe that many in industry and many in universities wish to see it repaired.

The leadership, however, must come from government.

REFERENCES

[1] FAIRBAIRN (David), "Orchestrating computing" in Computer Management (Nov 1980)

[2] TEBEKA (Jacques), La formation des specialistes informaticiens,
         typescript report to the Prime Minister of France (Mar 1980)

[3] BARRON (Iain) and Ray CURNOW, The future with microelectronics,
         Open University Press (1979)

[4] ACARD, Technological change: threats and opportunities for
         the United Kingdom, HMSO (1980)

[5] ACARD, Information technology, HMSO (1980)

[6] ELECTRONIC COMPUTERS SECTOR WORKING PARTY OF THE NATIONAL
     ECONOMIC DEVELOPMENT OFFICE, Computer manpower in the 80s: the
         supply and demand for computer related manpower to 1985,
         HMSO (1980)

[7] COMMITTEE OF INQUIRY INTO THE ENGINEERING PROFESSION, Engineering
         our future, HMSO (1980)

[8] BROWN (John), "Engineering courses in the 1980s" in Electronics
         and power (Jan 1980)

The Importance of Educational Computing Resources for Individuals, Local Communities and Society

Christine Disney

Consultant, F International Limited, UK

During the last ten years, the provision of educational computing resources has been ignored in some cases, obtained limited funding in others and only been adequately financed where training for formal computing qualifications necessitated the provision of appropriate resources. Thus developments have varied according to geographical and institutional location and levels of individual expertise and personal motivation, rather than from any National Objective or need to train and educate people to live with future technology.

With the impact of micro-electronics during the last few years, the Government has focussed attention upon two areas. First the Department of Industry Microprocessor Applications Project in 1978 and more recently the Department of Education Micro-electronics Education Programme.

Although this funding will provide the stimulus for new developments, it will not provide a complete solution. It will remain the responsibility of all professional computer staff to inform and assist with increasing general public awareness about computers, the new technology and its implications.

Reminiscences

The reminiscences of some people are unfortunately the current
experience of many new computer users today whether education,
commerce or industry orientated.   The availability of new cheaper
hardware and communication techniques has quickly brought more
flexible processing power without the chance to build up
administration, operational and software expertise.   To help fill
this information and skills void, the educational system will need
to introduce more computers and train more teachers in order to
provide effective education for the general public and future
generations of school children.

A brief look at the background to the current situation will help
to emphasize the requirements for the successful development of
comprehensive facilities.

Stumbling through the 1970's

The introduction and expansion of educational computer resources on
a national basis has not depended upon need but upon apparently
random arrangements for funding and availability of manpower and
equipment.

The Universities, providing learning resources for a large
community, have been able to finance central computing power for
many years although primarily as an administration and research
facility.   Most institutions now have a central mainframe computer
complex with microcomputers sited in specific research areas e.g.
high energy physics, astronomy, electronic measurement and control,
statistical laboratories, and an increasing number of micro-based
instruments and microcomputers as calculational aids.

Meanwhile, amongst the Polytechnics, a growth of computer science
undergraduate courses during the 1970's ensured that certain
Polytechnic institutions were able to install comprehensive student
computer services and encourage all students and academic staff to
use the computer as a teaching resource.   Gradually as the hardware
became cheaper and demand for computer qualifications increased,
more institutions installed or extended facilities to satisfy CNAA
examination requirements.

During this phase the Department of Education and Science provided
advice and helped to influence decisions by ensuring that the large
capital outlay required for new computer hardware would be
subsequently supported by appropriate levels of professional staff.
In this way hardware could be utilised for the maximum community
benefit with encouragement to provide a service for all academic
departments/schools of study and external institutions such as local
colleges and secondary schools.   Thus provisioning generally moved

away from the experimental computer science/technology tool
supporting specific courses, to a central provision of hardware and
support staff for general use.

In the secondary education sector there were isolated individuals
battling with donated obsolete equipment and geographical pockets of
development based around those Local Education Authorities with the
foresight to provide funding, advice and staff during the 1970's.
Many different ways of administering these resources were found.
In particular processing facilities could be at the Local Authority
computer installation Polytechnic/University site or from Open
University services.   Similarly support services and advice could
be non-existent, available from the hardware site and/or
supplemented by special units with responsibilities for advising
and developing computer skills in computer science and across the
curriculum.   Initially these facilities were based upon data
preparation and conventional remote batch processing but gradually
on-line terminals became available and 'live' demonstrations with
interactive student work could be encouraged.   Now the microcomputer
provides a powerful local resource with access to more comprehensive
facilities (including software libraries) from terminal links into a
central mainframe.

The Local Authorities and schools which have followed this
development pattern over the last five to ten years have the
advantage of:-

1. Organised links between resources and individuals.

2. Administration procedures which have evolved to serve the
    variety of different remote sites.

3. Experience in assessing the value and potential of central
    facilities which can house expensive equipment, hardware/
    software expertise and advisory services.

4. Providing policy guidance for microcomputer developments which
    can benefit from links to a mainframe service and access to
    central library facilities for distribution of software.

So until the late 1970's, the range of computing facilities depended
upon the following historical developments:-

The University sector provided mainframe services for
predominantly research facilities.

The Polytechnics and colleges provided a greater emphasis on
undergraduate facilities with computing centres to support
computer science courses and a range of educational aids for other
disciplines.

The secondary school sector relied upon mixed services from local
authority, local college or independent installations and primary
school developments were virtually non-existent.

Changes of Emphasis

It would be wrong to assume that developments have been at a regular
steady pace.   During the mid 1970's the government funded National
Development Programme for Computer Assisted Learning (NDPCAL) gave a
much needed boost to the use of interactive terminal work and the
application of computers as a learning resource across the
curriculum.   Many University departments participated in the
Programme and provided some of the first resources for undergraduate
work in the University sector.   Often the learning curve on these
projects was slow and at least one year was spent by project staff
becoming familiar with hardware and software aspects of their
proposed computer assisted learning work.   However those staff
remaining within the educational sector did provide a valuable
nucleus of expertise for subsequent development work.   It is still
true that the major shortage is in qualified, educationally
experienced staff.

The Programme could have extended its influence if the funded
projects had spread their ideas from the original participating
departments and project centres to foster collaboration across
disciplines and between different institutions during the post
NDPCAL years.   However it is the chip revolution and availability
of cheap hardware which is influencing and motivating developments
now and it is to be hoped that Government funds will help to make
the initial contact and familiarisation phase more rapid and less
isolated.

The organisations and institutions who are best able to meet the
challenge of cheap hardware are those who have attempted to provide
comprehensive hardware, software, advisory and programming services
to a variety of users.   Although the provision of the 'right'
hardware has been fundamental, it was the ancillary services which
enabled the varied user populations to succeed in new activities.

In particular, lessons from the past include:-

1.   An installation should provide a centre for technical
     excellence and a community focal point for:-

     1.1   general computer awareness e.g. guided tours,
           demonstrations, open days,

     1.2   technical seminars and advisory services for local and
           remote users,

     1.3   analysis and programming facilities,

     1.4   systems support to tailor conventional operating
           systems for specific educational use and maintain new
           systems, languages and special packages for different
           teaching commitments.

2. The computer should be a general resource, not specifically allocated to one teaching discipline.

3. There should be user-group participation in the provision of facilities.

4. The professional computing staff should be encouraged to participate in educational activities and attend working parties for developing computer materials for teaching.

In the future the hardware will be a mixture of isolated microcomputers, network links, minicomputers and mainframe equipment but the need for a variety of technical expertise will remain and it will not be practical to have the full range of skills at each computer site i.e. in each school or college department.

Impact of the Chip

The all pervading influence of microtechnology will affect the daily activities of the total population and it is vital that the next generation of the working population understand the implications of the technology and have a chance to use and evaluate different aspects in the course of normal schooling.   Apart from providing a general awareness from as young an age as possible it would be a pity not to exploit the versatility and educational opportunities now available with microcomputers.   This would include student motivation, presentation of new materials via simulation modelling and games, remedial exercises and automation of selected administration procedures as well as training people to work with computers and introducing keyboard, visual layout, programming and analysis skills.   (See Appendix C)

So the wider use and provision of computers is vital to the education process.   Various aspects are common to all age groups and these will be considered in the context of equipment and staff/student involvement.

It is accepted that expensive resources, whether equipment or specially trained personnel, should be shared.   Thus a large comprehensive school can afford a modern well equipped science laboratory whereas a smaller educational unit would not necessarily be able to provide a complete range of aids.   Similarly the most successful developments in general computing resources occurred where funding was able to supply substantial shared computing power and, more importantly, enough trained staff to advise and help individuals, schools or departments.

Although the need for large amounts of money to finance local processing power via terminal links is diminishing, it is essential that the organisation and support services available under the central facility system are maintained and expanded to help the increasing numbers of new users.

For several years, the Association of Computer Users in Higher and
Further Education (ACUCHE) has helped to provide a national forum
for exchange of information, growth of self-help policies and
specialist skills, and software development in several disciplines
for computer assisted learning.   At school level some authorities
have appointed advisors with responsibility for purchasing policy,
teacher training and student development via examinable courses or
extra mural activities.   In other parts of the country an
individual school or teacher must develop their own abilities and
class contact with a computer as best they can without formal
guidance.   So mutual help and co-operation on a National basis is
vital to the efforts of each individual teacher.

Fortunately for the school user population, it is now clear that the
£9million Micro-electronic Education Programme will primarily
support about 14 regional facilities covering centres for
information, in-service training and curriculum development.   In
some cases the regional activities will be based on existing work
but the new centres will help to distribute and co-ordinate the
currently active areas with the multitude of new users and their
efforts to fill the knowledge, software, experience gap.   Although
the ME Programme is directed towards school age groups, hopefully
some of the new centres will be based or linked to the further
education sector.

Both would benefit from collaborative projects and when formal
government funding is removed there could be a more co-operative
attitude towards maintaining the services from a combination of
Local Authority, College, Polytechnic and University resources.

Hardware Dilemma

The Micro-electronic Education Programme will not be providing much,
if any, hardware and therefore any hardware policy will remain with
individuals.   There is always debate over this controversial topic
and although there is not a single correct view it is important for
groups, authorities, colleges etc. to develop a hardware policy for
the good of the local community rather than leave the hardware
decision to the end user.   The following paragraphs outline some of
the factors affecting hardware provisioning.

The more established organisations provide a range of facilities
such as batch processing, on-line access to a large mainframe
computer and local hands-on experience via microcomputers which can
act as remote terminals.   Large numbers of student jobs whether
program development or application packages can best be served by
data preparation and rapid turnround batch processing.   This has
the advantage of removing initial major keyboard input, leaving the
student free to study the implications of the work and later perform
on-line editing for program development.   Similarly package work

involving large amounts of computation with minimal interaction would waste valuable on-line facilities and are best processed as background or batch jobs.   The value of on-line facilities to a large processor is usually in terms of variety of computer languages, access to large application packages and increased file storage. In particular this latter aspect can enable large quantities of teaching material to be stored for efficient down loading to a microcomputer for class use as required.

As more microcomputer hardware is installed and teachers are trained in the use of a computer laboratory the emphasis will change to individual student use of a stand alone microcomputer or a network of computers to provide a system controlled by the teacher in the manner of a language laboratory.   However for training students in the use of large mainframe computer systems there is no substitute for on-line access to a similar hardware system.

For those parts of the country without access to central mainframe facilities, national developments for Prestel and software distribution via television networks (telesoftware) will help to provide co-ordinating material although there is likely to be incompatibility between software and local hardware.   And so we arrive at the basic argument for a hardware policy..........For the forseeable future there will be deficiences and non-standardisation of operating systems and language compilers/interpreters such that without a co-ordinated hardware policy too limited staff resources will be spending valuable time amending and adjusting software for their computers instead of creating new materials.   Similarly the justification of a single expensive, more advanced microcomputer system with terminal capabilities is appropriate for those users with previous computer experience whereas several cheaper systems may be a better buy for new users to gain experience.

The most important aspect of any hardware policy will be its group-help potential but the final decision will depend upon all the following criteria:-

1. Available money

2. Educational objectives

   2.1 Support for CSE, O Level, A Level qualifications

   2.2 Student awareness

   2.3 School/Department administration

   2.4 Computer managed learning

   2.5 Computer assisted learning

   2.6 Remedial Aids

3. Staff experience

4. Availability of software

5. Organisational arrangements for using the hardware

6. Local computer experience

> 6.1 Other schools/departmental use
>
> 6.2 Resources from other institutions, local authorities, colleges

7. National user experience.

Teaching Impact

Much hardware in the school sector is being financed by parent/
teacher organisations and provided advice and assistance is
available from a central resource (Information Centre, College,
Polytechnic, University), school staff members should be able to
start immediately with computer awareness. This is met by
introducing the equipment and demonstrations preferably including
student interaction with package programs of either educational
subject relevance or general information manipulation.
Unfortunately, in these days of educational cutbacks, a tremendous
strain is placed upon one or two individuals who 'take charge' of
computing facilities. This means that apart from normal teaching
commitments the equipment needs organising, schedules for use need
specifying and individual training is required in the new hardware
and aspects of programming. If there was a good supply of
educational packages, an immediate impact in the classroom would be
possible whilst staff coped with retraining and possibly building up
to provision of examinable computer science subjects. However
most staff are enthusiastic and often spend many hours of their own
time in learning to program the computer, often believing that this
new tool cannot be used without a knowledge of programming skills.
It is to be hoped that the training aspects of the Micro-electronic
Education Programme will help to ensure that this familiarity phase
is eased and that a teacher can use a microprocessor more
effectively, sooner. It is inevitable that specialist training
will centre around the equipment and programming techniques at the
moment; but ultimately it is important to provide the subject
teacher with confidence to use the equipment in a classroom
situation. They should be able to cope with package use and the
implications of the tool for demonstrations, individual student use
and specially its remedial powers. If teachers of any subject do
not become confident in the use of the technology they will not use
it in the classroom despite the beneficial effect this could have
upon a group of students or any individual. Generally this
requires positive support from the Head Teacher/Head of Department
who must provide and demonstrate enthusiasm and leadership to
encourage a build up of familiarity and expertise amongst all the
teaching staff. This includes good interstaff relationships,
appropriate in-service training and promotion of extra curricula

activities e.g. hobby clubs, research projects.   However a lot more
material will need developing before the teacher will be able to
draw from a library of packages for a specific topic.

Student Involvement

As is usual with new concepts, children adapt sooner than adults and
often become very proficient with equipment, wanting access at all
available times.   In a college/university environment, facilities
are usually available for longer periods of time during the day and
week than is practical at school.   However, if teachers were to
share computer club evenings with parents or other local computer
people interested in the developments of microcomputers, the
resources could be safely supervised.   It would also provide a
valuable local amenity for the general public and local businessmen
to take an interest in and examine the potential of this powerful
tool.   A number of schools and colleges have provided those kind of
facilities and found a tremendous response and co-operative effort
between all ages in the community.   Until the quantity of suitable
software increases, the power of the computer for all age groups
will be in developing:-

1.   Familiarity, ease of use

2.   Demonstrations of information retrieval and calculational
     powers

3.   Limited hands-on experience

4.   Elementary programming skills

5.   Screen, keyboard, computer interaction.

Eventually, as more hardware is installed and micro-laboratories
and/or terminal classrooms are established with a good supply of
educational software, there will be resources for individuals to
learn about new topics, exercise skills in preparation for
examinations and reinforce traditional teaching and learning methods
via computer managed remedial work.   This provides scope for
extending the bright students and yet still enables the slower
student to gain a minimum level of expertise in specific areas
(e.g. at junior school level work and character manipulation and
elementary number handling.)

Also with established administration packages as an aid to
timetabling, student record keeping and class work statistics, the
teacher can offer more time to a class and provide the valuable
person-to-person contact required at so many different stages.

Into the 21st Century

The one area which can most revolutionise the use of the microcomputer and/or other computer terminal links is software.

Appendix B provides a list of some of the types of software currently
used in the educational system.   Because of the variety of hardware,
operating systems and languages, much of the development to date is
not portable and requires large manpower resources to convert it for
each different set of computer hardware.   Attempts have been made
to set up libraries of information, publish material and standardise
on approaches to subsets of the languages and user interface for
computer assisted learning.   The main problem has been lack of
money which might be partially solved for the school sector by the
Micro-electronics Education Programme.   However if local commercial
interests were to sponsor the development of software on the basis
that material would be freely available to all educational
establishments and helping to train employees of the future, the
financial load could be shared.

Industry is being encouraged to think of technological improvements
to business and certain funding is available from the Department of
Industry Microprocessor Application Project.   But how much better
if industry, education and local community relations could benefit
from joint activities in learning about microprocessors, using them,
providing software expertise/resources in some areas and receiving
help in others.   Many children/students would welcome the change to
work on real projects but the specification process must be provided
first.   A lot of computer professionals are unfamiliar with using
the microcomputer yet could contribute a wealth of experience and
expertise in software skills.   Also it will still be important for
people to understand about mainframe computers and to be reassured
about privacy and the security of large information banks.   Having
used microcontrolled devices or even a small microcomputer will not
have prepared them for the role of data collection and information
processing which will still remain hidden, secretive and therefore
dangerous in some people's view.

Users of computers with the educational resources at their disposal
must provide public confidence over the next few years until the
next generation comes along with its more detailed knowledge about
computers.   If we do not concentrate on educating the public,
children and adults alike, the development of appropriate computer
tools will be handicapped in the future.   The learning process must
encompass the technology as soon as possible.

One of the most exciting new areas of computer use is with primary
and junior school pupils but like other areas it suffers from lack
of software.   Authorities with many years experience of computing
in schools are tending to restrain the primary and junior school
sector from buying hardware until their objectives and suitable
software have been developed more thoroughly.   Despite this
approach a number of experiments are in progress and some teachers
are allowed to bring their own equipment into school for a club-time
session.   The areas with most potential at the moment seem to be

the use of number and spelling work which is able to bring slower
children along through the play/game aspect. Obviously this can be
achieved more cheaply with specific devices such as "Speak and
Spell" or "Little Professor" type toys but these devices do not
have the versatility to deal with different age ranges, difficulty
of questions and flexibility of various exercises.   So the
microcomputer with a range of software can serve more widely varying
abilities.   In some cases using the computer is a good behaviour
reward which has helped mischievous bright youngsters to develop
their skills and eventually gain responsibility for helping others.
In other cases where reading and number work has lagged through
communication problems (e.g. in immigrant communities) the computer
has helped by the choice of simple visual instructions.

One of the most interesting exercises was carried out by a school
without a computer where the teacher built up an awareness programme
to develop the relationship between pupil and equipment.   This is
especially important when a young child spends most of its early
life relating to one or two individuals and then learns about
manipulating and handling other forms of communication.   By moving
from personal interaction to audio aids, working from recorded
instructions, then visual aids using projectors to jumbo typewriter
keyboards to learn key controls, the teacher introduced the basic
communication processes between computer and individual.   In the
absence of a real computer, a cardboard box with a face provided an
input slot for questions and output slot for replies supplied by
one of the children.   If these skills are developed at a young age,
a child will be able to use learning aids in the future, to read
signs/instructions, push buttons and interpret results which could
open a completely different set of experiences in school and future
life.

References and Useful Addresses

The following organisations provide a variety of advice, assistance
and publications.

A.1   British Computer Society Computer Education Group,
      c/o Computer Centre,
      North Staffordshire Polytechnic,
      Blackheath Lane,
      Stafford.

A.2   Council for Educational Technology,
      3 Devonshire Street,
      London.
      WIN 2BA

A.3   ACUCHE (Association of Computer Users in Higher and Further
              Education)
      c/o Computer Centre,
      Leicester Polytechnic,
      P.O. Box 143,
      Leicester.
      LE1 9BH

A.4   Mr. R. Fothergill,
      Director,
      Micro-electronic Education Programme,
      Cheviot House,
      Coach Lane Campus,
      Newcastle-upon-Tyne.
      NE7 7XA

A.5   MUSE (Microcomputer Users in Secondary Education)
      Freepost,
      Bromsgrove,
      West Midlands.

A.6   Hertfordshire Advisory Unit for Computer Based Education,
      Endymion Road,
      Hatfield,
      Hertfordshire.

A.7   ILEA Schools Computer Service,
      City of London Polytechnic,
      139 Minories,
      London EC3

A.8   Birmingham Educational Computer Centre,
      The Bordesley Centre,
      Camp Hill,
      Stratford Road,
      Birmingham.
      B11 1AR

Appendix A 2

A.9   Merseyside Schools Computing Centre,
      Liverpool Polytechnic,
      Byron Street,
      Liverpool.
      L3 3AF

Educational Software

B.1 Examples of commercial packages which are required to train
     students in Further and Higher Education

PAFEC	Finite Element Calculations for Engineers
GINO	Graphics Software
ECSL	Event Orientated Simulation Language
IMAGE	Continuous Simulation Package
SPSS	Statistical Package for Social Scientists
DBMS	Database Management System
BIPS	Highway Design Suite
2CL	Numerical Control for Industrial Engineers
ECAP	Electrical Control and Analysis Design Package
PROSPER	Financial Modelling for Accounting and Business Studies

Also various CAL packages have been developed primarily for
scientific and engineering disciplines.

B.2 Examples of Secondary School Computer Aided Learning Materials

DIET	Nutritional Analysis of Food/Diets
COXIST	Simulation of Population Growth Curves for Different Species
POND 1	Pond Ecology including Pollution Effects
SPREAD	Simulates Spread of Disease through a Population
STATS	Statistics for Biologists
ELEMNT	Chemical Element Game
GASCR 1	Gas Chromatography Analyses
EQUILA	Chemical Equilibrium
RKINET	Reaction Kinetics
ESCAPE	Escape Velocity and Gravitational Fields
HEAT	Home Heating (percentage heat loss with different building materials etc.)
NOISE	Analysis of Sound Reverberation as a Function of Room Size, Furnishings etc.
SCATT 1	Particle Scattering

ORBIT 1   Planetary Motion

RADACT   Radioactive Decay

NEWTON   Satellite Orbits

TIMAP   Geographical Topology

HIKE   Exercise in the Use of Bearing Notation

SYMAP   Map Drawing to Produce Contours, Intensity Levels
            or Three Dimensional Representation

PEOPLE   Population Studies

ROUTE   Motorway Siting Simulation

AGCOM 1   Simulation of EEC Common Agricultural Policy

ELAST   Price Elasticity in Relation to Demand Curves

KING 3   Role Playing Exercise to Manage a Primitive
            Economy as 'King' of a Small Community

COORDV   Game to Practise Plotting by Co-ordinates

PLOT   Demonstration Graphs for Simple Equations

SWAPV   Visual Representation of Number Sorting

QUEUE   Computer Simulation to 'Control' Queues and
            Provide Management Information

QUERY   Information Retrieval Package which can be used
            with a variety of databases for History,
            Geography, Biology and English lessons

SPORT   Monitoring of any Competitive Sports Fixtures

STARS   Produces a Map of the Star System according to
            user defined date and time and place

PAYROLL   Exercise to Demonstrate the Operation of a
            Computer Managed Payroll System

B.3   Examples of Materials Suitable for Primary School Level

JANET and JOHN   Associated with first school readers

WORD ORDER   Testing alphabetic knowledge

STORY TELLER   Generates random situations for children
                     to create a story about

CAT and MOUSE   Shape matching

NUMBER CHECKS   Simple arithmetic, relative size of
                     numbers.

Microcomputing Should be Helping Teachers to Meet the Educational
Challenge of the 1980's

The following list provides a comprehensive set of objectives, many
of which could benefit from the use of a computer.   It is a result
of a brainstorming session at Upwood School in June 1978, reported
by R. Jones in the CET Publication March 1980, Microcomputers : Their
Use in Primary Schools.

C.1 Education for leisure

C.2 Ability to evaluate new technology

C.3 Pupils' practice in community skills

C.4 Alternative skills and hobbies

C.5 Politics of technology

C.6 Awareness of ethics

C.7 Discussion and debating skills

C.8 Define technology and alternatives

C.9 Emphasize the teaching process

> thinking
> evaluating
> valuing
> perceiving
> decision making
> knowing
> organising
> patterning
> communicating
> caring

C.10 Individuals matter

C.11 Outlets for creativity and problem solving

C.12 Morals and values emphasized

C.13 Create an interest in automation, alternative technology

C.14 Technological literacy (terminology and vocabulary)

C.15 Educate for technical change

C.16 Decision making skills

C.17 Worthwhile enriched relevant experiences

C.18 Teach children to live with technology

C.19 Teach children the importance of power and control

C.20 Emphasize the importance of human relationships

C.21 Help children to be selective and make the right choice

C.22 Emphasize effective side of school philosophy

C.23 Develop in children social conscience e.g. pollution

C.24 Teach processes involved in technical revolution

C.25 Cope with basic needs i.e. self reliance, initiative and resourcefulness

C.26 Doomwatch and balance

C.27 Motivation

C.28 Balance future orientation with interest in the past

C.29 Understand physchological problems

C.30 Need cultural background to fall back on.

Industrial Placement For Computer Science Students

B. A. Wyld

Consultant, Urwick Orr & Partners Ltd, UK

S. I. McClinton

Senior Lecturer, Ulster Polytechnic, Northern Ireland

This paper outlines the course structure of the BSc Computer Science at Ulster Polytechnic. An essential aspect of this course is the third year's industrial placement. In an attempt to obtain the most suitable pairings of student capability with employer requirements a battery of tests was introduced.

Having now completed four year's placements sufficient statistical data has now been assembled to make an assessment of the tests that have been employed and their usefulness, not only in the placement sphere but to judge their validity in relation to the programming examination results and eventual degree classification.

The Polytechnic

The Ulster Polytechnic came into being as a direct result of the Lockwood Report. There are currently 7,000 students registered with the Polytechnic.

The philosophy of the Polytechnic is based on certain fundamental principles. These are that higher education should be sensitive to the personal and career needs of students, that courses reflect the diverse needs of today's society, and that the Polytechnic should be positive in its commitment to teaching. Transfer between different levels of the same subject area and even different disciplines is also an important part of course planning. Stress is laid on the professional and applied aspects of the course being studied, there is a strong vocational emphasis.

All the degree courses are validated by the Council of National Academic Awards (CNAA). CNAA degrees are of equal standard to those awarded by Universities in the UK. Many of the degree courses offered by the Polytechnic are of a "sandwich" nature where periods of full time study alternate with periods of relevant industrial experience. For example, a "thick" sandwich degree course has two years of academic study followed by a year out in industry with a final year of academic study. The BSc degree with Honours in Computer Science (Data Processing) is an example of the "thick" sandwich course.

BSc Computer Science – Honours

In common with most Polytechnic degrees students are normally 18 years of age and possess two passes of the General Certificate of Education at the Advanced level. English and Mathematics are prerequisites at the Ordinary level of the GCE. But a pass in Mathematics at "A" level is not specifically required.

First Year Syllabuses

Information, Storage and Processing
Computer Architecture and Organization
Algorithms and Data Structures
Quantitative Techniques
Business Organization and Accounting
Behavioural Science I
Communication Studies

Second Year Syllabuses

Computer Organization and Operating Systems
Algorithms and Data Structures II
Quantative Techniques II
Information Storage and Processing II
Systems Analysis
Behavioural Science II

Third Year – Industrial Training Placement

Fourth Year Syllabuses – Honours Stream

Systems Programming
Data Management Systems
Systems Design
Systems Development and Evaluation
Related Topics – i.e. Data Processing Control, Micro-processing,
Data Communication Systems.
Project

Fourth Year Syllabuses – Degree Stream

There are certain common features between the Honours and Degree
streams, namely Systems Programming, the Related Topics and the
Project, however the emphasis between the two streams is slightly
different. The following subject areas are distinctly unique to the
degree stream.

Information System Design
Systems Implementation

Industrial Training/Placement

The prime objective of the industrial training period is to enable the
student to study the "real life" applications of the principles
previously learnt at the Polytechnic through participation over a
substantial time period. The active placement period can last from
12 to 15 months. The secondary objectives are to provide a stimulus
for the final year project and to give exposure to other relevant
aspects of industrial activity which cannot be adequately dealt with
in the classroom situation. The major proportion of the students
time is spent in the programming and analysis departments of a
computer installation. Although this phase of our degree course is

officially called "Training" we prefer our placement organizations to look upon the student as one of their own employees for the period that they remain with them. We find that employers gain considerable benefit when they adopt this approach.

The first placements were made in 1975 and were of a hit and miss nature; in fact we learnt a lot through our mistakes. Since 1976 the same senior member of the School has been responsible for the total placement routines. A gradual process of change has evolved from our initial subjective approach to one that now contains a high element of objective testing. We have developed a method of trying to match the student with the correct, for him, industrial organization. The process of putting round pegs into round holes now hinges on five elements:-

i)   A series of tests;

ii)   Students programming ability.

iii)   Students own personality.

iv)   Having a good working relationship with our industrial clients.

v)   Searching our new industrial contacts.

The actual placement cycle starts in the first term of the second year and usually by November the preliminary soundings are made with employers trying to judge their requirements. Prior to this students complete the tests, also completing a background profile and listing preferred locations. Hopefully by the end of the first term we have completed all the necessary spade work.

At the beginning of the second term the students sit their mid-sessional examinations. Once these results are available a preliminary match is made of students with the industrial organization. Shortly afterwards the Head of the Department and Senior Course tutors meet to discuss and agree or perhaps disagree with the proposed preliminary matching process.

From early February it is then a matter of arranging interviews and tying up all the administrative details that will safely deliver the student to the host organization by the middle of July.

Indicative Statistical Data

Table I - Total Intake

Year of Entry	Students Male %	Female %	Total Number
1974	73.3	26.7	15
1975	85.7	14.3	14
1976	80.0	20.0	15
1977	73.7	26.3	19
1978	81.8	18.2	22
1979	93.1	6.9	29

Table II - Academic Qualifications of Intake

Average Nos. for GCE passes

Year of Entry	"O" Levels over Grade "C"	"A" Levels	Average grade of ** GCE "A" Levels
1974	N/A	N/A	N/A
1975	5.5	2.0	1.79
1976	5.4	2.4	2.18
1977	7.4	1.8*	2.02
1978	8.6	2.3	1.60
1979	8.9	2.2	1.87

* Included students who entered with other classified qualifications.

** GCE "A" Level passes are graded "A" through to "E", a 5 in this column indicates a pass average at grade "A" down to a 1 which indicates a pass at grade "E".

Table 3 - Summary of GCE "A" Level subjects at entry 1975-79

Subject	% of Students with this GCE "A" Level
Maths (all categories)	74.4
Physics	33.7
Geography	24.4
Chemistry	17.4
Economics	16.3
Biology	11.6
Geometric and Eng. Drawing	12.8
French	8.0
Computer Science	7.0
English Literature	5.8
History	3.5
Irish	3.5
Art	2.3
Domestic Science	2.3
Geology	2.3
English Language	2.3
Sociology	1.2
Statistics	1.2
Latin	1.2
German	1.2
Spanish	1.2
Economic History	1.2
Technical Design	1.2
Accounts	1.2

Tests Employed

Since 1976 the number of tests being administered to students has gradually increased from two to a total of five, in an attempt to get a more accurate matching procedure. The following tests are currently being used:

1)   Group Tests of High-Level Intelligence AH6 AG and AH6 SEM.

2)   Two computer manufacturer aptitude tests.

3)   Computer Programmer Aptitude Battery.

The Group Tests AH6 comprises two separate tests of general reasoning SEM and AG. They are designed for use with selected, highly intelligent subjects such as candidates for and students at places of Higher Education. Both tests include problems with verbal, numerical and diagrammatic biases but the proportions of these biases differ.

The two computer manufacturer's tests are of a very similar nature. They both take approximately one hour to complete and are basically designed at ascertaining "programming" aptitude. These tests form part of the manufacturers actual job selection procedures. The tests are divided into three separate elements, letter series, diagrammatic problems and arithmetic reasoning. Approximately 50% of the allowed time is allocated to the arithmetical section, 30% the diagrams and 20% on the letter series.

The Computer Programmer Aptitude Battery (CPAB) was first developed by J M Palormo and published in the USA by Science Research Associates Inc. in 1967. This test was designed with the specific purpose of selecting computer programmers and systems analysts. These subtests aim at measuring the following aptitudes and skills; verbal meaning, reasoning, letter series, number ability and diagramming.

Analysis of Results

All the available data for the four years intakes 1975-1978 was input to calculate Pearson Correlation Coefficients. A summary and an analysis of these calculations is given below.

1975 Intake

P E A R S O N   C O R R E L A T I O N   C O E F F I C I E N T S

	PROG1	PROG2	PROG4	DEGREE	AG	I1
PROG1	1.0000	0.5535	0.5237	0.3417	-0.6164	-0.2920
	(0)	(10)	(9)	(9)	(10)	(10)
	S=0.001	S=0.048	S=0.074	S=0.184	S=0.029	S=0.206
PROG2	0.5535	1.0000	-0.0035	-0.0457	-0.5426	-0.4847
	(10)	(0)	(9)	(9)	(10)	(10)
	S=0.048	S=0.001	S=0.496	S=0.454	S=0.053	S=0.078
PROG4	0.5237	-0.0035	1.0000	0.8229	-0.4735	-0.3786
	(9)	(9)	(0)	(13)	(13)	(13)
	S=0.074	S=0.496	S=0.001	S=0.001	S=0.051	S=0.101
DEGREE	0.3417	-0.0457	0.8229	1.0000	-0.4086	-0.3295
	(9)	(9)	(13)	(0)	(13)	(13)
	S=0.184	S=0.454	S=0.001	S=0.001	S=0.083	S=0.136
AG	-0.6164	-0.5426	-0.4735	-0.4086	1.0000	0.3223
	(10)	(10)	(13)	(13)	(0)	(14)
	S=0.029	S=0.053	S=0.051	S=0.083	S=0.001	S=0.131
I1	-0.2920	-0.4847	-0.3786	-0.3295	0.3223	1.0000
	(10)	(10)	(13)	(13)	(14)	(0)
	S=0.206	S=0.078	S=0.101	S=0.136	S=0.131	S=0.001

(COEFFICIENT / (CASES) / SIGNIFICANCE)

(A value of 99.0000 is printed if a coefficient cannot be computed)

The data under the headings "PROG1-4" is the result of the
Programming examination for those particular years, whilst "Degree"
gives the final classification obtained. This intake only received
two tests, the High Level Intelligence AH6 AH and the first
manufacturer's test which we have coded "I1". The main features
of the results would appear to be:

a fairly strong positive correlation between year 1 and year 2 and
also between year 1 and year 4 programming results.

There is a weak negative correlation between programming in year 1 and the first manufacturer's test. This may be due to the "classical structure" of the test.

The virtual absence of any correlation for the programming year 2 results with the programming year 4 results or the final degree classification.

The negative correlation of the programming results and the manufacturer's tests becomes stronger for the year 4 results and stronger still for the year 2 results. It is interesting to note that the AH6 AG scores are negatively correlated with every other variable except the manufacturers test.

<u>1976 Intake</u>

P E A R S O N   C O R R E L A T I O N   C O E F F I C I E N T S

	PROG1	PROG2	AG	SEM	I1
PROG1	1.0000	0.4771	0.3842	0.2692	0.3562
	(0)	(15)	(15)	(15)	(15)
	S=0.001	S=0.036	S=0.079	S=0.166	S=0.096
PROG2	0.4771	1.0000	0.4174	0.4122	0.4794
	(15)	(0)	(15)	(15)	(15)
	S=0.036	S=0.001	S=0.061	S=0.063	S=0.035
AG	0.3842	0.4174	1.0000	0.8386	0.8533
	(15)	(15)	(0)	(15)	(15)
	S=0.079	S=0.061	S=0.001	S=0.001	S=0.001
SEM	0.2692	0.4122	0.8386	1.0000	0.7246
	(15)	(15)	(15)	(0)	(15)
	S=0.166	S=0.063	S=0.001	S=0.001	S=0.001
I1	0.3562	0.4794	0.8533	0.7246	1.0000
	(15)	(15)	(15)	(15)	(0)
	S=0.096	S=0.035	S=0.001	S=0.001	S=0.001

(COEFFICIENT / (CASES) / SIGNIFICANCE)

(A value of 99.0000 is printed if a coefficient cannot be computed)

This intake will shortly be taking the final year 4 examination. A further test was undertaken by this year, the AH6 SEM, in addition to the two tests previously sat by the 1975 intake. An analysis of these results indicate the following observations:

Again there is a strong correlation between the year 1 and year 2 programming results.

Although they did not reach "statistical significance", it is interesting to note the correlation co-efficient for the programming results year 1 with the AG test and the manufacturers test.

The programming year 2 results show a moderate positive correlation with both AH6 AG and SEM and a much stronger positive correlation with the manufacturer's test.

The AG test shows highly significant positive correlations with both the AH6 SEM and manufacturer's tests which themselves are strongly correlated.

1977 Intake

P E A R S O N   C O R R E L A T I O N   C O E F F I C I E N T S

	PROG1	PROG2	AG	SEM	I1	I2
PROG1	1.0000	0.7053	0.0071	0.2820	0.1773	0.4897
	(0)	(16)	(17)	(17)	(17)	(17)
	S=0.001	S=0.001	S=0.489	S=0.136	S=0.248	S=0.023
PROG2	0.7053	1.0000	-0.2244	-0.0455	-0.1651	0.3675
	(16)	(0)	(18)	(18)	(18)	(18)
	S=0.001	S=0.001	S=0.185	S=0.429	S=0.256	S=0.067
AG	0.0071	-0.2244	1.0000	0.7934	0.6709	0.6010
	(17)	(18)	(0)	(19)	(19)	(19)
	S=0.489	S=0.185	S=0.001	S=0.001	S=0.001	S=0.003
SEM	0.2820	-0.0455	0.7934	1.0000	0.7736	0.7091
	(17)	(18)	(19)	(0)	(19)	(19)
	S=0.136	S=0.429	S=0.001	S=0.001	S=0.001	S=0.001
I1	0.1773	-0.1651	0.6709	0.7736	1.0000	0.5149
	(17)	(18)	(19)	(19)	(0)	(19)
	S=0.248	S=0.256	S=0.001	S=0.001	S=0.001	S=0.012
I2	0.4897	0.3675	0.6010	0.7091	0.5149	1.0000
	(17)	(18)	(19)	(19)	(19)	(0)
	S=0.023	S=0.067	S=0.003	S=0.001	S=0.012	S=0.001

(COEFFICIENT / (CASES) / SIGNIFICANCE)

(A value of 99.0000 is printed if a coefficient cannot be computed)

For this intake an additional test was set, a second manufacturer's test which was to all intents and purposes very similar in its construction. The following points are worthy of note:

The programming year 1 result is strongly correlated in a positive direction with each of the Programming examination of year 2 and the second manufacturer's test.

The second manufacturer's test is also strongly correlated with both of the AHG tests and to a lesser degree the first manufacturer's tests.

There is an absence of correlation between the programming year 2 and the AH6 SEM test.

Programming year 2 and the second manufacturer's test are moderately correlated.

The AH6 AG test scores have a strong positive correlation with all the subsequent tests carried out for that particular intake.

The AH6 SEM scores have a strong positive correlation with each of the manufacturer's tests.

<u>1978 Intake</u>

P E A R S O N   C O R R E L A T I O N   C O E F F I C I E N T S

	PROG1	AG	SEM	I1	I2	BATTERY
PROG1	1.0000	-0.2200	0.0632	0.0054	0.1187	-0.0119
	(0)	(22)	(22)	(22)	(22)	(22)
	S=0.001	S=0.163	S=0.390	S=0.490	S=0.299	S=0.479
AG	-0.2200	1.0000	0.6325	0.6620	0.6213	0.5937
	(22)	(0)	(22)	(22)	(22)	(22)
	S=0.163	S=0.001	S=0.001	S=0.001	S=0.001	S=0.002
SEM	0.0632	0.6325	1.0000	0.6214	0.5352	0.4766
	(22)	(22)	(0)	(22)	(22)	(22)
	S=0.390	S=0.001	S=0.001	S=0.001	S=0.005	S=0.012
I1	0.0054	0.6620	0.6214	1.0000	0.5266	0.7605
	(22)	(22)	(22)	(0)	(22)	(22)
	S=0.490	S=0.001	S=0.001	S=0.001	S=0.006	S=0.001
I2	0.1187	0.6213	0.5352	0.5266	1.0000	0.5930
	(22)	(22)	(22)	(22)	(0)	(22)
	S=0.299	S=0.001	S=0.005	S=0.006	S=0.001	S=0.002
BATTERY	-0.0119	0.5937	0.4766	0.7605	0.5930	1.0000
	(22)	(22)	(22)	(22)	(22)	(0)
	S=0.479	S=0.002	S=0.012	S=0.001	S=0.002	S=0.001

(COEFFICIENT / (CASES) / SIGNIFICANCE)

(A value of 99.0000 is printed if a coefficient cannot be computed)

This intake sat the Battery test bringing the total number of tests up
to five. The programming year two examinations will be completed
at the end of this academic year. We have the following comments
to make on the results obtained so far:

The AH6 AG test scores have a strong positive correlation with each
of the other variables except the examination results for programming
in year 1. This observation also applies to the AH6 SEM scores.

The programming results have no statistically significant correlation
with any other results.

It will be noted that the two manufacturer's tests display a strong
positive correlation but each is more strongly correlated with the
Battery results.

Conclusion

In the first instance the raison d'etre for using any type of
Intelligence or Aptitude tests was to try and organize our industrial
placement methods for our third year students in a more logical and
scientific way. The tests were brought into use as a device for
cutting down mis-matches between the students and employers,
saving time, building up the confidence of our employers where our
recommendations could be acted on with a high degree of confidence.

But within a relatively short period we found out that more and more
of our employers were starting to use their own tests as an
essential element of the recruitment cycle. With this being the case
we could ill afford to send a relatively weak student to such an
organization.

The policy of the School of Computer Science has been to gradually
expand the intake numbers in line with the number of industrial
placement positions that come on to the market. We now have the
happy position of having more employers than actual students,
although this situation tends to enhance our reputation, it does
bring about a different set of problems. In the foreseeable future
it is unlikely the annual intake will expand beyond say 30 students.
The various tests used so far have achieved their original intention,
saving time, effort and money. If the testing procedure is to
continue in the future, purely as a guide, to the industrial placement
problem, then it is felt that the total number of tests could safely
be reduced to two. At this stage we feel the AH6 AG and Battery

would suit our needs.

We have produced a set of Pearson Correlation coefficients for all the intakes between 1975-1979 and made several observations on the results for each year. We would however doubt the computer industry's general acceptance of manufacturer's tests. The relevance between actual programming performance and test results is, to say the very least, doubtful. The actual manufacturer's tests we have used do not prove "a high score means a capable programmer". In no way can it be said that such tests reflect the various job requirements of any programmer but merely establishes a certain level of measured intelligence. The major job entry point within the computer industry as a whole is simply that of programming. It is surprising that manufacturers have not as yet been able to construct a more meaningful test vehicle. Perhaps the ideal test should include the following features or elements -

- spatial reasoning,

- verbal reasoning,

- arithmetical capability,

- flow chart type problems that reflect the programming function,

- some aspect of comprehension and communication.

Although we have made various comments on the correlation of the tests we have used and the results obtained under examination conditions, namely programming in years 1 and 2. It must be appreciated that no course, however well managed, can be organized and run in exactly the same manner year in and year out. We are after all dealing with human beings not machines!

We have not yet established a sufficient data bank of information to make any judgements on the various tests, GCE "A" Level results and the final degree classification. But it is our hope and intention to publish such information some time in the future.

This polytechnic and other similar institutions are currently going through a phase where the total number of applications to join computer courses is increasing at an alarming annual rate. We are currently running at a 50% increase this year as against last year. With this being the case then it does become very important to select the "right" student. The days of a casual interview are long

past. It is felt that we should attempt to test all those potential
students who we consider suitable, having seen their application
form and references. In the past we have only tested the
borderline cases or where a special situation existed, i.e. a mature
student. As it will be appreciated there are problems with testing
every suitable candidate, the administrative problems, time involved
and not least of all using the most appropriate test in the selection
procedure.

We consider that none of the tests we have used so far matches up
with our ideal requirements namely:

- the test should take no longer than 40 minutes,

- be very easy to administer,

- not be over complicated and yet somehow forecast the
  future requirements of the course, i.e. to make efficient
  and workable programs,

- to be completely acceptable and fair to all categories of
  potential students, Arts and Sciences, without giving
  only one group a built-in advantage,

- we are attracted to the inclusion of the "flow chart"
  type of problem but these questions do pre-suppose
  some previously learnt knowledge that is not commonly
  taught,

- to adequately cover the communication/verbal aspect.

It is our intention to continue our testing procedures and it is hoped
to report on our findings at some future date.

Part 7
Methodology

Experience in the Use of an Overall
System Design Methodology

A. L. Freedman

*Head of System Studies, Plessey Radar Limited,
Addlestone, Weybridge, UK*

Work on a major project was carried out following a system design methodology which addresses the system as a whole and aims to cover all aspects of system design.

The work done to derive a requirements definition, and from this, a performance specification, is described.

1. THE METHODOLOGY

1.1 NEED FOR A SYSTEM METHODOLOGY

By no means all computer based systems are completed on schedule and within budget. Even then performance does not always live up to expectation. When development costs are analysed at the conclusion of the project it is usually found that the greatest overrun is on software development. From this it is often concluded that what is needed is a software methodology. But is this where the problem really is?

Considering first specially designed, one-off systems one finds that, typically a contract will be signed that states only vaguely what capabilities the system will have, but which specifies quite precisely what hardware will be in it, when the system will be ready and also the price. Because the schedule is tight, design work starts immediately, possibly even the actual writing of software, before there is a design for the software as a whole. As the capabilities required of the system are gradually settled and detailed they filter through to the software writers. Since the hardware is fixed, the detailed specifications call for changes in the software as it is produced, probably in an unstructured manner to a still incomplete design, without a discipline for controlling changes or the software build state. Furthermore, as the hardware is fixed, the software may have to be shoehorned into computers which are not powerfull enough and if there is one way of spending lots of money fast, it is trying to shoehorn software into inadequate computers. Given this lack of a design approach to the system as a whole it is not surprising that work on the software still goes on, at great expense, long after it should have been finished.

When one turns to systems which are designed to be standard products, one sometimes finds that in the event it turns out that significant special engineering is required for every order, making the product unprofitable. It is even more disappointing to find that potential customers prefer to buy a competitor's system even though the competing system is much more expensive.

A customer for a system will sometimes team up with some of his suppliers for a joint design. In one such case the system didn't work at all and had to be carted away. This particular system was not stored program controlled and therefore had no software.

Where then is the real problem? It is mostly inadequate specification of what should be designed or insufficient design expertise or both.

1.2 REQUIREMENTS WHICH A SYSTEM METHODOLOGY HAS TO MEET

This being so, it means that any design methodology which aims to ensure that systems projects are successfully completed on time and within schedule, must have at least the following three properties:

(1)   It has to ensure that the designers know what it is they should design.

(2)   It has to ensure that they know how to achieve this.

        and as a corollary

(3)   It has to provide the designers with a means of finding out whether or not they have achieved what they set out to achieve.

So far so good, but how do we find out what it is that needs to be designed? To answer this question one must first realise this: to specify what the proposed system has to be capable of, that is what facilities it would have to provide, it is necessary to go outside the system and investigate what it will be used for and how it will be used. In other words:

The starting point of the whole design exercise, the definition of the requirements which the system had best meet can only be derived from a knowledge of its use when it is designed, produced and put into use.

If follows from this observation and from other considerations that a general format for a requirements definition has to meet the following four requirements:

(1)   It has to be capable of expressing the requirements of a data processing system for any type of application (universality).

(2)   It has to do so unambiguously in terms which will be understood both by experts in its use and by system designers, two groups of people who normally inhabit two separate worlds. (unambiguous common language).

(3)   It has to define fully all the requirements which the system will have to meet (completeness).

(4)   It should not unnecessarily preclude any possibilities
which may exist for the design of the system
(implementation independence).

1.3   THE METHODOLOGY USED

It turns out that it is in fact possible to create such a
general format, based in part on the following blinding flash of the
obvious:

The facilities provided by a system are outputs from the system.

This fact allows us to specify all the required facilities of
any data processing system unambiguously in terms understood by both
system specifiers and system designers, by specifying fully for all
the outputs all their operational parameters as listed in Table 1.1.

TABLE 1.1   OUTPUT DEFINITION PARAMETERS

1   Identity

2   Information contents

3   Stimuli causing the output

4   Forms and formats

5   Tolerances and resolutions

6   Response times

7   Freshness of information

8   Speeds

9   Sizes

10   Occurrences

11   Interfaces on which output is available

12   Variabilities

13   Any other requirements which the output may have to meet

---

Explanations of the data which have to be included for a
complete statement of each of these parameters are given in Appendix
1.

We haven't finished yet. A data processing system outputs information derived from the data provided to it as inputs. The requirements definition must therefore provide full information on all the inputs available to the system, as shown in Table 1.2.

TABLE 1.2 INPUT DEFINITION PARAMETERS

1   Identity

2   Information content

3   Recoverability of information

4   Forms and formats

5   Tolerances and resolutions

6   Periods for which input is available

7   Freshness of information

8   Speeds

9   Sizes

10   Occurrences

11   Interfaces on which input is available

12   Variabilities

13   Any other constraints

Explanations of these parameters are given in Appendix 2.

There are also constraints on the system as a whole. Such constraints are most likely in the areas listed in Table 1.3. Details are given in Appendix 3.

TABLE 1.3 GENERAL CONSTRAINTS

1   Acceptable price

2   Time scales

3   Environmental requirements

4   Services capabilities

5   Operators' capabilities and requirements

6   Maintenance capabilities and requirements

7   Adaptabiity requirements

8   Security

9   Mandatory design requirements

10   Mandatory implementation requirements

A complete requirements definition is thus seen to consist of three parts:

(1)   Complete definitions of all the outputs.

(2)   Complete definitions of all the inputs.

(3)   A complete statement of all the general constraints under which the system will have to operate.

Furthermore - this is all there should be in the performance specification. For instance, it will be observed that there is nothing about system availability. This is because there is usually no such thing. There are only availabilities of individual facilities, i.e. outputs. Within the same system there may be an output which a user could afford to loose for a day, say, but another one which he will not want to loose even for a second. Further more, the tolerable length of loss may well depend on the percentage of interfaces providing that output on which it is lost. The required availability of each output is in fact specified by its response times. Similarly there is usually no such thing as system integrity - only integrities of outputs, defined by the tolerances and resolutions and response times and of the output. (In some cases part of this information may be more conveniently given under the 'interfaces' heading).

The requirements definition as described specifies fully the boundary between the system and the rest of the world, and only this boundary. It is therefore implementation independent (except for the mandatory design and implementation requirements). It is derived from purely operational considerations, so that it can be prepared by experts in the use of the system. These definitions are expressed either as parameters of inputs or outputs or as general constraints as defined in Appendix 3, both of which can be understood by system designers. The format in itself does not guarantee that all the inputs, outputs and constraints will be included but it does virtually ensure that those which are not overlooked will be fully specified.

Are we saying that all this work, and it is a lot of hard work, needed to produce the requirements definition as described, is to be done without any reference at to whether it is feasible to meet the requirements? Yes, we are. In fact, we go further and say that until there is such a complete requirements definition we cannot even start to determine whether it is feasible to meet the requirements. As with some legal documents, the small print is what matters. The feasibility or otherwise of meeting the reqirements within the specified price and time scale may very well depend on what response times, tolerances or interfaces have been specified, or details of other parameters or details of the general constraints, which is why quantification is essential. A definition demanding a 'fast' response time is as useless as it is meaningless.

This does not mean that the system will necessarily be designed to meet the original requirements definition. The document which specifies what requirements the system will actually be designed to meet is another document, called the performance specification, the format of which is very similar to that of the requirements definition. The relationship between the requirements definition, the performance specification and the design and test specifications (which provide the answers to questions (2) and (3) in Section 1.2) are indicated in Diagram 1.1

The same four part process of requirements definition and performance, design and test specifications needs to be successively repeated throughout the design and implementation of the system. However, rather than go on explaining the methodology it would be better to report at this point on the work done in deriving first a requirements definition for a particular system, and then from it, a performance specification.

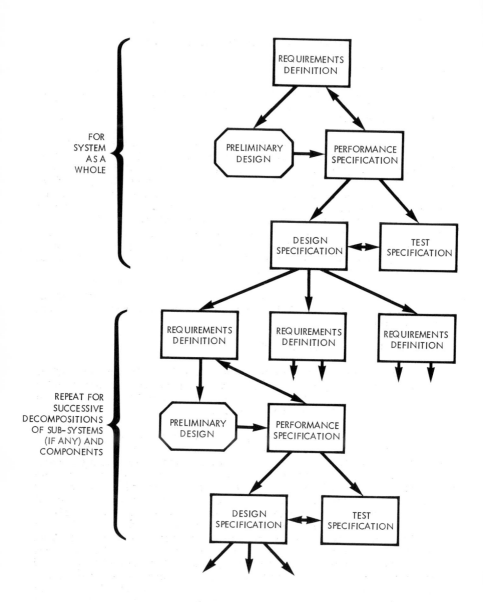

Diagram 1.1 Principle of the Methodology

2. APPLICATION OF THE METHODOLOGY

2.1 THE PRODUCT

The methodology was applied to the design of a full range of display and data processing systems for Air Traffic Control. This requires some explanation.

Air traffic control centres vary greatly in size and function. The display and data processing system displays data to air traffic controllers. In addition it may or may not have to process radar from one or more radars, carry out flight plan processing, combine the results of the radar and flight plan processing or interchange data with a variety of communications networks. The air traffic control centres served by these systems vary not only in the mix of functions which they perform but also in size: from two control positions to, say, a hundred control positions. The processing power required may vary from one mini-computer to over a hundred computers, some of them powerful mainframes.

The product design objective was to design a range whose configurations will span this spectrum of requirements in a cost effective manner.

2.2 THE REQUIREMENTS DEFINITION.

The requirements definition was prepared by a former air traffic controller assisted by a number of people experienced in air traffic control, the provision of air traffic control facilities and in the marketing of air traffic control systems.

The work of preparing the operational requirement started out with the compilation of a list of all the outputs which would be required to provide the operational facilities which a user might require from the system in the next ten years. For this purpose some half dozen specifications for air traffic control systems were scrutinized. Visits were made to air traffic control centres of different types and discussions held with air traffic controllers. Those familiar with the diversity of opinions amongst air traffic controllers will not be surprised to hear that all the facilities requested were carefully evaluated as to why they should be there and how they would be used. When completed the list of outputs was found to contain over five hundred outputs. There were operational inter-dependencies between many of them. Therefore the list of outputs takes the form of a configurator; that is, against each output are listed any outputs which have to be available before the output in question can be used and also any outputs which cannot be provided together with the output in question. Sometimes the conflict can be between two outputs in the same system and sometimes the outputs will conflict only if it is attempted to provide them on

the same display.   Obviously the complete list of outputs is too long
to be presented here.   Table 2.1 presents an extract from the
configurator.

2.3 FROM REQUIREMENTS DEFINITION TO PERFORMANCE SPECIFICATION

To see how the performance specification is derived from the
requirements definition compare the secondary radar output
definition, shown in part in Table 2.2 with the corresponding items
in the performance specification in Table 2.3.   The first difference
is in the information content.   It is not technically feasible to
provide the information requested in the requirements definition from
a single radar with present day radars and the alternative in the
performance specification is acceptable.   Under 'Forms and formats'
a choice of two brightness levels has been substituted for the
pulsating facility.   The present state of the art does not permit to
guarantee a given accuracy.   It is only possible to measure the
accuracy achieved under specified circumstances.   The response times
in the performance specification are very much a case of "you pays
your money and you takes your choice".   It should however be noted
that they define only the availability of the particular output.
Other, more essential, outputs may still be available when this
output is not.

In this instance the reasons for the difference between the
performance specification and the requirements definition were mostly
technical feasibility.   In other cases differences may arise due to
cost or time considerations.   The design team may offer an
alternative facility which will be cheaper to provide but still
acceptable, or it may request the removal of the facility because the
development work required to provide such a facility would exceed the
timescale within which the system is to be supplied.   Many of the
figures in a requirements definition, such as, response times, can
only be approximate ones, because they are of necessity guesses as to
what will be good enough.   There may therefore be significant
lattitude there to allow for design, cost or time considerations.

Yet other considerations may cause differences between the
performance specification and the requirement definition.   For
example, if one were to compare the list of inputs in the
requirements definition with that in the performance specification it
would be seen that the latter has additional inputs which do not
appear in the former.   The reason for these additional inputs is a
design decision to provide the controllers with a head-up menu
selection input method.

TABLE 2.1 EXTRACT FROM LIST OF OUTPUTS

		CONFLICTING OPTIONS		PRE-REQUISITE OPTIONS
(1)	GRAPHIC DISPLAY			
(1.1)	AIRCRAFT POSTIONAL DATA	Same Display	Same System	
(9.3)	Plot Extracted Radar			
(10)	Mono Radar			
11	Primary Plot: Position symbol corresponding to position in plan of target not yet declared as a track, as last extracted from primary radar	19		
12	SSR Plot: Position corresponding to position in plan of aircraft not yet declared as a track, as last detected by SSR.	20		
(13)	Tracking: Position symbol corresponding to predicted position in plan at successive time intervals, derived from:			
14	Auto Initiated SSR Tracking;	22-25		
15	Auto Initiated SSR Tracking with Primary Plot infill;	17-22-25		11
16	Auto Initiated SSR Tracking with Manually Initated Primary Tracking;	22-25		11
	Auto Initiated SSR Tracking and Auto Initiated Primary Tracking	14-22-25		17

TABLE 2.2   ABBREVIATED EXTRACT FROM MONO SECONDARY RADAR OUTPUT
DEFINITION IN REQUIREMENTS DEFINITION

Identity: Auto Initiated Mono Secondary Radar Tracking

2   Information content: Position of a target declard as an SSR
track at time of display on plan position indicator as predicted
by secondary radar tracking, whether target is steadily tracked
or coasted and whether target is normal or urgency, i.e.
emergency, radio failure or hi-jack; see also variabilities.

3   Stimulus: receipt of SSR plot message confirming track or
causing new track to be declared, or alternatively, expiry of
period within which such message should have been received.

4   Forms and formats: symbol drawn from preset vocabulary
definable by a 10 x 7 dot matrix, the symbol being (1) steady,
(2) pusating or (3) flashing:

5   Minimum accuracy: least stringent of:

(1)   3 millimetres

(2)   .5% range, 0.5^{o} azimuth at up to half range

(3)   .25% range, 0.5^{o} azimuth otherwise

6   Response times:

95% within 1 second

99.5% within 3 seconds

99.95% within 30 seconds

99.995% within 10 minutes

TABLE 2.3 EXTRACT FROM MONO SECONDARY RADAR OUTPUT DEFINITION IN
          PERFORMANCE SPECIFICATION

1	Identity: Auto Initiated Mono Secondary Radar Tracking.

2   Information content: tracked, (including coasted) smoothed or
     unsmoothed (see variabilities) position of aircraft as last seen
     by radar, displayed on plan position indicator, whether target
     is steadily tracked or coasted and whether target is normal or
     urgency, i.e. emergency, radio failure or hi-jack; see also
     variabilities.

3   Stimuli: receipt of secondary radar plot message confirming
     track or causing new track to be declared, or alternatively,
     expiry of period within which such message should have been
     received.

4   Forms and formats: position indicated by one, or overlay of
     two, of symbols shown under 'interfaces', symbols either normal
     or double brilliance, steady or flashing.

5   Accuracies: as per reports on tracking performance, available
     on request.

6   Response times: maximum period between completion of receipt of
     plot message and completion of output, as follows:

             95% of occurences - 1 sec
             99.5% of occurences - 3 secs
             99.95% of occurences - 30 secs
             except during periods as follows:

     Case 1 (see variabilities):
     1.1 On site maintenance,   0.15% of time - 3 hrs
                                        0.16% of time - 24hrs
     1.2 Maintenance within 12hrs,   0.75 of time - 15 hrs
                                        0.24 of time - 36 hrs

     Case 2 (see variabilities):
     2.1 On site maintenance,   0.0004% of time - 30 secs
                                        0.008% of time - 7 mins
                                        0.08% of time - 24 hrs
     2.2 Maintenance within 12hrs,   0.0004% of time - 30 secs
                                        0.15% of time - 15hrs
                                        0.1% of time - 36hrs

     Case 3 (see variabilities):
     3.1 On site maintenance,   0.0004% of time - 30 secs
                                        0.001% of time - 7 mins
                                        0.001% of time - 4hrs

The head-up menu selection device consists of a small keyboard with blank keys. On a display in front of the controller is a corresponding presentation with the keys labelled with whatever functions would be of interest to the controller at the time. Also on the presentation of the keyboard is an indication of where the controller's finger rests. The controller performs input functions by pressing the appropriate key. Not all the possible input functions appear all the time. In order to enter a specific function the controller may have to do a page selection to get the page offering that function displayed. Hence the page selection inputs which do not appear in the requirements definition. For the same reason there are also in the performance specification additional outputs which do not appear in the requirements specification. These are pages from which the controller selects the function he is interested in.

These examples illustrate the point that further inputs and outputs over and above those in the requirements definition may well appear in the performance specification because of decisions on the design. An area where such additional inputs and outputs typically occur is the system maintenance area. It is quite likely that in order to achieve the required availability, outputs giving maintenance data will have to be added and inputs for maintenance actions provided. It is thus seen that while operational facilities imply outputs, the converse is not necessarily true.

It follows from this that the performance specification may not be wholly implementation independent. Even so it is still all 'what' and no 'how' in its form, thus giving the designers the maximum freedom within the framework of the design decisions taken and explicitly recorded. This is important even when a designer executes a design to meet a performance specification of which he is himself the author, because the separation of the 'what' from the 'how' helps the designer to identify, hiw own, possibly non-optimum design pre-conceptions, opening the way for those flashes of lateral thinking which give more cost effective solutions. These may well make the difference between a profit or loss on a fixed price contract or between a competitive and non-competitive product.

The process of transition from the requirements definition to the performance specification obviously requires a design team capable of carrying out sufficient preliminary design work to determine feasibility, cost and timescales.

It should not be deduced from the description of the transition from the requirements definition to the performance specification that communications between the system specifiers and the system designers were limited to the interchange of the formal definitions of inputs and outputs. On the contary, the system specifiers and the system designers were members of the same project team. In addition to the formal definitions the system specifiers also produced background notes for the benefit of the system designers and the latter were also taken to visit Air Traffic Control Centres. None of this however is a substitute for the interchange of formal definitions. Only the latter can ensure the completeness and correctness of the transfer of information between users and designers.

2.4 RESULTS ACHIEVED

The most important question is: 'How good is the requirements definition?', that is, to what extent does it really cover all the facilities which may be required in an air traffic control system in the course of the next ten years. By the very nature of the question one would have to wait ten years for the answer. Since the work was completed several requirements for air traffic control systems have become known. All of these would have been satisfied with configurations out of the range as defined by the requirement definition. This still does not prove much. However, there is an encouranging pointer. The requirements definition introduced a new facility which as far as is known has never been provided in or proposed for, an air traffic control system. It so happens that the very first requirement for an actual system which then became known demanded this facility.

The work done on the requirements definition and on the performance specification made it possible to produce figures for the cost of the development, production costs for sample configurations and the timescale for the development with a fair degree of confidence. It also enabled the marketing department to forecast a sales profile together with income from the sales. The two together then made it possible to forecast the return on the investment.

3. DISCUSSION OF METHODOLOGY

3.1 THE COMPLETE METHODOLOGY

No attempt is made on this occasion to present the whole of the methodology, just enough to provide the necessary background for reporting on the work done on a particular system. However, it has been indicated earlier that the four part process has to be repeated for the successive decompositions of the system into sub-systems, if any, and then successively smaller components. These successive decompositions constitute the design process. The need for requirements definitions throughout the successive decompositions may seem surprising. Consider however the following:

The design team may well contain practitioners in a number of disciplines who may have almost as little in common as system users and system designers. Also, some parts may be sub-contracted outside.

When a major system is divided into sub-systems and the requirements for these sub-systems defined, it is by no means certain that the sub-systems actually designed will be those originally defined. Preliminary design work may show a better split into sub-systems.

The same may well happen at subsequent decomposition levels. A requirement definition may be prepared for what is assumed to be a software component. In the event it may turn out to be that, or a combination of a software package and some special hardware or a micro-computer with firmware in it and a performance specification differing substantially from the original requirements definition.

3.2 FEATURES OF THE METHODOLOGY

The most important feature of the methodology used is its comprehensiveness, in the sense that it covers all aspects of system design, where the word 'system' is used in the widest one of the several senses in which it is used in the computer field. In this it differs from some other methodologies which are in fact mainly software methodologies, is spite of claims to the contrary.

The details of the parameters making up the definitions of the inputs and outputs, and of the possible general constraints, as given in the appendices, are effectively questionnaires which have to be filled in for the system as a whole and successively for all its components. This feature of the methodology yields a number of advantages. Questionnaires are easy to use and they can ensure completeness. They are also suitable for data capture for possible computer aiding in the use of the methodology. They have the further important advantage that the same questionnaires are also a management tool in that they can, and should, be used by reviewers to assess both the quality and the progress of the work.

The preparation of a complete requirements definition demands a lot of work. Note however that this is work which has to be done anyway, and does in fact get done. At present however it is done piecemeal, during design, production and commissioning, sometimes even after commissioning. The insistence on a complete requirements definition before design decisions are taken is really only saying "get this work done at the stage at which it will enable you to choose the best possible design rather than at a time when it will cause repeated, often major, disruptions to the design and the design process, perhaps leaving you with a design which is far from optimum".

The formalism of the methodology described contrast with the graphic presentations advocated by other methodologies, but there is really no conflict here. Pictures are excellent for explaining and understanding, including explaining to oneself. To achieve completeness and correctness, however, an adequate formalism (which may itself be in part pictorial) is required.

The work done so far on the methodology has been confined to requirements definitions and performance specifications. For this reason it is still more of a framework for a methodology than a fully worked out one. In the process of establishing design specifications to meet the specified performance specifications and producing test specifications to determine whether the design specifications have been met there is room in this framework for many of the good methods that have been developed in the various methodologies currently being proposed. At this juncture it is worth pointing out a crucial gap which we still have in all our methodologies, namely the almost total absence of tools for determining the amount of processing power needed to provide a given system facility.

The author is grateful to the Directors of the Plessey Company for permission to publish the work. He sincerely thanks the many colleagues who have worked on the project and its documentation.

APPENDIX 1

OUTPUT DEFINITION PARAMETERS

1   Identity

A unique identification of the output.

2   Information content

A statement of all the information provided by the output. There may
be a number of versions of an output depending on circumstances.

3   Stimulus or stimuli

The stimulus or stimuli which will cause the output, typically an
input or the expiry of a specified period.

4   Form and formats

The outputs from a real time system have a wide variety of forms,
e.g. electrical voltages, mechanical displacements or the display of
data. Following a statement of the form, all the parameters required
to fully define and quantify the form of output are stated. For
instance in the case of an electrical voltage the function by which
the voltage represents the information, e.g. whether linear,
logarithmic etc and the range. In the case of a data display, all
the formats in which the data may be displayed.

5   Tolerances and Resolutions

Quantifications of all the acceptable deviations of the actual output
from its perfect presentation as defined in 2 and 4 above. The types
and quantities of operationally acceptable inaccuracies vary from
wholly wrong numbers being no more than a nuisance in a telephone
exchange to a single incorrect digit in an air traffic control system
possibly causing a collision between two jumbo jets if it persists
long enough. This last instance illustrates the fact that the period
for which the inaccuracy lasts may have to be included in
quantification. For certain types of outputs the required
resolutions have to be specified.

6   Response times

The periods between a stimulus which causes the output and the
output. Typically it will be the period between the completion of
the stimulus and the completion of the output, but not necessarily
always so. There is therefore a definition of the response time in
this particular instance, followed by a distribution of the response

times. The reason for quoting a distribution rather than a single reponse time is that, while on the one hand a real time system cannot provide the optimum response time all the time, on the other hand, certain proportions of extended response times are usually acceptable operationally.

7   Freshness

The periods between an output and the point in time when the world outside the system was in a state corresponding to that represented by the output. For example, in an air traffic control display and data processing system the position of an aircraft may be displayed within a second from the arrival of the radar message at the input to the system, but the position of the aircraft displayed may be that where the aircraft was at some time prior to te receipt of the radar message at the system input. The period stated will usually be to the completion of the output, but not always so. As with the response time it is therefore necessary to give first a definition of the period and then, for similar reasons, a distribution of the freshness periods.

8   Speeds

The speed or speeds at which the actual output will occur. This is not necessary in those cases where the response time and freshness are defined as the periods to the completion of the output, but may be relevant in other cases, e.g. where there is a continuous output or where messages of varying lengths are to be displayed or printed out.

9   Sizes

A distribution of the sizes of individual outputs, e.g. the lengths of messages transmitted or displayed.

10   Occurences

The distribution of occurrences of the output, coupled, if relevant, with any other parameters which are a function of this distribution. For instance, if it is known that messages during a peak period do not exceed a specified length, this is included in the data on the distribution of occurrences.

11   Interfaces

This is a statement of the interfaces to the outside world at which the output is available together with complete definitions of these interfaces. The contents of the definition are again heavily dependent on the interface. It, for instance, the output is an electrical voltage this will give such data as the impedance and voltage levels. If the output is on a Cathode Ray Tube display it will give such data as screen size, brightness, character repertoire etc.

The number and locations of the interfaces are also stated. Location may refer to geographical locations or to the maximum allowable distance between the interfaces and other parts of the system.

12   Variabilities

The choices which are available for all the above parameters. The variabilities are of three types. Initial choices, made by the customer at time of purchase (e.g. differences between models), off-line changes, introduced during use, usually for ever after to adjust to changed needs and on-line adjustments by, usually, the operator, to suit the circumstances of use and which are reversible. Examples of the three types of variabilities in an air traffic control system are as follows:-

Initial choice:- whether the positions of aircraft are shown purely as last reported by the radar (unsmoothed) or whether they are adjusted as a pre-determined function of the positions as previously reported (smoothed).

Off-line changes:- a change of the symbols by which the positions of various aircraft categories are indicated. (If for instance a further category of aircraft is introduced.) Initial choices may also be offered as off-line variabilities.

On-line adjustment:- the brightness of the various categories of symbols on a display.

It is mainly the off-line variabilities which determine the adaptability of the system, i.e. the extent to which it will adapt to future changes in requirements.

13 Any Other Requirements

Anything else which, on the one hand, affects or may affect the suitability of the system for its intended operational use and which, on the other hand, affects or may affect its design. This does not include explanations of how the system will be used or how it may be designed. Such information is provided in separate documents. However, definitions will be included of any terms used whose meanings may not be clear to both system designers and users.

APPENDIX 2

INPUT DEFINITION PARAMETERS

1   Identity and
2   Informaton content:- as 1 and 2 in App 1.

3   Recoverability:- A statement of the possibilities of obtaining
the information provided by the input, or informaton in lieu, in case
of failure to capture the input when it was available for capture.
For instance, when the input is an alphanumeric message which was
lost either because it was garbled in transmission, or because the
system was overloaded when it arrived, it may be possible to request
a re-transmission of the message. On the other hand, in the case of
a display and data processing system for air traffic control it is
not possible to have messages from the radars giving the positions of
aircraft re-transmitted. However, a new message giving the position
at the time of the following sighting of the aircraft by the radar
will normally be received within approximately one revolution time of
the radar.

4   Forms and formats and
5   Tolerances and resolutions:- as in 4 and 5 of App 1.

6   Availability periods:- The period or periods within which an
input or its constituent parts are available for capture. In the
simplest case this is the period during which an input like a voltage
level is available at the system interface; however, there may be
more complicated cases, for instance, one in which there is a warning
signal (in itself an input which has to be captured) that a message
in the form of a string of bits will arrive within a specified period
(with tolerances on it) with the bits themselves then lasting for
specified periods with specified intervals between them (both with
given tolerances on them).

7   Speeds,
8   Freshness,
9   Sizes,
10   Occurrences,
11   Interfaces
12   Variabilities and
13   Any other constrainsts:- as the corresponding items in App 1,
except that:

<u>10   Occurrences</u>:- This also states the conditions under which the input can occur and also the conditions under which, though it may occur, it will be illegal.

<u>11   Interfaces</u>:-   The locations, numbers and definitions of the interfaces at which the inputs are available to the system.

APPENDIX 3

GENERAL CONSTRAINTS

<u>1   Acceptable prices</u>:- The maximum price at which the system will still be worth procuring, or in the case of a system designed as a standard product, the maximum price at which the product will still find a worthwhile market.   There may be a distribution of prices, depending on such factors as the facilities provided or the time at which the system will become available or the times at which various models will come on the market.

<u>2   Time scales</u>:- The times at which the system, or sometimes parts of it, have to become available.   The times may be dependent on the facilities provided.

<u>3   Environmental Requirements</u>:-   These define the environment in which the system may have to operate, (including in some cases that in which it may have to be stored).   For military systems the appropriate standards are usually specified.   The environmental requirements should also specify maximum weights and sizes, any further transportability requirements, appearances, noise levels and so on.   If, say, certain materials are not to be used because they may be hazardous in the given environment this should be stated.

<u>4   Services Capabilities</u>:- Complete specifications of any services available which may be required, e.g. electrical power, heat removal and so on.   The specifications should state tolerances, including periods for which they may last.

<u>5   Operators capabilities and requirements</u>:-   Qualifications and experience of the operators and any requirements or constraints which they may impose on the system.   This includes information such as, for instance, the fact that higher pay will be demanded if the operators are required to operate keyboards; that space is to be provided on the working surfaces for coffee and magazines; any assistance which may be required from the supplier with the training of operators; requirements for, and contraints on, users' manuals.

<u>6   Maintenance capabilities and requirements</u>:-   The qualifications and experience of the maintenance personnel, tools available, and periods of availability with possible variations in the level of expertise available at different periods; any requirements for assistance with the training of maintenance personnel; requirements for, and constraints on, maintenance manuals.

<u>7   Adaptability</u>:- Means for ensuring adaptability and extension capability beyond that which can be specified, at the time, under other headings. Classically, specification that the processing load should not exceed n% of that available in the system and that store capacity should be expandable by m%.

<u>8   Security</u>:- Anything, other than outputs and inputs, to support the required level of security, from ensuring that the system will not constitute a fire risk, to temperproofing.

<u>9   Mandatory design requirements</u>:- Any requirements which infringe the principle of implementation independence, typically that approved computers or approved high level languages be used.

<u>10   Mandatory implementation requirements</u>:- Any requirements or constraints imposed on the design and implementation process, e.g. quality assurance procedures; progress reports; meetings at specified stages in the process.

Reducing the Risk of Failure in Computer System Development Projects

A. A. Levene

Principal Consultant, Systems Designers Limited, UK

This paper describes an approach to the definition, selection and use of development standards which are one part of the set of mechanisms necessary for the successful operation of a computer-system development project.

The initial consideration of the requirements for a total project control system appears to be unusual but it is felt to be worth the effort since it makes it possible to define both what development standards <u>are</u> and what they <u>are not</u>. The notion of a set of standards that can provide for effective quality control and be readily adapted for use in a wide variety of applications and development environments is considered to be a vital contribution towards reducing the risk of failure in futire computer system development projects.

REDUCING THE RISK OF FAILURE IN

COMPUTER SYSTEM DEVELOPMENT PROJECTS

CONTENTS

1.   INTRODUCTION

2.   THE NATURE OF A DEVELOPMENT PROJECT

3.   SYSTEM AND SOFTWARE DEVELOPMENT STANDARDS

4.   USE OF COMPUTER-BASED TOOLS DURING DEVELOPMENT

Acknowledgements

The work on which the development standards, described in
this paper, are based was carried out by a group of
people at Systems Designers Limited. Recognition is made
of the efforts of M.G. Bailey, G.P. Mullery, and
K.E. Stangroom.

1. INTRODUCTION

This paper describes the nature, form and use of
DEVELOPMENT STANDARDS which are one of several classes
of mechanism necessary for the efficient execution of a
computer system development project.

The background to the development of the set of standards
and the problems they are intended to overcome, is
explained below in this chapter (1.1 and 1.2).

Chapter 2 discusses the general nature of a development
project and the risks to which it is subject. An
overview is given of a project control system which
serves to indicate what development standards are, what
they are not, and to emphasise that they can only
usefully exist in conjunction with other components of
the project control system.

Chapter 3 represents the body of the paper and is a
comprehensive description of a set of development
standards that has been developed by Systems Designers
Limited.

Chapter 4 introduces the idea of using computer-based
tools to assist with the requirement and design
specification activities and discusses the form of
available tools.

Indication of the scope of content for a useable set of
development standards can be judged from Appendix 2
which is the contents list of Systems Designers
Limited's System and Software Development Standards
Reference Manual.

1.1 Background

Software development (or maintenance) projects have the
following characteristics which are the major influences
on their ultimate success or failure.

-        Software Development activities generate a
         large amount of information in the form of
         functional specifications, design
         specifications, code listings, test
         specifications etc.

- Software Development information needs to be processed and controlled in order to ensure that it is current, complete and accurate whenever it is needed.

- Software Development activities need to be organised in a systematic manner, so that responsibilities and functions are clearly defined.

- Software Development activities need to be supported and audited in order to ensure their proper functioning.

Of course, similar characteristics are equally relevant to a broad spectrum of non-software development tasks. However, failure to recognise their importance and to provide for their needs in software projects are major factors contributing to time and cost overrun, and unsuitable and unreliable systems that are difficult and expensive to maintain and modify.

In the last decade or so there have been many attempts to bring a more disciplined approach to the development of computer based systems. Notable amongst these are,

- Documentation Standards
- High Level Programming Languages
- Structured Programming
- Design Reviews/Structured Walkthroughs
- Project Management techniques such as PERT, CPA etc.

In the Defence sector great emphasis has been placed on "quality planning" with the introduction of various guidelines (1,2,3,4,5) and the need for contractors to show evidence of certain project control practices which conform to those guidelines.

Over the last four years Systems Designers Limited have been developing and evolving STANDARDS by which QUANTITATIVE quality control and evaluation can be applied throughout the development cycle.

These standards (6), which have been evolved with the co-operation of a number of clients e.g. (7), are not intended to replace techniques such as those mentioned above: rather, they are intended to supplement otherwise subjective measures of quality.

1.2   Potential Standards Problems

In many organisations, often despite significant
expenditure, the introduction of standards has failed
to make a significant impact in reducing the life-cycle
costs of software based systems. Such failure can
usually be attributed to one or more of the following
types of shortcoming in such standards,

- they are inappropriate for the particular
  project
- they are incompatible with other
  techniques in use
- they are deficient even for the subset of
  topics that they do cover
- they are difficult and/or costly to apply
- they are over-restrictive in the
  limitations that they place on the
  individual or project

Particular attention has been paid to avoiding these
particular problems in order to produce standards that
will provide assistance both to Management and to the
project team. For Management the benefits would be in
the form of better project status information leading to
more reliable project control. For project teams the
benefits would be in the form of more coherent working
practices - i.e. for each task, clear definition of what
is to be produced, what information is supplied, what
criteria will be used to judge the acceptability of
products. Additionally, there is the possibility of
collecting valid statistics which may be used to assess
the need for improvement to current practices
(including the standards themselves).

2.   THE NATURE OF A DEVELOPMENT PROJECT

A Development Project can be simply defined as - an
undertaking established for the specific purpose of
producing an acceptable Target System, given some
statement of requirement or need. As such we can equate
a Development Project to a system and can expect to be
able to define that system in terms of - functions, and
mechanisms for their performance; information, and media
for its storage and transmission; and a structure
(organisation).

In order to define a suitable system - in this case, an
effective project control system - we must clearly
understand the requirements that it must fulfil. We have
already mentioned the obvious functional requirements -
to produce a Target System - but in this chapter we
consider vital additional requirements, primarily in
terms of the need to identify, control, and eventually
eliminate, risk.

Since we are concerned with development rather than
mass-production, by definition a Target System is not
an exact copy of an existing system; therefore there
are always a new set of values for the risk elements
associated with each project. We argue that in fact the
risk elements are characteristic of the risks to which
all projects are subject.

2.1   Development Project Risks

The risks to which a Development Project is subject are
most clearly manifest as both business and technical
failures. That is to say, projects are very prone to
overrun of both timescale and budget and to producing
the "wrong" system (see Fig. 1 below).

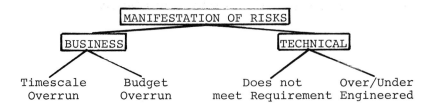

FIGURE 1 : MANIFESTATION RISKS

Whereas there is normally little disagreement on risk manifestation there appears to be ample scope for discussion regarding the sources, or components, of risk. However, a closer look at the situation suggests that, whilst different authorities prefer to categorise these components in different ways, with different terminology, there is probably a strong concensus as to what are the prime components. Our rationalisation of the situation, which recognises three major components of risk, is shown below in Table 1.

One major risk component arises directly from the nature of any development (as opposed to mass-production) undertaking: the ever present risk of things changing unexpectedly, i.e. PERTURBATION.

A second major risk component arises from the 'man-month' syndrome (8) that implies that there is a simple, linear relationship between the amount of time needed (or available) for a development task and the man-power available (or needed). That is to say we put a project at risk if we do not recognise the particular problems of PERSONNEL.

The third major risk component is largely self-inflicted in that,

- we fail to recognise some of the basic technical features of a development project (e.g. that errors in design are far more easily and cheaply corrected the sooner that they are detected);
- we allow a 'black art' syndrome to persist rather than formalising our methods of working and insisting on common standards.

In summary we often pay insufficient attention to establishing the correct PROJECT ENVIRONMENT.

PERTURBATION	PERSONNEL	PROJECT ENVIRONMENT
"The best laid plans ...." Requirement Changes - Genuine change of mind by customer - Hidden implication emerges Failure to Meet Requirement - Cannot produce a feasible design - Acceptance test fails Problem or Error Detected - Design inconsistent - Missing component - Inadequate computer time for testing	"Though all men be made of one metal, yet they be not cast all in one mould" Wrong People Available - Not the right grade - Not the right training - Not the right expertise Wrong Availability - Too many people for current tasks - Too few people for current tasks	"It is best to do things systematically, since we are only human, and disorder is our worst enemy". Undefined Responsibilities & Authorities Undefined Procedures Unknown Quality of Development Products Inadequate Control of Development Products Problems/Errors Detected Late Inadequate Technical Approaches Inadequate Support Facilities/Services Lack of "visibility"

TABLE 1 : MAJOR COMPONENTS OF RISK

2.2   Development Project Functions and Organisation

In this section is explained a basic definition of a
project control system which is relevant to the previously
discussed major components of risk. The main purpose of
this definition is to establish - as one part of a
project control system - a scope and role for
DEVELOPMENT STANDARDS which are the main subject of this
paper (see chapter 3).

The definition, given here, of a project control system
comprises three main functions - Project Management,
Development Management, Configuration Management - plus
one "extra mural" function - Quality Assurance, and an
organisation which clearly defines responsibilities and
authorities so that the various functions may be
properly executed.

a)   Project Management

This function is conceived of as a closed loop control
function which can be put into operation at any 'level'
within the project organisation (i.e. its basic
operation is as relevant to the control of a team which
is a sub-division of the overall project organisation as
it is to the overall control of the project).

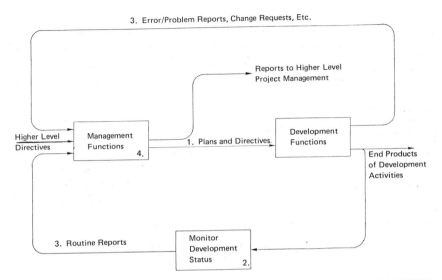

FIGURE 2 - BASIC OPERATION OF PROJECT MANAGEMENT FUNCTION

The purposes of this function are to deal with the problems of "perturbation" and to ensure timely detection and correction of errors: leading to control of both timescale and budget and to minimising the technical risks.

Examples of components of this function are shown in Table 2, below, keyed to figure 2, above, which illustrates the basic operation of the function. The component, Development Functions, is expanded in b), below. A useful discussion on some project management issues can be found in reference (9).

1. PLANS & DIRECTIVES	2. MONITOR DEVELOPMENT STATUS	3. REPORTS	4. MANAGEMENT FUNCTIONS
Progress - Time	Reviews	Weekly	Estimate Resources
Cost - Time	Progress Meetings	Monthly	Estimate Effort
Progress - Cost	Analyse Achievements versus plans	Minutes of Meetings	Estimate Cost
Staff/Resources - Time		Review Reports	Estimate Timescale
Dependencies		Phase End Reports	Produce Plans
Task Definition		Problem Reports	Produce Directives
Work Breakdown Structure		Error Reports	
		Change Requests	
		Progress Variance	
		Cost Variance	

TABLE 2 : COMPONENTS OF PROJECT MANAGEMENT FUNCTION

b)   Development Management

As can be seen in figure 2, above, Development Functions
are the "process" which is "controlled" by the
Management and Monitor Functions. Development Management
comprises the "internal" functions of this process.

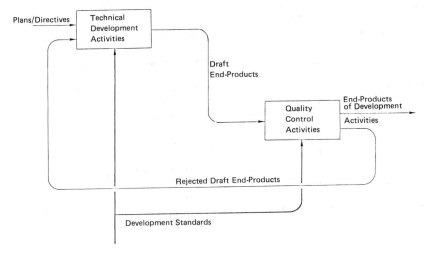

FIGURE 3 - BASIC OPERATION OF DEVELOPMENT MANAGEMENT
                              FUNCTION

Separation of the concerns of Development Management from
those of Project Management enables us to consider
technical issues of the Target System without the
confusion of other important, but essentially
non-technical, issues such as how to subdivide the
project into phases, how to staff it, and so on.
Definition of such items form part of the directives
which are an essential input to this function.

The basic operation of this function as shown in Figure 3,
above, which can be put into operation for any technical
development task: the development standards, which
define the scope of the particular task, will vary from
phase to phase of the project (as determined by Project
Management).

The intentions of this function are to ensure that the
correct technical approach is followed and that all
end-products of development activities are of KNOWN
QUALITY.

There is no further discussion here on the component parts of the Development Management function since this is the overall subject of this paper (see Chapter 3). However it is emphasized here that the use of appropriate technical METHODS is vital to the correct operation of this function during all project phases (formal methods are particularly relevant during Requirements Analysis - e.g. CORE (10), System Design, - e.g. JSD (11) and Program Design - e.g. JSP (12)). Discussion of such methods is beyond the scope of this paper.

c)   Configuration Management

Traditionally, formal Configuration Management (possibly in the form of a Project Librarian) in conjunction with change control procedures has only been involved during the latter stages of a software development project. In our model of a project control system change control is part of the Management functions (see Project Management, above), whilst Configuration Management should be put into operation in all phases of the project.

The purposes of the Configuration Management function are to ensure that at all times all development products are of known status and that the location of all copies is known. This paper contains no further discussion on this function. A full discussion on the various options for the necessary standards and procedures is contained in reference (6).

d)   Quality Assurance

Whereas the previous three functions define a self-contained project control system, in reality any project will normally exist as a sub-division of the Contractor organisation (and possibly also of the Customer/User organisation) - see Project Organisation, e) below. Therefore it is to be expected that there will be a need for accountability by the project to the parent organisation: equally a project may reasonably expect assistance from other parts of the parent organisation.

The Quality Assurance (QA) function is defined as a function of the parent organisation (not of an individual project) which provides a means for accountability and assistance.

QA is not discussed further in this paper save to
exemplify three distinct "services" that it may usefully
perform for each project,

- auditing

   i.e. formal checks that the project is
   operating according to its own prescribed
   standards, etc.

- advising

   i.e. provision of independent expertise
   to provide an opinion of any aspect of a
   project.

It is recommended that each of the above two services is
invoked as many times as necessary during the course of a
project at the discretion of a Company (not Project)
appointed authority (sometimes referred to as the Quality
Manager).

- monitoring

   e.g. regular receipt and inspection of the
   standard plans and reports produced as a
   result of the Project Management function
   (see above) in order to provide regular
   independent reports on the state of the
   project to Company Management.

e)   Project Organisation.

In order to ensure that every participant in a project is
aware of his (and other people's) responsibilities and
authorities an appropriate organisation must be defined.
It is not possible to conceive of a 'standard'
organisation relevant to all projects but certain
principles can be set down. A full discussion of the
subject is beyond the scope of this paper.

The basic principle is to establish a hierarchical
organisation for each project which, wherever appropriate,
involves members of the customer/user organisation (with
defined responsibilities and authorities).

Thus, for example, the top of the hierarchy (referred to in Figure 4 as the Project Board) might be "manned" by the Developer's project manager and a person from the Customer organisation with certain executive powers (often referred to as User Executive or Project Officer).

Reporting directly to the Project Board would be one or more "Project Leaders" appointed by the Developer organisation who might also usefully have a direct technical liason with members of the Customer organisation (e.g. to resolve technical queries, rather than have executive powers).

Each Project Leader would have an organisation beneath him which reflects the current structure of the system being developed - following the principles of "work breakdown structure" e.g. (13), and which provides for proper execution of the different sub-functions of Project management, Development management and Configuration management. Again certain principles apply e.g. staff with both technical development and quality control responsibilities are not normally permitted to check their own work; a discussion on quality control is contained in Chapter 3.

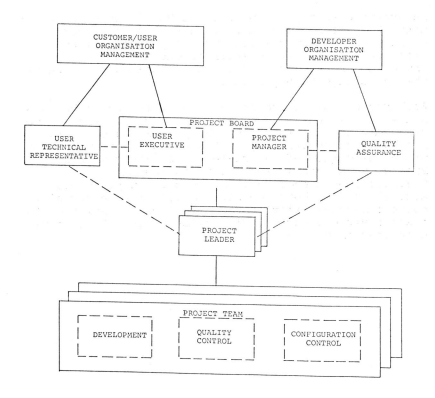

```
            ┌──────────────────┐                    ┌──────────────────┐
            │  CUSTOMER/USER   │                    │    DEVELOPER     │
            │   ORGANISATION   │                    │   ORGANISATION   │
            │    MANAGEMENT    │                    │    MANAGEMENT    │
            └──────────────────┘                    └──────────────────┘
```

— = Functional Responsibility for the purposes of the project

--- = Advisory Communication

Note: Project management functions, as described in 2.2a), are performed by the Project Board, Project Leader and within the Project Team.

FIGURE 4 - BASIC PROJECT ORGANISATION

3.   SYSTEM AND SOFTWARE DEVELOPMENT STANDARDS

The application context for the Development Standards described in this Chapter, is defined in Chapter 2.2,b).

3.1   Terminology And Key Concepts

One particularly unfortunate feature of the software industry at large is the terminology problem - not only in terms of jargon which confuses the outsider but more insidiously in the lack of standardisation of terminology within the industry. The problem hardly needs any further discussion but for the would-be provider of standards it is a potential nightmare.

We tackled this problem in two ways.

a)   Rationalisation of Documentation

A study of a number of widely used documentation standards e.g. (14,15,16) led us to the conclusion that any document required during, or as a result of, a development project can be classified into one of only three basic types - Specification, Evaluation, Instruction.

b)   Use of Entity/Relationship Model for System Description

We explored the notion that a simple entity/relationship model could be used as a basis for system descriptions to be recorded in various documents. We chose the model that is inherent in the requirement specification method, CORE (10) and have satisfied ourselves that commonly used terms (e.g. process, task, program module,) are just specific instances of one of five basic entity types - as shown in table 3, below.

3.2   Quality Control

Quality Control is defined as the act of checking for conformity (of a product) with pre-defined standards.

The standards in question are derived by choosing an appropriate set of attributes for each instance of the five entity types illustrated in Table 3, below.

ENTITY TYPES	ACTIONS	MECHANISMS	DATA	EVENTS/ CONDITIONS	MEDIA
	SUB SYSTEM	PROCESSOR	MESSAGE	STARTED	PAPER
	PROCESS	PERIPHERAL	SYSTEM DATA	STOPPED	CARDS
	TASK	OPERATOR	PROGRAM DATA	FAILED	DISK
ENTITY INSTANCES	PROCEDURE		PARAMETER	MODE CHANGE	MAGNETIC TAPE
	SUBROUTINE		FILE	MAINTENANCE DUE	BUS
	MODULE				
	TEST*				

* Test has been included as an instance of ACTION. Tests (e.g. module tests, integration tests, acceptance tests) do not form part of the final system; they are included because their definition and the record of test results are major factors in the confidence that can be expressed for the final system.

TABLE 3 — SAMPLE INSTANCES OF ENTITY TYPES

Attributes cover both intrinsic properties of the entity and relationships with other entities. The standards exist in the form of a "checklist" of attributes for each instance.

Of course, the mere existence of an entry for each attribute is no guarantee of quality. Therefore, a set of criteria for acceptability of such entries has been drawn up and incorporated into each checklist. When applied, the criteria ensure certain qualities in the system descriptions, such as consistency (e.g. of relationships). Criteria may also be defined which are related to particular methods of analysis or design, such as enforcement of top down description (e.g. item defined only after definition of parent).

It must be noted that this approach to quality control is essentially "clerical" - i.e. it is mechanistic and requires a minimal amount of expertise to apply it. The adoption of this clerical quality control scheme provides an otherwise unachievable <u>basic quantitative</u> assessment of quality. However, in addition it is usually essential to supply both more complex quantitative checks and also subjective assessments of quality.

<u>Complex Quantitative Quality Control</u> is often typified by simply expressed rules which cannot be checked consistently and reliably by non-expert staff (e.g. "check for adherence to structured programming rules"). Reference (17) contains a discussion on application of this type of quality control.

<u>Subjective Quality Control</u> is often typified by the inability to express precise rules e.g. "is the solution <SUBJECTIVE WORD>?", where SUBJECTIVE WORD might be one of the following, Complete, Enhanceable, Flexible, Maintainable, Feasible, etc. It is clear that in such circumstances the quality (technical expertise/ judgement) of the reviewer is the major factor determining the success of applying Subjective Quality Control.

An example of a "clerical" quality control checklist is shown in Figure 5.

COMPONENT FIELDS	QUALITY CONTROL CHECKS													
IDENTIFICATION	INVALID ENTITY TYPE (i.e. NOT ONE OF THE TYPES SHOWN)	INCONSISTENT CROSS REF	UNDEFINED ENTRY	PREMATURE DEFINITION	TOO MANY COMPS (>THAN SHOWN)	TOO FEW COMPS (<THAN SHOWN)	NAME CLASH	NAME UNDECLARED	ALREADY DEFINED	OUT OF BOUNDS	UNAUTHORISED ENTRY	N/A NOT PERMITTED	TBD NOT PERMITTED	BLANK ENTRY NOT PERMITTED
NAME							F	F	F			F	F	F
CATEGORY	ACTION											F	F	F
DEFINED BY					W(1)						F	F	F	F
DESCRIPTION										W(10)		F	F	F
DOCUMENT REFS			F									W	W	F
DATE												F	F	F
PROPERTIES														
FREQUENCY										F		W	W	F
TIME LIMITS										F		W	W	F
PRIORITY												W	W	F
OTHER													W	F
RELATIONSHIPS														
PART OF	ACTION	F	F	F	W(1)			F	F			W	W	F
PARTS ARE	ACTION	F				W(2)		F				W	W	F
BEFORE/AFTER	ACTION	F	W					F	W				W	F
	EVENT	F	W					F	W				W	F
PERFORMED BY	MECHANISM	F	W					F	W			W	W	F
STARTS/STOPS	MECHANISM	F	W					F	W			W	W	F
USES	DATA	F	W					F	W			W	W	F
SETS	DATA	F	W					F	W			W	W	F
CAUSES	EVENT	F	W					F	W			W	W	F
CAUSED BY	EVENT	F	W					F	W			W	W	F
TESTED BY	TEST DEF	F	W					F	W			W	W	F
STORED IN	MEDIA	F	W					F	W			W	W	F

The example checklist demonstrates how the identification, property and relationship attributes that have been selected may be presented with the selected checks in an easily readable format.

The error messages are cross-referenced to the attributes by the characters F or W. "F" means an outright failure, "W" means that there may be an error but a more technically expert member of staff must decide whether the error really exists.

FIGURE 5 - "ACTION" CHECKLIST

3.3   Development Standards Overview

The approach, described in this paper, to System and
Software Development Standards - and their selection for
a project - is a distinct departure from the "traditional"
approach.

In the first instance, certain items such as Project
Phase Model and Project Management Standards which might
otherwise have been considered an inbuilt part of such
standards have been removed.

Standard Forms have not been considered as they are
strongly governed by individual/local preference. The
standards described contain the expected content of such
forms but leave the representation to local preference.

This separation of concerns has produced a much clearer
picture of what System and Software Development Standards
really are - standards for the content, and criteria for
the acceptability, of the End-Products of a Development
Project.

The term END-PRODUCT is used to denote any material
produced as a result of carrying out any designated
project task. The concern of System and Software
Development Standards is in End-Products which are
documents, or parts of documents (regardless of
documentary media). A clear distinction is made between
Administrative End-Products and Technical End-Products.

Administrative End Products are the means by which
project staff interface with project management functions
and handle technical end-products. They may be produced
according to pre-defined schedule (e.g. Progress Reports)
or as and when needed (e.g. Error Reports). Note, that
although Administrative End Products are not regarded as
instances of the Entity/Relationship Model they do have
corresponding quality control checklists. Standards for
Administrative End-Products are not discussed further in
this paper, but are exemplified in Figure 6 below.

Technical End-Products are documents which describe
different aspects of the system under development. They
are produced according to a pre-defined schedule which
at its highest level is represented as the chosen
Project Phase Model (as defined by the Project
Management function). The User may require delivery of
all or only some of the Technical End-Products produced.

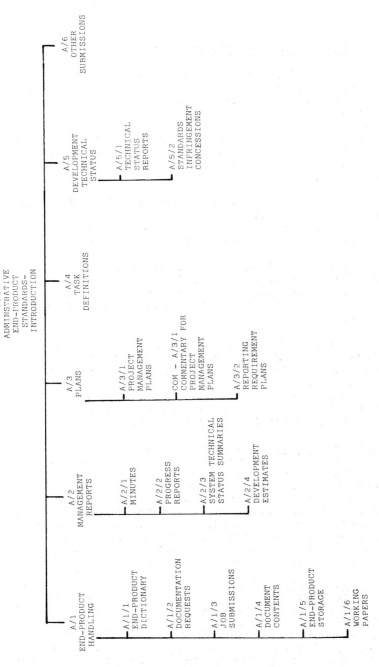

FIGURE 6 – SCOPE OF ADMINISTRATIVE END–PRODUCT STANDARDS

In order to facilitate the subsequent discussion a
distinction is made between Phase End-Products (documents
to be available at pre-determined project milestones) and
Component End-Products which are constituent parts of
Phase End-Products.

Standards for Technical End-Products are arranged into
three groups of "Major" End-Products (which will, in many
cases, correspond to Phase End-Products), see Figure 7,
below.

These groups are End-Products of type:-

- Evaluation: end products dealing with the
  assessment of situations (e.g. feasibility;
  completed tests etc).

- Specification: end-products which define the
  various requirements for the development
  process to continue (e.g. Requirement
  Specification, Program Module Definition etc).

- Instruction: end-products which provide the
  information necessary to utilise other
  end-products successfully (e.g. User Manuals,
  Operator Manuals etc).

End-Products are arranged in these groups especially to
facilitate selection of standards.   That is to say, to
enable any Selector to identify with any given standard.
To further this intention, the Standard for each
End-Product is identified not only by a "reference" name for
it, but also with other commonly used names where
relevant (e.g. Requirement Specification, but also
Functional Specification, System Specification etc).

Below this highest level, end-products are successively
decomposed into lower level component End-Product
standards.   The lowest level of component End-Product is
the documentation for the occurence of an "entity".
The occurence of an entity is a specific named instance
of any one of 5 general Entity types,(see Table 3, above).

3.4   Standards Selection and Introduction

It is a necessary precursor to the start of a project that
standards are selected for it.   If more standards are to
be used than is absolutely necessary it may well
jeopardise the success of the project and even bring the
standards into disrepute (and ultimate disuse!).

```
T/0                 Technical End Product Standards Introduction
         T/1        EVALUATION End-Product Standards
                    T/1/1    Feasibility Study Reports
                             T/1/1/1 Existing System Evaluation
                             T/1/1/2 Proposed Solutions
                             T/1/1/3 Cost-Benefit Analysis
                    T/1/2    Test Evaluations
                    T/1/3    System Audit Reports
         T/2        SPECIFICATION End-Product Standards
                    T/2/1    Requirement Specification
                             7/2/1/1 Management Report
                             7/2/1/2 User Specification
                             7/2/1/3 Technical Specification
                                 T/2/1/3/1 ...................
                                 ...........................
                    T/2/2    Design Specification
                             T/2/2/1 System Design
                                 T/2/2/1/1 ...................
                                 ...........................
                             T/2/2/2 Program Module Design
                             T/2/2/2 ...........................
                                 T/2/2/2/1...................
                                 ...........................
         T/3        INSTRUCTION End-Product Standards
                    T/3/1    Source Code
                             T/3/1/1 Code Presentation
                             T/3/1/2 Code Production
                    T/3/2    System Integration
                    T/3/3    Conduct of Tests
                    T/3/4    System Changeover
                    T/3/5    Operations Manual
                    T/3/6    User Manual
```

FIGURE 7 - SCOPE OF TECHNICAL END-PRODUCT
STANDARDS

Selection of standards is achieved by the selector
following a Standards Leaflet hierarchy down to the
desired level of detail (e.g. see Figures 6 and 7). This
desired level of detail depends on the current intention
of the selector. For example, if the selector is
preparing a proposal for carrying out a project, it
may only be necessary to show the intention of standards
use by highlighting standards at a high level. Similarly
it may not be realistic to define all the detailed
standards for later end-products very early in a project.
Naturally, such considerations are affected by the size
and duration of the project.

A part of the standards selection process may be to "edit"
individual standards checklists e.g. to cater for local
project preferences.

The selection process is not one to be undertaken
lightly since it requires a comprehensive understanding
of the project environment in which the standards are to
be employed. In fact, a complete chapter of the Systems
Designers Limited System and Software Development
Standards Reference Manual is devoted to the selection
process. The contents of this manual are shown in
Appendix 1 in order to illustrate this point.

Factors influencing choice of the appropriate sub-set
of standards for a project include:

- Type of project (e.g. feasibility study,
  requirements analysis, full development)

- Potential cost of failure

- Security requirements

- Staff experience

- Availability of automated aids

Successful introduction of standards is influenced by
such factors as:
- Form of Standards manuals
- Ease of use and interpretation of standards
- Allowance for training
- Existence of a standards monitoring/management
  function independent of a particular project.

4.   THE USE OF COMPUTER-BASED TOOLS DURING DEVELOPMENT

There is a healthy trend towards making more and more use
of computer-based tools during development. The current
emphasis on the use of such tools is in the programming
environment, but use is design and analysis activities is
growing - See e.g. references (18,19).

A survey recently carried out by Systems Designers
Limited for the Ministry of Defence (20) revealed the
existence of a number of practical tools for the storage,
analysis and retrieval of specification information in
the form of an entity-relationship model. Perhaps the
best-known and currently most widely used tool of this
type is PSL/PSA - Problem Statement Language/Problem
Statement Analyser (21,22). The functional form of this
tool is shown in Figure 8, below. A tool of this type
should not be confused with the typical data-dictionary
which, in general, offers only a very restricted sub-set
of facilities. However, some of the more advanced data-
dictionaries may well be able to provide a practical tool
for this type of application.

Use of this type of tool allows the specification
"database" to be built up piece-meal (i.e. information
is entered as and when it is acquired/generated by
analysts and designers). Application of "clerical"
quality control checks can be achieved as and when
required by means of available analysis and query
programs.

As well as providing a reliable means of performing
the clerical type of quality control the use of this
type of tool helps enforce use of standard terminology,
greatly assists in performance of certain Configuration
Management functions and provides a source of authentic
development progress status information.

PSL/PSA and other, like, tools of its generation
require reasonably large computing resources (e.g. DEC
VAX 11/780, IBM 4300 series, and upwards) and may be an
"overkill" in some situations - PSL/PSA has available
about 50 standard reports, complex query facilities and
a word-processing package. As awareness grows of the
benefits achievable with this type of tool even on
quite small projects it is inevitable that mini and
micro-based tools will become widely available.

A word of warning however: Without the selection and
introduction of relevant development standards and
well defined and properly used methods (for analysis,
design, etc) the use of such tools will at best be
pointless, and at worst a hindrance to progress.

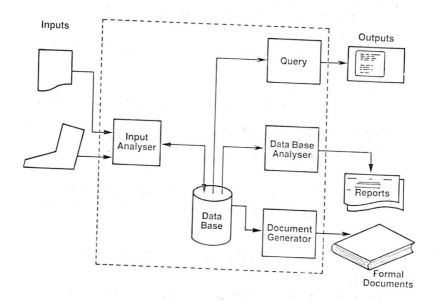

FIGURE 8 - FUNCTIONAL FORM OF COMPUTER-BASED
SPECIFICATION AID

APPENDIX 1

REFERENCES

1. Ministry of Defence
    Defence Standard 05/21 "Quality Control System
    Requirements for Industry", 1973.

2. Ministry of Defence
    A Guide to the Management of Software Based Systems
    for Defence, 1978.

3. Ministry of Defence
    OTM1 "Planning to Achieve Quality", 1975.

4. Ministry of Defence
    QTM6 Quality Assurance in the Programming and Use
    of Computers, 1976.

5. Electronic Engineering Association
    Guide to the Quality Assurance of Software, 1978.

6. Systems Designers Limited
    System and Software Development Standards
    Reference Manual, 1981.

7. G.P. Mullery
    Standards for the Production of High Quality
    Systems. Proceedings of IFAC Workshop, SAFECOMP,
    1979.

8. F. Brooks
    The Mythical Man Month. Addison Wesley, 1975.

9. P.M. Haine
    Tackling the Intractable Problems of Project
    Management. Computer Bulletin, March 1981.

10. G.P. Mullery
    CORE: A Method for Controlled Requirements
    Expression: Proc. 4th International Conference
    of Software Engineering, 1979.

11. M. Jackson
    Principles of Program Design. Academic Press,
    1975.

12. Michael Jackson Systems Limited
    Jackson System Development.

13.   R.C. Tausworthe
       The Work Breakdown Structure in Software Project
       Management. The Journal of Systems and Software,
       Vol. 1 No. 3, 1980.

14.   National Computing Centre
       Data Processing Documentation Standards, 1977.

15.   Guidelines for Documentation of Computer Programs
       and Automated Data Systems, FIPS PUB 38. Federal
       Information Processing Standards Publication, 1976.

16.   I.B.M.
       HIPO - A Design Aid and Documentation Technique,
       ref.

       GC20 - 1851 - 1, 1974.

17.   M.E. Fagan
       Design and Code Inspections to Reduce Errors in
       Program Development. IBM Systems Journal, No. 3,
       1976.

18.   EDP Analyser
       Programming Work-Stations.
       Vol. 17, No. 10, 1979.

19.   Systems Designers Limited/ISDOS Project
       Proceedings of Conference, Use of Computer Aids
       in Systems Development, London, June 1980.

20.   Systems Designers Limited
       A Survey of Automated Techniques for System
       Description. Working Paper 5, C0789, August 1980.

21.   D. Teichroew, E.A. Hershay III
       PSL/PSA: A Computer Aided Technique for Structured
       Documentation and Analysis of Information
       Processing Systems. IEEE Trans. on Software
       Engineering, Vol.SE-1, No. 1 January 1977.

22.   Systems Designers Limited.
       A Technical Overview of the PSL/PSA Software
       System, 1980.

APPENDIX 2

CONTENTS LIST FOR DEVELOPMENT STANDARDS REFERENCE MANUAL

1.   SYSTEM AND SOFTWARE DEVELOPMENT STANDARDS MANUAL

    1.1   PURPOSE
    1.2   STRUCTURE
    1.3   USE

2.   INTRODUCTION TO SYSTEM AND SOFTWARE DEVELOPMENT STANDARDS

    2.1   WHERE STANDARDS FIT IN A DEVELOPMENT PROJECT
    2.2   OVERVIEW OF SYSTEM AND SOFTWARE DEVELOPMENT STANDARDS
    2.3   END-PRODUCT DEVELOPMENT - QUALITY CONTROL OPTIONS

3.   PREREQUISITES TO SYSTEM AND SOFTWARE DEVELOPMENT STANDARDS USE

    3.1   INTRODUCTION
    3.2   PROJECT PARAMETERS
    3.3   QUALITY ASSURANCE
    3.4   PROJECT ORGANISATION
    3.5   PROJECT PHASE MODEL
    3.6   MEANS OF IMPLEMENTATION
    3.7   OTHER PROJECT STANDARDS
    3.8   PROJECT PROCEDURES

4.   SYSTEM AND SOFTWARE DEVELOPMENT STANDARDS SELECTION

    4.1   INTRODUCTION
    4.2   STANDARDS SELECTION OVERVIEW
    4.3   EFFECTS OF OTHER PROJECT COMPONENTS
    4.4   THE COMPOSITION OF A STANDARDS LEAFLET
    4.5   THE STANDARDS LEAFLET HIERARCHY
    4.6   THE STANDARDS SELECTION PROCEDURE
    4.7   STANDARDS USE
    4.8   SUMMARY

5.   SYSTEM AND SOFTWARE DEVELOPMENT STANDARDS' LEAFLETS'

    CONTENT LISTED AT PART 4, Chapter 5   for

    ADMINISTRATIVE END-PRODUCT STANDARDS' ('A' series)
    TECHNICAL END-PRODUCT STANDARDS' ('T' series)

APPENDIX 1   GLOSSARY OF TERMS
APPENDIX 2   SAMPLE PHASE MODEL
APPENDIX 3   ENTITY TYPES FOR SYSTEM DESCRIPTION
APPENDIX 4   SYSTEM AND SOFTWARE DEVELOPMENT STANDARDS' SELECTION CHECKLIST

A Query Language as the Prime Reporting Technique on a Codasyl Database

G. O. Jones

Data Administrator, Constructors John Brown Ltd, UK

A major plant contracting company, faced with the problem of volatile demands for computer reporting, are making extensive use of a query language for user access to databases.

Successful use of a query language depends upon an appropriate database design to ensure that the query language is user friendly and economically viable and to accommodate restrictions in the capabilities of the query language.

This paper discusses some of the design considerations for query language access and reviews the economics of its operation.

For many years Data Processing departments have controlled access to companies' data held on computers. Reports have been produced by carefully and expensively written programs which print fixed format outputs, frequently in large quantities. How useful these reports have been has depended upon the quality of the original design and specification of the system and the stability of the organisation's structure, function and information needs.

When changes or new reports are required they are usually expensive and often take a long time to develop. Frequently users hesitate to request changes, and make do with large and comprehensive tabulations when they would prefer small exception reports. When this occurs the systems are no longer serving their proper purpose, and the computer cannot be described as 'User Friendly'.

At CJB we are solving this problem by providing our users with query language access to all databases, thereby giving them virtually unrestricted access to their data.

The success of this technique can be attributed to several factors:

- Query language access has been regarded as central to our database design strategy from the start. All databases are, therefore, designed to support query language access.

- The nature of the company's business results in very volatile user reporting requirements which has resulted in the enthusiastic acceptance of the techniques by users.

- Univac's QLP (Query Language Processor) has proved to be a flexible package meeting most of our requirements.

- We run our own in-house user training programme geared to the requirements of users, with a training database available for 'hands on' practice.

- Access to QLP is entirely controlled by job control macros to protect the user from job control required by the operating system.

CJB

CJB, a member of the John Brown Group, is a major international plant contractor servicing the Oil and Gas, chemical, petrochemical and offshore industries. Contracts are very varied and include such projects as North Sea oil production platforms, polymer plants, ethylene, oil and gas pipelines, chocolate and pharmaceutical plant. The scope of projects is equally varied, some contracts are management only, some engineering only, whilst others may be complete turnkey jobs with CJB handling the entire project from initial design through to final commissioning.

Although the company operates extensive computer procedures, the principal database developments have been in the key area of Materials Progress and Cost Control. A major project will typically require anything from 10,000 to 20,000 individual items to be ordered. Many of these items are known as 'bulk'; typically piping and electrical materials. 1000 metres of six inch pipe may be only one line on a purchase order, but the pipe may be used in twenty different parts of the plant.

The reporting requirements of the Materials Management system are very varied. This is due to two main causes:

- CJB handle a wide range of projects with differing information requirements. 'Design and Procure' for an Eastern Bloc country is totally different from a 'Management Only' contract for an offshore oil platform.

- Within a project, even when its needs have been defined and accommodated, there are still frequent urgent demands for special reports arising from unforseen circumstances. For example, a decision to move part of the fabrication work from one sub-contractor to another would require the production of numerous schedules of material quantities and costs; all of them outside the scope of the normal project requirements.

In the past we have attempted to satisfy these requirements on conventional systems by conventional methods with varying degrees of success, always however, to the detriment of our development programme. A project's need for information is almost always urgent, and talk of ruptured development schedules and other priorities cuts little ice with project managers at the 'sharp end' of the business.

It is hardly surprising, therefore, that when we installed our UNIVAC 1100 series machine in 1977, as a replacement for an aging second generation machine, we looked hard at the possibilities of DMS 1100, Univac's Codasyl Database Management System, and its associated Query Language Processor, (QLP).

DEVELOPMENT PHILOSOPHY

We had already decided that we should use database techniques in
order to handle our information requirements. We, therefore,
implemented a pilot project to evaluate QLP in terms of its
acceptability to users and its ability to satisfy our dynamic
reporting requirements.

We chose a materials progress and cost information system which
used serial files and had extensive but fixed reporting
facilities. The database implementation was 'quick and dirty' -
we simply copied the main serial file onto a database everytime
it was updated. The operational overheads for this arrangement
are obviously high: two sets of files and a database load to run
as well as the serial file update. But it only required about
two man-months of effort for initial implementation, and the pay
off has been high; and, since we did not make a single change to
the existing system, we were able to implement the database
immediately on existing projects with few of the usual problems
of parallel running and system proving which normally accompany
such developments.

Our users took to QLP and the database with gratifying
enthusiasm, using not only the simpler commands but also the more
complex Report Writer facilities. The cries of anguish which
occurred whenever we had problems with the database indicated all
too clearly the importance which it had assumed in their
operations. During this 'quick and dirty' exercise we were in
constant touch with the users to monitor both their method of use
and acceptance of the query language; the information obtained
from this exercise providing an essential input to the design
phase for a new materials database and other related developments.

The success of this 'quick and dirty' pilot study prior to the
main development was considerable and it has now become our
standard procedure where older systems are to be converted to
database. The higher running costs of such temporary systems
being amply justified by the gains in user experience and
improved design of the final system.

DMS 1100 & QLP

DMS 1100 is a CODASYL database management system which runs on the
Univac 1100 series machines and supports Cobol, Fortran, PL1 and
Query Language Processor (QLP).

QLP operates under the 1100 Operating System, Exec 8, as either
an interactive program in Demand mode (Univac's name for Time
Sharing) or as a Batch program. It differs from normal database
programs in having a special type of sub-schema, which not only
identifies the particular entities on the database which are
available to the QLP user, but also specifies the paths through
the database which enquiries can follow. These paths must be
linear and non-recursive and, since an enquiry will not be
actioned unless there is a path encompassing all the necessary
data-items, the sub-schema provides a level of privacy control
since confidential parts of the database can either be completely
omitted from the sub-schema or not included in any path
definition. The sub-schema can also be used to give data-items
more user friendly names than those to be found in the schema.

The QLP command language offers the user three operating levels:

- Basic non-procedural commands.
- Report Writer with procedural commands for the
  manipulation of the retrieved tuples.
- Advanced facilities which allow the user to determine his
  own navigation around the database.

In addition there are macros, procedures and library facilities,
which allow the user to save and edit command sequences for later
re-use.

The principle non-procedural command is:

    LIST data-items WHERE conditions

The data-items in the command are the names of those data-items
which are to be listed in the output. The conditions in the
WHERE clause specify the criteria which are to be used during the
selection process on the database. An unlimited number of
data-item names can be specified; and the WHERE condition can be
any logical combination of arithmetic, comparative and Boolean
operators.

Examples:

1. List the purchase order numbers for the orders placed with
   the vendor SMITH

   LIST PO-NO WHERE VEND-NAME = 'SMITH'

2. List equipment numbers and descriptions for items planned for
    ex-works delivery before 1st July 1981.

    LIST EQ-NO, EQ-DESC WHERE ITEM-EXW-PLAN LT 810701

3. Tabulate in sequence, equipment numbers and estimated and
    committed costs for items where the committed cost exceeds
    the estimated cost by more than 10%, exclude items in area 50.

    LIST BY COLUMN EQ-NO, COST-EST, COST-COMMIT;
    SORT ON EQ-NO;
    WHERE (COST-COMMIT - COST-EST)*100/COST-EST GT 10;
    AND AR-NO NE 50;

In its most basic form LIST uses default layouts and headings,
however, a FORMAT command is available which permits the user to
predefine very simple tabular reports. Options are also
available to SORT the data and to display totals, minima, maxima
and averages.

The LIST and FORMAT commands are simple to use and are easily
assimilated by users with no previous computer experience. Their
simplicity, however, results in a very limited layout capability;
and the user who requires something more than a simple tabular
layout must use the Report Writer.

The Report Writer is an integral part of QLP and uses the same
WHERE clause for data selection but writes the retrieved tuples
to a hit file for sorting followed by printing.

Within the printing phase the user can specify control breaks,
procedural processing with IF and COMPUTE commands and locally
defined variables, printing with Cobol pictures for editing, and
virtually unlimited layout capabilities.

If a user needs to control the way in which QLP navigates the
database then he must have recourse to an altogether more complex
set of procedural commands than those available in the Report
Writer; usually this will be when he needs to access a branched
network. These commands are intended by Univac for use by
professional data processing staff to supplement the basic
facilities. However, although we have users who are successfully
applying these facilities, we fully endorse the view that they
are not generally suitable for non data processing staff.

Using this technique QLP can navigate most forms of database structure with the important restriction that the route traversed must be non recursive. This, therefore, excludes the classic bill of materials implosion/explosion structure.

DESIGN CONSIDERATIONS

As our first database was designed purely to support a query language, and had no other purpose - apart from giving some data processing staff experience in designing and operating a database before the more critical applications were handled - it was given a reasonable structure for this purpose. Had we being concerned about the problems of transaction processing and batch updating we would probably have given less priorty to the query language. It is now clear to us that the requirements of the query language have to be considered very carefully during the database design phase if users are to get a satisfactory service. Inappropriate design can result in three main problems:

- Poor performance with long response times and unacceptably high use of machine resources.

- A database structure in which some data is either inaccessible or, at best, accessible only by complex procedures.

- Specialised space saving storage formats resulting in unreadable data.

The database designer's problems are already extensive so that the additional demands and constraints to accommodate query language will not be welcomed; particularly as they frequently conflict with the requirements of updating by transaction processing systems, most notably those requirements affecting performance.

Some of the points which the database designer must consider are discussed below:

Encoded Data

A query language generally presents the user with data as it appears on the database. Standard edit functions similar to COBOL PICTURE may be available, but at the simplest level defaults will be used. Program encoded data will therefore not be decoded by the query language and will be presented to the user in an unacceptable form.

Implied Decimal Point

Implied decimal points should be specified at the schema level
whenever this is appropriate so that the query language can
present the user with the data as he would expect to see it. Do
not, for example, define a price field as PIC 9(7) (PRICE IN
PENCE), but rather as PIC 9(5)V99 (PRICE £.PP)

Dates

Dates are particularly difficult numbers for users if the query
language does not include modulo date arithmetic and comparative
facilities.

When specific date manipulation facilities are not available, the
ISO format of year-month-day is the most convenient. This seems
to be reasonably acceptable to users and is unambiguous in
situations where both American and European conventions are
likely to be encountered. Selection criteria of the form:

   'List orders placed since 1st May'
are readily handled, but date separations such as:

   'List deliveries which were more than 20 days after promised
date'
cannot be handled conveniently. This latter enquiry may need
dates to be duplicated in some modulo 10 Julian form such as the
number of days since 1st january 1900. This form is economical
of storage but is obviously unacceptable for display purpose.

Derived Fields

Values derived from data items held on the database and likely to
be used frequently for selection criteria should be considered
for inclusion in the database in their own right particularly if
the derivation involves processes other than very simple
arithmetic.

Variable Length Records

Variable length records will not always be accepted by a query
language as they cause problems of definition for output. Points
to consider before specifying variable length records are:
whether the sub-schema permits adequate redefinition to give
acceptable user data names (OCCURS DEPENDING and subscripted

variables are not attractive concepts to thrust onto unsuspecting
users), and how output is defined, particularly for variable
length narrative fields.

Cross Tuple Selection

Query languages which operate in single tuple mode cannot select
data if the selection criteria depend on the examination of more
than one tuple.

If such queries are to be satisfied summary or count data must be
held at suitably high levels in the database. The following are
examples from the schema in fig.1 which would all require such
treatment:

    List Employees who have had less than 5 jobs
    List Departments with more than 10 women
    List Employees with average salary over last 5 years greater
    than half present salary

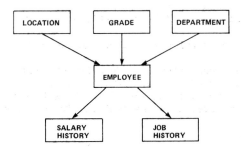

FIGURE 1   STAFF DATABASE

Linear Access Mode

Many query languages only provide linear access mode and those
which do offer branched access do so at the cost of complex
syntax which can only be considered for advanced users.

Unnecessary branched structures such as single occurrence
subsidiary records should be avoided whenever possible.

When the designer cannot avoid such situations some assistance to
the user can be given by duplicating some data from high records
into lower level records and holding summary data such as totals,
maxima, minima, latest dates etc. in high level records.

Recursive Sets

Recursive sets occur particularly in bill of materials systems to
define parts explosions, but can also occur in other areas, for
example to define supervisor - subordinate relationships between
employees.

Many query languages will not handle this structure to access
subordinate part numbers since the enquiry must pass through the
same record more than once.

Data Inversion

The effectiveness of a query language is generally dependent on
having a schema which allows the first stage selection of most
enquiries to be actioned at a level where there are relatively
few record occurrences. If the schema does not provide for this,
then massive searches will be needed to satisfy enquiries,
resulting in long response times and unacceptably high volumes of
mass storage I/O.

To provide the user with these access paths inversions are
necessary on the fields likely to be needed for first stage
selection. In many cases these inversions will be provided
solely to service the query language. In the example in fig.1
three inversions are provided on the assumption that users will
normally be able to restrict their enquiries to a specific
Department, Grade, or Location.

An enquiry such as:
    LIST EMPLOYEES WHERE DEPT = 'ENGINEERING' AND EMPLOYEE-AGE GT
    '50'
can be satisfied after a search of only a fraction of the
database.

Whereas enquiries such as:
    LIST EMPLOYEES WHERE EMPLOYEE-AGE GT '50' AND EMPLOYEE-SEX =
    'MALE'
would require a search of the whole population of employees on
the database.

The additional records which these inversions require will
generally occupy little space on the database, but the pointers
associated with them will occur at the lower level and may well
make a significant contribution to the size of the database.

Where inversions are provided, the data held in the entry records
so created should always be duplicated in the lower level
records, otherwise it may be inaccessible when access is through
another root.

Inversion on Multiple Fields

Savings of mass storage can sometimes be achieved by inverting on
multiple fields. For example, in fig.1 Department and Location
could perhaps be combined to provide a single path root. It will
probably be necessary to allow FETCH NEXT RECORD OF AREA (FNA)
searches on root records of this type. (See below). Careful
balance in the design will be necessary to ensure that these FNA
searches are at least an order of magnitude smaller than the
lower level searches which they are replacing.

Inversion on multiple fields is a particularly valuable technique
when some degree of correlation exists between the grouped fields.

Fetch Next Record of Area (FNA)

If a user specifies the complete key for a root record with a
direct access location mode such as CALC the query language can
gain immediate access to the record, and the I/O can be minimised.

If, however, the user wants to specify selection criteria in the
root record and not a complete key, then the query language must
retrieve all occurrences of the root record. This will involve a
search through the entire area or areas in which the record may
be stored. Thus, although there may be only a trival number of
occurrences of the root record, access to it by FNA can involve
massive I/O if there are large numbers of other record types
stored in the same areas.

Three solutions may be considered:
- Lock out FNA access and force the user to specify a
  complete key. This may be too restrictive on the user,
  but it does have the advantage of automatically preventing
  massive searches at lower levels on the database.

- Permit FNA and store the root records in a very small area
  so as to restrict the initial search to acceptable limits.

- Provide a higher level single record as a root. First
  level searches will then be restricted to the apparent
  root records even if they are stored in a large area (fig.
  2).

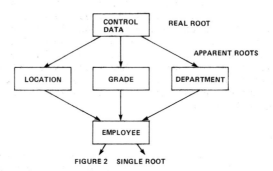

FIGURE 2   SINGLE ROOT

If large searches are permitted the users should be made aware of
the potential cost of blanket selection criteria which may search
the entire population of low level records on the path.

Multiple Similar Areas

A somewhat different approach to the problem of reducing first
stage searches is to divide the database into similarly
structured areas at the highest possible level in the data
hierarchy. In the example in fig.1 this might be at Division
level; indentically structured areas being created for each
division in the company. Each query language sub-schema would
only give access to one area although a sub-schema including all
areas might be necessary say, for use by head office personnel
department.

TRAINING

Our first QLP users started work with only the most basic
training session and pointers to the principle sections of the
User Manual. Luckily they were pretty smart, and strongly
motivated to use the database. They needed a fair amount of
support during this initial period, but they quickly established
the viability of QLP. We therefore set up a more formal training
scheme which has now been running for some two years. The course
is aimed at users who have no experience whatsoever of data

processing and consists of three half-day sessions to cover the
basic facilities. Each session is a mixture of lecture and
tutorial and the lecturer always circulates around the students
to monitor and assist, where necessary, with the exercises.
There is a further half-day session on the Report Writer. We
maintain a training database, which uses the structure from our
original materials database and only contains a few hundred
record occurrences. This is used as the basis of all examples
and exercises in the course, and it is available to the students
for practice between sessions. The sessions are at weekly
intervals to ensure that the students have ample opportunity to
get 'hands on' experience and can come back to subsequent
sessions with their problems.

ACCESSIBILITY

The virtue of easy user access to data, which a query language
gives, also holds the seeds of its greatest potential danger:
unauthorised access to data.

We have combined part of our defence against this unauthorised
access with procedures to simplify authorised access.

The Univac Exec 8 Operating System is popular with data
processing and technical staff since the JCL for both batch and
demand modes are identical. This, however, results in a user
interface at a terminal running in demand mode which is less than
ideal for a non specialist user. He does not know any JCL,
doesn't want to know any and shouldn't need to know any. We
therefore provide a job control macro which is automatically
invoked at log-on for a QLP user. This macro calls up procedures
which select the appropriate database and sub-schema for the
user. It is therefore acting as both a user friendly front-end
and a privacy processor. We only permit access to the databases
through this procedure. Schema and sub-schema names and access
control keys required by DMS and QLP are incorporated into the
procedure and are not displayed, so that the user is not aware of
their existence. The log-on procedure to the computer which
invokes the macro is protected by a password which is very
readily changed by the user himself.

ECONOMICS

Detailed economic assessments of query language use are difficult
to make since the availability of a query facility permits
working methods which cannot be considered in another environment.

Two factors can be considered:

- The increase in storage and update costs resulting from a database structure suitable for query language access.

- The cost of running enquiries with a query language compared with the cost of producing the information by other means.

Both factors are heavily dependent on local considerations. For the purposes of this study we have considered the CJB materials database. For a project there is a fairly stable population of large records with a high incidence of modifications to the contents of records (but not to their set occurrences).

Approximate increases in storage to accommodate QLP are as follows:

Entry Records	1%
Pointers in data records for entry sets	1%
Provision of Julian format dates in addition to ISO format	10%
Total	12%

Dates are an important constituent of this database and the storage overhead could obviously be much reduced for a query language which provided modulo date arithmetic facilities.

In addition there is an increase in I/O processing during updates to maintain the additional sets. This amounts to approximately 12%. This figure is very sensitive to the ratio of inserts to amendments and in a database with a more volatile record population could be much higher.

With regard to query performance it has been our experience that a QLP enquiry will carry out an identical volume of I/O to a Cobol program extracting the same information. CPU time is generally a little higher, but, since CPU cost for this type of job is normally only about 5% - 10% of the total run cost, the remainder being I/O, this is hardly significant.

Comparisons of the cost of producing reports by manual techniques and with QLP show that manual techniques are cheaper for small searches with very small quantities of information extracted.

Under all other circumstances QLP is more economical and with a
complex report the cost of producing it with QLP may be as little
as 1% of the cost of manual techniques.

Other less tangible factors influence our use of database and
QLP. With older systems materials controllers spent a large
proportion of their time, probably as much as 50%, answering
queries which now take perhaps as little as 10%, leaving the
balance for them to concentrate on their real function of
expediting the purchase, inspection, and delivery of materials.
A major intangible factor is the ready availability of the
information needed to run a contracting business, where accurate
and timely information is increasingly necessary to ensure
successful completion of projects. The ability to provide more
complex reports to clients is also affecting the award of
contracts and a contractor without good computer systems is
unlikely to survive in these harsh economic times.

A Corporate Human Resource Information System

J. M. Myszko

Corporate Information Systems,
International Computers Ltd, UK

ICL's Corporate Information Systems have constructed a system which
is a true hybrid of local and central computing facilities, in
which differing requirements of management information about
personnel at different levels throughout have been met with equal
success.

The combination of these facilities has proved oustanding in speed
of implementation, savings in development expenditure and running
costs, and complete acceptability to non-technical end-users.

"CHRIS - A Corporate Human Resources Information System"

In many organisations Personnel Systems have to satisfy two very
different sets of requirements:

- at the local level, Personnel Officers and local
  management need to be able to manipulate complete
  details of the records of their local staff; much
  of the work involves only one record at a time -
  adding this new joiner, noting this man's promotion;
  recording this girl's married name, etc.

- at the corporate level, manpower planning involves
  surveys of large bodies of data, to establish trends
  and patterns, to highlight anomalies and to facilitate the formulation of policy.

Many implementations favour one aspect above the other, and a truly
balanced system is not only rare, but, with conventional means,
unduly expensive to develop.

ICL's Corporate Information Systems have constructed a system which
is a true hybrid of local and central computing facilities, in
which both sets of requirements are satisfied with equal success,
and which has established remarkable new standards for ease and
cheapness of implementation.

Background

The data processing systems used in ICL's UK Personnel operations
had developed in entirely conventional form with the Company having
a parallel pair of master files, one containing personnel details,
the other concerned with payroll information.

The master files were based on magnetic tape and were updated in
batch mode on a weekly basis with the data provided by local
personnel offices from many different UK locations. The data
preparation load was fairly heavy, and each updating cycle produced
the usual list of errors and inconsistencies which were fed back to
local office for corrections. Since the data was manipulated
centrally the local offices, although provided with reports on a
regular basis, felt the service was inflexible and lead times for
response prolonged. Effort in correcting the errors tended

naturally to be concentrated on payroll data and it was acknowledged generally that the personnel records were becoming progressively less reliable. In all these respects the system was typical of its time and it was agreed that it had outlived its usefulness and that it ought to be replaced.

Nevertheless, very heavy use was being made of reports extracted from the existing files. For normal administrative purposes an extensive family of regular reports was generated and distributed, and managers throughout the Company received details enabling them to maintain local files of data sheets relating to all the employees in their departments. Further reports were produced from time to time to assist in one-off administrative procedures, such as helping managers to decide how to apportion permitted merit increases among their staff while remaining within budgetary and other limits.

But the stage had been reached by early 1979 where the most extensive - and certainly the most burdensome - type of output from the personnel files was the generation of statistical reports in response to ad hoc queries. A typical ad hoc would require the creation of a matrix of totals with, say, salary scale code along one axis and geographical location on the other. The increasing proportion of management time which was having to be devoted to manpower planning and all other aspects of personnel management made it clear that the top priority was to provide a system which would give much more rapid response to such unpredictable reporting requirements.

Software Environment

The situation within a data processing environment had reached the stage where large software developments were lengthy in timescales, labour intensive and the results risky.

The cost of manpower had been rising rapidly and the costs of hardware, as ever dropping. The constraints placed on system development were now resulting from hardware requirements which were allied to the cost of manpower needed to operate the system.

The load placed on the communication network supporting on-line and RJE systems was so high, that distributing hardware to where the processing power was required, was a prime consideration.

On the user side there was a need for user friendly, easy to operate and change, systems which could be responsive and flexible.

Emphasis was being increasingly placed on systems that could be quickly adapted to meet changing business needs.

ICL Personnel Database and User Requirements

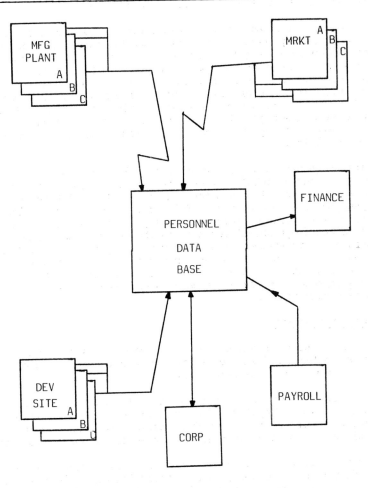

Fig 1. Personnel Database

Examination of the Personnel database and user requirements
identified <u>local</u> and corporate or central requirements.
Manufacturing plants, marketing regional offices or Product
developments sites each had their individual requirements for
data processing power as well as data about their employees.
Centrally Corporate and Management requirements specified the
need to look at all the employees mainly for analytical and
statistical information required towards policy decisions.
Reference Fig. 1.

The personnel functions within ICL, generated a user requirement
specification which had the following as its main points.

    * Flexible Enquiry and Reporting

The prime requirement was to provide a mechanism which would cater
for unspecified output requirements and gave the control of the
enquiry completely to the user of the system. Essentially,
personnel did not know what they would ask of the System or how
it was to be presented until the moment when they wanted to use
it.

    * Rapid Response

Due to the large volumes of data required to be interrogated and
the nature of personnel's business, rapid response was essential.
Interactive "question-answer" mode of operation suited personnel
for a large number of enquiries.

    * Simple Enquiry Syntax

As the system was to be operated by non-data processing staff a
simple "English language" Syntax was required for eas of learning
and operation.

    * Total Privacy

The very nature of personnel business means that privacy of
information and security of unauthorised access is most important.

Personnel Data and Business Functions

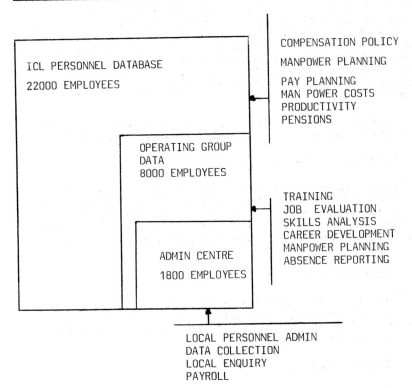

Fig 2. Personnel Data

Investigation of the relation between data required and business function performed identified three levels of operation. Reference Fig. 2.

1.   Corporate level which concerned itself with policy implications and related to ICL's 22,000 employees.

2.   Operating Groups like Manufacturing or Marketing needed to plan their actions related to perhaps 8000 staff. Functions like Job Evaluation and skills analysis needed to be performed at that level due to the different nature of each group.

3.   Administration Centres were identified as the levels
       at which the day to day problems occurred and where
       the individual was of the greatest importance.
       Certainly at this level data collection was most
       evident and the whole quality of the complete data-
       base depended on the integrity of data gathered here.

Resulting from the above analysis the concept of a local system was
developed. A "Local system" could exist at administration centre
level, group level or even at corporate level. The distinguishing
identification was the need to perform repeated and frequent
operations on the same sub-set of the overall database.

The Initial Proposal

It was at first intended that a single replacement system should be
built from the group up, combining the data which had previously
existed separately into a single database covering the whole of
ICL's operations in the UK. In accordance with the technical
guidelines for new systems in force within Corporate Information
Systems, this would have used IDMS as the fundamental software.
Online data collection would be used to eliminate the errors and
delays inherent in the previous transcription and data preparation
methods. Online enquiry would certainly have been provided.
And online updating was considered as a further facility to be
introduced at a later stage if it proved to be fully justified.

However, several problems arose when this solution was more
thoroughly investigated:

   * so many data elements were identified as potential entry
     points to the database that the data model came to be
     known as the 'starfish' - there was only one main record
     type, containing the details of an individual's personnel
     record; but this was surrounded by large numbers of
     pseudo-records whose only function was to permit multiple
     CALC accesses. It was therefore judged that we would not
     be gaining significant advantage from the navigational
     facilities inherent in IDMS, and at the same time there
     was some question as to whether we could create a
     sufficiently flexible reporting system if we based it
     wholly on IDMS.

* an inverted file solution was briefly considered. It
  undoubtedly offered a better match to the requirements,
  but it was rejected on the combined grounds of
  unfamiliarity to the development staff, probable
  excessive demands on mainframe capacity, and incompatibility with the prevailing standards governing the
  development of online applications.

* despite the urgency of the need for improved end-user
  access to the data, the scale of the development effort
  required was too great when measured against the
  resources budgetted for personnel systems development
  and maintenance.

Personnel Local and Mainframe Systems

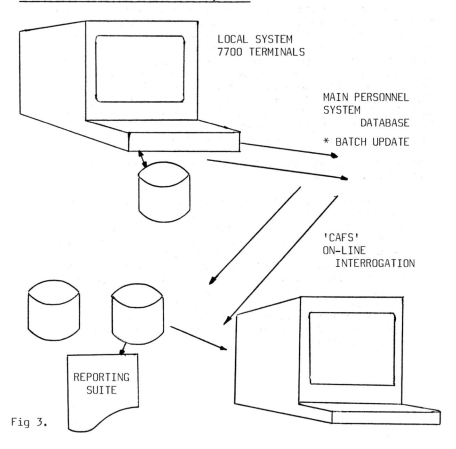

LOCAL SYSTEM
7700 TERMINALS

MAIN PERSONNEL
SYSTEM
            DATABASE
* BATCH UPDATE

'CAFS'
ON-LINE
        INTERROGATION

REPORTING
SUITE

Fig 3.

The solution adopted recognised that several different techniques could be combined to make up a System which though more complex than any single technical approach would be easier and cheaper to implement, would be more efficient in operation and would give users exactly what they were needing.

Two main elements constituted the design:

* use of 7700 intelligent terminals for local data collection validation and local enquiry.

* a CAFS enquiry service was implemented as a most striking feature because of the perception of the need for flexible on-line enquiries coincided with a decision by ICL to seek a further practical demonstration of the importance of content addressing by integrating CAFS into a real live data processing application. Reference Fig. 3.

7700 Terminal based Local Systems

The heavily loaded state of the existing mainframes was already causing us to consider off-loading work of this class. It is obviously preferable to devote mainframe capacity to providing good data response to enquiries rather than checking the accuracy and validity of new data often inadequately submitted.

The Local System applications were developed using ICL's Terminal Programming Language TPL and had the following main objectives.

* Systems had to be capable of effectively on-line data collection and validation to mainframe standards, so that the user was aware of errors immediately and could effect correction.

* Data needed to satisfy the local business need was held on the 7700 terminal and applications like Job Evaluation, Training etc. (see Fig 2), could be satisfied using the processing power of the terminal.

* Enquiry on the local and mainframe files could be performed using the same 7700 terminal.

* Operation of the system using simple English language compounds was possible as well as performing word processing.

* The system was designed so that stringent privacy and security facilities were available.

Throughout the UK, the records of individual employees
are held on 7700 Intelligent Terminals. The use of the
Terminal Programming Language (TPL) applications has
given each local Personnel Officer a wide range of
facilities for interrogating, displaying and amending
the records of the staff in his own local personnel
unit. These facilities are effectively owner-driven,
allowing the user complete control over the choice of
functions to be performed. A feature which has proved
particularly successful is the ability to initiate
processing in either of two modes: when a standard
function is to be invoked, an automatic mode is used,
in which a predefined series of screens is presented to
the user in the required sequence; where the requirement is more particular, the user can nominate the
preferred screen, which is then presented and used,
without the processing being complicated by the presentation of unwanted formats.

From the point of view of the D.P. professional, TPL,
though a relatively low-level language, has proved to
be a most efficient vehicle for the rapid generation
of powerful end-user facilities. These include
comprehensive validation of input data, including
format checking, code table look-up, within-record
consistency checking, in addition to format conversion
and general editing. On the output side, facilities
include not only standard displays, but also user-
generated special displays, sorting before output,
and output either to the VDU or, via a spool-file,
to a line-printer.

Any data input via the local facilities is retained in
a spool-file until end of day, and then transmitted to
a central mainframe. The central personnel file is
remarkable for being permanently resident on CAFS.
Changes transmitted from the local level are applied
to this file in a weekly updating cycle.

CONTENT ADDRESSABLE FILE STORE (CAFS)

The development of the central database system was based on the
availability of the CAFS 800 product to ICL's internal data
processing functions. The CAFS device is an intelligent hardware
based information retrieval sub-system with sophisticated hardware and software techniques for accessing data by its
attributes and values.

The fact that information could be made available based on content
rather than pre-defined keys meant that the system related to human
behaviour when enquiring for information. As a result the
personnel officers in ICL found that using CAFS for enquiries on
large databases was satisfying their prime requirement for
non-predefined enquiries and unspecified output requirements.
The capability to read 2 million records in 60 seconds was a
major contribution towards an interactive system that responded to
non-predefined enquiries in a matter of seconds.

The use of mnemonics to identify data on the files that
was embodied into English Language type commands ensured that the
users quickly and easily learnt how to operate the system.

The CAFS enquiry service depends on the data files being in CAFS
format and loaded onto CAFS discs. The creation of a data
description capable of being used by the CAFS general enquiry
package and creation of suitable entries in the CAFS System
file was the other areas covered by the data processing personnel.
Creating the data description turned out to be relatively simple
and as experience was gained a number of CAFS files were created
which reflected the personnel database. Reference Fig. 4.

The ability to look at a number of CAFS files simultaneously was
achieved by enhancing the general enquiry package to give
software driven file correlation routines. The end result was the
capability to look at a large database with simplicity and ease of
use that the end users of such a system had not experienced
previously.

The main function of the central CAFS file is to support a wide
variety of enquiries which can be loosely classified under the
heading of Manpower Planning. The topics forming the basis for
enquiry can be as varied as the full range of management's
personnel interests - the planning of training, maintenance of
consistency in pay policy, analysis of staff experience, prediction of retirement, patterns of turnover etc.

The CAFS enquiry facilities have proved to be very acceptable in
that senior personnel managers are obtaining answers to their
questions entirely through their terminals, and very economic,
in that the machine time previously expended on report
generation - both regular and ad hoc - is now saved.

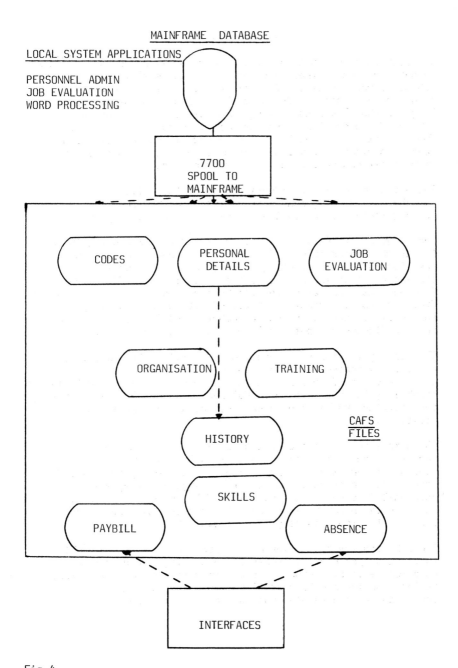

Fig 4.

BENEFITS

User Advantages

The use of the personnel system has shown that the approach
described can give users processing power related to their
geographical needs and in a way that is consistent with a database approach to satisfy central and corporate requirements. The
main points which emerged from such an implementation were:-

* The use of simple free-standing intelligent terminals with
  limited processing capabilities can satisfy user local and
  corporate needs if the data distribution permits this
  approach.

* Such systems can be developed quickly and cost effectively
  especially if based on a packaged approach.

* With user driven and operated systems like the 7700 and
  CAFS substantial cost reductions are possible without the
  involvement of expensive D.P. Staff.

D.P Advantages

In a situation where data processing staff are becoming a very
scarce resource and thus a very expensive commodity, increasing
pressure will be applied to use their skills more cost effectively.
Currently many computer departments have to cope with the development of strategically important systems whilst satisfying the day
to day pressures for tactical developments to existing systems. In
such situations the following points are important and have
resulted from the system development experiences on the CHRIS
project.

* Domestic and tactical systems can be satisfied quickly and
  cost effectively using the type of approach described in
  the 7700 and TPL implementations.

* The use of devices like CAFS 800 eliminate the risk of
  extended timescales and possible high costs on technically
  complex systems.

* Data processing staff could be deployed more effectively
  and concentrate on satisfying Strategic Systems.

* The use of simple intelligent terminals exposes the users
  to the disciplines necessary to run large distributed
  systems which now make the practical reality of such
  systems feasible.

The relationship between costs, timescales and project size and
complexity is shown in Fig. 5.

TIMESCALES AND COSTS

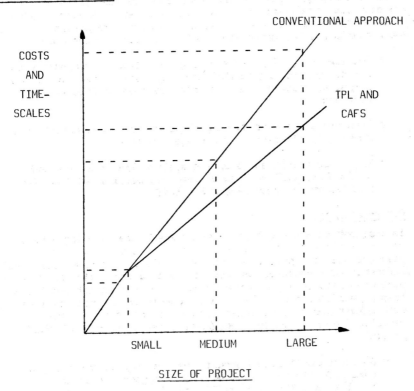

SIZE OF PROJECT

Fig 5.

A Fast Optimising Algorithm for Solving the Dynamic n Job on One Machine Scheduling Problem

B. Adamczewski
Director, Harris Computers Limited, UK

This paper proposes an algorithm which completely solves the dynamic n operations on one machine scheduling problem. It does so with a method that can be computed simply and quickly. It achieves the optimum solution by minimising the sum of the total (or the average) delays under all circumstances. The algorithm has been implemented on a microprocessor based finite capacity scheduling system.

1. Introduction.
================

The algorithm this paper proposes has been implemented on a
micro-processor based finite capacity scheduling system
marketed under the name of PLANSTAR by my company Harris
Computers Ltd.

The PLANSTAR system was developed by me personally in 1980.
The programs were originally written in BASIC and are now
partly converted to assembler language routines. The system
has been used to schedule several hundreds of operations for
several tens of machines (works centres) and even the original
unimproved BASIC version achieved scheduling throughputs of
between 12 and 25 operations per minute. Typically 500 operations
on 25 resources would take about 35 minutes, whereas 1000
operations over about the same number of resources would take
about 50 minutes. These times include all the time required for
startup, floppy disc input/output and the printing of the
schedule.

Figure 1 illustrates the principal files, jobs and reports on
PLANSTAR. Figure 2 shows a typical scheduling report. Naturally
the system deals with the whole of the data handling, filing and
retrieval requirements related to works order processing as
required in production control departments. The system does not
handle material requirements.

In the past 20 years a large number of papers have been devoted
to the solution of the n jobs on one machine problem. Many
algorithms, mostly heuristics of various kinds have been
proposed. Instead of listing examples as references let me
quote Professor R. Wild of Brunel University (6):

"Many of the techniques .... offer optimum solutions to
sequencing problems, but a question that should be asked is
whether or not optimum solutions are necessary or even
desirable. Clearly, if a solution to a problem can be obtained
only after excessive computation (e.g. linear programming) or
through oversimplification (e.g. the early algorithms, or even
the branch and bound method) then there is little to recommend
it.
Furthermore, all of these methods have dealt only with the static
rather than the dynamic problem. When the dynamic situation
arises there is no practical and general method of ensuring
an optimum solution. If this fact is accepted, then it is
reasonable to consider such problems in simpler "dispatching"
terms, i.e. considering the immediate priority of jobs on one
facility, rather than attempting explicitly to consider several

facilities at once. The efficiency with which dispatching is
performed determines to a large extent the overall operations
efficiency, since it can effect such crucial things as
operations time, work-in-progress, facility loading etc."

The algorithm proposed can readily be built into a system
which deals with precedence constraints and is quite unaffected
by the dynamic arrival of new operations to be scheduled.

THE PLANSTAR SYSTEM ITS PRINCIPAL FILES, JOBS AND REPORTS

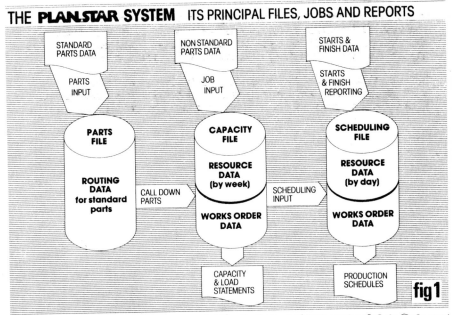

fig 1

JOB NO.	OP NO	ST	ERLY ST	PRES ST	ERLY FIN.	LATE FIN.	TIME HRS.	SLACK DAYS	QUANT	NO. OPS	NO. LIN	LINES: 1 2 3 4	STATUS	RESOURCE NO.	as at: 41 - 2
100009	1	1	41-1	41-1	41-1	41-5	5	4	100	5	1	X	Started early	9	CONLATHE
100018	1	1	41-3	41-3	41-4	42-2	11	3	120	2	1	X	Schedld early	9	
100068	1	1	41-3	41-4	41-5	42-3	6	3	110	5	1	X	Schedld early	9	
100061	2	2	41-2	41-5	41-5	43-3	5	8	90	7	1	X	Schedld	9	
100066	2	2	41-5	41-5	42-1	42-1	2	0	60	7	1	X	Schedld early	9	
100011	2	2	41-5	42-1	42-2	42-5	8	3	70	3	1	X	Schedld early	9	
100048	2	2	42-1	42-2	42-2	42-5	3	3	60	7	1	X	Schedld LATE	9	
100015	3	3	41-2	42-2	42-3	42-1	5	-2	55	5	1	X	Schedld early	9	
100092	2	2	42-3	42-3	42-3	43-3	6	5	120	5	1	X	Schedld early	9	
100086	1	1	42-4	42-4	42-4	43-2	6	3	90	2	1	X	Schedld early	9	8 more ops filed
100039	1	1	42-5	42-5	45-1	45-5	89	4	60	10	1	X	Schedld early	9	
100030	3	3	41-1	41-1	41-2	41-4	9	2	240	4	1	X	Started early	10	UNIVGRND
100027	3	3	41-3	41-3	41-4	42-2	10	3	150	4	1	X	Schedld early	10	
100002	8	8	42-2	42-2	42-2	44-4	7	12	60	13	1	X	Schedld early	10	
100002	7	7	41-5	42-2	42-4	44-2	16	8	60	13	1	X	Schedld early	10	
100036	7	7	42-4	42-4	43-1	44-2	16	6	60	13	1	X	Schedld early	10	
100036	8	8	43-1	43-1	43-2	44-4	7	7	60	13	1	X	Schedld early	10	11 more ops filed
100077	2	2	43-5	43-5	43-5	44-5	5	5	55	5	1	X	Schedld early	10	
100003	7	7	42-4	42-5	45-1	13	11		60	19	1	X	Schedld early	11	SURFGRND
100003	6	6	42-3	42-5	43-1	44-3	7	7	60	19	1	X	Schedld early	11	
100038	6	6	42-5	43-1	43-2	44-2	7	5	60	19	1	X	Schedld early	11	8 more ops filed
100038	7	7	43-1	43-2	43-4	44-5	13	6	60	19	1	X	Schedld early	11	
100033	3	3	40-4	40-5	40-5	41-3	5	3	60	6	1	X	Finishd early	12	DRILL
100060	3	3	41-1	41-1	41-2	43-4	8	12	120	6	1	X	Started early	12	
100056	4	4	41-4	41-4	41-4	43-1	2	7	60	7	1	X	Schedld early	12	
100067	2	2	41-5	41-5	41-5	42-4	4	4	60	5	1	X	Schedld LATE	12	
100015	2	2	42-2	42-2	42-2	41-4	3	-3	55	5	1	X	Schedld early	12	
100057	3	3	42-2	42-2	42-2	42-3	4	1	60	6	1	X	Schedld early	12	
100032	2	2	42-2	42-2	42-3	42-4	5	1	100	5	1	X	Schedld early	12	
100014	2	2	42-3	42-3	42-3	43-1	3	3	90	5	1	X	Schedld early	12	
100058	5	5	42-1	42-3	42-4	43-3	3	4	60	8	1	X	Schedld early	12	
100002	6	6	41-4	42-4	42-5	43-4	7	4	60	13	1	X	Schedld early	12	
100003	5	5	42-2	42-5	42-5	44-1	5	6	60	19	1	X	Schedld early	12	13 more ops filed
100036	6	6	42-3	42-5	43-1	43-4	7	3	60	13	1	X	Schedld early	12	
100011	1	1	41-1	41-1	41-1	42-3	3	7	70	3	1	X	Finishd early	13	BENCHWK
100005	4	4	41-5	41-5	41-5	42-3	5	3	60	7	1	X	Schedld early	13	
100015	4	4	41-3	41-3	41-3	42-3	6	5	55	5	1	X	Schedld early	13	
100002	10	10	42-4	42-4	42-5	45-3	6	14	60	13	1	X	Schedld early	13	

fig 2

2.   The Problem Statement.
===========================

In this paper

n = the number of operations considered for scheduling on 1 machine;

e_i = the earliest start of the i-th operation;

t_i = the time (set-up + working) required for the execution of the i-th operation;

d_i = the due date of the i-th operation;

$d'_i = d_i - \sum\limits_{1}^{s} t_i$ = the due date offset from current time reached after s operations have been scheduled;

$r_k = \max.[\ 0;\ \sum\limits_{1}^{k} t_i - d_k]$; the delay of the k-th operation;

s_i = the slack left between the due date offset and the completion of the i-th operation for any sequence of operations if that sequence is followed;

$s_k = \max.[\ 0;\ d'_i - \sum\limits_{1}^{k} t_i]$;

l_i = the larger of either the due date offset (from current schedule time reached) or the earliest finish offset for the i-th operation;

$l_k = \max.[\ d_k - \sum\limits_{1}^{s} t_i;\ t_k]$

or

$l_k = d'_k + r_k$

R = the sum of delays suffered by all operations in a given sequence.

Trivially

[1] $R = \sum\limits_{1}^{q} r_i = \sum\limits_{1}^{q} \sum\limits_{1}^{a} t_i - \sum\limits_{1}^{q} d_a$

where

q = the number of delayed operations;

a = the sequence number of the delayed operations.

Also, as can be shown easily

$$[2] \quad R = \sum_1^n (n + 1 - i)t_i - \sum_1^n d_i + \sum_1^n s_i$$

and

$$[3] \quad R = \sum_1^q (q + 1 - j)t_j - \sum_1^q d_j + \sum_1^p c_f \cdot t_f$$

where

p = the number of operations not delayed; $n = p + q$;
t_j = the operation time of the j-th delayed operation;
d_j = the due date of the j-th delayed operation;
c_f = the number of delayed operations that the f-th undelayed operation precedes;
t_f = the time of the f-th undelayed operation.

If in [2] above $\sum_1^n s_i$, the sum of the slacks, is always zero, i.e there is no sequence of operations in which any one or more operations do not have to suffer a delay then R is a minimum if the operations are arranged in order of ascending operation times (for all j $t_j \leq t_j + 1$). This is the well known shortest processing time (SPT) rule, discussed in almost every elementary text on the subject. It is worth repeating that the SPT rule does not neccessarily produce an optimum solution if there is any operation at all that could be completed before due date if it went first.

Lawler (1) has shown that <u>if a sequence exists</u> in which no operation is delayed then sequencing operations by increasing due dates (for all j $d_j \leq d_{j+1}$) is such a sequence. This is the well known due date rule.

These two rules cover the extreme ends of the scheduling problem: the case where no operation at all need suffer a delay and the case where all operations must suffer a delay. In practice the middle ground between these two extremes is naturally most common.

At any time $a = \sum_1^j t_i$, after j operations have been scheduled, the due date offset for the k-th operation (k>j), as yet unscheduled is $d_k - a$.

If $d_k < a + t_k$ then operation k will be delayed. The earliest possible finish offset (from a) for operation k is its operation time t_k.

As will be immediately clear, it seems reasonable to propose a scheduling rule which schedules (sequences) operations by increasing values of

$$l_k = \max. \; [\; d_k - \sum_1^{k-1} t_i \; ; \; t_k]$$

If for all j

$$l_j = d_j - \sum_1^{j-1} t_i$$

and we schedule by increasing values of l_k then we are scheduling by increasing values of due dates as required by the due date rule.

If for all j $l_j = t_j$
and we schedule by increasing values of l_k then we are scheduling by increasing values of operation times, as required by the SPT rule.

Scheduling by increasing values of l_k - the larger of either the due date or the earliest finish - also provides us with a scheduling rule for those cases where some operations are delayed and some are not.

Unfortunately, as will be shown below, this rule does not always achieve an optimum schedule. It is interesting to note however that of all the "primitive" scheduling rules it appears to be one of the best.

K.R. Baker (2) has published 16 test cases of 8 operations each, giving values for t_i and d_i as well as the optimum (minimum delay). He claims the following results:

Algorithm	Optimising Performance	Ratio of Solution to Optimum Averaged over all 16 Problems
Wilkerson-Irwin (3)	14 out of 16	1.004
Neighborhood Search (4)	14 out of 16	1.0002
For comparison (not in Baker's table):		
By increasing l_k	14 out of 16	1.066
The proposed algorithm	16 out of 16	1.0

The computional effort required for l_k scheduling is trivial and certainly well below that for either of the two algorithms quoted above, yet it achieves the same number of optimum solutions. It performs somewhat worse, by some 6%, when its results are averaged over all 16 test cases.

To illustrate this point further, and to show how l_k sequencing does not guarantee an optimum solution, consider one of the test cases published by Baker (5); his case 1 for which he quotes a minimum possible delay of 755.

Op. No.	e_i	t_i	d_i	Schedl. Start	Schedl. Finish	Selectd on l_k	r_i	s_i
1	0	121	260	0	121	260	0	139
4	0	79	266	121	200	187	0	66
6	0	83	336	200	283	136	0	53
3	0	102	400	283	385	117	0	15
5	0	130	337	385	515	130	178	0
2	0	147	269	515	662	147	393	0
8	0	88	719	662	750	88	31	0
7	0	96	683	750	846	96	163	0
Totals:		846	3270				765	273

The algorithm proposed in this paper achieves the optimum as shown below

Op. No.	e_i	t_i	d_i	Schedl. Start	Schedl. Finish	Selectd. on l_k	r_i	s_i
1	0	121	260	0	121	–	0	139
4	0	79	266	121	200	–	0	66
6	0	83	336	200	283	–	0	53
3	0	102	400	283	385	–	0	15
5	0	130	337	385	515	–	178	0
7	0	96	683	515	611	–	0	72
8	0	88	719	611	699	–	0	20
2	0	147	269	699	846	–	577	0
Totals:		846	3270				755	365

Just so as to complete the picture compare the above with pure due date sequencing, as shown overleaf:

Op. No.	e_i	t_i	d_i	Schedl. Start	Schedld. Finish	r_i	s_i
1	0	121	260	0	121	0	139
4	0	79	266	121	200	0	66
2	0	147	269	200	347	78	0
6	0	83	336	347	430	94	0
5	0	130	337	430	560	223	0
3	0	102	400	560	662	262	0
7	0	96	683	662	758	75	0
8	0	88	719	758	846	127	0
Totals:		846	3270			859	205

3. The Algorithm.

The algorithm proposed in this paper involves:

    1. an absolute start initilisation procedure;
    2. a selection pass initilisation procedure;
    3. a single pass over the operations data for operations as yet unscheduled to select the next operation.

The procedure works only on the operations as yet unscheduled at any time in that no operation once assigned a position in this scheduling run's sequence need be reconsidered for another position. The procedure is therefore very fast.

1. Absolute Start Initialisation.
    The n operations to be considered for scheduling on one machine are sorted into the order of both increasing due date and increasing operation time.
    In effect 2 lists in due date order and in operation time order are created.

2. Pass Initialisation.
    The total delays that would result if one followed either due date order or operation time order are calculated for any operations still unscheduled.
    Let
        R_t = the delay inherent in the operation time (SPT) order for the operations as yet unscheduled;
        R_d = the delay inherent in the due date order for the operations as yet unscheduled.

3. Next Operation Selection.

    1. For $R_t > R_d$:

        Select the operation with the smallest l_k next.

    2. For $R_d > R_t$:

        Select the operation with the smallest E_k next, where

$$E_k = l_k - \sum_1^k t_i + \sum_1^{k-1} \max.[0;t_k-s_i] - s_k$$

      and k = the sequence number of the operation in
             operation time (SPT) order; i.e. $t_i \le t_{i+1}$

Provided that we exclude any operation k which delays
another operation e where the following applies:

    1. $E_k < E_e \le 0$; and $k > e$.
    2. $t_k + t_e - l_e > 0$; i.e. operation e is delayed
                    by scheduling operation k.
    3. $s_k = 0$; $s_e \ge 0$; the slack of k is zero the
                    slack of e need not be.
    4.   there is an operation j, with e < j < k, for
        which $s_j > 0$.

And provided that if there are several operations
with equal values of E_k we select amongst them the
operation with the smallest due date.

Before proceeding to show why this works it is perhaps useful to
express the proposed algorithm in words:

1. For any list of as yet unscheduled operations find out
   whether due date order or operation time order would produce
   the smaller delay on that list.

2.1. If due date order sequencing produces the smaller total
    delay (at present) select next the operation with the
    smallest l_k - i.e. the larger of either the due date or the
    earliest finish.
2.2 If operation time (SPT) order sequencing produces the
    smaller total delay (at present) select next the operation
    for which the delay which it would incurr in an SPT sequence
    is bigger than the reduction in the slacks it would cause if
    it were scheduled now; subject to the above provisos for the
    case were scheduling such an operation causes a delay to
    another.

4. Proving the Algorithm.

To deal with the trivial cases first:

1. If for all j $l_k = d_k - \sum_1^{k-1} t_i$

    then
    $$R_t > R_d \quad \text{and}$$
    the algorithm proposed sequences in due date order, which
    gives the optimum result.

2. If for all j $l_k = t_k$

    then
    $$R_t \leq R_d.$$

2.1 If $R_d = R_t$
    then the algorithm proposed schedules in order of l_k which
    is the same order as operation time order, which gives the
    optimum result.

2.2 If $R_t < R_d$
    then the algorithm proposed schedules in order of smallest
    E_k where
    $$E_k = kt_k - \sum_1^k t_i \; ; \quad \text{as all slacks are then zero.}$$
    i.e. SPT order as $t_j \leq t_{j+1}$.

    Therefore the algorithm works for these boundary conditions.

From [2] above let R_m for any arbitary sequence of operations be
the sum of the delays inherent in that sequence for the m
operations as yet unscheduled after the first (n-m) operations
have been scheduled. Let R_{m-1} be the sum of the delays left
after the next, the (n-m+1)-th, operation is scheduled.

$$R_m = \sum_1^m (m+1-i)t_i - \sum_1^m (d_i - \sum_1^{n-m} t_p) + \sum_1^m s_i + \sum_1^{n-m} r_p$$

$$R_{m-1} = \sum_1^{m-1} (m-i)t_j - \sum_1^{m-1} (d_j - \sum_1^{n-m+1} t_q) + \sum_1^{m-1} s_j + \sum_1^{n-m+1} r_q$$

Let R_{m-1} be derived from R_m by removing the k-th operation
from the sequence of operations making up R_m.

$$F = R_m - R_{m-1}$$

Taking the above factors one at a time we find:

1. $\sum\limits_{1}^{m} (m+1-i)t_i - \sum\limits_{1}^{m-1} (m-i)t_j = (m+1-k)t_k + \sum\limits_{1}^{k-1} t_i$

2. $\sum\limits_{1}^{m} (d_i - \sum\limits_{1}^{n-m} t_p) - \sum\limits_{1}^{m-1} (d_j - \sum\limits_{1}^{n-m+1} t_q) = d_k + (m-1)t_k$

3. $\sum\limits_{1}^{n-m} r_p - \sum\limits_{1}^{n-m+1} r_q = -r_k$

4. $\sum\limits_{1}^{m-1} s_j = \sum\limits_{1}^{m} s_i - s_k - \sum\limits_{1}^{k-1} \min.[s_i;t_k]$

$\sum\limits_{1}^{m} s_i - \sum\limits_{1}^{m-1} s_j = s_k + \sum\limits_{1}^{k-1} \min.[s_i;t_k]$

i.e. the sum of the slacks left after removing the k-th operation in the sequence i is the sum of the slacks before that removal, less the slack of the k-th operation, less the slacks remaining for those operations that preceded the k-th operation. Any slack of an operation that, in the sequence i, followed the k-th operations is obviously unaltered as

$$s_i = \max.[0;d'_i - \sum\limits_{1}^{i} t_i]$$

and both d_i and $\sum\limits_{1}^{i} t_i$ are reduced by t_k for $i > k$.

The slacks of operations that preceded the k-th operation in the sequence i are either reduced by t_k, by virtue of the reduction of d_i or are eliminated if they are smaller than t_k.

From this

$$F = (m+1-k) + \sum\limits_{1}^{k-1} t_i - d_k - (m-1)t_k - r_k + s_k + \sum\limits_{1}^{k-1} \min.[s_i;t_k]$$

Without any loss of generality we can replace d_k, the due date with d'_k, the due date offset, and as $l_k = d'_k + r_k$ we get

$$F = \sum\limits_{1}^{k-1} t_i + \sum\limits_{1}^{k-1} \min.[s_i;t_k] - (k-2)t_k - l_k + s_k$$

or for $\qquad E_k = -F_k$

$$E_k = l_k + (k-2)t_k - \sum_1^{k-1} t_i - (\sum_1^{k-1} \min.[s_i,t_k] + s_k)$$

Generally

for k=1 $\qquad E_1 = l_1 - t_1 - s_1 = 0$

also

for k=2 and $s_1 > t_2$; $\quad E_2 = l_2 - t_1 - s_2 - t_2 = 0$

i.e. the due date plus any delay or minus any slack is equal to the sum of the operations times that precede it. Or $E_1 = 0$ is the somewhat pompous mathematical way of expressing the obvious; namely, that for any arbitary sequence the sum of the delays inherent in that sequence will not be altered if we choose as our next operation the first operation in the sequence, that is we follow the sequence as given.

To achieve $R_m > R_{m-1}$ we must find an operation k for which $E_k < 0$.

Let us first prove that sequencing by l_k - the larger of either the due date (offset) or the earliest finish (offset) - is better than scheduling purely by due date.

Assume our operations are arranged in due date order, and that at some time a

$$d_1 < d_2 \ldots.< d_{k-1} < d_k < d_p + r_p$$

with

$d_p + r_p = l_p$ and l_p being the smallest value l_i for any i in the range from 1 to (k-1)

d_k = the due date (offset) of the first operation in this due date sequence not yet subject to delay.

Because operations 1 to $(k-1)$ are already subject to a delay

$$\sum_{1}^{k-1} \min.[s_i;t_k] = 0$$

and also because

$$d_k < d_{k-1} + r_{k-1} = l_{k-1} \leq \sum_{1}^{k-1} t_i$$

it follows that $s_k = 0$, and therefore

$$E_k = l_k + (k-2)t_k - \sum_{1}^{k-1} t_i$$

By definition

$$\sum_{1}^{k-1} t_i > (k-1)(d_k-a) = (k-1)l_k \geq l_k + (k-2)t_k$$

as a = the current time. Therefore $E_k < 0$.
But also, by definition, for any $p < k$, including the operation
with the smallest possible t_p

$$l_p = t_p > l_k > t_k \qquad \text{from which we get}$$

$$l_p + (p-2)t_p - \sum_{1}^{p-1} t_i > l_k + (k-2)t_k - \sum_{1}^{k-1} t_i$$

$$l_p + (p-2)t_p + \sum_{p}^{k-1} t_i > l_k + (k-2)t_k \qquad \text{and as}$$

$$\sum_{p}^{k-1} t_i > (k-p)t_p \qquad \text{we find}$$

$$l_p + (p-2)t_p + \sum_{p}^{k-1} t_i > l_p + (k-2)t_p > l_k + (k-2)t_k$$

Therefore

$$E_k < E_p \qquad \text{for any } p < k$$

which proves that l_k sequencing is better than due date
sequencing.

For our algorithm to work we need to show that l_k sequencing will
always achieve the maximum possible reduction of the sum of
delays given a due date sequence.

Let there be $(q+1)$ operations which are not yet subject to delay
and for which

$$d_1 < \dots < d_{k-1} < d_k < \dots d_{k+q} < d_p + r_p$$

where again
d_k is the first operation not subject to delay yet, and
$d_p + r_p = l_p$ with l_p being the smallest value for the
operations already delayed.
then, by definition, scheduling in order of k, $(k+1)$, ... $(k+q)$
will not cause any of the $(q+1)$ operations to be delayed.

We know from [3] (page 407) that the sequence in which operations not subject to a delay are scheduled has no effect on the final sum of delays.

Therefore, even if there was some operation (k+s), with s < q+1 for which

$$E_{k+s} < E_k$$

and if we scheduled operation k with the smallest l_k first we will still achieve the maximum possible reduction of the sum of delays for a due date sequence. For, all as yet undelayed, (q+1) operations will be scheduled before any of the operations already subject to delay, as each time one of undelayed operations is scheduled time moves on for all the unscheduled operations by a constant amount.

Scheduling by the smallest current value of l_k therefore reduces the delay inherent in a due date sequence by the maximum possible amount for a due date sequence.

Loosely speaking l_k sequencing achieves this by delaying operations with " relatively" early due dates and "relatively" large operation times.

We know from the SPT rule that there are schedulng sequences in which ordering operations by operation times produces the minimum delay.

At any time before we select the next operation we can easily establish whether SPT or due date sequencing would give us the better result.

Assume SPT sequencing gives a smaller total delay than due date sequencing. Then

$$R_m = \sum_1^m (m+1-i)t_i - \sum_1^m d_i + \sum_1^m s_i$$

Given an SPT sequence we know that

$$\sum_1^m (m+1-i)t_i \quad \text{is the minimum value possible;}$$

$\sum_1^m d_i$ is always a constant for any sequence.

If therefore there exists an $R_0 < R_m$ then there must be a sequence j for which

$$\sum_{1}^{m} (m+1-i)t_i + \sum_{1}^{m} s_i > \sum_{1}^{m} (m+1-j)t_j + \sum_{1}^{m} s_j$$

verbally expressed: we must increase $\sum_{1}^{m} (m+1-i)t_i$ by some amount and reduce $\sum_{1}^{m} s_i$ by greater amount when doing so to arrive at the j sequence.

Let

$$K = \sum_{1}^{m} (m+1-i)t_i + \sum_{1}^{m} s_i$$

and

$$K' = \sum_{1}^{m} (m+1-i)t_i + \sum_{1}^{m} s_i + mt_k + g_k - (m+1-k)t_k - \sum_{1}^{k-1} t_i - s_k -$$
$$- \sum_{1}^{k-1} \min.[s_i; t_k]$$

where

g_k = the actual slack left if we schedule operation k first.

and K' is the original value of K plus the change that results from letting the k-th operation go first.

After simplification we find

$$K' - K = g_k + (k-1)t_k - \sum_{1}^{k-1} t_i - s_k - \sum_{1}^{k-1} \min.[s_i; t_k]$$

but as $g_k = l_k - t_k$

$$K' - K = l_k + (k-2)t_k - \sum_{1}^{k-1} t_i - s_k - \sum_{1}^{k-1} \min.[s_i; t_k]$$

which of course is our old friend E. By choosing that operation with the smallest E_k we reduce the delay inherent in an SPT sequence by the maximum that is possible with each selection.

If it were impossible for the maximum reduction in the delay inherent in an SPT sequence to be followed by an increase when we schedule the k-th operation before the j-th, with $j < k$, then following such a rule would produce the maximum possible reduction in the inherent sum of total delays.

The inherent delay of no successor operation is altered by scheduling a preceding operation.

If scheduling an operation with a larger operation time before an operation with a smaller operation time simply means that the slack of the preceding operation is reduced, but not eliminated then no delay is imposed on the preceding operation.

But assume there is an operation j, with $j < k$, for which $s_j < t_k$ where $E_k < 0$ and is the smallest value E_j. Then scheduling operation k before operation j will eliminate its slack, s_j, and increase its inherent delay.

But as the slack, s_j, is defined as the slack assuming an SPT sequence, the mere elimination of that slack need not mean that operation j will be definitely delayed; it could, for instance, be scheduled immediately after operation k and still not suffer a delay.

For if $t_k + t_j - l_j < 0$ operation j need not be delayed by scheduling operation k.

From $s_j > 0$ we know

$$s_j = l_j - \sum_1^j t_i$$

therefore $E_j = (j-1)t_j - \sum_1^{j-1} \min.[s_i;t_j] \geq 0$

i.e. no reduction in the delay inherent in an SPT sequence is possible by scheduling an operation which still has slack.

Therefore if $E_k < 0$ then $s_k = 0$.

Before examining the question of whether a delay can be caused by scheduling the operation with the smallest E_k to an operation that precedes it in an SPT sequence let us find a more convenient expression for E_k.

$$E_k = l_k - \sum_1^k t_i - s_k + \sum_1^{k-1} \max.[0; t_k-s_i]$$

because

if $t_k > s_i$ $\sum_1^{k-1} \min.[s_i;t_k] = s_i$

and $\sum_1^{k-1} \max.[0;t_k-s_i] = t_k-s_i.$

if $t_k < s_i$ $\sum_1^{k-1} \min.[s_i;t_k] = t_k$

and $\sum_1^{k-1} \max.[0,t_k-s_i] = 0$

Therefore

$$\sum_1^{k-1} \min.[s_i;t_k] + \sum_1^{k-1} \max.[0;t_k-s_i] = (k-1)t_k$$

from which we can derive the above expression for E_k.

As we know we can replace l_k with $(d_k + r_k)$ in our formula.

$$E_k = d_k + r_k - \sum_1^k t_i + \sum_1^{k-1} \max.[0;t_k-s_i]$$

as

$$d_k + r_k = \sum_1^k t_i \qquad \text{if } r_k > 0$$

we get $\quad E_k > 0 \quad$ for any operation already permanently delayed for any $k > 1$.

Assume

$$E_k < E_{k-1} < E_{k-2} < \ldots < E_{k-n} \leq 0$$

and therefore $s_i = 0$ for any i from k to k-n.

Let E_k be the smallest E_i not only of the above series but of all values for operations as yet unscheduled.

Then

$$E_{k-1} = l_{k-1} - \sum_1^{k-1} t_i + \sum_1^{k-2} \max.[0;t_{k-1}-s_i]$$

$$E_k = l_k - \sum_1^k t_i + \sum_1^{k-1} \max.[0;t_k-s_i]$$

$$E_{k-1} - E_k = l_{k-1} - l_k + t_k - t_k - A$$

where

$$A = \sum_1^{k-2} \max.[0;t_k-s_i] - \sum_1^{k-2} \max.[0;t_{k-1}-s_i] = \sum_1^{k-2} a_i$$

If $t_{k-1} > s_i$ then $t_k > s_i$ and $a_i = t_k - t_{k-1}$
If $t_k < s_i$ then $t_{k-1} < s_i$ and $a_i = 0$
If $t_{k-1} < s_i$ and $t_k > s_i$ then $a_i = t_k - s_i < t_k - t_{k-1}$
Therefore $A \geq 0$ and as,

$$l_{k-1} - l_k > A$$

it follows that if $E_k < E_{k-1}$ then $l_k < l_{k-1}$.

Therefore should scheduling operation k force a delay on any of the n operations immediately preceding it, and for all of which $s_i = 0$, then this is an unavoidable delay as operation k has the smallest due date and no operation which were better scheduled than it can be found.

As $E_1 = 0$, however many operations we have scheduled, we need not consider any operation for which $E_j > 0$ for scheduling, as at least this first operation will be schedulable without increasing the inherent delay.

Now assume we have a sequence such that e < j < k. And

$$E_j > 0 \qquad \text{and} \qquad E_k < E_e \leq 0.$$
Therefore also $\qquad s_j > 0;\ s_e \geq 0;\ s_k = 0.$

And assume further that $s_e < t_k$ and $t_k + t_e - l_e > 0$; i.e. the slack of operation e is smaller than operation k's time and

that scheduling operation k would definitely cause operation e
to suffer a (permanent) delay.

For clarity let us also define our sequence in words: operation e
which will be delayed if we scheduled operation k, is followed by
operation j which has a slack, s_j, and only after that do we
reach operation k, which seems to promise to decrease the total
inherent delay by more that operation e does.

If $E_j > 0$ and $s_e \geq 0$ it follows that $s_j > s_e$
as

and $l_j - \sum_1^j t_i - s_j = 0$

$$\sum_1^{j-1} \max.[0; t_j - s_i] \geq t_j - s_e > 0.$$

Let

$$D_k = E_k + t_k + t_e - l_e$$

i.e. the reduction possible in the total delay by scheduling
    operation k increased by delay imposed by it onto operation
    e.

Let D'_k be the value of E_k after scheduling operation e.

$$D_k = l_k - \sum_1^k t_i + \sum_1^{k-1} \max.[0; t_k - s_i] + t_k + t_e - l_e$$

$$D'_k = l_k - t_e - \sum_1^k t_i + t_e + \sum_1^{k-1} \max.[0, t_k - s_i] - t_k + s_e + \sum_1^{e-1} x_i$$

$$D_k - D'_k = 2t_k + t_e - s_e - l_e - \sum_1^{e-1} x_i$$

where

$$\begin{aligned}
x_i &= 0; & \text{if} \quad t_k &\leq s_i - t_e \\
x_i &= t_k + t_e - s_i & \text{if} \quad s_i &> t_k > s_i - t_e \\
x_i &= t_e & \text{if} \quad t_k &> s_i > t_e \\
x_i &= s_i & \text{if} \quad s_i &< t_e
\end{aligned}$$

If $D_k - D'_k > 0$ we must not schedule operation k, as this
would definitely cause operation e to be delayed, whilst D'_k the
of E_k on the next round will be even smaller than it is now.
Whether we should schedule operation e must depend on whether
there are other operations for which E_i is smaller than E_e and
which do not cause a delay to operation e. In other words we
must simply remove operation k from current consideration.

But assume $D_k - D'_k < 0$ then this must mean that the slack

19

of an operation p, for $p < e$, would be reduced by scheduling operation e below t_k. And therefore $t_k + t_p - 1_p > 0$ as

$$1_p = s_p - \sum_1^p t_i$$

so that scheduling operation k, rather than operation e, would impose an even greater delay on operation p, as $t_k > t_e$.

As $\sum_1^{e-1} x_i \leq (e-1)t_e$

and therefore $D_k - D'_k > 0$ for any $e < 3$ our above considerations for $D_k - D'_k < 0$ must eventually lead to a $p < 3$. Therefore operation k must be barred from being scheduled whether or not the potential reduction it offers for the total delay is further reduced or increased.

Finally we must determine what to do if there are several operations for which E_i is equal. Quite simply choose the one with the smallest due date.

We have proved:

    1.   for a sequence with a due date bias scheduling by smallest 1_k is best.

    2.   for a sequence with an SPT bias scheduling by smallest E_k, subject to the exception just dealt with, always reduces the total delay inherent in that sequence by the maximum possible. And given that the rule about barring operations which delay preceding ones is observed the inherent total delay is never increased.

Therefore this method always minimises the total inherent delay.

5. Postscript.
================

Next to no computation is required for scheduling by smallest
l_k - the larger of either the due date or the earliest
finish. Yet it is this scheduling rule that will apply to the
bulk of all real factory data.

                            *****

Whilst testing the proposed algorithm it appeared to me that
even when scheduling by E_k, on a sequence with an SPT bias, the
best sequences deviated from a sequence that would have been
produced by l_k scheduling by only a few selections in very
many cases.

The following suggestion for a possible improvement in the
algorithm occurred to me:

This algorithm or any variant of it will always require the data
to be sorted into operation time order.

The present requirement to sort to due date as well derives
purely from the need for a marker to indicate when to switch
from l_k to E_k sequencing.

The computation required for E_k scheduling is higher than for
l_k based scheduling.

It therefore seems desirable to find a method to determine when
to switch between these two procedures, which

    1.   does not require the data to be sorted into due date
         order, and

    2.   allows the switch into and back out of E_k
         scheduling to be made more quickly responsive; i.e.
         allows the algorithm make an even greater number of
         its selections on the basis of l_k scheduling.

                            *****

Practically all my studies of the literature were dependant on the excellent facilities and the friendly co-operation of the BIM Library in London. I am not a BIM member, yet they allowed me the use of their facilities. I would like to thank the BIM for that.

Finally I would like to apologise to any reader who has born with me thus far, particularly for the trudging cumbersomeness of my proof of the algorithm; the only excuse I can offer is that I am not a mathematician, the only comfort that the algorithm seems easier to put into a computer program than to prove.

                    *****

References:

1   Lawler, E.L.   "Optimal Sequencing of a Single Machine
                     Subject to Precedence constraints"
                     Management Science, USA, Vol.19 No.5
                     January 1973
2   Baker, K.R.   "Introduction to Sequencing and Scheduling"
                     page 68
                     John Wiley & Sons, Inc. New York
                     1974
3   Wilkerson, L.J. & Irwin, J.D.
                     "An Improved Algorithm for Scheduling
                     Independant Tasks"
                     AIIE Transactions Vol.3 No.3
                     September 1971
4   Baker, K.R.   as above 2   page 67
5   Baker, K.R.   as above 2   Appendix A.
6   Wild, R.   "Production and Operations Management"
                     page 267
                     Holt, Rinehart and Wilson, Eastbourne 1980.

Electronic Funds Transfer Systems

Enio Presutto

Department of Computer Science, York University, Canada

The cashless society predicted in the early sixties may not have materialized, however Electronic Funds Transfer Systems do exists and are in use today. This report will discuss the evolution of EFT systems, their components, social impact, government regulations, and future direction.

* This research was supported in part by a Government of Canada NSERC Grant, 1980.

As we enter the 1980's it is obvious that the cashless society predicted in the early sixties has not materialized. The money presses have not yet been dismantled and we have not been completely depersonalized and numbered. However, we can not pretend that these things will not occur, for they will; they already exist but at the moment are lurking in the shadows.

Funds Transfer Systems have evolved over the centuries from primitive payment systems based on precious metals to modern payment systems using computers and telecommunications. A payment system is the mechanism established for the safe and orderly transfer of funds between financial institutions. All exchanges of funds, except cash exchanges, are made using written requests directing a financial institution to transfer funds to another financial institution. In our banking systems, cheques, money orders, and bank drafts all represent written instructions directing a transfer of funds.

Electronic Funds Transfer System (EFTS) is a term used to represent the payment systems using computers and telecommunication facilities, such as microwave, lasers, and satellites. The introduction of computers into our payment systems has resulted in a dramatic increase in the number of transactions which can be processed daily, and has also reduced significantly the time required for a transaction to be completed. The financial institutions have also made use of computers to improve their customer services, by providing 24 hour banking facilities and multibranch banking. Hence, Electronic Funds Transfer Systems are in use right now in various parts of the world and the 80's will witness the spread of their availability and use, particularly by means of international computer networks.

Brief History

Automation came to the financial institutions in the late 1950's with the development of the Cheque Reader/Sorter, a device capable of reading the Magnetic Ink Character Recognition (MICR) encoding at the bottom of the cheques. Once the amount had been added by an operator through an encoding device, the cheque could then be processed entirely by the Reader/Sorter. The amount of the cheque and customer account information would be recorded and customer account files updated automatically. Given the enormous volume of cheques processed daily (four to nine million cheques daily (2)) the financial institutions were quick to employ these Reader/Sorters in an effort to reduce the time requirement and cost of processing cheques.

As computer technology advanced, the financial institutions saw the benefits to be gained by automating many of their other functions. The computer could be used to perform many repetitive functions quickly and efficiently. The savings achieved by using the computer to process cheques lead to the development of batch

systems aimed at financial analysis and money management. Also,
many financial reporting systems were implemented in order to
increase the availability of management reports.

Other batch services included: consumer lending portfolio
analysis, certificate of deposits, commercial lending, capital
stocks, loans analysis, payroll services.(3) Even though the
automated batch services mentioned above were in the forefront of
technology, they required overnight processing and did not fully
exploit the power of the computer. These batch services were
acceptable for commercial customers, but not for the general public.

In an effort to reduce costs and paper handling, Online Savings
Accounts were introduced, enabling customers to make deposits and
withdrawals and get accurate up-to-date information on the status of
their accounts. Today, we are all quite familiar with the online
teller terminals and passbook printers that are in use. Online
Savings Accounts proved to be quite acceptable to the general
public, who appreciated the reduced manual processing of their
accounts and the speed at which inquires regarding their account
status could be answered. Large corporations with many offices and
bank accounts also benefited from the Online Savings Accounts. It
was now possible for the rapid transfer of funds in order to meet
financial commitments, and for companies to obtain immediate
information regarding their financial status.

Customer Bank Communications Terminals

Online Savings Accounts have been made possible through the use
of Customer Bank Communications Terminals connected to a centralized
bank computer via a telecommunications network. These terminals are
subdivided into three major groups, Online Teller Terminals,
Automated Teller Machines (ATM) and Point of Sale (POS) terminals.
The Online Teller Terminal is used by the tellers in the servicing
of customer accounts. Through the keyboard/display the customer's
accounts can be updated or inquiries taken. The printer provided
with these terminals is used to update passbooks and to print daily
totals and teller totals. These terminals however, are solely for
the use of the bank staff and are not designed for public use or
maximum security. The only security is that which is programmed in
by the financial institutions. The most accepted form of security
is requiring tellers to enter a password.

Automated Teller Machines (ATM)

The Automated Teller Machines allow the customer to receive the
same services as with a teller, but at the customer's own
convenience. The customer is provided with a plastic card
containing a magnetic strip upon which has been recorded the
individuals account identification information. The card is
inserted into a slot on the front of the machine, and once the

information on the card has been validated, the customer is required to enter his Personal Identification Number (PIN) which acts as the customer's private password and is used to validate the card and customer. Once this sequence of steps has been performed the customer is allowed access to his accounts. Deposits are allowed through the use of special envelopes, into which the customer places the deposit, and inserts the envelope into a slot on the machine. A simple and specialized keyboard is provided through which the customer can indicate the amount of deposit or withdrawal.

When withdrawing money, the customer is usually allowed to withdraw only a certain maximum amount on any one day. In the event that more money is needed then the customer is forced to enter the bank and withdraw cash via the teller. The customer is also allowed to transfer money from one account to another as long as he is authorized to access both accounts. The ATMs available today reflect the rather primitive stage of our EFT systems. Primitive because the customer is provided with a limited withdrawal and deposit service. In most cases the number of withdrawals and the total amount withdrawn on one day is limited. The Automated Teller Machines, unfortunately are not designed to recognize currency and therefore when a deposit is made, the machine can not verify the true amount tendered. In order to provide some security against fraudulent deposits and withdrawals the financial institutions have had to impose these restrictions. These restrictions however, have not detered the general public and the ATMs have been gradually accepted as a convenience and are growing in popularity. ATMs can now be found in most large cities and are generally available 24 hours a day. (4)

Point of Sale Terminals

Point of Sale Terminals (POS) are merchant operated terminals located in retail outlets replacing the conventional cash register. The merchant registers the goods purchased by the shopper (just as would be done with a cash register) and rather than receiving cash or cheques for the goods, the POS terminals communicate directly with a bank computer, credit the merchants account, and debit the shoppers account. This is done by the shopper placing an identification card into a card reader and the clerk entering the amount. This transaction must, of course, be validated by the shopper's PIN. Point of Sale Terminals provide the consumer with many conveniences. The shopper can deposit funds into his account, deposit or cash cheques, pay for goods purchased, and withdraw funds from his bank account. The role of the teller in this case is assumed by the cash register operator. Point of Sale Terminals are currently not as widely used as ATMs and hence are not as widely known by the shopping public. However, given the convenience that they offer, it is certain that financial institutions in conjuction with the large retail outlets will eventually provide this service. (5,6,7)

Telecommunications Network

The Customer Bank Communications Terminals discussed above are usually located in heavily populated areas, or at locations convenient to the public. However, these are not the people who will benefit most from the use of Electronic Funds Transfer Systems. These customers are located near banking centers, where payment settlements were done manually in the past and can survive without EFT. However, the consumers who will benefit the most are those located in remote areas. Through the use of modern telecommunications facilities, it will be possible for Canadians living in the far north, or in our Rocky Mountain region to receive the same banking services as customers in large cities.(8)

Bank networks fall into two categories: local EFT networks and international EFT networks. Both local and international networks make use of telecommunications technology such as satellite, micro wave, laser, fiber optics, and packet switching. However, the local or regional networks are used to link financial institutions with their branches. The transactions may be transmitted across communications channels operated by common carriers or privately leased lines. It is important that these local networks be secure, fast, efficient, error free and able to route transactions to and from the appropriate banks. International networks are used in the transfer of large amounts between financial institutions on either side of the Atlantic ocean. Such a network was used to transfer funds from the U.S.A. to Europe in order to secure the release of the American Hostages from Iran.

SWIFT (Society for Worldwide Interbank Financial Telecommunications)

SWIFT, a message switching network operated by the Society for Worldwide Interbank Financial Telecommunications (9,10,11), was formed in the early 1970's to reduce the problems encountered by the banking community in handling international payments. The increase in international trade and travel caused an increase in international payments. Previous to SWIFT, the transactions were described on paper and transmitted by mail. Exchanges of large sums or time critical payments were sent via TELEX. This of course was a slow and inefficient way of settling international payments. The SWIFT network was designed to:

1. replace the services performed by TELEX and the mail,

2. eliminate the high rate of clerical errors, and

3. most importantly, reduce the tedious manual checking.

The benefits derived from the above design considerations were primarily a result of the standardization of the format in which transactions would be sent.

The SWIFT network has proved to be a success and is in use by 683 member banks in 26 countries. This international network provides the financial institutions with an efficient and fast way of transferring funds across the Atlantic. The normal speed for transmitting payment messages is about 10 minutes (under one minute for priority messages.) The network has a capacity of 250,000 messages per day, with two levels of security in the coding and authentication of messages by the sending and receiving banks. Additionally, the cost of sending an overseas message has been reduced from approximately $2.75 per message before the introduction of SWIFT to below 50 cents with SWIFT. All messages going over the network adhere to rigid formats, which is mandatory where transactions involving huge sums are concerned.

The SWIFT network provides a complex system of alternative paths and redundant equipment, in order to maintain a very secure and reliable message handling network with minimal inconvenience to the financial institutions.

Visa

The second message switching network currently in use today by many financial institutions is the VISA network. VISA is an international network used by member credit card issuing institutions to authorize purchases made by customers. Further, once the purchase data is captured by the processing centres it is transmitted to the central VISA centre, which in turn sends the information to the financial institution which issued the card.

In addition the VISA network allows merchants to obtain authorization on any credit card purchase. The merchant calls the authorization centre run by the financial institution to which he subscribes. The operator enters the request into the VISA network and the information is transmitted to the card issuing institution. Here the request is validated and the customers credit card limit is lowered by the respective amount. Approval is then given to the requestor. The VISA network is not a true EFT system, but simply a message switching network used for authorization requests on credit card purchases. It is however, a step towards a more automated system in the future.

SOCIAL IMPACT OF EFT

Society is usually quite slow in accepting major technological advances and changes in life styles. Hence, when introducing Electronic Funds Transfer Systems to the public it must be done very slowly and carefully. Public reaction will decide whether a new technology will survive. If the majority of people do not accept the service, then it will never be cost effective and will most likely fail. It is for this reason that most financial institutions have proceeded very slowly in installing ATMs and POS terminals.

Full EFT systems are technically feasible today, but the financial institutions are beginning by pursuading individuals to accept ATMs by highlighting their advantages such as; convenient, fast efficient service with extended hours, and ideal in case of banking emergencies. The key to introducing EFT services such as ATMs and POS terminals, is to stress that they are optional. Hence, at this point the decision to try an automated teller machine rests solely with the individual, and no one else. This approach will convince the consumer that he has chosen the service and at the same time the way is being paved for future acceptance of full EFT services. There must exist a growing acceptance by the people who are to make use of this service before any large scale implementation can take place.

The public are becoming very skeptical when confronted with new technology, thus it is difficult to say whether it is better to continue advancing our technology or whether we may be advancing too quickly for our own good. The financial institutions may be as skeptical as the consumers, but they must remain competitive so if one bank does fully automate and is successful then the other banks will lose their competitive edge and must follow. However, if they rush into automation and EFT is not successful, then considerable investment and reputations can be lost.

In the February 5, 1981 edition of Computing, an article by Peter White indicates that the Barclays Bank has earmarked 35 million pounds to introduce a new generation of automation to its services. Peter White continues to report that "the move is designed to further Barclay's ambitions to be the first UK bank to take automation right to the counter and could pull its rivals behind it." (12) Here is the case of one bank increasing its use of automation, soon to be followed by its competitors.

Consumer acceptance of banking automation varies from total denial of a new service, to conditional acceptance until they get more comfortable with it, to total acceptance. At the individual level, which category a person falls into can depend on the person's age, education, income or profession. Generally, people tend to fear things they don't understand. Therefore a person with a combined appreciation and understanding of computers is more likely to feel more comfortable and have a better acceptance of EFT, than a person who has a natural dislike or less of an understanding of machines. The latter might feel that he does not like the idea of trusting his money to a machine he does not understand. This of course, is a valid fear which should be considered when evaluating social reaction.

At the group level the category which the majority of the people tend to fall into would probably be the conditional acceptance. Unless a customer is highly concerned with the dehumanizing issue that arises from replacing people with machines, or the security issue, he or she would tend to give EFT a chance and try to adjust to the service before adoption of it.

Certainly full EFT services will not achieve universal acceptance until a future generation, where the individuals are computer literate and who are comfortable with computers and telecommunications. One of the first and most critical steps leading towards acceptance of EFT services is to educate the consumer -- EFT Literacy. Many people today are very skeptical when confronted with ATMs. Much of this fear is caused by a lack of education regarding the principles behind the ATMs. We must also consider that introducing ATM and POS terminals will cause many individuals to alter drastically their banking habits and possibly also their spending habits. The average person will likely make one trip a week (excluding emergencies) to the bank and will usually set themself a spending limit for the week. However, many individuals fear that ATM and POS terminals will make money considerably more accessible and may increase their temptation to overspend.

Another concern about full EFT services is the effect that it will have on our society . How important will this new service become once it is fully implemented and more importantly to what extent will people depend on it as an essential part of their life. If EFT services are to eventually replace all current payment systems; what happens if suddenly something happens to disrupt these services severly; will people be able to cope? Will we forget how to handle cash? Will we remember how to write cheques? Will the banks still know how to cash it? The question is should EFT services be built to such a height that they become as essential as the telephone, electricity, airplanes and automobiles? Should the consumer back himself into such a corner knowing that if something goes wrong it will probably result in a major social upset.

Two particularly good examples of system collapse are the New York blackout in 1978 and the California gasoline shortage which occurred in 1979. When New York was blacked out for a period of time, people simply could not cope with the lack of electricity. Mass rioting and looting were results of this upset. In 1979, Southern California experienced a shortage of gasoline and since people had become so dependent on their automobiles as a means of transportation, this shortage resulted in a severe disruption. The rationing of gasoline forced people to do such things as:

getting in line at gasoline stations at such hours as two o'clock in the morning, and resorting to

violence, such as, pushing, shoving, hitting people who try to beat others to the gasoline pumps. There we reports of murders over suspected queue-jumping and gasoline robberies.

Does society want the same problems in the case of an EFT crisis?
It is something to consider carefully!

Another important point to consider under social implications
is the human engineering ATM or POS terminals and what it involves.
Canada is a multicultural country with diverse ethnic groups in
different geographical areas. Toronto alone is rich in ethnic
groups. It is estimated that 60 ethnic groups speaking 75 languages
live in the city. What happens for example, in a primarily Italian
neighbourhood where a good part of the population does not speak
English well enough to read the instructions on the terminals.
Should the terminal instructions and keys also be provided in
Italian and what of the literature to educate the customer, should
that also be provided in Italian? This difficulty could also apply
to our large chinese population. This point should be considered in
detail. It should be noted that there are people who can not read
at all, what are they to do? A solution that might help a good part
of these people could be to use symbols to represent the transaction
keys. However, there is still a problem concerning instructions.
Should someone else do their banking if they can not remember how to
use the terminal? This affects the consumer's privacy and security.

While in the area of types of terminals one must also design it
to conform to the type of consumer environment. A residential area
consisting of the average consumer should most likely provide
terminals with very straightforward services ie. deposits,
withdrawals, transfer of funds between accounts, balance inquiries,
etc. A thriving business area would probably consist of, in
addition to the average consumer terminals, a multitude of private
terminals within corporate offices with more complicated services
involving corporate cash management. (13)

Legislation

Our financial institutions, because of their importance in our
society are regulated by national governments. The regulations
imposed by the various governments differ greatly due to the unique
internal bank structure within each nation. Canada for example has
financial institutions chartered by the Federal government and these
institutions are allowed to operate branches in all provinces.
Several of the chartered bankks have over 3000 branches
coast-to-coast. While the United States has two major types of
financial institutions, commercial banks and savings banks
legislated by Federal and State governments. The charters issued to
these institutions severly limit the number of branches that they
may operate and in which States they may operate. (It is possible
to have a bank which is allowed only one branch.) There are no truly
national banks in the USA as there are in Canada. The banking
systems of other nations may be similar to the Canadian or U.S.A.
model or may be quite different. Differences in internal bank
structure will mean differences in legislation required. Canadian

banks for example need not be concerned about the status of an ATM, while banks in other countries will have to argue against outdated legislation. In some countries bank charters may be worded in such a way that an ATM could qualify as a separate branch if not housed within the actual bank building. This type of charter would severly limit the growth of EFT systems for banks allowed only one branch.

The United States has introduced legislation (commonly referred to as Regulation E (14)) to regulate EFTS activities. This legislation is concerned with:

1. ATMs -- deposits, withdrawals, third party funds transfer

2. POS terminals,

3. Telephone transactions -- bill payment, telephone transfers,

4. Preauthorized credits -- payroll, social security direct deposits,

5. Preauthorized debits,

6. Credit/debit cards -- liability, privacy, stopping payments.

The United States by establishing this legislation has taken the lead in modernizing Banking laws for the introduction of EFTS.

Another concern which must be considered when discussing EFTS is the difficulty in controlling movement of funds across national borders. Most nations are quite concerned about the amount of money entering and leaving their country and have established strict Custom laws about importing and exporting funds. However, with the introduction of EFTS networks using satellites, the mechanisms currently in use to control funds movement will no longer be effective. This is a particular concern which is currently being investigated at York University by Prof. J.R. McBride.

The Laws of most countries have not kept pace with the quick growth of EFT systems over the last decade. However, in the 1980's we can expect to see much more debate regarding EFT regulations and the possible introduction of legislation similar to Regulation E, in other countries.

Just the Beginning

In this report we have discussed the evolution of EFTS from early batch systems to our present highly sophisticated networks. What does the future hold in store for us? Most financial institutions in the world today make use of computers for internal

processing and also for running local, limited, EFT systems. Japan,
for example makes extensive use of ATMs (15) and most European
countries also provide ATM services. In some countries national EFT
networks have been established to handle the flow of funds. (The
SICA in Spain and STACRI (16) in Italy are operated by the Savings
banks with in each country.) In Canada and the United States ATMs
are also in use with the POS terminals lurking in the shadows.
However, no financial institution has yet adopted a full EFT
service. The closest to a full EFT service offered in Canada is the
Bank of Montreal's MultiBranch banking, and it is not that close!

What the future holds is very difficult to predict at this
point in time due to the rapidly changing computer and
telecommunications technology. Financial institutions in the United
States are experimenting with a personal computer service, which
allows subscribers to bank at home. The subscriber, through the use
of a microcomputer and the standard telephone system, can
communicate with the bank's central computer, and can currently
initiate a few limited query transactions. The next decade will
tell if this service is found to be acceptable by the public and it
will interesting to watch its impact upon our society. Another
recent technological breakthrough is the "CHIP CARD" (17) introduced
in France. The "CHIP CARD" has the appearance of a regular credit
card, but instead of the conventional magnetic strip on the back it
has a microcomputer memory which can store about 1000 bits of
information about the card owner. It is predicted that this new
device will alter significantly the services provided by the
financial institutions. With the development of the two-way
television systems such as Videotex and TELIDON, we can expect some
future link-up with the banking system. These new innovations must
be introduced into our banking systems slowly and carefully, if
their use is to be successful.

Further concerns include:

1. Who will control and police future international networks
    established for transferring funds,

2. Standards will have to be established and accepted by the
    nations of the world, if we are to make use of the "CHIP
    CARD" as a replacement for currency,

3. The impact which the introduction of full EFT services will
    have upon our society and economies.

4. The impact on privacy of the individual.

Unfortunately space does not permit a more indept discussion of
Electronic Funds Transfer Systems and their impact. However, the
reader is urged to consider the concerns raised in this report and

consult the articles listed in the partial bibliography.

REFERENCES

1. Crean, J.F., Automation and Canadian Banking, The Canadian
    Banker and ICB Review, July-August, vol. 85, No. 4, 1978,
    pp. 16-21.

2. Crean, J.F., The Canadian Payment System, The Canadian
    Banker and ICB Review, October, vol. 85, no. 5, 1978, pp.
    20-28.

3. Crean, J.F., The Canadian Payment System, The Canadian
    Banker and ICB Review, October, vol. 85, no. 5, 1978, pp.
    20-28.

4. Crean, J.F., Contrasts in National Paments Systems, The
    Canadian Banker and ICB Review, Feb. 1979, pp. 18-26.

5. Streeter, B., Battle in Beantown, ABA Banking Journal, May
    1980, pp. 64-68,71.

6. Streeter, B., Renewed Interest in Point of Sale Banking,
    ABA Banking Journal, Sept. 1980, pp. 101-102,104,106,109.

7. White, P., Point of Sale causes Chain Reaction, Computing,
    Jan 22, 1981, p. 12.

8. Streeter, B., Winning the West with a Shared ATM Network,
    ABA Banking Journal, Sept. 1979, pp. 86,89,90,93.

9. ------, New SWIFT Network gives Banks Instantaneous Link --
    World Wide, Banking, July 1977, pp. 48-49,98.

10. Newman, S., International Messages are Moving SWIFTly,
    Telecommunications, Feb. 1979, pp. 75-77,99.

11. -----, What's Ahead for the Wire Sevices?, ABA Banking
    Journal, Feb. 1980, pp. 96,99,102-105.

12. White, P., Barclays Starts its 35 Million Pound Revolution,
    Computing, Feb. 5, 1981, pp. 1,3.

13. Kling, R., Electronic Fund Transfer Systems and Quality of
    Life, National computer Conference, 1978, pp. 191-197.

14. Dunkin, A., Massive Cost Feared for EFT Compliance, ABA
    Banking Journal, May 1980, pp. 200,202,205-206,208,210.

15. Howard, M., World Computer Banking Systems, The Bankers'
     Magazine of Australasia, Feb. 1979, pp. 10-12.

16. Pesant, J-M., The Third force in International Banking, The
     Banker, May 1980, pp. 193-195.

17. Orr, B., The Chip Card is Here, But Where is it Going?, ABA
     Banking Journal, Sept. 1980, pp. 93,95.

                            BIBLIOGRAPHY

 1. Vandeven, W.J., Communications Standards for Banks, Bank
     Administration Institute, Park Ridge, Illinois.

 2. Takayanagi, A. and Hiratsuka, K., On-line Real-time
     Banking System of NTT, First USA-JAPAN Computer Conference,
     1972.

 3. Kodama, T. and Hirayama, Y., Data Telecommunication system
     of All Banks in Japan, First USA-JAPAN Computer Conference,
     1972, pp.341-349.

 4. Ege, S.M., Electronic Funds Transfer: A Survey of Problems
     and Prospects in 1975. Maryland Law Review, Vol 35, no.
     1, 1975.

 5. Lee, R.E., Dialing for Dollars: Communications Regulation
     and Electronic Fund Transfer Systems, Maryland Law Review,
     vol 35, no 1, 1975, pp. 57-73.

 6. Schuck, P.H., Electronic Funds Transfer: A Technology in
     Search of a Market, Maryland Law Review, Vol 35, No. 1,
     1975, pp. 74-87.

 7. -----, Electronic Funds Transfer and Branch Banking - The
     Application of old Law to New Technology, Maryland Law
     Review, Vol 35, no. 1, 1975, pp. 88-114.

 8. Pipe, G.R., Work Paper on Transborder Information Flows:
     Requirements for a New International Framework, Law and
     Computer Technology, 1st Quarter 1976, pp. 17-26.

 9. Mazzetti, J.P., Design Considerations for Electronic Funds
     Transfer Switch System Development, National Computer
     Conference, 1976, pp. 139-146.

10. Kaufman, D. and Auerbach, K., A Secure, National System
     for Electronic Funds Transfer, National Computer

Conference, 1976, pp.   129-138.

11. Backman, F., Are Computers Ready for the Checkless
     Society?, National Computer conference, 1976, pp.   147-156.

12. Monosson, S., Is There a Used Computer in your Future?,
     Banking, Journal of American Bankers Association, May 1977,
     pp.   115-116.

13. Asher, J., Five Cards for one Bank?, Banking, Journal of
     American Bankers Association, May 1977, pp.   39-41, 130.

14. Donaldson, C.W., Why Telecommunications has become the Hot
     new Trend in Bank Operations , Banking, Journal of American
     Bankers Association, May 1977, pp.   90-94.

15. -----, The New Wild Blue Yonder of Bank Communications,
     Banking, Journal of American Bankers Association, May 1977,
     pp.   42-43,82,86.

16. -----, New SWIFT Network gives Banks an Instantaneous Link
     - Worldwide, Banking, Journal of American Bankers
     Association, May 1977, pp.   48-49,98.

17. Fabry, J., Computerized Transfer of Legal Information
     between Nation-- Possibilities and Necessities, Law and
     Computer Technology, 3rd Quarter, 1977, pp.   56-65.

18. Simon, L.S., Advances in Electronic Funds Transfer, The
     Banker, October 1977, pp.   79-85.

19. -----, Decentralizing Microfiche Capacity, Banking, Journal
     of American Bankers Association, November, 1977, pp.
     46-47.

20. -----, Changing how Managers Manage, Banking, Journal of
     American Bankers Association, Novermber, 1977, pp.   44-45.

21. Dewey, R., Systems Auditablity and Control in an EFTS
     Enviromnent, Nation Computer Conference, 1978, pp.
     185-188.

22. Rose, P.S. and Bassoul, H.G., EFTS: Problems and
     Prospects, The Canadian Banker and ICB Review, May-June
     vol. 85, no. 3, 1978, pp.   24-28.

23. Crean, J.F., Automation and Canadian Banking, The Canadian
     Banker and ICB Review, July-August 1978, vol.85, No. 4,
     pp.   16-21.

24. Crean, J.F., The Canadian Payment Systems, The Canadian
    Banker and ICB review, October Vol. 85, No. 5, 1978, pp.
    20-28.

25. Macmillan, J.H., Thy Servant - A Computer (A Personal
    View), Scottish Bankers Magazine, November 1978, pp.
    143-149.

26. Crean, J.F., EFTS and the Canadian Payments System, The
    Canadian Banker and ICB Review, December, Vol. 85, No. 6,
    1978, pp. 18-23.

Part 9
Data Communications

Using Databases Through Networks

W. B. Cousins

Managing Director, Computel Limited, UK

There is a growing requirement to share information through communications networks.

The minimum architecture that will support such an information processing environment has the following essential components:-

1. Network architecture standards to facilitate and govern communications between the centre and the various subscribers to the system.

2. A Data Base Management System to control shared data and allow administrative operations to be carried out effectively and regularly.

3. New database machines that allow new ways of using information, in particular content addressable file stores.

4. Good communications facilities in minicomputers that can widen the subscriber base and so achieve economies of scale.

5. Computer aids such as a data dictionary system to document, and give some control over the computerised and non-computerised parts of the overall information system.

Certain of these components already exist though in very diversified forms. This paper discusses the essential functions of these components in an information sharing environment and, by way of example, describes some currently available products that provide those functions. The paper concludes that the most likely agents to realise an information sharing environment will not be the manufacturers of current components, but intermediaries such as bureaux, whose interest is to sell a network and information service.

1. FUTURE NETWORKS

1.1. Structure

The aim of communication networks is to enable people to obtain
the information they want as quickly as possible. A number of
problems have prevented this being realised in the past, perhaps
the most crucial being the fact that computers and people have
viewed information in a different way. Computers view information
as a number of strings of bits, whose significance and likely
usefulness can be appreciated only by specifying many other
strings of bits that provide positional and hierarchical
information. To people, on the other hand, information can be
any of a wide variety of things: the name or description of an
object or of an idea, or the fact that some relationship exists
between two things. The need to reconcile the simplicity and
precision of the computer's view with the complexity and
vagueness of people's ideas has given rise to a new profession:
programmers and systems analysts whose sole function is to act as
translators between men and machines.

It is perhaps ironic that the most successful members of this
profession are those whose existence is least obvious. An example
would be a database designer who produces a data model that
corresponds so closely to the real world and to the information
needs of the end user that this end user can easily understand it
with no computer knowledge or experience. Another example would
be a communications specialist who defines a number of message
formats that can be used by someone inexperienced and
unsupervised to obtain some required information at a terminal.
Even in these cases, however, it could not be claimed that a
completely successful mapping had been achieved between human
needs and machine capabilities; in neither case, for example,
would it be possible for anyone to make an open-ended query or
one that conformed to no predefined format.

What, then, will be the shape of the networks of the future,
whose task will it be to solve these problems? At their centres
will be large mainframes that offer conventional batch processing
facilities, support database management systems capable of
handling complex data models, and can deal with a heavy
communications workload. Clustered round each such central site
will be a number of local sites, each with some processing power
and with a communications link to the centre. To increase the
scope and flexibility of the tasks that can be carried out, it
should be possible for a number of networks of this kind to
interlock with each other so that a user at a local site can
access any data and use any software that is available, centrally
or locally, through any network interlocked with his own.

1.2. Components

The essential components of a network capable of meeting the
requirements already discussed are:

1. A data dictionary system that can provide clear, accurate
    documentation for the information system as a whole, that is,
    for tasks and data that are still dealt with manually as well
    as for those that have been automated.

2. A database management system that can

    (a) Support complex network data models that accurately
         reflect the real world as it is seen by the user organ-
         isation.

    (b) Allow data to be made available to individual users
         while retaining central control over it to prevent its
         corruption or destruction.

    (c) Enable administrative operations and large-scale batch
         processing to be carried out regularly and efficiently
         without hindering or being hindered by interactive data
         access.

3. Minicomputers on local sites, providing sufficient processing
    power to allow small-scale operations to be carried out
    without making use of the central mainframe, acting as hosts
    to terminals at which users can take advantage of local or
    central facilities, and communicating with the central main-
    frame whenever system requirements make this necessary.

4. Network architecture standards to govern communications, and
    in particular to allow access to public networks and to
    networks based on other manufacturers' equipment and
    software.

5. Hardware or software, or a combination of both, that will
    allow data records to be retrieved by means of open-ended and
    imprecise queries that are based on vague search and
    selection criteria and do not presume any knowledge of the
    structure of the files in which the records are held.

The next section will discuss these components in more detail,
noting those that are already available and examining those that
are still at an early stage of development.

2. THE AVAILABILITY OF COMPONENTS

Some of the components listed in the previous section are
hardware products; some are software products. Others do not yet
exist as products at all, and still others never will, being
philosophies or concepts. If the widely available components are
to be used to the full as part of a communication network,
however, the following points should be borne in mind:

1. End users and their information requirements should always be
   kept to the fore when employing a data dictionary, so that
   the end product is a picture not merely of a computer system
   but of who is supplying information, however indirectly, to
   whom and for what purpose.

2. Databases must be neither remote and inaccessible nor so
   distributed as to be impossible to control; expensive
   resources such as mainframe hardware and skilled labour
   should be concentrated centrally, but access from elsewhere
   should be simple and flexible enough for inexperienced users.

3. Much effort has been devoted to boosting the processing power
   that can be made available locally by means of minicomputers;
   even more effort will be needed in the future to ensure that
   these become fully functioning network nodes, not processing
   islands restricted to simple operations and limited data
   resources.

This leaves two components to be considered: network architecture
standards and the capacity to handle imprecise queries. The two
following sections discuss these in the light of recent
developments that have taken place in the UK.

2.1. Network architecture standards

Computer manufacturers have always shied away from defining
communications standards. There are a number of reasons for
this, one of them being that technological developments have been
taking place at such a rate that any standard is likely to be
overtaken by events before it can be widely accepted or
implemented. Another possible reason is the domination of the
computing industry worldwide by a single company, IBM. At the
moment, the signing of a mainframe contract won ahead of IBM is
the signal for a manufacturer to heave a sigh of relief; if
industry-wide communications standards were agreed, however,
nearly every software package and system development contract
would be the occasion of a new battle.

In spite of this, International Computers Limited (ICL) publicly
dedicated itself some months ago to standardising all its
communications-related products under its Information Processing
Architecture (IPA), which recognises the seven level
communications model recommended by the ISO. This model divides
the total information processing and communications function into
seven well-defined levels, ranging from the low level functions
concerned with electrical signalling to high level functions such
as transaction routeing. Adherence to this model in systems
design would greatly increase the ability of systems to
communicate through networks; but, up to now only ICL has made
any practical attempt to design communications systems that
conform to it. IPA is a design philosophy rather than a product
or set of products, but it lays down a number of clearly defined
objectives that future ICL systems are to meet. Among these is
the provision of the following facilities:

1. RANGE REMOTE JOB ENTRY (RRJE) The ability to enter via one
   type of machine and under one type of system a job that is to
   be run on a different type of machine and under a different
   system.

2. REMOTE SESSION ACCESS (RSA) The ability to use one type of
   machine and system to initiate and participate in an interactive session using the facilities of a different machine
   and system; in particular, to use a minicomputer to gain
   access to the full range of facilities available within a
   virtual machine environment supported by a large mainframe.

3. FILE TRANSFER FACILITY (FTF) The ability to transfer files
   between systems, so that a file created for use on one type
   of machine can later be employed on a different type.

4. DISTRIBUTED APPLICATION FACILITY (DAF) The ability to break
   down an application into a number of parts, each of which can
   be carried out under a different type of system and on a
   different type of machine; in particular, to ensure that this
   distribution of functions is invisible and automatic, so that
   each part of the application is handled with maximum
   efficiency and minimum user effort.

5. MESSAGE TRANSFER FACILITY (MTF) The ability to route input
   messages through and between systems of different types so
   that access is obtained to all the necessary resources
   regardless of where they are located.

By concentrating on these objectives, IPA is at a sufficiently high conceptual level not to be overtaken by technological developments. It could, of course, be argued that concepts have a disturbing tendency to disappear when the time comes to put them into practice. One indication that this is not likely to happen with IPA, was ICL's simultaneous announcement of a new minicomputer, the ME29, dedicated to communications excellence and fully able to play its part in providing the facilities described; work on the large virtual machine environments to enable them to do likewise is already in progress.

Now that one manufacturer has provided a lead, others will have to follow. As users become aware of the wealth of information available through public and large private networks, the demand for machines and systems that can access all of these is certain to grow. Much remains to be done, but the way forward has been mapped out.

2.2. Handling imprecise queries

Queries handled by computers have always had to be precise and to conform to a predefined format; even the shift from batch to interactive processing and the emphasis on natural language in programming and communications has failed to change that. The prerequisite for handling open-ended and imprecise queries is that it should be possible to retrieve records from a file by means of their attributes and values rather than by means of their position in the file. This is the principle on which ICL has based its Content-Addressable Filestore System (CAFS).

The records in a CAFS file do not require any hierarchical structure for the purpose of administration or retrieval; each record consists of a number of fields containing identifiers that indicate the type and length of data the fields hold. When data is to be retrieved from a CAFS file, the CAFS controller is informed of the area of the file that should be searched. Such a logical search area is specified as one or more tracks in a given cylinder on a given disc drive. The data on each track is regarded as a cyclic sequence of 15 blocks, which enables content searching to begin as soon as the heads are on the required cylinder; there is no latency.

The unstructured stream of bytes read from a CAFS file is divided into self-identifying data fields and record trailer fields. The record evaluation process begins only when a record trailer, which indicates the end of a record's data fields, has been encountered. There are 16 identical key registers that operate in parallel on each field of disc data. Each contains a field value that is being searched for, with separate bytes indicating the identifier, length and required contents of the field. To allow more complex comparisons to be carried out, each key register has a mask register associated with it; this allows parts of data fields to be masked out as they are compared, so that partial matching or matching on subfield values can be achieved. The result of each field comparison is preserved until a record trailer is encountered, when a microprogram is executed to combine the results of the comparisons carried out on all the fields in the record. This combination of results indicates whether the record is a possible hit that should be passed on to the CAFS controller.

CAFS requires three items of information before it can respond to any information retrieval request:

1. The name of the file that contains the area to be searched.

2. A record selection expression that defines the criteria on which records are to be selected. Such an expression consists of a number of field names, each paired with a value by means of a logical operator that specifies whether the field value should be greater than, less than, or equal to that value. Rather than specify a new record selection expression for each query, it is possible to invoke predefined enquiry frames, or screen formats, which prompt the user by listing various field names; a full or partial value can then be input for some fields, and the system will combine the values supplied for use as a record selection expression.

3. The way in which the results of the search are to be presented. This may be a detailed layout specification, or simply a request for a count of possible hit records to be supplied, so that more stringent selection criteria can be specified if necessary.

Because most of the operations involved in searching a CAFS file are carried out by hardware rather than software, response times are decreased by up to two orders of magnitude; for the same reason, the number of mainframe instructions required for any search can be reduced by up to four orders of magnitude. Yet mainframe processor usage is also dramatically reduced. More important, though, is the fact that CAFS allows queries to be stated imprecisely and without any technical overtones. It also allows the scope of a search to be progressively narrowed; this not only increases the likelihood of success, but also mirrors the way in which people pursue the information they require.

A parallel development to CAFS, and one of almost equal
importance for the current discussion, is ICL's Personal Data
System (PDS). This is a relational database management system
that can not only handle imprecise queries but also implement
immediately updates that have been specified interactively.
Because it is a software package rather than a hardware-based
subsystem, it is slower than CAFS and is limited to handling
relatively small amounts of data. It is cheaper and much more
compact, however, and is therefore ideal for small local sites;
its query language is just as easy to understand and use, but the
fact that immediate updates are allowed greatly increases the
flexibility and degree of local control that is possible.

Finally, although it does not support complex network data
models, it allows tables to be defined whose entries, which
correspond to records, can be linked implicitly or in the course
of an interactive session.

3. Interface problems

This part of the paper is divided into two sections. The first
of these discusses how information defined and handled centrally
in a conventional way should correspond to that which is made
available locally in response to imprecise queries; the second
examines how far such correspondence can be ensured by means of
current technology.

3.1. Necessary correspondence

The correspondence between the central database management
system, say, IDMS, and CAFS will be handled centrally; this is
because CAFS is likely to be too large and expensive to be widely
available on local sites, though of course it is local sites that
will use it most by means of communications links. The aim must
be to ensure that the files supporting the database, which are
updated by means of application programs, are regularly dumped,
converted to a format in which they can be handled by CAFS, and
used to replace the obsolete CAFS versions of the same files.

Ensuring correspondence between IDMS AND PDS is rather more
difficult, since correspondence is required at a detailed logical
level, not merely file by file. A PDS database will generally
correspond to an IDMS subschema, and each of its tables to a
schema record type. Since IDMS sets cannot be explicitly
represented and named, they must be represented implicitly.
Finally and most importantly, immediate updates in the course of
interactive sessions must be reconciled with updates that are
carried out by means of predefined application programs.

3.2. Solutions currently available

Before dumping an IDMS file and converting it to a format in
which it can be used by CAFS, it is necessary to decide what to
do with all the administrative information included in the file.
Clearly, information that is used only by the system should be
eliminated if this is possible; space management pages and page
headers, for example, contain nothing that is likely to be of
interest to a CAFS enquirer. Other administrative information,
though, such as database keys, might well be included in CAFS
records; since database keys are used as pointers within sets and
between record roots and fragments, this would effectively make
many IDMS access paths available as well as direct CAFS access.
It would probably be useful to define a CAFS enquiry frame for
each schema record type, naming fields to contain the database
key, data item values and pointer values of each record
occurrence. Some CAFS administrative information will have to be
added during the conversion process: identifiers for the data
fields in each record occurrence, and a record trailer field to
terminate each occurrence. The result of conversion should be a
CAFS file that offers slightly worse retrieval performance than a
file specially designed for CAFS, but that obviates the need for
such design and may offer more access possibilities.

The first step in ensuring correspondence between a centrally-
held IDMS subschema and a small local PDS database is to define
equivalent logical elements in each. Defining a PDS table to
correspond to each IDMS record type is simple; the table has the
same name as the record type, and there is a table column for
each data item in the record type. There will then be a table
entry corresponding to each record occurrence. Finding some way
of using PDS to represent IDMS set types is more difficult. The
simplest way would be to take the tables corresponding to the
linked record types and join them to make a single large table
with the same name as the set type; this would, however, be so
cumbersome and waseful of space that its implementation would be
pointless in a small installation. There are two other
alternatives:

1. Including in each table corresponding to a member record type
    a column called OWNER; every entry in such a table would have
    the identifier of its owner record ocurrence (or the table
    entry corresponding to this occurrence) as its value in that
    column. In this way set types can be implicitly represented
    so that the access paths they provide are still available.

2.   Using the PDS facility that enables all or part of different
     tables to be combined in the course of an interactive
     session. This effectively allows individual set occurrences
     to be created and used as and when required.

Even with current technology, therefore, it seems possible to
ensure that the logical elements of IDMS and PDS correspond to
each other. If PDS is to be used only for retrieval, as CAFS is
now, only file conversion is necessary to ensure that both
systems can be used in harmony. The single most important
facility that PDS offers, however, is that updates can be
implemented immediately in the course of an interactive session.
Only if updates implemented in different ways by different
systems can be kept consistent will it be possible to use
databases to the full through networks. The next part of this
paper discusses how this may be achieved in the future; achieving
a solution is vital, and will become more so when the fast large-
scale access that is possible using CAFS is combined with the
updating capability of PDS.

4. The way forward

Three things are essential for any solution to the problem of
reconciling immediate interactive updating by means of natural
language dialogues with the central database control that is
necessary for security, integrity and resilience.

These are:

1.   The ability for systems, whether local or central, to
     identify specific record occurrences or table entries
     uniquely and rapidly.

2.   The ability to apply locks to individual record occurrences
     and table entries, and to apply locks simultaneously and on
     the same data locally and centrally.

3.   The ability for communications system software to initiate
     updating operations on the central database.

To ensure that entries in a table can be uniquely identified, it
is necessary for a column or group of columns to have a different
value in each table entry. If no such column or group of columns
is included in the original table definition, an extra column
must be defined for the purpose. Corresponding to this column or
group of columns there should be a data item or group of data

items defined as a record key for the database record type that
corresponds to the table; for rapid access, it would be best if
this record key is supported by an index. When retrieving a
table entry locally so that it can be updated, it would not, of
course, be necessary to specify its unique identifier, as this
would be contrary to the principle of access using incomplete or
imprecise information; the system will, however, require this
value so that it can identify the corresponding record occurrence
in the central database.

Achieving the necessary degree of precision in applying locks is
of crucial importance; locks applied at the subschema level are
of no use, and even page locks are likely to impose a significant
performance penalty by tying up too many record occurrences each
time a single occurrence is to be updated. It will therefore be
necessary to include in the database system software extra code
that will apply locks to the particular record occurrence to be
updated. There will be three update procedures: one for adding a
record, one for modifying a record and one for deleting a record.
Locks at the local level can safely be left to standard system
software.

Not much code will need to be added to the communications system
software to enable it to initiate updating operations. It is
necessary merely to ensure that the local system sends a message
to the central system, and that this message is used to activate
one of the predefined update procedures and run it using standard
transaction processing software.

The sequence of events during an update operation in such a
system would be as follows:

1. A local user at a terminal specified a new table entry that
    he wishes to add, or engages in a dialogue to find an
    existing table entry that he wishes to delete or modify.

2. The local system logs the update request and applies the
    necessary locks to the table entry.

3. The unique key value of the corresponding record occurrence
    is passed to the database system software, which FINDs the
    record and applies the necessary locks to it.

4. The local system implements the requested update and sends
    one of the following messages to the database system software

    (a) A request to add a new record occurrence, in
         which case the new record occurrence must also
         be sent.

    (b) A request to modify an existing record occurrence,
         in which case the updated record occurrence must
         also be sent.

    (c) A request to delete the record occurrence that has
         already been identified.

5. The appropriate update procedure is activated by the message
    and carries out a STORE, MODIFY or ERASE operation.

6. The database system software releases its locks and sends a
    message to the local system requesting it to do the same.

There will be a performance penalty, of course, for the local
user, but this will be far outweighted by the additional backup
and resilience provided by the facilities of the central system,
by its documentation and data modelling capability, and by the
access it offers to other databases and even other networks that
may be of use to him.

None of the additions and modifications described in this part of
the paper is particularly complex or difficult. Most could be
accomplished even using existing technology. What seems to be
lacking is the will to invest the effort necessary to bring them
about.

5. Conclusions

At the start of this paper I stated that the aim of communication
networks is to enable people to obtain the information they want
as quickly as possible. I qualified this by pointing out that
people in their quest for information are frequently vague or
even downright inaccurate, and that the computer-based
communication networks of the future should be capable of dealing
with this. Much work has already been done on individual
products aimed at meeting this need; some of these products, like
CAFS and PDS, are already in the market place. It cannot be
emphasised too strongly, however, that these products lose much
of their utility if they are seen in isolation. They are
complementary to conventional computing techniques, and should be
integrated with them and used in parallel with them, each
performing the tasks for which they are best suited.

The problems of integration does not apply only to using new
techniques and conventional techniques together, however; it
applies just as much when using different types of conventional
systems and machines. Computers will increasingly be used
interactively by means of networks, and these networks will have
to interlock to meet the demand for more information and for
different types of information. Users denied access to
information will no longer accept the excuse that it is
unobtainable because two systems or machines are incompatible.
IPA defines for one company a strategy for solving this problem;
unfortunately, there is little or no sign yet of other
manufacturers accepting the need to do the same.

Problems remain to be solved, certainly, but they can be clearly
identified and are far from insurmountable; most involve
providing interfaces between different types of system. Like all
problems, however, they require three things before a solution
can be achieved: skill, will and resources. Computer
manufacturers certainly have the resources and may well have the
skill, but the will is apparently lacking. Individual users may
have the skill, but only the largest of them are likely to have
the resources and none is likely to have the will. Software
houses also have the necessary skill and would be willing to use
it once potential customers had been identified, but the
resources required would probably be beyond them. This leaves
only large bureaux as the likely providers of a solution.

Bureaux tend to be privileged users, given advance warning of new
developments by manufacturers and sometimes even consulted about
such developments. On the other hand, though, they are closely
in touch with users and aware of their needs. Finally, the fact
that they handle a wide variety of tasks means that bureaux
programmers tend to have a range of experience denied to those
who work directly for a user or a manufacturer. It seems
probable, therefore, that bureaux will be the central sites for
many of the networks of the future, making resources available to
small local users and providing the expertise necessary to enable
such users to gain the maximum advantage from the network.

The future for the average user seems bright. Computer-based
communication networks will be able to provide more facilities
than ever before, but the expertise needed to take advantage of
these will be reduced to a minimum. Small users will be able to
have access to the power and resources of large systems without
having to invest a fortune in buying or leasing such systems. For
everyone with a need for information, the ability to use
databases through networks will provide a golden opportunity; for
the computing industry, it provides a challenge that can be and
must be met.

Micros and Local Networks

Lyndon Morgan

Senior Consultant, Standards Division,
National Computing Centre Ltd, UK

The convergence of computers and telecommunications
has long been established. This paper looks at the
effect microcomputers have had particularly the emergence of the microcomputer based local area network.

Two archietectures for local networks are discussed
and four currently available network systems described.

A few years ago the 'in' word in computing was
'convergence'. This term defined the true meeting of
telecommunications (voice and data) and computing.
Computing of course was the well identified field of
data processing and most of the advertising was directed
at the DP department and its manager. Their role was a
continuation of the historical role of controlling the
introduction of information processing technology within
their company. Convergence simply meant an expansion of
their empire into controlling the total information
processing and flow within their company.

However, at this time the DP department was being overtaken by an even newer revolution the microprocessor.
The microprocessor had been around for some time but
only known to electronic engineers in their more
advanced projects. However, through the hobbyist market
the microprocessor appeared as the free standing microcomputer. Very cheap, very versatile with a rapidly
expanding range of software that made it very easy to
use. Suddenly the ground was slipping from under the
DPM's feet. The in word was "micros". Everyone could
join in and far from an expanding empire some were
predicting the contraction of the DP department and in
many small companies there was computing but no DP
department as such.

So what happened to convergence? What happens to the
companies with hundreds of micros and word processors?

The application of a fresh mind to an established
problem often brings results. This is the principle
behind 'lateral thinking' which trains you to bring a
fresh approach to a problem you cannot solve. Many of
the microcomputer manufacturers were not scaled down
mainframe manufacturers. They were fresh minds on
computing coming out of the LSI component production
and they seem to have made a break-through in computing
that the traditional manufacturers cannot match. They
have produced a low-cost Local Area Network which has
the capability of linking to remote sites and remote
mainframes. Already such networks are available and
are challenging the traditional distributed or online
systems.

The requirement for local networking came about because
of an increasing need to find a coherent alternative
solution to piecemeal cabling for connecting distributed
user devices such as terminals, computers and word

processors, to shared resources such as printers, disc
storage and databases, and to each other, within the
same building.

The architecture of the interconnections on such systems
has centred on two major concepts; the 'ring' architecture and the single channel cable architecture. Both
these concepts are currently being actively
pursued by a number of manufacturers and research
organisations.

Ring Archietecture

The best know ring archietecture is the Cambridge Ring
which works in the following way. Data for transmission
is put onto the ring at one point, the source, and
pulled off at another, the destination. Points around
the ring need to have an identification of some sort and
are given a unique address. Each point has therefore
some means of recognising information destined for it,
and marking information so that the desired destination
recognises it. Destinations need to know who is sending
information, whether the transmission was successful or
not, or even if a destination is switched on. It is
also necessary to provide some error checking facility.
The ring provides all these facilities by using a transmission 'information packet'.

A working Cambridge Ring supports such a structure and
consists of four pieces of equipment (a 'monitor'
station, a 'workstation', a 'repeater', and a 'ring power
supply') and a length of twin twisted-pair cable.

The monitor station initialises the ring on starting and
then enforces the packet structure for the rest of the
time the ring is switched on. It also keeps watch on
the ring structure and detects and counts errors.

The workstation is used to transmit and receive packets
of information from the ring. Each workstation must
have a repeater connected to it to encode and decode the
data stream from the ring.

Packets transmitted on the ring make one complete revolution before they are freed for use by other workstations. When a packet is sent by a source it is
marked as being full and the response bits are cleared.
The source address bits are set by the workstation to
its own address as the source is sending the packet.
When the packet reaches its destination,response bits

are set depending on how the packet was received e.g.
correctly or rejected. The free packet continues round
the ring back to the source which sent it. The source
then checks to see if there are any errors and marks the
packet empty. The free packet continues round the ring.

At some stage the packet passes the monitor station
where the 'monitor passed once' bit is set. If a packet
arrives at the monitor station with this bit set then it
is an error packet as it has been round more than once
without any destination picking it up or any source
freeing it. The monitor station frees any packets in
this state, so that they are again available.

Single Channel Archietecture

The single channel archietecture most used in Ethernet-I
which was developed by Xerox Corporation.

Ethernet-I is a single co-axial cable (called the'ETHER')
run around a site to which devices are attached by means
of TV cable clamp connectors. Data is transmitted in
digital packets in the cable at 3 million bits per
second along a length up to I kilometre.

Unlike the Cambridge Ring, it does not rely on a control
device to referee what is going along the cable. Each
device listens all the time to passing packets which
have a common format in which there is a destination
device address. A packet of data is broadcast onto the
Ether and is heard by all stations. The packet is
copied from it at only those destinations selected by
the address bits on it.

The Ether is a totally passive broadcast medium with no
central control. All the stations contend for use of
the Ether until one of them acquires it for packet
transmission. A packet is detectable through the
presence of a carrier signal on the Ether. Thus a
station listens to the Ether as it transmits, to detect
any other carriers that appear on it. This situation
would indicate a potential collision of packets caused
by propogation delays in the Ether, ie. a distant
station may have seen a quiet state on the Ether and
started to transmit at the same time. If a collision
is detected the transmission is aborted and a jam signal
sent out to notify all other stations.

Micros and Local Networks

Although the Cambridge Ring is being used by Logica and
Prime it has been rejected by Acorn Computers. In
general it is the Ethernet-I approach that has been
selected by most microcomputer network suppliers. A
number of such networks are either available now or
under development. Companies involved include:

> Acorn Computers Ltd
>
> Zilog UK Ltd
>
> Zynar Ltd
>
> Research Machines Ltd
>
> Thame Systems Ltd (Agents for the USA
>
> > Ungerman-Bass system)

Also available is the CP/Net system. This is a software product developed by Digital Research Ltd to run
in conjuction with the CP/M and MP/M operating systems.
This is available in the UK on the Dynabyte range of
micros from Metrotech Management Technology Ltd.

Let us take a brief look at just 4 of these systems;
Econet, Cluster/one, Z-net and CP/net.

Econet

Econet is based on the Acorn Atom computer. It is aimed
at the low cost end of the market with a ten terminal
system costing around £3000. Each terminal is a Acorn
Atom connected to a file station which is an Acorn
System 3, 4 or 5 or a disc based Atom. Typically the
file station would have 400K bytes of storage. Econet
will support up to 255 stations on a twin twisted-pair
cable   over a maximum run of 1 kilometre. Nominal
data transmission rate is 210 kilbaud.

Cluster/One

Cluster/One is based on the Apple-II microcomputer.
One of the Apple-II micros acts as a file server controlling up to 33 million bytes of file store. Other
Apple-II micros provide typical facilities such as Basic
and UCSD-Pascal with a typical configuration of 48K bytes
of store and up to 1.2 megabytes of floppy disc store.

The communication link is a 16 wire cable with a maximum
run of 300 metres which can handle up to 65 Apple-II
stations. Typical cost for a 10 station system is about
£23,000.

Z-Net

Z-Net is Zilog's own networking system based upon the
MCZ-2 microcomputer. Z-Net implements the Ethernet
principle of a TV grade co-axial cable link. Each
station is linked into the cable by a "T" Tap. The
network can handle up to 255 stations with a maximum
run of 2000 metres. Each MCZ-2 station can have up to
4 megabytes on the master file controller. Each MCZ-2
runs the RIO operating system with COBOL, BASIC and
Machine Code facilities. Nominal data transfer rate is
800000 bits per second.

CP/Net

CP/Net is a software product produced by Digital
Research Ltd to complement its CP/M and MP/M operating
systems. The network itself has to be provided and can
be serial, parallel or telephone links. CP/Net works
on a master/slave principle. The slave sends information
to its master for transmission to another slave or
another master. A master CPU must be running the MP/M
operating system. The slave must be CP/M or MP/M.
CP/Net allows two masters to be connected and two slaves
thus a wide variety of configurations can be built up.
A CP/Net system running on the Dynabyte range of micros
is available from Metrotech.

Reference

Communicating with Micros   by J.E. Lane
                            NCC Publications 1981

A Local Computer Network

Eva Huzan

Head of Computing Division,
Slough College of Higher Education, UK

The Nestar Cluster/One, Model A local computer network is
described. This comprises a number of user work stations linked
to each other and to various network servers (file, printer and
modem). Each work station (Apple microcomputer) has an interface
card which has ROM based firmware executed in the work station's
CPU. The tasks which the network has to perform are detailed.
Users may access the central disk storage system and printers from
their work stations. Facilities are available for protecting
shared files by means of passwords and access rights. The use
of two Zynar software packages is described, for financial modelling (PLANET) and for electronic mailing (MESSENGER).

1. INTRODUCTION

Local computer networks (LCNs) can provide a viable, inexpensive
alternative to using multi-user, multi-tasking mini or microcomputers. Each user in the network has a work station (microcomputer) providing a local processing capability limited only by
the power and memory capacity of the work station. Access to
relatively expensive disk storage and printers is available to each
user in the network on a shared basis.

The restrictions experienced in early LCN implementations are
rapidly disappearing. Microcomputer work stations are becoming
more powerful, with the availability of 16-bit microprocessors, and
can have larger memories based on low-cost RAM. Winchester disk
capacities have increased and 66 megabyte stores can be used in networks. Back-up of such large capacity disks on to floppy disks is
inconvenient and slow. Improvements in this area include the
availability of low-cost magnetic tape units and associated software
for archiving. Users of the network may require more than one type
of printer, typically, a fast printer for general purpose computer
output and a high quality printer for letters and reports. Queue-
ing of jobs to the appropriate printer is an essential requirement
for many environments.

Lack of good software, particularly for business applications,
limited the usefulness of microcomputers when they were first introduced. Over the last two years there has been an increasing
expansion in microcomputer software products. Much of this software has been designed specifically for the first time business
user, and is easy to use, 'friendly' and requires very little
practice before it can be used in a meaningful way. For example,
integrated accountancy packages are available for small businesses
enabling microcomputer based systems to be implemented without any
programming effort.

The biggest impact, however, is arguably in larger organisations
where many departmental managers are finding that stand-alone microcomputers can give them processing power in their own offices for
financial modelling, word processing and various other planning,
scheduling and forecasting activities. As business users become
more sophisticated in their use of microcomputers, they find a need
to extend their applications to areas which involve the setting up
and updating of files and information retrieval either from their
own or external data bases. These extended activities require the
control traditionally applied by the company's data processing
department to the handling of corporate data. The control and
linking together of a diversity of microcomputers, data files and
applications may be extremely difficult if not impossible. The
installation of departmental local computer networks under the
control of the data processing department is a more rational

approach, which additionally gives the business user the support of
dp professionals without removing the independent processing capability from the user department.

Although an LCN may be set up for the reasons outlined above, there
are other important facilities that can be provided through the
LCN which not only increase the viability and usefulness of the
network, but indeed can be the prime reason for installing it. Much
of the paper work generated within a department comprises internal,
memoranda and reports. An LCN can give full electronic mail facilities to its users and, through gateways, to other LCNs in the
company or externally to other organisations. Access to external
data bases including Prestel is possible through appropriate
communication gateways. Since all work stations in an LCN can be
linked logically, further applications are made possible such as
teleconferencing.

The LCN that was investigated is the Nestar Cluster/One Model A,
market by Zynar Limited in Europe including the UK. This was
chosen because it isa practical implementation currently available
and installed in a number of office environments.

2. THE NESTAR CLUSTER/ONE, MODEL A SYSTEM

The network comprises a number of user work stations linked to each
other and to various network servers via 16-way ribbon cable which
forms the cluster bus (see fig. 1). The work stations are Apple
microcomputers, with their own printers and/or mini floppy disk
units if required. The file server consists of an Apple microcomputer which controls a combination of 8 inch floppy and hard
disk (14 inch Winchester disk, capacity $16\frac{1}{2}$, 33 or 66 megabytes).
The printer server similarly is an Apple which controls and drives
one or two printers. Communication to other systems is achieved
by a modem server, which comprises an Apple controlling a modem
connected to a telephone interface.

The system is based on the 'Ethernet' concept, but is not a full
implementation of this at present. Each work station has an interface card which has ROM based firmware used to transmit and receive
multiple byte packets of data. In addition to the ROM code, the
network interface card contains network bus drivers and RAM buffers
but no CPU, the ROM code being executed in the CPU of the work
station. Access to the network is implemented as a layered set of
protocols. Tasks which the network needs to perform include:

   bus allocation, bus contention resolution, address recognition,
   byte transmission   (protocol level 0)

   packet transmission - sending of multiple byte packages with
   error detection and transmission   (protocol level 1)

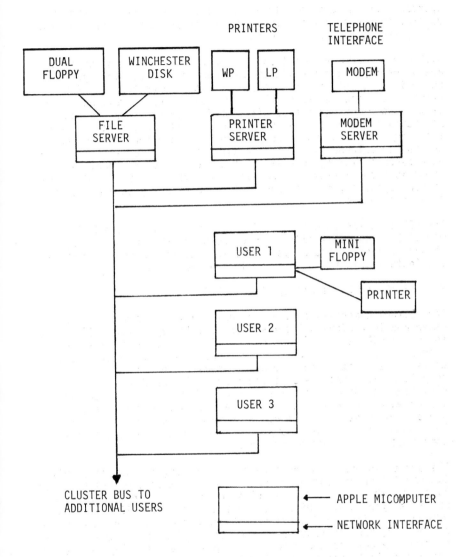

Fig. 1. A typical Nestar Cluster/One,
Model A system.

WP = Word processing printer
LP = Line printer

message transmission - multiple byte packets to be grouped for
interpretation as a single message   (protocol level 2)

interpretation of messages by software running on the communicating stations   (protocol level 3)

3. THE FILE SERVER

One of the requirements of the LCN is that the user is able to
process work at the local microcomputer work station, using existing software and different operating systems. Each user on the
network has access to the central disk storage system (back-end
storage network, BSN), via the file server. The BSN is viewed as
a set of virtual mini-disks which are indistinguishable from the
5¼ inch diskettes available with the stand-alone microcomputer
stations, except that possible file sizes are greatly increased
(the maximum size depends on the operating system used). The file
server, driving the BSN, provides users with two virtual channels,
one for file server metacommands and the other one for passing
I/O requests and data. The metacommands are used for creating,
deleting, mounting and unmounting files and locking shared data
during simultaneous updating.

The virtual I/O channel is used exactly the same as a local disk
facility. The file server interprets the file access control
blocks of the work station's operating system and additionally gives
the user improved I/O facilities. For example, extra disks can be
'mounted' simultaneously. The advantage to the user is that larger
files, with a more sophisticated structure, can be used, at faster
transmission rates. The files can be shared by more than one user,
but this implies a need for access control to protect the consistency and privacy of the data.

4. FILE STRUCTURE AND PROTECTION

Each physical unit which is part of the central disk system has a
unique number assigned to it, and also can be given a name when
formatted. The root directory on each disk unit points, directly
or through sub-directories, to every virtual diskette, utility
program or sub-directory on that unit, but not to files on other
physical units. The identity (pathname) of each virtual diskette
is defined by its hierarchical pointers.

A typical system would have sub-directories for its Users, for the
various Operating Systems and for System Utilities, as shown in
Fig. 2. Each user has a sub-directory, under the sub-directory
'Users', giving the user's name or initials. The printer server

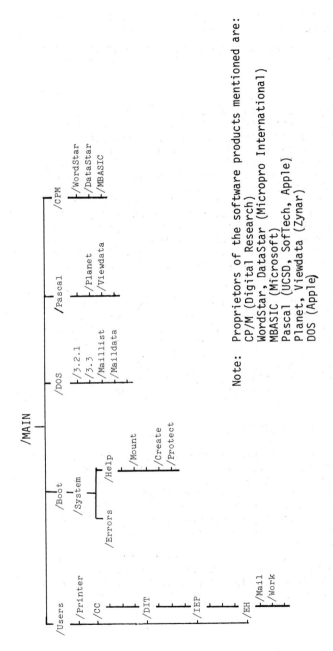

Note: Proprietors of the software products mentioned are:
   CP/M (Digital Research)
   WordStar, DataStar (Micropro International)
   MBASIC (Microsoft)
   Pascal (UCSD, SofTech, Apple)
   Planet, Viewdata (Zynar)
   DOS (Apple)

Fig. 2   Directory structure of a typical system

is a special type of user that runs a dedicated program. The DOS, Pascal and CP/M operating system sub-directories contain system utility libraries and application packages. The Boot sub-directory contains some items that are available to the user; for example, HELP is a program which assists the user in correctly using appropriate commands.

Only part of the pathname needs to be specified if a current default directory of the prefix to be used is set. Every pathname specified without a leading slash is prefixed by the default directory; this avoids unnecessary disk accesses, typing and processing.

The files the user sets up on virtual diskettes are structured in accordance with the operating system (DOS, Pascal, CP/M) being used at the local microcomputer station. File protection of whole cluster directories and virtual diskettes (cluster-files) is provided by a system of passwords and access rights. The password required and the access rights of each class of user is specified when a cluster-file is created.

Potential users of a particular cluster-file may be public users who do not know a password (PUB), group users who know the group password (GRP) or private users who know the private password (PRV). Each class of user (public, group or private) may be granted or denied certain access rights, such as the ability to:

    read the data part of a cluster-file (P)
    write on the cluster-file (W)
    erase the cluster-file (E)
    create a new entry in a directory (C)
    delete an entry from a directory (D)

In addition to specifying passwords and access rights when creating a cluster-file (by the CREATE command), the PROTECT command can be used to specify new protection requirements of an existing cluster-file. Default access rights allow public users to read the cluster-file, and private users to read, write and erase virtual diskettes, and to create and delete directories. Group and private passwords need only be set by a user once during a session, rather than specifying these every time a pathname is entered. It is possible to use passwords in a program and to prevent these appearing in the program listing.

Part of the justification of an LCN is the ability to share resources. For many applications it may be necessary to give several users access to the same data files. If more than one user has write access for updating a file, then the updating program should put a LOCK on the item being updated. The program will receive a message back to indicate whether updating can go ahead,

otherwise it has to wait and reissue the command at a later stage
when the LOCK has been removed (i.e. the other program has issued
an UNLOCK command).

Any shared resource can be locked while it needs to be used
exclusively. For example, a program may need to lock the printer
while it is using it, causing another program also requiring access
to the printer to wait. An alternative method is to spool to the
required printer. A user can determine the status of resources
and file access rights by using the SHOW command (SHOW LOCK, SHOW
PROTECT).

5. GATEWAYS TO OTHER SYSTEMS

The departmental user in a large organisation is likely to have at
least three different requirements for electronic communication to
other departments/organisations. Although up to 65 stations can
be linked in a single Nestar Cluster/One network, a more practical
configuration would be based on multiple LCNs. The users in one
department may need to use the network in a different way from those
in other departments. Each department can have an independent LCN
with work stations and servers configured according to the department's requirements. However, occasionally users on one network may
need to access data files held by other LCNs or use devices (e.g.
special printers) available on another department's network. This
can be achieved by gating the LCNs together using an Apple to direct
the information into the appropriate LCN.

Another requirement is for access to files and devices from an LCN
to the company's mainframe. The modem server allows access to
RS232C compatible devices so that information can be transferred
via the mainframe's TTY ports or to external data bases via public
or private telephone lines.

6. USER DEPARTMENT APPLICATIONS

Departmental LCNs allow managers to use microcomputers on their
desks for 'personal' computing (e.g. financial modelling) and for
electronic mail (sending and receiving of messages and memoranda).
Programs which give a variety of powerful facilities for financial
modelling are available from a number of different sources. The
Zynar PLANET package allows shared use of data on a Nestar Cluster/
One system. One of the main requirements of such a package is that
the manager finds it easy to use and that it has sufficient
facilities to avoid the need for further programming or for extensive support from the data processing department. The PLANET
system enables the user to carry out different financial calculations, row and column manipulations, and to display results in
graphical form, using simple commands. Since most of the processing
is local, apart from disk access and printing, use of the network

is light. Reports need only be printed when the user has finalised
them. The reports and graphic displays (in colour on appropriate
screens) can be shown in the form of a slide projector show to
other users on the network.

Electronic mailing is implemented on the Nestar Cluster/One using a
Zynar product called MESSENGER. Users can send messages or
memoranda (entered from the keyboard or from a previously prepared
file) by submitting the command SEND, which results in the following
type of 'conversation':

        TO:? DIT
        CC:? IEP
        SUBJECT:? "heading"
        ENTER MESSAGE OR %FILENAME, TERMINATE WITH A CONT.D
        "lines of message"
        D(ISPLAY), F(ILE), Q(UIT), R(ECEIPT), S(END), W(RITE)?S

The recipients of the messages can read their "mail" at any time by
submitting the command:

        READ or CHECK

CHECK causes the work station to wait for messages, bleep when a
message arrives and display the message heading. The user can
choose to read the whole message at that time or later.

The sender can request an acknowledgement, preventing the recipient
deleting the message until it has been read, at which time a receipt
is generated automatically and sent back to the originator. As
with any other use of the system, the privacy of the information is
protected by the use of passwords which prevent a recipient's
file being accessed by unauthorised users.

7. CONCLUSION

There is a current and growing demand from business users, particularly in large organisations, for a 'personal' computing facility
for many different applications. Local computer networks extend
the use that managers can make of their microcomputers by providing
local and external electronic communication facilities. More powerful and improved facilities will become available to match the more
sophisticated applications that business personnel will require in
the future. These include faster data transmission rates in
networks based on the full 'Ethernet' specification, using VLSI
devices for the interface logic, larger capacity disk stores
with data base management software, and improved microcomputer work

stations. Work is progressing in all these areas as well as in
improving system gateways to other networks and services. Application of advanced technology is likely to progress at a faster
rate if low-cost usable networks are made available to a wide
range of users.

REFERENCES

1.   Local microcomputer network system and back-end storage
     network, Zynar Technical Information, 1980.

2.   Cluster/One, Model A, User Manual, Nestar Systems, 1980.

3.   COLIN CROOK, Low cost local computer networks and their future,
     Communications International, March 1981.

The Disposition of Facilities
Within a Distributed Computer Network

P. W. Williams

Senior Lecturer in Computation, UMIST, UK

In the near future it will be feasible for some firms to
position their computing activity at any point in a
comprehensive computing network which contains large scale
remote computers, personal microcomputers, and local
minicomputers which are interconnected. The paper
discusses the factors which will influence the placing of
facilities within the computing network and illustrates
the possibilities by referring to work with a
microcomputer terminal enhancement which has been used to
improve the access to the international information
systems.

1. INTRODUCTION

1.1 THE FUTURE COMPUTER ENVIRONMENT.

The purpose of this paper is to discuss the situation which will exist in industry over the next few years as firms begin to acquire small computers. Many companies will soon be using a complete hierarchy of computers of various sizes ranging from the massive time-sharing computers accessed through the telecommunications networks to the microcomputer on the manager's desk, or even the small pocket machines which are now becoming available. This paper discusses the factors which influence the siting of the different computing activities in a network in order to obtain the most effective computing arrangements. The time-scale of the scenario is from the present time, when the facilities discussed are present in only a fragmentary fashion, to some years hence when the more forward-looking firms will have taken advantage of these technical developments.

The discussion is based on the following assumptions:
1. There will be substantial numbers of small computers, costing from a few hundred pounds to three or four thousand pounds, puchased by many different sections within an organisation and utilised for a variety of different purposes.
2. Many medium size firms will also have, or will acquire, computers of a more substantial size costing $40,000 to $400,000 at present prices. These may be on a local site or may be accessed through the public telephone network.
3. Some company activities will require large scale facilities which will normally be accessed remotely via telephone lines. These may be national or international systems or they may be owned by the company.
4. It is also envisaged that there will be increasing use of hand-held computers which operate on batteries and can be taken out of an office to the shop-floor or on a train or to a meeting. These will be plugged into a 'mother computer' when the more powerful facilities of the larger machine, such as printing and larger scale storage, are required.
5. In the medium term the low cost of local intelligence and storage in the form of a small microcomputer will make such a device an attractive purchase for individual managers or technologists and their use will multiply. Also the cost of an overall grand plan for distributed intelligence in a coherent network, and the inevitable delays of overall organisational discussions will make a central solution to the same problems far less likely in the near future.
6. It will be difficult in the near future to obtain

6. It will be difficult in the near future to obtain cheap
telecommunications access to large computers with a
response time equivalent to the personal microcomputer.
Access to remote computers in the next few years will
therefore be concentrated on computing which demands a
large scale resource or where the extent of the activity
justifies very large investment. The momentum in the near
future will be towards dispersion of computing power.

1.2 THE DIFFERENT APPLICATION AREAS

Microcomputers will be used in a wide variety of contexts
some of which are outlined here to set the framework for
the discussion. There is now considerable interest in the
concept of the manager's terminal. Since many scientists,
technologists, engineers, and research workers have
managerial functions there should be universal benefit in
a terminal which provides facilities to assist a manager
in his job. Facilities for such a terminal would include a
personal information system on appointments and meetings,
a name and address file, a word processing system for
producing or editing reports, and packages for accessing
systems placed elsewhere on the network such as local
company information or international public information
sources.

Also substantial number of scientists and technologists
will use microcomputers to carry out their technical
calculations.

A further application of microtechnology is the gathering
of data from laboratory apparatus and shop-floor
equipment. There will be an increasing trend towards
linking this type of apparatus with the computers which
are used by an organisation for financial accounting and
management planning.

The balance between intelligence at the terminal and the
central processing power needs to be determined for some
of the traditional tasks such as program preparation.
Modern terminals have introduced facilities for checking
each line of input before transmission but other checking
is still carried out centrally. Technology now exists for
carrying out syntax checking at the terminal so that only
correct statements are transmitted to the central
processor. Work is in progress at UMIST to develop a
system for producing structured programming at an
intelligent terminal without calling on central processing
power until the compilation and execution of the program
is desired.

Another environment where analysis is needed to assess the

optimum division of functions between a central site and
intelligent machines at the extremity of a network is the
typical medium size retail organisation which has several
retail sites and a main office in which the central
control and organisation is situated. Some function such
as daily accounts and stock control are more under the
control of the peripheral sites whereas overall financial
control and planning will rest at the main office. The
disposition of the facilities in such a situation needs
careful analysis.

The work which led to this study is concerned with the use
of an microcomputer attachment to provide a more powerful
terminal to access online information systems. Significant
simplification of the user interface can be achieved and
substantial savings in online costs can be made by using a
microcomputer instead of an ordinary terminal. However it
became clear that some of the features which can be
implemented would be more sensibly introduced at other
points in the network if there was an opportunity to
influence the user interface provided by the host computer
or the network. The advantage of the microcomputer
approach for modifying the user interface is that no
organisational change is necessary to introduce the new
methods whereas a change in the method of operation of a
large time-sharing service is not easily or quickly
achieved.

2. A CASE STUDY

2.1 THE ENHANCEMENT OF ONLINE SEARCHING USING LOCAL INTELLIGENCE

The author has recently been investigating ways in which a
microcomputer can be used to alter the facilities in an
information network by providing intelligence at the
user's terminal. Several ways were found in which the
system could be made more effective by transferring some
of the processing to the terminal. The benefits of a
microprocessor driven terminal for online contact can be
generalised under the following headings.

- The use of permanently stored messages for automatic
log-on to the system using a few keystrokes only.
- The preparation, checking and editing of statements in
the microcomputer memory before contacting the online
system so that the contact with the online system can take
place at the maximum speed of transmission, rather than
the 1 or 2 characters per second which is a typical typing
speed.

- The capture of the output from an online system to allow
further local processing and manipulation.
- The use of subsidiary information or computer programs
to make the online interaction more powerful or simpler
for unskilled users. In the case of online information
systems these facilities include artificial intelligence
interfaces to allow enquiries in natural language, systems
to translate from one command language to another and
systems to translate either the search commands or the
output to the national language of the requester. Systems
are also being developed to allow unskilled users to carry
out searches by answering a computer controlled dialogue
which determines the subject and character of the search.
- The keeping of records of computer sessions either in
the form of copies of transactions and results, or in the
form of statistics of usage and costs.
- For some systems the ability to carry out computation
locally on the results obtained from the remote system is
valuable.

2.2 THE USERKIT ONLINE TERMINAL ENHANCEMENT.

The author has been concerned for some time with the use
of microcomputers to access the international online
information systems. These systems are mainly situated
outside the United Kingdom, and in the Spring of 1981 the
cost of these systems was still approaching $2 per minute
for people outside London. Furthermore there is a
complicated logging on system through the International
Packet Switched Service or the Euronet network which is
both tedious and time-consuming. This gave a strong
incentive to try to improve the way in which the systems
were used.

The use of a microcomputer rather than an ordinary
terminal gives considerable scope for improving the
interface to the online system (Williams 1979). Initially
programs were developed on a full microcomputer system to
tackle the most significant problems, i.e. complex logon
procedures and the high cost of telecommunications access.
In order to make these facilities available to the library
and information science community who access these
systems, many of whom are not computer proficient, the
programs have now been transferred to a purpose-built box
which plugs in directly between any terminal and a modem
or acoustic coupler. This device, the USERKIT is now
available as a commercial product and has been
enthusiastically received both in this country and in the
USA.

The present version of the USERKIT provides permanently

stored messages which give rapid access to the online
systems using only 2 or 3 keystrokes and also allows
substantial savings in costs by formulating the search
statements before connecting to the online systems and
then sending them at the full transmission speed of the
terminal. More than 50% savings in connect time were
recorded for tests on standard searches carried out for
research workers at Manchester. The device is designed so
that no special action is necessary to type directly to
the host system in the normal way. The USERKIT is called
into action with a command key which then enables complete
lines to be sent to the remote system using 1 keystroke
only.

Other facilities include the ability to define new stored
phrases and the opportunity for the user to specify his
own permanently stored messages or search profiles. For
example, one user has included the STAIRS commands in his
permanent storage because some of them are rather long to
type. The new commands from Systems Development
Corporation, the "PRINT SELECT" and "SHOWSELECT", can be
entered using only 3 keystrokes and sent using 1
keystroke.

Work is progress on the storage of output from the system
for review, editing, and annotation. A translation system
is also being developed in which mixed commands from any
of the standard systems can be used for searching and the
program will transform them to a specified target search
system. Future facilities will include the ability to take
data from one system and use it as search input to another
system, the development of an interface to the Prestel
system and a study of the possibility of capturing
graphical data for chemical structures and representing
these on a standard terminal.

2.3 FURTHER IMPROVEMENTS TO THE SYSTEM

There are other more ambitious enhancements which online
searchers would like to see. There are many different
command languages used in the various systems and some
means of access is needed which avoids the difficulties
caused by the multiplicity of languages. In the USA some
attempts have been made to solve this problem, notably the
CAST system for chemical information developed by the
Computer Corporation of America which provides command
translation and re-formatting of computer output between a
number of information systems. The system, which was
supported by research funding, is based on a large
microcomputer and sells for around $30,000, which is 12
times the cost of the USERKIT. In contrast the European

Commission have provided funding for the modication of
some of the existing host computer systems to allow
searching via a common command language. This illustrates
the opportunities for implementing similar facilities
either on a local microcomputer or on the central computer
on which is mounted the online system.

Another more ambitious facility is a feed back system
which uses an initial search to provide information from
the system to improve the original search profile to give
a more effective search. Some investigations have been
carried out at Aston University by Jamieson and Oddy
(1980) based on the use of user judgements of relevance to
modify a weighted term search to try to improve the
quality of the search output. Alternative strategies have
been used by Doszkocs and Rapp (1979) at the National
Library of Medecine which are based on the frequency
information which is derived from the database dictionary.
The work by Doszkocs uses the judgement of the user to
choose the modification terms for a search profile rather
than an automatic algorithm based on adusting mathematical
weights in a formula. The other difference is that the
central processor for the information service is used to
carry out the iterative adjustment of the search profile
as opposed to the use of a microprocessor in the work by
Jamieson. This is another example of a facility which
different workers have implemented on local intelligence
or on the central mainframe.

There is some work which is inevitably based on the
central host computer. If facilities for automatic
translation into different national languages are required
then large scale storage and processing power is needed so
this should sensibly be situated at the mainframe. The
most that could be expected in a small computer is a
limited list of language equivalents which will be
inadequate as soon as the translation moved into the
context sensitive area. The systems which use artificial
intelligence to determine the requirements of a search
request also use large scale storage and processing. Work
such as that by Schank, which shows exciting prospects of
giving intelligent analysis of the information needs of a
requester, do need a large scale computer to store the
associations between words which is the basis of
intelligent analysis.

A development which is now becoming almost standard in
information systems is a help system which gives
assistance to those who are less skilled in the use of the
system. These systems take a great deal of space for the
text of the help messages and a decision must be taken

whether this type of system should be stored locally or on the remote computer which is being accessed.

3. THE POSITION OF COMPUTER FACILITIES IN THE NETWORK

3.1 THE FACTORS AFFECTING THE DECISION

There are complex factors which will determine whether computer facilities will be provided centrally or dispersed to the location where the activity is taking place. Some of these are technical or economic factors based on sound reasons and others are a reflection of the organisational forces which determine what changes will take place. These factors are first summarised and then discussed in more detail.

3.1.1 Cost factors

Telecommunications
The cost of telecommunications to access remote facilities is a major factor motivating dispersion of computer resources.

Distribution costs
Another force is the organisational cost of processing output centrally in order to sort it and disperse it to the component sections of a company.

3.1.2 Technical forces for large computers

Storage requirements
Some systems, such as the large scale information systems or an integrated company database require large scale storage and a central mainframe solution is required.

Large computer packages
Another situation where the large mainframe is required is where a user requires access to several computer packages each of which takes tens of kilobytes of storage.

3.1.3 Technical forces for small computers

Local selected information
In situations where there is a large comprehensive facility but only a small portion is used in a particular local unit, it is often advantageous to use a local solution. One example is the coding structure of the international host addresses for information systems. A local coding system is much shorter than one designed for international usage. The same arguments could apply to a

products coding system where the products were each
manufactured at different sites.

Frequency of access
Data or programs which are frequently used are also more
sensibly stored locally. The microcomputer with the built
in Basic compiler is an obvious example.

Independence from central organisations
A powerful force supporting the use of small local
computers is the urge of the manager to be independent of
external support. The wish to purchase equipment which is
at a low enough cost to avoid organisational arguments on
its desirability, and the opportunity to have computing
power which is not under the control of a data processing
department are strong forces leading to the introduction
of microcomputers.

Need for high quality printing
A rather suprising factor which is assisting the trend
towards dispersed processing is the need for high quality
printing. The high volume lineprinter is still a feature
of the central mainframe but letter quality printing is
now most easily obtained from a slow speed daisy wheel
printer. The dispersion of the printing function to the
ends of a network mean that the volume of printing is low
enough to use the slow speed daisy wheel printer.

3.1.4 Management control

Central management control
One of the strongest forces supporting the use of
centralised facilities is the management concern to avoid
duplication of activity and the dissipation of company
resources by unplanned computing activity. There is the
problem of the waste of company resources by several
employees all developing programs for the same purpose.

Dissipation of management information
There is also the waste of resources when company
information is developed at one point in an organisation
which could be useful to other sections of the
organisation.

Standardisation of volatile data
One application which provides strong arguments for a
centralised facility is data which is very volatile and
which is important as a common standard. This might be the
current state of airline bookings or the correct way to
fill in a company record form or the correct procedure for
assembling or repairing a product. The management effort

to control this situation if the information is dispersed
to many sites is considerable.

3.1.5 Privacy of data

Restrictions on access
The best strategy to safeguard data which is confidential
is not self-evident. Most large central mainframe have a
privacy system with passwords and restricted access to
prevent unauthorised access, but the number of people who
access the system is itself a threat. There is a good
argument to suggest that a small computer with a floppy
disk system offers greater protection for work under the
control of a single individual since the disk containing
the data can be locked in a secure place when it is not
being used.

Security of data
A large computer system will have much better security of
the data. There will be systems for keeping different
generations of a computer program and its data, and
dumping arrangements to keep copies of the work which is
in the computer at regular intervals in case of system
difficulties.

3.2 ALLOCATION OF FACILITIES IN AN INFORMATION NETWORK

3.2.1 Situations requiring a large central computer

There are some cases where the technical factors are
overwhelming and the decision on the disposition of
facilities is obvious. The large machine intelligence
programs, which understand natural language by storing
comprehensive associations between words to identify the
context of any given word, will clearly require not only
large scale storage but also heavy processing to discover
the appropriate frame of reference for any query to the
system.

Those applications which demand large scale storage are
also of necessity sited on a large mainframe. Examples of
this are the large information retrieval systems which
contain many billions of bytes of information or the large
company mainframe which contains all the details of
company products and sales.

Another situation which will result in the use of a
central mainframe is when a user requires a number of
packages which take tens of kilobytes of computer store.
If only one or two packages are required then it may be

possible to use a microcomputer (there are implementations
of Basic, Pascal and Cobol on microcomputers) but if a
comprehensive service is required this can be more
effectively provided on a larger computer.

The use of a mainframe for providing printing facilities
is no longer an inevitable solution. When dial-up
transmission speeds were restricted to 30 cps and
telecommunications costs were high, which is still the
case in many places in Europe, the printing was most often
carried out at the central site and then sent by mail to
the terminal site. However as access speeds have risen to
120 cps and with low telecommunications costs, as in the
US, there is a strong move towards printing at the local
site by transmitting the data over the telephone network.
This has been the case for some time in some distributed
systems using leased lines.

The advent of the daisy wheel printer is another force for
dispersing the printing function to the station which
requires it. A daisy wheel printer which gives typewriter
quality output is a slow speed device so that it is only
practicable for modest amounts of printing. An individual
can accept the slow speed of a daisy wheel for the limited
amount of information which he might need but for volume
output of a complete company site this is impracticable.

3.2.2 The case for local intelligence

A good example of the need for local intelligence is the
need for the storage of personal information for logging
on to various computers. The totality of computers to be
available on the international network necessitates a very
long address to be typed in whereas the average user will
only access a dozen or so addresses which could be
identified by one or two characters. The creation of a
personal list of such data with a set of codes to select
them will substantially reduce the effort in contacting
these systems. This facility must be local to the user
because a shared list requires a large number of codes
which increases the complexity of the coding system and
destroys the value of a local list. For example the
address codes used by British Telecom are from 16 to 24
characters long but comprehensive lists have been created
for individual users of the USERKIT using only two
characters for the mnemonic.

Another case where local storage of data is sensible is
for data which is accessed very frequently. The use of
telecommunications links when data is being constantly
used will often be wasteful. So for data such as telephone

numbers of colleagues, or personal appointments, it will
be uneconomic to have this stored in a remote computer. It
may be that a local minicomputer which is permanently
accessible through a local network could be an acceptable
solution if telephone contact were not needed. The key
factor in the decision between a computer available on a
local network and a desk-top microcomputer will be the
effectiveness of the particular system is saving time and
trouble in accessing the information.

In other case economic arguments will be the deciding
factor. At the moment the cost of telecommunications is
about $30.00 per hour. This level of charge combined with
the decreasing costs of small computers has given a
stimulus to the development of computing which is
distributed to the site where the activity is taking
place. There will be some modification in this situation
as PSS brings cheaper dial-up access at $4 to $6 per
hour.

There are other economic aspects as well as the cost of
telecommunications. It is more economic from the storage
point of view to have centralised facilities for
activities such as word processing which use large amounts
of storage over a period of time but these facilities have
in fact developed at local level not at the site of the
company mainframe. This is partly due to the economic
costs of the manual processing of the data for a
centralised operation. If a secretary has a word processor
in a local office then the operations of creating a letter
and sending and filing it can be done very quickly by the
person who knows all the details of the transaction. In
the case of remote facilities there has to be a tightly
controlled administrative arrangement to send the
information back to the correct destination and the
administrative work load has been multiplied.

One of the significant results of the low cost of
microcomputers is the ability of individual managers or
scientists to purchase equipment within their own budget
responsibility. This gives the individual unit within a
company the opportunity to develop the computing it
requires without an organisational discussion to produce a
corporate view. The immediate availability of computer
power also has a valuable educational effect in that staff
will use a piece of equipment which is immediately to
hand, and thereby extend the application of computer
methods, whereas a remote computer may be ignored. It has
also been a useful stimulus to research because
developments such as the USERKIT have been funded with
minimal resources.

3.2.3 The case for the local minicomputer

The obvious candidate for a local communal computer is a company message switching system. These have the important advantage that they mitigate the time mis-match which plagues so much personal contact. By allowing individuals to make contact via computer messages at a time which is convenient to them the contact between individuals is improved.

Other examples suitable for the local minicomputer are those which involve transfer between machines. An example of this is the need for translation between information retrieval command languages. The programs to achieve this are quite large but it is not feasible to have these based at the host computer because each host would need to create a full set of translators. The existence of a central computer would mean that only the translators from each language into some common standard and the translators from this common basis out to the target language would be needed. This considerably reduces the translation effort.

The same is true of national language translation facilities which are now being developed by the European Commission. Since the translation of output between languages is a universal requirement the repetition of such a facility at each computer centre would be foolish. Facilities such as these which satisfy a universal requirement should be available on a centralised basis. Ideally the facility should be local to minimise the telecommunications costs but the high capital cost of such a development will argue for a central facility accessed through telecommunications in the first instance.

There are several activities where the urge for a personal microcomputer solution should be resisted. Where individuals are recording data which is of company interest there should be central decisions on the collation of the data and the choice of format so that all the appropriate company personnel can benefit from the stored information. For example if one member of a company is creating an information collection on the research in a particular area it should be centrally available for all to access.

The same argument is true when the company resource is the man time involved in the creation of a program. Where there is a centralised computing facility the amount of time spent on creating programs is monitored and controlled but when managers, scientists, and

technologists all have the means to create individual
programs even the knowledge of the extent of company time
spent on programming is absent and there is certainly no
management decision on the use of manpower resources.

There is a particular danger that departments which carry
on computing activity outside the computer centre will
concentrate their activity on programming and ignore the
computer houskeeping standards which have grown up over
the years. It is equally important to create a program
which can be understood and modified in a year's time as
it is to ensure that the program works when the
calculation is needed.

4. CONCLUSIONS

The situations where a large scale computer is necessary
tend to be obvious. Where large scale processing or
storage is needed then the central mainframe will be
inevitable.

The balance between the local minicomputer and the
microcomputer on the desk is still not completely clear. A
key advantage of the local microcomputer is the
opportunity to involve those who will use the computer
system. The most difficult aspect of new computer systems
is the acceptability of the system to the personnel
involved. If they are themselves helping to create the
system it becomes more easily accepted.

It is equally clear that organisations cannot afford to
allow uncoordinated development of computing, both from
the point of view of creating company information which is
not available to all sections of the firm, and also to
make sure that any programs written are universally
available to prevent duplication of effort. The solution
to this problem is a clear policy of devolving computing
to the site of the activity to which it relates, if the
staff wish to participate, backed by an efficient central
administration which lays down standards for computing
activity and maintains good coordination between the
active groups.

Activities which are particularly suited to local
solutions are online contact with a high typing content,
which can be carried out more cheaply locally and then
transmitted at full line speed, and local coding systems
which can use far fewer characters than a comprehensive
global coding system.

REFERENCES

Doszkocs, T.E., and Rapp, B.A., Searching Medline in
English, Proceedings of 42nd ASIS Annual Meeting, Vol. 16,
1979.
Jamieson, S.H.,and Oddy, R.N., Low cost implementation of
experimental retrieval techniques for online users,
Proceedings of Fourth International Online Information
Meeting, Learned Information, Oxford, 1980.
Williams, P.W., Microprocessor assisted terminals for
online information, Proceedings of 3rd International
Online Information Meeting, Learned Information, Oxford,
1979.

Part 10
Expert Systems

Approximate Reasoning in Intelligent Relational Data Bases

L. J. Kohout

Man–Computer Studies Group,
Department of Computer Science,
Brunel University, Uxbridge, Middlesex, UK

W. Bandler

Department of Mathematics,
University of Essex, Colchester, Essex, UK

The purpose of this presentation is to outline briefly a conceptual framework of, and a methodology for, implementing an intelligent data base for expert systems, using the rules of approximate reasoning. The proposed approach is formally based on many-valued extensions of relational algebras [1]. These new extensions to a relational data base framework make it possible to deal meaningfully with queries formulated by imprecise questions, to deal with incomplete or imprecise data, as well as with data accompanied by probabilistic or fuzzy grades of relevance.

It is our contention, that the logic of intelligent data bases should attempt to match more closely the logic of human reasoning, in order to mitigate the problems of user-expert system interaction. An expert system ought to be a reliable technological system operating in realistic conditions with proper emphasis on engineering and man-computer interaction aspects. In particular we address the following problems in our approach:

a) protection

b) problem of information credibility and relevance

c) contradictions and incompleteness of information

d) vagueness and approximation in queries and statements

e) structural constraints imposed by the system implementation.

Available implementations of relational data bases are in terms of "hard", static, deterministic relations, whereas in the real-world applications data is often incomplete, imprecise, inherently dynamic and non-deterministic. The problem of incompleteness of data is usually avoided by the use of a "closed world" assumption. However, a wide variety of scientific, medical, sociological, etc., data is incomplete. Most query languages require the user to specify his query precisely. However, with an intelligent user-interface, it is often desirable too that the user need not, or need not even be able to formulate his information retrieval requests precisely. Several authors proposed the use of Zadeh's fuzzy logic and fuzzy set theory to deal with imprecision of information as well as to overcome the problems mentioned above [2], [3]. Zadeh himself described a fuzzy relational data base system [4]. As far as we are aware, no full implementation of fuzzy relational data bases exists at present because of the lack of suitable power-set theories that would play a role similar to the classical power-set theory in implementation of conventional relational data bases (e.g. Codd's normal forms, etc.). However, we have developed a range of fuzzy power-set theories, making the implementation now possible [5].

The possibility of combining the approaches dealing with dynamic consistency, stability, data-incompleteness, protection and approximate reasoning has been demonstrated in [6], [7]. These provide a unifying square and triangular relational product structure [8] that is the main building block utilised in the approach outlined in this presentation.

A distinguished feature of the outlined approach is its modularity. This makes it possible to switch between various logics of approximate reasoning (such as fuzzy, probabilistic, etc.) according to the requirements of a particular user area, without the need to change the major part of the data-base system implementation. This is made possible by the use of a relationship between various implication operators and new relational products developed by the authors [9].

REFERENCES:

1. Bandler, W. and Kohout, L.J. (1982). Relations in Systems Science, Book in preparation.

2. Chang, C.L. (1976). DEDUCE -- A deductive query language for relational databases. In Cheng, C.H., ed., Pattern Recognition and Artificial Intelligence. Academic Press, New York, pp. 108-134.

3. Chang, S.K. and Ke J.S. (1979), Translation of fuzzy queries for relational database system, IEEE Trans. on Pattern Analysis and Machine Intelligence, PAMI-1, pp. 281-294.

4. Zadeh, L.A. (1978), Approximate Reasoning. In Machine Intelligence 9.

5. Bandler, W. and Kohout, L.J. (1980). Fuzzy power sets and fuzzy implication operators. Fuzzy Sets and Systems, 4, pp. 13-30.

6. Bandler, W. and Kohout, L.J. (1979). Application of fuzzy logics to computer protection structures. Proc. 9th Intl. Symp. on Multiple-Valued Logic, Bath, England, May 1979. IEEE Computer Society, Long Beach, Calif., IEEE79CH 1408-4C, pp. 200-7

7. Bandler, W. and Kohout, L.J. (1979). Activity structures and their protection. Proc. Silver Anniversary Intl. Meeting of the SGSR, London August 1979, SGSR, Loouisville, Kentucky, U.S.A., pp. 239-244.

8. Bandler, W. and Kohout, L.J. (1980). Fuzzy relational products as a tool for analysis and synthesis of complex systems. In Wang, S.K. and Chang, P.P., eds., Fuzzy Sets: Theory and Applications to Policy Analysis and Information Systems. Plenum Press, New York, pp. 341-367.

9. Bandler, W. and Kohout, L.J. (1980). Semantics of implication operators and fuzzy relational products. Internat. J. Man-Machine Studies, 12, pp. 89-116. Reprinted in Mamdani, E.H. and Gaines, B.R., eds. (1981). Fuzzy Reasoning and its Applications. Academic Press, London.

A Survey and Critical Review
of Expert Systems Research

M. A. Bramer

Lecturer, The Open University, UK

An important development, arising largely from Artificial
Intelligence research, which has crystallised in the last few
years is the idea of an expert system.

An expert system has been defined as a computing system which
embodies organized knowledge concerning some specific area of
human expertise, sufficient to perform as a skilful and cost-
effective consultant.

This paper surveys the state of the art in this field, describing
the major systems currently in existence and the underlying
computational mechanisms. A number of associated theoretical
issues are also discussed.

1.   INTRODUCTION

An important development, arising largely from Artificial
Intelligence research, which has crystallised in the last few
years, is the idea of an expert system.

An expert system has been defined as a computing system which
embodies organized knowledge concerning some specific area of
human expertise, sufficient to perform as a skilful and cost-
effective consultant.

Thus it is a high-performance special-purpose system which is
designed to capture the skill of an expert consultant such as a
doctor of medicine, a chemist or a mechanical engineer.

Although the earliest acknowledged expert system - DENDRAL -
dates back to 1965, the term itself has gained common use in
Britain only in the last three or four years, culminating in the
holding of an AISB (Society for the Study of Artificial Intelligence
and the Simulation of Behaviour) summer school devoted to the topic
in July 1979 and the formation of a British Computer Society
specialist group on expert systems in the summer of 1980.

Although the definition quoted above places the emphasis firmly on
performance not methodology, expert systems typically make use of
heuristic rules relating to the domain in question, which are
acquired from subject experts and refined (either by expert human
users or by the systems themselves) in the light of experience.

Alternative terms with a broadly similar meaning are "knowledge-
based systems", "rule-based systems" and "expert consulting systems".
The skill involved in setting up an expert system is often referred
to as "knowledge engineering".

2.   TYPICAL FEATURES OF EXPERT SYSTEMS

Expert systems can vary considerably from one another in terms of
system design and capabilities - not least because the term 'expert
system' is not yet precisely defined - however, in practice, the
most important systems (especially those developed by the Stanford
Heuristic Programming Project) have many features in common.

Much expert knowledge is of an ill-defined and heuristic nature,
frequently at an unconscious level. It is most unlikely that even
standard textbooks will give sufficient detailed, precise and
accurate information to be suitable for direct use. Much of the
expert's skill will undoubtedly be in approximate 'rules of thumb',
which are seldom or never recorded.

It is the task of the "knowledge engineer" (system implementor) to
extract this knowledge and organize it, and to achieve this generally
involves a period of intensive discussion with one or more subject

experts and the analysis of a selected set of test cases. This may
seem to be a daunting task, but for an experienced knowledge engineer
it is perfectly feasible. As an example of the amount of work
involved, it is reported that the development of the PUFF system (for
diagnosing possible pulmonary function disorders) required less than
10 man-weeks of effort by knowledge engineers and less than 50 hours
of interaction with subject experts.

Subject experts' knowledge is generally encoded not procedurally (i.e
as procedures and functions in a particular programming language) but
in a declarative form (known as a "knowledge base"), which comprises
a modular set of rules of the form

> situation ⇒ action

for example 'if X and Y and Z then deduce A', which operate on
associated facts.

Each such rule is intended to correspond in a natural and direct
fashion to a " chunk" of knowledge meaningful to the domain expert.
If successful, this form of representation is likely to prove much
more amenable to analysis, modification and augmentation (at the
instigation of the subject expert rather than the knowledge engineer)
than would be, for example, a program written in Lisp.

Returning to the example of PUFF, the system's rules were derived
from an analysis of 100 test cases, with a further 150 cases being
used to validate the initial set of rules. The resulting system
(1978) originally comprised 55 rules which has subsequently grown
to over 250. Tests indicate a high level of diagnostic agreement
between the system and human experts.

In addition to a knowledge base of rules, a mechanism is needed for
manipulating these rules to form inferences, make diagnoses, etc.
This mechanism (which is essentially a form of theorem prover) is
often referred to as the "inference engine". As a design aim the
inference engine, which may be standard across a wide range of
systems or applications, will be kept entirely separate from the
knowledge base, which is domain-specific.

An important complication arises from the fact that expert knowledge
in many domains (especially medicine) is often not definite, but of
an inherently imprecise nature such as

"if symptoms A,B and C are present then it is probable/it is possible
/there is some reason to suppose that the cause is X".

Although, in principle, such rules might be extended with further
conditions to make them definitive, in practice these conditions may
not be known, or to determine whether they applied in a particular
case might be impossible in the time available, or without incurring
a prohibitively high cost or risk to life. Many systems permit
imprecise rules to be included and provide means of manipulating
combinations of them as necessary, often described as "inexact
reasoning", "plausible reasoning" or "reasoning with uncertainty".

The fact that expert systems are typically used in fields where both the experts who are essential to their development and, in most cases, those who will use them when developed are highly skilled and largely autonomous professionals, often with a strongly developed sense of professional responsibility, places a number of constraints on system design. In medicine, for example, the physician will have the final responsibility for his patient's treatment, and his profession- al reputation will be at stake, to some extent, each time he consults an expert diagnostic system. For this reason it is most unlikely that he will accept the recommendations made by the system (and probably undesirable that he should) unless he also understands and accepts the underlying reasons.

Many systems provide an 'explanation' facility which enables the user to consult the system interactively to ask for explanations of the system's decisions, diagnoses etc. and the 'lines of reasoning' used to obtain them. Such explanations (which may also involve listings of rules, etc) are themselves given in the form of English text meaningful to the user, not internal codes. Some systems, notably MYCIN, provide the capability for the user to examine the system's line of reasoning in detail and suggest modifications to rules or new rules, if appropriate.

A "user-friendly" design is of great importance to the acceptance of the use of an expert system. However, this does not necessarily imply the need to accept input in unrestricted natural language. Communication in a restricted form, in the jargon of the field, may be fully acceptable.

Although a number of impressive high-performance systems have been created along the lines described above, it is notable that very few are currently in regular use 'in the field'.

Some of the unresolved theoretical issues underlying expert systems development are discussed in Section 6. However, the psychological barriers to the acceptance of expert systems may also be high.

Ultimately expert systems will only gain widespread acceptance if the users come to view them as aids, which can be consulted in the same non-threatening way as a textbook or a colleague rather than as diminishing their own professional status.

3.   SUMMARY OF PRINCIPAL SYSTEMS

Figure 1 summarises the areas of application of the principal expert systems.

The great majority of these have been developed in the United States, most notably by the Stanford Heuristic Programming Project(H.P.P.) under the leadership of Edward Feigenbaum. Details of many of the Stanford H.P.P. systems are given in Feigenbaum (1979) and Heuristic Programming Project (1980).

In constructing this table, it has been necessary to apply a parti- cular interpretation to the definition of expert system given previously.

No restrictions were made in the definition on the form in which expert knowledge had to be embodied, and it could be argued that virtually any Artificial Intelligence system written in Lisp, for example, was an expert system if its performance was sufficiently good. The assumption has been made here that one requirement for an expert system is that subject knowledge should be embodied in it in declarative not procedural form (as discussed in Section 2). It is worthwhile to point out, however, that the comparative value of the two forms of representation is a long-standing source of controversy in Artificial Intelligence and the distinction can also be difficult to make precise in some cases.

The definition given also places no explicit restrictions on the 'area of human expertise' concerned, and thus a system which performed expertly on a task such as solving '0'-level Mathematics problems, or playing Chess, for example, would be included. Many practitioners in the field would suggest that such systems should be excluded, since these task areas are not ones for which professional consultants are usually employed, and this interpretation has been followed when selecting systems for inclusion in the table. However, it is clear that a system excluded for this reason may be very close, in terms of methodology, to 'acknowledged' expert systems.

Even with these reservations, the list given is not intended to be exhaustive. Nevertheless, it includes most of the best known and most important of what are generally considered to be expert systems.

It is important to note that the systems listed in the table by no means form a homogeneous group with respect to stage of development, frequency of practical use or level of performance attained.

Three of the most fully developed systems are DENDRAL, MYCIN and PROSPECTOR and these are discussed in detail in Section 4. A number of other systems, such as DART and RLL, are still at an early stage of development. Some of the systems in the table (for example, CENTAUR) are designed with more than one application area in mind. In such cases the major application area to date is given in the table.

FIGURE 1

NAME OF SYSTEM OR PROJECT	APPLICATION AREA	PRINCIPAL RESEARCHER(S)	BRIEF DESCRIPTION OF SYSTEM	COMMENTS
AGE	Knowledge Engineering	H P Nii N Aiello (Stanford H.P.P.)	Provides guidance on building expert systems and a set of tools for doing so.	'Attempt to Generalize'. Used for building PUFF.
AL/X	Fault Diagnosis	J Reiter (Intelligent Terminals Ltd./ University of Edinburgh)	Diagnoses causes of automatic shut-downs on oil production platforms.	
AM	Mathematics	D B Lenat (Stanford H.P.P.)	Conjectures new concepts in elementary mathematics	
BACON.4	Science	P Langley G Bradshaw (Carnegie-Mellon University)	Discovers empirical scientific laws.	
CASNET	Medicine	S Weiss, C Kulikowski (Rutgers University)	Long-term management of glaucoma	
CENTAUR	Medicine	J S Aikins (Stanford H.P.P.)	Interprets pulmonary function test measurements from patients with lung disorders.	
CONCHE	Science	I H Chisholm D H Sleeman (University of Leeds)	An intelligent aide for scientific theory formation.	'Consistency Checker'
CONGEN	Science	R E Carhart (Stanford H.P.P./ University of Edinburgh)	Aids the structural chemist in finding possible molecular structures for an unknown compound.	'Constrained Structure Generator'. Part of DENDRAL project

FIGURE 1 (Continued)

CRIB	Fault Diagnosis	T R Addis (Internation- al Computers Limited)	Diagnosis of faults in computer hard- ware and software.	
CRYSALIS	Science	E A Feigenbaum R S Engelmore (Stanford H.P.P.)	Infers the structure of a protein from a map of electron density derived from x-ray crystallo- graphic data.	
DART	Engineering	(Stanford H.P.P.)	Diagnosing hardware faults in computer systems. (Under development)	Joint project with I.B.M.
HEURISTIC DENDRAL	Science	E A Feigenbaum J Lederberg B G Buchanan et al. (Stanford H.P.P.)	Identification of organic compounds by analysis of mass spectrograms.	First and most success -ful expert system. Dates from 1965 (400 rules)
EMYCIN	Knowledge Engineering	W Van Melle (Stanford H.P.P.)	A domain-independent version of MYCIN, usable for develop- ing rule-based consultation programs for many fields.	'Essential MYCIN'. (Used for PUFF, SACON, ONCOCIN etc)
EXPERT	Knowledge Engineering	S Weiss C Kulikowski (Rutgers University)	A system for designing and building models for consultation.	
GAMMA	Science	D R Barstow (Yale University)	Interpreting gamma ray activation spectra.	
GUIDON	Education	W J Clancey (Stanford H.P.P.)	Case-method tutor designed to improve a student's ability to diagnose complex problems in medicine and science	(Designed to be usable for teaching about any domain re- presentable in EMYCIN.)
HEADMED	Medicine	J F Heiser	Psychopharmacology advisor.	Constructed using EMYCIN (270 rules)

FIGURE 1 (Continued)

INTERNIST	Medicine	J D Myers H E Pople (University of Pittsburgh)	Diagnosis in internal medicine.	
LOGIN	Engineering	E A Feigen- baum H P Nii (Stanford H.P.P.)	Development of tools to complement or supplement signal processing programs (initially by adding geological information).	
MACSYMA Advisor	Mathematics	M R Genesereth (M.I.T.)	An automated consultant for MACSYMA (an algebraic manipulation system)	
MDX	Medicine	B Chandra- sekaran (Ohio State University)	Performs diagnoses related to cholestasis.	
META- DENDRAL	Science	B G Buchanan (Stanford H.P.P.)	Induces rules for determining mole- cular structure from mass spectro- metry data.	Part of DENDRAL project
MOLGEN	Science	J Lederberg N Martin P Friedland M Stefik et al (Stanford H.P.P.)	Provides intelligent advice to a mole- cular geneticist on the planning of experiments invol- ving the manipulation of DNA.	
MYCIN	Medicine	E Shortliffe (Stanford H.P.P.)	Diagnoses certain infectious diseases and recommends appropriate drug treatment.	(400 rules)
ONCOCIN	Medicine	E Shortliffe A C Scott (Stanford H.P.P.)	Assists in the management of cancer patients on chemo- therapy protocols for forms of lymphoma.	'Oncology Protocol Management System'. Constructed using EMYCIN.
PROS- PECTOR	Geology	P Hart R Duda (SRI Inter- national)	Aids geologists in evaluating mineral sites for potential deposits.	

FIGURE 1 (Continued)

PSYCO	Medicine	J Fox (Imperial Cancer Research Fund,London)	Diagnoses dyspepsia	Experimental Production System compiler. (Initial application)
PUFF	Medicine	J C Kunz (Stanford H.P.P.)	Analyses results of pulmonary function tests for evidence of possible pulmonary function disorder.	In routine use at Pacific Medical Center Hospital, San Francisco. Constructed using EMYCIN (250 rules.)
R1	Computing	J McDermott (Carnegie-Mellon University)	Configuring the VAX/780 computer system.	
RAFFLES	Fault Diagnosis	T R Addis (International Computers Limited).	Diagnosis of faults in computer hardware and software.	
RITA	Knowledge Engineering	R H Anderson (Rand Corporation).	Provides the user with a language for defining intelligent interfaces to external data systems.	'Rule-directed Interactive Transaction Agent'.
RLL	Knowledge Engineering	R Greiner, D B Lenat (Stanford H.P.P.)	Provides user with a flexible set of facilities as a tool for building his own knowledge representation language.	'Representation Language Language'. (Developed from UNITS.)
RX	Medicine	R L Blum (Stanford H.P.P.)	Derives knowledge about the course and treatment of chronic diseases from a database of patient information.	

FIGURE 1 (Continued)

SACON	Engineering	J S Bennett R S Engelmore (Stanford H.P.P.)	Advises structural engineers in using the structural analysis program MARC.	'Structural Analysis Consultant'. Constructed using EMYCIN (170 rules)
SECS	Science	W T Wipke	Proposes schemes for synthesising stated organic compounds.	
SU/X	Engineering	H P Nii and E A Feigenbaum (Stanford H.P.P.)	Forms and updates hypotheses about location, velocity etc. of objects from primary signal data (spectra).	
TEIRESIAS	Medicine	R Davis (Stanford H.P.P.)	Knowledge acquisition program used with MYCIN.	
UNITS	Knowledge Engineering	M Stefik (Stanford H.P.P.)	Interactive language providing general-purpose facilities for knowledge representation. Used for MOLGEN plus other small applications.	(Originally developed as part of MOLGEN.) (Now being superseded by RLL.)
VLSI	Engineering	(Stanford H.P.P.)	Assistance in the design of very large scale integrated circuits. (Under development.)	Joint project with Stanford Centre for Integrated Systems.
VM	Medicine	L M Fagan (Stanford H.P.P.)	Provides diagnostic and therapeutic suggestions for critical care patients needing mechanical assistance with breathing.	'Ventilator Management'. Operates in real-time, with time-dependent relations (120 rules). Used in the intensive care unit of the Pacific Medical Center, San Francisco.

4.   CASE STUDIES : DENDRAL, MYCIN and PROSPECTOR.

4.1   DENDRAL

The DENDRAL project includes three programs: DENDRAL, CONGEN and
META-DENDRAL. The major program, HEURISTIC DENDRAL was the first
and is probably still the best-known and most successful expert
system. The program is designed for use by organic chemists to
infer the molecular structure of complex organic compounds from
their chemical formulas and mass spectrograms. (Mass Spectrograms are
essentially bar plots of fragment masses against the relative
frequency of fragments at each mass.) It is claimed to rival expert
human performance for a number of molecular families.

DENDRAL was developed as part of the Stanford Heuristic Programming
Project by Edward Feigenbaum, Bruce Buchanan and others from 1965
onwards, in collaboration with the Stanford Mass Spectrometry
Laboratory. The lengthy period of development and use of the
program no doubt helps to explain its considerable success. The
DENDRAL system is now in daily use by chemists at Stanford as well
as by others in universities and industry.

The program makes use of rules which relate physical features of the
spectrogram (high peaks, absence of peaks etc.) to the need for
particular substructures to be present in or absent from the unknown
chemical structure. Using these constraints, CONGEN (CONstrained
structure GENerator) produces a list of all acceptable candidate
structures. For each of these the corresponding spectrogram is
then computed, and a matching algorithm ranks the candidates in
order of the best fit between their spectrograms and the spectrogram of the unknown compound.

HEURISTIC DENDRAL removes the need for a large amount of difficult
and error-prone work from the chemist, but itself has required a
considerable amount of subject expert time to set up and refine
the system's knowledge base of rules. META-DENDRAL aims to extend
the automation process a stage further by containing 'higher-level'
rules which are used to examine data and discover rules for
determining molecular structures from mass spectrometry data.
Plausible rules are generated from an analysis of experimental data
and these are then refined (e.g. by merging or by eliminating
partial redundancies) with the most plausible rules being selected
as the final rule set. Some new rules have been discovered and
previously known ones successfully rediscovered in this way.

4.2   MYCIN

MYCIN is a system developed by the Stanford Heuristic Programming
Project by Edward Shortliffe and others from 1975 onwards, in
collaboration with the Infectious Diseases group at the Stanford
Medical School.

The program diagnoses blood and meningitis infections and recommends appropriate drug treatment, on the basis of an interactive dialogue with a physician about a particular case. The
questions asked vary according to the answers previously given.

MYCIN is said to perform at above the level of a human specialist for the limited areas of meningitis and blood infections, but is not yet in routine clinical use.

The knowledge base of the system comprises over 400 rules of the form
        IF   <condition>   THEN   < implication>
each of which has an associated 'degree of certainty' or 'certainty factor' indicating the subject expert's level of confidence in the rule. A <condition> can comprise a number of components linked by logical 'AND' and 'OR' connectives.

As an example, the following is given by Feigenbaum (1979) for blood infections :

Rule 85
IF :
1) The site of the culture is blood, and
2) The gram stain of the organism is gramneg, and
3) The morphology of the organism is rod, and
4) The patient is a compromised host
THEN :
There is suggestive evidence (0.6) that the identity
of the organism is pseudo-aeruginosa.

The above is the form in which the rule might be printed out for the user. Note that the degree of certainty (0.6) is given as a probability-like value in the range 0 to 1, but is accompanied by a more meaningful descriptive term : "suggestive evidence". Degrees of certainty are, in fact, supplied by the subject expert as numbers in the range 1 to 10 and automatically converted to "probability" values.

In order to test whether an <implication> is justified, MYCIN tests whether the components of the associated <condition> are satisfied. The truth values of the components are either determined directly from patient data entered by the user (physician) during the consultation (and also have associated certainty factors) or are themselves the <implication> parts of other rules.

Thus MYCIN effectively uses 'backward chaining' through an implicit AND/OR tree, linking medical diagnoses ('goals') to user-supplied data ('leaf nodes'). This form of reasoning has the additional value that it helps to ensure that groups of questions asked by the system appear "focussed" towards evaluating a particular hypothesis. Once a hypothesis is found to be justified, or refuted, further questions relating to it do not need to be asked. This form of information gathering is probably much more acceptable to most users than a random gathering of facts, followed by "forward" deduction from them (especially if establishing the facts involves, say, performing repeated tests on a patient).

A simple model of inexact reasoning is used to propogate certainty factors through the tree. Thus for example, at an 'AND' node i.e. one where <condition> is composed of a number of logical 'AND' operations, the smallest of the certainty factors of the constituent parts of <condition> is multiplied by the certainty factor of the entire rule, to give the certainty factor of <implication>. A more complex formula is used at each 'OR' node. Computed certainty factors less than some threshold such as 0.2 are automatically reset to zero. Further details are given in Shortliffe and Buchanan (1975).

MYCIN examines the evidence for approximately 100 possible diagnoses by backward chaining; the output from the program is a list of possible alternative diagnoses, above a suitable threshold of certainty, and recommended treatments to cover all the identified possibilities.

TEIRESIAS is a knowledge acquisition program used in close conjunction with MYCIN. At any stage of a consultation, the user (expert) can ask WHY (to query the significance of a request by MYCIN for information) or HOW (to ask how deductions so far considered as established by MYCIN were arrived at). After the consultation the user can also ask why alternative diagnoses were ruled out. Such queries are handled by the TEIRESIAS program, which maintains a record of MYCIN's search tree for this purpose. If the user disagrees with a diagnosis he is led back through the chain of reasoning which led to it until the reason for the disagreement is found. The user can then interact with the system to change existing rules or add new ones and test the outcome. A simplified version of 'medical English' is used for input to the system and the output is also in a form intended to be clearly understandable to the user.

The following fragment of dialogue between the user and MYCIN-TEIRESIAS is also taken from Feigenbaum (1979) as an example of the system's explanatory capabilities. The dialogue begins with a question from MYCIN to the user. After each question asked by the user, TEIRESIAS prints an explanation of its understanding of the meaning of the question as a means of avoiding any possible misunderstandings.
MYCIN: Is the patient's illness with ORGANISM-1 a hospital-acquired infection?
USER: WHY
TEIRESIAS: (i.e. WHY is it important to determine whether or not the infection with ORGANISM-1 was acquired while the patient was hospitalized?)
[1.0] This will aid in determining the category of ORGANISM-1.
It has already been established that
[1.1] the gram stain of ORGANISM-1 is gramneg, and
[1.2] the morphology of ORGANISM-1 is rod, and
[1.3] the aerobicity of ORGANISM-1 is facultative
Therefore, if
[1.4] the infection with ORGANISM-1 was not acquired while the patient was hospitalized then there is strongly suggestive evidence (.8) that the category of ORGANISM-1 is enterobacteriaceae
Also: there is weakly suggestive evidence (.1) that the identity of ORGANISM-1 is pseudomonas-aeruginosa
[RULE 37]
USER: HOW 1.3
TEIRESIAS: [i.e. HOW was it established that the aerobicity of ORGANISM-1 is facultative?]
The following were used :

[3.1] RULE 27 indicated there is strongly suggestive evidence (.8) that the aerobicity of ORGANISM-1 is facultative
[3.2] RULE 27 indicated there is weakly suggestive evidence (.2) that the aerobicity of ORGANISM-1 is anaerobic
Since this gave a cumulative CF of (.8) for facultative, and (.2) for anaerobic, it has been established that the aerobicity of ORGANISM-1 is facultative.
USER: WHY DIDN'T YOU CONSIDER STREPTOCOCCUS AS A POSSIBILITY FOR ORGANISM-1?
TEIRESIAS: The following rule could have been used to determine that the identity of ORGANISM-1 was streptococcus: RULE 33
But clause 2 ('the morphology of the organism is coccus') was already known to be false for ORGANISM-1, so the rule was never tried.

Although DENDRAL is doubtless the most successful of the various Stan-ford H.P.P. systems, in many respects MYCIN is closer to exemplifying the essence of a typical 'expert system'.

In summary, its most important features are as follows
(i) a backward-chaining inference system to reason 'backwards' from diagnoses to symptoms.
(ii) the use of rules with 'certainty factors' and a corresponding method of 'inexact reasoning' to manipulate logical 'chains' of such rules.
(iii) an 'explanation' facility to justify the inferences made by the system, combined with a means for the expert user to refine the system's knowledge base if deficiencies are found.

Item (iii) is no doubt of particular importance in helping to ensure the co-operation of subject experts and their acceptance of the system. (DENDRAL does not have such a facility, but the information contained in the system is of a highly technical nature, which would not be easily amenable to a natural language explanation.)

As an extension of the MYCIN project, a subject-independent version known as EMYCIN ('empty MYCIN' or 'essential MYCIN') has been set up, by removing the detailed medical information from MYCIN, whilst leaving the overall 'backward chaining' framework, explanatory capabilities etc. intact. In principle, therefore, EMYCIN can be used as a general-purpose framework from which an expert system for any domain can be created simply by adding a domain-specific knowledge base. In practice, of course, it is possible that the EMYCIN framework may not prove sufficiently general outside a fairly narrow set of domains. However, several EMYCIN-based expert systems have successfully been created, in particular PUFF in medicine and SACON for structural engineers. These two systems contain approximately 250 and 170 domain-specific rules, respectively.

An "automated tutor" system known as GUIDON has also been built with the aim of teaching about any domain representable in EMYCIN. An operating version of the program now uses the MYCIN knowledge base and a set of 200 tutorial rules.

4.3 PROSPECTOR

PROSPECTOR is a system developed by R Duda, P Hart and others at SRI
International in California, which is intended to aid geologists in
assessing the favourability of a given region as a site for exploration for ore deposits of various types. The user provides the program
with a list of rocks and minerals observed 'in the field' and other
information expressed in a rudimentary form of English. The program
then conducts a 'dialogue' with the user, requesting additional
information where needed. At any point, the program is able to
provide the user with an explanation of the intent of any question,
or its geological rationale or a current trace of the conclusions it
has reached so far. The eventual output from the program is an indication of the 'level of certainty' to which the available evidence
supports the presence of a particular form of deposit in a given site.
The system has a number of different knowledge bases, corresponding
to different classes of ore deposit, including porphyry copper,
nickel sulphide and uranium. These are held as data structures independent of the PROSPECTOR program itself, and the program is designed so that other knowledge bases can readily be used with it when
they become available. The program's knowledge for a particular ore
deposit is held in the form of an 'inference network' of relations
between field evidence and geological hypotheses, the top level
assertion being that the available evidence matches the presence of
the deposit in question and the 'leaf' nodes corresponding directly
to field evidence. In general, even the field evidence will not be
definite. The user expresses his certainty about a piece of evidence-
on a scale -5 to 5, where 5 denotes that the evidence is definitely
present, -5 that it is definitely absent, and zero indicates no
information. These are converted automatically into probability-like
values. As each piece of field evidence is collected, assertions
which depend directly on it become established more or less definitely (i.e. their probabilities are modified). There will generally
be further assertions which depend on these, and their probabilities
will also be changed, and so on as each new piece of information
propogates through the network.

There are three kinds of relation used in the inference network.
(i)   Logical relations indicate that the truth value of a hypothesis
      depends entirely on those of the assertions which define it,
      using the standard AND, OR and NOT connectives of Boolean logic.
      Since the truth of the constituent assertions is only known (in
      general) as a probability value, the methods of fuzzy logic are
      used to determine the resulting probability of a hypothesis
      defined by means of logical AND   or   OR   connectives.   In
      practice, logical relations are not always appropriate. For
      example, it may often not be possible to determine the truth
      or falsity of some component of an AND relation.

(ii) Plausible relations are used for the more general case where the
      establishing or the refuting of an assertion (i.e. a change in
      its thus far established probability) provides evidence to
      support a change in the probabilities of a number of related

hypotheses. (These may be further adjusted if other assertions are later established and so on.) In this case, methods derived from Bayesian probability theory are used to determine the changes to make to the probabilities (i.e. the current probability estimates) at each stage. Each hypothesis has a 'prior probability' associated with it (i.e. the probability of its being true in the absence of any evidence for or against). These values are assigned by the system designer. Plausible relations are then specified by inference rules of the form

IF <u>evidence</u> THEN (to degree LS,LN) <u>hypothesis</u>.

Here <u>evidence</u> can refer to either field evidence or evidence established by a chain of reasoning, i.e. the <u>hypothesis</u> part of another rule. LS and LN are measures of the 'sufficiency' and 'necessity' of the evidence, i.e. they determine the adjustment to be made to the current probability estimate of the hypothesis if the evidence is found to be definitely established or definitely refuted, respectively. (An interpolation formula is used for the more normal case where only some intermediate level of certainty is available for the evidence.)

(iii) Contextual relations are used to express any necessary conditions that must be established before an assertion can be used in the reasoning process.

The smallest knowledge base in PROSPECTOR comprises 28 assertions and 20 inference rules, while the largest contains 212 assertions and 133 inference rules. Although the system is not yet fully evaluated, initial results are very promising. The cost of a typical consultation session with PROSPECTOR is also remarkably low, approximately $10 at commercial computer rates (Duda, Gaschnig and Hart (1979)).

5. PRODUCTION SYSTEMS AS A KNOWLEDGE – HANDLING FORMALISM

A number of the underlying computational methods used in expert systems have already been described, in particular the use of a knowledge base of rules of the form 'situation $\Rightarrow$ action'.

An important way in which such rules can be incorporated into a working program is in the form of a Production System, and it is this formalism which is the basis of most expert systems to date. It has been suggested, for example by Newell and Simon (1972), that the use of Production Systems has psychological significance for certain kinds of problem-solving activity, but they can equally well be used outside a 'psychological modelling' context. The description below corresponds to the standard forms of Production System; many variants and extensions of this are to be found in practice.

A production system is a collection of rules of the form 'conditions $\rightarrow$ actions', where the conditons are statements about the contents of a global database of 'facts' and the actions are procedures which may modify the contents of the database.

Program execution consists solely of a continuous sequence of <u>cycles</u> terminating when some 'halting' action is executed. At each cycle,

all rules with conditions that are satisfied by the contents of the
database are determined. If there is more than one such rule, one
is selected by means of some suitable 'conflict resolution' strategy
(e.g. the first in some pre-determined priority sequence is taken).
All the actions associated with the selected rule are then performed
and the database changed accordingly.

Such a Production System is said to have a <u>condition-driven</u> (or
pattern-driven) architecture, an important example of an expert
system with this form of architecture being META-DENDRAL. An alternative architecture which is probably more commonly used in expert
systems is the action-driven, goal-driven or <u>consequent-driven</u> production system. In this case, rules can usefully be thought of as
having the form 'antecedent → consequent'. For example, A&B&C→D can
be interpreted as 'the logical conjunction of A,B and C implies D'
or 'to prove D, it is necessary to establish A,B and C'. The system
is given, in effect, a 'goal' to prove through deductive inference.
The consequent parts of rules are examined to find one which could
make the goal true. When such a rule is found it is examined to
see if all its conditions are true. If they are the rule is 'fired',
if not the process continues recursively in an attempt to show that
each condition of the rule is true. The following simplified
example and description is taken from Waterman (1977). Letters are
used for database elements and they are considered true if they are
in the database.

          Database: A F
          Rules 1 :   A&B&C→D
                2 :   D&F→G
                3 :   A&J→G
                4 :   B→C
                5 :   F→B
                6 :   L→J
                7 :   G→H

"If the goal is to show that H is true, the system first checks the
database to see if H is there. In this case it is not, so the system
tries to deduce that H is true using the rules that have H on the
right-hand side. The only one applicable is rule 7. The system
now attempts to show that G is true, since if G is true then H is
also true. Again it checks the database; G is not there, so it
looks for rules that have G on the right-hand side. Conflict
resolution for this example is considered to be rule ordered, thus
the first (highest priority) rule that is applicable is used. This
is rule 2, so now the goal is to show (or deduce) that D and F are
true. This is accomplished by showing that A is true (from the
database), B is true (from rule 5), and C is true (from rule 4).
Since D and F are true, G is true and thus H is true, and the goal
has been accomplished. As the applicable rules are fired the
appropriate elements are added to the database. In this case the
database ends up with the elements : H G D C B A F, inserted by rules
5,4,1,2 and 7, in that order."

MYCIN is an example of consequent-driven Production System architecture (also described as using 'backward-chaining' through rules, to pass successively from 'implications' to their corresponding 'conditions').

A system which combines the two forms of architecture, condition-driven and consequent-driven, is RITA.

A much fuller description of Production Systems is to be found in the papers by Davis and King and by Young, which are listed in the bibliography.

6. DISCUSSION AND CRITICAL REVIEW

In such a recently established area, where the emphasis is essentially on high-performance systems, it is inevitable that an understanding of theoretical issues and problems involved in building expert systems should lag behind the development of working systems. Apart from one large project (the Stanford Heuristic Programming Project) most systems have been developed as independent efforts, mostly as academic research projects. Few attempts have been made by researchers to relate their work to that of others, particularly in terms of the programming techniques used. Detailed performance information in a form suitable for evaluation by non-subject specialists is difficult to obtain and little attention has been given to identifying the degree to which the underlying subject-independent representation, rather than 'fine tuning' of the knowledge base, contributes to the level of performance achieved. The field of expert systems should therefore probably be seen as principally a growing body of practical experience, from which underlying principles are slowly beginning to emerge. Some of these principles were discussed in Section 2.

If expert systems are ultimately to become widely used, it is important that they are not only useful in practice, but soundly based in theory. A problem of particular importance concerns the choice of representation to adopt for encoding expert knowledge. The use of Production Systems, as described previously, is by far the most common method at present, but it is not clear that this situation will continue indefinitely. Other declarative forms of representation can be envisaged, and one such form that has been advocated strongly in some quarters is a restricted form of first-order predicate logic.

The programming language PROLOG permits such "logic programs" to be executed directly. A PROLOG program consists of a collection of logic statements (of a restricted form). Execution corresponds effectively to performing a controlled deduction from the constituent clauses of the program. The following is a very simple example of a program which performs deductive reasoning over a database.

```
parent-of (X,Y)←mother-of (X,Y).
parent-of (X,Y)←father-of (X,Y).
grandfather(X,Y)←father-of(X,Z), parent-of (Z,Y).
mother-of (martha,henry).
mother-of (susan, ronald).
mother-of (jane, louise).
```

```
father-of(john, henry).
father-of(mark, jane).
father-of(michael, ronald).
father-of(ronald, frances).
```

The above is the complete program. (The first three lines are rules,
the others are facts.) The program has a declarative meaning (taking
the 'natural' interpretation of the names used). Thus line 1 can be
read: for all X and Y, X is the parent of Y if X is the mother of Y.
Line 3 denotes: for all X and Y, X is the grandfather of Y if, for some
Z, X is the father of Z and Z is the parent of Y.
Line 4 denotes: martha is the mother of henry. In addition to the
declarative meaning, the program has a procedural interpretation,
e.g. (line 3) "to prove that X is the grandfather of Y, find a Z such
that X is the father of Z and Z is the parent of Y". To satisfy a
goal (left-hand side) the system tries to satisfy the conditions
(subgoals) on the right-hand side, one at a time, in left-to-right
order. If a goal cannot be satisfied the system backtracks. Thus
program execution is effectively a left-to-right, depth-first search
through an AND/OR tree of logical relations, chaining backwards from
goals to be established to given facts.
Entering the question
? - grandfather-of (michael,Y)
will produce the answer Y = frances.
To find all   grandfather/grandson   relationships it is only
necessary to enter
? - grandfather-of (X,Y).
This will return the solutions
       X = mark, Y = louise
and   X = michael, Y = frances,
in that order.
The potential value of the idea of "logic programming" is considerable, offering an extremely compact means of representing complex
logical relations and a database of relevant facts, together with a
built-in means of performing deductions, which is firmly based in
the theory of mathematical logic. Unfortunately, it would seem that
no non-trivial expert system has so far been constructed in this way,
so no practical evaluation is possible. Advocates of logic programming have so far paid little attention to a critical evaluation of
its strengths and weaknesses or to comparisons with the use of Production Systems. This is, however, an important area to pursue in
the future.

If expert systems are to be used as a medium for formulating,
accumulating and transferring expert knowledge, perhaps over several
generations, rather than as 'one-off' high performance systems, it is
extremely important to establish a standard framework, at least for
all the systems in a particular field. EMYCIN represents a valuable
step in this direction. However, it is vital that standardization
(de facto or otherwise) should be preceded by a fundamental examination of representational issues.

Another area in which basic research seems to be needed is that of inexact reasoning. The MYCIN model of propogating certainty factors of both rules and facts through a network of relationships has been analysed by Adams (1976).

Although the MYCIN model is presented as an alternative to standard probability theory, Adams proves that a substantial part of the model can be derived from and is equivalent to probability theory, with assumptions of statistical independence, although there are also important differences. By this means a number of shortcomings in the MYCIN model are identified. In particular, there are interdependence restrictions which need to be applied to the estimation of certain parameters ('measure of belief' and 'measure of disbelief' in a hypothesis, supplied by the physician) to maintain internal consistency, but which are not included in the MYCIN model. In addition the use of certainty factors as a means of ranking hypotheses is also suspect, since examples can be given of cases where, of two hypotheses, the one with the lower probablity would have the higher certainty factor. On the basis of Adams' analysis, it would seem that the MYCIN model has serious limitations. With the development of EMYCIN as a domain-independent expert system building tool, this matter is potentially of great importance.

It is interesting that such an apparently flawed method should give results which are apparently acceptable in practice. Adams comments: "empirical success of MYCIN ... stands in spite of theoretical objections of the types discussed. ... It is probable that the model does not founder on the difficulties pointed out because in actual use the chains of reasoning are short and the hypotheses simple. However, there are many fields in which, because of its shortcomings, this model could not enjoy comparable success".

An alternative critique of the MYCIN model is made by Fox, Barber and Bardhan (1980), from the viewpoint of comparison with human reasoning.

They comment "Tactically MYCIN depends heavily on the modus ponens style of reasoning. Psychological studies, however, have shown that human reasoning makes use of a range of inference schemata beyond modus ponens ... [MYCIN's] strategy is one of 'subgoaling'. This strategy is probably unlike that employed by clinicians. Firstly they are unlikely to depend upon a single reasoning strategy. ... Second, to set up goals the system works from the conclusions of rules to the premises in order to see which ones it should try to prove - this is tantamount to employing the modus tollens schema of logic which appears to be untypical of human reasoning". They propose an alternative rule-based system which is intended to be more closely modelled on clinical thinking, taking as the initial domain of interest the diagnosis of 'dyspepsia' (PSYCO). However, it is still too early to evaluate this model.

Other models of inexact reasoning have also been tried (notably by PROSPECTOR), but whether these avoid the problems of the MYCIN model is also not clear.

As the expert knowledge embedded in a system is allowed to grow (to several hundred rules in the case of some existing systems, stability

problems can arise, especially if the knowledge base can be augmented
by a user who was not involved in setting it up. Preventing contradictory items of knowledge entering the knowledge base is an
extremely difficult problem.

Moreover, the addition of more and more items of knowledge to the
system may lead to the overall operation of the system becoming in-
comprehensible to the user, even though each item is comprehensible
in itself. Unless the output from the system, especially in fields
such as medicine, can be explained and justified, it is most unlikely
that the user will even consider adopting its recommendations rather
than following his own professional judgement.

A problem associated with deductive reasoning systems which has been
identified by several researchers, but which does not appear to have
been taken into account in expert systems development, is the need
to make default assumptions when reasoning about incompletely
specified domains. Thus deductions may need to be made which are
consistent with the available information but are not provably
correct and may, in fact, turn out to be incorrect in the light of
information subsequently obtained. As an example of the problems
that can arise with "conventional" reasoning, given a rule such as:
if x is a bird then x can fly, and the knowledge that alpha is a
bird, one can conclude that alpha can fly. However, this may turn
out to be a mistake if alpha is an ostrich. Of course, the rule can
be modified to exclude the possibility that x is an ostrich or a
penguin etc., but then the further information that beta is a bird
(without any information of its species) will not allow of any
deduction about beta's powers of flight to be made, even though it is
extremely likely that beta can, in fact, fly. A means of 'default
reasoning' which enables tentative conclusions to be drawn which are
compatible with the evidence so far available is proposed by Reiter
(1979).

A final problem associated with expert system development is that of
automatically acquiring new information or refining existing information on the basis of experience gained, or accumulating "case lore".
As an extreme example, a particular set of symptoms may point to the
diagnosis of a rare disease only one time in a million, and the general practitioner may well be totally unaware of the possibility.
Nevertheless if a local epidemic of the disease occurs, he will
quickly learn to diagnose the disease with ease, that is his subjective estimate of the probability of it occuring will have greatly
changed. Similarly, a particular illness may be well known to be
prevalent in a particular geographical area. If a computerized
system is to be useful in changing circumstances and different
locations, it may be necessary to give attention to such contextual
factors.

The above discussion of unresolved theoretical issues is not intended
in any way to diminish the achievements of those who have implemented
working expert systems, but to indicate some of the areas in which
further research is needed. Such questions will become more pressing

as expert systems move further out of academic establishments into industry. There are considerable potential advantages to industry in being able to capture the knowledge of their key staff, to guard against their departure or death or to relieve excessive calls on their time. However there is clearly a possibility that in industry those who are required to use the systems will not always possess such well-developed judgement to support overturning the system's recommendations (or such a high level of professional autonomy to enable them to feel free to do so) as do, for example, general practitioners in medicine.

The rapid growth in the power and ready availability at a low price of microcomputers may soon mean that expert knowledge of a complex domain once encoded will rapidly become available very widely indeed, and inevitably to individuals with progressively less skill in the subject area themselves. From this point of view the need for well-designed explanatory capabilities and a sound model of inexact reasoning, in particular, is very real indeed.

REFERENCES

Adams, J. B. (1976). A probability model of medical reasoning
    and the MYCIN model. Mathematical Biosciences, Vol. 32,
    pp. 177 - 186.
Duda R., Gaschnig, J. and Hart, P. (1979). Model design in the
    PROSPECTOR consultant system for mineral exploration.
    In Michie, D. (ed.) Expert Systems in the Micro-electronic Age.
    Edinburgh University Press, pp. 153 - 167.
Feigenbaum, E. A. (1979). Themes and case studies of knowledge
    engineering.
    In Michie, D. (ed.) Expert systems in the Micro-electronic
    Age. Edinburgh University Press, pp. 3 - 25.
Fox, J, Barber, D. and Bardhan, K. D. (1980). Alternatives to
    Bayes? A quantitative comparison with rule-based diagnostic
    inference. Methods of Information in Medicine, Vol. 19, No. 4,
    pp. 210 - 215.
Heuristic Programming Project (1980). Stanford University Heuristic
    Programming Project.
Newell, A. and Simon, H. A. (1972). Human Problem Solving.
    Prentice-Hall.
Reiter, R. (1979). A logic for default reasoning. Dept. of
    Computer Science, University of British Columbia Technical
    Report 79 - 8 .
Shortliffe, E. H. and Buchanan, B. G. (1975). A model of inexact
    reasoning in medicine. Mathematical Biosciences, Vol. 23,
    pp. 351 - 379.
Waterman, D. A. (1977). An introduction to production systems.
    AISB European Newsletter, Issue 25, pp. 7 - 10.

BIBLIOGRAPHY

The following is a selective bibliography of books, papers etc. on
expert systems. The bibliography includes general/survey articles,
articles on Production Systems and "inexact reasoning", and
articles on over 30 specific systems.

At least one article is given on each of the systems listed in the
table in Section 3, together with some on other systems.

Unpublished research reports are only given when no references to
more accessible sources are known. Two particularly valuable
sources of information are Michie (1979) and Heuristic Programming
Project (1980), which are included under 'general/survey' below.

No references to the DART, LOGIN and VLSI projects are known
except for brief descriptions in the latter source.

Abbreviations

The following abbreviations are used throughout the bibliography.

ESMA: Michie, D. (ed.) (1979). Expert Systems in the Micro-
    electronic Age. Edinburgh University Press.
IJCAI75: Advance Papers of the fourth international joint conference
    on Artificial Intelligence, Tbilisi, USSR, 1975.
IJCAI77: Proceedings of the fifth international joint conference on
    Artificial Intelligence, Massachusetts Institute of
    Technology, Cambridge, Mass., 1977.
IJCAI79: Proceedings of the sixth international joint conference on
    Artificial Intelligence, Tokyo, Japan, 1979.
PDIS: Waterman, D. A. and Hayes-Roth, F. (eds.) (1978). Pattern-
    directed inference systems. New York, Academic Press.
GENERAL/SURVEY
Feigenbaum, E. A. (1979). Themes and case studies of knowledge
    engineering. ESMA, pp. 3 - 25
Heuristic Programming Project (1980). Stanford University Heuristic
    Programming Project. [A 'prospectus' of the various systems
    developed by the Stanford H.P.P.]

Michie, D. (ed.) (1979). Expert Systems in the Micro-electronic Age,
    Edinburgh University Press. [ESMA]
Michie, D. (1980). Expert Systems, Computer Journal, Vol. 23, No. 4,
    pp. 369 - 376.

PRODUCTION SYSTEMS

Davis, R. and King, J. (1977). An overview of production systems.
    In Machine Intelligence 8 (Elcock, E. W. and Michie, D. (eds.)),
    Chichester: Ellis Horwood. and New York: John Wiley, pp. 300 - 332.
Young, R. (1979). Production systems for modelling human cognition.
    ESMA, pp. 35 - 45.

INEXACT REASONING

Adams, J. B. (1976). A probability model of medical reasoning and
    the MYCIN model. Mathematical Biosciences, Vol. 32,
    pp. 177 - 186.
Duda, R. O, Hart P. E. and Nilsson, N. J. (1976). Subjective
    Bayesian methods for rule-based inference systems. Proc.
    National Computer Conference (AFIPS Conference Proceedings
    Vol. 45), pp. 1075 - 1082.
Fox, J., Barber, D. and Bardhan, K. D. (1980).
    Alternatives to Bayes? A quantitative comparison with rule-based
    diagnostic inference. Methods of Information in Medicine,
    Vol. 19, No. 4, pp. 210 - 215.
Shortliffe, E. H. and Buchanan, B. G. (1975). A model of inexact
    reasoning in medicine. Mathematical Biosciences, Vol. 23,
    pp. 351 - 379.

LOGIC PROGRAMMING

Warren, D. (1979). PROLOG on the DEC System - 10. ESMA, pp.
    pp. 112 - 121.

AGE

Nii, H.P. and Aiello, N. (1979). AGE (Attempt to Generalize): A
    knowledge-based program for building knowledge-based programs.
    IJCAI79, pp. 645 - 655.

AL/X

Reiter, J. (1980). AL/X: an expert system using plausible inference.
    Machine Intelligence Research Unit, University of Edinburgh.

AM

Lenat, D. B. (1977). Automated theory formation in Mathematics.
    IJCAI77, pp. 833 - 842.

BACON.4

Bradshaw, G. L., Langley, P. and Simon, H. A. (1980).
    BACON.4: the discovery of intrinsic properties.
    Proceedings of the third biennial conference of the Canadian
    Society for Computational Studies of Intelligence. Victoria,
    British Columbia.

CASNET

Weiss, S. et al. (1978).
    A model-based method for computer-aided medical decision making.
    Artificial Intelligence, Vol. 11, pp. 145 - 172.
Weiss, S., Kulikowski, C. and Safir, A. (1977).
    A model-based consultation system for the long-term management
    of glaucoma. IJCAI77, pp. 826 - 833.

CENTAUR

Aikins, J. S. (1979). Prototypes and production rules: an approach
    to knowledge representation for hypothesis formation.
    IJCAI79, pp. 1 - 3.

CONCHE

Chisholm, I. H. and Sleeman, D. H. (1979).
    An aide for thoery formation. ESMA, pp. 202 - 212.

CONGEN

Carhart, R. E. (1977). Re-programming DENDRAL. AISB Quarterly,
    Vol. 28, pp. 20 - 22.
Carhart, R. E. (1979). CONGEN: an expert system aiding the structural
    chemist. ESMA, pp. 65 - 82.

CRIB

Addis, T. R. (1980). Towards an 'expert' diagnostic system.
    ICL Technical Journal, May 1980, pp. 79 - 105.

CRYSALIS

Engelmore, R. and Terry, A. (1979). Structure and function of the
    CRYSALIS system. IJCAI79, pp. 250 - 256.

DENDRAL

Buchanan, B. G. and Feigenbaum, E. A. (1978). DENDRAL and Meta-
    DENDRAL: their applications dimension. Artificial Intelligence,
    Vol. 11, Nos. 1 - 2, pp. 5 - 24.
Buchanan, B. G. et al. (1976). Applications of Artificial
    Intelligence for chemical inference, XXII , automatic rule
    formation in mass spectrometry by means of the Meta-DENDRAL
    program. J. Amer. Chem. Soc., Vol. 98, pp 6168 - 6178.
Feigenbaum, E. A., Buchanan, B. G. and Lederberg, J. (1971).
    On generality and problem solving: a case study using the DENDRAL
    program. In Machine Intelligence 6, Edinburgh University Press.

EMYCIN

Van Melle, W. (1979). A domain-independent production rule system
    for consultation programs. IJCAI79, pp. 923 - 925.

EXPERT

Weiss, S. and Kulikowski, C. (1979). EXPERT: a system for
    developing consultation models. IJCAI79, pp. 942 - 947.

GAMMA

Barstow, D. R. (1979). Knowledge engineering in nuclear physics.
    IJCAI79, pp. 34 - 36.

GUIDON

Clancey, W. J. (1979). Dialogue management for rule-based tutorials.
    IJCAI79, pp. 155 - 161.
Clancey, W. J. (1979). Tutoring rules for guiding a case method
    dialogue. Int. J. Man-Machine Studies, Vol. 11, pp 25 - 49.

HEADMED

Heiser, J. F., Brooks, R. E. and Ballard, J. P. (1978).
    Progress Report: A computerized psychopharmacology advisor.
    Proceedings of the 11th Collegium Internationale
    Neuro - Psychopharmacologicum, Vienna.

INTERNIST

Pople, H. E, Myers, J. D. and Miller, R. A. (1975). DIALOG: a model
    of diagnostic logic for internal medicine.
    IJCAI75, pp. 848 - 855.

MACSYMA Advisor

Genesereth, M. R. (1979). The role of plans in automated
    consultation. IJCAI79, pp. 311 - 319.

MDX

Chandrasekaran, B., et al. (1979). An approach to medical diagnosis
    based on conceptual structures. IJCAI79, pp. 134 - 142.

META-DENDRAL

Buchanan, B. G. and Mitchell, T. (1978). Model-directed learning
    of production rules. PDIS, pp. 297 - 312.

MOLGEN

Martin, N., et al. (1977). Knowledge-based management for
    experiment planning in molecular genetics. IJCAI77,
    pp. 882 - 887.
Stefik, M. (1978). Inferring DNA structures from segmentation data.
    Artificial Intelligence, Vol. 11, Nos. 1 - 2, pp. 85 - 114.

MYCIN

Davis, R., Buchanan, B. G. and Shortliffe, E. H. (1977). Production
    systems as a representation for a knowledge-based consultation
    program. Artificial Intelligence, Vol. 8, No. 1, pp. 15 - 45.
Shortliffe, E. H. (1976). Computer-Based Medical Consultations:
    MYCIN. New York: American Elsevier/North Holland.

ONCOCIN

Scott, A. C., Bishoff, M. B. and Shortliffe, E. H. Oncology
    protocol management using the ONCOCIN system: a preliminary
    report. HPP Working Paper.

PROSPECTOR

Duda, R., Gaschnig, J. and Hart, P. (1979). Model design in the
    PROSPECTOR consultant system for mineral exploration. ESMA,
    pp. 153 - 167.

PSYCO

Fox, J., Barber, D. and Bardhan, K. D. (1980).
    Alternatives to Bayes? A Quantitative Comparison with Rule-
    based Diagnostic   Inference. Methods of Information in
    Medicine, Vol. 19, No. 4, pp. 210 - 215.

PUFF

Kunz, J. C. et al. (1978). A physiological rule-based system for
    interpreting pulmonary function test rules. Heuristic
    Programming Project Memo HPP - 78 - 19.

R1

McDermott, J. (1980). R1: a rule-based configurer of computer
    systems. Computer Science Department, Carnegie - Mellon
    University.

RAFFLES

Addis, T. R. (1980). Towards an 'expert' diagnostic system.
    ICL Technical Journal, May 1980, pp. 79 - 105.

RITA

Waterman, D. A. (1979). User-oriented systems for capturing
    expertise: a rule-based approach. ESMA, pp. 26 - 34.

RLL

Greiner, R. and Lenat, D. B. (1980). A representation language
    language. Proc. of the first AAAI conference.

RX

Blum, R. L. (1980). Automating the study of clinical hypotheses on
    a time-oriented data base: the RX project. MEDINFO80
    proceedings.

SACON

Bennett, J. S and Engelmore, R. S. (1979). SACON: a knowledge-based
    consultant for structural analysis. IJCAI79, pp. 47 - 49.

SECS

Wipke, W. T. (1974). Computer-assisted 3-dimensional synthetic
    analysis. In Computer Representation and Manipulation of
    Chemical Information (eds. W. T. Wipke, et al.), London and
    New York: Wiley Interscience, pp. 147 - 174.

SU/X

Nii, H. P. and Feigenbaum, E. A. (1978).   Rule-based understanding
    of signals. PDIS , pp. 483 - 501.

TEIRESIAS

Davis, R. (1977).   Interactive transfer of expertise I: acquisition
    of new inference rules. IJCAI77, pp. 321 - 328.
Davis, R. (1979).   Interactive transfer of expertise - acquisition
    of new inference rules. Artificial Intelligence, Vol. 12,
    No. 2, pp. 121 - 157.
Davis, R. and Buchanan, B. G. (1977). Meta-level knowledge:
    overview and applications. IJCAI77, pp. 920 - 927.

UNITS

Stefik, M. (1979).   An examination of a frame - structured
    representation system. IJCAI79, pp. 845 - 852.

VM

Fagan, L. M., Shortliffe, E. H. and Buchanan, B. G. (1980).
    Computer-based medical decision making: from MYCIN to VM.
    Automedica, Vol. 3, No. 2.

OTHER SYSTEMS

De Dombal, F. T. et al. (1972).   Computer-aided diagnosis of acute
    abdominal pain. British Medical Journal,   Vol. 2, pp. 9 - 13.

Gorry, G., Silverman, H. and Pauker, S. (1978).
    Capturing clinical expertise: a computer program that considers
    clinical responses to digitalis. Amer. J. Med., Vol. 64,
    pp. 452 - 460.

INFOLEX as a Videotex Gateway to Full Legal Information Retrieval

Stephen Castell

Director, Infolex Services Limited, UK

INFOLEX, the UK's first commercially-available computer-
assisted legal information retrieval service, offers a
non-full-text database CLARUS to practising lawyers via
Prestel. One of the possible limitations of CLARUS is
that it is impossible for a user to request further
details through his Prestel TV set terminal of items of
information identified as of interest on the CLARUS frames.

This paper sets out several approaches to overcoming this
limitation, by presenting alternative designs for a Prestel-
based 'gateway' into commercially-available computer-
resident legal databases which do store the full text
of the precedents abstracted in CLARUS.

INFOLEX AS A VIDEOTEX GATEWAY TO FULL TEXT LEGAL INFORMATION
RETRIEVAL

1. INTRODUCTION AND OVERVIEW

INFOLEX, launched in November 1978 as the UK's first commercially-
available computer-assisted legal information retrieval service,
provides through Prestel, British Telecom's public viewdata system,
access to a unique database CLARUS: Case LAw Report Updating
Service (see references (1) to (6) for background details).

For the purpose of this discussion, the essential characteristics
of CLARUS to note are:

- it is a non-full-text service, offering simple references to
  and abstracts of the standard published law reporting sources
  by way of a proprietary printed 400-term CLARUS Index covering
  all areas of the law from Admiralty, by way of Crime.....
  Employment...Land...Revenue...etc., etc...to Workmans
  Compensation;

- the CLARUS Index, made available on a private subscription
  basis to Infolex subscribers, lists precise end-frame
  numbers of Infolex's Prestel database, enabling viewdata
  'direct jumps' to be carried out simply and accurately. This
  affords rapid access to the end-frame information (some
  typical examples of which are shown in Figure 1.);

- being hosted on Prestel, the service is comparitively cheap
  to use (typically at a cost of perhaps less than £1,000 per
  annum, uncluding subscription, Prestel TV set terminal
  rental, telephone charges and frame access usage at 5p per
  end-frame);

- using viewdata retrieval software, which relies only on a
  simple 12-button calculator-like keypad for operation, no
  computer expertise is required of the non-technically-
  trained 'general practitioner' lawyer user;

- like all non-full-text indexed systems, Infolex is subject to
  the potential limitations of a) the skill of the abstractor/
  indexer (Infolex in fact uses only trained lawyers for this
  purpose), and b) the inability to present more detail on a
  particular reference or abstract retrieved (the impossibility
  of "getting any closer to the verbatim source" of the prime
  published information).

```
Infolex (Copyright 79)  3711354d      5p
        CRIME - EVIDENCE (Contd.)
        ======================================

MAY80 R v Murphy (CA)
        Recklessness. .......  80 2 WLR 743
JUN80 R v Andover JJ Ex P.
        Rhodes (Bankers books
        evidence Act s.7- order
        made against husband not
        party to proceeding. . TLR 17/6/80
J N80 R.v Fenlon (CA)
        (Barristers duty in
        defending - if it is
        intended to allele co-
        defendant is not
        truthful counsel should
        cross-examine and make
        it clear what evidence
        is unacceptable)..... TLR 25/ 6/80



            PRESS # TO CONTINUE
```

```
    Infolex (Copyright 79)  3711354e     5p
        CRIME - EVIDENCE (Contd.)
        ======================================

    MAY80 Barker v Wilson
        bankers books include
        microfilm records ... 80 2AER    81
    JUL80 R v Air India (HL)
        (Death of parakeets
        on aircraft out of
        jurisdiction - held
        as act not committed
        in UK the case not
        triable in UK)....... TLR  4/ 7/80
    AUG80 R v Watson (CA) power
        to reconsider admiss-
        ibility.............. 80 1WLR  991
    JUL80 R v Chatwood (CA) Con-
        fession as to nature
        of drug.............. 80 1WLR  874
    ■
```

Figure 1.   Examples of CLARUS frames on Prestel.

With respect to a) - the observation that Infolex may be
constrained by the skill and approach of the abstractor/indexer -
three comments may be made:

- Infolex, as a matter of database update policy, errs on the
  side of extensive multiple- and cross-referencing under/
  between CLARUS Index headings;

- each case referenced will, in the printed source text from
  which it has been abstracted, invariably make further
  reference to other cases, statutes, and points and principles
  of legal precedent, so that there is frequently a large 'fan
  out' from even a single reference, mitigating the effects
  of a possibly rigid Index;

- the CLARUS Index is itself in a continual state of evolution,
  with index terms being revised, added and sub-divided at
  frequent intervals (the Index itself is issued to subscribers
  in a durable loose-leaf wallet folder in order to facilitate
  update).

The objective of this discussion is to address the second possible
limitation of Infolex, b) referred to above - the lack of an 'in
depth' research capability for any particular item of information -
and to outline how this might be overcome by the operation of a
commercial Infolex 'gateway' into a full-text computer-assisted
legal information retrieval system (of which there are now two
commercial services, EUROLEX and LEXIS, offered in England).

Alternative technical approaches to providing such an enhanced
Infolex service are described with some assessment of their
relative advantages and shortcomings. A focus is made on the
existing CLARUS, Prestel and full-text systems as presently
commercially available, with the intention of showing how a
practical and simple-to-use 'gateway' service could currently
operate.

It is assumed the reader is familiar with the basic technical
aspects of Prestel, videotex and on-line retrieval systems
generally - reference (7) may provide a good overview.

2.   DESIRABLE DESIGN FEATURES OF AN INFOLEX 'GATEWAY' TO
     FULL-TEXT RETRIEVAL.

Simplicity:- the use of the standard simple viewdata keypad
              should be preserved. If a full alphanumeric
              keyboard is to be allowed, the user should not
              have to become skilled in the full-text software
              dialogue;

Speed:- the speed of retrieval must be considerably higher than that of searching manually through a library, without an uncompetitive cost penalty. On the other hand, an instant business decision based on the information retrieved is not normally required in the environment of a lawyers office, so that instant, 'real-time' response to a retrieval request is not neceessary;

Hardware redundancy:- to avoid proliferation of information technology equipment in the lawyers' office, the system should use a 'common terminal' approach ;

User interaction:- the user should be able to go on requesting further details dependent on the results of the retrieval so far;

Utilisation of resources:- since full-text information will be established on Prestel frames, this implies that frames will quickly be used up. Thus a rapid turnover of individual frames with information requested among many users will have to be ensured, with implications also for the pricing structure of such frames and the use of a printer attachment to the individual user's Prestel TV set terminal (note that all Figures showing system designs illustrated in the remainder of this paper do not, for simplicity, show the printer attachment which would undoubtedly improve the cost effectiveness of such a gateway service);

Record structure of information on Prestel frames:- there should be a means of accurately identifying an individual item of end-information (viz, a case reference) on which further details are required to be retrieved. This implies an extension of the current static CLARUS database structure to ensure unique indexing of individual items.

3. ALTERNATIVE SYSTEM DESIGNS

3.1 Fully manual system using human 'mid-user'

As shown in Figure 2, this relies crucially on the expertise of a skilled human 'mid-user' who moves freely between a Prestel editing terminal A and a full-text retrieval terminal B in response to verbal, real-time telephone communication and discussion with the Infolex gateway user. A and B are located physically next to each other (probably in the same office), but would be remote from both the "Duke" Prestel Update Centre (PUC) in London C and the full-text database housed on a timesharing mainframe facility D

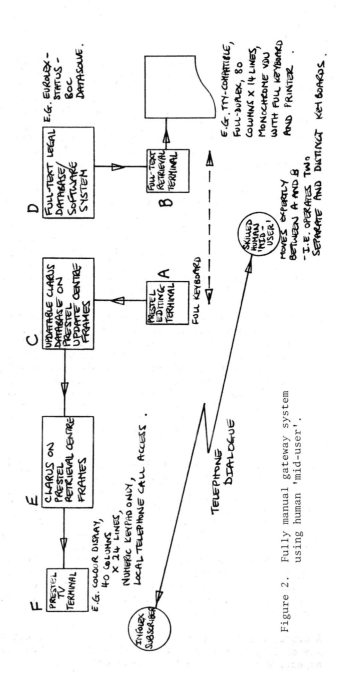

Figure 2.   Fully manual gateway system using human 'mid-user'.

(e.g. EUROLEX on BOC Datasolve's London computers). The
Infolex subscriber, also physically remote from the mid-user,
essentially need access only his local Prestel Retrieval Centre E
(PRC) - 16 of which spread round the UK now give local telephone
call access to over 60% of the telephone-subscribing population -
via his standard Prestel TV terminal F. With this, he accesses
Infolex frames on Prestel giving the fruits of his telephoned
requests for more details on items identified within CLARUS to
be extracted from D through B.

This design provides great comfort to the essentially non-
technical lawyer user (assumed unskilled in both computer
technology generally and the use of powerful full-text legal
retrieval software, e.g. STATUS, in particular), who may carry
out free and easy dialogue by telephone with the human mid-user.
He in turn would ideally be as skilled in assisting the lawyer
to formulate his legal research and retrieval problem as in the
purely technical manipulation of the keyboards of both the Prestel
editor and the full-text on-line terminal.

In this simple manual gateway system design, the mid-user
operator has the somewhat tedious, time-consuming and possibly
error-prone task of physically re-keying the text retrieved from
the on-line full-text service, and printed at its terminal, into
the PUC via the standard Prestel keyboard and editing software.
This further implies that, for simplicity and speed, the mid-
user enters the text in free sequential form, probably spread
across a series of successive Prestel frames of the same page
number, with little attempt at a high-quality layout, text
justification or indexed structuring and 'routing'.

3.2   Semi-automatic system: human mid-user assisted by all-in-one 'intelligent' Prestel editing/full-text retrieval terminal.

This design, as sketched in Figure 3, is essentially the same as
the manual system of 3.1, the significant difference being that
the skilled mid-user now has a single keyboard to operate. This
controls an 'intelligent' terminal capable of acting both as a
retrieval terminal for the full-text database and as a Prestel
editor. More importantly, the design of this intelligent
terminal configuration includes hardware for temporary storage
of data and software to re-format this data from the structure
of the on-line text retrieved into that suitable (and effective)
for input to Prestel.

A dramatic improvement in throughput over a purely manual system
may obviously be expected from this design. The 'user comfort'
aspect, with direct verbal communication and discussion over a

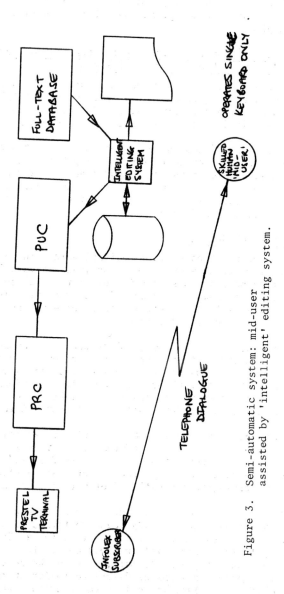

Figure 3.   Semi-automatic system: mid-user assisted by 'intelligent' editing system.

telephone link between the Infolex subscriber and human mid-user
is, however, maintained, and for this reason this design is likely
to prove the most acceptable and attractive in the legal
marketplace.

3.3 Fully-automatic system: intelligent editor/terminal driven by Prestel response frame.

With this design, illustrated in Figure 4, the human mid-user is
now no longer required to be a skilled full-text/Prestel editor
'consultant', but merely a keyboard operator who can at intervals
start required jobs at the intelligent terminal.

This terminal system is an enhancement of that used in 3.2:
it automatically collects Prestel response frames completed
by Infolex subscribers and in-gathered to the PUC and, driven
by the information contained therein, initiates the required
full-text retrieval, re-formats and inputs to the PUC using
Prestel editing software.

3.4 Prestel Gateway

Prestel UK and Prestel International were both launched as
'end information' sources in themselves. Bildschirmtext (Btx),
the Deutsche Bundespost version of British Telecom's Prestel
service, was, however, conceived from the start as, rather, a
'high-level selector' system into other existing 'Third Party
Databases' (TPD's) and computer systems.

Systems Designers Limited (SDL) enhanced the basic Prestel
viewdata software to create the Btx 'gateway' system, and
British Telecom has now re-purchased the software from Btx
which, with further UK-oriented technical amendments, and
possible improvements gained in the light of the Btx Market
Trial experience to date, will form 'Prestel Gateway' (PG).

It is understood that a PG Market Trial is anticipated to begin
late 1981-early 1982: the Information Providers who take part
will evidently have not only to possess Prestel/electronic
publishing skills and experience, but also mainframe computer
data processing/communications/software resources.

Very large database access, such as bibliographic databases
and timetables, have already been identified as a possible
application area for PG. The use of PG for an Infolex videotex
gateway to full-text legal information retrieval can thus be
seen as a natural, and ultimate, step in the development of
possible gateway designs as described so far in this paper. The
use of PG would also, it would seem, provide a neat way of meeting

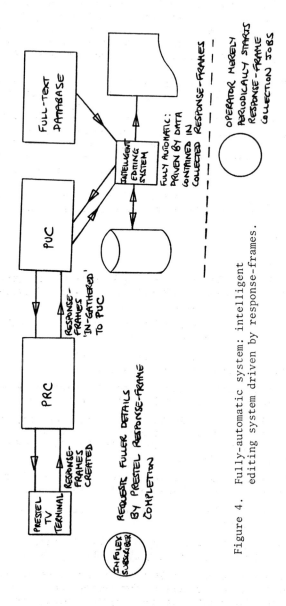

Figure 4. Fully-automatic system: intelligent editing system driven by response-frames.

the desirable objective of a single 'common terminal' approach
to on-line computer-based legal databases, an objective often
identified by The National Law Library (see (8) for example). Thus,
whilst EUROLEX uses a TTY-compatible terminal and LEXIS its own
special dedicated terminal, both databases could now in principle
be accessed via a Prestel TV set receiver, using PG.

The general network configuration envisaged for PG is sketched in
Figure 5. As reference (9) puts it "...TPD computers will be
owned and operated by organisations other than Prestel but they
will have to conform to a standard interface specification. In
particular the connection between the Prestel Information
Retrieval Centre and a TPD computer will be via PSS (Packet
Switched Service) and so the TPD will have to support the X25
protocol. In addition to X25 a higher level protocol called
the BT protocol (level 4-7 of the ISO Open Systems Architecture)
is also defined. As a matter of principle, international
standards will be adhered to wherever this is practical...."

REFERENCES

(1) "Infolex - Computerised Legal Information Retrieval on
Prestel, the Post Office's New Viewdata Service".
Law Society's Gazette, 29 November 1978.

(2) "Prestel - The Post Office's Viewdata Service".
Computers & Law, No.19, February 1979.

(3) "The Infolex 'National Law Library'".
The Law Librarian, 10, 2, August 1979.

(4) "Prestel and the law". Paper delivered at Viewdata '80
Conference, March 1980. Online Conferences Limited.

(5) "CLARUS, a Case LAw Report Updating Service, available on
Prestel, British Telecom's national viewdata service".
Proceedings of the "Lawyers in the 80s" Conference,
July 1980. Society for Computers & Law.

(6) "Viewdata and Teletext". The Solicitors' Journal,
27 June 1980. Office Technology Supplement.

(7) "Update on Prestel". Market Report No.23, June 1980.
ECC Publications.

(8) "A National Law Library - The Way Ahead".
Society for Computers & Law, February 1979.

(9) "Prestel Gateway to Third Party Databases". Proceedings
of a one-day conference for senior management held on
18th. March 1981, London. Systems Designers Limited.

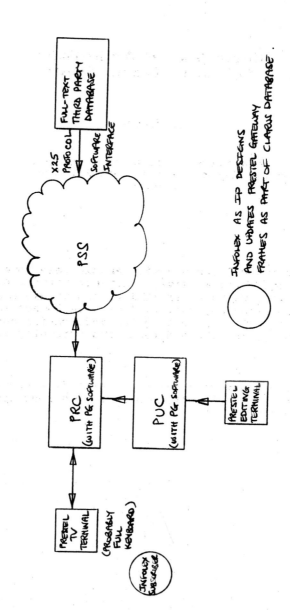

Figure 5.   Prestel Gateway.

Use of a Dedicated Machine Within
the Electronic Directory Project

J. Harivel

Technical Supervisor, Electronic Directory Project,
Cap Sogeti Logiciel, 5 rue Louis Lejeune, 92128 Montrouge,
Cedex, France

The Electronic Directory will enable telephone subscribers to consult a massive, fully-organized fund of
information. Using a terminal placed within reach of an
ordinary telephone, they will be able to access a collection of data duplicating the information contained
il all paper telephone directories currently in existence.

System implementation makes use of a disk subsystem and
transfers the host machine's screening function to the
disk subsystem.

INTRODUCTION

The Electronic Directory Service is designed for
gradual replacement of the use of paper directories
with - cost aside - are growing in information content
from year to year, making consultation by the user a
difficult and discouraging task.

When fully installed, the Electronic Directory should
offer a service which is at least equivalent to that
provided by present-day paper directories.

Videotex terminals, installed on subscriber's premises,
should also be accessible in post offices and selected
public places.

The network infrastructure and data processing resources employed are designed to offer a quality of service
surpassing levels currently available to subscribers.

The basic service offers the following features :

- subscriber search by name,
- subscriber search by profession or business
- subscriber search by telephone number
- billing information
- telephone company information
- multiple access to the most frequently-called emer-
  gency-service téléphone numbers.

This service is characterized by :

- information updating
- rapid response time
- inquiry assistance, particulary to help obtain information contained in the paper directory, but hard to
  find at present.

The Electronic Directory Service will also permit a decrease in information service personnel requirements.

1. SYSTEM SEARCH OPERATIONS

The system handles the following operations :

- Search for a known subscriber by use the following
  Level 1 criteria :

  1) Place   Place location consists of the determine
                of a geographic region for inquiry. This
                region may be a township, an urban pre-
                cinct or district, a group of towns sur-
                rounding a given city (county, region) or
                a rural crossroads site.

  2) Name   This may be either the exact or approxi-
                mative name of a person or the legal name
                of a business.

  These criteria may be supplemented by the following
  Level 2 criteria :

  3) Address

  4) Profession

  5) Given name

  These criteria will be used only to screen the
  response if the scope of preselection is too broad.
  They will be useable only if the relevant information
  is provided in directory listings by the telephone
  company (or PTT).

- Search for a known subscriber by the following Level
  1 criteria :

  1) 8 digit national telephone number.

- Search for a professionnal or business subscriber by
  use of the following Level 1 criteria :

  1) Place   Given in the form of locality or dis-
                trict. Locating accuracy depends on the
                region in question : city, town or rural
                area. The search is extended by inquiry
                in neighboring areas associated with the
                locality.

  2) Activity   Activity is given by an overlap of mul-
                tiple criteria :
                . element(s) from the list of professions
                  or trades
                . qualifier
                . trade name

On the basis of the location indicated in the request,
the Inquiry Center determines the Documentation Center
to be queried and sends on the inquiry information to
it. When the Docmentation Center receives a query, then
it is provided with inquiry-dependent information including :

- subscriber's name, as captured by the Inquiry Center
- subscriber's given name, as captured by the Inquiry
  Center
- location, fully coded for places with catalogued
  streets, and partially coded in other cases (township
  coded, streets non-coded)
- telephone number (8 digits)
- profession, coded
- trade name, coded
- qualifier, coded.

The query is completely formalized on the basis of the
selected search type prior to interrogation of the
database associated with the Documentation Center.

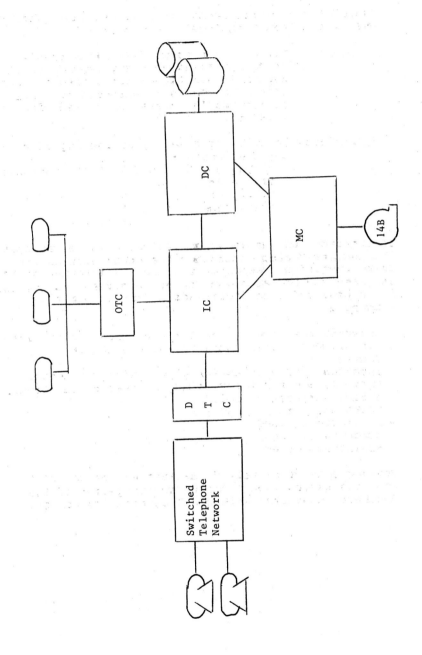

2. SYSTEM ORGANIZATION

The Electronic Directory's data processing system is made up of elements with logically share system functions and are interconnected via the directory network.

From the function standpoint, the Electronic Directory's DP system consists of the following components :

- directory terminal concentrator : DTC
- operator station terminal concentrator : OTC
- inquiry center : IC
- documentation center : DC
- management center : MC.

Directory terminal concentrator (DTC)

This component implements the link between the Directory system and the swithed telephone network.

It accepts subscriber calls and manages exchanges between directory terminals and the Electronic Directory DP system.

The DTC also manages the echo to the directory terminal on the basis of instructions received from the Inquiry Center.

During subscriber assistance by an information operator over a voice link, the DTC dials the operator station number.

Operator Station Terminal Concentrator (OTC)

This component manages exchanges between the Directory system and the information operator stations.

Information operators perform a twin function within the system :

- assistance to subscribers in case of difficulty in subscriber-system,

- updating of local documentation managed within the Directory system.

Inquiry center (IC)

This component is the element which dialogues with the subscriber. It helps the subscriber to formulate his request fully and correctly, i.e., to provide all information required to insure successful retrieval from the database. In particular, it not only acquires information, but also checks its validity. In case of ambiguity, it requests additional information from the subscriber. In case of difficulty, this component manages the information operator-subscriber link.

After having obtained the desired information, the Inquiry Center formats it before displaying it on the subscriber's screen.

The Inquiry Center also manages a local documentation base complementing that of the Documentation Center.

Documentation Center (DC)

This component is the Directory system's core element. It manages a database whose information corresponds to that contained in conventional paper directories (official listings, additional spacial listings provided by the telephone company or PTT marketing service).

Queries are submitted to the Documentation Center by the Inquiry Centers after validation and codification of subscriber requests.

Search operations performed by the Documentation Center are :

- alphabetic search
- professionnal search
- search based on known telephone number.

The Documentation Center also manages the pages of videotex information associated with listings.

Managments Center (MC)

This component provides the interface between the Directory system and the telephone company (or PTT) marketing services.

It accepts the listings and videotex information supplied by the "14 B" application, the PTT and telephone
company marketing services, formats them to meet system
requirements and updates information at relevant Documentation Centers.

It manages inter-center transactions.

It also manages and updates reference files, and transmits them to the relevant centers.

3. DOCUMENTATION CENTER

3.1 General description

The Documentation Center contains two MINI 6 processing
units operating in duplex mode and providing access to
a disk-based distributed database.

A processing and database-access chain includes :

- a front-end porcessor
- a duplicated MINI 6 computer.

interconnected by a high-speed link.

The front-end processor supports exchanges with the
external environment, IC and MC, via a transmission
network up of leased lines and TRANSPAC.

The MINI 6 processes inquiry transaction and updates
system databases.

The DC database is stored on :

- disk (capacity 256 megabytes)
- high-performance MOX disk subsystems.

The conventional disks support the videotex advertising
pages and their "pointer" modules. A disk is accessible
only by a single MINI 6.

The remaining disks support the kisting files. A duplicated access system permits access to the files from
either processing chain.

3.2 COPERNIQUE disk subsystem

3.2.1 General subsystem goals

The disk subsystem is designed to optimize apparent
times to the SMD-interface magnetic disk, in order to
enhance the performance of applications which are limited by these access times (and not by CPU performance).

This goal is achieved by the installation of the following functions :

- management of a high-capacity (1 to 16 megabytes)
  cache memory incorporated in the disk subsystem. At
  any given moment, this cache memory contains a subsystem of the sectors belonging to the various disks
  managed by the controller.

- optimization of information transfers as a function
  of the angular position of disks relatives to read-
  /write heads.

- simultaneous updating capacibility of two dishs with
  a single write request, for automatic save management.

- volume save/restore function using a save volume
  provided by the controller (n tracks by n tracks),
  using the cache memory as a buffer. Save/restore time
  is optimum - 10' for 60 useful megabytes - and is
  limited only by intrinsic disk characteristics
  (rotary speed, seek time).

3.2.2 Cache memory management

The cache memory is logically partitioned into a management area and a frame and segment area.

Upon system initialization, all non-defective segment
frames are free, and are chained in a free-frame queue.

Upon volume mounting, segments whose addresses are
memorized in a volume file are automatically transferred to the cache memory. These segments constitue the
"static" portion of the cache memory, and include all
segments subject to very frequent access (VTOC, index
tables, etc.).

Following this initialization, the free segment frames
are used for dynamic recopying of segment chains.

Two options are available for input to the cache memory
upon each read request. If "n" is the number of segments requested by the host computer :

a) Transfer of no less than 2 x n segments and no more
   than n + m segments into the cache memory.

   The actual number of transferred segments equals n =
   1 (1 $\leqslant$ m).

   The value of "l" depends on the waiting disk
   transfer requests and the angular position of the
   disk : if a disk is ready to perform a fresh
   transfer and the number of segments transferred into
   the cache memory for the current transfer operation
   is 2 n, the current transfer is halted and the new
   transfer is initialized. This option provides a
   continuous anticipatory effect, without
   significantly delaying another possible transfer.

b) Transfer of no less than n segments and no more than
   (n + m) segments to the cache memory.

   This option ensures that performances will never be
   degraded (in comparison with a cache-less solution)
   regardless of the circumstances, but does not
   garantee the anticipatory feature.

The cache memory very significantly enhances the average transfer rate in both cases. Option 1) and 2)
provide different responses to match special cases.

When the cache memory is full, an algorithm (LRU)
permits detertmination of the segment chain to be ele-
minated.

Segment chains to be rewritten are rewritten to disk in
deferred mode in ordre to optimize arm travel.

3.2.3 Active modules

Concepts

   Goals :

The active modules are designed to facilitate information retrieval from a set of data stored on magnetic
disk. Retrieval is performed by content according to a
"criterion".

   Search region :

A retrieval operation is performed on a search region
consisting of a number fo areas of a single disk.

Each of these areas is defined by segment number, with
a quantity of consecutive segments constituting the
area.

   Criterion :

The disk memorizes "listings", containing two types of
information :

- non selectable information, to which retrieval operations are hot applicable,

- selectable information, forming the object of retrieval operations. These retrieval operations
  consist in seeking in listings which comply with a
  given criterion.

The selectable information and criterion are broken
down into fields, each identified by a name. Fields
having identical criteria and selectable-information
names are compared character by character. The criterion contains function characters used when only a
portion of the field to be retrieved is known, or when
multiple-value fields are being sought.

Sample criterion :

DURAND / = DUPON%
end of work or joker

where / % = are function characters :
    / indicated an end of work
    % replaces one or more characters
    = indicates that DURAND/ and DUPON% are being si-
multaneously.

DURAND, DUPON, DUPONT, DUPONTEL match the criterion ;
DURAN, DURANDAL, LEDURAND or LEDUPON do not.

Retrieval :

Three function types are provided for active modules :

a) Read search

   The active module searches for listings in the
   search region which comply with the criterion.

b) Locating search

   The active model searches for a listing in the
   search region which complies with the criterion, and
   indicates its location within the area.

c) Blank search

   The active module searches for a blank of given
   length in the search region, and indicates its location.

Programming interface

General operating principles :

A retrieval operation performed by an active module covers a search region and is concluded by the transmission of a result.

The active module performs its retrieval operation in a concetenation of successive phases :

- loading of all or part of the region into the active module,
- search by criterion,
- transmission of results, as applicable.

This succession of phases may be repeated a number of times. When the area is exhausted or the results buffer is full, an interrupt is generated and send to the host computer processing retrieval results. At this stage, all information concerning the retrieval operation is consolidated in the host computer so that the retrieval operation may be resumed from the breakpoint upon a request sent to the active module.

The information will be :

- either fixed data (for all information defining the retrieval operation)
- or the result, together with information permitting its analysis (status words)
- or variables masked from the computer (from all information permitting resumption of an interrupted retrieval operation).

In the following schematic representation of the
retrieval operation, everything inside the dashed box
is internal to the MOX subsystem (disks + active
modules) ; the remainder is contained in the MINI 6
software.

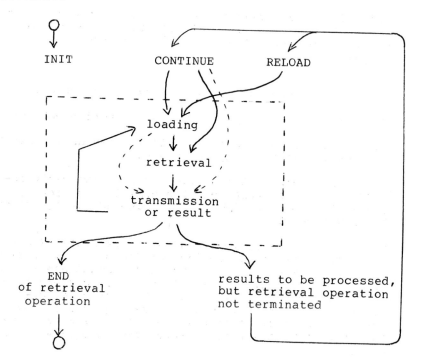

Active module programs :

The programs to be loaded into the active modules and constituting the various retrieval procedures are located in a file on one of the disks supported by MOX.

This file is initialized and updated by the host computer. Commands are also available to enable the host computer to load one of the file programs to an active module.

Mutual independence of disks and active modules :

The MOX subsystem supports disks and active modules.

Each disk and each active module is seen as a separate peripheral, each having an interrupt.

Commands issued to the active modules implicitly include disk read operation. The disk in question is physically (but not logically) occupied during the necessary read time.

Disk drivers and active modules are separate. Nonetehless, system software must handle problems or disk concurrency when a "active module" command and a "disk" command are acting on a single unit. Concurrent transfer requests are possible, but the controller does not guarantee the order in which these requests are executed. In case of updating, conflicts are managed by the host computer, which ensures the integrity of disk data.

Recognition commands are available for determination of the number, adress and size of active modules.

CONCLUSION

Retrieval by content, performed directy on disk read heads, presents numerous disadvantages :

- System design must be substantially reworked if the disk model is changed, or in case of very rapid technological development.

- A continuing adaptation of performances must be carried out between disk capacity and the processing capability of the associative system, and these two technologies are evolving in an independent manner.

- "On-the-fly" retrieval can be performed in a single pass only, or require a number of disk rotations.

- Data <u>integrity</u> can be guaranteed only in a <u>very</u> <u>expensive</u> manner by ECC, as the preparation/control/-correction system cannot be brought into effect.

The architecture adopted by COPERNIQUE is not subject to any of these disadvantages :

- Retrieval by content may be performed concurrently in the active modules, in one or more passes.

- The system guaranteeing data integrity may be very sophisticated and is implemented only once per system.

- Full buffering is provided between the disk and the retrieval systems. A number of disk models may be used.

- The cache memory substantially reduces arm travel and consequently increases apparent speed.

The directory system is being developed in two phases :

- a MOX simulation phase on MINI 6 (active module simulation)
- a phase with full utilization of MOX.

This technique will make it possible to validate the contribution, from the performance standpoint, of a dedicated machine for selective magnetic-disk retrieval operations.

BIBLIOGRAPHY

Electronic Directory System Specification - DGT/DAII, november 1979.

Information Retrieval for Cancer Therapy: Problems and Prospects

A. S. Pollitt

Senior Lecturer in Information Systems,
Huddersfield Polytechnic, UK

A large number of sources of information are available to the physician which may provide useful material to help in the treatment of cancer. This paper seeks to review the availability and modes of access to these sources, investigating the problems that exist and the prospects for improving information provision, concluding that the bibliographic systems, although more technically advanced and available than the recorded data, such as patient records, could still be better utilised.

1. INTRODUCTION

Many medical topics are emotive, none more so than Cancer which caused over 128,000 deaths in England and Wales in 1979(16) where the nature of the disease and the side effects of treatment are often distressing in the extreme. The variety of forms and manifestations of cancer and the historic division into medical specialities results in a wide range of different treatment methods. The three main divisions being Surgery, Radiotherapy and Chemotherapy with different combinations of treatment providing what some regard as the most promising results (8). The treatment may be palliative where the disease has progressed beyond the prospect of a cure, or it may be aimed at cure with a predictable measure of success, to imagine no prospect of recovery on the diagnosis of cancer is a myth which is slowly being dispelled.

In the United Kingdom, as in other countries, there are specialist treatment centres which seek to bring together facilities and expertise. Regional organisations have also been established which provide an appropriate administrative framework which can be used to foster collaboration on treatment methods, patient care, and the dissemination of information both within the profession and to the general public. There are large charities devoted solely to research into cancer, its nature, causes and possible treatment and in the United States there is a National Cancer Institute which concerns itself with all aspects of cancer.

The individual clinician, or a panel of clinicians where a multi-modal form of treatment is being considered, has the unenviable problem of prescribing appropriate treatment, monitoring the changing condition of the patient and modifying the treatment as necessary. The choice of treatment method is determined by relating patient history, presenting symptoms and the results of tests to information either immediately at the clinicians disposal, from training and experience or potentially available from a great variety of sources. The problems and prospects for improvement in access to these sources form the basis for this paper.

2. INFORMATION SOURCES

Identifying the possible information sources may not be too difficult (see Fig. 1). To assess the extent and utility of the different sources is however a task of much greater magnitude and to determine what would be the appropriate circumstance and level of use of each source for each individual is close to impossible. The education and experience of a clinician give rise to strong views on treatment methods and attitudes to the application of treatment as well as opinions on the utility of information sources and the need to search for information. Whilst efforts are made in the better provision of information it must be recognised that provision is not necessarily the nub of the problem of seeking to improve treatment which may lie in the very nature of the disease and the difficulty in defining better treatment or even in the educational processes and the traditional approach to identifying a disease and then treating according to that identification. To quote Gabrieli (5)

"Transition from the memory-based clinical medicine of the Gutenberg culture to the electronic information system may be closer to revolution than evolution. Values cherished for centuries such as rapid memorisation and effective recall will be replaced by judicious evaluation, rational decisions and crisp logic."

In the same paper Gabrieli identifies a "medical knowledge deficit" which he defines as "a difference between existing published knowledge and actual use of the knowledge in bedside decisions".

LIBRARIES (Local & Remote)	SPECIALISED INFORMATION SERVICES	DRUG INFORMATION SERVICES & COMPANIES
Journals, Books Reports Indexing & Abstracting Journals	Oncology Information Service Bulletins N.C.I. Cancergrams	Reports Company Reps. Newsletters
COMPUTER HELD DATABASES Cancerlit/Cancernet Clinprot/Medline Cancerproj/ Excerpta Medica and others		CANCER REGISTRIES Distillation of Patient Record Data
PERSONAL INFORMATION COLLECTION Journals Photocopies Bulletins Reports	COLLEAGUES Personal Collection Experience not documented	PATIENT RECORDS Hospital Case Notes Special Records Hospital Activity Analysis

Fig.1. Information Sources

Unfortunately this revolution is a long way off for practitioners
in the United Kingdom, perhaps not as far away for those in the
U.S.A. where the circumstances are more conducive to the
establishment of electronic information systems. There is in any
case an imbalance in the application of computer based systems
to the different sources that the clinician may wish to consult
which reflects the relative difficulties in bringing such systems
into being. A crude division of the information sources could be
made into Recorded Data (Patient Records, Cancer Registries) and
Literature (Libraries, Computer Held Bibliographic Databases,
Selective Dissemination of Information) where the latter finds
itself using a higher level of technology for access and consultation than the former.

Investigation into the nature and content of the recorded data
sources reveals various problems many of which are traditional
disadvantages of paper against electronic data storage, such as
limited access and difficulties in extraction and processing. In
addition there are problems of missing data either because at the
time it could have been recorded its future use was not anticipated,
or the effort required to complete all possible information was
deemed too onerous a task or simply that it was overlooked, basic
items such as sex of patient have been omitted from some records.
Extraction from patient records to provide data for an existing
computer system, the Hospital Activity Analysis, is selective on
an already limited amount of data and as such will not provide an
appropriate base for treatment review.

Entries to the various Cancer Registries do not necessarily include
treatment information and so may limit the use made to epidemiology
and mortality statistics although the potential role of the
registries is seen as the means to achieve treatment reviews (10) .
The follow-up of cases recorded in a registry may not be fully
achieved even when details of treatment are recorded leading to the
missing data problem mentioned above.

These problems do not in themselves inhibit the conversion into
computer based systems from paper files or from Batch systems to
Online although they will have an effect on the eventual utility
of the resulting sources. This situation may be different from
one part of the U.K. to another and markedly different to some
parts of North America. What is clear is that the revolution to
provide some form of integrated information system will only come
about with substantial investment and development. Examples of
what is technically possible are well described in the literature
(6,12,13) , but the global availability of such facilities faces
distinct economic stumbling blocks where the cost benefit equations
are illusive. Accounting procedures for medicine in the U.S.A. have
been one important factor behind the more advanced state of
electronic medical information systems in that country.

There are technical and intellectual problems which do confront the
developer of medical information systems and there is work which
seeks to confront these problems. One area of work is in
linguistics and the coding of medical information (9) , although in
cancer particular work has been done on classifying the nature,
site and stage of the disease (7) . A further problem area which
should not be ignored being that of privacy and confidentiality
 (17) and the related question of medical audit and peer comparison.

Access to the literature sources provides a marked contrast to
what has just been described in that there is ready access in an
interactive mode to large universal information collections (3)   ,
and the rest of this paper will concern itself with the problems
and future developments in this area.

3. BIBLIOGRAPHIC DATABASES

There is no single collection of references to all written articles
on cancer therapy and its related topics as several organisations
have been involved in collecting, indexing and providing independent
collections which display different characteristics of coverage
and access methods. The well established medical collections based
on paper abstracting and indexing journals such as MEDLINE from
Index Medicus and EXCERPTA MEDICA from Excerpta Medica are
supplemented by special cancer collections such as CANCERLIT which
may not have a paper equivalent. Six of these databases which
are probably the most important for searches on cancer therapy
topics are presented in Table 1. together with the originators of
each database and the suppliers who host the computer based
collections. It can be noted that no single supplier provides
access to all six collections although he may provide access to
several. The list of databases is certainly not exhaustive as
there are a number of related databases which may occasionally
prove useful such as TOXLINE from the National Library of Medicine.

3.1 COSTS OF SEARCHING

Table 1. also provides details of costs and reveals cost differences
between databases and,for a given database, between suppliers. It
does appear that those wishing to search for medical information in
the U.K. are at an outstanding disadvantage compared with their
counterparts in Germany or, even more strikingly, in the U.S.A..

The costs given in the table concern the time linked to the
supplier's computer and the amount of print-out generated during
and at the conclusion of a search. There have been some moves to
shift charging from the time spent connected to the computer onto
the amount of output in recognition of the great advantage of
interactive searching which is the ability to react to the response

Database Name & Producer	Subject	Supplier	Start Year Online	No Commitment MAX H($)	No Commitment MAX P(c)	No Commitment MIN H($)	No Commitment MIN P(c)	With Commitment MAX H($)	With Commitment MAX P(c)	With Commitment MIN H($)	With Commitment MIN P(c)
CANCERLIT National Cancer Inst. (N.C.I.)	Cancer	BLAISE	1963	86	29	31	29	72	29	24	29
		DIMDI	1963	20	05	20	05	-	-	-	-
		NLM	1963	15	15	8	15	-	-	-	-
CANCERNET Institut Gustave-Roussy	Cancer	QUESTEL	1968	57	13	49	13	48	13	43	13
CANCERPROJ N.C.I.	Cancer Ongoing Research	BLAISE	1977	86	29	31	29	72	29	24	29
		DIMDI	1974	20	05	20	05	-	-	-	-
		NLM	1976	15	15	8	15	-	-	-	-
CLINPROT N.C.I.	Clinical Protocols	BLAISE	-	86	29	31	29	72	29	24	29
		NLM	-	15	15	8	15	-	-	-	-
EXCERPTA MEDICA Excerpta Medica	Medicine	DIALOG	1974	65	20	50	20	60	20	50	20
		DIMDI	1978	54	15	54	15	-	-	-	-
MEDLINE National Library of Medicine (N.L.M.)	Medicine	BLAISE	1978	86	29	31	29	72	29	24	29
		BRS	1977	-	-	-	-	10	13	10	13
		DIMDI	1978	20	05	20	05	-	-	-	-
		NLM	1977	15	15	8	15	-	-	-	-

Supplier Key:- BLAISE - British Library Automated Information Service, London
BRS - Bibliographic Retrieval Services Inc., New York
DIMDI - German Medical Information Centre, Koln.
NLM - National Library of Medicine, Bethesda, U.S.A.
QUESTEL - Telesystemes Questel, Paris.

Table 1. Databases and Costs of Searching for Information on Cancer Therapy. (1)

to a prepared search statement which may result in the modification
of the search strategy,so for any given search the value to the
searcher may be more appropriately judged against the amount.
A basis for appropriate charging is,however,difficult to establish
using measures of time spent at a terminal and the amount of output
generated,as the same characteristics - e.g. long search time with
no output - may be found to represent satisfaction for one user -
not wanting to find references - and dissatisfaction for another
- under the impression that there is a key reference in there
somewhere.

It may not be possible to compare manual with computer searches on
a cost basis as often there is no manual alternative available,
access to the computer held collections requiring access to a
terminal and telephone facility. It is nevertheless interesting
to pose the question "What does it cost a doctor to perform a
limited manual search?" and the more interesting but sensitive
question "What does it cost for a doctor not to perform a search?".
The latter question enters the realms of continuing education
and the problem of appreciating when a computer or in general an
extensive literature search would be required. The earlier question
has been tackled in different subject areas with firm conclusions
as to the cost effectiveness of online searching (4)   . The more
highly paid the doctor or consultant the more cost effective the
online search. The second question requires a much more detailed
study that some doctors might consider to be too much of an
intrusion.

3.2 THE USE OF INTERMEDIARIES

Most searches of online bibliographic databases are performed by
intermediaries either in a library or information service where
the skilled intermediary endeavours to translate the stated
requirements of the doctor into suitable search statements and to
put these to appropriate databases. The skills of the intermediary
are based on several categories of knowledge acquisition, this may
be a haphazard or a deliberate process but in either case can rarely
be described as complete.

Knowledge of the subject domain of the search is the province of the
clinician who is unlikely to permanently exchange his stethoscope
for the computer terminal with present comparative rates of
remuneration let alone undergo a course in information science into
the bargain.

Knowledge of the controlled vocabularies such as Medical Subject
Headings (MeSH) for MEDLINE acts as a great boon to the intermediary
who is less able to converse with the enquirer on a given search
topic as this may act as the medium for interpreting the user

requirements and help in search expansion or contraction. The free
vocabularies used to access such as CANCERLIT,which has no
controlled vocabulary,allow the intermediary to return relevant
references without comprehension or any great effort, often to the
great delight of the clinician who sees a direct match between his
stated requirement and the retrieved references, all this in
deference to the enormous effort invested in controlled indexing
to improve search performance. An increased knowledge of the
subject area and the role of controlled and free vocabularies can
at one and the same time raise the quality of the search and cause
the user difficulties, in that the simplistic view of the
information store taken by a naïve intermediary is replaced by a
more profound appreciation of the scope of the systems as a whole
resulting in a better qualified but probably more involved response
to the user's original requirement.

Knowledge of terminal commands helps in the development and
execution of a search strategy as even a rudimentary search would
be impossible to perform without such knowledge. A careful choice
in the options available in such as printing can help in the
assessment of the progress of a search. These commands differ from
one system to another but as they contain many common features one
common command language is possible and such a language has been
implemented on Euronet.

One last category of knowledge is that which enables the intermediary to determine which of the available databases to search. This
category is probably the hardest to acquire as each search can be
different from any previous search and there may be no scientific
approach to selection based on anything other than a general idea
of the contents of each database. Very often it is not a matter of
coverage but of the availability of appropriate indexing and
retrieval features that dictates which database is to be searched.

The reluctance to search more than one database, given the costs
involved, is understandable yet studies have shown (14) that
multiple database searches retrieve extra relevant references for
a number of reasons. In retrieving information concerning patient
treatment what price do we pay for the relevant reference not
retrieved. The coverage aspect requires further illustration so
Fig 2. provides Venn diagrams representing the references added to
two of the major databases in Table 1 since 1978. Whilst the
number of articles added to CANCERLIT over this period is over
10 per cent. higher than those added to MEDLINE, considering only
articles concerning cancer therapy, there can be no assumption
that all the articles added to MEDLINE were also added to
CANCERLIT. The difference between the sets displayed in Fig 2.
may serve to illustrate the effect of indexing where the less
discriminating free text indexing takes no account of the main
subject of any article whereas controlled indexing does, which

suggests that quite different search results could be expected for the same question posed to each database.

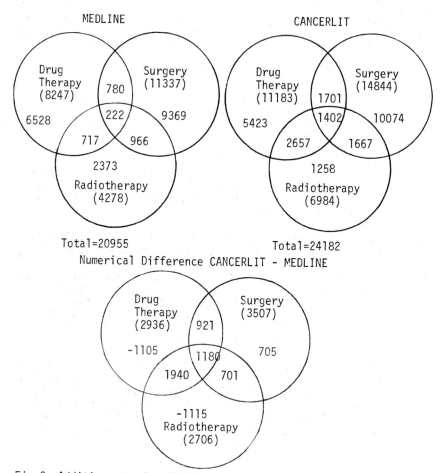

Fig.2. Additions to the MEDLINE and CANCERLIT databases of references to literature on cancer therapy made between February 1978 and February 1981.

The main conclusion about multiple database searching is that the results are better than single database searching, although there is yet only limited experience, due to the small number of searches, as to the cost-effectiveness of multiple searches. This problem may be more approachable with better host computer searching facilities when multi-file searching could be allowed where the order of cost is not simply a straight multiplication by the number of databases to be searched but some more acceptable figure. There are, of course, problems in translating between free and controlled vocabularies and to other controlled vocabularies which have been investigated (11).

3.3 THE COMPUTER AS INTERMEDIARY

The problem of deciding when an online search should be performed has already been mentioned. What is evident is that there are numerous occasions when a quick scan of the core journals in a subject area is performed by a clinician who seeks information to a pressing problem, this provides a poor substitute for the more comprehensive online search and could well be more expensive in real terms.   If this is the case then why are these scans made in preference to online searches.

There are several reasons why these scans are preferred, firstly the clinician has confidence in the core journals and is of the opinion that anything of note will have appeared in them, he also has confidence that a scan has been completed from having turned the pages and seen with his own eyes and finally the answer is immediate, if there is a relevant article it does not have to be sent for. This scan may well be less effort than putting the question, which may not be easy to specify, to an intermediary at a reasonably local information service.

All of the above reasons seem quite valid but we are confronted by the fact that not all relevant information is bound to be contained in a given number of core journals and secondly that the clinician should have better ways to spend his time compared with scanning journals in a retrospective search. One way of combining a more effective search with efficient use of the clinician's time may be to provide him with a local searching facility using the computer as intermediary.

Several developments are underway to help put the clinician in direct contact with the retrieval systems, probably the most notable is the introduction of a natural language input facility, using statements from the clinician instead of the usual boolean combination of search terms (2)   . This may well increase the acceptability of these systems, but the power of the formal systems in limiting or extending the search must suffer without some emulation of the skilled human intermediary. One particular area of development could be directed to building what may be termed an expert system as an intermediary which was able to acquire the knowledge, or part of the knowledge, of the human intermediary, with the potential to extend that knowledge at a personal level for each individual clinician.

Whilst these systems are only in the form of ideas there are certain features, such as handling the communications requirements of dialling and connection to remote systems which could be, and to some extent have been (18), automated or made easier. To incorporate some personal features onto a terminal such as the notification of articles held in a personal collection (15), does not require very much in the way of new technical development, yet the overall impression made on the searching clinician could affect the scope the powerful searching systems that already exist.

4. CONCLUSION

Eventually the recorded data collections referred to earlier will be searchable in the same manner as the bibliographic systems, only with much more powerful processing alternatives to allow statistical studies to be undertaken. For the time being, however, it is in the traditional writing of results to be published in journals, reports or conference proceedings and the subsequent indexing and maintenance of reference collections that provides what is generally accepted to be the most useful collection of information in the area of cancer therapy. To provide powerful online searching facilities is not enough to ensure that these facilities are used whenever they should be to, do that may require further levels of sophistication

ACKNOWLEDGEMENTS

Acknowledgements are due to Ann Whitcombe of the Oncology Information Service at the University of Leeds for work in deriving Figure 2., to Learned Information for allowing the use of the figures presented in Table 1., extracted from Online Review, and to the numerous doctors and surgeons who provided the background information for this paper.

REFERENCES

(1) Databases Online. Online Review 5(1) 61-83, 1981

(2) Doszkocs T.E., Rapp B.A.: Searching Medline in English. A prototype user interface with natural language query, ranked output and relevance feedback.
Proc Am Soc Inf Sci 16 131-137 1979.

(3) Doszkocs T.E. et al : Automated Information Storage and
Retrieval in Science and Technology
Science 208   25-30, 1980.

(4) Flynn T. et al : Cost Effectiveness Comparison of Online and
Manual Bibliographic Retrieval
Journal of Information Science 1(2) May 1979

(5) Gabrieli E.R. : Medical Information Systems, Health Records and
Knowledge Banks
Med Instrum 12 245-247, 1978

(6) Glicksman A.S., McShan D.: Interactive Computer Supported Tumor
Registry in the State of Rhode Island
Computer Programs in Biomedicine 8 274-283, 1979

(7) Harmer M.H. (Ed.) : TNM - Classification of Malignant Tumours.
UICC - International Union Against Cancer, Geneva 1978

(8) Israel L. : Conquering Cancer Penguin Books, London, 1980

(9) Kostrewski B.J., Anderson J. : Structural Considerations for the
Encoding of Medical Data: A Formalism for Medicine
Medinfo 79   841-852, 1979

(10) Maclennan R. et al : Cancer Registration and its Techniques
IARC Scientific Publications 21
International Agency for Research on Cancer, Lyon , 1978

(11) Marcus R.S. : A Translating Computer Interface for a Network
of Heterogeneous Interactive Information Retrieval Systems
SIGPLAN Not (U.S.A.) 10 (1) 2-12, 1975

(12) McShan D. et al : A New Interactive Computerized Data Base
and Retrieval System
Computer Programs in Biomedicine 9 284-292, 1979

(13) Meyers A. et al : A Technique for Analyzing Clinical Data to
Provide Patient Management Guidelines
Am J Dis Child   132   25-29, 1978

(14) Pollitt A.S. : Cancerline Evaluation Project Final Report
BLRDD Report Series No 5377 , University of Leeds 1977

(15) Pollitt A.S., Whitcombe A.C. : Personal Reference Collections
and Online Searching
Journal of Information Science 3 (1981)

(16) United Kingdom in Figures 1980 Edition, Government Statistical
     Service.

(17) Vuori H. : Privacy Confidentiality and Automated Health
     Information Systems
     Journal of Medical Ethics 3 174-178, 1977

(18) Williams P.W. : Microprocessor Assisted Terminals for Online
     Information Systems
     3rd. International Online Information Conference, London
     Dec. 1979

The Use of Distributed Data Bases in Libraries

M. Agosti

Lecturer, University of Padua, Italy

F. Dalla Libera

Lecturer, University of Padua, Italy

R. G. Johnson

Senior Lecturer, Thames Polytechnic, UK

Many libraries in both the public and academic sectors are organised in groups for purposes such as administration and the sharing of book stocks. This results in extensive sharing of information between a number of geographically separated libraries. From a study of the user requirements and library organisation the paper outlines the facilities required from a library computer system. It then shows that these facilities could be provided using a distributed data base. The paper surveys existing computer projects using distributed data bases and a classification is proposed for these projects.

1. Introduction
   This paper contains general observations on the application of
   distributed data base management systems (DDBMS) to libraries.

   The authors have examined two libraries in detail – those of the
   University of Padua in Italy and of Thames Polytechnic in
   London. The present organisation of these libraries is
   described in section 2.

   From these studies and other work, the user requirements outlined in section 3 have been obtained. The possible provision
   of these requirements by a computer is described in section 4.
   A survey of the existing research projects on distributed
   library and information retrieval systems is given in section 5.

2. The Environment: two different library systems
   2.1 The library system of the University of Padua
   The library system of the University of Padua consists of
   the central University library together with several other
   types of libraries. In decreasing order of size these are:
   (1) the central libraries of Faculties, (2) the multi-
   Institute libraries, whose aim is to collect in one
   physical place many documents of interest to several
   related Institutes, (3) the libraries of the individual
   Institutes, and finally (4) the libraries built-up by
   small groups of teachers and scientists inside the
   Institutes, without any official recognition.

   Geographically, all these libraries are within a 4 mile
   radius of the city centre. A more detailed description
   of the whole library system is in (Agosti et al, 1980).
   No institutional connections and cooperation exist among
   the libraries except for a union card catalogue of books
   and a union list of the scientific periodicals (a union
   list of the humanistic periodicals is under development).
   At present 68 libraries contribute to the maintenance of
   the card catalogue, consisting of almost one million cards.
   These libraries include the Padua Municipal and County
   libraries which also take part in this organisation. The
   catalogue is held in alphabetic name order, using photo-
   copies of the cards coming from each library. One card
   only is included in the catalogue, with the marks of all
   the libraries where the item can be found. Only one copy
   of this very large catalogue exists, held in the University
   library. Consequently the user has to go into that library
   to consult it. However, the union list of periodicals is
   available in every library.

   2.2 Thames Polytechnic library organisation
   The Polytechnic has three main sites each with a library,
   holding in total 165,000 volumes. There are two libraries
   in Woolwich, about $\frac{1}{2}$ mile apart and another 7 miles away

at Dartford. In addition small specialist libraries exist
in individual departments but books in these libraries are
not publicly available and will not be considered further.

The book stock is divided into two, the collections at
Woolwich and Dartford being regarded as independent.
Naturally, however, the proportion of books in different
subject areas reflect the topics taught at the different
sites. However, at Woolwich, the books are divided between
the two libraries, by allocating certain ranges of Dewey
numbers to one library and the remainder to the other.
This is done by the subjects taught on each site. However,
major difficulties exist in areas, such as computing,
which are on a very large number of syllabuses.

A union catalogue exists on microfiche of all acquisitions
since 1977. Books acquired prior to that exist on a card
catalogue, copies of which are held in both libraries in
Woolwich. A separate card catalogue exists at Dartford.

2.3 Union catalogue: advantages and disadvantages

The union catalogues developed by groups of cooperating
libraries are relevant to this discussion because they
represent a first attempt to make available the catalogue
information to the users of the "network" of libraries.

The principal advantage is that the user can find out
whether a specific item is held by a library, without
having to examine that particular library's catalogue.
The disadvantages of the union catalogue depend on the
way in which it is compiled rather than on its conception.
Two specific disadvantages are, firstly, that it does not
contain the information about all the books of the
institution (the information of the books in the unofficial
libraries are not inserted in this catalogue) and secondly
that the cataloguing work is not always correctly shared,
delaying some material entering the union catalogue.

There are several examples of cooperative library
organisations, which make available to the users machine
readable union catalogues. One of the most important is
the OCLC (Ohio College Library Center) in the United
States of America (Allison et al, 1979).

3. User requirements

The library users can be divided into four groups, the
librarians, the academic staff, the students and the institutional administrators.

3.1 The Librarian

The librarian is requested to interact with:
a) the institutions administration for:
  - management of the inventory

      - accounts for books and journals
      - renewal of current subscriptions
      - acquisition of books and other material.
  b) users including lecturers, researchers and students
     inspection copies
      - planning of acquisition: purchases, end of subscript-
       ions
      - interface between document archives and user require-
       ments
      - management of loan and documents for examination
      - management of photocopy service.
  c) the library catalogues
      - acquisition and examination of general documentary
       material
      - different types of cataloguing, taking into account
       the requirements of the priveleged users such as
       scientists and students as well as indicating basic
       and advanced research documents. Moreover a strong
       coordination is required among the individual
       libraries to get a uniform type of classification of
       similar disciplines, thereby ensuring the creation of
       a useful union catalogue
      - allocation
  d) other libraries within the institution
      - periodical production of bibliographic references
      - coordination for acquisition and loan schedule
       national and international library organisations
      - acquisition and exchange of reference books, for both
       general and specific information
      - dissemination of bibliographic information

3.2   The lecturer
     These users interact with:
     a) the librarians
       - collaboration on the acquisition programme
       - acquiring of material for examination, borrowing of
        books and photocopies.
     b) Catalogues and other library services
       - retrieval of documents relevant to some specific
        topics, inside a single library or the whole library
        system (not deterministic retrieval)
       - the use of general or specific references of national
        or international organisations
       - use of online bibliographic data bases services
        (Hall, 1977; Hall et al, 1981).
     The research student is similar to this user.

3.3   Students
     The student, like the lecturer interacts with the librarian
     and the catalogue. Nevertheless his retrieval work is
     mainly oriented towards his course, rather than research

material.

3.4 Central Administration

The central administration determines local regulations for the operation of the libraries, and oversees their implementation. In addition, there are often requirements for the maintenance of an inventory of the library and its contents for the purposes of auditing.

4. Technical requirements for DDB in libraries

In a distributed library contect:

1) data is distributed over different sites,
2) users need local access to the information in each library, and also should have easy selective access to the material on different fields of knowledge, held in other libraries. Union catalogues of books and periodicals are maintained for this purpose,
3) the central Administration has to control and oversee the whole library collection.

In this contect it seems natural to plan the application of a DDBMS to manage the local application and the global access to the information in a transparent way to the different types of user. In fact a DDBMS is a system which manages data physically stored in different sites connected by a communication network. The data in the system should be logically integrated to enable global access to be made to the information. The data allocation should be transparent to the user. The consistency and the availability of data must be guaranteed in the event of a crash of a local system or a network failure (Draffan et al, 1980). In this particular kind of application the DDB has to support the administration of the local library, global access from each library to the bibliographic information, and a unified inventory. However, the design of the global architecture of the system may be affected by the previous existence of heterogeneous local computer systems already running at some sites. For the integration of these existing systems it will be necessary to create a mapping schema with which to translate each local schema.

4.1 Distributed and replicated data

A bibliographic DDBMS has to manage data of two different types: data for administrative purposes and data for information retrieval purposes. This functional partition of the whole record representing each document can affect the physical data distribution and replication.

A lossless vertical fragmentation can be used in the data distribution (Dayal et al, 1978): the administrative fragment is specific for each document at each owner site, while different copies of the information fragment can be allocated to different nodes.

It will normally be more efficient for a copy of the file of a specific discipline to be allocated to the node where the users have most frequent access to the information. In systems with too many inquiries relative to the number of updates the amount of communication among nodes can be minimised in this way. To improve system performance, particularly when using small computers, it is possible to choose to delay updating multiple copies of a file, such as catalogue details. The updates are then carried out altogether when the system is not busy.

4.2 Query language

The main facilities required of a query language for such a system are:

1) the user query language has to be independent of the site, while the format of the answer should be the same at each site,
2) the answer should indicate at which libraries the document is available,
3) the user should be able to reserve the selected document or to obtain a photocopy.

The queries for bibliographic information retrieval are likely to be mainly casual, while the queries for administrative information will be mainly recurrent.

4.3 Operative aspects

The operative aspects mainly concern the maintenance of the consistency and availability in a multi-user/multi-site environment. One characteristic of the application is the need for only periodic updates of data rather than simultaneous update of all copies. A periodic strategy can be to use off-line update and refresh (i.e. during the night). In this context specific mechanisms of concurrency control do not have to be implemented.

Only authorised users should be allowed to access administrative information, since without developing sophisticated algorithms, it is difficult to restrict access to only parts of records. No privacy mechanism are normally required for bibliographic information.

5. Study of the projects on bibliographic DDB

A classification scheme has been developed for the current bibliographic DDBMS projects. The classification takes particular account of the architectural characteristics of these systems.

The proposed classification scheme is:

A - Information Retrieval Systems (IRS)
    A1 - Distributed access to centralised data.

A2 - Distribution of an IRS.
A3 - Systems integrating heterogeneous IRS.
A 4 - DDBMS designed for IR purposes.
B - Data Base Management System (DBMS)
    B1 - General-purpose DDBMS used in an IR context.

A - Information Retrieval Systems (IRS)
    A1 - Distributed access to centralised data
    The closely-coupled multiple mini-computer system, which
    has been implemented at the Scicon Limited of London (Bird,
    1978), can be inserted in this class, because its config-
    uration to the outside world may resemble a single large
    computer but in this system there is a degree of functional
    separation between different machines and individual
    machines have specialised functions.

    This implementation consists of seven PDP-11 computers
    connected together by short lines with high data transmission
    rates, where the data base is distributed over the three
    file processing machines to enable parallel retrieval
    functions to be executed.

    A2 - Distribution of a particular IRS
    The SYSIDORE system can be included in this class (Karmouch,
    1980a; Karmouch, 1980b; Le Bihan et al, 1980). It is an
    experimental system, developed at the University of
    Toulouse in France, for interactive retrievals in a
    distributed environment consisting of a set of local
    homogeneous data bases managed by the MISTRAL information
    retrieval system (MISTRAL, 1978). The SYSIDORE prototype
    runs on IRIS 80 computers connected to the CYCLADES network.

    The node user has a global view of information, even if
    that information is distributed on several sites. The end
    user can have this global view of information, because the
    distributed access system is replicated in every node, and
    the distributed access system is connected to a user inter-
    face managing a catalogue of all available data bases in
    every node. When the end user wants to retrieve information
    from a global file on a particular subject, for example
    Computer Science, he has to supply only the name of this
    file. The distributed access system will then connect the
    user to the pertinent local data bases. In fact the data
    base catalogue avoids making connections to nodes which
    have no pertinent local data bases. End user queries
    containing an incorrect data base name are not processed
    since the error is detected in the local system. The data
    base catalogue must be regularly updated, but this update
    does not seem to be very heavy.

    At present a second SYSIDORE multi-user version is being
    developed.

A3 -<u>System integrating heterogeneous IRS</u>
An example of such a system is the SCOttish Libraries
Co-operative Automation Project (SCOLCAP) (Gallivan, 1978;
Royan, 1977; Royan, 1978; SCOLCAP, 1979).

The replication, fragmentation and partitioning approaches
to the distribution of data can be seen within SCOLCAP. An
example of replication is the treatment of the Potential
Requirements File (PRF). The PRF is the body of data most
likely to be utilised in any new cataloguing. An example
in SCOLCAP of fragmentation is in the treatment of local
data, where the information on a book which is of interest
only to one library is only held at that site. The example
of partitioning is the separation of the conceptual
catalogue into the cataloguing in process data base and the
computer output microfilm sequences.

SCOLCAP will be a star network and it will be connected to
the star network of BLAISE (British Library Automated
Information SErvice) to form part of a hierarchical network
(Holmes, 1978). In fact if a user search fails on the
SCOLCAP files, it will be automatically switched to BLAISE,
without any need for user intervention. The mechanics of
the distributed data base will remain transparent to the
user. On request the user will be connected directly to
BLAISE.

Three other projects can be included in this class. They
are very different in their design characteristics but the
final result of each one is an interface, implemented as a
separate computer system, which connects heterogeneous
centralised IRS into a network through which information is
readily retrieved by hiding system differences and providing
other user aids. The end user attempting to retrieve
information uses the same query language from each node.
The stand-alone interactive systems are utilized without
modifications. The computer interface is intended to
achieve compatibility among systems of heterogeneous hardware and software components.

One of these projects has been developed at the Laboratory
for Information and Decision Systems of M.I.T. The
experimental interface CONIT, (COnnector for Networked
Information Transfer), has been implemented on the M.I.T.
MULTICS computer system(Marcus et al, 1979; Marcus, 1980).
The systems included in the network were ORBIT (Systems
Development Corporation), DIALOG (Lockheed), and MEDLINE as
implemented at two locations: the National Library of
Medicine and the State University of New York.

The second project has been developed at the "Laboratoire
de Recherche en Informatique" of the University of Paris-Sud.

This software has been planned for the co-operation of
information retrievel systems and centralised bibliographic
DBMS (Bassano, 1979). Currently, an experimental single
site system is working with an ADABAS implementation on an
IBM 370/168.

The last is the standard language CCL (Common Command
Language) defined in the EURONET context to make easy the
communication with each IRS in the European network. Each
host has to develop an interface between his system and
CCL. For example, ELISIR (EURONET Language Interface
Software for Information Retrieval) is the preprocessor
which implements the interface between the CCL and the
IRS SEARCH for UNIVAC 1100 computers (Schreiber et al, 1980).

A4 - DDBMS designed for IR purposes
The MAGIDOC REPARTI system, which has been designed at the
University of Toulouse in France (Karmouch, 1979), can be
inserted in this class, because all the parts of this
system have been designed to constitute a new distributed
data base management system used solely for IR purposes.

The basic aim of the project is that the on-line user sees
the system as a global one, but the system is formed by
local homogeneous data bases at several geographic
locations. Each data base is updated only by the owner,
therefore all other access will be read only, thereby
avoiding the problem of deadlocks.

The local DBMS is the MAGISTRAL system, which has been
specially developed and which runs in batch mode. The
software for communication between the different nodes of
the network is not available.

B - Data Base Management Systems (DBMS)
B1 - General-purpose DDBMS used in a IR context
The prototype application of the general-purpose FRERES
system can be inserted in this class (Bosc, 1980a;
Bosc, 1980b; Le Bihan et al, 1980).

This application is concerned with the management of a
distributed union catalogue of periodicals. The user can
retrieve detailed lists of journals currently held by each
library.

The FRERES system has been developed at the Institut de
Recherche en Informatique et Systèmes Aléatoires (IRISA)
of the University of Rennes in France and it runs on IRIS 80
computers within the CYCLADES network. The common data
model chosen is the hierarchical model. The contents of
the local data bases are expressed in hierarchical schemas.
These local data bases are assumed to contain information
concerning the same data objects. So, the distribution can

be expressed by simple rules. Both a user query language and an intermediate language are processed by every local and heterogeneous DBMS.

The IRISA, the Orsay library, the Institut de Programmation of Paris VI University and the INRIA Documentation Centre have taken part in this prototype application.

6. Conclusions

This paper has analysed the requirements of two academic libraries, but the principles can be applied to many types of libraries and indeed to other types of organisations with similar information needs.

In our opinion, a bibliographic information retrievel system, similar to those described above, will not be realised in the immediate future. This is due more to coordination problems among libraries (even within the same University) than to lack of suitable data management systems, which are being developed at present. A discussion of the coordination problems of different libraries can be found in (Salton, 1979).

Work has to be done also on user requirements. However, it should be noted that more and more attention is being paid to this subject by computer scientists, (Marcus et al, 1979).

In spite of the present difficulties we believe that the technologies of distributed data base could represent, in the future, a significant support for the efficient use and management of bibliographic information.

Acknowledgments

The research of M.Agosti and F.Dalla Libera was supported by the Italian National Research Council (C.N.R.), "Progetto Finalizzato Informatica", sub-project DATANET; Distributed Data Base, under Contract No.80.01889.97.

References

(Agosti et al, 1980) M.Agosti, F.Crivellari, F.Dalla Libera, F.Gosen, G.Gradenigo. 1979 Report of the Scientific Computer Centre Team of the University of Padua for the Italian National Distributed Data Base Projects, DATANET (PFI, C.N.R.). February 1980, pp.96 (in Italian).

(Allison et al, 1979) A.M.Allison, A.Allan (eds.). OCLC: A National Library Network. London, England, Mansell, 1979, pp.248.

(Bassano, 1979) J.C.Bassano. Logiciel autoadaptatif pour un reseau de systemes documentaires correles. Rapport de Recherche No.50, L.R.I., Universite de Paris-Sud, Septembre 1979, pp.39.

(Bird, 1978) B.D. Bird. A Distributed Data Base and Information Retrieval System. EUROCOMP 78 (Proceedings of the European Computing Congress 1978), Uxbridge, England, Online, 1978, pp.565-580.

(Bosc, 1980a) P.Bosc. An Overview of FRERES: A System to Interrogate Distributed Data. Report EVA-I-005, IRISA, University of Rennes, France, January 1980, pp.13.

(Bosc, 1980b) P.Bosc. The Distributed Interrogation System FRERES. Distributed Data Bases, C. Delobel and W.Litwin (eds.), North-Holland, 1980, pp.361-363.

(Dayal et al, 1978) U.Dayal, P.A.Bernstein. The Fragmentation Problem: Lossless Decomposition of Relations into Files. Cambridge, MA, Computer Corporation of America, Technical Report CCA-78-13, November 15, 1978, pp.80.

(Draffan et al, 1980) I.W.Draffan, F.Poole (eds.). Distributed Data Bases. Cambridge, England, Cambridge University Press, 1980, pp.x+378.

(Gallivan, 1978) B.Gallivan. SCOLCAP and its Role in the Emerging National Network. PEEBLES 78 (Proceedings of the 64th Annual Conference of the Scottish Library Association), A.G.D. White (ed.), Glasgow, Scotland, Scottish Library Association, 1978, pp.77-87.

(Hall, 1977) J.L.Hall. On-Line Information Retrieval Sourcebook. London, England, Aslib, 1977, pp.xii+267.

(Hall et al, 1981) J.L.Hall, M.Brown. Online Bibliographic Databases: An International Directory (2nd ed.). London, England, Aslib, 1981, pp.xxx+213.

(Holmes, 1978) P.Holmes. BLAISE and its Role in the National Library Network. PEEBLES 78 (Proceedings of the 64th Annual Conference of the Scottish Library Association, A.G.D. White (ed), Glasgow, Scotland, Scottish Library Association, 1978, pp.67-76.

(Karmouch, 1979) A.Karmouch. Exploitation en conversational (sous temps partage) de bases documentaires reparties sur un reseau d'ordinateurs. These 3e cycle Universite Paul-Sabatier, Toulouse, France, June 1979, pp.x+201 et annexes.

(Karmouch, 1980a) A.Karmouch. SYSIDORE: Systeme de selection d'information documentaire repartie. Distributed Data Bases, C.Delobel and W.Litwin (eds), North-Holland, 1980, pp.365-367.

(Karmouch, 1980b) A.Karmouch. Le systeme de selection d'information documentaire repartie: SYSIDORE. Project SIRIUS, INRIA, rapport, June 1980, pp.v+85.

(Le Bihan et al, 1980)   J.Le Bihan, C.Esculier, G.Le Lann,
W.Litwin, G.Gardarin, S.Sedillot, L.Treille.   SIRIUS: A French
Nationwide Project on Distributed Data Bases.   Sixth International
Conference on Very Large Data Bases, Montreal, Canada, 1-3 October,
1980, pp.75-85.

(Marcus, 1980) R.S.Marcus.   Search Aids in a Retrieval Network.
Proceedings of the 43rd ASIS Annual Meeting, A.R. Benenfeld and
E.J.Kazlauskas (eds), White Plains, NY, Knowledge Industry
Publications, pp.394-396.

(Marcus et al, 1979) R.S.Marcus, J.F. Reintjes. Experiments and
Analysis on a Computer Interface to an Information Retrieval
Network. Report LIDS-R-900, Laboratory for Information and
Decision Systems, M.I.T., Cambridge, MA, April 1979, pp.iv+127.

(MISTRAL, 1978) MISTRAL. Manual d'utilisation. Paris, France,
La Documentation Francaise, 1978, pp.52.

(Royan, 1977) B.Royan. SCOLCAP - "But I Thought that was an
Online System". MICRODOC, Vol.16, No.3, 1977, pp.82-89.

(Royan, 1978) B.Royan. Distributed Data Base in a Library
Context: the SCOLCAP System. Preprint of ICMOD 78 Conference
Proceedings, Milano, Italy, 29-30 June, 1978, pp.305-315.

(Salton, 1979) G.Salton. Suggestions for Library Network Design.
Journal of Library Automation, Vol.12/1, March 1979, pp.39-52.

(Schreiber et al, 1980) F.Schreiber, C.Difilippo, M.Zagolin.
Un preprocessor per l'interfacciamento di distemi eterogenei di
Information Retrieval su una rete di calcolatori. Proceedings of
AICA '80 Conference, Vol.II, Bologna, Italy, 29-31 October, 1980,
pp.1245-1263.

(SCOLCAP, 1979) SCOLCAP. On-Line in the North. Report No.118,
SCOLCAP, National Library of Scotland, Edinburgh, 1979, pp.17.

Part 12
Computers in Developing Countries

A Profile of the Application of Computers in ASEAN Countries

K. Venkata Rao

Senior Lecturer, National University of Singapore, Singapore

There has been an increasing awareness of the potential role of computers in the economic development of the ASEAN region during the last few years. The liberal and bold policies of the ASEAN governments have largely contributed to the transfer of computer technology from the developed countries. The successful completion of the computerisation plans and the growth of software industry during the decade of 1980s depend on the availability of adequate number of qualified and trained computer professionals.

2. BACKGROUND OF ASEAN ECONOMY

The ASEAN (Association of South East Asian Nations), comprising of Indonesia, Malaysia, Singapore, Thailand and Philippines, was established in 1967 as a regional group with the stated objective, amongst others, of accelerating the economic growth, social progress and cultural development of the region through joint ventures.

The ASEAN countries (except Singapore) with their rural oriented agricultural economies believed in the early years of their independence, that industrialisation would lead to rapid economic development. After some initial disappointments, they realised that agricultural output and productivity must be increased, so that the surplus labour could be deployed for industrialisation. The early industrialisation consisted of simple manufacturing industries based on agricultural raw materials - saw milling, sugar and copra drying, rubber processing, rice milling, etc. In Singapore, however, the industries are more sophisticated and technologically advanced - oil refineries, ship building, electronics, precision instruments, etc. Subsequently, more modern and large scale import substituting industries were set up, and by the end of 1960s, due to the liberal policies adopted by the ASEAN governments towards foreign enterprises, creating a healthy investment climate, more sophisticated industries - automobile assemblies, machine building, electronics, etc. - were established by the foreign companies under different forms of ownership and control. The efforts of ASEAN as a whole towards industrialisation has been quite impressive, which is evident from the table below (Table 1).

Table 1

	1960-70 average annual growth rate %	1970-78 average annual growth rate %	1978 % distribution of GDP			
			A	I	M	S
Indonesia	3.5	7.8	31	33	9	36
Malaysia	6.5	7.8	25	32	17	43
Philippines	5.1	6.3	27	37	25	38
Singapore	8.8	8.5	2	35	26	63
Thailand	8.2	7.6	27	27	18	46

(Legend):

A = Agriculture
I = Industries
M = Manufacturing
S = Services

(Source: World Bank, World Development Report 1980)

The ASEAN countries embarked on new policies and strategies, following the international and internal economic environment after the oil crisis in 1973. They are aimed at generating more employment and greater income re-distribution, and lay emphasis on self-reliance, greater use of domestic resources and indigenous technology. The development strategies concede that the economic problems transcend national interests and hence the need for regional and international co-operation. The ASEAN governments believe that the economic growth and development are important for the region's social and political stability and the well being of its nationals.

The ASEAN economic background is presented as a backdrop in order to consider the role of computer technology and the prospects of exploiting this new and exciting field for a rapid economic growth and development of the region. One of the reasons for the slow economic growth of developing countries is the information gap, which is largely responsible for their inability to make timely adjustments and the restructuring of economic policies. The effective role that computers can play in bridging the information gap, in terms of timely availability of interpreted economic data relating to the various sectors of the economy for the policy/decision makers, was not well recognised until late sixties. A more sustained approach to the harnessing of computer technology for better management of economic resources is more evident since 1975.

3.   DAWN OF THE COMPUTER ERA

The early 1960s marked the beginning of the computer era in ASEAN. During the first decade, the number of computers in each of the ASEAN countries hardly crossed the single digit figure. Since 1975, there is a marked increase in the number of computer installations in all the ASEAN countries. The phenomenal growth in the number of computer installations in the last three years can be seen from the following table (Table 2).

Table 2

	1978	1979	1980
Indonesia	15	102	195
Malaysia	70	175	420
Singapore	98	228	350
Thailand	75	112	300
Philippines	196	286	409

(Source: Asian Computer Year Book 1979-80 for the data relating to 1978 and 1979. Data for 1980 obtained from the presentations at the 3rd Conference of SEARCC at Jakarta by the Presidents of Computer Societies in ASEAN).

The mini computers account for a large number of the total
installations during the last two years. The increase in the number
of computers do not appear to have any relationship to the size or
the economic resources of each country. In the wake of increasing
number of installations, computer related activities, such as,
computer and software consultancy services, data preparation
services, ancillary equipment and stationery supplies and services,
service bureaus and computer training services have emerged in a
large measure. The following table (Table 3) summarises the number
of establishments offering these services.

Table 3

	Computer Manufacturers/ Representatives	Equipment Supplies/ Services	Service Bureaus	Computer Consultancy Software houses	Data Preparation Centres	Computer Training Centres
Indonesia	13	5	5	8	2	7
Malaysia	12	8	5	4	3	3
Singapore	23	14	5	10	5	4
Thailand	14	5	3	3	1	4
Philippines	19	11	19	7	8	2

(Source: Asian Computer Year Book 1979-80)

The early computer applications in all the ASEAN countries comprised
the routine accounting and administrative tasks on batch processing
basis. Over the years, the range of computer applications has
increased to include more sophisticated and dedicated applications -
project management and control; automated mainframe engineering and
maintenance; Discrete Simulation for Refining Plant Scheduling;
Vessel Management Information System; Remote Entry Shipping System;
Reservoir Simulation System; On-line Banking System; Logistics, etc.
A survey of the current computer applications in ASEAN indicate that
industry, transport, communications, banking and trade are the main
sectors of the economy which employ computer technology in varying
degrees of sophistication. The impact of the computers is evident
only in the urban centres; the agriculture-oriented ASEAN countries
are yet to tap the computing power for improving agricultural
productivity and output.

4.   COMPUTERISATION PLANS FOR THE 1980s

ASEAN's computerisation plans for the 1980s cover a wide spectrum of
the sectoral applications. The Institute of Agriculture at Bogor in
Indonesia, in conjunction with USAID, has initiated steps for using
computers in the various developmental projects - agricultural
research, plantation management and livestock breeding. The projects
in the area of environmental control include natural resources
management, population control, energy planning and management,
regional planning and oceanographic studies. Indonesia, with the aid

of the domestic satellite PALAPA, plans to expand its telecommunications using computer technology. The Malaysian government has set up MAMPU (Malaysian Administration Modernisation and Planning Unit) to evolve a proper program for the computerisation of the various developmental activities in the different sectors of the economy. It has identified the need for improving data communication facilities which is considered vital for the use of computers on a wider scale.

The future plans, in Thailand, emphasise the on-line applications in the manufacturing and service sectors. The accent, in Philippines, is on more progressive use of computers in its various developmental projects through a more rational use of its present computer resources. In Singapore, the government has set up several system study teams to identify specific computerisation plans in the ministries of National Development, Finance, Environment, Communications, Home Affairs, Health and Social Services. Similar studies are already in progress in the ministries of Trade & Industry, Defence and Education. The national airline (SIA) has installed two large mainframe computers (IBM 3031 and Itel AS/5) for cargo reservation & handling, control engineering maintenance, and inventory planning & control. It also proposes to use the computer system to support a communication network of some 2000 visual display units all over the world. The Telecommunications Authority of Singapore (Telecoms) plans to expand its current uses of computer for improving its telephone services. The future plans aim at computerising all its information processing systems with extensive use of the most sophisticated technology, and a beginning has already been made with the introduction of computer-oriented Telefax and Telepac services. In the long term, Telecom's objective is to integrate voice, image (video) and data (computer) services in a total communications network, employing fibre optic technology. The multi-airline reservation system is another long term project.

Banks and financial institutions have exploited the computer technology for providing efficient customer services. The immediate future plans include the extension of the installation of more and more Automatic Teller Machines (ATM) by the various major banks, a computerised inter-bank cheque clearing system, and to develop eventually a national banking network which can be connected to similar banking networks in other countries. This is expected to enable the banks to exploit the time zone advantage. In the private sector, widespread computerisation plans are under various stages of implementation in the hotel, manufacturing, trade and other service organisations.

5.   TRANSFER OF TECHNOLOGY

The liberal policies of the ASEAN governments towards foreign investors and the presence of multi-nationals in this region has largely contributed to the transfer of computer technology. The choice of the hardware technology is practically dictated by the

computer manufacturing firms, and the major computer manufacturing
firms of the developed countries are represented in the region.
Thus, the computer hardware available in this region represents the
latest hardware used in the developed countries. There is no
evidence of any major efforts to manufacture computers in the ASEAN
countries except Singapore.

The transfer of software technology, however, is largely related to
operating systems and language compilers, which are usually supplied
by the computer manufacturers along with the hardware. Since
majority of the computer applications are of 'bread-and-butter' type,
the applications using Data Base Management Systems and Data
Communication Systems account for a small proportion. The use of
standard application software packages is also not common.

A broadening of the applications base is important for the transfer
of software technology. The development of system-oriented and
technique-oriented software packages allows the users to shorten the
development process and extend the use of computers to more
sophisticated areas of their operations at low cost. With the
increase in demand for computer usage and the widening of the base
of computer applications, there will be a great demand for 'ready-to-
use' software. There is, therefore, an immense scope for the growth
of software industry in the ASEAN region in general, and Singapore,
in particular. The latter, which depends for its economic survival
on the provision of services, is ideally suited for developing its
brain services which is so essential for the software industry. In
order to provide quality software, the software industry in ASEAN
must absorb the latest software design tools and techniques, such as,
Structured Design, Structured Programming, Programmer Walkthroughs,
etc. The growth and development of software industry, however,
depends on the right type of training and education in the various
areas of software; and this must be undertaken jointly by the
national governments, computer manufacturers, professional computer
societies and the users.

6.   GOVERNMENTAL POLICIES

The ASEAN governments, in general, have liberal policies for
importing computers and related equipment. There is no evidence to
show that computers have adversely affected the employment opportunities in this region. The Indonesian government has established
Bakotan by a Presidential decree, for overseeing and directing the
computer activities in the country. From the beginning, Bakotan
suffered from lack of funds and full-time experts. As the computer
usage increased in the last few years, there is urgent need for
reconstituting Bakotan to achieve its objectives. The Malaysian
government views computerisation as a means to achieve better socio-
economic development and the constitution of MAMPU is a first step
towards this effort. In Philippines, the government has formulated
guidelines for implementing a nationwide computer development plan,
which includes: equipment-sharing structure program; integrated EDP

education and training program; information processing standards; and
national information systems development program. The government, in
view of the tight foreign exchange resources, has imposed a ban on
the acquisition of computers and related equipment by the government
departments to prevent proliferation of computers and the consequences of under utilisation. The government's policy favours
minicomputers over large mainframes. The Thailand government has
issued guidelines for the use of computers in the public sector. A
working group was set up with the task of developing a national
computer plan for the purposes of data collection, evaluation and
control of governmental projects for development.

In 1979, the Singapore government restructured its economic policies,
under which both public and private sector units are encouraged to
introduce automation (including computerisation) to attain higher
levels of productivity. To permit greater use of computers, the
government allows accelerated depreciation on computer equipment for
three years. The software houses are granted tax holidays on all
software developed in Singapore for the export market. The Committee
on National Computerisation, in its report to the government, has
recommended concessional tax rates to the computer software industry
for a period of 5 to 10 years, a concession allowed to industries
enjoying the pioneer status. It also recommended income-tax reliefs
to the expatriate 'high calibre' software experts to allow the
transfer of software technology, and a liberal release of grants from
the Skills Development Fund for training computer personnel both at
Singapore and overseas. The government proposes to set up a National
Computer Board as a statutory body responsible for developing
concrete computerisation plans in the civil service, providing
computer consultancy services to the various government departments
and other statutory boards.

7.   COMPUTER EDUCATION AND TRAINING

A major factor for the late and a slower pace of computer usage in
ASEAN countries is the lack of computer education and training
facilities, resulting in shortage of trained and qualified computer
personnel. The increase in the number of computer installations
towards late seventies, partly brought about by decreasing hardware
costs and partly due to growing awareness of the potential of
computers in improving the productivity of the economic resources,
has created a sudden spurt in demand for properly qualified and
trained computer staff.

In the early years, the computer education and training was in the
form of short term courses provided by the computer manufacturers
to their client EDP staff. These courses covered one or two
programming languages. The programmers with one or two years of
experience emerged as systems analysts and later as EDP managers.
As a result, most of the analysts and EDP managers had no formal
qualifications and training in the areas of systems analysis and
design, management of systems, programming and operations. As the

computer technology advanced with new concepts, tools and techniques, such as, Data Base Management Systems, Data Communications, Distributed Processing, Structured programming, analysis and design, an acute shortage of personnel with knowledge and skills is acutely felt in all the ASEAN countries. At the recent 3rd Conference of the South East Regional Computer Confederation (SEARCC) held at Jakarta in October 1980, the Presidents of the Computer Societies of all the ASEAN countries unanimously voiced concern at the tremendous shortage of qualified and trained computer manpower to meet the requirements of computer installations and the software industry in the 1980s.

The various Universities in Indonesia have started establishing Computer Science Departments to provide computer education, covering both the theoretical aspects of computer science and the practical aspects of systems analysis and design, software programming and DP management through Computer Aided Instruction (CAI). The Universities in Philippines, offer courses in FORTRAN and COBOL programming languages; the University of Philippines offers a post-graduate program in Information Science. In addition, vocational type courses are offered by a number of commercial EDP Training institutions. The Philippines Computer Society feels that the education and training programs are not only inadequate but are sub-standard. The Philippines government proposes to entrust the task of providing quality education and training in computer technology to the National Computer Institute. The scenario in Malaysia is not very much different from that in Philippines. The Malaysian Computer Society views the Computer Science programs offered by the Universities in Malaysia as unsuitable to train the kind of computer personnel required to man the computer installations. The Malaysian government has constituted a study team to consider the proposal for setting up a National Institute of Computer Training, which will be the single most important education source for the training of computer professionals in the country. Besides, some private EDP training institutions conduct courses to prepare the students for the examinations conducted by the British Computer Society and the Institute of Data Processing in U.K.

One of the first two computers installed in Thailand is at the Chulalongkorn University in 1964. Thailand, among the ASEAN countries, has very good computer facilities for training and education. Almost every university and college in Thailand has a computer which is used for teaching computer courses at the undergraduate/graduate level. The Asian Institute of Technology, which has an IBM 3031 system, offers a wide range of programs in computer science, computer applications, operations research and industrial engineering at advanced level leading to M.S. and Ph.D degrees.

The blue print of the Singapore's master plan for computerisation in 1980s, envisages various measures to overcome the current shortage of qualified and trained computer professionals. The short term measures include accelerated training of manpower by sponsoring

suitable men and women to training programs conducted by accredited
institutions both locally and overseas, financed by liberal grants
from the Skills Development Fund. The Japan-Singapore Institute of
Software Technology and the Institute of Systems Science are two
specialised computer training institutes proposed to be set up by the
government. The Japan-Singapore Institute will train about 50
programmers each year, and about half of them will be upgraded to a
senior level through an additional year of training. The Institute
plans to offer programs in systems analysis and related areas besides
training programmes. The Institute of Systems Science to be set up
at the National University of Singapore with IBM assistance, will
conduct programs for graudates and working professionals, besides
undertaking software research. The long term measures aim at
providing computer education right from the school level. Last year,
computer science is introduced as an 'A' level subject in three
junior colleges, and this will be extended to all the junior colleges
in the course of next three years. In addition, students in
secondary schools will be encouraged to study computer as a hobby
subject. It is also proposed to restructure the computer science
course at the National University of Singapore and increase the
intake of students by 100. A Professional Examinations Syndicate is
proposed to be set up, whose main responsibility is to maintain the
quality standards of the computer education and training programs.

8.   CONCLUSION

The rapid increase in the number of computer installations in the
last five years in the ASEAN countries clearly establishes the
potential of computer technology for a better management of the
economic resources leading to a rapid economic development of the
region. To achieve this, it is necessary to identify clearly the
sectoral applications and their priorities.

In formulating the computer master plan based on each country's
unique features and priorities, through a set of deliberately
conceived policy measures, the services of the professional computer
societies must be enlisted. This is important to ensure that the
appropriate technology and an intelligently conceived governmental
measures are properly dovetailed into the implementation strategies.
The problems, and the prescriptions for their solution, are bound to
differ from country to country, and each of them must evolve their
own strategy suited to their genius, as in the case of Singapore.
And, through co-ordinated efforts, ASEAN can achieve a higher
economic growth with the use of computer technology, and can possibly
emerge as a leading centre of computer software industry by the end
of this decade.

9.   REFERENCES

1.   Highlights of the ASEAN Economy - Published by Singapore
      Airlines Ltd., 1977.

2.   ASEAN Economies in Perspective by John Wong - The Macmillan
      Press Ltd., 1979.

3.   The Asian Computer Year Book 1979-80 - Published by Computer
      Publications Ltd., Hongkong.

4.   State of Computer Technology in Indonesia by Rudy J. Pesik -
      3rd Conference of SEARCC'80, Jakarta.

5.   Computer Technology in Malaysia by C.F. Lau - 3rd Conference
      of SEARCC'80, Jakarta.

6.   State of Computer Technology in the Philippines by Vince P.
      Vargas - 3rd Conference of SEARCC'80, Jakarta.

7.   State of Computer Technology in Thailand by Dr Srisakdi
      Charmonman - 3rd Conference of SEARCC'80, Jakarta.

8.   State of Computer Usage in Singapore and Future Possibilities
      by Mr Robert Iau - 3rd Conference of SEARCC'80, Jakarta.

9.   Software Technology and South East Asian Countries by F.L. Ng -
      Proceedings of SEARCC'76, published by North-Holland Publishing
      Company, Amsterdam.

10.   How South-East Asia can close the Technological Gap by D.W.
      Davie - Proceedings of SEARCC'76, published by North-Holland
      Publishing Company, Amsterdam.

11.   Problems in Transferring Computer Technology to the Countries
      of South-East Asia - Some Answers? by G.P. Mead - Proceedings
      of SEARCC'76, published by North-Holland Publishing Company,
      Amsterdam.

12.   Computer Technology and National Development in Developing
      Countries by T. Sumantri - Conference Proceedings of 3rd
      Conference of SEARCC'80 at Jakarta.

13.   Survey of Computers in Singapore 1976.

14.   Survey of Computers in Singapore 1980.

The Delicate Role of the Consultant Adviser Within Successful Computer Development in Third World Countries

Victor P. Lane

Head of the Management Information Centre,
North East London Polytechnic, UK

The paper starts from a consideration of the computing needs of developing countries, reviews the involvement of international bodies such as the United Nations and then examines the contribution which can be made by computer advisers from developed nations to assist Third World countries.

Computing technology, if correctly harnessed, can help to improve social and economic conditions. This is only achieved through a correct blend of innovation and technology combined with an appreciation of a country's objectives. An adviser from a developed country, who attempts to add to his computing skills an understanding of the culture in which he is operating, can help to stimulate a professional approach and so be a catalyst for evolution and change. Therefore it is essential that the expert uses to advantage knowledge brought from the developed world, but realises the limitations of this knowledge because of the different local cultural socio-economic environment.

1.   INTRODUCTION

The paper starts from a consideration of the computing needs of
developing countries; outlines the involvement of international
organisations and the commitment of professional bodies; and
finally examines the contribution which can be made by computer
advisers from developed nations to assist Third World countries.

In order to understand the difficulties which the visiting adviser
may face, the paper considers the problems of technology transfer
and the possible contribution that computing can make to national
development in a Third World country.

Computing development is not an end in itself, but is only of
significance if it helps to support or accelerate enhancement of
the social, cultural and economic environment. It is generally
accepted that computing is able to contribute in this way, and the
United Nations have suggested that this is best achieved via:

- local education and training;

- each country having its own unique
  broad national policy;   and

- international co-operation.

Opinions of observers differ as to whether computing will widen or
reduce the gap between the economic performance of the
industrialised nations and the primary producers of the Third
World. As computing will not disappear, this point is only of
academic interest compared with the more important and immediate
problem of changing the pace of the introduction and development
of computing and its application. This requires a concerted
national effort to use computing as an aid to develop and exploit
natural resources and so shape the future. However the specific
objectives and strategic plan for each country must be a unique
plan and a distinct reflection of that country's needs.

The consultant's role is not necessarily to initiate change but to
be a catalyst and to help the right climate for progressive
development. The major difficulty for the adviser is that of
acclimatization to a country's needs; as opposed to transplanting
solutions from developed countries which may be inappropriate, or
perhaps even alien, without serious modification if they (the
solutions) are to be accepted and useful.

2. THE COMPUTING OBJECTIVES OF A DEVELOPING COUNTRY

The prime objective of all countries is to improve their social,
cultural and economic standards. On the assumption that computing
can make a significant contribution to these goals i.e. to national
development, there have been numerous initiatives by international
agencies and by the more advanced countries to assist the
developing nations.

For many years, the United Nations have been aware of this objective
and have been discussing the need to improve computing capabilities
of the developing countries. It has been acknowledged that each
country has its own special needs; nevertheless it has been
suggested by the United Nations $/ 1 /$ that this is best achieved
via:-

- each country having its own unique
  broad national policy;

- local education and training;

- international cooperation.

The principle advantage of transferring computer technology is not
in providing the physical device itself, but more in the
advantages that accrue to other disciplines from the provision of a
powerful intellectual tool. The degree of computing which is
necessary, how such a transfer should be achieved and how the
essential supporting human infra-structure is developed, are
always open to debate.

3. METHODS OF ACHIEVING THE OBJECTIVES

The tactical methods to encourage the use of computers to support
the strategic objective of national development have been
considered by the United Nations and the Inter-Governmental
Conference on Strategies and Policies for Informatics; their
recommendations are described in $/ 2 /$. In addition, associations
of computer professionals have also tried to help e.g. the Ad-Hoc
Committee on Computing in Less Developed Countries of the
Association of Computing Machinery (ACM) was set up to achieve the
aims shown in Table 1; the Specialist Group for Developing
Countries of the British Computer Society (BCS) has similar goals.

4. THE RELEVANCE OF COMPUTING IN A THIRD WORLD ENVIRONMENT

Computing development is not an end in itself, but is only of
significance if it helps to support or accelerate enhancement of
the social, cultural and economic environment.

Table 1

The aims of ACM group on Computing in Less Developed Countries

1.   to foster communications between individual computing
     professionals and organisations interested in computing
     in less developed countries

2.   to publish and distribute reports on topics related to
     computing in less developed countries

3.   to help presentation of papers at conferences on topics
     related to computing in less developed countries

4.   to exchange information and experience of computing in
     less developed countries between

              (i)   individuals

              (ii) organisations

5.   to maintain registers of individuals and organisations
     who are interested in helping less developed countries

6.   to maintain a list of organisations in less developed
     countries who need assistance

It can be argued that computing contributes little to overcome the problems of the poor in the Third World and therefore funds should not be used in this way but devoted to the immediate needs of the population. Support for this case can be found in a survey undertaken by the Ad-Hoc Group of ACM $\underline{/\ 3\ \underline{/}}$ in which many expressed concern about the proper application of computers, computers being used for the benefit of the poorest people and the need for compatibility with the local cultural socio-economic environment. Certainly the case for technology in general and for computing in particular can be overstated. In the mid-sixties, it was optimistically assumed that technology, in all its guises, could solve the world's problems. New and miracle seeds could solve hunger, and nuclear power would similarly contribute to energy problems. Nothing seemed impossible and computing was showing its potential. Computing still retains some, if not all of this pioneering enthusiasm, but it is essential that lessons are learned. The aim of assisting national development by means of computing is huge, daunting and complex. It is dangerous to approach the problem with an arrogance which underestimates the potential complexity of the problem.

In some less developed countries there is little or no computer training and education, computer industry or associated industries and little Government involvement. In such cases it often appears that "the organisational model that lies behind that concept (installing a computer in a Third World country) and the technology involved are light years removed from the needs of the poor in Third World countries". This was the view expressed by Brian W Walker, the Director General of Oxfam. However the more important point is that of appropriate technology $\underline{/\ 4\ \underline{/}}$ for a given situation in a specific country at a specific time or to quote Mr Walker again, "the concept of appropriate technology and the importance of the social development of people within that context is of prime importance".

The appropriate level of computing for a country should be closely related to its social, political and economic climate. Computing will serve the community if it is applied through areas which are of significance to that society; then the evolution of computing applications is achieved through an appropriate balance $\underline{/\ 5\ \underline{/}}$ of innovation, participation and current technology tempered with an appreciation of the culture in which the computer is to operate. The designer of computer-based systems must have an empathy for the culture for which he is designing because as there is an optimum management style for each country $\underline{/\ 6\ \underline{/}}$ similarly there is an appropriate level of computer technology which will vary with time and country.

5. WILL COMPUTING BRING PROGRESS?

Opinions of observers differ as to whether or not computing will
widen or reduce the gap between the economic performance of the
industrialised nations and the primary producers of the Third
World $\underline{/}$ 2, 7, 8 $\underline{/}$. As computing will not disappear, this point is
only of academic interest compared with the more important and
immediate problem of attempting to introduce computing to help
Third World countries.

The success of a computing implementation may be measured by:-

(i) the effect on local industries, or

(ii) the achievement of say a major national development (e.g. a
     fisheries project) to which computing makes a small but
     significant contribution.

There is no doubt that computing can assist in specific industries
in less developed countries to improve their effectiveness and to
help maintain the countries' economic competitiveness. However it
is predicted that in the long-term computers and micro-electronics
in particular $\underline{/}$ 8 $\underline{/}$ must work to the advantage of the more
developed nations, i.e. to the disadvantage of the less developed
nations, simply because automation will erode the labour cost
advantage of the less developed country. In $\underline{/}$ 8 $\underline{/}$ it is suggested
that the impact of micro-electronics will adversely affect (a) the
textile and clothing manufacture and (b) the electronics industry
within developing countries because automation in the more
developed countries will become competitive with cheap labour in
the Third World.

With respect to major projects for the country's infrastructure
(e.g. roads, water supply and sewerage) computing can play only a
small part, even though this may be a very important part. Aid in
developing countries tends to be used mainly for major projects
related to the country's infrastructure (consequently aid for
computing is of a much lower priority). Therefore if computing is
used as a tool within a project for national development, it is
possible for:-

          - the computing to be excellent

          - but unsuccessful, because the major
            project is inappropriate.

For example, the British computing expertise related to the design
of highways and transport is equal to the best in the world.
Similarly, the British highway designers are world-leaders.
Nevertheless in some cases it is possible for expensive highways

to be built in situations where they are not required.   John Howe in
$\underline{/9\underline{/}}$ suggests that money has been poured into overdesigned road
projects.   This example is described simply as a note of caution.
On the other hand, the Developing Countries Specialist Group of the
BCS has shown that computing can make successful contributions in
the primary activities of developing countries, that is in:-

- agriculture

- fisheries

- sanitation

- transportation

- energy

- health care

- water resources

Within these primary activities which are vital to that society,
there are many design problems and resource management, planning
and project management tasks for which there are computing aids.

6.   THE DIFFICULTIES FOR THE VISITING ADVISER

In this section, the difficulties are considered with relation to:-

- the host country i.e. the less developed
  country which is in need of help;

- the weaknesses inherent in the principle
  of an expert from one culture (probably
  a more developed country) trying to work
  and help in another country;

- implementation of computer projects;   and

- the use of most up-to-date technology.

In Section 5 above, reference was made to the manner in which
inappropriate technology can be suggested and possibly implemented.
This was done as a warning.   If other technologists can fail
occasionally, the computer professional must also take care.

There are many factors which impinge upon the work of the visiting
adviser:-

(i)   The host country: there is often a considerable gap in terms
      of organisations and systems, educational facilities,
      technology and applications of computing $\underline{/2\underline{/}}$ when comparing

a developing country with a more developed country.
Additionally, there is often a shortage of skilled manpower
and possibly foreign currency. For a visiting adviser, this
may be an unusual situation for which previous experience is
not necessarily appropriate. Therefore if and when the
adviser conceives a solution, the adviser must consider if
the solution is appropriate to the existing local cultural
socio-economic environment.

(ii) The visiting adviser: the consultant's role is not
necessarily to initiate change but to be a catalyst and to
help create the right climate for progressive development.
The adviser must approach the new situation with an open mind,
even if the area of application is not a new one; and take
care not to transplant solutions from another country which
may be inappropriate or perhaps even alien, to that situation,
without serious modification if they (the solutions) are to be
accepted and useful. The major difficulty for the visiting
adviser is that of acclimatization to a country's needs, and
to this end the visitor must develop an empathy for the culture
in which he operates. This is not at all easy and straightforward for the visiting consultant and in the final analysis
the adviser must attempt to find a solution which incorporates
technology which is appropriate at that time for that country.

(iii) Implementation of computer projects: one of the major
difficulties in designing systems in the USA and the UK $\sqrt{10}$ 7
is that of the successful management of projects to achieve

- cost targets   and

- implementation schedules.

It is apparent that the effect of working in an environment
which is unusual for the visiting adviser, can only compound
the implementation problems.

(iv) The most up-to-date technology: it is the intention of every
person when helping another organisation to attempt to
provide the best solution. The most recent or the current
state-of-the-art technique may not necessarily be the best.
It is very important that we give the best to less developed
countries but over-enthusiasm must not be indulged in the
manner described by Negroponte $\sqrt{11}$ 7 where self-centred and
self seeking aims take precedence over the project aims.
With a technology like computing which is continually changing
and advancing, it is essential that a situation is not
approached with the viewpoint "The latest computing technique
is the answer..... Now tell me, what is the question?"

The situation is extremely complex. Many of the applications fall largely into the public sector e.g. health, water resources, mineral resources, energy, telecommunications and transportation. The desirability of many of these major projects related to National development is not simply one of technological evaluation and assessment; they also fall squarely in the centre of political debate — not necessarily of political controversy — and the computer consultant must be aware of the need to advise the decision-makers of the possible impact of new technology.

7. CONCLUSIONS

The principle advantage of transferring computer technology is not simply in providing the physical device itself, but more in the advantages which accrue to other disciplines from the provision of a powerful intellectual tool. The degree of computing which is appropriate in a less developed country and how such a transfer is best achieved are questions which will always be open to debate.

The computer by its inherent logic and efficiency exposes the frailties and illogicalities of organisations, procedures and even societies. The correct level of computing for a country is closely related to its social, political and economic climate. The evolution of computing applications is best achieved through an appropriate balance of innovation, participation and latest technology tempered with an appreciation of the culture in which the computing is to operate.

An adviser to a developing country may bring previous experience from another country but must use this without prejudice on the areas of study in the host country. Often visiting advisers have current expertise in latest technology and techniques. A developing country, per se, is not necessarily the best place or even an appropriate place to practise such methods. The essence is to incorporate computing methods which are appropriate to the particular situation such that computers become tools which serve to shape the future in a desirable and planned way.

REFERENCES

1. United Nations "The application of computer technology for development", United Nations Report, New York, 1971.

2. Bogod, J L, "The role of computing in developing countries", British Computer Society, 1980.

3. Mazlack, L J "A Non-institutional focus for computing in less developed countries". A progress report of the Ad-Hoc committee on computing in less developed countries of the ACM, University of Cincinnatti, USA, 1981.

4. Moyes, A "The poor man's wisdom - technology and the very poor", Oxfam, Oxford, 1979.

5. Lane, V P "Organisational, management and communications implications of distributed computing" Euro-IFIP '79, London 1979.

6. Wellens, J "Management Style", Training, May 1980.

7. Laver, M "Computers and social change", Cambridge University Press, London, 1980.

8. Rada, J "The impact of micro-electronics", International Labour Office, Geneva, Switzerland, 1980.

9. Howe, J "Engineers must return to basic to meet the Third World needs", New Civil Engineer, 12 March 1981, pp. 16-17.

10. "The Urwick Report", Computer Publications, Ashford, UK, 1980.

11. Negroponte, N "Being creative with cad". Information Processing 77, The conference proceedings of IFIP '77, North Holland Publishing, 1977.

The BCS Developing Countries Project

J. L. Bogod

*Director, Developing Countries Project,
The British Computer Society, UK*

The Developing Countries Project is sponsored by The
British Computer Society, the Department of Industry
and ICL. It was set up to examine the feasibility of
establishing a UK Council to coordinate and direct
support for developing countries in computing and,
if appropriate, to establish the Council. The paper
considers the case for the Council and reports on
progress.

The objective of this project has been to explore the
desirability and feasibility of setting up a body to
coordinate and direct UK support for developing
countries in their development of computing capability.
If found to be viable, the project was to be extended
to implement the proposals made. At the time of preparing the written form of this paper, the first phase
has been completed, viability has been predicted and
the implementation phase has been started. By the
time the paper is presented at BCS 81, the organisation
will have been set up and work will be under way: the
paper will then describe the organisation and plans
which will have been established.

The roots of the project lie in the identification of
an unsatisfied and growing need, and the proposal
provides a means of satisfying that need.

THE NEED

As early as 1971, the United Nations Organisation
identified a close connection between computing
capability and the rate at which national development
can take place. A report was published on the subject
which came to four conclusions:-

1.   Education and training for the application
      of computers to accelerate the process of
      economic and social development must receive
      first priority.

2.   Each developing country needs a broad national
      policy, consistent with its national goals, on
      the application of computer technology.

3.   International co-operation needs to be increased
      in activities relating to the application of
      computer technology to development.

4.   Computer technology will increase in importance
      in the developing countries .... and its
      diffusion and sound application can make a
      significant contribution in accelerating the
      rate of their economic and social development.

Nowadays, in the same context, we are more likely to speak of 'Information Technology' or 'Informatics' rather than 'Computing', but the message is clear. During the 1970's, the need demonstrated by the first and fourth conclusions has become increasingly apparent. The 'Inter-Governmental Conference on Strategies and Policies for Informatics' (SPIN), held in 1978, was designed to enable national delegations to consider the relationships between computing and national development and to identify how this development could be achieved, particularly for those states in the greatest need. The conclusions reiterate more strongly those in the UN report.

The UN Conference on Science and Technology for Development strengthened the argument yet again, albeit for the field of Science and Technology generally. This Conference called for substantial funds to be made available for concentration on the development of scientific and technical capability, and an Interim Fund has been set up and is in operation.

The fact remains that progress is very slow and, with the notable exceptions of Brazil, Singapore and India none of the national policies called for by UNO in 1971 have been established. Nor has there been a marked increase in the level of international cooperation in this field except through the activities of the Inter-governmental Bureau for Informatics (IBI). This body was set up in 1974 by UNESCO to concentrate effort in computing development in the third world. Initially it sought to achieve its purposes by multilateral cooperation - an activity which led to a highly theoretical approach to the problem. Since the SPIN conference it has become realised that practical help can only be provided by bilateral cooperation. IBI identifies tasks to be carried out and then acts as a broker to establish a cooperative venture with a developed country.

The UN agencies themselves do not appear, in general, fully to appreciate the link between Information Technology and national development. Nor do they yet appreciate the problems which developing countries have in establishing their own competence. I.T. to them is a means of establishing internal information and administration systems. Computing is just another management tool at project level.

This last set of comments is, of course, a very
simplistic appraisal of a very complex problem. The
response of international agencies is ultimately
dependent upon the pressures applied by the nations they
represent. And if those nations are unable to present
their needs effectively, the agencies are not easily
able to respond.

MEETING THE NEED

For any developing nation, the satisfaction of its need
for developing computing competence lies in the second
and third UN recommendation - formation of a national
policy or strategy supported with cooperation from the
developed nations. Without this, progress will be slow
and will take unproductive paths which will have to be
retraced in time. It is true that similar paths will
also be followed with good planning, but they should be
less in number and identified earlier.

How will the developing countries set about this task?
Except for a few countries they cannot since they do
not have the technical competence or management
appreciation to do so. They are in a vicious circle
from which they cannot escape without help.

But, apart from IBI, no mechanisms exist to enable them
to get the support they need; and IBI support tends to
be project rather than national strategy orientated.

The vicious circle is likely to remain unless someone
is prepared to break into it and this the Developing
Countries Project proposes to do by the formation of
The UK Council for Computing Development.

THE COUNCIL

It is proposed to form an organisation with the title,
tentative at present, of The UK Council for Computing
Development. The Council will be an independent non-
profit making body incorporated under guarantee and
with charitable status. It will be directed by a Board
of Management whose members will act voluntarily. They
will be senior influential members of the computing
community or prominent figures concerned with
improving North-South relationships generally. They
will collectively direct the activities of the Council
and be available individually for advice and
influence.

There will be a small Executive under the management of
a Director General with two or three senior consultants
having expertise in Training, Education and Systems,
and some administrative support.

The objectives of the Council will be:-

> To foster, coordinate and, where necessary,
> direct support by the UK for developing
> countries in computing.

> By applying UK resources most effectively,
> to improve the recipients computing capability
> and thus improve their social, economic and
> cultural environment.

> To improve the North/South political relationships
> of the UK.

> To give the UK computing community a better
> appreciation of the state of computing development
> in developing countries.

The Council will establish links to the UK computing
community, government and funding agencies, building up
a register of individual and corporate expertise.
Through diplomatic and other governmental channels, the
Council will approach governments of selected developing
countries and seek formal agreements to the UK assisting
them in the formulation of a national computing
strategy. This will lead to programs of work commencing
with appropriate studies and moving on to specific tasks
within the national strategy. The Council will not
expect to be a development funding agency nor will it
expect to be an executive body, i.e. it will not itself
undertake project work. Rather it will act as a broker
and, after helping to define the projects, will help
to create funding packages through the various development agencies. When asked it will help to identify
potential UK contractors but will not negotiate on
their behalf.

The Council's activity will not be confined to those
countries with whom a formal agreement has been reached.
It is expected that many ad hoc requests for
cooperation may be expected from other countries and
from the development agencies.

Projects which arise from this activity will include:-

1. Establishing a national training institute.
2. Curriculum development.
3. Creation of a professional structure.
4. Setting up a National Computing Centre.
5. Application development in a strategic sector
    eg. agriculture.
6. Developing an indigenous computing industry.
7. University twinning (either permanent or
    project based) to improve education exchange.
8. Creating programmes of on-the-job training
    for foreign nationals with UK users.
9. Creation of training materials orientated to
    the country of use.
10. Creating a programme of individual correspondents
    (eg. D.P. manager in country X to D.P. manager
    in UK).

Services to members depending on category, will
include:-

1. Provision of a newsletter.
2. Information about developments in particular
    countries.
3. Information about government organisation and
    the indigenous industry in particular countries,
    and introductions where appropriate.
4. Obtaining exchange correspondents for individuals.
5. Information about UN and other agency mechanisms.
6. Publications resulting from specific study work.
7. Invitations to participate in conferences and
    seminars organised by the Council.
8. Invitations to participate in inward missions
    organised by the Council.

Organisations and individuals wanting to support the
Council will be invited to become members through
payment of a subscription. Individual membership
will appeal to professionals who simply want to make
a contribution in this area and also to consultants
who see some increases in business opportunities.
Organisations will want to join for a variety of
reasons. In every case there will be significant moral
motivation, but in addition the following groups will
see additional justification.

The industry:- Growth in business opportunities
overseas. Access to information about overseas markets.
Availability of advice on the international agency
network and how to access it.

Users:- Improved operating environment in other
countries where they may have business ventures with
computing support. Opportunities for training overseas
personnel. Opportunities for the employment of foreign
nationals on secondment.

The Financial Institutes:- Investment opportunities.
Long term improved economic climate.

The Government:- Increased opportunity for Industry.
Improved cooperation within the industry (a common
cause). Improvement in North-South relationships.
More efficient investment of development funds. A
focal point for links to international agencies.

Educational Institutions:- Opportunities to increase
contribution to education generally. Potential
increase in foreign student intake. Project work
providing staff with wider experience.

Charitable Foundations)
Government Agencies   ) An authoritative and
independent point of contact with the computing
community to provide advice and consultancy.

A scale of charges, appropriate to these categories,
will be drawn up. The costs of the Council will be
met from these subscriptions.

Part 13
Computing and the Disabled

Use of Computer-Based Facilities for the Dissemination of Information to Disabled People

Carmen Saiady
(*Research Student*)
and
Adrian V. Stokes
(*Senior Lecturer in Computer Systems*)

The Hatfield Polytechnic, Herts, UK

One major problem confronting disabled people is obtaining access to relevant information. There are a considerable number of statutory and voluntary bodies who function as information providers, often by using classical methods of information dissemination. However, this is an area where computer-based technology could be of considerable use. This paper examines applications of this technology, paying particular attention to videotex systems and to communication networks. The "Disability Database" on Prestel is also discussed in detail.

INTRODUCTION

A nationwide survey, carried out by Amelia Harris [1] at
the beginning of the 1970s for the Office of Population
and Censuses and Surveys, indicated that in Great
Britain, there were over three million people who were
classified as "handicapped and impaired", of whom over
one third needed a significant amount of support and care.
It is likely that the current number, in this the
International Year of Disabled People, is appreciably
higher.

The problems confronted by disabled people are many and
varied but a significant number arise from lack of
adequate information. Information is a key factor in all
people's lives but this is particularly true in the case
of disabled people and, in many cases, it can help to
alleviate the hardships caused by their disabilities.
Various projects carried out (e. g. at the Institute of
Consumer Ergonomics [2]) suggest that many disabled
people are further handicapped by their lack of awareness
of certain facilities or benefits that may be available
to them.

General lack of information can in many ways prevent
disabled people from taking a full role in society. The
kind of information that is needed by all people daily
may prove to be not so readily obtainable by disabled
people. For example, it is important for a disabled
person to know whether a specific building caters for, or
offers, special facilities to suit his/her disability.

The importance of information in the lives of disabled
people and its provision and dissemination, has recently
been of much concern. At present, this task is undertaken
by various voluntary and statutory bodies with some
degree of success. Much of this information is collated
and disseminated using classical methods, e. g. card
indexes and news-sheets. The various information
providing agencies are constantly seeking effective
methods for disseminating information to the end user,
i. e. the disabled person. Disabled people vary, not only
in their disabilities, but also in their intellectual and
educational abilities, their outlook to life and their
social background. Therefore, to presume that the needs
of all disabled people can be satisfied by using one
particular method for disseminating information is indeed
inaccurate. It is essential that information is
disseminated in the greatest possible number of ways to
suit all types of disability.

CURRENT METHODS OF INFORMATION DISSEMINATION

The need to identify methods that can be used most
successfully for disseminating information to disabled
people is evident. At present, a great deal of
information is in the possession of a number of
organisations which provide services, either directly to
disabled people or to the organisations which are
concerned with helping them. Most of these organisations
compile and provide information independently of each
other and this has been shown by a recent survey in the
field [3]. Lack of some measure of co-operation or coordination between these organisations can lead to
various problems, such as duplication of effort and
confusion on the part of disabled people caused by the
sheer abundance of information available in various
(often contradictory) forms. For example, many
organisations, in an attempt to outline the various cash
benefits to which disabled people are eligible, produce
leaflets publicising such entitlements. However, lack of
co-operation between information providers, often results
in a great amount of information being made available to
disabled people which often causes more confusion rather
than clarifying the issue. Certain printed literature,
such as Government publications, can also be too
difficult to be assimilated. The Department of Health and
Social Security prints leaflets publicising their own
benefits to disabled people; the fact that many voluntary
organisations have to produce further literature to
clarify the Department's literature is further proof of
the complexity of the information available. On the other
hand, it must be pointed out that the statutory
authorities must not provide misleading information and,
since the relevant legislation is complex, the leaflets
are similarly not easy to follow.

Not only are there problems with the information that is
disseminated but also with the medium for its
dissemination. For example, a deaf or partially deaf
person may experience considerable difficulties while
trying to communicate by telephone.

At present, there are a few different approaches adopted
for disseminating information to disabled people. These
are:

   *   Mass media, which are the more effective methods
       of conveying information to disabled people.
       Newspapers, radio and television provide direct
       means for disseminating the information.

* Publications, which can be very useful if updated
  and printed frequently. Handbooks and directories
  comprise a general source of information for
  disabled people and particularly for organisations
  which are information providers.

* Information providing organisations, which consist
  of voluntary and statutory bodies and which
  comprise the most established method of
  disseminating information. In recent years, there
  has been an increase in the number of such
  organisations.

Disseminating information through all the above methods
relies greatly upon the information being kept up-to-date.
Dissemination of out-of-date and hence often wrong
information can be more harmful than provision of no
information at all.

A useful tool in this case is the computer. With a
(potentially) vast storage capacity and high performance,
computers can be used to reduce the overheads incurred in
the provision and dissemination of information. An
information retrieval system, for example, can enable
certain tasks to be performed which would otherwise be
impossible. Advances in telecommunications and computer
technology have reached a stage such that they can be
applied with success in this area. For example, a
centralised database to which information providing
organisations might contribute could be established. Such
a database could then be made available for use by those
organisations and by any others with means of access to
it. There is no doubt that developments in computer-based
technology have not yet been fully exploited. However,
there is evidence of greater usage of computers as, for
example, information providing systems.

The most important single factor behind this growth is,
of course, the steadily declining cost of electronic
technology. The basic cost of micro-processor hardware
has fallen in price by as much as 20% in most years and
by half in 1980 [4]. Initially, micro-computers were
considered to have two disadvantages. First, they were
quite difficult to program. Secondly, there was a
shortage of ready-made applications software. In
addition, there were few, if any, standards. The
development of simplified programming techniques has gone
a long way towards solving the first of these problems,
while an increasing number of standard "application
packages" have become available at a reasonable cost in
recent years. The emergence of (often de facto) standards

such as the S-100 bus and CP/M [5] have gone a long way
to obviating the quite significant problems of sharing
software. Nevertheless, despite the achievements in
computer technology and advances in telecommunications,
it is evident that the application of such technology to
the specific problem of retrieving and disseminating
information to disabled people has been very slow.

As mentioned above, one of the tasks best performed by
computers is information retrieval. The best known system
pertaining to disabled people is, perhaps, the "welfare
benefits computer information system" devised by David du
Feu of Edinburgh University during the joint project
between the University, Inverclyde District Council and
IBM (UK) Ltd in 1976 [5]. This project arose from concern
over the large number of people not getting their full
entitlements to the benefits because of the complexity of
welfare benefits provision which was particularly true in
the case of disabled people. The Inverclyde package, as
it is best known, indicates to the user the best
combination of claims to make in cases where a variety of
alternative claims could be made, for example, the
alternatives of rent rebates or supplementary benefits.
At present, various Welfare Rights Departments make use
of the Inverclyde package. An example is that of the
Gateshead Welfare Rights Department which has used this
package as the basis for their own on-line welfare
benefits system. They have computerised their clients
notes and are developing a system where a person asking
for free school meals, for example, will be told,
automatically, of the other Local Authority benefits to
which they are entitled, for example, housing, education
and social services.

A similar system is being developed in Wales to provide a
computer-based information service for three locations in
Cardiff, each of which will be connected to the system
via the public telephone network. It is expected that the
introduction of this service in itself will increase the
number of CAB enquiries and hence the number of benefit
claims. The proposed system is expected to overcome the
limitations of the Inverclyde system which has restricted
applications and has to be extended in its scope to cover
all relevant benefits. The new computer package is being
tested at University College Swansea.

VIDEOTEX

Britain is one of the leading countries in videotex
technology. Videotex is generally used to describe on-

line information services available to the general public
[7], characterised by the use of adapted television sets
as terminals connected to remote computers and databases.
Generally, however, videotex refers to viewdata and
Teletext facilities.

The Teletext services, such as the BBC's Ceefax and IBA's
ORACLE, developed in the early 1970s are now each
transmitting more than one hundred pages of information
from the latest news to specialised material and even
computer programs ("Telesoftware"). So far, there are
100,000 television sets in Britain adapted to receive
Teletext. The service is "free" but the cost of the
adaptations is about £ 150.

ORACLE was initially the product of a team of IBA
engineers, the name being an acronym for "Optional
Reception of Announcements by Coded Line Electronics".
The first ORACLE system, early in 1973, allowed up to 50
pages, with text in only one colour. The system now
conforms to the joint viewdata/Teletext standard [8]
allowing seven colours and simple (alphamosaic) graphics.
As the pages are transmitted cyclically, their number is
restricted by the delay incurred before the selected page
is obtained (each page taking about a quarter of a second
to transmit) and, in practice, a maximum of about 100
pages is observed.

Basically, ORACLE is used to provide up-to-date
information "free of charge" to users. Originally,
Teletext was designed as a means of enabling hearing
impaired people to enjoy television programs by using the
facility to provide sub-titles. This facility is
currently available on the broadcast systems, although now
only as a small part of a much wider service. Although
superimposed sub-titles are not yet widely available, at
present only being broadcast for a few hours a week, a
great deal of work and research has been carried out in
this field and it is expected that this service will
shortly be available for longer period broadcasts.
Despite new equipment, however, the BBC suggests that it
still takes twenty hours of work to produce one hour of
sub-titling.

The potential for Teletext services is enormous. At
present two of the 625 lines used for television
transmission are used for Teletext. ORACLE has already
asked the Home Office to allow it to use two more lines.
One line will be used to improve the response time in
obtaining the page while the other will be used as a
means of inserting local data as a result of users demand

for this information.

The broadcast services, collectively known as Teletext (or "broadcast videotex") are restricted in the number of pages of information transmitted but, conversely, are insensitive to the load factor. There is no interaction at all between the user and the Teletext computer.

At the other end of the spectrum, there are the non-broadcast videotex services, usually known in this country as "viewdata", where a suitably adapted television set is connected via the public switched telephone network to a remote computer database. British Telecom's pioneering "Prestel" was set up in 1974 and it has been in full operational service for the last two years. To access the system, the user selects viewdata on his television and an auto-dialler in the set connects automatically to the Prestel computer. A "log-on" request appears on the screen; the user then keys in his identifying user number, although newer receivers have the facility to log on automatically. Once logged onto the system, information pages can be accessed directly using a very simple protocol. The telephone link has to remain set up for the duration of the enquiry.

At present, the Prestel computers are capable of offering up to 220,000 pages of information of which 1,200 pages comprise the "Disability Database".

It is clear that Prestel provides a facility, the need for which we have just described. Perhaps its major disadvantage is the cost and this is especially pertinent in the case of disabled people who, in general, rely more on State benefits than non-disabled people (for example, the unemployment rate among disabled people is between two and three times the national average) and hence have a lower income.

Information retrieval is currently the most important service on Prestel, but a message facility, called the "Response Frame" is also available. This enables a user to order services or goods through the system, his name and address being automatically supplied (and this may later be extended to a credit card number). Thus it is possible, by means of Prestel, to obtain a wide variety of information and to order goods without leaving home, thus removing many of the obstacles described above.

Using videotex for disseminating information is an area which still needs a great deal of study, as it is in an early stage of development. Prestel is the only existing

viewdata system in the UK which offers information about
disability. However, there is clear evidence that it is
not being used as widely as one might expect. This is
believed to be due to various factors, such as the
expense incurred in using the system and the limited
range of information provided for disabled people. There
is also the factor of people's general attitude towards
the new technology, which seems to be a feeling of
mistrust and uneasiness. Many of those who were
interviewed in our survey [3] explained that they
preferred to use books and directories when dealing with
an enquiry as they know exactly where to look. One
criticism of most of those involved in videotex is that
its various forms have been presented to the public in
such a patchy manner as to contribute to the confusion
which still exists about the technology. At present,
there are less than 8,000 Prestel sets sold. They cost up
to £ 900 and the service also has to be paid for. There
is no doubt that videotex provides a new method for
disseminating information and has many potential users,
although it is evident that full use has not yet been
made of this medium. Studies carried out of the
Disability Database on Prestel indicate that, to improve
the information retrieval, much improvement and
reorganisation in the content of information stored and
the efficiency of operation is needed.

COMMUNICATION NETWORKS

Advances in telecommunications and networks provide
opportunities for users to make use of information stored
on various databases irrespective of the distance
involved. A good example is EURONET/DIANE which started
operation in Europe in February 1980 and, in April that
year, the London link within the network was formally
opened. EURONET is a high-bandwidth packet-switched
network linking the various countries within the EEC.
EURONET is the term used to describe the
telecommunications network, whereas the databases
attached to that network are collectively described as
DIANE (Direct Information Access Network for Europe).
There are twenty principal sources of data throughout the
network constituting DIANE. These are called hosts and,
between them, offer 150 databases on a large variety of
scientific and socio-economic subjects. When connected to
EURONET, Prestel users will have the opportunity to access
DIANE and all the information stored on European
databases. Clearly, this has a great potential in many
fields, not least of which is that of information related
to disability.

A similar idea to the establishment of an international
database for disabled people, which is being examined by
various European countries, is being considered by
representatives of the national information providing
organisations, such as the Disabled Living Foundation
(DLF) and the Royal Association for Disability and
Rehabilitation (RADAR) for implementation in the UK. The
plans are to set up a national co-ordinating body which
will perform all the central processing and disseminating
functions relating to information.

It is expected that information from all the national
information providing bodies will be stored and hence
processed by one central computer. Information will then
be shared between the bodies concerned. It must be
pointed out that there are problems associated with this
proposal which concern the lack of willingness of a
number of national organisations to make available their
publications to be processed and distributed differently.
Although there are many problems in setting up such a
database, these are mainly political and current
technology is adequate for this purpose.

CURRENT INTERNATIONAL PROPOSALS

In 1975, a proposal was made to the EEC by two member
countries for the establishment of a large-scale European
database for disabled people. The proposal indicated the
need for a database which could be accessed by the
majority of European countries through their public
switched telephone or data networks. No further
developments took place concerning this proposal until, at
a recent meeting in Belgium between the EEC countries,
the importance of establishing a better information
centre in the field of "information on technical aids for
the aged and disabled" was emphasised [9]. As a result of
extensive research in this area, it was recommended to
undertake immediately the first phase which is a
feasibility study.

This study is intended to:
    *   Establish major features and requirements of the
        system and analyse long-term cost/income
        implications.

    *   Study the possibilities for satisfying the
        requirements by encouraging the extension of the
        proposed system to associated fields, such as
        product databases on medical equipment.

    *   Investigate the feasibility of additional
        desirable features of the information system.

This co-operation between European countries is expected
to achieve an improvement in dissemination of information
concerning the technical aids that are already available
to disabled people. Thousands of aids exist but most are
made only in small quantities and are known only to a
small circle. Establishment of such a database, which
would be accessible on-line, is envisaged to serve two
purposes; first, it would provide material for the
compilation of a printed catalogue and secondly, if
linked to EURONET/DIANE, it would be accessible to any
DIANE subscriber and thus provide another on-line channel
for disseminating information. Each aid included in the
catalogue will be diagrammatically represented and
accompanied with information concerning its purchase and
service. The establishment of this database would provide
access to a continuously up-to-date source of information
and enable rapid information retrieval. This is an
effective way of disseminating information as it can be
directly aimed at disabled people or health care and
social service professionals concerned with disabled
people.

Naturally, international co-operation gives rise to many
difficulties such as language problems and agreed
vocabulary on technical aids. The feasibility study
period is intended to support the development of a multi-
lingual thesaurus on technical aids and provide a list of
vocabulary which will include names of all devices and
their components, of all disabilities and all terms
needed for disability research.

The closest attempt at producing an international
catalogue has been achieved jointly by the International
Commission on Technical Aids (ICTA), and the Housing and
Transportation and Rehabilitation International operating
from Sweden, which also published data sheets on new
technical aids. However, this operation has now ceased.

The Registration of Nordic Projects [10] relating to
disabilities is another example of international co-
operation between non-EEC countries, namely, Denmark,
Finland, Iceland, Norway and Sweden. This publication
assembles information on research into disability and
technical aids, including testing and adaptation of aids
as well as investigation of needs. The register is issued
annually (now in its fifth edition) and lists the names
of the ordering agent of institution, principal
investigator, funding agency, starting date, estimated

date of completion and estimated cost, but,
unfortunately, very little on the evaluation of completed
projects.

Another international information system is being
developed by the Swedish Institute for the Handicapped
and is called TALDOC [11]. This is a computer-based
literature retrieval system in some fields of
rehabilitation, one of which is technical aids for the
speech impaired. The system contains about 800 references
to books, reports, journal articles and data sheets on
aids for the speech impaired.

In addition to databases which specifically provide
information for disabled people, there are various
services, based on the concept of packet switching, which
allow users to access another country's databases and
information systems, for example, International Packet
Switching Service (IPSS) which was introduced in 1978 by
British Telecom (then the British Post Office) and
operates between the UK and USA (since extended to
various other countries). It enables its users to access
databases and remote computing systems throughout the two
countries. There is also the Dutch Public Communication
Service which is similar to IPSS and is called Data Base
Access Service (DABAS). This service provides the user
with large quantities of information in a wide range of
fields such as literature abstracts. It is accessible via
the public data network of any country, for example, PSS
in the UK.

A CASE STUDY - THE DISABILITY DATABASE

Reference has already been made to the "Disability
Database" on British Telecom's Prestel service. In this
section, we examine briefly the facilities available on
this database at the present time and indicate possible
extensions.

The database consists of a maximum of 1200 frames, of
which about a quarter contain information. The concept of
the database is that it should provide a first line of
enquiry for disabled people and, as such, contains a
significant amount of detail about relevant organisations.

In addition, it provides as much information as possible
on "standard" enquiries - for example, the rate of Social
Security benefits (although it is hoped to remove them
from the database in the near future and merely provide
pointers into such a list provided by the Department of

Health and Social Security).

The database is structured in such a way as to (attempt to) minimise the time taken to obtain the required information while, at the same time, providing multiple routes to the same information, wherever this is deemed necessary.

In addition to the standard Prestel routing choices, it is intended to provide a keyword index, although this is not currently available. The database is being extended at present and, in the light of experience, restructured and it is expected that it will provide a useful service for, not only disabled people, but also professionals in the field.

In the case of certain disabilities, there will be problems in the use of Prestel. To take a simple example, the use of contrasting colours would be of little help to someone who is colour-blind. Similarly, the use of a medium such as Prestel is of little use to someone with a visual impairment. In these, and many other, cases, it should be possible to enhance the Prestel receiver to perform functions to obviate these difficulties. For example, in the case of colour-blindness, the receiver could determine that the contrasts were not adequate and modify one colour accordingly. Similarly, but technically more difficult, the text of a Prestel page could be input to a speech synthesiser so that the information would be spoken. These, and other enhancements, are currently under study.

CONCLUSIONS

There are a large number of people who have various disabilities and lack of access to suitable information provides an additional handicap. The use of computer-based technology can do a great deal towards removing this extra handicap and this has already been demonstrated in the area of videotex systems. The use of such technology will undoubtedly increase in the next few years and will thus be of considerable value in this area.

REFERENCES

1. Harris, A. I. , "Survey of Handicapped and Impaired in Great Britain", HMSO, 1971.

2. Cooper, S. E. , "An Investigation into the Provision

of Information to Disabled People in
Leicestershire", M Lib dissertation, Loughborough
University of Technology, 1980.

3. Saiady, C., "The Application of Computer Based
Technology to the Problems of Information
Dissemination for Disabled People - An Initial
Survey", Report TR-25, The Hatfield Polytechnic,
February 1981.

4. de Jonquieres, G., "Big demand creates huge
variety", Financial Times, 2 March 1981.

5. Stokes, A.V., "Characteristics of Micros and their
Applications", Proc. Joint BCS/IIS Conference on
"Minis, Micros and Terminals", 52-59, 1980.

6. Du Feu, D., "A Computer Based Welfare Benefits
Information System", The Inverclyde Project, IBM
(UK) Ltd., 1975.

7. Stokes, A.V., "Viewdata: a Public Information
Utility (Second Edition)", Input Two-Nine Ltd.,
1980.

8. --, "Broadcast Teletext Specification",
BBC/IBA/BREMA, September 1976.

9. --, "Information on Technical Aids for the Aged
and the Disabled - Short Analysis and
Recommendations for Community Action", The
Commission of the European Communities, 1980.

10. Petren, F., "Classification and Registration of
Technical Aids for the Disabled", The Nordic
Committee on Disability, 1978.

11. --, "The TALDOC Thesaurus", The Swedish Institute
for the Handicapped, 1980.

ACKNOWLEDGEMENTS

We wish to acknowledge the help of the many organisations
who have contributed the information discussed in this
paper. We would also like to thank Telemachus Ltd. for
their very significant help in connection with the
Disability Database and Savant Research Studies for
funding the project which is the basis of this paper.

An Information Service for the Disabled

Helen M. Townley

About a year ago, the BCS Committee for the Disabled
heard about the pages of PRESTEL on aids for the disabled
and appointed a Sub-Committee to look into it. We were
not very happy with what we saw and very little later
heard that it was being abandoned for the time being.
We suggested to the Committee that it might give
consideration to establishing its own database on all the
aids now being developed and based on the micro-computer
revolution and others made possible by The Chip.
Unfortunately the Committee was not able to proceed with
the matter at that time.

Only a few weeks later, however, the BBC TV programme
'Tonight' gave an extensive presentation of the rapid
developments being made in what I came later to call
Disablement Technology. I got in touch with the author
of that progrmme, visited him and was inspired with his
enthusiasm. I decided that since the BCS was not in a
position to establish such a service I would jolly well
'go it alone'....and so DEARS was born.

DEARS: Disablement, Electronic Aids, Reference Service.

Not 'retrieval service' because it will not give out
information on the actual aids:

(i)   because without knowledge of a suffer's actual
        condition I ought not to seem to recommend a specific
        aid: I shall tell him that A,B or C may have a
        siutable aid and tell him to get proper (usually
        medical) advice, telling also the name and address
        of the appropriate body - R.N.I.B., Spinal Injuries
        Association, etc. - and sending a copy of my letter
        to that body.

But so far enquiries have mainly fallen into the 2nd class:

(ii)   designers want to know if any other worker on such-
        and-such an aid has tackled the problem of........
        and found a way round it. Most of these workers are
        only too willing to share their knowledge, skill and
        experience. But there have been cases of the one
        seeking help then stealing and patenting the idea,
        (not just in Disablement Technology), so I just give
        a name and address, saying "you might find help by
        getting in touch with..."

So DEARS is not an information service in the accepted
sense of I.S.& R.

Frank Dale, who originally started me off on this trail,
went so far as to find a potential sponsor. We met last
October. Now, I was not then able to say that the idea
was feasible or even justified by the volume of information;
so I said that I would carry on unsupported for the next
few months and get in touch with him when I had proved the
validity of the idea. He advanced me £200 and a subsequent
well-wisher gave £50, and that £250 - and my overdraft -
is all DEARS has run on to date. With the sponsor, I met
a mini-computer manufacturer who promised that if I was
sponsored, he would provide the hardware. Pro. tem., I hold
the information on edge-notched cards.

At the time of that meeting I only knew of some 20-30 aids.
Obviously, then, my first task was to collect information.
Most of my time towards the end of last year was spent in
writing descriptive articles for the computing, medical
and paramedical, and general science periodicals. It paid
off hansomely. By December I was adding about 40 new aids
a week to the base, and though the main flood has dropped
I am still adding a dozen or so a week; I take a press-
cutting service from which I pick up a lot of reports about
aids developed 'for the kid next door','for himself' and
so on. Visits to hospitals and laboratories also produced
novel aids.

The most important thing to have happened is that my idea
was borne out - most aids are made by either a lone worker
at home or in the engineering and computing labs of
hospitals. AND THEY DO NOT GET GENERALLY REPORTED!

This failure in communication is appaling. A civilization
depending, like ours, on its communication skills, failing
like this!

That one person should invent a wheel is entirely laudable;
that two should simultaneously invent it, separately, is
ridiculous. Yet this is happening in Disablement Technolog
Here is an example from early in the life of DEARS - soon
after my first attempt at publicity: 'A' , a worker in
Northern England was helping a girl able to move only her
head, but with a talent for composing music; he was
trying to design a means of getting it written down.
I got in touch with 'B' who might, I thought, help.
When enquiring, 'A' had mentioned that he had designed a
wheel-chair controller for this girl. 'B' was able to
answer the music-writing question but was immediately
interested in the single-switch controlled wheel-chair,
being at that moment trying to develop one. So I put
them in touch with each other. To that extent, even if
it had done nothing else, DEARS has justified itself.

But, as you know, it was pure luck that lead them both to
contact me. And it aws pure luck again that they told me
about their work and so were able to help each other.
But it was pure luck... and are we to depend, in so
important a field as this, on pure luck? We need a
proper information service. And to make a proper
imformation service, you need information. So my
contribution today is primarily an appeal for information,
the life-blood of any science.

This is not to say that there are no existing information
centres. The specialist organisations for each of the
various disabling afflictions - the R.N.I.B., The Spastic
Society, the Society for Head Injuries and for Spinal
Injuries - all have collections of information about aids
for the people they serve; and the general ones, like the
Disabled Living Foundation, try to cover the entire field
of disabilities. But part of the problem here is that a
device designed to aid sufferers from 'A' may also be
useful to sufferers from 'B' and yet get reported to and
recorded by 'A' only.

It took me a long time when I started DEARS, to persuade
such specialised information centres of the utility of a
centralised information centre; but most now accept the

idea. Not all support the concept whole-heartedly; and
their argument that they are in a better position to advise
sufferers than an 'outsider' is perfectly valid (and is
why I do not give out information to sufferers). But at
least DEARS has got off the ground.

It was only in mid-April that I tried to estimate the
number of aids recorded within DEARS; till then I had
thought it was about 350 but I found it over 550. I
cannot give a definite figure, for I have still not decided
what is an aid. My record, for instance, for British
Telecom - a single record - shows 15 different kinds of
modification to the basic telephone handset. One aid,
therefore, or 15 ?

Nor, till I get properly sorted records, am I certain that
I have not got an aid once in its own right and once in a
catalogue. For instance, the DHSS in April 1980 published
"Aids for the Speech Impaired", listing 111 aids:
        to assist speech
        to produce speech from artificial sound generation
        to replace speech for those who can't use a
                              written language
        to replace it for those who can use a written language
A few of these aids I have, I know, recorded elsewhere in
DEARS, but without a properly organised system, I am not
sure how many.

Other compendia are the DHSS's similar one on environmental
control: others are 'Microprocessors for the Disabled' by
Sunderland Polytechnic workers and the resource book
updated regularly by the Trace Research and Development
Centre at the University of Wisconsin. Some of the devices
in this last I have, I know, collected elsewhere: but there
are others not in any of my records. For instance, the
Communimate, a micro-computer which can be used for
communication, environmental control, assessment and other
educational applications, entertainment and vocational
training; it was designed for the multiply-handicapped
(cerebral palsy, muscular distrophy, multiple sclerosis and
the like). With publications like these available, I am a
little hard put to it to defend the establishment of a
centralised information service. All I can say is that
many individuals and organisations in disablement technology
support me, and that the majority of aids are unrecorded
elsewhere.

I am concerned that there seems to have been very little
on games for disabled children. The London Borough of
Hillingdon has recognised this and developed POGO a
computer language for controlling animated puppets by
severely disabled children.

A recent visit to the Medical Engineering Unit of a local
children's hospital brought to my attention 11 devices
novel to DEARS yet none published in any literature.
(Actually none of these was computer-based, so in a way
they are not relevant to this meeting). But multiply this
by the number of such labs throughout the country - there
must be dozens of new aids being developed all over, and
of them unsung outside hospital walls.

The information sought for each program or device is:

- the name of the system (for identification)
- a name and address from whom more information can be
  obtained
- the disablilty or disabilities for which the aid was
  designed
- other disabilities for which it might be adapted, even
  though it was not developed with those specifically
  in mind
- the objectives

       first, in nice broad terms - communication,
       entertainment, mobility - or any combination of them

       second another set of keywords, much more precise
       (but using the designer's own terminology) to
       specify just what the device can do for a disabled
       user

and then briefly, something about:

- the hardware for which it was designed

       the computer; the configuration - for instance that
       it needs 2 line printers, or need access to 8k
       characters; the language in which it is written.
       And, of course, any charge made for it
- the extent to which the system has been evaluated -

       from fully tested down to just on the drawing board.
       Even the bright idea you had last night as you were
       falling asleep is worth recording

I would like to emphasise this last point. Your idle ideas
might prove a suitable project for, for instance, a degree
or post-graduate thesis. I think that it is important that
we encourage the younger entrants to our profession to think
of data processing not just along conventional lines.
(And you can always check with DEARS to find out if
anyone else has worked on it!)

Here is one more of the general purpose programs. It is
an aid to satisfy most physical disabilities. It is
controlled by a simple switch - any mechanical closing
can be used. The broad aims are education, communication
and environment control. Individual programs now
available are:-

- spelling, builds up messages from individual letters

- building up messages from stored vocabulary

- examination suite - 2 programs, = to set and = to take
  a multi-choise examination

- a drawing program allows the users to draw on an APPLE
  screen

- environment control operates remotely up to four devices
  such as light, fan, tape recorder' TV

- three games

Under preparation are a maths teaching package and
program to play tunes on the APPLE speaker. It was
designed for APPLE II with 48K disc; a printer is of
course needed if printed output is required. A special
mains switching unit has to be added for the environmental
control. Program is in BASIC and 5602 machine code.
Programs now available from the unit and shortly from
APPLE dealers. All these programs fully tested.

Now a set of programs aimed at a specific disability,
dyslexia. There are two main groups of programs - the
diagnostic, to pinpoint the genuine dyslexics from poor
spellers and calculators, and the structured lessons.
There are four units in the diagnostic set. The teaching
set comprises programs to

- overcome left-right confusion

- improve bad short-term memory

- overcome sequence confusion

- overcome spelling difficulties

  All these are on PET only. But on PET and 38OZ are
  programs to

- teach multiplication of large numbers and the so-called

Egyptian method of doubling and halving

- practice the points of the compass

- convert from volume to moles (the largest program to date, needing a 16K machine)

- teach the sequence of months

(all the programs except conversion of volume can use an 8K machine.) The programs were designed originally for a PET 8K cassette-loading computer, most of them now expanded to 380Z with twin disc drives and high definition graphics, though low-definition graphics can be used. The programs are freely available on receipt of a Commodore disc or cassette, or, for 380Z machines, a double-sided compatible disc.

Getting the information files organised, is going to be a sticky problem. I shall deal shortly with the thesaurus for DEARS, but pause for a moment to consider what an aid is as the principal subject of a record. Is the function the subject of the record; and if so what about a device which is multi-function? If one function can be operated by four different kinds of input device, there is, presumably, only one record. If different functions are executed by the same input, do I make 4 different records? It must be remembered that very seldom will retrieval be a straight look-up; almost certainly the main use of DEARS will be to retrieve devices which can be used to perform such-and-such by someone with such-and-such disabilities.

. . . .

I still hope ultimately to run DEARS on some sort of computer: the amount of information to be stored in respect of an aid (however I define it) is very large and will need a detailed and intricate thesaurus. For the time being, the best I can do is 94-hol e edge-notched cards. Which limits me to a total vocabulary of 94 descriptors - but at least some form of co-ordinate indexing is possible.

DEARS is using the Classification of Impairments, Disabilities and Handicaps produced for the W.H.O. by Dr. Wood of the Arthritis and Rheumatism Council Epidemiology Research Unit at Manchester. This distinction between the three facets is worth attention.

Impairment ... any loss or abnormality of physiological,
psychological or anatomical structure or function ...

Disability ... any restriction or lack (resulting from
an impairment) of ability to perform any activity in the
manner considered normal ...

Handicap ... a disadvantage for a given individual
resulting from an impairment or disability that limits
or prevents the fulfillment of a role that is normal ...
for that individual.

   Fig 6.. gives the first-digit classes in each of these
three broad classes:

Like most faceted classifications, at least one term from
each of these three classes pin points most accurately
what, with much less precision, we call simply "a
handicap". And since I can get every concievable
handicap for which an aid is designed in 50 holes, DEARS
is using the 2-digit codes for Impairment and Disability
and the first digit of the codes for handicap.

Another set of holes is used to indicate the part of the
body which has to be used to operate the aid. This is
not implicit in the 3 classes I have just shown you:
many hemiplegics, for example, can just move a finger;
people with exceedingly brittle bones can exert pressure
with some parts of the body more easily than others,
seriously paralysed cases can only suck and bow, or move
the head, and so on; so another 13 locations are used
for this.

Implicit in this same set of codes has to be the form of
input to the device. Once DEARS is computer-based, and
this limitation no longer applies, descriptors can for a
wide range of mechanical, electrical, eletronic terms
will be feasible; for the time being just one hole
indicates whether the information in the files does nor
does not cover the "technique of aid". A small set of
holes is allocated to how the aid makes its effect -
micro-computer, other computer, dedicated computer etc.
and whether the information relates primarily to the
computing or to the aid aspect of the problem (though
each record is primarily concerned with the aid per se.
The remaining holes are for retrieval of an aid by its
name, or the name of the individual concerned with it.

So far I have only talked about DEARS as retrieving
information about the physical things - the aids

themselves. There is not, in fact, a great deal of
published literature on aids (in fact, that is one
reason why DEARS is justified..) but there is some:
INSPEC scans the world literature on electrical and
electronic engineering and on computing. Now, the
Director of INSPEC has been very kind to us: he has
agreed to present, without charge, a "profile" run and
a print-out, on 'Computing' and 'Disability', for the
Group for Technology and Disability for their quarterly,
ACE. So far, ACE has been too short of space to cover
the results of the search of a 10-year backlog and will
only give author, title and source (but since the
advent of computer-based information retrieval systems
titles are becoming much more informative!)
Fig 9.. shows the total printed-out information on a
single document (selected literally at random - just
the first document of the list). We hope that the periodic
search, covering a much shorter period, will produce a
less massive result.

In addition to appearing in brief in ACE, I am hoping to
carry the literature, too, on DEARS, using a lot of
additional terms which I feel will be needed for the
highly specific retrieval needed for our purposes. So
I shall be able to point to relevant literature as well
as to actual aids when answering an enquiry.

(There is already one organisation publishing bibliographies
and effecting retrieval on aids - the Handikappintitutet
in Stockholm. Their thesaurus is not very specific.
But DEARS is not in any way competing with them;
nothing could be further from my intention.)

One of the problems I have still to come to terms with is
the distinction between mental and physical handicap.
Are sufferers from brain damage mentally or physically
handicapped? I am myself definitely physically
handicapped, t` rou jh brain damage affecting control over
my limbs, so in a way I am mentally handicapped. Hundreds
of children grow up deaf, and, because this is not
recognised early enough, dumb and, much worse, may be
treated as mentally handicapped. On the other hand,
mental handicap may cause a person not to be able to
learn the physical skills and to be physically
handicapped as well. There is not a well-defined border
between the two. DEARS is clear that it is about aids
to physical handicap. And I have written in large
letters over my desk "DEARS IS NOT CONCERNED WITH CAUSES
BUT WITH THEIR EFFECTS" But I've got to take causes
into account in drawing up the thesaurus. In fact, how

to index DEARS items is taking up a lot of my attention
at the moment.

A multi-disciplinary base is much better served by a
structured thesaurus than by retrieval based on words
naturally occurring in the texts being processed. In
addition to being multi-disciplinary, DEARS is dealing
not with texts but with objects, so there is all the
more reason for a proper thesaurus.

Sources of potential words are:

words from the INSPEC printouts (as they occur, natural
text, but in fact taken from a highly structured
thesaurus)

words drawn out of my own head, for the more specific -
for DEARS - indexing of the INSPEC output (natural text)

words from the Excerpta Medica thesaurus (drawn by me
from the unstructured index to the Rehabilitation and
Physical Medicine section to volume 22, though - again -
the descriptors are taken from a structured thesaurus)

words from the TALDOC thesaurus of the Handikappintitutet

words selected (not very methodically, but as the need
arose in indexing) from Butterworth's Medical Dictionary.

If any of you has access to another relevant collection
of words and could make it available to DEARS, I should
be most grateful.

Now, an information base that is not comprehensive
cannot be trusted. Most I R services start with their
information already acquired. DEARS started with the
idea of an information service and then set about
getting the information. So on of the reasons why I
leapt at the chance of presenting this paper was that it
would give me the chance of asking each of you who has
any likely - or even unlikely - contacts please to find
any one is doing any work on any kind of electronic aid
for any kind of disability, to let me know. If the
work is not relevant to DEARS I can always disregard it,
but I'd rather hear 50 times about the same irrelevant
thing than never once about one that is relevant.

And this brings me to my final point. Those programs
for teaching dyslexics. Might they not point a way in
designing a suite of teaching programs for children with

other learning difficulties?   They might be relevant to
teaching a differently handicapped child to spell - or
at least give pointers even if not directly useful
themselves. But of course, they could not even do that
if the teaching program people did not know about them.
I hope that this simple example has made my point.

There is still, of course, heaps still to be done of
DEARS quite apart from the major task of compiling the
thesaurus but speaking to you here today has been my
first step in making it publicly known that DEARS is
ready to accept an enquiry, for it is quite possible
that by now it has on its data base something at least
which is relevant.

This is going to cost money - postages and stationery,
typing and copying, proper office facilities - for all
these I will have to get money from somewhere. But
should DEARS depend on a sponsor? It is repugnant to me
to charge for information needed for socially useful
work - especially since most of the people working on
such projects in hospital or research units are not
what you might call well-paid anyway, and the disabled
themselves are certainly not well-off - but would it
not be reasonable to make a charge, and if so, on what
basis is it to be assessed.

Is an organisation that at present consists of me and
one volunteer 1 day a week, right to be controlled only
by my ideas of what should be done, and how? Ought I
not to have some sort of controlling body to oversee
DEARS? And from whom is such a body to be chosen?

If I don't have a sponsor, how am I to afford the
hardware and software.

I mention these because I don't want you to leave with
the idea that DEARS has sprung fully formed out of my
head, like Athene from the brow of Zeus. Since I'm
not supposed to work more than 45 minutes in any 60,
and on alternate days, I'm going to need help eventually.

But I am by now convinced, from what I have seen, and
the support I have had from the many professionals
concerned, that there is a place for DEARS and I would
like to take this opportunity of thanking them all for
their encouragement. In particular I would like to
express my special thanks to Martin Carrington, my
invaluable helper on DEARS, to INSPEC for the abstracts,
to Excerpta Medica not merely for help with the thesaurus

but for putting me in touch with useful contributors to
the data base, to Frank Dale without whom DEARS would
never have been born, and to Computer Age which published
my first attempt at making it known. And thanks to the
BCS through which I have this magnificent opportunity
of enlisting the aid of every one of you in getting
information for DEARS. Please remember the disabled
and remember all that the BCS is doing for them - and
remember that DEARS' needs information.

NEWSCLIP/APCUT

**ELECTRONICS
WEEKLY**

Weekly　　　　18,493

- 3 DEC 1980

TESTING a speech synthesiser developed by Matchless
Machines Ltd, Horsham, on behalf of the Manpower Services Commission, for use by blind people in industry who
are eligible under the Special Aids to Employment Scheme.
The headphones in use here are plugged into a digital
speakout which converts the binary coded digital readout
of a TESA electronic measuring system into synthesised
speech.
In addition to its use by the blind, the system is expected to
have many applications where electronic measurements
are transmitted by binary code in the electronics, avionics,
defence and security industries.
Standard vocabulary consists of numerals, mathematical
symbols, units of measurement or computer words. Languages are English, German or Arabic. The portable unit
weighs only 2kg and may be battery powered.

Steel News launches an appeal to aid children suffering from cerebral palsy

CAN YOU HELP?

SARA Miller is eleven years old. She cannot walk, move her arms or even talk. Her only way of communicating with the outside world is with a series of 'secret' signs with her feet she has devised with her parents.

But now all that may change because of the determination of a band of dedicated 'miracle workers' based in her own city of Swansea and led by Dr Alun Armstrong, principal research officer, Welsh Laboratories, based at Port Talbot Works.

Thanks to technology designed, ironically, for missile guidance systems aimed at creating bigger and better ways of blasting the human race out of existence, Sara may be able to talk with the aid of a computer.

However, it has cost the group in the region of £3,000 to give Sara this chance of a lifetime, and there are five other children in her school with similar disabilities, who

continued on page 2

CAN YOU HELP

continued from page 1

could also be helped in the same way, given that the cash is readily available.

Clearly it doesn't take a computer to work out the ultimate cost, and so Steel News is to launch an appeal, which we hope will culminate in Sara's five school chums being helped in the same way.

The group responsible for helping Sara is the West Glamorgan branch of the Rehabilitation Engineering Movement Advisory Panel (REMAP). A recent South Wales edition of Steel News told Sara's story and this sparked off the interest in REMAP.

Dr Armstrong, after learning about Sara's problems and then studying them in detail, was sure he could help her.

He found help forthcoming from a brilliantly gifted Port Talbot schoolboy, David Walker, considered to be a budding genius in the field of computers.

After many months of painstaking work, the group have already developed some pro-

ware can be bought virtually off the shelf. The hard work is writing the programs (software), which tailor the equipment to behave in the exact way for each individual child. That takes time. A ten minute teaching program can take as long as 10 hours to program. But I'm sure there are many people in BSC with this type of specialised knowledge who would be only too pleased to help us.''

A delighted Mrs Miller told us: ''We have just lived in anticipation since Dr Armstrong told us about the plan.

''Sometimes Sara comes home from school and she is itching to tell us what has gone on during the day. The frustration she suffers at not being able to communicate with us is unbelievable. Now, we hope, with the use of the computer she will be able to tell us.''

If you wish to help, please send your donations to Ron Jiggins, treasurer, West Glamorgan Branch, REMAP, c/o Ford Motor Company, Swansea.

Dr Alun Armstrong shows Sara and her family the new 'toy'.

grams for Sara and as our picture (taken on the very day she received her new 'toy') shows, she was over the moon!

Eventually the desk-top computer will be linked to a special speech synthesiser and by operating pedals with her feet, Sara will be able to select symbols or words on the television screen and have them spoken by the synthesiser.

Dr Armstrong told Steel News: ''What makes this system so perfect is that the hard-

Sara is suffering from cerebral palsy. It is a term covering many varieties of spastic child. It is thought to be due to brain damage at birth or in early infancy, and is depressingly common. Although a great deal can be done for the spastic (they are often of normal intelligence), the only sat: factory approach is prevention and this means expensive research into the causes.

Fig.3

INFORMATION SOUGHT

Name of system

Name and address from which information can be sought

Disabilities for which designed

Other disabilities to which it could be adapted

Objectives
        In broad terms
        Specifically

Hardware
        for which originally designed
        Configuration limitations
        availability to other users (e.g. remote access)

Program language(s)

Extent to which evaluated

Though information on each of these heads is required in
respect of computer-controlled devices, the same classes
of information are sought in respect of any aid.

Fig.4

A GENERAL PURPOSE PROGRAM SUITE

Aid designed for   Most physical difficulties. Driven by
a single-switch; any mechanical closing
can be used to drive the system.

Broad aims   Communication; educational; environment
control from displays on a domestic TV

Specific aids   A. Main Package

to write messages from individual letters

to build up messages from a vocabulary

to set and take a multi-choice exam

to control the environment - e.g. radio,
TV, tape recorder, light, door, telephone

B. Under Preparation

maths teaching package

play tunes on APPLE speaker

Hardware   APPLE II with 48K disc

Printer if paper output required

Special mains switching unit for
environmental control (may need slight
adaption for TV channel changing)

Program language   BASIC
6502 Machine Code

State   Main package fully tested. New programs
being added constantly.

Fig.5

PROGRAM SUITE FOR A SPECIFIC DISABILITY

Aid designed for   Dyslexia

Might also be used for   Slow learners with mathematical
                            and spelling difficulties

Broad aims   Diagnosis

                            Education

Sepcific aims   To pinpoint dyslexics as distinct
                            from bad spellers

                            Lessons to help pvercome right/
                            left confusion

                               bad short term memory

                               sequence confusion

                               spelling difficulties

Hardware   PET 8K cassette loading, originally.
                            Expanded to 32K PET with twin disc
                            drives.

                            Some programs will be available on
                            380Z on disc only, with high resoluti
                            graphics.

                            Nearly all programs will run on 8K
                            (except one special teaching program)

State   All programs fully tested and freely
                            available on pre-payment of postage.

Fig.6

W.H.O. 1st Digit Classes

IMPAIRMENTS loss of or abnormality of structure or function:

      Intellectual and psychological impairment

      Language impairment

      Aural impairment

      Ocular impairment

      Visceral impairment

      Skeletal and corporal impairment (including limb
                                    deficiency)

      Disfiguring impairment

      Generalised, sensory, other impairments

DISABILITIES restriction or lack (resulting from an impairment)
of ability to perofrm an activity in the manner considered
normal:

      Behaviour disabilities

      Communication disabilities

      Personal care disabilities

      Body disposing disabilities

      Dexterity disabilities

      Special skill disabilities

      Other actitity disabilities

HANDICAP disadvantage for a given individual resulting
from an impairment or disability that limits or prevents a
role that is normal (for that individual):

      Orientation

      Physical independence

      Mobility

      Occupation

      Social integration

      Economic self-sufficiency

Fig.7

AID OPERATED BY

Jaw

Face

Head, other than jaw and face

Throat

Body, trunk
      shoulder and upper arm
      elbow and fore-arm
      metacarpals and hand
      finger (inc. thumb)

Leg, hip and thigh
     knee and lower leg
     ankle and foot
     toe

Fig.8

OPERATION OF AID

Technique indicated

Micro-computer   Not computer controlled
Computer, other
dedicated computer
general purpose computer
input device indicated
output device indicated

PAGE   1
AIDS FOR DISABLED

-1-
AN - C80036463
TI - MICROCOMPUTERS FOR DEAF COMMUNICATIONS [IN PROCEEDINGS OF THE
       IEEE COMPUTER SOCIETY WORKSHOP ON THE APPLICATION OF PERSONAL
       COMPUTING TO AID THE HANDICAPPED, LAUREL, MD, USA, 2-3 APRIL 1980]
AU - RINALDO, P.L.; BRUNINGA, R.E.
OS - AMATEUR RADIO RES. AND DEV. CORP., MCLEAN, VA, USA ; IEEE
SO - IEEE, NEW YORK, USA, 78 PP., PP.22-7, 1980
DT - PA (PAPER); AP (APPLICATIONS)
LA - ENGLISH
CC - *3C7830; 3C7410F
IT - PERSONAL COMPUTING; COMMUNICATIONS COMPUTING
ST - DEAF COMMUNICATIONS; DEAF TELETYPEWRITERS; COMPUTER NETWORKS;
       MICROCOMPUTER; PERSONAL COMPUTERS
AB - MICROCOMPUTERS OFFER POTENTIAL FOR EQUIPPING THE DEAF WITH
       EQUIPMENT CAPABLE OF COMMUNICATING WITH BOTH EXISTING DEAF
       TELETYPEWRITERS AND COMPUTER NETWORKS. IN ADDITION, A
       MICROCOMPUTER MAY BE USED FOR OTHER PERSONAL OR BUSINESS
       APPLICATIONS. THE AUTHORS DESCRIBE THE WORK BEING UNDERTAKEN BY
       THE AMATEUR RADIO RESEARCH AND DEVELOPMENT CORPORATION (AMRAD) TO
       INTERFACE PERSONAL COMPUTERS FOR COMMUNICATION WITH DEAF
       TELETYPEWRITERS. IT ALSO OUTLINES THE USE OF A MICROCOMPUTER AS A
       MESSAGE SYSTEM THAT IS ACCESSIBLE BY BOTH ASCII AND BAUDOT
       TELETYPEWRITERS. IT DETAILS A PROTOCOL FOR SHARED USE OF A SINGLE
       PHONE LINE FOR BOTH ASCII AND BAUDOT SUBSCRIBERS. FURTHER, IT
       SUGGESTS A HIERARCHICAL STRUCTURE FOR MAJOR, REGIONAL AND LOCAL
       NODES TO SERVE DEAF AND OTHER USERS OF DATA COMMUNICATIONS OVER
       THE TELEPHONE NETWORK.

-2-
AN - C80036206
TI - MICROCOMPUTER AIDS FOR INDIVIDUALS WITH SEVERE OR MULTIPLE
       HANDICAPS...BARRIERS AND APPROACHES [IN PROCEEDINGS OF THE IEEE
       COMPUTER SOCIETY WORKSHOP ON THE APPLICATION OF PERSONAL
       COMPUTING TO AID THE HANDICAPPED, LAUREL, MD, USA, 2-3 APRIL 1980]
AU - VANDERHEIDEN, G.C.
OS - UNIV. OF WISCONSIN, MADISON, WI, USA; IEEE
SO - IEEE, NEW YORK, USA, 78 PP., PP.72-4, 1980
DT - PA (PAPER); AP (APPLICATIONS); PR (PRACTICAL)
LA - ENGLISH
CC - *3C7330
IT - MEDICAL COMPUTING
ST - HANDICAPS; REHABILITATION AIDS; ASSISTIVE PROGRAMS; MICROCOMPUTER
       AIDS
AB - THE POTENTIAL FOR USING MICRO-PROCESSORS AS A LOW-COST COMPONENT
       IN REHABILITATION AIDS IS A NEW AND VIABLE APPROACH, BUT IS MORE
       DIFFICULT THAN MIGHT BE IMMEDIATELY APPARENT. MANY PROGRAMS HAVE
       BEEN WRITTEN WHICH HAVE ALLOWED HANDICAPPED INDIVIDUALS TO USE
       MICRO-COMPUTERS TO PERFORM SINGLE FUNCTIONS. THESE PROGRAMS ARE,
       HOWEVER, GENERALLY WRITTEN AS FOREGROUND PROGRAMS, AND THUS
       CANNOT BE USED IN CONJUNCTION WITH OTHER, EXISTING SOFTWARE.
       SINCE IT IS NOT COST-EFFECTIVE TO RE-WRITE ALL OF THE SOFTWARE

Part 14
Software Engineering

Programs Without Programming

I. R. Wilson

*Department of Computer Science,
University of Manchester, UK*

This paper reviews the software production problems encountered and some of the solutions applied, during the MU5 project at Manchester. The difficulty of producing a large volume of software with a small but changing team of programmers has been overcome by use of automatic design documentation and code production tools. These tools have been largely diagram based and have developed from flowchart aids to more sophisticated and structured techniques.

The design technique most recently implemented at Manchester embodies a diagramatic representation of structured programming principles. The associated software documents the design elaboration and provides automatic generation of structured code listings in a choice of languages, including Pascal. A users view of this software tool and some experience of its use are presented within the paper.

HISTORICAL DEVELOPMENT AT MANCHESTER

The programming effort required to implement the basic system of
a new computer has been a problem which system designers have had to
face for some time. At Manchester University in particular, the
sixth successive new computer hardware design is currently being
implemented [1]. Heavy use of software tools during the most
recently completed of these projects, has been necessitated by the
small size and changing composition of the software team. Though
staff turnover is not a problem peculiar to university departments,
it is more certain when research students, by definition, stay for a
limited period.

On earlier Manchester machines, software emphasis was placed on
compilers, as typified by the provision on Atlas [2] of the Compiler
Compiler [3]. While this tool greatly simplified the production of
compilers, their efficiency suffered to some extent [4] and CC was
not so effective in tackling the problems of operating system
production. This resulted in a series of system programming
languages evolving [5,6,7,8] in scope and sophistication.

Despite improved languages, it was apparent early in the MU5
project [9], that further computer assistance was desireable. Figure
1 demonstrates the scale of the software aspect of this project.

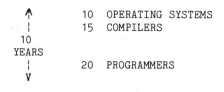

FIGURE 1   MU5 SOFTWARE

The frequency of staff changes, the need for communication amongst the team and the engineering background of the department at that time, caused a preference for diagrammatic documentation. Accordingly, the first software tools were aimed at automating the production of such diagrams during the software design. The necessity for a high degree of efficiency in operating systems and the use of highly machine dependant system programming languages, prolonged the life of flowcharts, discarded elsewhere at an earlier date.

Flocoder [10] was the first software tool to be provided for MU5 software development. This tool processed flowchart specifications to produce lineprinter and pen plotter diagrams for binding with descriptive narrative documentation. Attaching code specifications to each of the flowchart boxes permitted the system to generate programs in a linear 'machine coding' style. Most of the MU5 system software was developed using this tool. The disadvantage of the use of flowcharts and the unreadable nature of the generated code were accepted as the price for efficiency and detailed documentation.

EMERGENCE OF MORE POWERFUL SOFTWARE TOOLS

Several iterations of the flocoder software included an attempt [11] to make it more relevant to current generation languages. However, it is clear that the laudable principles of such languages are incompatible with the use of flowcharts and a wider view of the design process became desirable. Algorithm design may be an important part of this process, but it is generally accepted that consideration must be given to the modular nature of a problem solution and the information flow / data structures to be used. Retaining a diagrammatic base in this wider view, a 'programmer work station' might be envisaged as in figure 2.

DIAGRAMMATIC
DESIGN SPECS

⇓

CODE ⟸ | SOFTWARE
TOOLS | ⟹ HARD COPY
DOCUMENTATION

⇕

INTERACTIVE
DISPLAY

FIGURE 2. A PROGRAMMER WORK/STATION

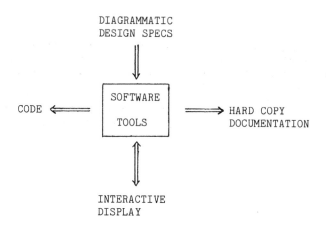

RED	Y	Y	–	N	N
AMBER	N	Y	–	Y	N
GREEN	N	N	Y	N	N
STOP()	1			1	
GET.READY()		1			
GO()			1		
TRAFFIC.SIGNALS()	2	2		2	
GIVE.WAY()					1

```
$IF GREEN $THEN
GO()
$ELSE
$IF RED $THEN
$IF AMBER $THEN
GET.READY()
TRAFFIC.SIGNALS()
$ELSE
STOP()
TRAFFIC.SIGNALS()
$CONTINUE
$ELSE
$IF AMBER $THEN
STOP()
TRAFFIC.SIGNALS()
$ELSE
GIVE.WAY()
$CONTINUE
$CONTINUE
$CONTINUE
```

FIGURE 3 A DECISION TABLE AND GENERATED CODE

636

Software tools were developed, under the guidance of the author, to support this idealistic picture. In an attempt to diversify the algorithm representations, a decision table processor [12] was implemented. It was hoped that the more state dependant parts of, for example, compilers, could be expressed more conveniently in this form. Figure 3 demonstrates how these diagrams were drawn and, in a local system programming language, how code could be automatically generated.

The importance currently placed on data, as opposed to algorithm, is illustrated by the data flow approach [13] to computation, by the respect paid in Britain to the commercial programming techniques of Michael Jackson [14] and the advent of languages such as PL/1, Algol 68 and Pascal [15,16,17]. This importance was partially recognised during the MU5 project, and a tool called Datadraw was produced, again under the guidance of the author, to provide documentation of data structures [18]. The diagrams produced were heavily used in the operating system design and their nature may be seen in figure 4. In fact, this is a relatively simple diagram and they were often more structured and complicated. However, Datadraw could document dynamic data structures only to a limited extent.

Clearly the approach   taken by all of the tools described above, is basically one of a linear view of the problem   solution. Accompanying textual descriptions and self discipline imposed by programmers themselves, generated a heirarchical flavour to the software on MU5. However, no significant assistance was given by software tools to demonstrate modularity and algorithmic structure.

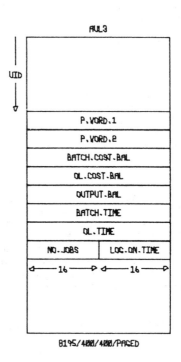

FIGURE 4. A DATADRAW DIAGRAM

STRUCTURE AS A DESIGN PRINCIPLE

The importance of data structures and modularity in recent developments, has been overshadowed only by overlapping advances in the use of the structured programming techniques, first proposed by Dijkstra [19]. This technique has since evolved in use in different communities in the computing world but is typified by

a) the construction of a program in terms of descending
heirarchical levels of abstraction.

b) the placing of a limit on the type of control structures used in
constructing the program.

The technique is embodied in languages such as Pascal. The author
of this language, Wirth, advocates the use of 'stepwise refinement'
associated with formal program verification [20]. This is a
basically textual approach, in which the statement of a solution is
written (perhaps proved) and rewritten, in more and more detail,
until it consists entirely of acceptable program. The validity and
popularity of this technique is not denied - indeed the author has
published a textbook advocating it to newcomers to the Pascal
language [21]! However, it does have a significant disadvantage for
a large scale problem, such as that of a new computer software
system. This is, that no documentation is produced, other than the
resulting program text. The many refinements are not easily related
to each other and may be obscured in the program text by its very
length. This difficulty derives from the fact that program text is,
unfortunately, only marginally more than linear and the difficulty
is only partially overcome by the use of procedures/modules.

The need for documentation to assist design, for communication
within a team and to assist in subsequent modifications, is not
precluded by the use of structured programming. This is well
demonstrated to anyone who has, for example, modified a large Pascal
program significantly - as has the author when porting Pascal
compilers written at Professor Wirth's college at Zurich.
Documentation is, of course, only as good as its accuracy in
representing both the intended solution and the actual program. This
accuracy may only be guaranteed if the program is not written, but
generated automatically from design documentation. It is assumed
that the undesirability of generating documentation from the program
is self evident!

The structured programming approach may be represented by a
nested diagram or 'structure chart' [22], where the level of
refinement corresponds to the depth of nesting, see Figure 5. This
technique is a valid means of demonstrating the form of an existing
program, but may not be helpfull during the design phase. One cannot
know in advance how big a box to draw and is therefore forced into
undesireable cross references or writing in character sizes which
appear to simulate perspective by their decreasing size.

```
┌─────────────────────────────────┐
│                                 │
│   PROBLEM SOLUTION              │
│   DESCRIPTION                   │
│      ┌──────────────────────┐   │
│      │ DESCRIPTION OF        │   │
│      │ FIRST HALF           │   │
│      └──────────────────────┘   │
│                                 │
│                                 │
│      ┌──────────────────────┐   │
│      │ DESCRIPTION OF        │   │
│      │ SECOND HALF          │   │
│      └──────────────────────┘   │
│                                 │
└─────────────────────────────────┘
```

FIGURE 5   FORM OF A STRUCTURE CHART

These problems might be overcome by provision of sophisticated on-line graphics, but the author has preferred the approach of representing the design by a tree structure. This form has been advocated by Michael Jackson and R. Witty[23], amongst others The essence of the use of a tree, is that each node of the tree gives a description of some part of the solution and the depth of the tree gives the degree of elaboration of the design. However, unlike the trees of Michael Jackson's technique, for example, the author draws them horizontally left to right in increasing depth and also demonstrates clearly the type of control structure elaborations applied.

ELABORATION AND TRANSLATION

The EAT system [24] has been developed by the author, to assist in the digestion of non trivial programming problems. It consists of

a)   a recommended tree diagram notation for elaborating the solution

b)   supporting software.

The notation is intended to assist the design and modification of a solution by localising the area tackled to the elaboration of one step. The software produces documentation diagrams and translates them into a program to perform the solution.

The diagram notation may be illustrated by considering the, admittedly trivial, version of the problem of a tax calculation. The most general statement of the steps in the solution are written one below the other, with a vertical line joining each to the next and a * symbol at the bottom, as in figure 6.

FIGURE 6 BASIC FORM OF AN EAT DIAGRAM

The steps may now be considered individually. Some steps may already be specified in sufficient detail, others may require some elaboration. This is written as a new column connected at the top to the step which is being elaborated, as in figure 7.

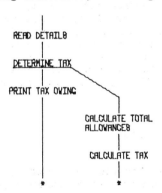

FIGURE 7   ELABORATION

This process is repeated for each step of any new columns, until every step is given in sufficient detail. Note the conventions of underscoring the steps which are elaborated and of drawing the * symbol at least as low as that of any subsidiary column.

If any step has several different elaborations, they are given in separate parallel columns. These are drawn with a line joining the tops of all the columns and with * symbols at the same level. Thus, since no one pays negative tax, however great their allowances, figure 8 is arrived at.

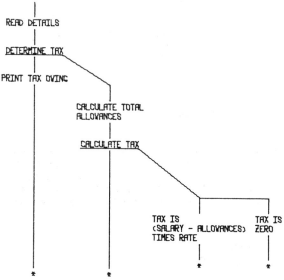

FIGURE 8   PARALLEL STEPS

CONTROLLING THE STEPS.

Clearly, the elaboration of the CALCULATE TAX step does not make sense, unless whatever controls the choice involved is also specified. There are three types of controlled elaboration - CHOICE, SELECTION and REPETITION.   Such 'control' over the steps may be exercised in two ways. Firstly, by use of special step types to be described later. Secondly, by specifying the type and form of the control of an elaborated step. This is written beneath the underscoring, as in figure 9.

Choice may be between two alternative elaborations, or a choice of whether or not a single elaboration is to be invoked. The control information should begin with the keyword IF and the first (or only) column is chosen if the condition given is true, see figure 9.

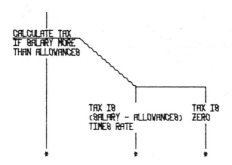

FIGURE 9   STEP CONTROL - CHOICE

A step may have several alternative elaborations, one of which is to be selected. In this case the step is controlled by writing the keyword SELECT followed by an object or calculation whose value governs the selection. Thus, considering the problem of implementing an arithmetic calculator on the computer, one step might be as in figure 10.

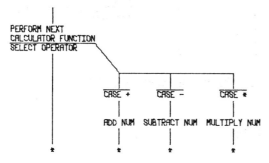

FIGURE 10   SELECTION

The special step type CASE normally only has control information. It is used to distinguish the various elaboration columns of a SELECT step.

Repetition is denoted by the control keyword LOOP. For a loop which is repeated a calculable number of times, the control information is given after the keyword. Otherwise the repetition should be controlled by one or more EXIT step types, as in figure 11.

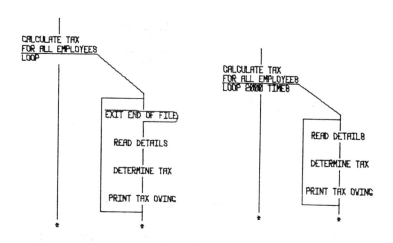

FIGURE 11   REPETITION

Note the drawing conventions of surrounding a loop elaboration with a line to the left and an EXIT step control with a line to the right.

Seven other step types are provided to assist in the control and layout of a diagram:

a) Each diagram should be given a name. This follows the word TITLE and appears at the top of the first column.

b,c,d) Where a procedure (or function) declaration is to be given, the control should be given as the keyword PROC (or FUNC) followed by the name of the procedure (or function) and any parameter information. The elaboration of this step is normally written as a separate chart, with the procedure (or function) name as its TITLE, as in figure 12. This also applies to an XREF step, in which the TITLE of a cross-referenced diagram follows the keyword XREF.

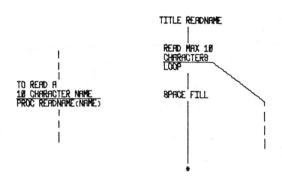

FIGURE 12   PROCEDURE DEFINITION

These three steps can be particularly effective in further localisation of sections of a solution, with a meaningful title. An XREF step implies an inline substitution, whereas a PROC/FUNC step would be invoked by procedure/function calls elsewhere.

e,f,g) Further control may be exercised over the solution by use of WITH, JUMP and LABEL step types. The WITH type opens up the scope of record data structure accesses, for all of the elaboration of the step. The keyword is followed by record selection information, as in figure 13.

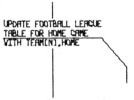

FIGURE 13   RECORD SCOPE

The JUMP and LABEL steps give, after the keyword, some identifying characters. They specify a direct jump from one part of the diagram to another. Their appearance would normally be infrequent or nil.

DIAGRAM SPECIFICATION

The EAT software accepts a file of commands and a file of diagram specifications. It may be directed to produce documentation drawings, on lineprinter or plotter, or to generate a program The notation used for batch specifications may be seen in figure 14.

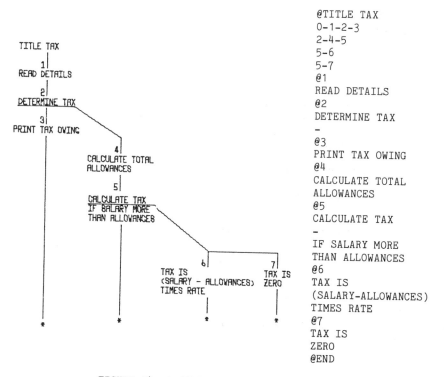

```
                                        @TITLE TAX
                                        0-1-2-3
    TITLE TAX                           2-4-5
        1|                              5-6
    READ DETAILS                        5-7
        2|                              @1
    DETERMINE TAX                       READ DETAILS
        3|                              @2
PRINT TAX OWING                         DETERMINE TAX
                                        -

                         4|             @3
                     CALCULATE TOTAL     PRINT TAX OWING
                     ALLOWANCES          @4
                         5|              CALCULATE TOTAL
                     CALCULATE TAX       ALLOWANCES
                     IF SALARY MORE      @5
                     THAN ALLOWANCES     CALCULATE TAX
                                        -

                                        IF SALARY MORE
                                        THAN ALLOWANCES
                       6|        7|     @6
                    TAX IS     TAX IS   TAX IS
                   (SALARY - ALLOWANCES) ZERO  (SALARY-ALLOWANCES)
                    TIMES RATE           TIMES RATE
                                        @7
  *         *          *        *       TAX IS
                                        ZERO
                                        @END
```

FIGURE 14   A COMPLETE DIAGRAM AND SPEC

The EAT software will generate a program from a set of diagrams.
The program will be of a high stylistic quality. This includes,
appropriate indentation, comments, cross-references to the diagrams,
use of language constructs wherever possible, creation of required
label declarations and definitions etc. In addition, the program may
be in one of several languages.

The high structural and stylistic quality of generated programs
may lead some users to treat the diagram as a design tool only. In
this case, the step specifications may be cast or re-cast in the
notation of the required language. No further specification is
necessary to generate the program.

However, if the English style step description is to be retained
as documentation, a new set of step descriptions, must be given for
each language required, as shown in figure 15. Where a step is
identical in both sets of descriptions, it need only be given once.

```
@TITLE TAX
0-8-9
9-1-2-3
2-4-5
5-6
5-7
@0.1
CONST rate = 0.35;   (*35P IN POUND*)
      alloweach = 150; (*150 POUNDS PER DEPENDENT*)
VAR salary,expenses,allowances : real;
    dependants,num,i,n : integer
@1.1
readln(salary,expenses,dependants,num)
@2.1
(* DETERMINE TAX *)
-
@3.1
writeln('TAX FOR EMPL',num,'IS',tax)
@4.1
allowances := expenses + dependants*alloweach
@5.1
-
IF salary > allowances
@6.1
tax := (salary-allowances) * rate
@7.1
tax := 0
@8.1
read(n)
@9.1
-
LOOP i := 1 TO n
@END
```

FIGURE 15a A PROGRAM SPEC

```
PROGRAM tax(input,output);
CONST rate = 0.35;    (*35P IN POUND*)
      alloweach = 150; (*150 POUNDS PER DEPENDENT*)
VAR salary,expenses,allowances : real;
    dependants,num,i,n : integer;
BEGIN
read(n);
FOR i := 1 TO n DO
    BEGIN
    readln(salary,expenses,dependants,num);
    (* DETERMINE TAX *)
        allowances := expenses + dependants*alloweach;
        IF salary > allowances THEN
            tax := (salary-allowances) * rate
        ELSE tax := 0;
    writeln('TAX FOR EMPL',num,'IS',tax)
    END
END.
```

FIGURE 15b THE GENERATED PROGRAM

A flavour of the options available in the system is given in figure 16. The FILLXREFS command is of interest, as this causes one large diagram to be drawn, for each starting chart specified, by bodily inserting each chart at its point of crossreference. The wall size charts produced prove useful in team discussion of a design. The NUMBERED option causes the drawn steps to be numbered as in figure 14 and comments in the textual program to be inserted to demonstrate the relation of the code to the diagram.

CODE n	DRAWALL	LANGUAGE i
CUESYM symbol	END	MONITOR i
DEVICE i[,i]	FILLXREFS	NUMBERED
DRAW n	INDENT i	VERSION i

FIGURE 16 COMMAND OPTIONS (n = name, i = number)

CONCLUSIONS

The primitive software tools available during the MU5 project
proved invaluable in documenting and controlling the software
production. Design effort could be encouraged and assessed before
programmers committed the design to implementation. Commissioning
and subsequent modification were facilitated by the certainty that
generated software corresponded to the available documentation.

EAT is a more recently available tool and has not yet stood the
test of large scale use. However, it has been implemented and used
on three machines. Porting it to the second and third machines was
eased by self-generation and the use of the Pascal programming
language. Several non-trivial items of system software have been
generated using EAT and it forms part of the standard library
facilities on MU5. Its advantage over previous tools is that, during
the design phase, it relates the purpose to the controlled
elaboration of each step, while maintaining a visual separation
between these two facets.

Clearly a knowledge of the control constructs of each available
language must be built into EAT, at least in a parametric form,
before it may generate code in that language. Only Pascal and
MUPL[7] are currently available, but the author is intending to
include FORTRAN 77, which has limited forms of control constructs.

Two serious criticisms of the system might be, that as much
effort is required to encode the steps as to write the program, and
that producing the batch specifications is an overhead on the
designers effort. The latter point is invalidated if interactive
graphics is available and it is, in any case, effort which could be
assigned to lower grade staff. The former point is closer to the
truth, regarding the number of symbols written, but the programmer's
mind is concentrated on the coding of one step as he codes it,
confident of its purpose, context and relation to existing
documentation. Indeed, the system has proven useful as a purely
design documentation tool, when an item of Z80 microprocessor
software was machine coded.

ACKNOWLEDGEMENT

The author wishes to acknowledge R. W. WITTY of the Rutherford
Laboratory, Chilton, England, as the origin of some of the ideas
presented and to thank him for the personal encouragement he
provided.

References

[1] D.B.G.EDWARDS, A.E.KNOWLES, J.V.WOODS (1980). "MU6-G. A new design to acheive mainframe performance from a mini-sized computer", the 7th. International Symposium on Computer Architecture, La Baule.

[2] T.KILBURN, D.B.G.EDWARDS, M.J.LANIGAN, F.H.SUMNER (1962). "A One-level storage system", IRE trans EC-11, No.2, p223.

[3] R.A.BROOKER ET AL (1963) "The Compiler Compiler". Annual Review in Automatic programming Vol.III p229.

[4] R.A.BROOKER ET AL (1967) "Experience with the Compiler Compiler", Computer Journal, Vol.9, No.4, p345.

[5] D.MORRIS, I.R.WILSON and P.C.CAPON, "A system program generator", Computer Journal, Vol.13, No.3, p248.

[6] P.C.CAPON, D.MORRIS, J.S.ROHL, I.R.WILSON, "The MU5 compiler target language and autocode", Computer Journal, Vol.15, No.2, p109.

[7,8] MUPL and MUDL manuals (1979). Internal technical documents of Department of Computer Science, University of Manchester.

[9] D.MORRIS and R.N.IBBETT (1979) "The MU5 Computer System". Macmillans.

[10] D.MORRIS, T.G.KENNEDY and L.LAST (1971) "Flocoder", Computer Journal, Vol.14, No.3.

[11] P.J.SCOTT (1973) "The Design and Implementation of an Automatic Coding System", MSc Thesis, University of Manchester.

[12] P.R.SAMBROOK (1974) "A Decision Table Processor", MSc Thesis, University of Manchester.

[13] R.M.KARP and R.E.MILLER (1966) "Properties of a model for Parallel Computations: Determinacy, Termination, Queuing", SIAM Journal, Vol.11, No.6, p1390.

[14] M.A.JACKSON (1975) "Principles of Programming Design" Academic press.

[15] ANSI X3-53 "Programming Language PL/1".

[16] A.VAN WIJNGAARDEN ET AL (1976) "Revised Report on the
Algorithmic Language Algol 68", Springer-Verlag, New York.

[17] K.JENSEN and N.WIRTH (1976) "Pascal User Manual and Report",
Springer-Verlag, New York.

[18] G.J.WHITE (1973) "Data Structures and an Automatic
Documentation System", MSc Thesis, University of Manchester.

[19] O.J.DAHL, E.W.DIJKSTRA and C.A.HOARE (1972) "Structured
Programming", Acedemic Press.

[20] N.WIRTH (1973) "Systematic Programming: An Introduction",
Prentice Hall.

[21] I.R.WILSON and A.M.ADDYMAN (1978) "A Practical Introduction to
Pascal", Macmillan.

[22] C.H.LINDSEY (1977) "Structure Charts - A Structured
Alternative to Flowcharts", ACM SIGPLAN Notices, Vol.12,
No.11, p36.

[23] R.W.WITTY (1977) "Dimensional Flowcharting", Software Practice
and Experience, Vol.7, No.5, p553.

[24] I.R.WILSON (1978) "EAT", MUSS Libraries Manual, internal
technical document University of Manchester.

SAVIOUR: A Tool to Assist in Constructing Large Software Systems

M. F. Bott

Lecturer, Department of Computer Science,
University College of Wales, Aberystwyth, UK

M.D. Tedd

Principal Consultant, SPL International Research Centre,
Abingdon, Oxfordshire, UK

Saviour is a tool which provides a unified environment for
the development of large software systems, without imposing
any specific design methodology.   It controls the source
code of the system, administers the relationship between
the source modules and supervises the construction of the
system from its component parts.

1. INTRODUCTION

Saviour is a software tool which has been developed by SPL's
Research Centre at Abingdon in collaboration with the Department of
Computer Science at the University College of Wales, Aberystwyth.
It was originally developed to satisfy clearly identifiable internal
needs but it rapidly became apparent that there was an important
external demand for such a product.

Saviour provides a unified environment for the development of a
software system. It controls the source code of the system,
administers the relationship between the source modules and
supervises the construction of the system from its component parts.
Furthermore, it provides a uniform and friendly interface to the
user. Many of the ideas in the system were inspired by SCCS [1]
and MAKE [2]; we have also been influenced by the Pebbleman and
Stoneman requirements [3].

2. BACKGROUND

Before describing Saviour in more detail, let us look at the
environment for which it is intended and, in particular, the problems
which it helps to solve.

Although the development of large software systems still presents
many difficulties, not the least of which is the amount of highly
skilled and scarce manpower required, there can be little doubt that
software engineering today is much healthier than it was ten years
ago. We have more experience of the problems we are tackling; we
have more experienced and more productive programming staff; we
have better programming languages, operating systems and utility
programs; and we have a much more mature understanding of the
principles of software engineering. As a consequence of this
overall improvement, we can implement software systems with far
smaller resources than would have been necessary a few years ago,
the failure rate of software projects is much lower, and we can
tackle projects of a more ambitious nature.

One of the key factors in this improvement has been our appreciation
of the benefits to be gained from modularity. Today's software
systems are built from comparatively small modules, individually
tested and developed, and we are tending more and more to re-use
these modules in systems other than the ones for which they were
originally developed. This re-use of modules is particularly
evident, of course, in the development of portable compilers, such
as RTL/2, but it is also becoming increasingly evident in such
application areas as process control. However, modularity brings in
new difficulties. In particular, the task of administering a large
collection of modules and ensuring that, when a system is built, the
appropriate versions of all the component modules are used, is

becoming increasingly onerous.

As an example of this difficulty, we can consider the case of RTL/2.
There are now over 20 different RTL/2 compilers and SPL Abingdon is
responsible for maintaining most of them.   Each compiler is made up
of some modules that are common to all the compilers, some modules
common to two or three compilers, some modules that are common to
several compilers but have to be slightly changed for each one, and
some modules that are unique to the particular compiler.   It is
clear that this situation can lead to considerable difficulties in
organising such a database of software.

It is to overcome precisely these difficulties that Saviour has been
developed.

3.   SAVIOUR - STRUCTURE AND FUNCTIONS

Saviour is built around the idea of the version store - a database
which contains the different versions of the modules which go to make
up a software system and which holds information about the way in which
these modules depend on each other (e.g. module B calls a procedure
which is defined in module A).   The most fundamental facilities in
Saviour are those concerned with manipulating the version store:
creating modules, editing them, creating new versions, etc.

Above this basic level, Saviour provides several groups of facilities
which may or may not be used in any particular application.   They
are:

-   access controls, by means of which Saviour can be used to control
    the level of access which individual users have to the various
    modules;

-   module preprocessing, which permits the source of a module to be
    processed in various ways before it is used (e.g. copying in
    material from other modules or including or excluding material
    according to the settings of parameters);

-   system building;   Saviour has facilities to support and control
    the complex job of putting together a software system from its
    component parts;

-   language specific features;   Saviour has some facilities designed
    specifically to help the construction of systems written in
    particular languages.   The first such facilities will be to
    assist RTL/2 users.   The language specific facilities are very
    self contained, so that users of arbitrary languages can still
    use all the other facilities of Saviour.

These facilities are described in more detail in the subsequent
sections.

4. THE VERSION STORE

The version store is a database containing a set of named modules
known as units.   In general the units contained in a particular
version store will all belong to the same project, but Saviour does
not attempt to enforce this in any way.   Each unit is a string of
text, and at the level at which the basic version store facilities
operate, no assumptions are made about the significance of the text.
Thus a unit may contain source program statements, data, command
store is analogous to a normal utility filing system such as the
George 3 filestore or the Files-11 system.

Saviour provides the obvious facilities for creating units from
external files, for copying the contents of a unit into an external
file, for listing units and for editing them.   Most importantly,
however, Saviour differs from a conventional utility filing system
in the facilities which it provides for handling versions of units,
for handling dependencies between units and for controlling access
to units.

4.1 Versions

Saviour handles three levels of versions — major versions, minor
versions and development versions.   These are numbered using the
usual decimal notation (e.g. 3.6.1);   the first digit refers to the
major version, the second to the minor version and the third to the
development version.   Although Saviour handles the different
version levels in different ways, various patterns of usage are
possible.   One example is the following:

At any given time, three major versions of a software system are
likely to be of interest;   suppose that these are major versions 2,
3 and 4.   Version 3 is the current version which most users of the
system are using.   A few users are, however, still using version 2
and this is still maintained.   Version 4 is a new version which is
still under development.   For each major version, one of the minor
versions will be marked as 'preferred', i.e. the one which most
users of that major version should have, Development versions are
those currently being worked upon;   Saviour regards them as less
permanent.

Saviour retains all major and minor versions of every unit in the
version store.   Furthermore, whenever a new minor version is
created, its creator must supply an explanation of the changes which
have been incorporated.   Saviour thus holds a complete history of
the new development of each unit.   Clearly this could make

unreasonable demands on the online storage available.   Saviour uses
several techniques to overcome this problem:

- text is held in a compressed format;

- most versions are stored as a set of changes from the previous one

- little used or older versions are held off-line.   (In the example
  given above, it would be likely that all information regarding
  version 1 would be off-line although Saviour would know on which
  disc or tape volume it was stored).

The first two of these are completely transparent to the user.

4.2 Dependency

A unit A is said to depend on a unit B if a change in B requires that
A be reprocessed in some way before being used to build the system.
In the simplest case, for example, A might be a source program unit
which required that some text from B be included before compilation.
Clearly a change in B would require that A be recompiled before
being used to build a new version of the whole system, even though
A itself had not changed since it was last compiled.   Provided the
Saviour conventions are adhered to, Saviour is able to detect
dependencies automatically, save this information in the version
store and make use of it to avoid unnecessary compilations or other
processing (e.g. macro processing) when the system building facilities
are invoked.

4.3 Access Control

Saviour provides facilities to allow a project manager, who is
regarded as the owner of a particular version store, to control the
extent to which users are allowed access to the units within that
version store.   At the top level, he can provide a list of users
who are allowed access to the version store at all;   no other users
will then be allowed to obtain any information from the version
store.   Below this, he can specify the right of access of each
user to a particular unit, e.g:

- read only access to preferred versions only;

- read only access to any version;

- the right to create new versions;

- no access right.

5. PREPROCESSING CAPABILITIES

One aspect of Saviour's preprocessing capabilities has already been
mentioned, namely the fact that Saviour allows a unit, A, to specify
that the text of another unit, B, is to be included at some
specified point in the text of A, before A is processed.   Such
inclusions may be nested, i.e. B may itself call for the text of
another unit C to be inserted, and so on.

It has become an accepted principle of good software engineering
that if an object such as a data structure has to be referenced
from a number of places, its definition should only be given once,
in order to avoid the errors which might result if one copy of the
definition were changed while another copy was left unchanged.
Unfortunately the requirements of many compilers and linkers are at
variance with this principle.   The simple inclusion facility
provided in Saviour overcomes this difficulty.   For example, a
Fortran COMMON block structure can be placed in a unit by itself
and then called into all the units containing subprograms which
need to reference that COMMON block.

A second type of preprocessing facility in Saviour is analogous to
the facilities provided in many assemblers by means of assembly time
variables and conditional assembly directives.   Saviour has its own
text variables and the values of these variables may be tested to
decide whether a part of the text is to be included or excluded.
This facility is intended to handle the need for slightly different
versions of units which may be needed in differing environments,
without the overheads and updating problems that would arise from
creating and maintaining independent copies.

It is at the preprocessing level also that the RTL/2 specific
facilities are provided.   The user may specify for example that a
data brick or procedure brick from another unit will be referenced in
the current unit and Saviour will then extract the ENT definitions
from the other unit, make the syntactic changes necessary to convert
them to EXT definitions and include these EXT definitions in the
current unit.

6. SYSTEM BUILDING

Modularity makes the job of constructing a system from its
components more complicated.   One has to arrange that all the
necessary compilations, assemblies, utility processing, etc are
carried out using the correct versions of the correct source files.
The final outcome of a system building operation may consist of many
things, each separately built, such as pieces of object code and
programs ready to run.   For reasons of efficiency, since system
building often takes a long time, one must try to avoid unnecessary

operations, e.g. recompiling a source file for which a correct
object file already exists.

Saviour can supervise this building process. The user describes
the structure of his system, supplies the commands needed to perform
each step in the building process and defines which versions of the
units are to be used. This last can be done in a variety of ways,
e.g. by giving a default version number and a list of exceptions.
Saviour then uses this information and its knowledge of what has
previously been constructed to ensure that all necessary operations,
and no others, are carried out. Any system which is being built is
regarded by Saviour as a collection of objects; objects are constructed
from source units (e.g. by compilation) or other objects (e.g.
by linking). Saviour does not handle the objects themselves
directly; they are stored in files external to the version store
but Saviour holds information about them within the version store.

Objects, like units, have version numbers but only a single level of
numbering is maintained. A new version of an object is always
created as the next higher version number. The user can create
and delete objects at will provided he has the necessary access rights.

For each object, Saviour holds a derivation which describes the
conditions under which it was constructed, i.e. names and version
numbers of the source units or objects which were used and the
settings of the various parameters. This means that if the
external file holding the object is deleted, Saviour has all the
information necessary to reconstruct the object. Saviour can thus
optimize the system building process by only constructing a new
version of an object if no existing version has the required
derivation.

The method of constructing a given object is specified in a command
unit; command units are held in the version store in the same way
as any other unit. Command units consist of a mixture of Saviour
commands and commands to the host operating system. Since they
are held in the version store they can be pre-processed in the same
way as other units. This means that the user can set up a hierarchy
of command units which reflects the structure of the complete system.

Saviour also recognizes the concept of a package, which is a group of
units, objects and, possibly, other packages which are in some way
related. Packages are similar to objects in that they have a
single level of version numbering and are constructed from within
a command unit; they also have derivations. The facility is
intended primarily for use in an environment where software is
delivered to customers but may also be useful in other contexts.
Saviour allows a package to be released; the customer receiving the
package, the version number of the package and the date of delivery
are then recorded by Saviour. This information can be interrogated

later to obtain, for example, the names of all customers who have
received some given version of the package.

7.   CURRENT STATUS

Saviour has been implemented on the PDP 11 computer under the
RSX11-M operating system.   It is programmed in RTL/2 and machine
and operating system dependent features are confined to a few
routines.

At the time of writing, the first version of Saviour is in use at a
number of sites; this version includes all the facilities described
here except for system building.   A second version incorporating
system building should become available during the summer.   It is
expected that a version of Saviour for the VAX computer will
become available within the next twelve months.

Full details are the facilities provided in the first version
of Saviour are given in the User Manual [4].

8.   BIBLIOGRAPHY

[1]   M.J. Rochkind (1975). 'The Source Code Control System'.
      IEEE Transactions on Software Engineering. SE1, 4 pp364-370.

[2]   S.I. Feldman (1979). 'Make – A Program for Maintaining Computer
      Programs.' Software-Practice and Experience. 9 pp255-265.

[3]   US Department of Defense (1979). 'Requirements for Ada
      Language Integrated Computer Environments.' (Preliminary
      Stoneman).

[4]   SPL International (1980). 'Saviour User Manual.'

A Compiler-Compiler for COBOL on Micros

A. E. Sale

Director, Angusglow Ltd, UK

The use of a compiler-compiler using the COBOL Metalanguage and using Metalanguage descriptions of the Target Machine Architecture is shown to result in a fast, robust and compact COBOL compiler for micros, with clear plain text error messages and a capability for tailoring the compiler to various dialects of COBOL.

1. Introduction.

This paper describes the design factors involved in producing a commercially viable COBOL compiler running on a micro-computer. The choice of a compiler-compiler approach is described together with the selection of a Metalanguage and the use of Target Machine Architecture Metalanguage descriptions.

2. The Multi-user problem and choice of a compiler-compiler.

A requirement arose for a compact, robust and easily maintained Multi-user COBOL compiler for compiling COBOL on micros.

One very effective way of achieving a Multi-user capability within the restricted addressing space of 16bit micros is to use the Bank Switch memory technique. In this technique the operating system resides in a fixed lower 32kbyte memory bank and each user has a dedicated bank of memory (up to 32kb). A hardware switch controlled by the operating system, connects as required one user bank as the upper portion of memory. The CPU thus "sees" a contiguous 64kb of memory at all times.

To be usable in such a bank switch system the COBOL compiler must either be completely contained within a 32kb user partition or be disected into 32kb of non-sharable code and tables and sharable code and tables which can reside either in fixed memory or in a shared pseudo user bank. Since a full implementation of COBOL was required it was not considered feasible to fit the compiler and user synbol table into 32kb. The use of overlays was also rejected on performance grounds. Thus the sharable tables became a necessity and this led to the compiler-compiler solution described below.

The compiler-compiler solution is particularly suitable because the final compiler is data driven by data sets produced by the Meta-compile phase of compiling the COBOL language specifications written in the Metalanguage. These data sets are pure read only data and are thus sharable by many users.

Previous experience with compiler-compilers had also shown that this approach produced very robust reliable compilers. This is because a relatively small set of primitives are required to implement a compiler-compiler since by definition it is mainly data driven. These primitives can be exhaustively tested thus ensuring high reliability and robustness.

Critics of the compiler-compiler approach have claimed that the resultant compilers run very slowly. This implementation shows that if care is taken in the design of the data sets driving the compiler and if a high level of target machine architectur is chosen then that very fast compilation speeds are possible.

The compiler-compiler approach considerably eases the maintenance and enhancement problems since in most cases only the Metalanguage source has to be changed and data sets recompiled.

3. The Structure of the Compiler-compiler.

Any compiler can be viewed as an information transformation between statements in a source language and statements in a target language, which may be machine code. In the compiler-compiler concept the Meta-compile phase compiles source in the Metalanguage into data sets used to drive an interpreter at source compile time. It is however also useful to view the compiler-compiler as two interpreters having a common interface data area and driven on one side by the Meta-compiled data sets representing the source language syntax and semantics and on the other side by Meta--compiled data sets representing the target language or machine syntax and semantics. See Fig 1.

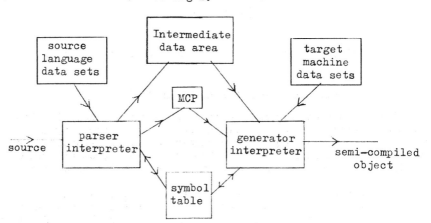

Fig. 1   Compiler-compiler architecture as a compiler.

In the Meta-compile phase the data sets on the input side represent the syntax and semantics of the Metalanguage itself and on the output side, the structure of the data tables. These Meta-compile data sets are hand coded to start the system off. The Meta-compile architecture is shown in fig 2. Because the final compiler is not in this case required to be extendable, the Meta data sets cannot be added to at final source compile time and are in fact pure read only.

As the similarities between fig 1 and fig 2 show, in principle the same syntax parser "engine" and generator "engine" could be used at Meta-compile time and source compile time. However in a final working source compiler, better performance is acheived if certain functions such as data allocation and picture parser are embedded in the compiler rather than being data driven.

In figs 1 & 2 MCP is the master control program controlling the synchronisation of the two interpreters.

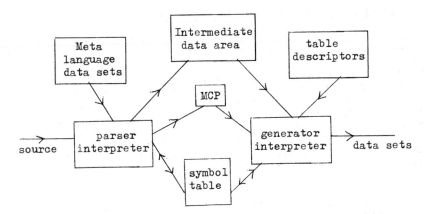

Fig. 2 Compiler-compiler in Meta-compile phase.

4. Choice of Metalanguage and Parsing Strategy.

The essence of a compiler-compiler is that it compiles into executable data sets the specification of the source language written in a Metalanguage. In designing a compiler-compiler two interacting factors have to be taken into account, namely, which Metalanguage to use and the coice of parser and the data sets driving it.

Most previously described compiler-compilers use the Metalanguage known as Backus Naur Form or BNF (sometimes refered to as Backus Normal Form), first used in the formal specification of Algol. (Gries, 1971). There are a number of objections to BNF as Metalanguage for a compiler-compiler for COBOL. Firstly BNF is very difficult to read at the best of times and almost impossible to read as a specification for COBOL. Secondly BNF translates most easily into data to drive a top down parser which would almost certainly be too slow for a working compiler. (Hopgood, 1969).

The COBOL language does however already posses its own Metalanguage namely the specification language for COBOL as used in the ANSI Standard, see fig 5. This COBOL Metalanguage is not formally complete since many important rules are specified in plain text outside the Metalanguage.

The COBOL Metalanguage does however have one overriding plus factor namely that it is very easy to read and clearly indicates to the human user of COBOL what are correct and acceptable source constructs in COBOL. It is thus very easy to maintain and enhance.

The choice of Metalanguage came down heavily in favour of the COBOL Metalanguage provided that its deficiencies could be overcome and provided that a machine readable form could be devised.

In choosing parsing strategy, speed of compilation was highest priority. Previous experience over a number of compilers had shown that a "matched pieces" approach called prototypes, was very fast and that "pieces" or prototypes could easily be generat--ed at Meta-compile time from the COBOL Metalanguage descriptions of COBOL. This technique is similar to SAG (Simpson,1969). The prototype approach is particularly appropriate to the COBOL language where the only open ended syntax structures occur in the COMPUTE statement. In COBOL the prototypes correspond to statements or phrases in the COBOL language. The syntax tree for COBOL can be arranged as single track and the parsing strategy is bottom up with no back tracking.

The data sets produced at Meta-compile time and used to drive the parser interpreter at source compile time, consist of a table of prototypes, a representation of the complete syntax tree for COBOLwhich shows the context of each prototype,a reserved word dictionary and tables relating semantic assignments and actions to specific prototypes. In the reserved word dictionary the entries are classified as delimiters, key words, verbs etc.

5. Rearrangement of the Specification of COBOL.

The ANSI X3.23-1974 Standard for COBOL contains the complete specification for COBOL mostly in the COBOL Metalanguage form but partly in written text form. Before the standard can be used as data input to a compiler-compiler all these written text rules have to be put into the Metalanguage where they really belong. The existing standard is very annoying to work from since these written rules are usually to be eventually found in some quite remote part of the standard manual.

A particularly bad example of these written rules is in the Format 1 specification of the General Format for Data Description Entry on page I-119 of the standard manual, reproduced in part in fig. 5. On reading through the texts on REDEFINES and VALUE in the NUCLEUS and texts on OCCURS in the TABLE HANDLING modules, a number of exclusion rules come out of hiding; such as for REDEFINES:-   "(3) This clause must not be used in level 01 entries in the File Section (See page IV-12, the DTAT RECORDS clause, general rule 2) "

or for VALUE:-   "(2) The VALUE clause must not be stated in a data description entry that contains an OCCURS clause ......   "

and for OCCURS:-   "(8) The OCCURS clause cannot be specified in a data description entry that has an 01,66,77 or an 88 level-number"

Figs 6,7 & 8 show in outline form how these and other similar rules have been incorporated into the revised specification of COBOL in the extended Metalanguage.

<u>GENERAL FORMAT FOR DATA DESCRIPTION ENTRY</u>

FORMAT 1:

level-number $\left\{ \begin{array}{l} \text{data-name-1} \\ \text{FILLER} \end{array} \right\}$

$\left[\; ;\quad \underline{\text{REDEFINES}} \quad \text{data-name-2} \right]$

$\left[\; ;\; \left\{ \begin{array}{l} \underline{\text{PICTURE}} \\ \underline{\text{PIC}} \end{array} \right\} \quad \text{IS} \quad \text{character-string} \right]$

$\left[\; ;\quad \underline{\text{USAGE}} \quad \text{IS} \quad \left\{ \begin{array}{l} \underline{\text{COMPUTATIONAL}} \\ \underline{\text{COMP}} \\ \underline{\text{DISPLAY}} \\ \underline{\text{INDEX}} \end{array} \right\} \right]$

$\left[\; ;\; \left[\underline{\text{SIGN}}\;\; \text{IS}\right] \left\{ \begin{array}{l} \underline{\text{LEADING}} \\ \underline{\text{TRAILING}} \end{array} \right\} \left[\underline{\text{SEPARATE}} \quad \text{CHARACTER} \right] \right]$

$\left[\; ;\quad \underline{\text{OCCURS}} \quad \text{integer-2} \quad \text{TIMES} \right]$

$\left[\; ;\; \left\{ \begin{array}{l} \underline{\text{SYNCHRONIZED}} \\ \underline{\text{SYNC}} \end{array} \right\} \left[\begin{array}{l} \underline{\text{LEFT}} \\ \underline{\text{RIGHT}} \end{array} \right] \right]$

$\left[\; ;\; \left\{ \begin{array}{l} \underline{\text{JUSTIFIED}} \\ \underline{\text{JUST}} \end{array} \right\} \quad \text{RIGHT} \right]$

$\left[\; ;\quad \underline{\text{BLANK}} \quad \text{WHEN} \quad \underline{\text{ZERO}} \right]$

$\left[\; ;\quad \underline{\text{VALUE}} \quad \text{IS} \quad \text{literal} \right]$

Fig 5.   Extract from ANSI X3.23-1974 Standard Manual

```
1   DATA DIVISION
2      [FILE SECTION
4          [COPY   text-name]
3      FD  file-name
4          [; BLOCK  CONTAINS     etc]
4          [COPY   text-name]
4          level-01  undeclared
7                        index-group-pic-level-88-clauses
5             [level-number  undeclared
7                        index-group-pic-level-88-clauses-
                         -with [OCCURS  integer  TIMES]
6                  [REDEFINES  declared
7                        index-group-pic-level-88-clauses] ]

2   [WORKING-STORAGE SECTION
4          [COPY  text-name]
4          [level-77  undeclared
7                        {index-pic-level-88-clauses}
7                        {pic-clauses-and VALUE    }
6                  [REDEFINES  declared
7                        index-pic-level-88-clauses]]
4          [level-01  undeclared
7                        {index-group-pic-level-88-clauses}
7                        {group-pic-clauses-and-VALUE    }
6                  [REDEFINES  declared
7                        index-group-pic-level-88-clauses]
5             [level-number  undeclared
7                        index-group-pic-level-88-clauses-
                         -with [OCCURS  integer  TIMES]]
5             [level-number  undeclared
7                        {index-group-pic-level-88-clauses}
7                        {group-pic-clauses-and-VALUE    }
6                  [REDEFINES  declared
7                        index-group-pic-level-88-clauses]]]
```

Fig. 6   Revised specification of COBOL

The aim has been to produce a single unique path through the complete syntax tree for any valid COBOL source construct. This eliminates back-tracking and results in very fast compilation speeds at the expense of a relatively large data set representing the complete syntax tree. It also provides for very clear error diagnostics and allows error correction for certain types of missing nodes in the syntax tree.

The major enhancement to the COBOL Metalanguage is the

inclusion of level numbers to show the syntax tree level at which
a construct is to be attached. These level numbers are shown
explicitly on the left hand side of the Metalanguage source,
although they could be inferred from tabbing rules if so desired.

An extension to the COBOL specification is to include more
semantic classes. Some of these like level-01 are specific to a
particular value, namely 01, of the more general class of level-
-number. Others are purely used to label nodes of the syntax tree
for attachment of other sections of the tree , such as
index-group-pic-level-88-clauses. Yet others such as declared
and undeclared are neede for error checking by the parser.

Further levels of expansion of the syntax tree outlined in
fig 6 are shown in figs 7 & 8. In fig 8 the empty class null
ensures that the default is USAGE IS DISPLAY. The picture string
analyser returns the classes alphanumeric, numeric etc.

```
         index-group-pic-level-88-clauses

              group-clause-level-88
                    level-88   undeclared VALUE IS literal
              pic-clause-level-88
                    level-88   undeclared VALUE IS literal
              group-clause
              pic-clause
              index-clause
```

Fig 7.   Expansion of a semantic class in fig 6.

```
     group-clause
                null
                [[USAGE] IS DISPLAY]
     pic-clause
              PIC IS alphanumeric
                     [[USAGE] IS DISPLAY]
              PIC IS alphanumeric-edited
                     [[USAGE] IS DISPLAY]
              PIC IS numeric-signed
                     [[USAGE] IS computational]
                     [[SIGN] IS] {LEADING } [SEPARATE        ]
                                 {TRAILING}  [        CHARACTER]
```

Fig 8.   Expansion of semantic classes in fig 7.

6. Machine readable form of the COBOL Metalanguage.

Since the specifications of COBOL written in the COBOL
Metalanguage are required to be used as input to the Meta—compile
phase of the compiler—compiler, they have to be in machine
readable form. This has been acheived as shown in fig 9.

	COBOL standard	machine readable
Reserved word	MOVE	"MOVE"
Optional word	IS	IS
Optional phrase	[USAGE IS]	["USAGE" IS]
Alternatives	{ LEADING / TRAILING }	("LEADING")/ ("TRAILING")
Semantic classes	literal	< LITERAL >
Ellipses	...	...

Fig 9. The machine readable form of the COBOL
Metalanguage

The machine readable form uses characters from the ASCII set
and the only real problem was simulating the vertical curly
brackets used in the COBOL Metalanguage to indicate alternatives.
If round brackets are used as shown in fig 9 and alligned
vertically then acceptable human readability is maintained.

7. Extensions to the Metalanguage to link to action routines and the interface data area.

Having arrived at a more complete Meta description of COBOL
by re—writing to include the text type rules, it was then
necessary to provide for mapping of the semantic information from
the source into the interface data area and for the initiation of
special actions, for instance at PROCEDURE DIVISION etc. This was
acheived by introducing two extra Meta symbols $=>$ and ! .
The equals greater than sign is used to show assignment of a
semantic value to a named location in the interface data area.
The exclamation mark is used to surround an action name. An
example of the use of these extensions is as follows:—

"MOVE" < IDENT > $=>$ P1 "TO" < IDENT > $=>$ P2   ! ISTAT !

At Meta-compile time each prototype is given a unique number which is used as a key for any assignment or action records associated with the prototype. The assignment record is generated from the list of assignments to intermediate data areas within the Meta statement, ie from   IDENT   Pl. The action record is derived from the list of actions, if any, following the Meta statement.

The COBOL compiler will work with any data set produced by the Meta-compile phase. This means that various data sets can be configured by editing the Meta COBOL source to match various dialects of COBOL. Data sets can also be produced which restrict the allowed COBOL constructs thus, if required, enforcing inhouse DP standards.

The Meta-compiled data sets for the COBOL language occupy about 12k bytes.

8. Target Machine Architecture.

It was decided at an early stage that the compiler would produce code for a pseudo machine which would be constructed in software. The reasons for this were twofold, firstly that the code generation phase of the compiler was made easier and secondly that the compiler was made more portable. The choice of target machine architecture (TMA) can vary from a very high level architecture matching the COBOL architecture, to a much lower level nearer to the hardware architecture. The subject of TMA is discussed in Elsworth(1979) in the context of compilation via an intermediate language (IL). Elsworth classifies IL's on the basis of relation to hardware architecture and match to source language. On his classification the TMA/IL chosen for this compiler is high level and highly machine independent. The main reason for choosing a high level is that it was not intended to compile the TMA/IL code down to hardware machine instructions but to interpret the generated code at run time by a soft or pseudo machine. In this case the software overhead of decoding the soft machine OP codes has to be made as small as possible compared to the time taken to execute the high level instructions. Thus by making the TMA match COBOL this interpretation overhead is minimised.

Doubts have been expressed about the speed performance of soft machines. It is however the authors experience that with the COBOL source language, careful design of the OP code fetch and decode and choice of high level architecture, that only 10-20% speed loss results over generated hardware machine code; which is usually only subroutine calls anyway.

The choice of nearly one to one correspondenc of TMA to COBOL verbs also has a number of other advantages. Firstly the code generation phase of the compiler is greatly simplified. Secondly since there is a nearly one to one correspondence between the TMA OP code and the COBOL source statement in the PROCEDURE DIVISION,

test and trace debugging becomes very easy to implement; just on
the OP code fetch routine in the soft machine run time
interpreter. This has the added advantage that special compile
switches are not required for debugging and that any COBOL object
program can be run under test and trace. Symbolic debugging is
achieved by saving the symbol table at the end of a source COBOL
compile and reloading it at test and trace time. Thirdly the size
of object program is considerably reduced, to an average of just
over 6 bytes per COBOL statement in the PROCEDURE DIVISION. This
small COBOL object size means that the full COBOL subprogramming
features can be easily implemented, especially since all TMA code
is program zero referenced ie is position independent in core.

9. Specification of Target Machine Architecture and code generation.

As discussed in section 2 above, data sets can also be used
to control the code generation and semantic error checking side
of the compiler. It is also possible and desirable to use Meta
descriptions of the TMA and to compile these descriptions at
Meta-compile time. Such an approach can also lead to semiautomatic
code generation.
    Boulton & Goguen(1979) describe a machine description
language which is for machine architecture at a lower level than
the TMA envisaged for COBOL. Since it also does not have any
embedded "hooks" for automatic code generation it was not
suitable for this compiler-compiler.
    The solution adopted for this COBOL system was to use a
COBOL-like Metalanguage in which to write the machine
descriptions together with the generator instructions and to use
the Meta-compile phase of the compiler-compiler to produce data
sets used to drive the final code generation phase of the COBOL
compiler. The format of a TMA description is shown in fig 10.

OP code	Variant	COBOL verb	semantic param. list	semantic actions
36	1	"MOVE"	$\langle$INTEGER$\rangle$ $\langle$INTEGER$\rangle$	INTEGER P1 INTEGER P2.

Fig 10.   Format of TMA description.

An outline of the complete machine description source is
shown in fig 11. This shows firstly the action list which
corresponds to the primitives in the generator interpreter. Then
comes the description of the interface data area used in the
compiler to interface between the parser and the code generator

interpreters. Next come the descriptions of the semantic classes used together with their assocciated code generator routines, if any, written in terms of the action names and the interface data area names. Finally the machine code specifications are presented in terms of the TMA OP code, variant, COBOL verb, semantic parameters and code generation routine invokations.

In this example in fig 11, if the parser had resulted in MOVE IDENT TO IDENT being on the prototype stack and MOVE INTEGER INTEGER being on the semantic stack, then when the prototype was validated and recognised, the symbol table addresses for the actual names of the IDENT's would be placed in locations P1 and P2 in the interface data area (see section 6). Control then passes to the generator interpreter which first searches for a match on the contents of the semantic stack. This when found points to the TMA OP code 36 and the compile routine INTEGER P1 and INTEGER P2. The OP code is then automatically generated and execution of the code generation commences.

       ACTION-LIST.
          .
       GEN16T1
          .
       END-ACTIONS.

       INTERMEDIATE-DATA-AREA.
          .
       240 PADDR
       260 P1
       300 P2
       END-INTERMEDIATE-DATA-AREA.

       SEMANTIC-CLASSES-AND-COMPILE-FUNCTIONS.
          .
       <INTEGER>   ....   GEN16T1 PADDR ....
          .
       END-SEMANTIC-CLASSES.

       MACHINE-CODE-SPECS.
          .
       36 1 "MOVE" <INTEGER> <INTEGER>   INTEGER P1
                                        INTEGER P2.
          .
       END-MACHINE-CODE-SPECS.

Fig 11. Machine Specification Input to Meta-compiler.

Code generation first links to the INTEGER semantic routine
taking the symbol table pointer placed into the interface data
area at location P1. The INTEGER sequence contains among others,
the invokation of GEN16T1. This, for instance, generates a 16 bit
value corresponding to the contents of the interface data area
location PADDR.

The size of the Meta-compiled data sets for the machine
descriptions are about 4k bytes, including keeping the literal
names of the semantic classes for error message generation.

10. The Lexical phase of the compiler-compiler.

At character level, when processing source, the compiler-
- compiler uses the usaul FETCH character routines which also
handle the production of a listing file together with error
messages and DATA and PROCEDURE division addresses.

The Get-Next-Word routine is driven by a character class
vector for the COBOL character set and a set of class precedence
rules. These are basically binary precedence with exceptions to
handle decimal point etc. All words are given tokens, usually
addresses in a table, and placed on various stacks. Identifiers
are dealt with as encountered including any qualification,
indexing or suscripting. If a PICTURE definition is encountered
then control passes to a separate picture analyser module. This
is basically binary precedence with some context rules to deal
with certain picture anomolies.

The compiler-compiler accepts source text produced by the
AMOS editor program VUE.

The main parser forms two stacks for each prototype, one
of reserved words and semantic classes and the other of semantic
values. On reaching a major or minor delimiter word, an attempt
is made to find a match for the prototype built so far on the
prototype stack by looking it up in the prototype table. If no
match is found then the parser carries on building. If a match is
found then control passes to the interpreter which assigns
semantic values to the interface data area and obeys any actions
specified. The prototype key number is then placed on a context
stack and this is then checked for validity.

11. The semantic phase and code generation.

On acceptance against a prototype of a piece of source text,
if the PROCEDURE DIVISION is being compiled then control passes
to the interpreter used for code generation and semantic checking.
The first thing that occurs is that the semantic stack built by
the parser is pulled through the table of TMA specifications. If
a match is found then the code generator interpreter runs against
the compile sequence pointed to by the TMA specification. This
code references items or tokens which have been assigned to
locations in the interface data area by the parser interpreter.

The code generated is semi-compiled tagged code relative to
data, literal, constant and code datums. An overlayed
consolidator routine reads back the semi-compiled code, resolves
all addresses and produces the final object module.

12. Error detection, correction and the generation of error messages.

Five basic types of errors are recognised by the compiler
namely:-

1.	ommissions	missing ---------
2.	syntax	no syntax for ------
3.	semantic	can't have ----------
4.	sequence	can't have -------
		after --------------
5.	specific lexical errors	

Within the first four catagories all messages are
constructed at compile time from the contents of the prototype
and/or semantic stacks built up as far as the error abort point.
This provides a very powerful and flexible method of error
reporting.

Because the complete syntax tree for COBOL is held in the
data sets produced by the Meta-compile phase, it is possible to
infer ommissions. If an ommission did not contain any vital
semantic information then the compiler can report the ommission
and then act as if it had been present by placing it on the
context stack. The error report just says:-

missing FILE SECTION

For syntax errors if the compiler fails to find a
prototype match then it reports the contents of the prototype
stack:-

no syntax for MOVE IDENT TO LITERAL

A semantic error arrises when no match is found in the table
of TMA specifications. A message might be:-

can't have MOVE NUMERIC-EDITED NUMERIC

Errors in sequence usually occur when the wrong COBOL phrase
is used to modify a construct:-

can't have ACCESS RANDOM
after ORGANISATION SEQUENTIAL

The specific lexical errors are such things as invalid
characters, missing quotes, duplicate names etc.

13. Performance.

The compiler—compiler has been implemented on an Alpha
Microsystems computer running on the Alpha Micro Operating
System (AMOS). It is written in Macro Assembler and takes
about 3,000 lines of source. The final COBOL compiler also
contains the Data Division allocation routines and picture parser
also written in assembler. The two read only data tables can be
placed either in System memory or in a pseudo user bank of Bank
Switch memory.
Compilation speeds are typically up to 400 lines/minute on
a 3 Mhz CPU clock speed and pseudo code density averages just
over 6 bytes per COBOL source statement in the Procedure Division.
In a 32kb user partition the compiler has symbol table room for
up to about 2,000 lines of COBOL source program. The level of
COBOL accepted by the compiler is very nearly full Level 2.
The compiler has proved to be very robust, as expected from
the compiler—compiler approach. One Technical College user with
9 concurrent student terminals doing mixed compiling and running,
has failed to crash the system in 7 months of very heavy usage.

14. Conclusions.

The compiler—compiler approach to producing a COBOL compiler
to run on a micro has resulted in a fast, compact and robust
compiler which allows, through the Metalanguage, easy maintenance
and enhancement of the COBOL language specifications.
In particular the ability to access parts of the Metalanguage at
compile time allows clear and aposite error messages to be given.
By editing the Metalanguage sources and re—running the
Meta-compile phase, data sets can be produced corresponding to
various dialects of COBOL. It is also possible by this method
to restrict the COBOL language features accepted by the compiler
in order to enforce in—house DP standards.

References.

ALPHA COBOL manual, Angusglow Ltd, 1980
ANSI X3.23—1974 Programming Language COBOL, FIPS PUB 21—1
Boulton P I P & Goguen J R, A Machine Description Language,
                     The Computer Journal, Vol 22 pg 132, 1979
Burgess C J, Compile-time error diagnostics in syntax-directed
                compilers, The Computer Journal, Vol 15 pg 302,1972
Elsworth E F, Compilation via an intermediate language,
                     The Computer Journal, Vol 22 pg 226, 1979
Gries D, Compiler construction for Digital Computers,
                     John Wiley & Sons Inc, 1971
Hopgood F R A, Compiling Techniques, Macdonald 1969
Simpson H R,   A compact form of one-track syntax analyser,
                     The Computer Journal, Vol 12 pg 233, 1969

A Logic of Correctness for Top-down Analysis and Synthesis of Programs

C. M. P. Reade

Brunel University, UK

A logic system is given for proving the correctness of incomplete programs relative to appropriate conditions for the unfinished parts. Such incomplete programs are termed 'conditional contexts' and arise quite naturally during the intermediate stages of development in top-down program design.

By interpreting the conditions as non-deterministic state transitions, the process of substituting programs or further contexts for conditions can be seen as narrowing the non-determinism. Derivations in the logic are based on 'correct substitution'.

INTRODUCTION

In this paper we show how it is possible to provide a logic system
for proving the correctness of programs which are incomplete,
relative to appropriate conditions for the unfinished parts. Such a
program can be termed a conditional context and arises quite
naturally during the intermediate stages of development in top-down
program design.

The usual Hoare logics for proving partial and total correctness of
programs are designed for bottom up proofs, requiring the constituent
parts of a program to be complete in order to combine their correctness formulae for verifying correctness of the composite program. It
is shown that with careful treatment of the conditions or inner
specifications, a small extension of the familiar Hoare method
suffices for verifications of these incomplete programs.

After introducing some basic definitions including a simple non-
deterministic programming language L_1 with its formal semantics,
section (2) deals with the introduction of conditions to make this
language to a language of Conditional contexts C_1. The central
definition in this section is the semantics of conditions as program
statements - instructions to achieve a desired goal (postcondition)
from the given precondition. In section (3) a proof system for
partial correctness of C_1 programs is described showing how the
'refinement' of a specification by substitution of 'appropriate'
contexts ensures a correct result. Section (4) deals with the soundness and completeness of the proof system and extensions to other
languages. The conclusions and possible future work from the last
section.

1. BASIC DEFINITIONS

We begin with a very simple programming language L_1 which has block
structure and local variables.

The syntax and denotational semantics of L_1 are described below using
a notation which closely follows that of DeBakker in [3] (see also
[11], [13]).

The dots, as for example in 'e,...' signify that subscripted versions
$e_1, e_2, \ldots$ etc. may be used.

L_1 Syntax: The language has the following syntactic categories:-

>   *Exp*   with variables e,...   (expressions)
>   *Bexp* with variables b,...   (boolean expressions)
>   *Prog* with variables P,Q,...   (program statements)
>   and the following sets:-
>   *Var*   (of variables) with x,y,... arbitrary elements of *Var*
>   *Cons* (of constants) with c,... arbitrary elements of *Cons*
>   *Fbase* (of function symbols) with f,... arbitrary elements
>   of *Fbase*
>   *Pbase* (of predicate symbols) with s,... arbitrary elements
>   of *Pbase*
>   and in particular = is included in *Pbase*

The syntax is then given by

$$P ::= x \leftarrow e \,|\, P_1; P_2 \,|\, \underline{\text{begin}}\ \underline{\text{new}}\ x; P_1\ \underline{\text{end}} \,|\, b? \,|\, (P_1) \cup (P_2) \,|\, (P_1)^*$$

$$b ::= \underline{\text{true}} \,|\, \text{false} \,|\, b_1 \supset b_2 \,|\, \neg b_1 \,|\, e_1 = e_2 \,|\, s(e_1, e_2, \ldots e_n) \text{ for each n-ary}$$

predicate symbol s in *Pbase*.

$e ::= c \,|\, x \,|\, f(e_1, e_2, \ldots e_n)$ for each n-ary function symbol f in *Fbase*.

Note the 'regular' constructs:- 'U' for choice and '*' for loop any number of times along with assertions of the form 'b?'. These are described in [7] and are essentially just non-deterministic versions of the more familiar branch and loop constructs which can be introduced as special deterministic cases. For example we can define

$$\underline{\text{if}}\ b\ \underline{\text{then}}\ P_1\ \underline{\text{else}}\ P_2\ \underline{\text{fi}} \triangleq (b?;P_1)\ \cup\ ((\neg b)?\ ;\ P_2)$$

$$\underline{\text{while}}\ b\ \underline{\text{do}}\ P_1\ \underline{\text{od}} \triangleq (b?\ ;\ P_1)*\ ;\ (\neg b)?$$

Before giving the semantic equations, we note some useful notation ommitting a formal definition.

Def$\underline{\underline{n}}$. The function <u>free</u> when applied to a program statement, expression or boolean expression produces the set of free variables in the statement (expression).

(Note that $\text{free}(\underline{\text{begin}}\ \underline{\text{new}}\ x; P_1 \underline{\text{end}}) = \text{free}(P_1) - \{x\}$
$\text{free}(\overline{b?}) = \overline{\text{free}}(b)$
$\text{free}(x \leftarrow e) = \text{free}(e)\ \cup\ \{x\}$ while in expressions and boolean expressions, all occurences of variables are free).

We also make use of a similar function <u>sets</u> which applies only to program statements producing the variables which are set by the program.

(Note $x \not\in \text{sets}\ (\underline{\text{begin}}\ \underline{\text{new}}\ x\ ;\ x \leftarrow e\ \underline{\text{end}})$
$\overline{\text{sets}}(b?) = \phi$
$\text{sets}(x \leftarrow e) = \{x\})$

Interpretations

An interpretation for L_1 is a set D (the domain) along with an assignment of (i) an element of D to each constant in *Cons*

(ii) n-ary functions over D to each n-ary function symbol in *Fbase*

(iii) n-ary relations on D to each n-ary predicate symbol in *Pbase*

with the equality relation assigned to =.

For interpretation I we write c_I, f_I, s_I for the interpretations of c,f,s respectively. In addition to fixing an interpretation for L_1 we will also need to introduce a set *Addr* of addresses which we take to be denumerably infinite and well ordered.

Def$\underline{\underline{n}}$. Σ the set of states with typical elements $\sigma, \ldots$ is the set of all functions from $Addr \rightarrow D$

Def$\underline{\underline{n}}$. *Env* the environments with typical elements $\rho, \ldots$ is the set of partial, one-one functions from $Var \rightarrowtail Addr$ with finite domains.

As we are dealing with partial functions, it is useful to have $\text{dom}(\rho)$ and $\text{range}(\rho)$ giving the domain and range of environment ρ respectively, and to augment D with an extra element($\perp$) to convert partial functions to total functions (writing $D_\perp$ for $D_\cup\{\perp\}$).

We will also use the notation $\sigma[d/a]$ to denote the state which is the same as σ except possibly on argument a which now gives result d. Similarly we use $\rho[a/x]$ with environments.

The semantic equations can now be given for interpretation I.

L_1 Semantics: The meaning of expressions is quite straight forward
$E : Exp \to Env \to \Sigma \to D_\perp$

$E[\![e]\!]\rho\sigma = \perp$ if free(e) $\not\subseteq$ dom(ρ), otherwise
$E[\![c]\!]\rho\sigma = c_\perp$
$E[\![x]\!]\rho\sigma = \rho(\sigma(x))$
$E[\![f(e_1,e_2,\ldots e_n)]\!] = f_\perp(E[\![e_1]\!]\rho\sigma , E[\![e_2]\!]\rho\sigma,\ldots E[\![e_n]\!]\rho\sigma)$

We omit details of the analogous semantics of boolean expressions except to note that $B : Bexp \to Env \to \Sigma \to \{tt,ff,\perp\}$. For the main syntactic category of program statements, we have

$$M : Prog \to Env \to 2^{\Sigma \times \Sigma}$$

(Thus the meaning of a program in an environment is to be a binary relation over states).

(i) $M[\![P]\!]\rho = \phi$ if free(P) $\not\subseteq$ dom(ρ), otherwise

(ii) $M[\![x \leftarrow e]\!]\rho = \{(\sigma,\sigma')|\sigma' = \sigma[E[\![e]\!]\rho/\rho(x)]\}$

(iii) $M[\![b?]\!]\rho = \{(\sigma,\sigma)|B[\![b]\!]\rho\sigma = tt\}$

(iv) $M[\![P_1;P_2]\!]\rho = (M[\![P_1]\!]\rho) \circ (M[\![P_2]\!]\rho)$ (usual composition of

(v) $M[\![P_1 \cup P_2]\!]\rho = (M[\![P_1]\!]\rho) \cup (M[\![P_2]\!]\rho)$ relations)

(vi) $M[\![(P_1)*]\!]\rho = (M[\![P_1]\!]\rho)*$ (reflexive transitive closure of

(vii) $M[\![\underline{begin}\ \underline{new}\ x\ ;\ P_1\ \underline{end}]\!]\rho = M[\![P_1]\!](\rho[a/x])$ relations)

Where a is the next new element in $Addr$ - range(ρ) (in the well ordering).

We note from (iii) that the meaning of 'b?' is a guard ensuring that computation down this branch only continues when b is true.

Also (vii) means that care must be taken to exclude, as we do from now on, those programs which use declared variables before they have been set (see for example [3] for reasons).

Assertions and Formulae

The class $Assert$ of assertions with p,q,r,... arbitrary elements of $Assert$ is given by p::= $\underline{true}|\underline{false}|p_1 \wedge p_2|\neg p_1|\exists x p_1|e_1 = e_2|s(e_1,\ldots,e_n)$ (s an n-ary predicate symbol in $Pbase$)

Extending free to apply to assertions (details ommitted), their meaning is given by the semantic function $A : Assert \to Env \to \Sigma \to \{tt,ff\}$ $A[\![p]\!]\rho\sigma = ff$ whenever free(p) $\not\subseteq$ dom(ρ), otherwise the equations are straight forward and the usual notation p[y/x] is used for substitution.

Assertions are used as pre-and post-conditions of programs to form logical formulae with which we describe partial correctness of programs. Initially we take $Form$ with variables $\delta,\ldots$ as, the set of partial correctness formulae defined by

$f::= p|\{p\}\ P\ \{q\}|\delta_1 \wedge \delta_2$

then extending free again so that free($\{p\}P\{q\}$) = free(p) $\cup$ free(P) $\cup$ free(q), the semantic function $F : Form \to Env \to \Sigma \to \{tt,ff\}$ gives the meaning of formulae as

$$F[\![\delta]\!]\rho\sigma = ff \text{ if free}(\delta) \not\subseteq \text{dom}(\rho), \text{ otherwise}$$

$$F[\![p]\!]\rho\sigma = A[\![p]\!]\rho\sigma$$

$$F[\![\delta_1 \wedge \delta_2]\!]\rho\sigma = \begin{cases} \text{tt if } F[\![\delta_1]\!]\rho\sigma = \text{tt and } F[\![\delta_2]\!]\rho\sigma = \text{tt} \\ \text{ff otherwise} \end{cases}$$

$$F[\![\{p\}P\{q\}]\!]\rho\sigma = \begin{cases} \text{tt if for all } \sigma' \\ (A[\![p]\!]\rho\sigma = \text{tt and } (\sigma, \sigma') \in M[\![P]\!]\rho) \Rightarrow \\ (A[\![q]\!]\rho\sigma' = \text{tt}) \\ \text{ff otherwise} \end{cases}$$

2. CONDITIONAL CONTEXTS

The Hoare-like correctness formulae {p}P{q}([8]) are used to make statements about a completed piece of program P. This P may form only part of a larger program Q, but it is still 'internally' complete when such formulae are applied. If now we wish to consider programs which are unfinished (- programs with 'holes' in them -) which we call contexts, then naturally questions of their partial or total correctness will usually depend on how the context is likely to be finished by supplying programs for the holes. However, by imposing conditions on the allowable completions, such as requiring them to satisfy another logical formula, we may be able to assert the validity of a formula involving the context. This brings us to the notion of conditional contexts, which are programs involving conditions at points where they are unfinished. For example, if α is a condition, we might have C = while x<0 do α od as a conditional context. Then if α expresses the condition that negative x are increased in value, we may show {x<0} C {x≥0} and that each of the programs x ← x+1 , x ← x+2, x ← -x satisfy the condition α. So substituting any of them for α would result in a 'correct' program for the specification x<0 precondition, x≥0 postcondition.

In general, we may wish to substitute further contexts for the conditions resulting not necessarily in an L_1 program, but possibly another conditional context. Beginning with the original specification, which can be treated as a condition and hence a conditional context, the process of substitution can be repeated, producing conditional contexts at each stage until eventually an L_1 program (a conditional context with no conditions left is produced).

Conditions and specifications we will treat as synonyms, and they will be, essentially, a precondition and postcondition which are assertions. However we will need to somehow 'control' which variables are to be altered in any program used to achieve a specification, and also, where blocks are involved, pass on some environment information (which variables are in scope) at the point in a context where a condition might appear.

For the language L_1, we can cover both requirements by incorporating into the conditions two sets of variables. One contains the variables which may be set in order to achieve the goal, while the second set contains all the other variables which are in scope and can therefore be used without declaration. Information about the values of such variables at a point in the context wouly only be assumed if it is explicitly mentioned in the precondition assertion.

Syntax of Conditions and Contexts

Letting $X, Y, \ldots$ range over finite sets of variables we give the syntax of conditions or specifications $Spec$ with arbitrary elements $\alpha, \ldots$
$\alpha ::= [p,q]_{X,Y}$ (where $X \cap Y = \phi$) and we call p, q, X, Y the pre-condition, postcondition, name-accessible variables and value-accessible variables of α respectively.

These are incorporated into L_1 to form a language of conditional contexts C_1. The class $Contexts$ with variables $C, \ldots$ and given by
$$C ::= x \leftarrow e \mid b? \mid C_1 ; C_2 \mid (C_1) \cup (C_2) \mid (C_1)* \mid \alpha$$
The functions free and sets will be extended to contexts by adding
$$free([p,q]_{X,Y}) = X \cup Y$$
$$sets([p,q]_{X,Y}) = X$$

which do not depend in any way on the free variables occuring in p and q since the X and Y 'control' the variables allowed in substituted programs while p and q may involve variables not to be used in any such substitution. For example the α described earlier stating that negative x are increased in value, could be written as
$$[x<0 \wedge x=z , x>z]_{\{x\},\phi}$$
Then the ommission of z from the subscripts, precludes the possibility of substituting programs which achieve the postcondition by changing z.

Semantics of Contexts

Perhaps surprisingly, we will not treat conditional contexts as partial functions over programs in L_1, but deal with them more directly as 'programs' in their own right.

The meaning of $[p,q]_{X,Y}$ in environment ρ will be a non-deterministic transition if p is true in the old state then q will be true in any new state, with the restriction that the new state can only be achieved by altering values of X.

The following notation is used in the semantic definition.

$\underline{def}^n$. $\sigma \xrightarrow{A} \sigma'$ (where A is a set of addresses, σ, σ' states) means $\sigma(a) = \sigma'(a)$ for all $a \in Addr - A$.

$\underline{def}^n$. $\rho(X)$ means $\cup \{\rho(x)\}$ i.e. the environment applied to a set of
$\qquad x \in X$
variables gives the corresponding set of addresses.

$\underline{def}^n$. ρ' extends ρ over X means $dom(\rho') = dom(\rho) \cup X$ and $\forall x \in dom(\rho)$
$\qquad \rho'(x) = \rho(x)$

Now we can define $\quad M : Contexts \to Env \to 2^{\Sigma \times \Sigma}$
using the same definition as before for $Prog$ (C replacing P) and in addition

$M[\![[p,q]_{X,Y}]\!] \rho = \phi$ if $free([p,q]_{X,Y}) \not\subseteq dom(\rho)$, otherwise

$= \{(\sigma, \sigma') \mid \sigma \xrightarrow{\rho(X)} \sigma' $ and $(A[\![p]\!] \rho' \sigma = tt \Rightarrow A[\![q]\!] \rho' \sigma' = tt)$ for all ρ'
extending ρ over $free(p) \cup free(q)\}$

Note that for states σ in which p is false, (σ, σ') will be included for all σ' such that $\sigma \xrightarrow{\rho(X)} \sigma'$. The use of an environment ρ' rather than ρ means that $[p,q]_{X,Y}$ will not be regarded as an undefined program (ϕ) should there be free variables in p and q which are not in $X \cup Y$ and therefore not going to be used in achieving the goal q but only to describe it.

Modified definition of Formulae

We will add subscripts to formulae to make the distinction between
auxilliary and input/output variables explicit as well as using
contexts for programs.

The syntax of $Form$ is now $\delta ::= p \mid \{p\}C\{q\}_{X,Y} \mid \delta_1 \wedge \delta_2$

For their semantics we note the use of the modified definition of free

$$free(p) = \text{as before}$$
$$free(\delta_1 \wedge \delta_2) = free(\delta_1) \cup free(\delta_2)$$
$$free(\{p\}C\{q\}_{X,Y}) = free(p) \cup free(q) \cup X \cup Y$$

and now

$$F[\![\{p\}C\{q\}_{X,Y}]\!]\rho\sigma = f\!f \quad \text{if either sets}(C) \not\subseteq X$$
$$\text{or } free(C) \not\subseteq X \cup Y$$

In future we will write $\models \delta$ (or $\models_I \delta$ if the interpretation I is not
obvious) instead of $F[\![\delta]\!]\rho\sigma = tt$ $\forall\sigma$ and $\forall\rho$ such that $free(\delta)\subseteq dom(\rho)$

3. A PROOF SYSTEM

The proof system which we use to derive properties of contexts will be
based on substitution. More specifically, the inference rules are
essentially just substitutions of contexts satisfying conditions α
for occurences of these conditions in another context. The more
familiar inference rules associated with Hoare logics of program
correctness are expressible as axioms and this is how they appear in
this system.

Substitution

Although the notion of substition is quite simple, a full formal
notation allowing both simultaneous substitutions and the selection
of a particular instance of a condition for substitution can be
unwieldy. Accordingly, we make the following assumption that each
occurence of a condition in a context is unique.

Writing $C(\alpha)$ to express that C is a context in which α occurs, we then
use the notation $C(C')$ to express the context arising by substitution
of context C' for condition α in C.

In the axiom for conditions (spec) the following notation is also
used:- $\forall X(p)$, where X is a finite set of variables, to indicate
universal quantification over each of the variables in X, the order
being unimportant. In addition we need to indicate for some
formula δ containing X, a set of new variables $\bar{X}$ (occuring nowhere in
δ), which is the same size as X and such that each element of X is
paired with a corresponding element in $\bar{X}$. Then a substitution such
as $p[\bar{X}/X]$ will naturally mean substitution of the appropriate element
of $\bar{X}$ corresponding to $x \in X$ for each such x.

Axiom System S

Axioms: All first order formulae valid in the interpretation I in
addition to

assign 1) $\{p[e/x]\} \ x \leftarrow e \ \{p\}_{X,Y}$ whenever $x \in X$ and $free(e) \subseteq$
     $X \cup Y$

guard 2) $\{b \supset p\} \ b? \ \{p\}_{X,Y}$ whenever $free(b) \subseteq X \cup Y$

concat 3) $\{p\} \ [p,q]_{X,Y} \ ; \ [q,r]_{X,Y} \ \{r\}_{X,Y}$

union 4) $\{p\}([p,q]_{X,Y}) \cup ([p,q]_{X,Y})\{q\}_{X,Y}$

loop 5) $\{p\}([p,p]_{X,Y})^* \ \{p\}_{X,Y}$

block 6) $\{p\}$ begin new x ; $[p[x'/x],q[x'/x]]_{X\cup\{x\},Y-\{x\}}$ end
$\{q\}_{X,Y}$

whenever x' $\notin$ X $\cup$ Y $\cup$ $\{x\}$ $\cup$ free(p) $\cup$ free(q)

extension 7) $\{p\}[p,q]_{X',Y'}\{q\}_{X,Y}$ whenever X' $\subseteq$ X and
Y' $\subseteq$ X $\cup$ Y and X' $\cap$ Y' = ϕ

spec 8) $\{\forall\overline{X}(\forall Z(p' \supset q'[\overline{X}/X]) \supset q[\overline{X}/X])\}[p',q']_{X,Y}\{q\}_{X,Y}$
where $\overline{X}$ are new variables for X and Z are
free elements of p' and q' not in X or Y.

Rules of inference:

MP (Modus Ponens) $\dfrac{p,\ p\supset q}{q}$

EXT (Extension) $\dfrac{p\supset p'\ ,\ q'\supset q}{\{p\}[p',q']_{X,Y}\{q\}_{X,Y}}$

SUBS (Substitution) $\dfrac{\{p\}\ C(\alpha)\ \{q\}_{X,Y}\ ,\ \{p'\}\ C'\ \{q'\}_{X',Y'}}{\{p\}\ C(C')\ \{q\}_{X,Y}}$

where $\alpha = [p',q']_{X',Y'}$

The requirement that all first order formulae valid in I are axioms
is quite strong since these may well not form a recursively
enumerable set (e.g. in the case of the integers with addition subtraction and multiplication). However the results of Cook [5]
demonstrate that we cannot expect more than relative completeness in
a reasonable logic of correctness.

Axioms 1 and 2 are standard apart from the addition of the subscript
restrictions X,Y which ensure x is allowed to be set (x $\in$ X) and that
all the variables in e and b are also accessible.

Axioms 3,4, and 5 take the place of the corresponding inference rules
from a system without contexts (see [1] , [3])which can be derived
from the given axioms using substitution.

Axiom 6 makes use of a new variable x' to describe the specification
after a declaration of new variable x, but note that the subscripts
X,Y exclude x' preventing its use in any valid substitution, while
x is available as a name-accessible variable in X $\cup$ $\{x\}$ (whether or
not it was already in X).

Axiom 7 is simple but important, as it ensures that programs which
may set variables in X' are still valid where the requirement is that
only variables in X may be set (X' $\subseteq$ X). Similarly, variables
accessible by value only could be any subset Y' of X $\cup$ Y.

Axiom 8 seems far from simple, but is necessary for completeness.
Most proofs should not need to make use of this axiom, which derives
from the expressibility of weakest preconditions. Roughly speaking,
the precondition is a property of those states σ such that when the
specification $[p',q']_{X,Y}$ takes us to another state σ', then q will
hold in σ', and this completely characterises the meaning of the
specification. The '$\forall Z$' ensures that the postcondition is achieved
whatever the value of the free elements in p' and q' which are not
accessible in the program, while the $\overline{X}$ stands for the desired new

elements of X.

The rules of inference are very simple, the main one (SUBS) being based on the substitution of a context C' satisfying condition α for an occurence of α in another formula while EXT corresponds to the usual Hoare rule

$$\text{EXT}' \quad \frac{p \supset p' \;,\; q' \supset q, \; \{p'\}P\{q'\}}{\{p\}P\{q\}}$$

With the usual definition of proof in S, we will write $\vdash \phi$ to mean that a proof of ϕ exists in S.

Some derived Rules

The following formulae for 'deterministic statements' can be proved when free(b) $\subseteq X \cup Y$.

WHILE $\qquad \{p\}$ $\underline{\text{while}}$ b $\underline{\text{do}}$ $[p \wedge b, p]_{X,Y}$ $\underline{\text{od}}$ $\{p \wedge \neg b\}_{X,Y}$

and IF $\qquad \{p\}$ $\underline{\text{if}}$ b $\underline{\text{then}}$ $[p \wedge b, q]_{X,Y}$ $\underline{\text{else}}$ $[p \wedge \neg b, q]_{X,Y}$ $\underline{\text{fi}}$ $\{q\}_{X,Y}$

which are probably more familiar as the rules (also derivable whenever free(b) $\subseteq X \cup Y$)

$$\frac{\{p \wedge \overline{b}\} \; C \; \{p\}_{X,Y}}{\{p\} \; \underline{\text{while}} \; b \; \underline{\text{do}} \; C \; \underline{\text{od}} \; \{p \wedge \neg b\}_{X,Y}} \qquad \frac{\{p \wedge b\} \; C_1 \{q\}_{X,Y}, \{p \wedge \neg b\} \; C_2\{q\}_{X,Y}}{\{p\} \; \underline{\text{if}} \; b \; \underline{\text{then}} \; C_1 \; \underline{\text{else}} \; C_2 \; \underline{\text{fi}} \; \{q\}_{X,Y}}$$

More importantly, we need to derive rules which are particularly suitable for the top down approach. In a sense, this is rather like taking a Hoare rule of the form $\frac{\{p\} \; P \; \{q\}}{\{p'\}P'\{q'\}}$ where P' somehow incorporates P, and applying it upside-down to find out what P should look like starting with a P' with its inner use of P missing (i.e. a context).

For example, we need a 'top-down' rule for loops, which tells us what to look for as a suitable loop assertion, given that p,q are pre- and postconditions. Compare the following with the above formula WHILE

$$\text{WHILE}' \quad \frac{p \supset r \;,\; r \supset q \vee b}{\{p\} \; \underline{\text{while}} \; b \; \underline{\text{do}} \; [r \wedge b, r]_{X,Y} \; \underline{\text{od}} \; \{q\}_{X,Y}}$$

whenever free(b) $\subseteq X \cup Y$

This then shows how the decision to use a while loop to reduce the specification $[p,q]_{X,Y}$ needs to go hand in hand with the discovery of loop assertion r satisfying $p \supset r$ and $r \supset q \vee b$, as we would expect.

Similarly $\qquad \dfrac{p \supset r, r \supset q}{\{p\}([r,r]_{X,Y})^*\{q\}_{X,Y}}$ is a useful derived rule.

Axiom 8 in the special case where free(q) $\cap X = \phi$ along with EXT allows us to derive $\qquad \{q\}[p',q']_{X,Y}\{q\} \qquad\qquad$ free(q) $\cap X = \phi$.

From this we can establish that for any Context C

$$\vdash \{p\}C\{p\}_{X,Y} \qquad \text{whenever sets (C)} \cap \text{free(p)} = \phi.$$

The need to use axiom 8 can be reduced further, by adding this as an axiom along with some more rules (whose soundness is not hard to check). In particular the rules

$$\frac{\{p\}C\{q\}_{X,Y}, \{p\}C\{q'\}_{X,Y}}{\{p\}C\{q \wedge q'\}_{X,Y}} \quad \text{and} \quad \frac{\{p\}C\{q\}_{X,Y}, \{p'\}C\{q\}_{X,Y}}{\{p \vee p'\}C\{q\}_{X,Y}} \quad \text{are useful.}$$

4. SOUNDNESS, COMPLETENESS AND OTHER LANGUAGES

The axiom system is said to be sound if $\vdash\!\delta$ implies $\models\!\delta$ which follows if firstly the axioms are all valid in the interpretation (i.e. $\models\!\delta$ for each axiom instance δ) and secondly, the rules of inference preserve validity (i.e. if $\dfrac{\delta_1,\delta_2}{\delta}$ is an instance of an inference rule and $\models\!\delta_1\wedge\delta_2$ then $\models\!\delta$).

The system is said to be complete if the valid formulae are all theorems, i.e. $\models\!\delta$ implies $\vdash\!\delta$. Such a completeness is actually relative to the interpretation, since we chose all valid assertions as axioms. For many important interpretations, this infinite class cannot be finitely generated (Gödel's incompleteness theorem) and so we have to assume the existence of some sort of oracle which can answer questions about the validity of assertions. As pointed out by Cook in [5] however, such questions about the underlying first order logic can and should be separated from questions about programs for which the system is designed, and the incompleteness of the underlying logic need not distract us from an investigation of the relative completeness of the system.

A proof of both soundness and completeness can be established from the following lemmas but we need to assume at this point that the interpretation is arithmetic (see [7]).

This assumption is necessary to establish the expressibility of weakest preconditions in the case of the loop construct (*) which requires a "Gödelization" of programs into arithmetic.

Lemma 1 For every context C, assertions p and q, disjoint finite sets of variables X and Y and variable x' not in free(p) $\cup$ free(q) $\cup$ X $\cup$ Y $\cup$ free(C) $\cup$ {x} we have

$\models\!\{p\}\ \underline{\text{begin}}\ \underline{\text{new}}\ x\ ;\ C\ \underline{\text{end}}\{q\}_{X,Y}$ if and only if

$\models\!\{p[x'/x]\}C\{q[x'/x]\}_{X\cup\{x\},Y-\{x\}}$

Lemma 2 For any contexts C_1 and C_2, assertions p,q and disjoint sets of variables X and Y, we have

i) For any assertion r

$\models\!\{p\}C_1\{r\}_{X,Y}$ and $\models\!\{r\}C_2\{q\}_{X,Y}$ implies $\models\!\{p\}C_1;C_2\{q\}_{X,Y}$

ii) There exists assertion r such that

$\models\!\{p\}C_1;C_2\{q\}_{X,Y}$ implies both $\models\!\{p\}C_1\{r\}_{X,Y}$ and $\models\!\{r\}C_2\{q\}_{X,Y}$

Lemma 3 For any context C, assertions p,q, disjoint sets of variables X and Y we have

i) For any assertion r

$\models\!\{r\}C\{r\}_{X,Y}$ and $\models\!(p\supset r)\wedge(r\supset q)$ implies $\models\!\{p\}(C)*\{q\}_{X,Y}$

ii) There exists assertion r such that

$\models\!\{p\}(C)*\{q\}_{X,Y}$ implies $\models\!\{r\}C\{r\}\wedge(p\supset r)\wedge(r\supset q)$

Lemma 4 For all contexts C_1 and C_2 assertions p,q, disjoint sets of variables X and Y, we have

$\models\!\{p\}(C_1\cup C_2)\{q\}_{X,Y}$ if and only if $\models\!\{p\}C_i\{q\}_{X,Y}$ (i = 1,2)

The soundness of the inference rule SUBS and completeness of the system can both be proved by structural induction on contexts. The details are ommitted here but as an example we take the case where C

is of the form $C_1;C_2$ in showing completeness ($\models\{p\}C\{q\}_{X,Y}$ implies $\vdash\{p\}C\{q\}_{X,Y}$). Using lemma 3 and $\models\{p\}C_1;C_2\{q\}_{X,Y}$ we know that there is a q_1 such that $\models\{p\}C_1\{q_1\}_{X,Y}$ and $\models\{q_1\}C_2\{q\}_{X,Y}$. By induction hypothesis we have $\vdash\{p\}C_1\{q_1\}_{X,Y}$ and $\vdash\{q_1\}C_2\{q\}_{X,Y}$.
It is now easy to see that using axiom 3
$\{p\}[p,q_1]_{X,Y}$; $[q_1,q]_{X,Y}\{q\}_{X,Y}$ and substitution twice, we have the desired result $\{p\}C_1;C_2\{q\}_{X,Y}$.

<u>Other Languages</u>

In L_1, the variables could be declared locally, and so the main interest in this language was to do with environments and the meaning and rules associated with blocks for which the subscripts X,Y of sets of variables in formulae were used. The subscript X will be a necessary part of the specification for other languages as well, but the second subscript Y contains the additional environment information, so in the simpler language with global variables only, one subscript X (variables which can be set) is all that is required. On the other hand, if we were to introduce procedures and procedure calls we might expect that the more sophisticated environments (associating procedure bodies with procedure names) would require further changes to the information contained in the second subscript. For global declarations, each procedure name in scope along with its associated body, would be needed.

Taking procedures which are declared globally and with ordinary variables also global, we look at the simplest case where we have a procedure declaration of the form $P \Leftarrow C_0$, P being a program variable and C_0 its associated body. C_0 may involve occurences of P thus giving a recursive procedure definition. We now consider conditional contexts C which may involve calls to this procedure. We need an appropriate rule of inference for the occurences of P in C in order to prove e.g. that $\models\{p\}P\{q\}_X$.

Usually the Scott induction rule requires an extension to the class of formulae (allowing $\delta_1 \to \delta_2$), but using contexts we do not need to do this, and simply use the rule

$$R1 \quad \frac{\{p\}C_0[\alpha/P]\{q\}_X}{\{p\}\ P\ \{q\}_X} \quad \begin{array}{l}\text{where } \alpha = [p,q]_X \\ \text{and } X = \text{sets } (C_0)\end{array}$$

The soundness of this rule is easy to establish using the following definition for the extended semantics. (M is now a function $M:\mathcal{Contexts} \longrightarrow 2^{\Sigma\times\Sigma}$ as we are no longer using environments)

$$M[\![P]\!] = \bigcup_{k=0}^{\infty} M[\![C_0^{(k)}(\underline{\text{false?}})]\!]$$

where for any C' $\quad C_0^{(0)}(C') = C'$

$$C_0^{(k+1)}(C') = C_0[C_0^{(k)}(C')/P]$$

note that $M[\![\underline{\text{false?}}]\!] = \phi$ (the empty set) making $\underline{\text{false?}}$ correspond to the 'undefined' program. None of the $C_0^{(k)}(\underline{\text{false?}})$ involves P and their meanings give a monotonically increasing chain of relations on Σ

corresponding to a recursion of depth k for $k \geq 0$.

In order to prove the soundness of the rule R1 we make use of the soundness of SUBS for contexts C,C' without calls to P

$$\models \{p\}C(\alpha)\{q\}_X \quad \text{and} \quad \models \{p'\}C'\{q'\}_{X'}, \quad \text{implies} \models \{p\}C(C')\{q\}_X \tag{1}$$

where $\alpha = [p',q']_{X'}$.

We also need the 'monotonicity' of contexts $C_0^{(k)}(P)$ i.e. that

$$M[\![C_1]\!] \subseteq M[\![C_2]\!] \text{ implies } M[\![C_0^{(n)}(C_1)]\!] \subseteq M[\![C_0^{(k)}(C_2)]\!] \quad k \geq 0$$

which can be shown by induction on n and the structure of C_0.

<u>Theorem</u> R1 is sound.

<u>Proof</u> Suppose $\models \{p\}C_0[\alpha/P]\{q\}_X$ ($\alpha=[p,q]_X$ and $X = \text{sets}(C_0)$) $\tag{2}$

Using (1) where $C=C_0$ and $\alpha=[p,q]_X$ along with (2) we can show by induction on k that

$$\models \{p\}C_0^{(k)}(\alpha)\{q\}_X \quad \text{for all } k \geq 0 \tag{3}$$

Now let $(\sigma,\sigma') \in M[\![P]\!]$ such that $A[\![p]\!]\sigma= \text{tt}$. This means that (σ,σ') $\in \overset{\infty}{\underset{k=0}{\cup}}M[\![C_0^{(k)}(\underline{\text{false?}})]\!]$ and thus $(\sigma,\sigma') \in M[\![C_0^{(k)}(\underline{\text{false?}})]\!]$ for some $k \geq 0$

By monotonicity we can show that for all k

$$M[\![C_0^{(k)}(\underline{\text{false?}})]\!] \subseteq M[\![C_0^{(k)}(\alpha)]\!] \quad \text{and so by (3) we know}$$

$A[\![q]\!]\sigma' = \text{tt}$, and hence $\models \{p\}P\{q\}_X$ as required.

For more complex languages, involving both local variables and more general procedure calls and allowing parameters to be passed (by reference, value or otherwise) the 'copy rule' determines the semantics which in turn governs the appropriateness of a rule of inference and the form of the specs in Contexts. Results concerning the completeness of Hoare like systems for languages (without specs) and whether they exist or not, can be found in both [4] and [9].

5. FURTHER WORK and CONCLUSIONS

Approximation ordering

It is more common, with non-deterministic programs to have for the semantic domain not all subsets of $\Sigma \times \Sigma$ with the ordering determined by the subset relation, but to use functions $\Sigma_\perp \rightarrow P_B(\Sigma_\perp)$ where $\Sigma_\perp$ contains an undefined state $\perp$, and $P_B(\Sigma_\perp)$ is a restricted class of subsets of $\Sigma_\perp$ suitable for 'bounded' non-determinacy. The ordering of $P_B(\Sigma_\perp)$ is the Egli-Milner Ordering, and does not treat for example $\{\sigma_1\}$ as below (an approximation to) $\{\sigma_1,\sigma_2\}$ because $\{\sigma_1\}$ indicates a completely determined result which could never continue to produce $\{\sigma_1,\sigma_2\}$. On the other hand $\{\sigma_1,\perp\}$ <u>is</u> below $\{\sigma_1,\sigma_2\}$, the undefined state $\perp$ indicating possible further computation which could produce σ_2.

In this paper, however, the non-determinism is present for a particular purpose. Namely to allow for algorithms which are not completely defined in that a particular deterministic method of solving a subgoal may not be available.

An algorithm which produced as resulting state $\{\sigma_1\}$ (starting in state σ say) would be an acceptable alternative or even a better solution to a problem than an algorithm which produced more possible results ($\{\sigma_1,\sigma_2\}$ say), so the subset ordering is of interest in this particular use of non-determism.

It is important to note that we are forced to abandon the restriction
of bounded non-determinacy, which only allows a finite set of choices
of next state, when we introduce specifications into programs, since
these usually allow an infinite set of choices.

Termination

So far, the term 'correctness' has been used in the sense of partial
correctness and does not take account of possible termination problems.
The program <u>false?</u> satisfies all specs α and thus could be substituted
into any context to give a (partially) correct solution, but of course
a non terminating solution ($M[\![\underline{false?}]\!] = \phi$).

To ensure that only totally correct solutions are constructed, it is
necessary to have additional formalism to express termination conditions (see [3]). A spec when taken out of a contextual while loop
may not provide any clue as to the 'value' which is to change each
time round in such a way that termination can be guaranteed. It would
therefore be useful to contain in a spec some further information
about the desired change. For example, we could make use of a new
variable 2 and a predicate '<' which is to be interpreted as the
ordering relation of a well founded set to indicate that expression e
must decrease in value $[p \wedge z=e, p \wedge z>e]_{x,y}$. Along with this, it may be
convenient if the semantics were to incorporate some sort of history
of computation steps such as computation trees (see [7]) and for the
case, where unbounded non-determinism is involved, a semantics based
on infinitely branching trees has been described by Back in [2].

Applications

A great deal of work is already being done in the area of computer
aided verification of programs and in particular the interactive
development of correct programs. It seems to be a sensible symbiosis
to have machines providing accurate checking of details while the
programmer directs or supervises development by providing the intuit-
ion.

The underlying theory or theories of the data types being used
(integers in the above examples) provides not only the language for
the formulae p and q of specs (predicates, functions and constant
symbols), but also axioms and useful theorems which could be provided
by a programmer, and possibly kept in a knowledge base for general use.
The knowledge base then gives us an approximation to the oracle mentioned earlier which answers questions about the integers for example.
The base could be put to further use by guiding the search for a
solution to a specification using its stored useful theorems and
solutions to equivalent problems, while at the same time generating
more theorems. Again much work is being done in the area of automatic
synthesis of programs, particularly with the use of first order logic
as a tool for expressing problems. Prolog ([12]) for example, allows
programs and specifications to be considered in a unified way by
treating certain logical formulae as programs. The formalism presented in this paper again mixes the two but allowing the use of more
familiar programming constructs. It is to be hoped that this mixture
will prove to be a useful tool for expressing partially developed
programs and for interfacing man and machine while they work on the

problem of 'completing' or rather <u>improving</u> the intermediate solution
represented as a conditional context.

REFERENCES

[1] K.R. Apt 1979. "Ten Years of Hoare's Logic, A Survey" in Proc. 5th
    Scandinavian Logic Symposium. Aalborg University Press.

[2] R. Back 1980. "Semantics of Unbounded Non-determinism" in 'Auto-
    mata, Languages and Programming', Lecture Notes in Computer
    Science No. 85 - Springer - Verlag.

[3] J. de Bakker 1980. "Mathematical Theory of Program Correctness"
    International Series in Computer Science - Prentice Hall.

[4] E.M. Clarke 1979. "Programming Language Constructs for which it
    is Impossible to Obtain Good Hoare-Like Axiom Systems" Journal
    A.C.M. <u>26</u> No. 1.

[5] S.A. Cook 1978. "Soundness and Completeness of an Axiom System
    for Program Verification", SIAM J. on Computing <u>7</u>.

[6] H. Egli 1975. "A Mathematical Model for Non-deterministic
    Computations", ETH, Zurich.

[7] D. Harel 1979. "First Order Dynamic Logic" Lecture Notes in
    Computer Science No. 68 Springer - Verlag.

[8] C.A.R. Hoare 1969. "An Axiomatic Basis for Computer Programming"
    Communications ACM <u>12</u>.

[9] H. Langmaack and E. Olderog 1980. "Present-day Hoare-like Systems
    for Programming Languages with Procedures: Power, Limit and Most
    Likely Extensions" in 'Automata, Languages and Programming',
    Lecture Notes in Computer Science No. 85 - Springer - Verlag.

[10] R.J. Lipton 1977. "A Necessary and Sufficient Condition for the
    Existence of Hoare Logics" Proc. 18th IEEE Symp. on Foundations
    of Computer Science.

[11] R.E. Milne and C. Strachey 1976. "A Theory of Programming
    Language Semantics" (2 Vols.) Chapman and Hall.

[12] P. Roussell 1975. "PROLOG: Manuel de Reference et d'Utilisation."
    Groupe d'Intelligence Artificielle, Universite d'Aix - Marsaille,
    Luminy.

[13] J. Stoy 1977. "Denotational Semantics : The Scott - Strachey
    Approach to Programming Language Theory" MIT Press.

[14] R.D. Tennent 1976. "The Denotational Semantics of Programming
    Languages" Communication ACM <u>19</u>.

Part 15
Performance Measurement

Monitoring CODASYL Database
Management Systems

Colin I. Johnston* and Aileen S. Stone

*Research Fellows,
Aberdeen University Computing Centre, UK*

* Present address: Atlantic Instruments Ltd., UK

This paper describes the development of monitoring tools for a CODASYL database management system. Monitoring information is collected at several different levels and stored in a data dictionary which also holds schema and subschema information about the database being monitored. The data dictionary can then be used in the analysis of the monitoring information, and in the assessment of likely effects of organisational and structural changes to a database. Ideally, all access to databases should be through a data dictionary such as the one described: however such an architecture is not essential to the use of the monitoring techniques described.

1.   INTRODUCTION

Many organisations make a major investment in designing a database
architecture to meet all their present and projected needs. However,
as these organisations evolve, their data processing requirements will
change, and the original database architecture may not provide the
best way of meeting the new requirements. With appropriate tools, an
organisation's database administrator (DBA) can monitor the state and
usage of a database. Using the information collected by these tools,
he can then determine how degradations in performance might be
alleviated by making changes to that database.

Many of the most widely used commercially available database
management systems (DBMSs) are implementations of the CODASYL model
and our material is presented in terms of this model, in particular as
implemented in Honeywell's I-D-S/II [7]. CODASYL recognises that for
effective long-term use of a DBMS, both the state and usage of a
database should be monitored [4]. The BCS/CODASYL DDLC Data Base
Adminstration Working Group (DBAWG) distinguishes two classes of
monitoring information in its report [1]:
  * Static statistics, describing the state of a database at a
    particular moment in time.
  * Dynamic or usage statistics describing the pattern of usage of a
    database.
The static statistics illustrate how well a database implements its
current schema design; for example the size and distribution of
clusters, the suitability of CALC keys, the accuracy of the sizing of
pages and areas. The usage statistics illustrate which parts of the
database structure are being accessed most frequently and enable the
DBA to assess how well the structure matches the usage. Most DBMS
implementors have provided some tools corresponding to the CODASYL
recommendations on monitoring [3], but few systems provide
monitoring information in sufficient detail for it to form a sound
basis for DBA decisions on reorganisation and restructuring.

For any database, the monitoring information collected relates to
operations performed on objects in that database and so it seems
sensible to hold the information in a meta-database together with a
description of the database. Data dictionary specialists at a recent
conference emphasised the desirability of storing monitoring
information in a data dictionary with a view to forecasting any need
for reorganisation [2]. We have therefore developed a data dictionary
in which we store   monitoring information together with schema and
subschema information on the monitored databases.

2.   IMPLEMENTATION OF MONITORING

In order to maintain an optimum service to users, the DBA needs to be
able to determine which organisational and structural modifications to
the database will lead to the greatest improvement in performance.
Static statistics will give some help here and should be collected

periodically, but usage statistics are also needed to show which parts
of the database are being accessed and the costs of access. Usage
monitoring may be implemented using either a hardware or software
monitor. Software monitors have the disadvantage of degrading system
performance while, with a hardware monitor, it is often difficult to
relate the information collected to a particular activity.
Accordingly, for monitoring a DBMS at the data manipulation (DM)
function level, a software monitor is ideal, since the results
produced can easily be related to the activity of the program being
monitored [6,9]. The overheads of a software monitor can be minimised
by the use of efficient coding techniques and by providing switches so
that the DBA need collect only those statistics for which he has a
definite purpose. Our implementation is conducted in a research
environment, where the overheads incurred by monitoring are less
important than in a commercial environment, and so we have implemented
all our monitoring by software.

Monitoring of the usage of databases can be carried out at various
levels, depending on the purpose for which the monitoring information
is being collected. We envisage a spectrum of usage monitoring and we
have paid particular attention to the following levels in the
spectrum:
* The intent level, where information is collected on the nature
  of complete transactions carried out on a database.
* The path and step level where we collect information on the
  usage of path and step (record->set->record) traversals through
  a database structure.
* The DM function level, where information is collected on the
  lowest level of DM operations directly available to a program.
* The storage level, where information is collected on the
  transfers between the Database Control System (DBCS) and
  storage.
Further levels in the spectrum can be identified: for example the
storage level could be subdivided into logical and physical storage
levels.

2.1 Intent level monitoring

This involves capturing the users intent in accessing a database
rather than monitoring the way in whcih he actually navigates through
the database structure. We felt that it was most practicable to
implement usage monitoring at this level by monitoring access to the
database through a high-level interface. An alternative strategy is to
attempt to extract the intent from the source of the program [10], but
this is not straightforward even for small programs. We developed a
simple high-level interface called NAVIGATOR, designed to relieve the
user of the problems of navigating through a database structure, and
to allow him to express his query as simply as possible [8]. NAVIGATOR
allows a user to view a database as a collection of data items and
submit a query using the following syntax:
        FETCH <data item name> [,<data item name>] ...
[:WHERE <data item name>=<value)> [,<data item name>=<value>] ...]

Thus the NAVIGATOR syntax itself represents the intent of the user in accessing the database. Query profiles are recorded in the data dictionary so that over a period of time, a picture can be built up of the use being made of the database. The query is characterised by:
* The data items requested
* The data items for which values were supplied in the AND selection conditions.

The current syntax of NAVIGATOR is somewhat limited, but we believe that it is sufficient to demonstrate the usefulness of monitoring at this level.

2.2 Path and step level monitoring

A step is a record->set->record traversal through a database structure. We have implemented monitoring at this level via the NAVIGATOR query interface described in the previous section. The code generated by NAVIGATOR to access the database includes CALLS to a subroutine which records, on a sequential file, statistics about each step taken through the database structure. Step monitoring is simplified by the stepwise way in which NAVIGATOR accesses a database; accessing all the required occurrences of each record type before progressing to the next record type. During execution of the program generated to process a user's query, the following information is recorded on a sequential file:
* The type of step - CALC entry, singular set entry, realm entry, owner-to-member step or member-to-owner step.
* The destination record of the step.
* Where applicable, the set involved in the step.
* The number of iterations of the step made on this execution - for all types of entry step this is defined to be one; for an owner-to-member step the number of owners; for a member-to-owner step the number of members.
* The number of records retrieved by executing the step.
* The number of records remaining after any appropriate selection conditions have been applied to the records retrieved.
* The number of page transfers made on each iteration of the step.

When query processing has been completed, a further component of NAVIGATOR, the step journaliser, processes the step level statistics recorded on the sequential file and updates the data dictionary.

A path consists of an entry step together with an arbitrary number of non-entry steps. In the present implementation of NAVIGATOR, a query submitted by a user implies a unique linking structure, at the subschema level, among the record types referenced or implied in the query. By selecting the most suitable entry point, the path selector component of NAVIGATOR determines how this structure is to be used. Thus for each query the path selector can determine a number of query paths, each identified by its entry point.

2.3 DM function level monitoring

There are various alternative methods of collecting statistics at this

level for example:
* Modifying the host language compiler to call a monitoring routine
  before or after each DM operation.
* Making use of CODASYL DDLC CALL functions where implemented [3].
* Building monitoring into the code of the DBMS.
As the source code of I-D-S/II was available, we chose the third
option. This enabled us to monitor programs in all host languages in a
way which was fairly transparent to the user. Whether or not to
collect these usage statistics is a decision which the user makes just
prior to loading his program by selecting the appropriate version of
the DBCS. I-D-S/II does collect some usage statistics but these are
grossed up over all record and set types so that it is not easy for
the DBA to identify slow paths through the structure. We currently
collect the following statistics for each DM function:
* DM function code.
* Set type name (where applicable).
* Record type name (where applicable).
* Database status value.
* Count of physical page read transfers.
* Count of logical page read transfers.
* Count of physical page write transfers.
* Count of logical page write transfers.
* Realm name.
* Target realm page number (for STORE and FIND <rse2>).
* Actual realm page number (except for READY and FINISH).
The statistics can either be written to a tape or sequential file, or
can be summarised and printed when the database is closed. Summarising
the statistics loses the sequentiality of the information, although
approximations to paths followed can be deduced from the summaries. We
do not collect timings for two main reasons:
* In our environment, it is difficult to collect accurate and
  reproducible timings at this level.
* We have shown by experimentation that timings are proportional to
  a weighted sum of the logical and physical page transfers.

2.4 Storage level monitoring

The distinction between DM function level and storage level statistics
is not always clear. This reflects the current confusion in the
CODASYL model which will be clarified when the Data Storage
Description Language (DSDL) is implemented thus removing storage
considerations from the schema DDL [3]. Some of the statistics
collected at DM function level such as page numbers, access costs and
realms could be said to be storage level.

Other storage level statistics are the static statistics concerning
the way in which the database is distributed over storage. These
static statistics include set distributions, chain lengths, percentage
fill and overflowing. An I-D-S/II utility calculates record
populations per area and the lowest and highest pages of an area on
which occurrences of a particular record type are found. This utility
also provides information for each area on the percentages of space

and database keys used per page. We have implemented two utilities; one to collect statistics on set distributions and populations and the other to monitor the lengths of CALC chains.

The set statistics utility is implemented by following set linkages using normal FORTRAN plus DML programs. Since I-D-S/II FORTRAN DML statements cannot be parameterised, the code which actually traverses the sets is generated automatically for the database which is to be monitored, by accessing the description of that database in the data dictionary. The set statistics collected are, for each set type:
  * The minimum, maximum and average costs of traversing a set occurrence.
  * The minimum, maximum and average population for each member record type.
  * The average cost of finding the owner record occurrence for each member record type.
Costs are measured in logical transfers rather than physical transfers so that they are independent of run-time parameters such as buffer sizes.

The CALC chain utility is implemented in the same way as the set statistics utility except that some low-level code is necessary in order to examine CALC header records and pointers. The statistics actually collected are, for each area:
  * The average length of a CALC chain in pages.
  * The average number of records in a CALC chain.
and for each record type in each area:
  * The minimum, maximum and average position of the record on a CALC chain.
  * The minimum, maximum and average number of page transfers required to reach a record in a CALC chain.
  * The lowest and highest page numbers on which an occurrence of the record type is to be found, and the total record population.

3. STORAGE OF MONITORING INFORMATION

We have developed a restricted data dictionary for the purpose of holding details of the structure and organisation of several databases along with relevant monitoring information. The data dictionary is implemented as a CODASYL database using I-D-S/II, and consists of two separate structures:
  * The dictionary directory, which indexes occurrences of the record structure.
  * The dictionary entry, for which there is one physical occurrence for each database known to the dictionary. Each entry includes the following information about a database:
      * Schema DDL information.
      * Schema DMCL information.
      * FORTRAN subschema DDL information.
      * Details of operating system files used.
      * Static and usage monitoring information.
Utility programs have been developed to load schema DDL, schema DMCL.

and FORTRAN subschema DDL information into the dictionary. This
information is used by NAVIGATOR to generate code to answer the
queries. Figure 1 illustrates that subset of the dictionary schema
diagram which contains the records and sets implemented to hold
high-level usage monitoring information. The usage statistics are held
at subschema level so that the usage of particular subschemas can be
assessed. Query profiles are represented by the record QPRFILE and
linked to the groups of items requested and supplied by sets QGRPREQ
and QGRPSUP. The information in QPRFILE consists of the following:
  * Usage count.
  * Cost of execution measured in page transfers.
  * Count of results obtained.
The path taken to answer a given query may vary from run to run as the
path chosen is optimised in line with the static statistics in the
dictionary. The paths taken may have different entry points and this
can be represented by the structure shown. Currently the only
information in the QPATH record is the type of path, the number of
steps in the path and a usage count for the path with the
corresponding QPRFILE.

For each step traversed during the execution of a NAVIGATOR query,
either a new STEP record is stored or an existing STEP record has its
data items updated. In an entry step, where no set relationship is
involved, there will be no set link between the STEP and SUBSET
records. The step record contains the following information:
  * The type of step.
  * A usage count for the step, initialised on the first traversal
    and incremented on subsequent traversals.
  * A running average of the iteration count for each usage of the
    step.
  * A running average of the number of page transfers made on each
    iteration using the step.
The reduction in the number of records retrieved which is achieved by
applying selection conditions, allows data item selectivities to be
updated for those items with values supplied. The data item
selectivity is defined to be the likelihood that a given data item
will have a given value.

The high-level usage statistics are collected as NAVIGATOR processes a
query and are entered automatically in the data dictionary by various
components of NAVIGATOR. The data dictionary is central to the
operation of NAVIGATOR and thus the correct dictionary entry is open
when a query is being processed. Ideally we see all access to a
database being made through a dictionary as high-level usage of
databases becomes more common with the users view becoming more remote
from the storage view.

However the collection of low-level usage statistics from the running
of normal application programs and the updating of the dictionary with
these statistics are currently two separate processes since the
dictionary is not permanently on-line.

The low-level usage statistics are also stored at the subschema
level. The sequential file of DM function level statistics is
analysed automatically and summaries of the statistics collected are
stored in the data dictionary in the records DM1STATS to DM5STATS
dependent on the DM function. For each DM function operating on a
particular record type, or record and set, record and realm or record,
realm and key combination, the following information is stored in a
DMSTATS record:
* Usage count.
* Running averages for the number of physical and logical page read
    and write transfers incurred in the execution of the DM function.
Thus the order of DM operations is lost but it should be possible to
deduce paths followed from the sequential information and relate this
to the QPATH records stored by the high-level usage monitoring. The
static statistics collected by utilities when the database is inactive
are stored in the dictionary as they are collected; they are stored at
the schema level.

4. USAGE OF STORED MONITORING STATISTICS

We distinguish two categories of changes which cam be made to a
database:
* Alterations in the mapping of the logical database structure to
    storage usually known as reorganisation.
* Alterations to the logical database structure itself, usually
    known as restructuring.
Figure 2 indicates DDL and DMCL parameters which affect the
performance of a database and shows both the usage statistics which
will suggest changes to these parameters and the static statistics
which will enable the DBA to estimate the feasibility and likely cost
of making these changes. In a self-organising system [5] the whole
process of monitoring, reorganising and restructuring is transparent
to the DBA but we feel that at the present time, it is more practical
to provide tools which allow the DBA to intervene at various stages in
the design-monitoring-redesign cycle.

We envisage an iterative process of design modifications, changing one
or two parameters at a time and then monitoring the effect of this
change before proceeding to the next one. In an environment with an
in-place restructurer [11], this may be quite feasible, but for the
presently available off-line restructurers which involve dumping and
reloading of the database, the DBA may prefer one major restructure to
several minor restructures. Therefore some sort of simulation of the
effect on all the other parameters in the database of modifying one
parameter would be desirable, so that a total restructure could be
planned.

A suggested strategy would be to first select the change to the
structure which promised the greatest cost saving and either initiate
a restructure to carry it out or simulate the change. Statistics would
be collected as before, and then the next most promising change would

be selected. This iterative process should gradually approach the best design for the measured usage although we would never expect to reach such an optimum design unless the workload remained constant. For a major restructure, we would select a point where sufficient cost saving is indicated to more than cover the estimated cost of the restructure.

Routines have been written to extract statistics from the data dictionary and present them to the DBA in a meaningful form. The statistics are tabulated in terms of record usage, set usage, realm usage and data item usage. The statistics which pertain to records are the static statistics on area populations, set populations and the majority of DM function level usage statistics. Record statistics can also be extracted from the STEP records although the step and DM function level statistics are kept separate in our implementation since path usage by NAVIGATOR is optimised. From the summaries of usage statistics, it is fairly easy to see whether suitable location modes have been chosen; for example if a record has a VIA location mode is it usually accessed through that set? If not, then estimates of the likely effect of relocating the record can be made using the static statistics to estimate the effect on cluster sizes and the usage statistics to estimate the cost of the measured usage given a different organisation.

We do not currently collect data item statistics via the low-level monitor. This is because the default forms of GET and MODIFY reference all data items and it would require monitoring of the source code to find out which data items are being used in the program and how they are used. However the intent level monitoring notes which groups of data items are used together and this is an indication of suitable clustering policies and candidates for record partitioning. Groups of data items which are frequently accessed together should ideally be in the same cluster if not the same record. The static statistics indicate which clusters are feasible and the usage statistics give information on which records and data items are accessed together.

Singular sets and non-singular sets are assessed separately. Whether or not a singular set is justified, is dependant on the following:
* Frequency of usage.
* Cost of using singular set compared with the alternatives.
* Overhead of using it in terms of space for pointers and extra
   updating costs.
Alternatives to a singular set traversal are realm searches or hierarchy traversals, although if the singular set is sorted, its removal may lead to overheads in sorting results. The alternatives to non-singular sets are repeating groups within the owner record, and replacement by data item values in the member records. The frequencies of usage of the various sets are a guide to where the largest performance improvements might be made.

Realm statistics are mainly storage and organisational statistics, concerning patterns of page usage, set usage between realms and the static organisation statistics. There should normally be a logical distinction between realms, with different realms or groups of realms being assigned to different subschemas.

The static statistics were initially collected to assist in the assessment of the effect of changes to the database structure and organisation. However we have also utilised these statistics to optimise NAVIGATOR access to databases and have demonstrated that considerable cost savings can be made [8].

5. OVERALL ARCHITECTURE

Figure 3 illustrates how the various implementations described in the preceding sections fit together to form a comprehensive monitoring scheme, in which the data dictionary plays a central role. DBMS operation is likely to become increasingly dependent upon the services of a data dictionary. We believe that advantage should be taken of this to make full use of the potential of the data dictionary and, in particular, to store monitoring information in the dictionary and exploit it in all possible ways. The dictionary directory, as its name implies, is not tied to any particular kind of structure in respect of the databases which it indexes. A dictionary entry, however, is presently designed to describe a CODASYL database. Additional types of dictionary entry could be designed to describe the structures of various kinds of non-CODASYL databases - for example hierarchical or relational.

The monitoring tools which we developed were designed after consultations with commercial database users on what they felt were the most appropriate statistics to collect. Any monitoring of database usage and performance will have some overhead and the DBA should be able to control the presence and range of monitors. The least expensive and intrusive monitor which we have developed is the step level monitor. This is because step level monitoring has been built in to the NAVIGATOR query interface and is closely linked to the method of implementation. Therefore we feel that manufacturers should consider building more monitoring into their database systems and query systems.

Static statistics utilities should be run at database load time so that the initial database organisation can be compared with the expected organisation. Ideally usage monitoring should be permanently switched on so that a complete history of the usage of the database can be built up. However commercial organisations may have a fairly constant workload so that periodic usage monitoring is sufficient.

ACKNOWLEDGEMENTS

We would like to acknowledge the help and encouragement we have derived from discussion with many people both at Aberdeen and elsewhere. Our work was supported by a grant from the Science Research Council.

REFERENCES

1. BCS/CODASYL DDLC DBAWG Report, June 1975.
2. BCS/DDSWP 'Discussion Session: Proceedings of the Conference on Data Dictionary Systems', BCS Computer Bulletin Series 2, No. 18, pp. 16-17, December 1978.
3. CODASYL DDLC: Journal of Development, January 1978.
4. CODASYL Systems Committee, Selection and Acquisition of Data Base Management Systems, March 1976.
5. Dearnley P., 'Monitoring Database System Performance', BCS Computer Journal, Vol 21, No. 1, pp. 15-19.
6. Dominick W.D., Penniman W.D., 'Automated Monitoring to Support the Analysis and Evaluation of Information Systems', Proceedings of the Second International Conference on Information Storage and Retrieval, ACM-SIGIR, September 1979.
7. Honeywell Information Systems Inc., DM-IV Data Base Administrator Reference Manual, DF77 Rev. 1, May 1978.
8. Johnston C.I., Stone A.S., 'Query Optimisation using a Data Dictionary', February 1981.
9. Loomis M.E.S., Allen F.W., 'Paging Behavior and Performance Optimization in a CODASYL DBMS', Proceedings International Conference on Data Bases, pp. 119-134, BCS/Heyden, July 1980.
10. Su S.Y.W., Lam H., 'Transformation of Data Traversals and Operations in Application Programs to Account for Semantic Changes of Databases', submitted to ACM Transactions on Database Systems.
11. Wilson T.B., 'Data Base Restructuring: Options and Obstacles', Proceedings of Euro IFIP 79, pp. 567-573, North-Holland, September 1979.

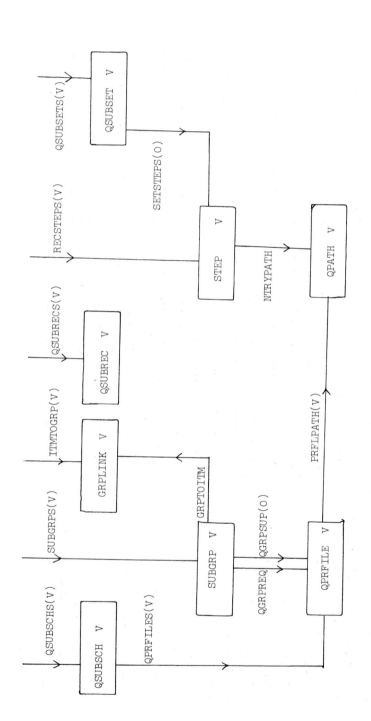

FIGURE 1: HIGH-LEVEL MONITORING PORTION OF DICTIONARY

DESIGN AND PERFORMANCE PARAMETERS	USAGE STATISTICS REQUIRED	STATIC STATISTICS REQUIRED
Grouping of data items into record	Which data items are accessed together	Relative item frequencies
Representation of relationships by sets or data items	Proportion of retrieval to update; Types of retrieval	Relative storage costs
Use of secondary keys, secondary indexes, pointer arrays	Ratio of retrieval to update; Types of retrieval	Data item selectivities and value distributions
Set selection and order	Number, costs and type of accesses	
Division of database into area	Which records are accessed together	Record and page size
DDL SOURCE and RESULT clauses	Number and type of data item accesses	
Use of singular sets	Type of access to record types	Cost comparisons
Location modes	Overall usage pattern for each record	Record and set populations
Prior pointers	Direction of set processing	
Page sizes	Amount of overflow from target page	Cluster sizes; chain lengths
Size of database; percentage fill	Degree of overflow and access costs; Usage pattern	Record and set distributions
Number of page buffers (application dependent)	Ratio of physical to logical transfers for varying buffer sizes	Cluster sizes and set distributions
Frequency clauses	Counts and types of accesses	
Relationships between schema records and storage records	Which data items are accessed together	Record sizes; physical storage parameters

FIGURE 2: DATABASE CHANGES AND RELATED MONITORING STATISTICS

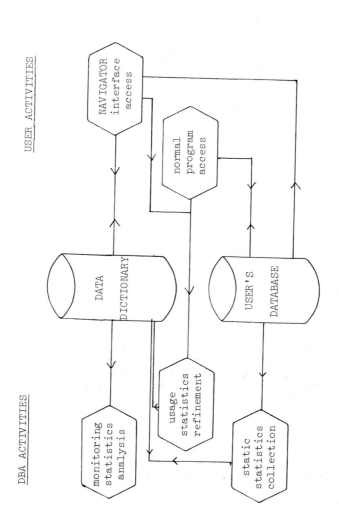

USER ACTIVITIES

DBA ACTIVITIES

FIGURE 3 : STATIC AND USAGE MONITORING IMPLEMENTATION

Sizing the Performance of Minicomputers

D. C. Menzies, FBCS

System Development Manager, Corporation of Lloyd's, UK

A simple linear model is described which may be used to predict minicomputer hardware configurations needed to meet specified requirements. Methods of calculation or assessment are specified for the major components of the minicomputer:

- terminals
- lines
- computer memory
- Disc capacity
- Disc input/output
- Disc controllers and channel capacity
- Processor
- other peripherals

1. INTRODUCTION

    Minicomputers are purchased for a price which ranges
    between £20,000 and £200,000. Many are supplied by O.E.M.
    companies and Systems Houses to relatively unsophisticated
    users : a specification of requirements is prepared and
    must then be used by the supplier to determine which
    minicomputer has the necessary power and what peripherals
    will be required to meet the requirements. The supplier's
    problem is that he must respond very quickly and accurately
    to the user's request, else the business will be passed to
    another supplier who does respond quickly and usually the
    response must be based upon incomplete or inaccurate
    information.

    It is possible to derive an accurate model which will
    reflect the behaviour of all aspects of a computer system :
    given accurate data, such a model would (eventually)
    produce an exact solution to the problem. This approach is
    totally impractical because of its complexity, and in any
    event is not worthwhile because the information upon which
    the performance assessment must be based is far too
    imprecise. This paper is concerned with a modelling
    approach, but the model which is proposed is (for those who
    are mathematically minded) a first order linear
    approximation to the system - in other words, it is a
    grossly simplified version of the true mathematical
    formulae which is easy to use and apply. Let's look first
    at the model and then at how it may be applied.

2. GENERAL APPROACH

    Figure 1 is a schematic diagram of a minicomputer.

    We need an approach which will determine the number and/or
    size of:

    - terminals
    - Lines
    - Memory
    - Disc Capacity
    - Disc input/output capacity
    - Channel capacity and Disc controllers
    - Processors
    - everything else that may be needed

We will consider each of these in turn. The general principle of the approach involves assuming that:

- Effects on the whole configuration may be calculated simply by adding together separate individual effects (technically, the "linear" part of the approximation). So, for example, total loading on telecommunication lines may be calculated by adding together the effect of all the separate messages which are transmitted over the lines.

- Queuing effects may be allowed for in response time calculations by using the first order approximation formula:

$$T_R = T_S / (1 - U)$$

where T_R = Response Time
T_S = Service Time
U = Utilisation

Examples will make the meaning of these terms clearer later as we consider each part of the system.

These approximation will permit an accurate assessment of performance when the utilisation of the equipment is low, and the queuing approximation extends the usefulness of the approach to practical utilisation levels (we'll see what that means in a moment) and allows an assessment of the effect of overloads. In practise, this is, of course, precisely what is required by the problem - a guide method which will ensure that the system is not under configured and provide an assessment of the available spare capacity.

Let's look at each component in turn.

3   MINICOMPUTER COMPONENTS

3.1 Terminals

There are several aspects which affect the requirement for terminals. As a first approximation, one may assume that each "transaction" (a very loose term - it means entry of an order, of a cash receipt, or whatever - a complete logical entry) will take about 2 minutes. The quick answer, then, takes the number of transactions in the client's peak hour, divide that by 30, and that is the number of terminals. If you don't believe that, let's look at the problem in more detail. The factors which determine the rate of working of a terminal operator are:

– The Keying Rate

A fast data-prep operator will enter data at about
18,000 key-depressions/hour, or 5 depressions/second.
VDU operation is seldom of a touch-typing nature, so I
prefer to assume 2 d/s for an experienced user and 1 d/s
for a typical unskilled user (like me!). In practise,
typical transactions usually involve entering a few
codes to identify and retrieve information – say 20
characters, taking 10 seconds.

– Transmission Rate

The rate of transmission depends on the line speed of
the lines and modems which have been installed. For a
simple calculation, assume 10 bits/characters, and a
2400 bps transmission line will transmit 500 characters
in 2 seconds – I realise that it isn't accurate, but the
time is about 10% of the keying time, so the error
doesn't matter.

– Thinking and Reading Time

The operator has now spent 10 seconds entering 20
characters, and the system has used 2 seconds
transmitting 500 characters (or so) back to the user's
screen. For a typical "transaction", the process will be
repeated two or three times. What takes the time, and
justifies my 2 minutes/transaction figure, is the fact
that each time a screen is returned, the operator must
read what has been returned to him (that is why it has
been returned by the system!), and that takes the time –
it takes about 30 seconds to read and digest a 500
character screen : add this to the 12 seconds for keying
and transmission, and multiply by 3, (for the number of
message exchanges in the transaction), and you end up
with my figure of 2 min/transaction. I was involved in a
review of the performance of a minicomputer system which
ignored thinking time with disastrous results on the
performance.

That is the general approach. Depending on the amount of
information available the calculation is done either on the
basis of 30 transactions/hour or on the basis of a careful
assessment of the operator's activities and of transmission
and reception lines. Where does queuing theory come into
the assessment? That depends upon what the operators are
doing:

- If they are working from a heap of documents, and have
  to get through the documents in a few hours (or a day)
  they will settle down to their load and work steadily
  till the job is finished – 100% utilisation, and
  thrashing away at the queue until it is cleared, and the
  basic calculation holds.

- The other situation is typified by the operator taking
  orders over the telephone : let's suppose that the syste
  requires the entry of 100 orders/hour, and assume 2
  minutes/order. Clearly we need at least 4 screens, and 4
  screens would be 80% utilised, so the service time would
  be:

$$T_S = T \: / \: (1 - U) = 2 \: / \: (0.2) = 10 \text{ minutes}$$

each customer who called would have to wait 8 minutes
before he could find a line which was free! If 10
screens were installed, each would be about 33%
utilised, and service time would be about 3 minutes – a
1 minute wait for a free operator for the customer. This
choice needs to be assessed by the user – he takes his
choice and pays his money for the appropriate number of
screens. The purists will point out that my formula is a
single-server formula while multiple screen is a multiserver problem. The calculation underestimates the
capacity of the multiple screens, but not seriously at
low utilisations – the "error" gives a useful safety/
contingency faster against errors in estimates of the
load.

3.2 Lines

From the screens and key-boards, we move to the lines. The
basis of the calculation here is that a certain number of
characters have to be transmitted from terminals to
computer. We have to chose :

- the number of lines
- line speed
- number of terminals chartered at each line
- protocol (bisynch, HDLC, asynchranous, etc)..

Most transmission codes use 8 bits for each character transmitted (if you plan something clever like code compression, you can calculate the effect), so we can make a crude gross simplification of the whole problem by allowing 10 bits for each character which is to be transmitted – this makes the calculation much simpler (unless you are a genius at octal arithmatic!), and also gives a margin which is more than adequate to cover the overheads of protocols and line turn-round. Looking back at the example of 100 transactions/hour and 1500 characters/ transaction (3 screens of 500 characters, we arrive at a bit capacity requirement of 1.5 million bits/hours, or about 400 bits/second : utilisation of a 2400 bps line would be about 17%. You will recall that we concluded that 10 screens would be required to provide an adequate service if the transactions arrive randomly : on this basis, all 10 screens could be served by a single 2400 bps line (using statistical multiplexans, an active controller on a t.d.m.), but it would be more usual to instal a second line for security reasons. It will be found that line capacity is seldom a problem – the communication line can transmit data much faster than the operator can enter it as read it when it is returned. Line speed is usually selected to meet the user's requirement for "instantaneous" filling of the screen – it takes about 20 seconds to fill a 2400 character screen at 1200 bps, and the fact that the operator can't read at that speed doesn't prevent him being distracted and frustrated by the slow scanning of data onto the screen while he tries to read the first few lines.

3.3 Computer Memory

Computer memory requirements depend very much upon the computer operating system and the way it manages the use of memory. Memory is required for:

- the system itself – this is usually a fixed figure for a particular system

- work being done from terminals – a fixed allowance for each terminal may be made

- other computer work – "batch" programs, spooling and house-keeping

Usually, the memory requirement may be assessed on the basis of the system need and the terminal space – the other computer work is scheduled at times when all the terminals are not in use and makes use of the space so released (if this is not so, additional memory is needed).

Effectively, we think of the memory being divided into a series of equal sized partitions. Then, depending upon levels of activity and the peculiarities of the particular system, we allocate each partition to a number of terminals. We are back with a queuing problem – when a message is received from a terminal, the system may seek a free partition from the set of all partitions (multiserver case) or may place the message in a queue for one case partition (single server problem). In either case, if the partition is not free or the code needed for processing is not held in the computer's memory, disk accesses are needed to make the memory available or retrieve the required code, and CPU power is needed to control the search for space and the disk accesses. A computer with insufficient memory will often waste CPU and disk power : the moral is to make sure that sufficient memory is available. Figures which have been found adequate for RSTS/Basic and CDMS/MUMPS DEC systems are shown in figure 2 : it boils down to an allowance of about 8K/terminal, plus 50-60K for the System.

3.4 Disc Space

It is usually possible to specify the amount of data which is to be stored fairly accurately at an early stage in the specification of a system, the calculation of the disc space which is needed is seldom difficult. However, an allowance must be made for

- packing density – space must be reserved for future data, else retrieval (or storage) will become less and less efficient as more data is loaded and changed.

- indices and links between one data entry and another

- house-keeping and other overheads, usually not very significant.

- future growth

Taken all together, an allowance of 50% on top of the basic calculated requirement is usually necessary and sufficient : more may be needed in particular cases.

3.5 Disc I/O Capacity

Each access to disc requires :

- time to move the read/write head to the correct
  position, usually between 0 and 100 mS with an average
  of about 35 mS for typical disc units.

- time for the disc to rotate until the data is under the
  head : typical rotation time is 25 mS, as the average
  rotation delay is 12.5 mS.

- a few mS to read the data and transfer it to the
  computer's memory

I have quoted typical figures which arrive at a total of
40-50 mS for a disc access - actual figures for any
particular disc are easy to obtain from the supplier.

Thus the upper limit to the number of disc transfers which
are possible is 20-25/S (for the "typical" disc I'm
considering). Suppose we try to retrieve data 24 times/
second from a disc which is capable of handling 25
accesses/second. The service time is 40 mS, so it will
take

$$T = .04 \, / \, (1 - 0.96) = 1 \text{ Second}$$

for each retrieval from the time at which the record is
requested, and the processing of a transaction requiring 20
disc accesses will take 20 seconds. The effect upon
response time of high utilisation can be very dramatic! The
practical limiting capacity of a disc drive is about 50-60%
of the theoretical capacity - beyond this level, the load
will have a significant effect upon response times.

So much for the capacity of a disc drive. The other part of
the problem is the assessment of the number of disc
accesses which are required to meet the user's
requirements. Disc accesses are required for:

- retrieval of code or overlaid pages : we've already said
  that there should be sufficient memory to minimise this
  factor, so for the present purposes we'll ignore it.

- storage and retrieval of data : the number of data entities or records which are to be retrieved or updated, together with any indices which must be accessed or chains which must be followed to reach the required information. The figures derived will, of course, depend upon the particular access method which is used : typically two disc accesses will be required to retrieve a record from an indexed file.

- security and back-up requirements : with an on-line system, it is usually necessary to carry the overheads of recording everything which is done (message logs) and traces of every update to the data (after images of updated records, and before images if down-dating to a previous check-point is a requirement).

Let's go back to our typical transaction of 3 message exchanges. We may either set out to design the database and use all its peculiarities to determine how many accesses are required under each of the headings, or we may take the simpler approach of assuming that data analysis and proper design techniques will allow us to design and implement a reasonably efficient access system. In the latter case, we assume:

- each input and output message is to be logged, but security requirements permit a single record for each transaction.

- each message requires the retrieval of one database record (two accesses), and the storage of a scratchpad record for retrieval and processing with the next message.

- each transaction results in a single update of the database which requires one database access, and a second access to record a before/after image for security purposes.

Our transaction of 3 messages then requires some 13 references to the database, and the 100 transactions/hour load will call for 1300 disc accesses - since the capacity of a drive is some 50,000 accesses/hour, this is unlikely to present significant problems! Again, the vast amount of spare capacity is a justification for the adoption of a fairly crude approach to the calculation. The approach will also identify a problem if it does exist : the answer will come out much closer to the actual disc capacity.

The calculation has one further significance. 13 references
to disc will take about 0.6 seconds : effectively, the disc
accesses are contributing about 0.2 seconds to the response
time in the processing of each message.

It should be stressed that a particularly simple case has
been analysed above. Processing may require access to a
number of master files for each message which is processed,
for example, order entry may require data to be examined
from the :

- customer master file
- outstanding orders file
- receivable file (for the state of the customer's
  account)
- stock master files
- stock holding file
- daily dispatch file

and others depending upon the precise functionality of
the system, and some files may be examined several times
for different data. The extension of the approach to more
complex situations is not difficult, and, of course, we
rely upon the linear assumption of the basic approach -
consider each requirement separately and add them all
together to arrive at the total load.

3.6 Channel and Controller Power

Disc controllers are usually supplied to control up to
eight disc drives. Two situations need to be considered:

- the controller does not separate the disc seek process
  from the data transfer process and is active throughout
  the 40-50 mS required for access to the disc : in this
  situation, the throughput capacity of the controller is
  the same as the capacity of a single disc drive, however
  many discs are attached to it.

- the data access process is separated into a seek request
  which causes the disk head to move and an access request
  which causes the data transfer when the correct track
  has been treated : the controller is active in
  initiating the seek and in controlling the transfer
  while the track is searched and the data is transferred
  - referring to the figures used earlier, that is about
  15 mS, with the result that a controller can control
  some 4 or 5 active discs which are being "heavily" used
  (remember that we set a practical limit of 10-15
  accesses/second for each disc drive).

It is sometimes surprisingly difficult to establish whether a controller operates with separated seeks or not. Most are capable of doing so, but many standard control programs which are provided with the controllers take the simpler approach of dealing with one request at a time and queuing any others which are outstanding. In practise, with minicomputers, the capacity of one disc is usually more than enough to cope with the demand, so the capacity of the controller is seldom a problem. If, however, the requirement is found to approach the capacity of a single disc (10-15 accesses/second), careful enquiries should be made about separation of seeks before it is assumed that the problem may be solved by splitting the load between several drives attached to the same controller.

Generally, minicomputers have a single channel for access to the computer's memory, with a capacity of the order of a megabyte/second or so. In the example we have been considering, we are concerned with 100 transactions/hour each involving 3 message exchanges of some 500 characters and 13 disc accesses of, perhaps 250 characters each, so the total data transfer rate is about 0.5 megabytes per hour, which is several orders of magnitude less than the channel capacity. Of course, this isn't the whole story - the channel will also be used for memory management, code overlays and a lot of other complicated purposes. However, my experience, whenever I've bothered to calaculate it, has always been that channel capacity is much greater than the requirement : the calculation is only worth doing if you have a very unusual requirement with a great deal of disc access and frequent transfers from one media to another (disc to disc or disc to tape).

3.7 Computer Processor

Computer power requirements may be calculated accurately by from the number of instructions which are needed for processing, feeding in the MIPS rate of the possible processor and completing the calculation. In practise, this is not usually a very useful process, because time for each instructions are different, and the only real way to determine the particular mix of instructions to meet a requirement is to write the programs and bench mark them, and even then the results are questionable for a variety of reasons.

There are two practical aspects which allow a quick
assessment of the size and power of the processor for a
particular problem:

- several minicomputer suppliers limit the amount of
  memory which is available with each size of processor -
  you calculate how much memory is needed, and the
  processor is decided for you by the supplier policy.

- experience shows that for typical minicomputer
  applications, a certain size of processor is needed to
  support the required number of terminals.

In effect, since the calculation of memory needs is based
upon the number of terminals, both the aspects assume that
the typical user wishes to do an "average" amount of work,
and then determines the size and power of processor which
is required.

3.8 Everything Else

The computer configuration will also require one or more
printers, perhaps a reader and/or a punch (card or paper
tape), magnetic tape, perhaps floppy discs, operator
console, or T-bar switch and so on. In general, assessment
of the load to be placed upon these devices is not
difficult and uses straight forward assessment and
calculation methods. I don't intend to go into this
further, but we can discuss items afterwards if there are
any particular problems which concern you.

4. SUMMARY

I've presented a crude linear model which permits a rapid
calculation of resource requirements. The model assumes
that we may simply add all the requirements together and
that the total requirement will be equal to the sum of the
separate requirements. The model is valid when utilisation
is low, and it is easy to predict when the model will
break-down - when utilisations start getting heavy :
justification of the approach is that, that break-down
point is exactly what we are trying to avoid!

I've discussed briefly how the approach applies to the
minicomputer components : we concluded that :

- terminals could handle about 30 transactions/hour (less
  with random processing), mainly because of the operator
  thinking time factor

- line capacity could reasonably be assessed by dividing
  the line speed by 10 to obtain the character capacity

- memory requirements could be estimated as 8K for each
  terminal plus an allowance for the operating system

- a 50% allowance should be added to the calculated file
  sizes to assess the disc storage requirement

- the practical limit to the capacity of a disc drive is
  about 10-15 accesses/second, depending on the drive

- disc controller capacity is approximately the capacity
  of 5 drives or the capacity of a drive depending upon
  whether seeks are separated from data retrieval by the
  controller or not

- the appropriate processor is usually determined by rule-
  of-thumb based upon the assessed memory requirements
  (because small processors are not supplied with a lot of
  memory) or the number of terminals

- calculation of the requirement for other components is
  seldom difficult

The approach is simple and direct : the state of knowledge
of future loads is usually such that a more detailed
calculation, even if it were possible, is not justifiable.
The objective must be to ensure that adequate allowances
are made for errors in predictions, and the approach does
make such allowances.

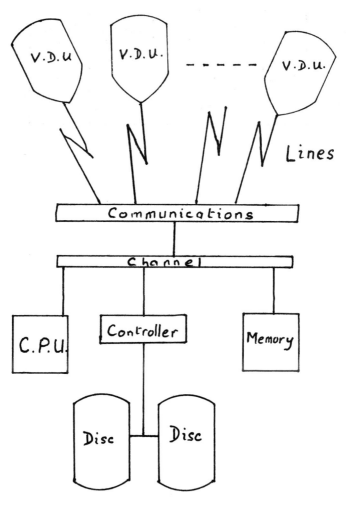

Figure 1   Minicomputer Schematic

Figure 2.   Memory Requirements

System	Partition Size	Screens/ Partition	Memory/ Screen	System Memory
CDMS/MUMPS	6-8 K	1	6-8 K	60 K
RSTS/BASIC	16 K	1-2	8-16 K	44 K

Is Your Installation Giving Value for Money?

Roger Townsend

Manager, Arthur Andersen & Co. London, UK

Effective performance measurement is the basis for assessing value received for money invested in the data processing function. Pre-requisites for an effective performance measurement approach are identified and key measures are examined in detail in each of four major areas of concern to data processing management. Finally, an overall system of reporting, together with an outline work programme for its implementation, are described.

INTRODUCTION

In the current economic climate many data processing executives are under pressure to reduce or contain their costs, while maintaining adequate service levels. Their job is complicated by the rate of technological change and the increasing dependence on the use of computers to contain rising personnel costs.

In an environment where there is increased use of shared data across departmental boundaries, brought about by the introduction of data base and distributed processing systems, the relationship between service and the cost of providing this service is complex and difficult to understand.

This paper sets out to demonstrate the importance and usefulness of a coherent system of performance measurement as an aid to providing an appropriate level of service at a reasonable cost. It will address problems which are most often encountered in mature installations, where the basic application systems are already in place.

BACKGROUND

Historically, many organisations have developed their systems on a piecemeal basis (piecemeal meaning: in the absence of a coherent long-range systems plan, and using a variety of development and maintenance standards). Often these systems have been considerably modified in order to meet changing user requirements. The end result of this approach is usually a collection of systems which may solve problems in specific components of the business, but fail to take advantage of possibilities which exist for the business as a whole. Ironically, although these systems are perceived to be badly structured and unduly expensive to maintain, it is often difficult to cost-justify a complete redevelopment. This is principally because the system of performance reporting, which could provide an early warning of the need for redevelopment or an assessment of the impact on costs and benefits, is not in place.

Further, an ability to identify inefficient systems, hardware bottlenecks, and personnel skill requirements can create business problems and prevent the company from taking advantage of the improved price performance of modern hardware and the availability of more powerful and flexible software.

What is needed is an overall, integrated approach to performance measurement which is well understood by technical and user management. Many organisations do not attempt to measure performance systematically. Those that do, often fail to communicate the results to senior executive management. This paper describes an approach which is practical and comprehensive, and which can produce results which are easily understood.

In describing this approach, each of the following areas will be
addressed in detail:

-    Pre-requisites for Effective Performance Measurement

-    Management of the Data Processing Function

-    Computer Operations

-    Systems Development and Maintenance

-    Technical Support

PRE-REQUISITES FOR EFFECTIVE PERFORMANCE MEASUREMENT

First, consider the pre-requisites for an effective system of
performance measurement.

1.   Systems Planning

The first pre-requisite is an overall plan. Without a mutually
agreed plan, data processing management has no real basis for
effective control.

The first step in the planning process is the preparation of
the business plan, which defines business objectives and
priorities in the light of the funds and resources available.

Many businesses recognise the need for a business plan; many
less for a systems plan, which quantifies the computer
production and systems development workload and identifies the
resources (in terms of equipment, facilities and personnel)
required to handle that workload, to an agreed level of
service.

The plan should contain details of costs and benefits for each
development project identified to enable senior executive
management to assign priorities and set the overall pace of
development.

The key element in the systems planning process is the
assessment of the return on investment which provides the basis
for these management decisions.

Historically, the most effective investment decisions have been
based on a formal evaluation of the return on that investment.
This is still the case in the data processing field today.
There are a number of factors which tend to re-inforce this
view: they include the rising cost of labour, the continuing
improvements in the price/performance of computer hardware and

the pressure on businesses to improve their cash flows and to
minimise the adverse impact of high interest rates and
inflation.

The major difficulty in assessing the return on investment is
the measurement of anticipated benefits. By definition,
intangible benefits cannot be quantified (although they should
be documented for comparison purposes), but tangible benefits
can and should be quantified and formally documented. However,
the key problem is how to ensure that the anticipated benefits
are clearly understood and accepted by the individuals who will
be responsible for achieving them (typically the users).

The solution, which must be reflected in the systems plan, is
to classify the benefits in clearly discernible ways, which
discourage arguments and help to ensure accuracy.

In the first place, we should recognise that there are two
primary sources of tangible benefits:

-     Reduced or deferred costs

-     Increased or accelerated revenue.

Cost reductions can generally be derived from:

-     Personnel costs

-     Operating expenses

-     Capital investment.

Accelerated revenue can generally be derived from:

-     Faster processing

-     Larger business volumes

-     Greater accuracy and completeness (e.g. more effective
      application of pre-determined rules such as credit
      terms).

In many cases, the tangible benefits should be fairly obvious:
an example of an obvious tangible benefit would be reduced data
storage costs resulting from the installation of more modern
disc drives. There are also occasions when benefits which
appear to be trivial, are worth quantifying. For instance, it
may be possible to achieve, say, a 5% improvement in
development efficiency as a result of the introduction of
interactive programming facilities. Here the benefit is made
obvious by the 'reasonable man' argument; namely, that it would

be difficult for any reasonably competent person to deny that a
4 or 5% improvement in almost anything could be achieved, as
long as it makes sense.

Both these examples involve a significant element of judgement
in quantifying the benefits. In all such cases the managers
most directly affected by the proposed project (in the examples
quoted, these would be the Computer Operations Manager and the
Systems Development Manager) must be convinced that the
predicted benefits are realistic and accept the responsibility
for achieving them.

The main purpose of performing the return on investment
analysis is to enable alternative options (including those
outside data processing) to be evaluated and to establish a
basis (the plan) against which the subsequent performance of
data processing, users and senior executive management can be
measured in implementing solutions and attaining benefits.

Lastly, we should recognise that the preparation of the systems
plan is not a once-for-all step. Adjustments will be necessary
as more experience is gained during implementation of the plan,
and priorities will change over the planning period, even in
the most stable organisations.

2.   Standard Practices

The second pre-requisite is the existence and use of
comprehensive standard practices and procedures.

The level of detail specified in the standards will vary
according to the size and nature of the installation. However,
in addition to normally available standards covering technical
matters such as program coding, there should, as a minimum, be
a generally agreed approach to the design, implementation,
operation and maintenance of systems.

These standards should provide for packaging work in clearly
defined phases, supported by standard work programmes setting
out the detailed steps to be included in each phase. This
approach should enable departmental management to verify the
estimates of effort for each phase, and to monitor the
completeness of each segment of work.

Standard procedures are also required to ensure that equipment
utilisation is monitored effectively and that equipment
capacity plans are prepared on a timely basis.

3. Adequate Staffing

The existence of a plan and standard practices and procedures does not remove the need for sufficient staff of the right calibre. Nevertheless, the existence of the plan should enable staffing requirements to be more accurately predicted, and as the annual revisions to that plan are made, it should be possible to match the workload more closely to the resources and skills available.

Subsequently, the training and effective utilisation of operations and development staff will be enhanced, if a standard approach has been adopted.

4. Effective Control

Adequate control mechanisms must exist to ensure that the standards are observed and that the plan is implemented as agreed. Typical control mechanisms would include a comprehensive system of time recording for development staff, a quality assurance programme covering development projects and an effective scheduling system for computer operations.

Another aspect which must be addressed and agreed in advance is the relationship between senior executive management, data processing management, and users. Some organisations have formalised the relationship and responsibilities by establishing a committee structure. In other organisations, a less formal approach is used in order to enable the interested parties to communicate with one another.

Whatever the precise nature of the mechanisms used, the responsibilities must be defined in such a way that:

- Senior executive management can influence the overall data processing strategy and control the total expenditure on data processing in relation to company objectives and user requirements.

- Data processing departmental management can support and control the data processing function on a day-to-day basis in order to implement the agreed strategy.

- User management can understand and approve the scope and cost of individual development projects and can ultimately accept the systems into production.

Having discussed the four pre-requisites for effective performance measurement (i.e. systems planning, standard practices, adequate staffing, effective control) let us now consider how the performance measures themselves can be applied in each major area of the data processing department, i.e.:

-    Management of the Data Processing Function

-    Computer Operations

-    Systems Development and Maintenance

-    Technical Support.

The discussion of each area will concentrate on:

-    problems which are typically encountered

-    how the necessary framework for meaningful performance
     reporting can be established

-    the key control factors which enable success or failure to be
     gauged.

MANAGEMENT OF THE DATA PROCESSING FUNCTION

The first area for consideration is the overall management of the
data processing function. The key problem with data processing, as
perceived by the senior executive management of many organisations,
is that it costs too much. In many cases the question of "How
much should data processing cost?" can only be answered on an
emotional or subjective basis.

In the absence of factual performance data for assessing current
activities and projected trends, the conviction grows on the one
side that the only way to control the data processing department is
to cut expenditure on automation, and on the other that senior
executive management is incapable of understanding the difficulty of
running a data processing department. Often characterised as a
'communications' problem, the real difficulty is the lack of
information on which to build effective communications.

Typically this problem arises because senior executive management
has no framework for assessing the return on investment and no
method of assigning priorities and quantifying progress on a
consistent and logical basis.

The first step must therefore be to establish a framework for
evaluation in data processing. As we have seen, it is at the
planning stage that the costs and benefits of the various competing
projects must be surfaced and evaluated, for it is here that
priorities are assigned to individual projects and that targets are
set in terms of costs and time scales.

Accordingly, the systems planning procedures and the method of assessing the return on investment must be agreed and established.

However, the effectiveness of future planning decisions will be enhanced if a formal procedure is also established as part of the framework, to account for the costs incurred and the benefits achieved once the system is fully operational.

The next step is to convert the first year of, say, a five year plan into the departmental budget. In subsequent years, the plan will be revised and updated in the light of experience and changed business priorities, as part of the budgetary planning exercise.

Having defined the overall framework, it remains to specify the key control factors which enable actual performance to be measured. The first and most important of these is the monthly comparison of actual costs against budgets. Given that the budgets have been prepared on a realistic basis (in the manner described) they should provide management with effective control over annual data processing expenditure.

A second key control measure is required, however, as an indicator of the work done or the benefit received, for this expenditure. One such measure is the overall data processing cost per business transaction processed. Of necessity this is a fairly crude measure, and it should be calculated for major transactions only. The figures should be indexed to remove the effects of general inflation and should reflect the trend over the preceding three to five years. The average data processing costs can then be compared with other overheads, or with staff costs per transaction as appropriate, in order to assess the effectiveness of the organisation's data processing investment.

The third key control measure is the recovery of data processing costs through transfer-charging. This is a particularly effective measure of the efficiency of Computer Operations, but it can also be applied usefully in some circumstances to Systems Development and Maintenance. Standard costs should be agreed with the users in advance (based on the overall budget for data processing) for standard units of work (e.g. the cost of processing an order, or an invoice in Computer Operations, and the average cost of a man-day in Systems Development and Maintenance). The costs should be set so as to allow for full recovery and should reflect planned levels of re-runs, and non-productive time.

These standards can then be applied to the actual units of work (e.g. number of invoices) processed for each user department as the basis of the transfer-charge. A monthly analysis of the costs recovered in this way should reveal both volume variances (which may

be useful for capacity planning) and efficiency variances (which
highlight potential weaknesses in the control of the data processing
function).

There will be other measures of performance in which senior
management will be interested but these three are the most readily
understood and commonly used.

COMPUTER OPERATIONS

Having considered the impact of three key performance measures (i.e.
budgets, cost trends and transfer-charging) on the overall
management of the data processing function, let us examine some
fairly common weaknesses in the computer operations function which
indicate the absence of effective performance reporting. For
instance, there may be a tendency within the installation for
additional computer equipment to be needed at short notice. If
there is, it probably suggests that equipment utilisation is not
properly measured and that capacity planning is inadequate.

Other typical symptoms which reflect the need for improved
performance measurement are:

-    user complaints about response times or the level of down-time

-    development project slippage attributed to a poor testing
     service

-    large amounts of unutilised capacity.

In summary, the service provided is poor and the cost is high.

In establishing the overall framework, the first requirement is,
therefore, to define and agree with user management the level of
service required and to ensure that the cost of providing the
required level of service is acceptable. There are several
generally accepted service level measures for the operations
function:

-    on-line system availability

-    on-line response times

-    batch system reporting deadlines

-    testing turn-around time.

In most installations the key constraints in terms of service level
and the capacity required to provide it, will be determined by one
or two major applications. Greatest effort should therefore be
devoted to analysing the requirements of these critical systems.

Historically, the key determinant of equipment capacity has been the overnight batch reporting deadline. However, with the development of more on-line applications and the introduction of interactive program testing facilities, the response time requirement of the peak hour of the on-line day has become the key factor in many instances.

Within this framework, key control measures over the continuing performance of computer operations are required at two levels. First, there should be a system of flash exception reporting to the executive responsible for the data processing function, which highlights user problems, down-time, etc. when the service level targets are missed by more than, say, 5%. The discipline upon operations personnel of knowing that management takes a keen interest in their performance is important. Furthermore, the data processing executive is in a better position to deal with user management, should complaints arise, if he is armed with the facts.

The second level of control is the routine reporting of equipment status and capacity utilisation. It is not the purpose of this paper to specify in detail how capacity utilisation statistics should be collected, since the most effective approach will vary according to the size and cost of the equipment involved, and the availability of measurement tools, such as hardware and software monitors. Nevertheless, measures should exist which show how the existing capacity is being utilised and what the trends are. Reports of this sort should be reviewed in detail by the Operations Manager once a month. In a large installation, senior data processing management might only review such reports quarterly.

In most installations there will be rather more performance reports than have been described here, but those that have been mentioned are among the more important.

SYSTEMS DEVELOPMENT AND MAINTENANCE

The third major area in which systematic performance measurement can prove beneficial is Systems Development and Maintenance. Here also, the scope for improved measurement and control is indicated by some of the problems which are commonly encountered. The most obvious example is a poor track record in the development of new systems, with projects typically being delivered late and over budget. There are other quite common pointers, however, such as:

-    user dis-satisfaction with the quality of existing systems

-    an inability to release sufficient development staff from maintenance to undertake new development work and vice versa

-    low development productivity.

Before we review how each of these problems can be addresed, let us
first of all define the objectives of an efficient development
service. They may be summarised as follows:

'The delivery and maintenance of systems to user expectations, to a
schedule and for a cost commensurate with management expectations.'

The first step in establishing the overall framework must therefore
be to discover what user expectations are, and to determine the best
approach to meeting those expectations. Typically, this will
involve deciding between full-scale redevelopment and continued
maintenance and enhancement of existing systems in each area of the
business. A large backlog of systems change requests for any given
system does not necessarily point to the need for redevelopment. It
may indicate a shortage of staff resources, or a very volatile area
of the business. Alternatively it may reflect the fact that changes
are very difficult to make because the system is badly structured or
the documentation is poor.

In these circumstances it is useful to analyse historic performance
data for each system, such as:

-    the level of production failures

-    the average number of man-days required to apply a change
     request

-    the average level of machine resource required to test that
     change.

The analysis should reveal those systems which are the most costly
to maintain, and hence provide a clear indication of whether or not
redevelopment is justified.

Having identified those applications where full-scale development
projects are required it remains to agree with user management the
level of maintenance service to be provided for the other applications. The maintenance service level can be defined in terms of:

-    the elapsed time to fix program bugs or implement high priority
     changes

-    the backlog of unactioned change requests.

The first step was to establish the level of user management
expectations, the second is to quantify the cost of meeting those
expectations and the time scales involved. For development
projects, the costs and time scales are based on the overall work
programme and the estimates of human and machine resources required.
These estimates should be derived from the detailed estimating
guidelines maintained as part of the development standards.

Not only do such guidelines assist the project manager in preparing
his estimates, but they also provide, as we shall see later, an
additional yardstick against which his own and his team's subsequent
performance can be measured.

For maintenance, the costs will depend upon the resources required
to provide the agreed level of service, based upon the historic
incidence of bugs and change requests.

It now remains to establish the key controls over the actual level
of development and maintenance service provided. For development
projects this will entail the preparation and review of conventional
weekly or fortnightly progress reports.

In a very large development department, management might wish to
review the detailed progress of individual projects on an exception
basis, such that only those projects which were over a certain size
or which were more than, say, 10% over budget would be reviewed at
the most senior level.

For maintenance, a similar system of progress reporting may be
required for significant enhancements. In addition, performance
against the service level targets discussed earlier (responsiveness
to user requests and the size of the maintenance backlog) should be
monitored routinely.

Control also depends on obtaining an understanding of how
efficiently resources are being applied. One key measure is the
ratio of productive time to total available time. A second is the
level of non-productive time (i.e. time recorded for holidays,
sickness and other absence, training and non-project related
administration). Targets should be set for the levels of productive
and non-productive time budgeted at each grade of staff, and actual
performance monitored monthly.

Another effective measurement technique is to compare, say, once or
twice a year, actual times for standard tasks with the estimating
guidelines. In this way, the guidelines can be kept up-to-date and
individual efficiency (especially of project managers) can be
gauged.

One productivity measure which is much canvassed is the number of
lines of code written and tested per day. Its effectiveness will
vary depending on how accurately the results are measured but it can
prove extremely useful in large departments which produce a lot of
code (and therefore make comparisons meaningful) or for large
projects where individual performance is some times hard to assess
objectively. It may not always be practical however, to use the
number of lines of code to make comparisons between development
efficiency in one organisation and another, since conditions and
standards vary so much.

For this reason, the exact nature of the performance measures used, will vary from installation to installation. The key to success, however, is to select those measures which gauge the effectiveness of the systems development and maintenance function in meeting its agreed objectives within the agreed costs and time scales.

TECHNICAL SUPPORT

We have reviewed the impact of an effective system of performance measurement on the Management of the Data Processing Function, on Computer Operations and on Systems Sevelopment and Maintenance. Let us now consider its impact on Technical Support. Once again, the need for improved performance measures is highlighted by some of the problems typically encountered in this area. One such problem is the tendency, prevalent in many organisations, for Technical Support to indulge in technical innovation while circumventing normal control procedures. As a result a great deal of money may be wasted on the provision of facilities which are not required to support the business, or the level of service to users may suffer because of the disruption caused by the abrogation of the normal controls.

Other examples which suggest the absence of effective measurement and control are:

-   The existence within the installation of several pieces of systems software which ostensibly perform a similar function.

-   An inability to take advantage of new hardware announcements, because of restrictions imposed by out-of-date systems software.

-   Evidence that proven techniques (such as structured analysis and design) have been ignored by those who could gain the most from their use.

In many cases, these problems arise because the technical support function is thought in some way to be special. The approach described in the earlier sections of this paper hinges on the establishment of an overall framework with clearly defined targets, which are agreed with management, and the subsequent measurement of how successfully those targets have been met and at what cost. This same approach can be used to direct and control the technical support function.

For example, the decision to introduce data base facilities should rest solely on the business needs identified at the planning stage. There are a number of reasons why the planning stage is the most appropriate point at which to address these issues. Firstly, it is at this point that the business needs of each application are reviewed. Secondly, since the cost of the necessary systems software is unlikely to be justified by any one application, it is necessary to analyse the overall requirements of all applications, before deciding to proceed. Thirdly, the installation of, say, data base management software is a major undertaking, requiring significant resources; this requirement needs to be reflected in the overall development plan. A further advantage of this approach is that it inhibits the duplication of software performing the same function.

If the approach described is adopted, it should be possible to identify the major undertakings of the technical support function as development projects which can be planned and controlled in the same way as application systems developments.

In addition to development, however, there is a requirement to provide a maintenance service. The same techniques used for determining service levels for applications maintenance can be applied to Technical Support. Service levels can be defined in terms of responsiveness to bugs, and the incidence of production failures.

Similarly the techniques for measuring performance will be broadly similar to those used for Systems Development and Maintenance.

CONCLUSION

This paper has attempted to demonstrate the importance of adopting a coherent approach to measuring the performance of the data processing function. There are several measures which can be used (some would suggest as many as fifty) but a few basic measures, say fifteen, can provide most of what is needed. The precise nature of those key measures will vary from organisation to organisation, but at a minimum they should include the major items that we have identified earlier. The method of presentation will also vary, but graphic presentation is usually more easily understood.

To summarise, the key measures in each area would include the following:

1.   Management of the Data Processing Function

     -    Actual cost comparisons with budget

     -    Data processing costs per transaction, compared with overheads, staff costs, etc.

     -    Actual costs compared with costs recovered by transfer-charging.

2.   Computer Operations

     -    Service levels achieved compared with target

     -    Capacity utilisation compared with plan.

3.   Systems Development and Maintenance

   -   Development project progress reports:

       • man-days against estimate
       • cost against budget
       • elapsed time against target

   -   Maintenance backlog compared with target

   -   Percentage of non-productive time compared with target.

4.   Technical Support

   -   Development project progress reports

   -   Maintenance backlog compared with target

   -   Percentage of non-productive time compared with target.

The recommended approach to installing a system of performance reporting such as the one described in this paper is as follows:

1.   Ensure that the four pre-requisites (systems planning, standard practices, adequate staffing, and effective control) are in place.

2.   Establish the overall framework in each area, by discussion with users and management.

3.   Agree the objectives in terms of service level and cost in each area and identify the key control factors to be reported.

4.   Agree the format of the control reports and assign responsibility for regular production of those reports.

In the initial stages, a considerable amount of attention will be required from data processing management to ensure that the reports are prepared accurately and promptly, and are reviewed by the appropriate levels of management inside and outside the department.

Once installed, the system of performance reporting should enable management to decide whether or not value for money is being provided. In the context of this paper, value for money is defined as: 'The delivery of the agreed level of service, at the agreed cost, within the agreed time scales'.

Part 16
Systems Design

IDMS and CAFS

J. W. S. Carmichael

*Systems Controller, ICL Corporate Information Systems,
London, UK*

The contrasting approaches to data management of IDMS
and CAFS are described. On the basis of existing data
layouts a compromise was constructed which allowed an
IDMS database to be scanned in CAFS mode while remaining accessible to IDMS navigation by conventional batch
and on-line programs. An experimental implementation
of the compromise structure, using a small pilot database, is reviewed. Some of the important implications
for the future development of data management practice
are outlined.

IDMS and CAFS

INTRODUCTION

The past 10 years have seen rapid development in software database management systems, which aim to serve an
organisation's data processing and information needs by
explicitly-defined structures built into the stored data.
IDMS, as an example of such a system, is highly effective
in providing navigational paths through the data for
those activities which are predictable. But it is of
the essence of such systems that the requirements must be
most carefully analysed in advance of system building, so
that appropriate paths can be built into the database.
Experience shows that this approach can give rise to
several difficulties :

- it remains hard to achieve an accurate and
complete picture of the navigational requirements during the data analysis phase.

- once built, a database cannot be easily
changed; there is a conflict between a
business' need for the ability to react
dynamically to changing circumstances,
and the database's preference for static
continuity.

- although efficient in handling predicted
processes, structured database systems can
be sadly inefficient in handling unexpected
information requirements.

By contrast, CAFS - the Content Addressable File Store -
encourages a very simple approach to the storage of data.
Self-identifying group-fields, each of which may contain
a number of primitive data elements, are combined into
records; these in turn are stored serially in "cells".
A distinctive feature of a CAFS file is that the cell is
many times larger than the bucket or page which is the
corresponding unit of access in a conventional index-
sequential or database file; cell sizes of half a
cylinder (76,800 characters) or a complete cylinder are
normal. There are no pointers built into standard CAFS
records. Each file normally has a primary index, which
is small and efficient. Secondary indexes can be added

(or deleted) with great flexibility, since applications
can take advantage of them without needing to be aware
of their existence. This organisation, together with
the specialised searching hardware of the CAFS
controller, provides an unrivalled ability to scan large
volumes of data and to extract relevant information.
Unpredicted enquiries are handled without difficulty.
And the performance is so good that traditional report-
generating processes can be progressively replaced by
on-line enquiries.

This paper describes an experiment undertaken by ICL's
Corporate Information Systems division (CIS) which
attempted to establish whether it was possible to
reconcile the two approaches. The experiment arose
because it has been CIS policy for some years that all
new major applications should be based on IDMS, but at
the same time 18 months of live running of a Personnel
system on CAFS had been very successful, in terms of
development effort, facilities provided, and user
satisfaction. Any mode of combining the discipline of
an IDMS approach with the flexibility of CAFS access
would, therefore, be extremely attractive.

Preliminary discussions soon showed that a simple-minded
approach might yield worthwhile initial results for
relatively little development effort, and the experiment
was therefore authorised.

OBJECTIVES

Figure 1 shows the target environment in outline. It
was required that an IDMS database should be established
on CAFS discs, and that it should be confirmed that it
was possible to access the database both in CAFS mode for
searching and enquiry processes using the CAFS content-
addressing techniques, and in IDMS navigation mode
following the connections between related records by the
standard use of IDMS set pointers.

Under this basic objective, it was also required :

- that the experiment should quantify the
  performance of programs accessing the
  database in both modes and, if possible,
  to determine how the performance differed
  from that of the same programs operating
  on non-hybrid versions of the database;

- that the development effort expended in
  the experiment be recorded, and used to
  assess the effect on development expenditure
  if the same techniques were adopted on a
  full-scale implementation;

- that any constraints be identified and where
  possible translated into guidelines to be
  followed in the design of future databases.

It was further decided that the experiment should be
undertaken in such a way that there was minimum change
to existing software, both in CAFS and IDMS, in user
programs and in utilities, though at the same time notes
were to be taken of any points where more extensive
changes to software would give significant additional
advantages if a decision was taken to follow this approach
with serious full-scale implementations.

STORAGE STANDARDS

The first step was to establish whether a viable
compromise could be made in the storage standards, so
that the same data could be accessed in both modes. The
next two sub-sections describe the standards followed by
CAFS data, and the standards observed in "conventional"
IDMS files.

CAFS Standards

A CAFS file consists of an integral number of cylinders
on EDS60. The first cylinder is reserved for various
red-tape subjects which need not be described here.
Data starts at the beginning of the second cylinder.
Thereafter, up to the end of the file, all areas must
be CAFS-scannable; this normally means that in the last
cylinder the end of real data will be followed by dummy
records in CAFS format. The next significant physical
unit below the cylinder is the track, which on this

hardware consists of 15 blocks of 128 words. The lowest
level of access, (corresponding to the "bucket" in normal
UDAS Housekeeping), is the "pail" of 5-blocks or 640
words. Pails never cross track boundaries, and there is
therefore never any occasion for a head-move in the
middle of a pail-read as can occur during bucket-read in
UDAS files with 2-block, 4-block, or 8-block buckets.
The first word of each pail contains a count of the
number of words used within the pail. The first byte
(bits 0-7) of the second word contains the value '1',
known as the "pick-up point" from which a CAFS scan can
begin.

In the description of a CAFS file, pails are grouped
into "cells". As the pail is the lowest unit of
reading or writing in direct access mode, the cell is
the lowest level of access in CAFS-scanning mode. The
smallest practical cell is a single track but, as stated
above, cells of half a cylinder (10 tracks = 30 pails =
19,200 words) or a complete cylinder (20 tracks =
59 pails* = 37,760 words) are usual.

(* Only 296 of the 300 blocks in a cylinder are avail-
    able for data storage, and on CAFS the 296th block
    is not used, leaving 295 data blocks arranged in 59
    pails).

Each CAFS record consists of a number of group-fields.
A group-field is introduced by a word having 0 or 1 in
the first byte, an identifier with value up to 239 in
the second byte, and a length in the third byte. The
maximum length of a group-field is 256 bytes. Within
the group-field there may be any reasonable number of
fixed-length primitive fields, followed optionally by
a single variable-length field. The variable-length
option is not used in the IDMS-on-CAFS experiment.

A CAFS record is terminated by a trailer word containing
zero in the first byte, an identifier greater than 239,
and a length of 2. Records may not cross pail-
boundaries.

Figure 2 shows these standards in diagrammatic form.

IDMS Standards

An IDMS database consists of 1 or more "realms", each of
which corresponds to a physical file of 1 or more areas.
(In the experiment we have confined ourselves to a database consisting of simple realms, so that each realm is
held in a single contiguous physical area).

Within the realm, data is held in "pages".   A page may
be any number of physical blocks from 1 to 31,
corresponding to 128 or 3968 words.   Typical databases
appear to consist of pages of between 2 and 8 blocks,
and the experiment confined itself to the more common
values within this range.

A page opens with a four-word page-header, and closes
with a two-word page-trailer.   Their contents and
functions are adequately documented in IDMS manuals
and, since they do not affect the experiment, they are
not further described here.

Records grow forwards through the page from the end of
the page-header, and an index in the form of a line
space inventory grows backwards from the beginning of
the page-trailer, so that any spare space will be
surrounded by significant matter.   The line space
inventory and page trailer are collectively known
as the page footer.

Each record consists of two parts - pointers and data.
The pointers, which are held in what is called the
record prefix, contain the database keys of other records
to which a record may be connected through the IDMS
"sets" defined in the schema.   A single set may give
rise to several pointers, depending on the choice of
"next", "prior", and "owner" connections.

In form, a databasekey is an integer, identifying the
record by its page number and by its line number within
the page.   Line number may be in the range 0 to 63, but
since line 0 is by convention the page header only 63
line numbers are available for data records in any page;
(these details refer to the specifications of the 1900
version of IDMS).

Each entry in the line space inventory occupies 2 words, and contains 4 critical factors : the record-id of the record to which the entry points; the displacement of the record within the page; the total record length; and the length of the prefix section of the record.

It will be observed that in IDMS a record does not normally contain its own database key, nor does it contain a note of its own identity. The former is found by appending its line number to its page number, the latter by extracting the record-id from the line space inventory entry.

Figure 3 shows these standards in diagrammatic form.

Experimental compromise storage standards

Since there was no way that CAFS could read data in IDMS form, it was obviously necessary to adopt a compromise format in which the IDMS data was dressed up in CAFS-readable form. The first element of this involved the conversion of IDMS records into CAFS records, by the identification of suitable CAFS-type group-fields, and the inclusion of the requisite CAFS header words and trailer words.

IDMS records tend to be fairly small in size. This allows the creation of a typical record consisting of a single CAFS header word, a single group-field, and a CAFS trailer word. The identifier byte in the header word can be derived directly from the IDMS record-id by calculation, or can be found from a translation table. Longer records are similarly constructed out of two or more CAFS group-fields, the identifier bytes increasing by 1 from field to field.

It was also decided, to facilitate various modes of correlation, that each record should contain its own database key. This decision ensured that the same numeric value would appear in a record containing a pointer and in the record at which that pointer was directed.

The IDMS Page header, line space inventory, and page
trailer were unlikely ever to be the objects of CAFS
enquiries, but they could not be eliminated without
making the data inaccessible to IDMS programs. They
were, therefore, similarly topped and tailed with CAFS
header and trailer words, and given identifier bytes
outside the range usable for normal data fields.

These standards are represented in Figure 4.

The edited pages had to be stored in suitable CAFS pails.
It was decided to bring all the "red-tape" data to the
front of the pail, and follow it with the data records.
This meant that any spare space would be at the end of
the pail, rather than, as with IDMS, in the middle.

The inclusion of CAFS header words, database keys, and
CAFS trailer words caused an expansion of the data, the
amount of the expansion depending on the number of
records in the page. It was, therefore, decided that
each IDMS page should be stored in the CAFS pail of the
next larger size or, if necessary, in a pair of pails.
Of the range of possible page-sizes, only the following
subset were considered in the experiment :

    3-block page to be converted into a 5-block pail

    4-block page to be converted into a 5-block pail

    6-block page to be converted into a pair of 5-block pails

    8-block page to be converted into a pair of 5-block pails

There is thus a very considerable expansion in the
storage space required. It was felt that this was
tolerable in experimental conditions, though in a
serious long-term implementation different standards
which avoided this degree of inefficiency would have
to be established.

CONVERSION SOFTWARE

Once the standards defined in the previous section had
been established, it was possible to build some items of
simple interfacing software to cope with the changes in
data format.   Three items were created and used in the
experiment :

- A conversion subroutine, provisionally named
  IDMSTOCAFS, which takes a standard IDMS page
  and edits it to the CAFS format.   This was
  designed to be used between IDMS and the disc;
  whenever IDMS issues a page-write command,
  this subroutine is called.   In addition to
  re-formatting the data, it also adjusts the
  physical address on disc to which the page
  will be written.   But as far as IDMS is
  concerned, all that appears to happen is a
  standard page-write.

- A companion subroutine, names CAFSTOIDMS, which
  performs the same functions in reverse.   Every
  time IDMS calls for a page to be read, this
  subroutine first adjusts the address on disc,
  then performs the read, and finally converts
  the data from CAFS format to IDMS format.
  IDMS receives a clean page in the format which
  it understands.

- A Conversion utility, designed to read an
  existing database and to write it out in
  converted form to CAFS discs.   This utility
  makes use of the IDMSTOCAFS subroutine for the
  format conversions.   For debugging purposes it
  was written to also re-convert pages into IDMS
  format, to compare the original and final form,
  and to print all three forms if any discrepancy
  arose.

These items were written in PLAN.   They contain, 300,
600 and 550 lines respectively, and were written in some
$2\frac{1}{2}$ man/weeks.

CAFS is unaware of the existence of these conversion
facilities.   As far as it is concerned, the data is in
standard CAFS format, and needs no conversion.

An IDMS program needs to be re-compiled, to include a
modified version of one module which is now able to call
the conversion subroutines, and re-consolidated to
incorporate the conversion subroutines. The modified
module was created in 1 man/week.

PRACTICAL EXPERIMENT

Conversion Activities

A test database was acquired for the purpose of the
experiment from the manufacturing systems development
team, who had created a suitable pilot database to
assist in the development of product costing applications.
This was chosen partly because it included a sufficient
degree of complexity to make the experiment realistic,
but partly also because it was already supported by a
number of simple navigation programs and extensive
documentation, which provided the evidence for confirming
the accuracy and completeness of any CAFS enquiries.
Moreover, the whole test database was reasonably compact,
which effectively minimised the time taken during
conversion, testing and proving.

This database was small enough to make very convenient
test data for checking the operation of the conversion
utility. About five attempts were made before a
successful translation was achieved, and in total they
did not consume a significant amount of either man-time
or machine-time. The final conversion of all 4 realms,
involving the re-formatting of 672 pages containing 5564
records, took only about 10 minutes on a small processor.

The CAFS data description was then created by manual
editing from the IDMS schema. The CAFS field-names were
closely modelled on the IDMS field-names, but partially
abbreviated in some cases to reduce the amount of typing
that would be necessary in the specification of CAFS
enquiries. Because the version did not contain any
provision for using a common name, with a subscript, to
address each instance of a repeated field, it was
necessary to allocate unique names to each instance;
this was tedious, naturally, but not difficult. It was
also necessary to allocate CAFS data-names to each IDMS
pointer, as it was clear that these would be used

explicitly in many CAFS enquiries.   Initially these
pointer names were very rudimentary, of the form "PTR1",
"PTR2", "PTR3", etc.;   as experience was acquired some
pointers were given more meaningful synonyms.   The
initial process of creating the data description details
occupied about 1 man/day, which was largely taken up in
typing.

All the ancillary set-up activities - creating a CAFS
System File, translating the raw data description into
a CAFS data model, generating CAFS file header data in
the first cylinder of each file - took only about 15
minutes using a set of appropriate utilities controlled
from a MOP terminal.   No CAFS indexes were created, so
that each enquiry necessitated a full scan of the target
file.   But apart from the fact that the file-sizes were
trivial, this simple approach was justified on the basis
that the experiment was chiefly concerned to establish
whether CAFS enquiries on a database were possible, and
performance considerations were secondary.

FINDINGS

Simple Enquiries

The experiment showed, as expected, that IDMS could be
successfully made available to enquiry in CAFS mode,
using the standard facilities of the CAFS General Enquiry
Package.   Enquiries where all the data, both selection
criteria and retrieval fields, co-existed within records
of the same type, could be answered directly by a single
pass through the appropriate realm at full CAFS reading
speed.   The response time for such enquiries was
delightfully fast, but hardly surprising since the
largest realm in the pilot database comprised only twelve
cylinders.   This small scale allowed another simplification which differed from practical real-life working,
in that no CAFS indexes - either primary or secondary -
were used.   Some ambiguity was observed in processing
questions containing a concealed correlation requirement,
where the data existed in the same file but in more than
one type of record;   such enquiries were accepted as
logically valid, but gave null results, since no one
record contained all the relevant data to enable it to
qualify as a hit.   These difficulties could have been
eliminated by specifying a more realistic CAFS data model.

Navigational Enquiries

Of course, much of the value of an IDMS database consists
in the links between records of different kinds, and the
intelligent exploitation of set relationships is the key
to effective information processing.   It was therefore
important to see whether the stored structural links
could be exploited in CAFS mode.

In the simple conditions of the experiment only the most
primitive facilities were available.   An enquiry that
involved navigation could be processed in several
stages : the first stage retrieved a list of database
keys or pointers from records of one type;   these were
then incorporated in a further stage of the enquiry to
read the records at the other end of the links.   This
was feasible as part of an experiment, but involved some
subtlety in manipulating data on the screen of the
enquiring terminal, and would not be satisfactory in
real life application conditions.   Furthermore, one
could not expect end users to be skilful in such
explicit pointer handling, and they would certainly not
enjoy it.

Meanwhile CIS have developed for use in other CAFS
applications software which permits data in different
files or records to be correlated as an automatic
process during the execution of a complex enquiry.   This
provides the degree of facility which end users require,
and makes the process suitably invisible.   It is clear
that this software will be the key to improving the run
times of batch applications of database material.   Its
performance in on-line working remains to be confirmed.

In due course the CAFS hardware File Correlation Unit
will provide the most effective solution to all
correlation requirements, whether in batch or on-line
mode.

IDMS Working

The experiment proved, as required, that it was still
possible to read an IDMS database held in the compromise
storage format on CAFS discs.   No change was needed to
any IDMS DDL or DML statements, and no change was needed

in any application code. The only extra work involved
was the reconsolidation of existing application programs
to incorporate the transformation subroutines. These
subroutines of course impose a performance penalty at
each page-read and page-write, which was roughly
quantified as involving $100 + 50n$ extra instructions per
transfer, 'n' being the number of records in the IDMS
page. The effect of this overhead will therefore vary
widely according to the space available for page buffers,
the volatility of the data, the frequency of page-
swapping, and the record population in transferred pages.
The balance between this overhead and the advantage of
extra flexibility in the making of enquiries could not
be established once for all by any experiment, but would
need to be separately assessed for each database and its
family of applications.

Further Work

The results of the initial experiment were judged to be
sufficiently encouraging for further work to be undertaken. Some of the topics in this category are :

- modifying the IDMS-on-CAFS format to give greater
  efficiency and better packing;

- loading a full-scale live product costing database,
  in place of the experimental pilot;

- exploration of the possibilities for exploiting CAFS
  indexing techniques on IDMS data;

- quantifying the improvement possible in some batch
  system run times;

- quantifying the effect of CAFS correlation techniques,
  initially in software mode and later with hardware;

- quantifying the effect of CAFS searching power as a
  means of providing the effect of multiple clustering
  in an IDMS database;

- making the experimental IDMS-on-CAFS database available as a demonstration.

CONCLUSIONS

It will be seen that the experiment described in this
paper is only the first stage in what may be a considerable development. The value of the simple facilities
developed hitherto has certainly been enough to justify
their relatively trivial implementation cost and to
provide confidence that the benefits of a full-scale
trial will be considerable. As required, several
pointers have been identified which will help to make
future implementations even more effective.

So far, all work has been conducted on databases which
already existed, and whose structure had therefore been
designed to operate in a purely IDMS environment. We
look forward with interest to the future design of
database systems designed ab initio to operate in the
hybrid CAFS and IDMS environment. The main hope for
such work is that it will prove possible to implement
databases with structures that are much closer to the
entity models emerging from data analysis studies, that
the difference between the real-world and the
implementation view of data will diminish, and that
thereby databases will become more readily accessible
to the whole population of end users.

FIGURE 1

THE EXPERIMENTAL OBJECTIVE

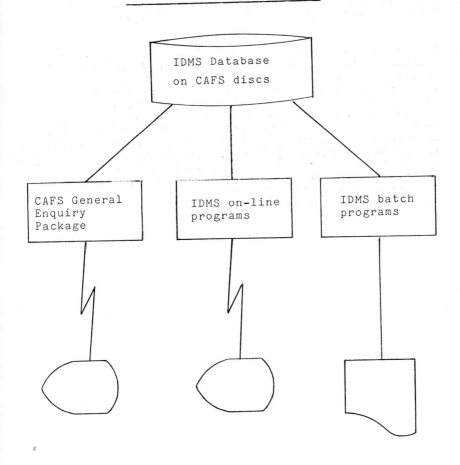

FIGURE 2

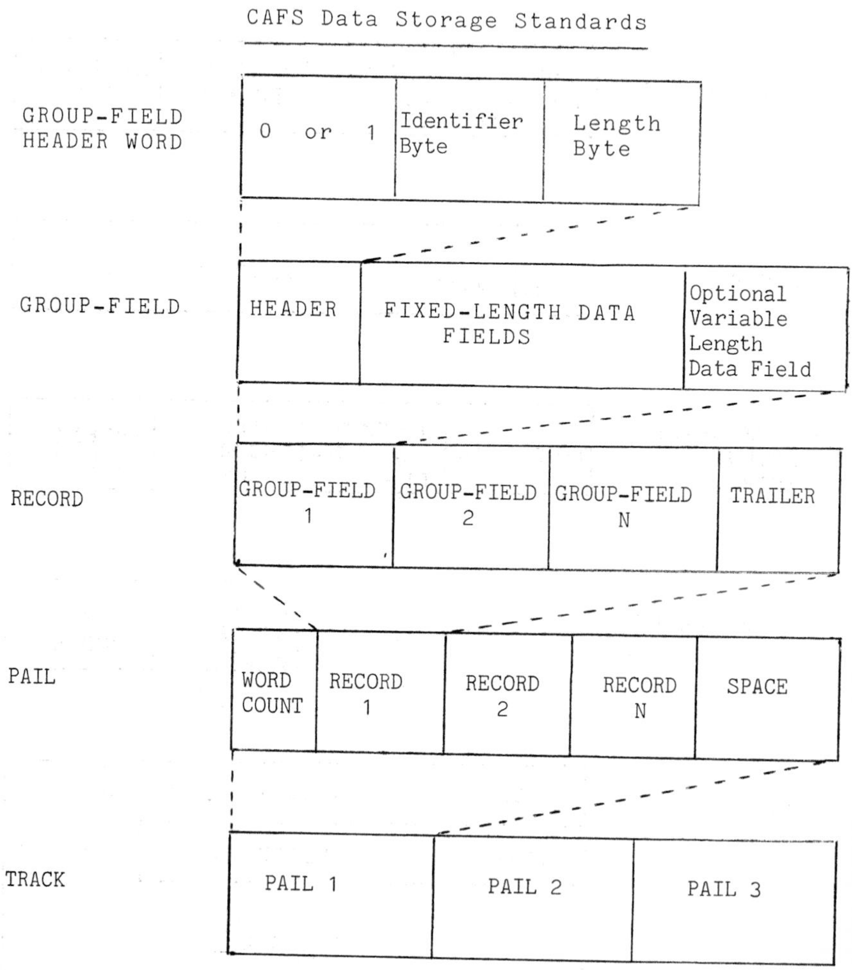

CAFS Data Storage Standards

GROUP-FIELD HEADER WORD	0 or 1	Identifier Byte	Length Byte

GROUP-FIELD	HEADER	FIXED-LENGTH DATA FIELDS	Optional Variable Length Data Field

RECORD	GROUP-FIELD 1	GROUP-FIELD 2	GROUP-FIELD N	TRAILER

PAIL	WORD COUNT	RECORD 1	RECORD 2	RECORD N	SPACE

TRACK	PAIL 1	PAIL 2	PAIL 3

FIGURE 3

IDMS Storage Standards

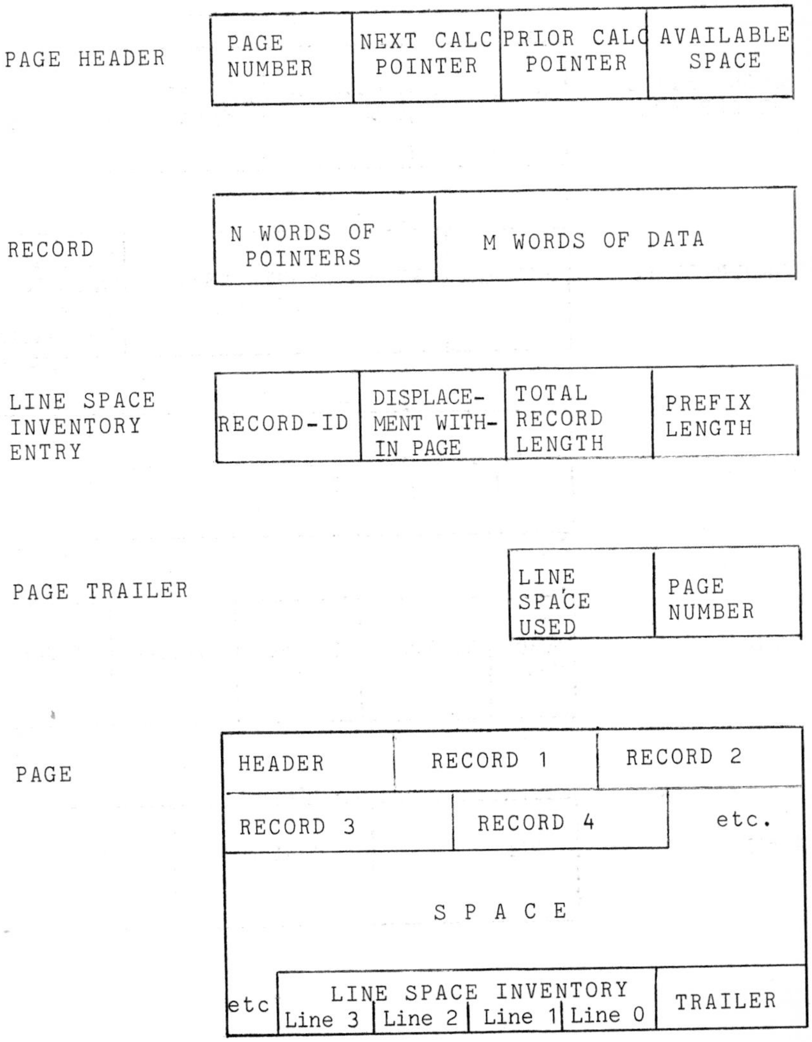

PAGE HEADER

PAGE NUMBER	NEXT CALC POINTER	PRIOR CALC POINTER	AVAILABLE SPACE

RECORD

N WORDS OF POINTERS	M WORDS OF DATA

LINE SPACE INVENTORY ENTRY

RECORD-ID	DISPLACE-MENT WITH-IN PAGE	TOTAL RECORD LENGTH	PREFIX LENGTH

PAGE TRAILER

LINE SPACE USED	PAGE NUMBER

PAGE

HEADER	RECORD 1	RECORD 2
RECORD 3	RECORD 4	etc.

S P A C E

etc	LINE SPACE INVENTORY				TRAILER
	Line 3	Line 2	Line 1	Line 0	

FIGURE 4

IDMS-ON-CAFS Storage Standards

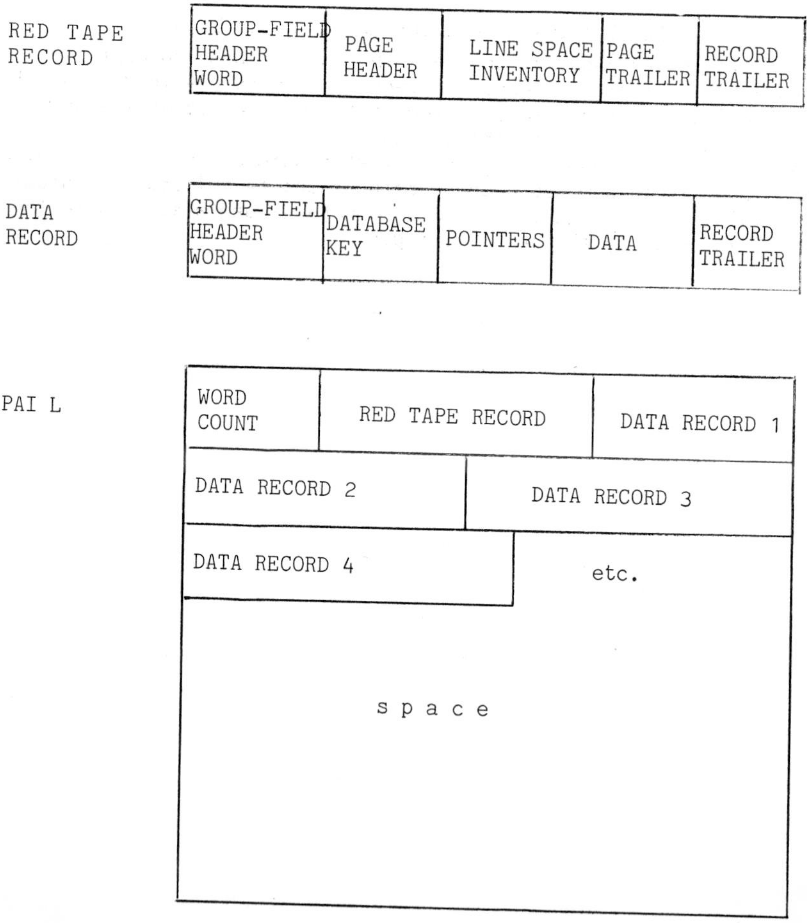

RED TAPE
RECORD

GROUP-FIELD HEADER WORD	PAGE HEADER	LINE SPACE INVENTORY	PAGE TRAILER	RECORD TRAILER

DATA
RECORD

GROUP-FIELD HEADER WORD	DATABASE KEY	POINTERS	DATA	RECORD TRAILER

PAI L

WORD COUNT	RED TAPE RECORD	DATA RECORD 1
DATA RECORD 2	DATA RECORD 3	
DATA RECORD 4	etc.	
space		

New Approaches to Systems Analysis and Design

J. Abbatt, C. Campbell, A. H. Jones and F. F. Land

BCS Business Information Systems Specialist Group, UK

The paper proposes that a number of accepted concepts in systems design are in danger of becoming too deeply ingrained while not in fact being entirely suited to the challenges we are now beginning to face. Both the concepts and their challenges are reviewed and the paper then investigates some of the many emerging developments in new approaches, methods and techniques in systems analysis and design which may prove to be valuable sources to the problems posed by the new challenges.

NEW APPROACHES TO SYSTEMS ANALYSIS AND DESIGN

BACKGROUND

The design and implementation of computer based information systems in the business environment has been a sufficiently repeated process to have acquired by now an accepted procedural methodology, at least at the general level. Although at specific levels, ranging from that of the broad organisational standards to the personal preferences of the individual practitioner, variations and differences of emphasis are still common we would expect a good systems analyst nowadays to be perfectly able to communicate with another across even organisational boundaries without excessive amounts of preliminary explanation of method, definition of terms, and so on. In other words, even though we might still have some difficulty in providing a succinct definition of business systems analysis for the non-practitioner, we do seem to have arrived at a reasonably common understanding of what comprises its essential practice.

This situation has not been achieved without some degree of painful experience. Projects developed under loosely or pragmatically defined procedural rules have often been inefficient and unpopular to the point of failure. Most data processing managers must be relieved to have nowadays some semblance of a manual of procedures together with a related guide to standards against which to monitor and measure the progress of projects of which they are responsible.

But we should be wary of complacency. As concepts gain general acceptance and become more deeply ingrained we lose our ability to be critical of them. A number of concepts about project development procedure have begun to be challenged in recent times however and we want to make the identifying of these the starting point of this paper. We see some five important concepts in particular that come into this category and these are shown in the first box of fig. 1. We shall now comment briefly on each.

The systems life cycle

Although, as we said earlier, emphasis does vary, there is reasonable current agreement that the stages of a project should follow the general sequence of, for example, feasibility study, problem analysis, system design, implementation, maintenance. (Other terms are in use, but these give a reasonable idea of the common ground).

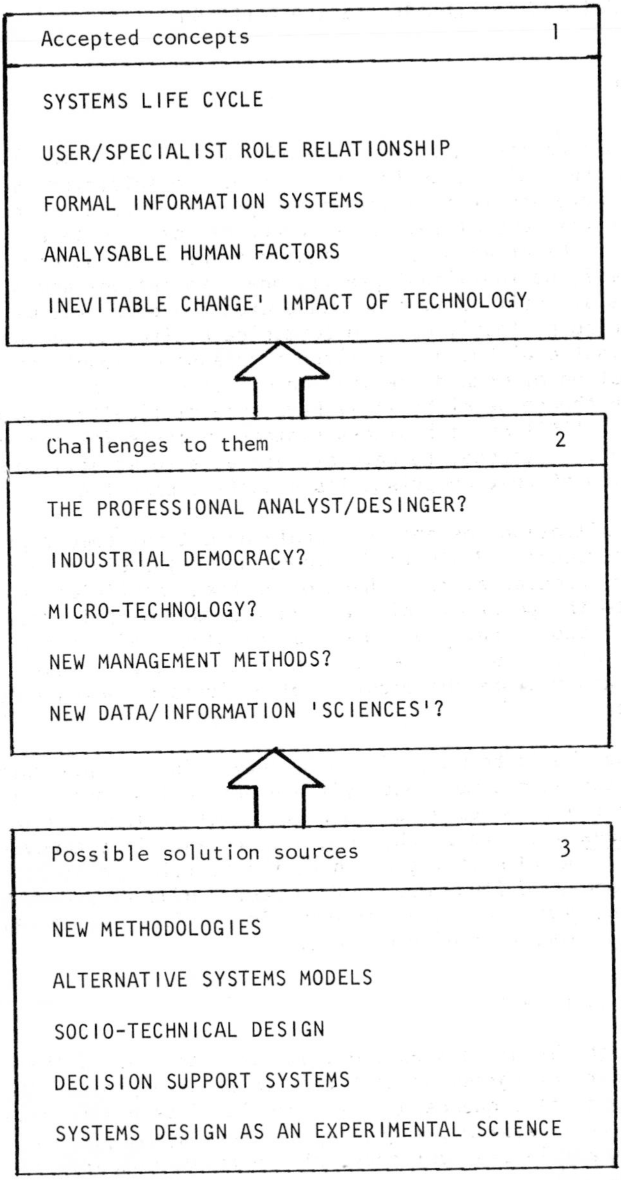

Accepted concepts	1
SYSTEMS LIFE CYCLE USER/SPECIALIST ROLE RELATIONSHIP FORMAL INFORMATION SYSTEMS ANALYSABLE HUMAN FACTORS INEVITABLE CHANGE' IMPACT OF TECHNOLOGY	

Challenges to them	2
THE PROFESSIONAL ANALYST/DESINGER? INDUSTRIAL DEMOCRACY? MICRO-TECHNOLOGY? NEW MANAGEMENT METHODS? NEW DATA/INFORMATION 'SCIENCES'?	

Possible solution sources	3
NEW METHODOLOGIES ALTERNATIVE SYSTEMS MODELS SOCIO-TECHNICAL DESIGN DECISION SUPPORT SYSTEMS SYSTEMS DESIGN AS AN EXPERIMENTAL SCIENCE	

Fig. 1.   An illustration of the structure of the paper.

The sheer pace of technological change has been strongly influential in encouraging the view that a project should aim primarily to produce something that works in the first instance. This has had a profound effect upon the way we organise the development tasks and even upon the ways in which we structure the designed system itself. The emphasis is upon the initial creation. Little attention, beyond lip-service, is given to the continuing robustness and to the long life of the system after its initial setting up.

The user/specialist role relationship

The user (the name itself somehow reinforces the non-specialist view of the role) is often seen as being merely the source of enabling-triggers at key points in the stages of the project. The specialist is seen to <u>need the user</u> to define requirements, to agree terms of reference, to approve the design proposals, and to take over the system at implementation. A good deal is said by both sides about the importance of good communications in these 'exchanges', and yet all too often we finish up complaining that communication has after all failed. It is this all too rigid division of functions between the two roles that is the feature which is now seen as being in need of re-examination.

The formal information system

In the early days of the use of computers in business it was natural that the procedures that were routine, documented and low in judgemental content should be the primary candidates for automation. As demands for greater sophistication grew so methods were stretched to incorporate greater volumes and complexity of data. But this effort seems always to have been applied to extending the automation of the <u>formal</u> features of the system. At worst, this has led the designer to squeeze out <u>informal</u> aspects of information usage and, at best, merely to neglect them. The non-routine, the poorly documented and the judgemental types of information are of course difficult and expensive to identify and define and their incorporation into software therefore even more so. And yet the reality is that they play major roles in the work of the skilled decision maker. Little wonder that data processing systems often prove a bitter disappointment to the middle to upper reaches of management.

The analysable human factors

We hear less nowadays than we did a decade ago about 'human engineering' and 'models of human behaviour', but this is due more perhaps to the language style being out of vogue than to a loss of faith in the ethos behind such phrases. This ethos leads designers to assume that users have common values, that managers' responses to information system access can be predicted, that the information needs related to a job title remain stable or are at least not too difficult to monitor, and so on. When these assumptions and predictions prove false, or at best highly inaccurate, designers are apt to wash their hands of human capriciousness and to appeal to 'terms of reference' or 'impossible expense' as reasons not to modify them. The ethos is that the human factor <u>should</u> be analysable while the evidence so often is that it certainly <u>is not</u>.

The 'inevitable change' impact of technology

Systems designers and management who have gained their experience of systems implementations over the last two decades have become accustomed to the idea of obsolescence in systems as a consequence of changing technology. It has seemed important to be using the latest 'generation' of machine type to support the information system and to consider it a matter of pride to have 'upgraded' the hardware at the opportune moment. Gradually, therefore it was accepted that the excellence of the information system was directly dependent on keeping up with the latest technology. This is fairly obviously a habit of expedience rather than of getting the priorities right.

2.   NEW CHALLANGES

The above then are we suggest some of the concepts that are showing signs of their weaknesses. They are coming up for some challenge from a number of directions. We cannot necessarily attach the challenges (and the associated suggestions as to how to meet them) uniquely to a single category of the concepts set out in the previous section. Usually the relationship is many-to-many. That is to say, that any one of the challenges that we shall now proceed to identify might attack more than one of the concepts, and that any one of the concepts will need ideas generated by the responses to more than one challenge.

The following is a brief summary of new challenges as we see them at present. The remaining sections of the paper will then comprise investigations of the new ideas, new approaches and new tools for systems analysis and design which comprise the responses and possible sources of 'solutions' to the problems set by these challenges. The second and third boxes of fig. 1 illustrate this.

Challenging the professional

The computer industry has in many respects been patently successful. The general public and the users of computer systems remain sceptical however of the view of the computer expert as a true professional. Why is this? Is it important? If it is what should be done about it?

The challenge of industrial democracy

Public attitudes and social trends in western industrial society show a distinct tendency towards expecting industry to be more sensitive to human considerations. In spite of severe economic conditions, few people expect a return to the 'work-slavery' of the industrial revolution and its inheritance. Work people at all levels of industry will expect more and more to be able to participate more closely in directing their own work and in influencing organisational objectives. Information is a vital factor in the distribution of power. What therefore will those responsible for computer-based information systems have to offer in providing for this growing need?

The challenges of microelectronic technology

There are developments in this field that can, and surely will, affect managerial thinking and practice profoundly. The more prominent of these are: new office technology, more powerful (yet smaller and cheaper) digital computers, communications technology and artificial intelligence (including robotics). How can these be brought into use with optimum effectiveness and minimum disruptiveness?

The challenge of new management methods

Irrespective of technological changes there are movements in managerial thinking that in themselves affect the ways in which data and information are to be used. These include, for example: profit centre accounting, management by objectives and the decentralisation of decision taking. Can the existing so-called MIS cope with these methods and others not yet introduced?

The challenge of new data/information sciences and technologies

A number of related developments are affecting our perspectives of the view we have of data and information as a resource. These include techniques for data analysis and data modelling, database management systems and, a very important special case of the latter, data dictionary systems. Will these facilities result

in more adaptable systems, in systems less constrained by the purely
formal aspects of the organisations they model?

3.   THE SOURCES FOR NEW IDEAS AND APPROACHES

     Although it is neither an exhaustive list nor one in which
the headings are completely distinct from one another we now direct
attention to some of the new approaches and new tools that we believe
can begin to provide answers to the problems outlined in the previous sections. (See fig. 1, box 3).

New analysis and design methodologies

     A sense of disappointment with the results of the use of each
generation of new computer technology has stimulated the search for
better ways of solving the problems of analysing and designing
systems. A variety of such new methods have evolved, sponsored by
both DP practitioners and academics, each with its own problem
definition and approach.

     The notion of the systems approach (33) is common to some of
these methodologies. This originated with the application of the
traditional scientific method to the solution of strictly quanti-
fiable organisational problems (e.g. the wartime development of
Operational Research in the U.K., the postwar work done by the RAND
Corporation and others for the U.S. Government). Unlike traditional
science, it emphasised a wide 'holistic' approach to problem solving.
Some of the early developments, particularly in the public policy
area, have themselves been severely criticised for their over-
enthusiastic reliance on mathematical modelling and for their lack
of contact with the real world (16). Newer systems approaches have
attempted to redress the balance by recognising the messy nature of
real problems, and the complexities of real organisations.

     The cybernetic approach developed by Stafford Beer and others
(3, 4, 14) views the organisation as a self-regulating organism
concerned primarily with it's own survival. In order to remain
viable, it must be able to match each relevant distinct state within
its environment with an appropriate response. This matching of
variety must also take place within the organisation to enable it
to function. The problem for management is thus one of designing
information systems which will effectively reduce the complexity of
the situation and amplify the managerial response. Traditional
computer applications very often exacerbate the control problem by
generating more information than management can absorb within the
time required to respond. The cybernetic approach identifies autonomous functions at different levels within the organisation and

develops indices of their performance which can adapt to changing
circumstances, and which thus constitute a system for learning about
the organisation's behaviour.

The systems approach developed at Lancaster by Checkland and
the Iscol consultancy (8) views organisations as human activity
systems within which many problems are ill-defined and have no single
solution. This approach seeks to enquire as objectively as possible
into the underlying views of the various participants, and to develop
a number of alternative models of the situation, drawing on a variety
of systems ideas. Comparison of these models with each other and
with the real world problem is then used to clarify the issues for
the participants and to suggest changes that are both feasible and
desirable. This approach has been applied by Iscol to the strategic
planning of information systems development, among other projects.

The need for more efficient and reliable programming gave rise
in the 1960's to 'software engineering' which developed more scientific <u>structured</u> methods of program design. The approach has been
applied to systems analysis and design by Jackson, Yourdon,
Constantine, De Marco and others (12, 18, 34). Structured analysis
seeks to take formal account of such problem areas as communication
with the user and changes to system requirements by the systematic
use of graphical methods of documentation (for example, data flow
diagrams), partitioned specifications, decision tables and data
dictionary software. The more recent emphasis on data structure
has led to the related use of data modelling and analysis techniques,
and structured design methods have demonstrated the virtues of the
so-called top-down approach, namely the partitioning of the proposed
system into manageable modules arranged in a hierarchy of dependencies.

Alternative system modes

There is surely little doubt that we are entering an era when
computerised information systems will be expected to survive longer
than in the past. Not only smaller packaged systems but also larger
custom-built systems (sometimes admittedly relying upon the packaged
aids such as database management systems and data dictionaries) will
be expected to have a recognisable continuity of existence of perhaps
thirty years or more.

Current design practice may try to acknowledge this by stress-
ing the importance of 'maintainability' as a feature of the design
stage of the life cycle model and in relying upon proper management
of the post-implementation stage to ensure that the maintenance
service is properly supported. In engineering this building-to-last
approach is rather dated, and in the design of social systems the
thought of neglecting the future (as yet unknown), life of the

system is surely unacceptable. "What about the all-important pheno-
mena of growth, learning, adaptation, and evolutionary development?"
the true systems engineer will want to ask.

Some attention to this question as it relates to software
design has appeared in recent years. For instance, d'Agapeyeff (10)
provided an interesting number of points covering such questions as
the excessive precision of some pre-programming analysis, the dis-
ordered collection of ideas on program reliability, the relative
obscurity of many structured and modular programming methodologies,
and so on. This was a timely plea for a reassessment and reorganising of software maintenance issues. More recently a whole
conference has addressed itself to the subject (17).

Software is however only one component of an information system
and however well it survives to meet defined objectives it will soon
become antiquated if the objectives themselves have not been modified to suit current demands upon the overall system. A 'properly'
designed total system would not be one that merely coped defensively
with such demands but one which recognised change as natural, and
adaptation as healthy in the longer, if not the shorter, term. The
rapid changes in technology in the computer-related field make such
a proper design both desirable and challenging at the same time.

Both the scale and scope of this challenge demand some radical
and long-term changes in approach to systems design. Systems must
have sensitivity to their environment, with high inner stability to
be able safely to afford that sensitivity and possessing an intelligence, a kind of consciousness even, so as to learn to adapt to the
trials of the changing environment. Thus a personnel records system
might develop into a human resources information system, an information retrieval system might get to recognise its users and adapt to
their needs and styles both as a group and as individuals, a production control system might recognise incipient weaknesses in its own
performance and alert those responsible of the need for sub-system
redesign. Such adaptable long-life systems are technically feasible
now, but the very system fabric would fail if designed purely on the
basis of the life cycle model. The main requirement for change in
approach must be the commitment to iteration of design rather than
a bland policy of post-implementation maintenance. Thus the whole
of the systems development stages must become involved with the
system-in-operation (see fig. 2).

This still does not tell us how the sensitivity, stability and
consciousness features can be satisfactorily incorporated in the
design stages of the iterative process. We don't yet have precise
models to help us to overcome this problem. The following are some
general suggestions as to how we might proceed in developing such
models. A more detailed examination is given in refs. 20, 21.

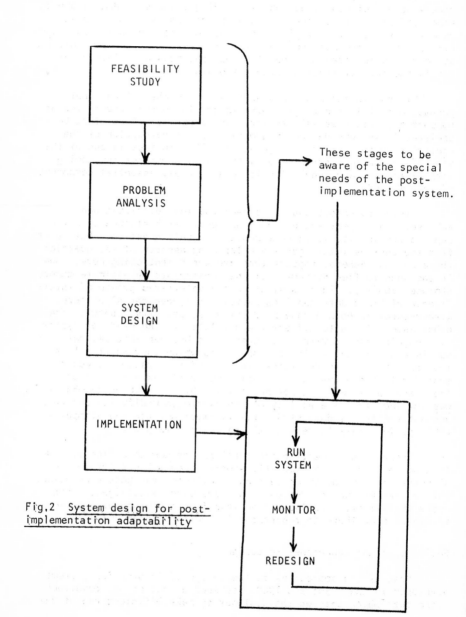

Fig.2 System design for post-implementation adaptability

Sensitivity might be described as the ability to maximise the receiving of relevant input while avoiding consequent damage due to shock effects. Crises need to be absorbed and used rather than merely survived. This implies the need for improved continual scanning of the environment combined with improved internal communication structures which transmit the all-important news of crisis to precisely the correct stations within the system.

Living systems achieve stability in a number of ways but perhaps a most interestingly imitable one is in the structuring of homeostats, nested as well as serially connected. This might be achieved in systems design by a more emphatic perception of the control structure at the design stage. This in fact is one of the aims of the various structured systems design methods now coming into wider use, and modularity is an absolutely essential component of such methods.

System consciousness is perhaps the most difficult goal to achieve. The expert systems approach dealt with elsewhere in the paper addresses itself in some measure to this question. But apart from the obvious intelligence and learning aspects of the question there are two general aspects that are worth mentioning here. One is the need to free systems from the constraints on ultimate memory storage capacity. This is vital to the unfettered growth of intelligence within a data handling system and indeed the signs here, with respect to both hardware and software, are very hopeful. The other aspect is quite different and relates to the need for systems to recognize the inevitable discrepancies between internal data models and the real-world information to which they refer. This implies a kind of self-critical ability of the system and would mean for instance that output design would always aim to inform the reader as to what it was not telling him as much as to what is was telling him. The ability of the system to modify its own rules and not simply its data structures is important too and Stamper's LEGOL project (31) is very promising in this respect.

Other ways of meeting the challenge of how to design systems that do not suffer the traumatic shocks of an unknown future are discussed in the following section. Designing for people as humans rather than as robots, designing systems more 'intelligent' than users themselves, treating design itself as a continuous experiment - all these contribute to robustness in their different ways.

Socio-technical approaches to design

Most of the approaches to the design of information systems developed in the 1950s and 1960s focussed attention and developed techniques which enabled the designer to make efficient use of the

technical apparatus available. Organisation structure and work
organisation were typically regarded as given, and it was supposed
that changes in the way tasks were organised, as for example, by the
introduction of teleprocessing and interactive systems, could be
introduced by the two processes of 'selling' the change to the user,
and providing appropriate training. Many of the design methods in
current use, and even some of the newer methods, such as top-down
structured design (12) are based on values and ideas which look at
problems in mainly technical/economic terms and tend to favour
technocratic solutions.

In the last few years, studies of the effectiveness of
implementing computer based systems have drawn attention to the
fact that many systems have not provided all that was expected of
them, and it has become clear that failure to perform at the
expected level is due as much to the failure to appreciate the
importance of organisational and social factors as to problems with
the technology. The recognition of the importance of social factors
in the successful implementation of systems led to a number of new
approaches to the management of the development phase of the systems
life cycle. In Scandanavia followers of Langefors (24) who as early
as the mid 1960s stressed the difference between an 'infological'
approach - an approach which saw the design of a system as the design
of an organisation - and the conventional 'datalogical' approach
which looked for ways of structuring solutions to human problems in
the context of a given organisation. Lundeberg (25) has developed
a design package - the ISAC method - which explicitly recognises the
need to identify social as well as technical/economic problems and
the need to find solutions which meets some social and organisational
criteria.

In the U.K., in the Checkland approach (8) mentioned earlier,
the techniques encourage problem recognition based on the concept
of an information system as a 'human activity system'. The method
attempts to find a 'root definition' of the problem to be solved
which encompasses (and reconciles) the views of the different
interest groups.

The approach known specifically as the socio-technical approach
is derived from methods developed at the Tavistock Institute for
Behavioural Research in the 1950s. This approach attempted to find
a way of introducing new technology in industry (new coal mining
methods in the U.K. coal mines) by analysing human (social) needs in
parallel with the identification of technical/economic needs. Its
underlying rationale is based on the value that change should improve
human conditions and that a system will only function effectively if
human needs, such as job satisfaction, are provided for. Hence it
seeks technical solution to problems which harmonise with social
solutions (in terms of, for example, work organisation).

In the 1970s the socio-technical approach began to be adopted for the design of computer-based information systems. In the USA, Taylor (32); in Italy, De Maio (11); in Finland, Saaksjarvi (30); in Denmark, Bjorn-Anderson (5) developed the socio-technical approach and adapted it for data processing and MIS. In the U.K. Enid Mumford, recognising that for a system to be successful it had to be approved by those who work with it, began to use the socio-technical approach. But she found that the approach worked best when the users of the system played a major role in the analysis and design of their own system, and in particular where they were given the opportunity to redesign the work organisation in such a way as to enhance social goals such as job satisfaction and technical goals such as efficiency of operation. Mumford and her colleagues (23) have developed a range of analysis, design and evaluation tools which aid those who participate in the analysis and design tasks. The principal tools help to analyse the problem situation (variance analysis), diagnose job satisfaction needs, assist in an information requirement analysis, provide a method for evaluation of objectives and alternative solutions, and help the design team to assess needs of the future (future analysis). The socio-technical methods, although still relatively new, have been applied to computer-based systems in a number of cases in various parts of the world.

Decision support and expert systems

In the 1970s the terms "Decision Support System (DSS)" and "Expert System" have emerged to describe new concepts and approaches for applying computers and information to the decision problems faced by business managers.

Although the label Decision Support System may not yet be in widespread use amongst data processing professionals in Europe, in the USA the label is rapidly becoming the vogue to replace the much maligned Management Information System (MIS) which has been given so many different meanings. However the concept of a DSS differs significantly from that of MIS.

According to the recent Addison-Wesley series of books on Decision Support (1, 19, 22) the concepts have evolved from two main areas of research: the theoretical studies of organisational decision-making done at the Carnegie Institute of Technology during the late 1950s and early 1960s and the technical work on interactive computer systems, mainly carried out at the Massachusetts Institute of Technology in the 1960s. Decision Support is defined as "a concept of the application of interactive technologies to management decision-making through the development of tools that:

address nonstructured rather than structured tasks

support rather than replace judgement

focus on effectiveness rather than efficiency in decision processes."

DSSs differ from the data processing systems that are commonly designed to automate the basic business operations such as order processing, inventory control and ledger accounting, and from the more sophisticated applications for management control using MIS, Management Science, and Operations Research techniques. Alter (1) argues that the basic EDP systems are designed to improve efficiency of clerical transaction processing and/or record keeping, whereas a DSS is designed to improve the effectiveness of individuals and organisations by helping people make decisions. The differences between the DSS concept and that of MIS or Management Science is explained by Keen and Scott Morton (22) as follows:

Management Information Systems

a   The main impact has been on structured tasks where standard operating procedures, decision rules, and information flows can be reliably predefined.

b   The main payoff has been in improving efficiency by reducing costs, turnaround time, and so on, and by replacing clerical personnel.

c   The relevance for managers' decision making has mainly been indirect, for example, by providing reports and access to data.

Operations Research/Management Science

a   The impact has mostly been on structured problems (rather than tasks) where the objective, data and constraints can be prespecified.

b   The payoff has been in generating better solutions for given types of problems.

c   The relevance for managers has been the provision of detailed recommendations and new methodologies for handling complex problems.

Decision Support Systems

a   The impact is on decisions in which there is sufficient structure for computer and analytic aids to be of value but where managers' judgement is essential.

b   The payoff is in extending the range and capability of managers decision processes to help them improve their effectiveness.

c   The relevance for managers is the creation of a supportive tool, under their own control, which does not attempt to automate the decision process, predefine objectives, or impose solutions.

In parallel with the development of Decision Support concepts, Artificial Intelligence (AI) researchers appear to have made significant progress in developing computing systems and tools which perhaps offer the greatest potential for supporting business managers in decision-making.

These systems are able to translate human knowledge and expertise in a given domain into codified machine forms, and to interact intelligently with a user in the manner of a consultant. The label Expert Systems is therefore used for such systems. A tutorial by Michie (28) on the development of Expert Systems appeared recently, and it showed that examples of such systems are no longer confined to the research laboratories. A significant finding has been that a system of this type can out-perform any single one of its human experts who tutor it.

Computer support for managers will be a key aspect of systems in the 1980s. Advances in technology will play a significant role in improving the computer support which managers receive. Perhaps equally significant are the advances being made in the areas of Decision Support and Expert Systems to create new tools for managers to increase their effectiveness. Further references are given at (6, 13, 27).

Systems design as an experimental science

The design of an information system is typically based on a model of the real world developed by an analyst in conjunction with a set of users. The model is the outcome of the analysis phase of the systems life cycle and is based on the classic techniques of 'fact' finding:

> interview
>
> questionnaire
>
> observation
>
> study of documents and procedure manuals

Empirical studies have shown that each of these techniques are suspect. For example, Argyris & Schon (2) have shown that there is a wide difference between what a person says he does - espousal - and what he actually does when he is faced with the situation. The well-known 'Hawthorn' effect (26) biases the results of observation and documents and procedure manuals tend to describe situations which may have been true some time ago but are no longer an accurate description of what is practised today. Hence the model of the real world based on the classic techniques of systems analysis is almost certainly inaccurate and biased.

If the model of the real world today is inherently inaccurate, the model of the real world in the future, when the system now being designed has to function, is likely to be even less accurate. In order to design systems which have to operate successfully in the future the designer has to model not only the state of the real world in terms of technological advances, economic parameters, changing attitudes, changing legal requirements, at points in the future, but he also has to provide a model of user behaviour in the face of new, often innovative, systems. The difficulty of building precise models of the real world into which the new information systems will have to fit, means that for most systems at least the designer cannot make deterministic assumptions, but must accept that he faces uncertainty. Nevertheless, the conventional approach to systems analysis and design has tended to rely on deterministic assumptions.

Neumann, Davis and McKeen (29) suggest that the uncertainty inherent in a situation can be assessed from four contingency factors.

1.   the size and complexity of the project. Large complex systems are inherently less certain as regards a good model of require-ments, than simpler smaller systems.

2.   the degree of structure in the object system. A highly struc-tured application can be modelled with greater certainty than a less structured application.

3.   the extent of knowledge and consensus the users have of the tasks to be performed by the information system. If users have a low understanding and do not agree on what the system is intended to do, the level of uncertainty is high.

4.   the skill and proficiency of the systems developers. Low levels of training and experience result in high uncertainty.

To these may be added:

5.   the time span the system is expected to survive, or the system's

planning horizon. In general the greater the expected life of
the system, the greater the uncertainty regarding the requirements for the system towards the later periods of its life.

6.   the extent to which the chosen design is innovative. The more
     the design departs from known practice the more uncertain is
     its effect on those who use the system.

Neumann and his colleagues propose a method for calculating an
uncertainty index as a guideline for the designer in choosing a
design strategy. They suggest that systems with a high degree of
certainty can be designed on the basis of the users requirements
statement, systems which have less certainty should use the coven-
tional life cycle approach of a sequence of design stages, systems
with high uncertainty should have an iterative design strategy, but
where the uncertainty is very high an experimental approach has to
be used.

In practice all systems have some attributes which are very
uncertain and where some techniqeus of uncertainty reduction has
to be built into the systems design process, if the design is to
stand a good chance of being successful.

There are many experimental techniques which a systems designer
can use to reduce uncertainty. Of these the most widely discussed
and most commonly used is the prototype approach. Brittan (7) sets
out the steps in a prototype based life cycle:

    1.   Project proposal

    2.   Preliminary study

    3.   Full study

    4.   Systems specification ◄─────────────────────┐

    5.   Systems construction   │

    6.   Implementation impact   │

    7.   Implementation   │

    8.   Monitor, review, evaluate ──────────────────┘

    9.   Project closure

    (N.B. "Implementation' here refers to the prototype)

The designer constructs a prototype using relatively crude but
cheap construction methods. The prototype is tested in the user
environment and, if necessary, further prototypes built. Only when
a prototype fits the user's needs, is it 'engineered' to perform at
a high efficiency level. (This may be contrasted with post-implementation monitoring mentioned under 'alternative system models' earlier).

The prototype approach is, however, only one of many possible experimental design strategies the designer can use. These include building simulation models of the system. For example, the LEGOL project of Stamper (9) can be used to simulate the operation of alternative designs of administrative or legislative rules prior to the implementation of such rules. In this way inconsistencies and unforeseen consequences of the application of the rules can be identified. Simulation models can also be used as part of a strategy exploring behaviour by means of management type games. Hawgood and colleagues (15) describe the construction of a game COMSI-COMSA which models, for example, the existing stock control system and proposed inventory control system. The game is played by the stock control management team, using the two models and the results of each game are compared against criteria for efficient inventory control. This enables the designer to choose the inventory control system which provides the best results in the game.

Other experimental techniques useful for the designer include field experiments with new systems components, or prototypes of such components, as for example, simulated exception reports and attitude surveys by questionnaire. It is becoming clear that systems analysts have to be educated in the use of experimental methods for the design of systems.

IN CONCLUSION

It would have been satisfying to have concluded the paper with a claim that we have shown clearly how the challenges to systems analysis and design are being met by a phalanx of well integrated methods of approach. We cannot at this point make the claim however, although there does seem to be an underlying similarity between many of the methods. A unifying theory for systems analysis still eludes us but perhaps there is now some evidence that we are not bereft of ways to meet the challenges, and we hope this review has contributed in a modest way to the assembling of that evidence.

REFERENCES

1.   Alter S.L.: Decision Support Systems, current practice and continuing challenges: Addison-Wesley, 1980.

2.   Argyris C. and Schon D.: Theory in Practice, increasing professional effectiveness: Jossey-Bon San Francisco, 1974.

3.   Beer S.: Brain of the Firm: Allen Lane, Herder, 1972.

4.   Beer S.: Platform for Change: Wiley, 1975.

5.   Bjorn-Anderson N. (ed): The Human Side of Information
      Processing: North Holland, 1980

6.   Blanning R.W.: Functions of a Decision Support System:
      Information and Management 2, pp 87-93, 1979.

7.   Brittan, J.: Design for a Changing Environment: The Computer
      Journal, Vol. 23, No. 1, Feb. 1980.

8.   Checkland P.B.: Towards a Systems Based Methodology for Real
      World Problem Solving: Journal of Systems Engineering,
      Vol. 3, No. 7, April 1972.

9.   Cook S. and Stamper R.K.: LEGOL as a tool for the study of
      bureaucracy, in The Information Systems Environment (eds:
      Lucas, Land, Lincoln, Inpper): North Holland, 1980.

10.   D'Agapeyeff A.: An Empirical Approach to Long-life Systems:
      Computer Bulletin, pp 24-6, June 1976.

11.   De Maio A.: Socio-technical Methods for Information Systems
      Design, in The Information Systems Environment, op.cit. 9.

12.   De Marco T.: Structured Analysis and Systems Specification:
      Yourdon Press, 1978.

13.   EDP Analyser: Tools for Building an EIS: Vol. 17, No. 8, 1979.

14.   Espejo R.: The cybernetics of a small company: Information
      and Management.

15.   Hawgood J., Mumford E., Land F.F., Readington C.M.: Evaluation
      and Management of Computer-Based Systems: North Holland, 1972.

16.   Hoos I.R.: Systems Analysis in Social Policy: IEA Research
      Monograph 19, 1969.

17.   Infotech: Life-cycle Management: State of the Art Report,
      1980.

18.   Jackson M.A.: Structural Design of the Information System:
      Academic Press, 1975.

19.   Johansen R., Valee J., Spangler K.: Electronic Meetings,
      technical alternatives and social choices: Addison-Wesley.

20.   Jones A.H.: Some Systems Design Principles for Longer-Life
      Information Systems: working paper.

21.   Jones A.H.:   Control Checking as a Dynamic Component of
        Operational Information Systems: Progress in Cybernetics
        and Systems Research, Vol. VII pp 195-9:   Hemisphere, 1980.

22.   Keen P.G.W. and Scott Morton M.S.:   Decision Support Systems,
        an organisational perspective: Addison Wesley, 1978.

23.   Land F.F., Mumford E., Hawgood J.:   Training the Systems,
        Analyst for the 1980s, in The Information Systems Environment,
        op.cit. 9.

24.   Langefors B.:   Information Systems Theory, in Information
        Systems Vol. 2, No. 4, 1977.

25.   Lundeberg M., Goldkuhl, Nilsson: Information Systems Develop-
        ment, a first introduction to a systematic approach: ISAC
        Group, University of Stockholm, 1978.

26.   Mayo E.:   The Human Problems of an Industrial Civilisation:
        Macmillan, N.Y.,. 1933.

27.   Michie D. (ed.):   Expert Systems in the Microelectronic Age:
        Edinburgh University Press, 1979.

28.   Michie D.:   Expert Systems: The Computer Journal, Vol. 23,
        No. 4, Nov. 1980.

29.   Neumann J.D., Davis G.B., McKeen J.D.:   Journal of Systems
        and Software, No. 1, 1980.

30.   Saaksjarvi M.:   Framework for Participative Systems Long Range
        Planning, in The Information Systems Environment, op.cit. 9.

31.   Stamper R.K.:   Information Analysis in LEGOL: Proc. Nordic
        Research Course on Conceptual Information Modelling for Data
        Bases, 1979.

32.   Taylor J.C.:   The Socio-Technical Approach to Work Design,
        in Designing Organisations for Satisfaction and Efficiency
        (eds.: Legge, Mumford): Gower Press, 1978.

33.   West Churchman C.:   The Systems Approach: Dell, 1968.

34.   Yourdon E. and Constantine L.L.:   Structured Design, funda-
        mentals of a discipline of computer program and systems
        design: Prentice-Hall, 1979.